THE MIDDLE EAST

The Arab-Israeli Arena

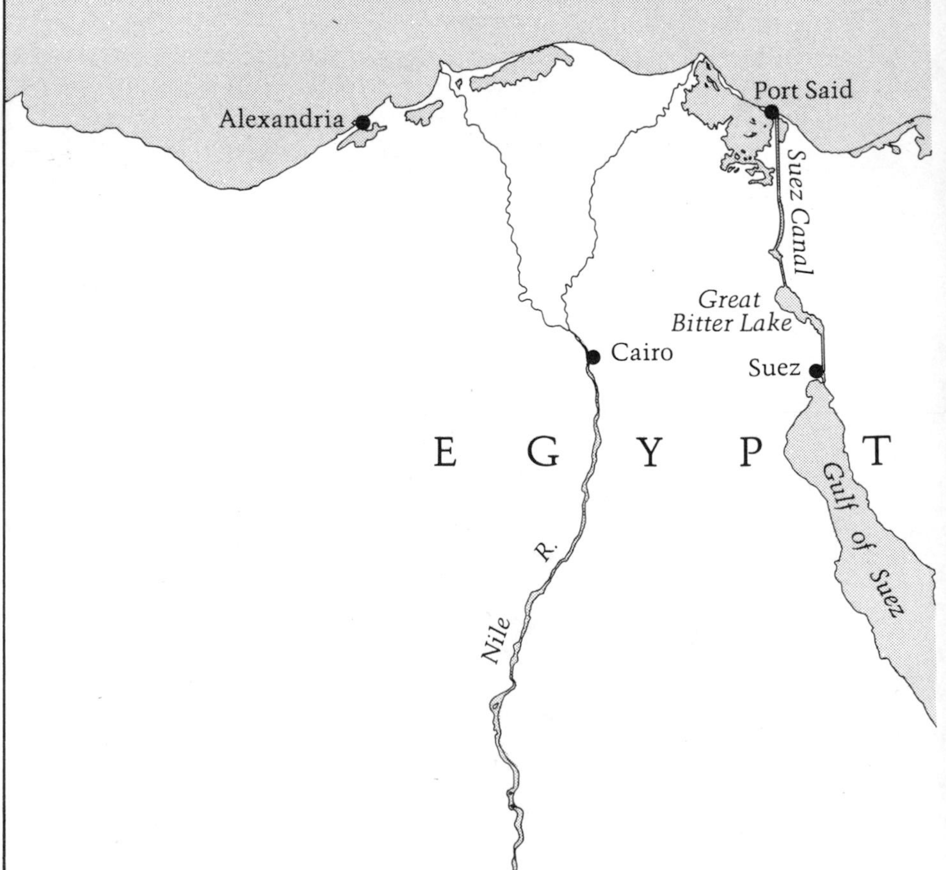

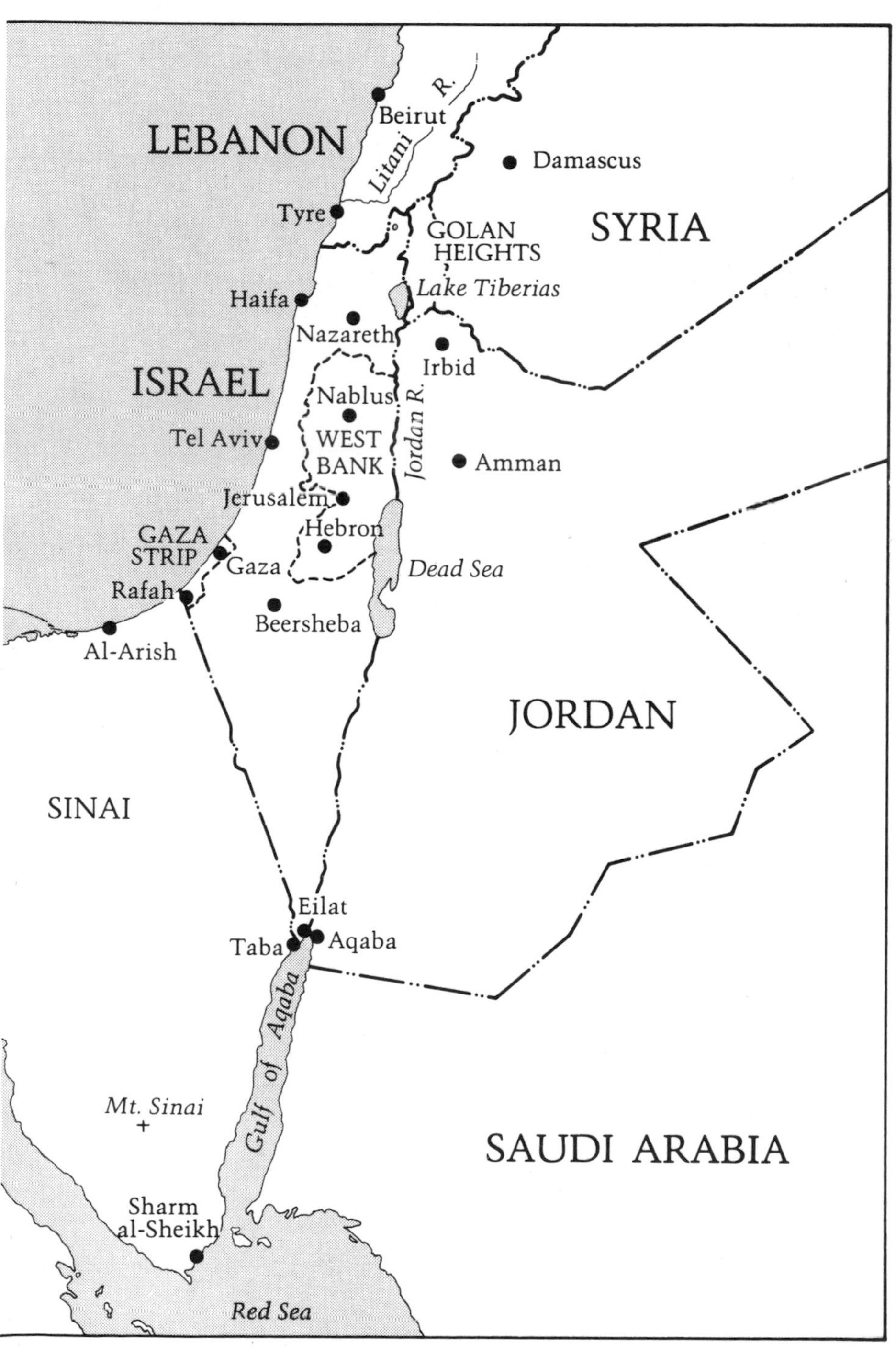
LEBANON
Beirut
Litani R.
Damascus
Tyre
GOLAN HEIGHTS
SYRIA
Haifa
Lake Tiberias
Nazareth
Irbid
ISRAEL
Nablus
Jordan R.
Tel Aviv
WEST BANK
Amman
Jerusalem
Hebron
GAZA STRIP
Gaza
Dead Sea
Rafah
Beersheba
Al-Arish
JORDAN
SINAI
Eilat
Taba
Aqaba
Gulf of Aqaba
Mt. Sinai
SAUDI ARABIA
Sharm al-Sheikh
Red Sea

THE MIDDLE EAST

Ten Years after Camp David

William B. Quandt
editor

THE BROOKINGS INSTITUTION
WASHINGTON, D.C.

1775 Massachusetts Avenue, N.W., Washington, D.C. 20036

Library of Congress Cataloging-in-Publication data

The Middle East : ten years after Camp David / William B.
Quandt, editor.
p. cm.
Includes index.
ISBN 0-8157-7294-7 (alk. paper) ISBN 0-8157-7293-9
(pbk. : alk. paper)
1. Israel-Arab conflicts. 2. Egypt—Foreign relations—
Israel. 3. Israel—Foreign relations—Egypt. 4. Middle East—
Politics and government—1945– I. Quandt. William B.
DS119.7.M473 1988
327.6205694—dc19 88-24234
CIP

9 8 7 6 5 4 3 2 1

The paper used in this publication meets the minimum requirements of the American National Standard for Information Sciences—Permanence of Paper for Printed Library Materials, ANSI Z39.48-1984.

Set in Linotron Trump with Trump Gravur display
Composition by Monotype Composition Co.
Baltimore, Maryland
Printing by R.R. Donnelley and Sons, Co.
Harrisonburg, Virginia
Book design by Ken Sabol

THE BROOKINGS INSTITUTION

The Brookings Institution is an independent organization devoted to nonpartisan research, education, and publication in economics, government, foreign policy, and the social sciences generally. Its principal purposes are to aid in the development of sound public policies and to promote public understanding of issues of national importance.

The Institution was founded on December 8, 1927, to merge the activities of the Institute for Government Research, founded in 1916, the Institute of Economics, founded in 1922, and the Robert Brookings Graduate School of Economics and Government, founded in 1924.

The Board of Trustees is responsible for the general administration of the Institution, while the immediate direction of the policies, program, and staff is vested in the President, assisted by an advisory committee of the officers and staff. The by-laws of the Institution state: "It is the function of the Trustees to make possible the conduct of scientific research, and publication, under the most favorable conditions, and to safeguard the independence of the research staff in the pursuit of their studies and in the publication of the results of such studies. It is not a part of their function to determine, control, or influence the conduct of particular investigations or the conclusions reached."

The President bears final responsibility for the decision to publish a manuscript as a Brookings book. In reaching his judgment on the competence, accuracy, and objectivity of each study, the President is advised by the director of the appropriate research program and weighs the views of a panel of expert outside readers who report to him in confidence on the quality of the work. Publication of a work signifies that it is deemed a competent treatment worthy of public consideration but does not imply endorsement of conclusions or recommendations.

The Institution maintains its position of neutrality on issues of public policy in order to safeguard the intellectual freedom of the staff. Hence interpretations or conclusions in Brookings publications should be understood to be solely those of the authors and should not be attributed to the Institution, to its trustees, officers, or other staff members, or to the organizations that support its research.

Foreword

THE Camp David Accords, signed by Egyptian President Anwar Sadat and Israeli Prime Minister Menachem Begin ten years ago, clearly marked an important watershed in the contemporary history of the Middle East. Not surprisingly, they continue to be debated within the Middle East region and in the United States as well. Most analysts see the durability of the Egyptian-Israeli peace treaty as the most important legacy of the accords. The most obvious shortcoming, in the opinion of many, was the inability of the Camp David negotiators to develop an acceptable formula for dealing with the complexities of the Palestinian dimension of the Arab-Israeli conflict.

In 1986 Brookings published a detailed account of the Camp David negotiations by William B. Quandt, a senior fellow in the Foreign Policy Studies program. Entitled *Camp David: Peacemaking and Politics*, the book set out the American side of the negotiations. Even as that book was being published, it was clear that other perspectives, especially those of Egypt, Israel, other Arabs, and the Soviet Union, could add a useful historical dimension. With this concern in mind, Quandt invited the authors of the chapters in this volume to participate in an effort to assess the impact of the Camp David Accords from a variety of perspectives. The authors met in November 1987 to discuss all of the chapters in draft. Each was aware of the perspectives of the others as they completed their writing in early 1988.

William B. Quandt is particularly grateful to a number of reviewers who commented on various chapters: Helena Cobban, Adeed Dawisha, Karen Dawisha, Raymond L. Garthoff, Dan Kurtzer, Madiha Madfai, Yahya M. Sadowski, David K. Shipler, and I. William

Zartman. Susanne E. Lane helped research and edit some of the chapters and provided invaluable assistance in organizing the authors' conference. Theresa B. Walker edited the manuscript, Amy R. Waychoff and Patricia A. Nelson verified it, and Susan L. Woollen prepared it for publication. Judy Buckelew provided essential administrative support at every step of the project.

Brookings gratefully acknowledges the financial support for this project from the John D. and Catherine T. MacArthur Foundation, the Zilkha Foundation, and the Rockefeller Foundation.

The views in this book are solely those of the individual authors and should not be attributed to the Brookings Institution, to its trustees, officers, or other staff members, or to the organizations that support its research.

Bruce K. MacLaury
PRESIDENT

September 1988
Washington, D.C.

Contents

THE MIDDLE EAST

WILLIAM B. QUANDT

Introduction

EVENTS OF historic significance can give new meanings to words. This was the case with "Camp David," words that for many years meant nothing more than the name of a private presidential retreat located in the hills of Maryland. On September 17, 1978, after twelve arduous days of negotiation, the president of Egypt, Anwar Sadat, and the prime minister of Israel, Menachem Begin, finally informed President Jimmy Carter that they were prepared to sign two "framework agreements" (see appendix C). One spelled out an approach to an overall Arab-Israeli peace settlement. The other specified principles that should govern the negotiation of an Egyptian-Israeli peace treaty. Henceforth, in the language of diplomacy Camp David was synonymous with the process that led to Egyptian-Israeli peace and with a particular formula for trying to deal with the Palestinian question. Camp David, in short, was redefined by events to connote a set of principles and processes.

From the moment of formal signature of the Camp David Accords, as they are commonly called, reactions were mixed—and strong. Everyone seemed to sense that a watershed had been crossed, for better or worse. Many were surprised, some pleased, others shocked and angry, but few in the Middle East, at least, were indifferent.

For most Americans, Camp David stands out as a proud moment in their recent history. Politicians regularly embrace the Camp David Accords as the centerpiece of American policy toward the Middle East. But elsewhere the reactions have been far less positive. Many in the Arab world see Camp David as the cause of their misfortunes. Israelis are, on the whole, more positively inclined, although arguments abound as to what Camp David implies for the future. The Soviets speak of Camp David as a model to be avoided at all costs, and Europeans have long since concluded that a new approach to Arab-Israeli peacemaking is required.

While the debate over Camp David will no doubt go on, the tenth anniversary of the accords provides an opportunity to gain some perspective on the consequences of the agreement forged by Carter and accepted by Begin and Sadat. No single perspective is adequate to assess the multiple effects of the Egyptian-Israeli peace that followed on the heels of Camp David. This book is meant to reflect a diversity of views as well as several levels of analysis—the effects of Camp David on the parties to the agreements, on the broader region, and on the policies of the superpowers.

PLACING CAMP DAVID IN PERSPECTIVE

Like any significant historical event, the Camp David Accords cannot be seen in isolation or frozen at a single point in time. Instead, they need to be seen in context, as part of a process that preceded September 17, 1978, and continued well beyond that date. An event of this magnitude, a peace settlement between two long-time belligerents, is also bound to have wide-ranging consequences, many of which could not have been anticipated. Finally, one should not expect a consensus among scholars on the significance of Camp David. The same events need to be examined under several different lenses, as the authors of this volume have done.

As used in this volume, Camp David has two distinct, though related, meanings. The broadest usage refers to the process of negotiation between Egypt and Israel that began in the early 1970s and culminated in the peace treaty that was signed on March 26, 1979. This usage emphasizes the strong continuity in Egyptian foreign policy throughout the decade following the death of former Egyptian President Gamal Abd al-Nasser. The Sadat era, it can be argued, gave priority to Egyptian national interests, to the recovery of the Sinai peninsula, and to a reversal of alliances with the superpowers. Sadat's Egypt was prepared to break with the prevailing Arab consensus on Israel. The logic of this stance was to pursue a separate peace with Israel if the Arab consensus could not be dragged along behind Egypt's lead.

Some analysts look at the pattern of Sadat's diplomatic efforts dating back to February 1971 when he first spoke of the possibility of peace with Israel. They see a determined policy of proceeding toward a settlement of the conflict with Israel. Even the October 1973 Arab-Israeli war can be seen as a bid by Sadat to break the diplomatic impasse. From this perspective, Egypt was an initiator of many of the major moves of the 1970s, perhaps evidenced most dramatically in Sadat's decision to visit Jerusalem in November 1977.

An alternative view sees Egypt as the victim of American and

Israeli manipulation. Sadat, it is argued, was sincere in wanting to achieve an overall settlement of the conflict with Israel, including a just resolution of the Palestinian question. Admittedly, he was prepared to go beyond the existing Arab consensus, but he wanted to lead it, not break with it. Once he distanced himself from the Soviets, however, he was heavily dependent on the United States to persuade the Israelis to move toward a comprehensive settlement. Unfortunately for Sadat, Israel turned out to be more intransigent than he had expected, and the Americans were less assertive. This reality left the power balance tilted heavily against Arab interests. In the end, according to this view, Sadat was forced to settle for a separate peace, since the alternative would have involved a return to a posture of belligerency from a very weak position. Egypt is seen as object, as victim, not as a full partner in the steps that led to the peace treaty with Israel. On the whole, this view is not widely supported by the analysis in this volume.

The second meaning of Camp David that will be found throughout this book refers more directly to the actual agreements signed on September 17, 1978, particularly the "Framework for Peace in the Middle East Agreed at Camp David," which set out a three-stage formula for dealing with the Palestinian question. This proved to be the most controversial part of Camp David. Many Arabs were angry at Sadat for breaking ranks, but they generally agreed that Egypt had every right to recover its national territory through diplomatic means. Classical *raison d'état* is understood—and practiced—throughout the Arab world. What most Arabs objected to, however, was Sadat's willingness to spell out in detail how the Palestinian issue should be addressed and to arrogate to himself a role in negotiating on behalf of the Palestinians, without their consent.

It was not just Sadat's presumption to speak for the Palestinians that angered most Arabs. After all, if he had been able to strike a very good deal on behalf of the Palestinians he would have been hailed as a hero. But there was a stark contrast between what Sadat achieved for his own country—a return of all occupied territory—and the formula for dealing with Palestinian demands. In addition, many Arabs saw Sadat as far too ready to capitulate to combined American and Israeli pressures.

In essence, the part of Camp David that dealt with the Palestinians spelled out a process, while leaving substantive questions mostly unresolved. Claims to sovereignty over the West Bank and Gaza were to be left in abeyance for five years. Egypt, possibly with Jordan, would negotiate guidelines with Israel for a transitional period of no more than five years. At the outset of this period, the Palestinians in the occupied territories would be able to elect a "self-governing authority" to manage local affairs. Israel, however, would continue to be responsible for internal and external security. Despite Carter's urgent plea, Begin had refused to agree to a freeze on establishing new Israeli settlements in the West Bank and Gaza. Palestinians would not be able to participate on their own behalf in negotiations until talks began on the "final status" of the disputed territories. Camp David stipulated that these talks should begin "as soon as possible but not later than the third year after the beginning of the transitional period." However, even for those "final status" negotiations, Israel was unwilling to commit itself to the principle of withdrawal in exchange for peace as envisaged in United Nations Security Council Resolution 242 (see appendix A).

To many Palestinians, Camp David offered little or nothing, and certainly the frail hopes embodied in the accords—the commitment to respect the "legitimate rights of the Palestinian people," for example—could not make up for the tangible sense of loss symbolized by Egypt's decision to make a separate deal. Henceforth, Palestinians were on their own or left to depend on the not always tender mercies of the Jordanians and Syrians.

The Israelis saw in the Camp David concept of a transitional period a chance to postpone the hard decisions over borders and sovereignty. The Arabs, with almost no exceptions, saw Camp David as a way of avoiding the crucial issues of territory and self-determination while doing nothing to keep Israel from proceeding with the de facto absorption of the occupied territories. The passage of time has done little to change these perceptions.

THE CAMP DAVID LEGACY

Ten years after the signing of the Camp David Accords, the Palestinian-Israeli dispute was no closer to resolution than earlier. Indeed, the Palestinian uprising, or *intifadah*, in the occupied West Bank and Gaza that began in December 1987 and continued into 1988 was a sharp reminder of how volatile and explosive the situation in the West Bank and Gaza remained. The Palestinians who felt they were treated as objects in the Camp David Accords were, a decade later, insisting on their centrality. Still, no acceptable diplomatic formula existed to break the Palestinian-Israeli impasse. Why was this the case?

The decade after Camp David witnessed many paradoxes. Some of the most ardent critics of Camp David on the Israeli side became its most stalwart supporters. This was particularly true for Israeli Prime Minister Yitzhak Shamir, who opposed Camp David in 1978, but who clung to it as a sacred text a decade later.

On the Arab side there were no such converts. But attitudes nonetheless evolved. Arabs got used to the idea that Sadat's decision to make peace with Israel was not just his idiosyncrasy. Even after Sadat's assassination in October 1981, the Egyptian regime continued to adhere to the terms of the treaty with Israel. And gradually the Arab attempt to ostracize Egypt for its apostasy crumbled. By 1988 most Arab countries had restored full diplomatic relations with Egypt.

With the realization that Egypt's peace with Israel was likely to last came the awareness among most Arabs that the military option of confronting Israel was not very promising. As a result, it became commonplace for Arabs to talk of a political settlement with Israel. The conditions for such a deal were still defined in terms of full Israeli withdrawal from occupied territory and Palestinian self-determination, but Israel's existence was almost taken for granted, as in the resolutions of the Arab League summit held in Fez, Morocco, in September 1982 (see appendix E).

The Arab parties also came to the realization that some form of transitional arrangement might be needed if they were ever to wrest the occupied territories from Israel. This point was also reflected in the Fez resolutions, although the formula used there was far from the Camp David concept.

Camp David could also be seen as having two other messages for the Arabs. First was the notion that the United States could play an important role in promoting Arab-Israeli agreement. Whatever one thought of the contents of the Camp David Accords, all saw that the United States had played an essential part. On his own, Sadat would probably have gotten far less from Israel, and indeed it is questionable whether a deal could have been struck at all. This realization raised the question of whether or not the United States could be brought back into the game to do for the Palestinians—and perhaps the Syrians as well—what it had done for Sadat.

In short, was Camp David a model of what could be expected of the United States in the right circumstances, or was it a one-time exception, designed to neutralize Egypt and thus prevent another Arab-Israeli war? Most Arab regimes chose to conclude that the United States might again lend its weight to the peace process. Certainly that was the message of the parade of Arab visitors who came to Washington in early 1985 to persuade the Reagan administration to be more active. But Arab leaders were also reluctant to rely exclusively on the United States and thus called for an international conference that would also include the Soviet Union and the other permanent members of the United Nations Security Council.

A second message, quite different in thrust, that could be distilled by Arabs from the Camp David experience was one of self-reliance. For years, many Arabs waited for the international community to produce a solution to the Palestinian issue. In Nasser's time they often looked to Egypt to define policy toward Israel. Then Sadat broke with prevailing expectations, first by going to war in 1973 and then by making peace with Israel. Sadat, of course, depended on the United States to help win concessions from Israel, but he was not a passive player in the diplomatic game. He made moves and countermoves, often suddenly and without much preparation, but at least he acted. And from the standpoint of Egypt's national interests, he did relatively well. One might conclude that the message to other Arab leaders confronting Israel would be that they should take initiatives rather than wait for others to do so. To some extent, the Jordanians and Palestinians in adopting their joint stance of 1985 seemed to be drawing this lesson (see appendix F). And in another sense the Palestinian uprising of 1987–88 can be seen as a deliberate attempt to shake off dependence, to challenge the status quo, and to pursue a policy of self-reliance. Although few Arabs would probably acknowledge it, these points are all valid conclusions that can be drawn from the Camp David experience.

THE BALANCE SHEET OF THE FIRST DECADE

Few of either the hopes or fears of the participants in, and observers of, the Camp David negotiations were fully realized in the subsequent decade. The Egyptians and Americans who professed to see Camp David as the first step toward a comprehensive peace were disappointed. This hope had been anchored in the belief that Israel, once its security was enhanced through the peace treaty with Egypt, would be flexible in dealing with the Palestinian question. Sadat, on occasion, even entertained grandiose schemes such as the diversion of water from the Nile to Israel as an incentive to the Israelis to relinquish the West Bank. All of these ideas foundered on the rock of Begin's deep conviction that Israel's destiny was to remain in perpetual control, in one form or another, of the West Bank. This was not just a bargaining posture. It was central to his beliefs.

The Egyptians and Americans were also overly optimistic about the potential of starting a process for resolving the Palestinian question that would acquire a momentum of its own. Sadat and Carter had both initially believed that Jordan, the Palestinians, and Saudi Arabia would have no choice but to go along with the Camp David formula. This proved to be a gross misjudgment. It was also hoped that somehow Begin could be maneuvered into a position of accepting transitional arrangements for the West Bank and Gaza that would eventually open the way for some form of Palestinian statehood, preferably in association with Jordan. Some Israelis who opposed Camp David did so precisely on the grounds that Camp David would inevitably plant the germ of a Palestinian state. After all, the concept of autonomy, as envisaged in Camp David, was to be applied throughout the West Bank and Gaza and could be seen as placing real power in the hands of Palestinians as a step on the way to governing themselves.

Within one and one-half months of the signing of the Camp David Accords, an Arab summit held in Baghdad set the tone for the Arab consensus. Camp David was condemned and Egypt was put on notice that it would be drummed out of the Arab League and its members would break diplomatic relations if Egypt proceeded toward peace with Israel. Undeterred, Sadat struck back by breaking relations with his Arab critics and publicly denouncing them for their cowardice. At times, Sadat seemed to be doing all he could to alienate the Saudis and Jordanians, referring to their leaders as jackasses and dwarfs.

As it became clear that Egypt was intent on making peace with Israel, many in the Arab world expressed the fear that Israel would become more aggressive once Egypt was neutralized. Evidence for this belief was soon in ample supply, especially in 1981 and 1982. In short order, Israel bombed the Iraqi nuclear reactor near Baghdad, extended Israeli law to the Golan Heights, accelerated the process of establishing settlements in the West Bank, and, most damaging of all, invaded Lebanon in June 1982 with the expressed intention of driving out the Palestine Liberation Organization (PLO). All of these events were consistent with the thesis that the removal of the weight of Egypt would free Israel to pursue very assertive policies in the Arab world. Most Arabs found it hard to believe that Israel would have behaved similarly if Egypt had not been neutralized.

But the evidence for this belief is ambiguous at best. If the events of 1981 and 1982 seem to offer confirmation, subsequent developments suggest that Egypt was certainly not the only restraint on Israeli behavior. For example, how can one explain the Israeli decision to disengage from Lebanon? That had nothing to do with

Egypt, but rather with the high costs, including domestic strife, of pursuing a poorly thought out policy in Lebanon. Even the West Bank, which seemed to lie open to Israeli absorption after the collapse of the so-called autonomy talks in 1982, was not so easily digested. Egypt, after all, had not stopped Israel from expanding its presence in the West Bank. It was only when the Palestinians launched their uprising in late 1987 that the prospect emerged of slowing the de facto annexation of these territories by Israel. From this perspective, Egypt was not the only available brake on Israel's aggressive policies. Even without the weight of Egypt on the scales, the local populations that Israel encountered as it tried to reshape Lebanon and absorb the West Bank were able to check Israeli policies, at least to some extent.

The Israelis also had their fears in the aftermath of Camp David. The most widely expressed was the belief that Sadat would renege on some or all of his commitments to Israel once Egypt had recovered Sinai. While many Israelis have been disappointed that the peace with Egypt has been relatively cool, the worst fears that Egypt would return to a posture of belligerency have not been realized. Despite Sadat's assassination in October 1981, Egyptian policy has remained wedded to the peace treaty, although with little enthusiasm for the idea of "normalizing" relations. Following the Israeli invasion of Lebanon, Egypt did feel compelled to withdraw its ambassador from Tel Aviv, but a new ambassador was eventually reassigned. And during subsequent moments of friction, such as the Israeli bombing of the PLO headquarters in Tunis in October 1985, the harsh repression of the Palestinian uprising, and the assassination by Israel of PLO leader Khalil Wazir (Abu Jihad) in April 1988, Egypt confined its protests to normal diplomatic channels. In addition, bilateral problems such as the Taba territorial dispute were handled with scrupulous respect for the procedures laid out in the peace treaty.

The Palestinian issue has proved more difficult to deal with through negotiations than many thought at the time of the Camp David Accords. Ten years after those agreements, Israel is still unwilling to deal with the PLO, which has not yet made an unequivocal statement that might reassure Israelis about the long-term intentions of the Palestinians. (See appendix L for such a statement by a close adviser of Arafat.) But at least the Palestinians, unlike the Syrians, were very much on the minds of the Camp David partners. In retrospect, the disregard for Syria's position seems hard to understand.

Since 1978, Syria has been the most adamant of the Arab parties in its opposition to Camp David. Almost alone among the Arab parties, it has held out against the move to bring Egypt back into the Arab fold. Syria has formally insisted that Egypt abrogate its peace treaty with Israel before reconciliation can take place.

From the perspective of Damascus, Camp David is a formula for dividing and weakening the Arab world so that Israel, with American help, can consolidate its position. Syria has seen each of the initiatives of the past decade as part of the Camp David conspiracy: the Israeli invasion of Lebanon was aimed at defeating the PLO and establishing a pro-Israeli regime in Lebanon; the Reagan plan of September 1982 was designed to lure Jordan into a separate deal with Israel; and the initiative launched in March 1988 by Secretary of State George P. Shultz, while marginally better from Syria's standpoint, continued to see the path to peace as based on a series of bilateral negotiations between Israel and its neighbors (see appendixes D and K).

Syria has consistently argued for a unified Arab stand as a precondition for confronting Israel, either diplomatically or militarily. Whatever one may think of the Syrian view, Damascus has been an important player in the regional political game, especially when Egypt was relatively isolated and Iraq was bogged down in an endless war with Iran.

For many Americans, the most surprising result of Camp David has been the effect on the positions of the two superpowers. Camp David was the high tide of American unilateralism. The Soviets seemed almost irrelevant to the diplomatic game between Israel and the Arabs. Some observers spoke carelessly of a Pax Americana in the region. Against this background, it is striking to find the Reagan administration, ten years after Camp David, dealing with the Soviet Union as a serious contender in Arab-Israeli diplomacy. Washington has even come to embrace the idea of an international conference, albeit one of limited scope. And the Middle East is now a regular item on the agenda of superpower talks. The Soviets have even launched a diplomatic offensive to improve relations with countries formerly seen to be in the American camp such as Egypt, Saudi Arabia, Jordan, and even Israel.

The watershed event in the decade after Camp David was, I believe, the Israeli invasion of Lebanon and its aftermath. The war in Lebanon affected all of the regional parties; it also influenced the policies of the superpowers. Lebanon revealed in a humiliating and costly way the outer limits of American and Israeli power in the region. The crisis also forced the Soviets to decide whether to back Syria in the crucial period of late 1982. The Soviets were not prepared to write off their heavy investment in Syria. They rearmed the Asad regime, and Syria then became a formidable Soviet ally in 1983 both in disrupting American plans in Lebanon and in challenging the Reagan initiative. The lesson was not lost. Those in the Middle East who witnessed this struggle of the superpowers through their respective clients saw that the Americans had not come out on top. Certainly this was one of the reasons that King Hussein was reluctant to move forward with the Reagan initiative after 1982.

The balance sheet on Camp David, then, ultimately depends in large measure on how one evaluates the war in Lebanon. If it is seen as an inevitable consequence of Camp David, then the balance sheet is likely to be tilted on the negative side. If instead one sees the Israeli decision to invade Lebanon as independent of Camp David, then one would assess Camp David in a different light. My own judgment is that the Lebanon war might have been avoided, but only with a significant and determined effort by the United States. Barring that, the Israeli leadership of the day was determined to strike at the PLO and might have done so even if Egypt had not made peace. But without the peace treaty with Egypt, it is hard to imagine that the Americans would have been so complacent, and it is hard to believe that the Israeli invasion would have gone on so long, including the siege of Beirut. At most, one might have seen a larger version of the so-called Operation Litani, the limited Israeli incursion into southern Lebanon in March 1978, right in the midst of the negotiations with Egypt. In sum, Camp David does bear some, but not all, of the blame for the tragic events in Lebanon in 1982 and 1983.

THEMES

The picture of the Middle East in mid-1988 could not have been painted by even the most prescient analyst when the Camp David Accords were signed a decade earlier. True, Egypt and Israel are at peace, as Camp David mandated, but the peace is a cool one and has not served as a model for others in the Arab world. The Palestinians are in revolt, but a diplomatic breakthrough is nowhere in sight. Israel is deeply divided as it heads toward national elections. The PLO, despite the multiple setbacks of the past decade, is still a player in the game, whereas Jordan has retreated to the sidelines (see appendix M). Syria is more obviously an important party to the conflict than anyone seemed to think a decade ago, while Egypt's role has shrunk. Still, Egypt has resumed relations with almost all Arab countries, without having to curtail its relationship with Israel. Saudi Arabia, once thought to be a significant regional power because of oil wealth, is now running sizable deficits and is preoccupied with the security situation in the Gulf. There, Iran and Iraq may finally be moving toward a truce in their eight-year-old war.

In this environment of the late 1980s, the Camp David Accords are still mentioned, but with decreasing frequency. They represent an echo of the past, not a model for the future. Some broad themes from Camp David have been absorbed, almost unconsciously, into the mainstream of political thinking, and the Egyptian-Israeli treaty does show that negotiations can produce lasting results. But Camp David is rarely seen today as a complete plan of action for future diplomacy.

The experience of the past decade suggests the futility of trying to predict the future in a volatile region like the Middle East. It is also a vain exercise to try to provide a definitive assessment of the Camp David Accords. The historical verdict cannot yet be rendered. But the authors of this volume do provide glimpses into the past and sketches of possible futures. Taken together, these chapters provide an interim report on the first decade after Camp David and lay the ground for thinking about the next decade.

Several broad themes deserve special attention. All of the authors agree on the strategic importance of Egypt's decision to make peace with Israel. Likewise, all see the Lebanon war of 1982 as a major event of the past decade, related in complex ways to the Camp David experience. A third theme that most authors dwell on is the importance of understanding domestic politics as part of the broader regional scene in the Middle East. For most of the actors in the Arab-Israeli conflict—and certainly for the Israelis, Egyptians, Palestinians, and Americans—political change within their societies has an immediate and often decisive impact on foreign policy.

A fourth point that emerges from the following chapters involves the ambiguous relationship between military power and political goals. Both Israel and the United States discovered the difficulties of translating military prowess into political gains in Lebanon and with respect to Syria. The Syrians also have been reluctant to commit their full military power in Lebanon. And the Palestinians, while still adhering to the policy of "armed struggle," have placed much more emphasis recently on the unarmed civilian uprising in the West Bank and Gaza as the central element in their quest for national self-determination. Even the Soviets, long reliant on arms transfers to advance their regional policy, seem to be pursuing their goals through more traditional diplomatic channels.

Finally, most authors would probably agree that American unilateral initiatives, which played such a large role in promoting the Egyptian-Israeli agreements, are no longer likely to play as large a part in future peace efforts. The parties to the conflict—especially the Israelis and the Palestinians—are likely to be the ones to take initiatives in future peacemaking; and a multinational framework of some sort now seems essential if formal peace talks are to take place.

The chapters focusing on Egypt show that Camp David has left an ambiguous legacy. The peace with Israel is widely accepted, although it enjoys little popular support, as Saad Eddin Ibrahim documents in detail. Abdel Monem Said Aly argues that President Husni Mubarak has been engaged in a serious restructuring of Egyptian politics while searching for a new basis of legitimacy. Arab nationalism and the struggle with Israel no longer provide the Egyptian regime with easy arguments with which to confront domestic critics. Ali E. Hillal Dessouki places the treaty with Israel in perspective and analyzes how it has affected Egypt's relations with the United States and the Arab world, the other two major issues in Egypt's foreign policy.

All of the Egyptian authors expect that the peace with Israel will last, but they do not foresee the "normalization of relations" that was envisaged at Camp David. They also express uneasiness about the U.S.-Egyptian relationship, in part because it remains so closely tied to relations with Israel. This point is also echoed by Hermann Frederick Eilts, who sees a continuing divergence of interests between Egypt and the United States but believes that the relationship can be managed if expectations on both sides are kept at realistic levels.

One might expect the picture of Israel to be considerably brighter. After all, Israel was widely seen as the big winner in the Camp David negotiations. But Naomi Chazan portrays a deeply divided country, still carrying the scars of the Lebanon misadventure and uncertain about how best to deal with the ongoing Palestinian challenge. Shimon Shamir also pictures an Israeli public that has been disillusioned by the experience of peace with Egypt. Normalization, which was sought both as a sign that Egypt was sincere in its commitment to peace and as insurance against a reversal of policy, has made little headway. Many Israelis now see peace with Egypt as little more than nonbelligerency. (Still, it is worth noting that Shamir is the newly appointed Israeli ambassador to Cairo, which shows that in the diplomatic sphere, at least, something more than nonbelligerency has been achieved.)

In one of the most upbeat chapters in the volume, Samuel W. Lewis assesses the U.S.-Israeli relationship and finds it strong and dynamic ten years after Camp David. Not only has the relationship withstood a number of strains and a freezing of the peace process, it has also acquired a substantial strategic dimension that gives it added strength. But Lewis notes the continuing differences between the two countries concerning further steps in the peace process. The future of U.S.-Israeli ties, according to Lewis, will depend greatly on the leaders in both countries and the quality of the relationship that develops between them.

The chapters of this book that deal with the other actors in the region—the Palestinians, Jordan, and other Arab parties—tend to emphasize the negative aspects of the Camp David Accords. Certainly for the PLO, Camp David came to be seen as an unmitigated disaster, as Rashid Khalidi argues. Lebanon was the setting for the most traumatic blow to the PLO in 1982, but the PLO survived as a powerful symbol of Palestinian nationalism and was given a lease on life by the *intifadah*, or uprising, that began in December 1987.

Jordan, by contrast, has had a difficult time forging a relationship with the Palestinians in the occupied territories, and, as Emile Sahliyeh demonstrates in his chapter, has found all its diplomatic options with respect to Israel heavily constrained. Jordan has no recognized claim to negotiate for the Palestinians, and its Syrian neighbor has been suspicious of any move toward separate negotiations. The closest Jordan came to entering the peace process was probably in 1985, in alliance with the PLO, but that effort reached an end by early 1986. Because of domestic stability and successful economic management, however, Jordan remains an important regional actor and is on good terms with most countries in the Arab world. Thus King Hussein cannot be written off, even though he may remain on the sidelines for an indefinite period.

Ghassan Salame, in his chapter on inter-Arab politics, calls attention to the emergence of regional blocs in the Arab world. This situation has coincided with a decline of pan-Arabism as the dominant ideology, although strong pragmatic links of interest still hold the Arab world together. Syria has played a particularly large role in the decade since Camp David, in part because of Egypt's isolation and Iraq's preoccupation. But Hafiz al-Asad's leadership skills are certainly also part of the reason. Still, Syria has not been able to prevent most Arab countries from restoring relations with Egypt, nor has it succeeded in its campaign to unseat the rival Baath regime in Baghdad. Even Lebanon continues to be a difficult problem for Syria, a reminder, if one is needed, of the limits of the power of all players in the Middle East game in the face of stubborn local realities.

The two chapters on the superpowers in the Middle East convey a sense of the evolution of their policies over the decade. Evgeni M. Primakov begins his analysis with the aftermath of the 1973 war and Henry A. Kissinger's determined effort to exclude the Soviets from the postwar diplomacy. With the exception of a brief interlude symbolized by the joint U.S.-Soviet statement on October 1, 1977, Primakov sees the United States following a consistent policy of trying to fragment the Arab parties and to isolate the Soviets, all with the goal of giving the Israelis the upper hand in negotiations (see appendix B). By implication, Primakov is saying that Soviet policy throughout much of this period was aimed at thwarting the American approach. Soviet policy may have been primarily reactive in the years after Camp David, but since Mikhail S. Gorbachev became general secretary in 1985, there has been a new tone to Soviet policy. Initiatives are taken and contacts have widened, including those with Israel and Saudi Arabia. A high-level dialogue with the United States has also begun on a range of regional issues, including the Arab-Israeli conflict. As a result, it is increasingly difficult to imagine negotiations taking place as they did at Camp David, with no contribution whatsoever from the Soviet Union.

Indeed, my own chapter on U.S. policy shows that the Reagan administration, having tried to consign the Arab-Israeli conflict to the back burner, and then having tried to revive the Camp David process with Jordan taking the role of Egypt as spokesman for the Palestinians, has been obliged to adopt a broader approach of supporting an international conference that would include the Soviet Union. As the Reagan administration approached its end, it seemed eager to leave as its legacy to the next administration an ongoing peace initiative, as well as the strong commitments to Israel and Egypt that grew out of Camp David. The most obvious gaps in the American position, in my view, are the continuing reliance on Jordan as the primary interlocutor on Palestinian issues and an unwillingness to develop extensive relations with representative Palestinians. In addition, the United States, having forged a remarkably strong relationship with Israel, has been unable to use its influence to support moderate Israeli elements who might be prepared to revive the peace process within an international framework and on the basis of the "territory for peace" formula of Resolution 242.

In the concluding chapter, Harold H. Saunders reminds readers that the peace process, if it is to amount to anything, must be conceived as a political effort, not just a formal exercise of organizing negotiations and getting parties to talk to one another. After such a prolonged pause in the search for Arab-Israeli peace, he believes that more effort must be made to build the political foundations necessary for a serious attempt at negotiations, not merely to find procedural formulas to convene a conference. His preference is to think of a series of interrelated steps, an agreed scenario, whereby leaders can build support for the compromises that must come. Statesmen, in short, are more essential to the process of peace than diplomats.

CONCLUSION

If there is a monument to the Camp David Accords, it is surely the peace between Egypt and Israel. With all its imperfections, it has lasted for ten years. And while it has not led to a wider peace, and it did not prevent the war in Lebanon, it has ensured that no full-scale Arab-Israeli conflict could take place similar to that of October 1973. For most of the world, that has been a welcome result.

By reducing the chance of all-out war, the Egyptian-Israeli treaty has increased the prospects that the remainder of the Arab-Israeli conflict will be seen in political, not military, terms. And in the Arab world, that realization has indeed spread, even if it is challenged at times, especially from the vigorous Islamic movements in the region. Still, for most Arabs and most Israelis, the Egyptian-Israeli peace is a fact of life that will not soon be changed. It therefore must be taken into account.

Few would claim that the Camp David formula for dealing with the Palestinian question has weathered the decade as well as the Egyptian-Israeli treaty. To be sure, some Israelis and some Americans continue to hold closely to the autonomy formulations of Camp David, but in the Arab world there are almost no supporters. Arab disenchantment is not hard to explain. From the outset, Camp David papered over rather than resolved the vital questions of sovereignty, Jerusalem, and Palestinian self-determination. This result did not stem from American or Egyptian preferences, but rather from the unwillingness of Prime Minister Begin to budge from his well-known positions. Since agreement on substance was out of the question between Sadat and Begin on these matters, all that remained was a procedural formula and some broad guidelines for the first step of negotiations.

During the Camp David negotiations, I recall a moment toward the end when it seemed as if the only way to get agreement on a particularly sensitive point would be to resort to ambiguity. In essence, Begin would be allowed to say that he had not agreed to withdraw from the West Bank under any circumstances, and Sadat would be able to say that Begin had accepted the withdrawal provision of Resolution 242 as governing the "final status" negotiations. At that point in the discussion, one of the Israeli negotiators warned that it would be a mistake to try to finesse the issue in this way. It would come back to haunt us, he warned. There would never be a better time to try to devise a serious formula for addressing the Palestinian issue and the question of Israeli withdrawal. But it would take hard work, imagination, and commitment. For his part, he said, he was prepared to stay at Camp David for another ten days or however long it took. None of the three heads of government, however, felt that the issue required such a commitment. So the problem was buried in incomprehensible verbiage. And, as predicted, it came back to haunt the negotiators when it became clear that the Camp David Accords did not mean that Israel was committed to the concept of withdrawal "on all fronts." Ten years later this issue was still a source of controversy between Israel and the United States.

The Palestinians' uprising is their answer, in a certain sense, to Camp David. As such, it shows both the strength and the limitations of what was achieved at Camp David. On the negative side, the Palestinians and Israelis remain locked in conflict, with no way out of the impasse in sight. But both parties acknowledge the need for a political settlement. And both parties realize that Egypt, despite its solidarity with the Palestinians, will not readily turn its back on peace with Israel. These realities could mean that the Palestinian issue, the source of so much bloodshed to date, will be seen by all parties as a political problem in need of a political solution. Then, if leaders from all sides, including the United States and the Soviet Union, are prepared to make a substantial commitment, it might be possible to revive the search for a comprehensive peace, thereby giving full meaning to what was begun at Camp David.

PART I

THE CAMP DAVID PARTNERS: EGYPT AND ISRAEL

SAAD EDDIN IBRAHIM

Domestic Developments in Egypt

> There is not a single pen in Egypt which has not cursed Israel. There is not a single voice in Egypt that has not disavowed its previous faith in the possibility of total peace with Israel. . . . The essence of peace is a Palestinian state . . . otherwise there is no peace even if every single Israeli carried an atomic bomb, and even if American space ships carried every Palestinian to the moon! . . . We had reconciled with Israel, looking forward to a comprehensive peace. . . . It turned out to be a mistake. . . . The most optimistic among us knows now that it will take another 34 years to correct that mistake.
>
> Anis Mansour
> *Al-Ahram,* July 17, 1982

ANIS MANSOUR is one of Egypt's most prominent authors and journalists. He was the editor-in-chief of one of Cairo's major dailies, *Al-Akhbar,* then of a major weekly, *October,* for years. He currently has a daily column in *Al-Ahram*. Between 1972 and 1981, Anis Mansour was a close confidant of the late President Anwar Sadat, and until mid-1982, the loudest advocate of peaceful coexistence between the Arabs and Israel. He opened the pages of his weekly magazine, *October,* to Israeli writers between 1979 and 1981—something that had not happened before and has not happened since. For nearly three weeks after the Israeli invasion of Lebanon on June 6, 1982, Anis Mansour kept silent. Then on July 17, 1982, he broke his silence with the above vehement condemnation of Israel in *Al-Ahram*.

Mansour is representative of a substantial constituency in Egypt that initially welcomed Sadat's peace initiatives toward Israel—the disengagement agreements of 1974 and 1975, the historic trip to

Israel in 1977, the Camp David Accords of 1978, and the Egyptian-Israeli peace treaty of 1979. This constituency, however, has steadily eroded in the decade since Camp David. Today an observer of the Egyptian scene would be hard-pressed to point to prominent voices that still publicly hail peace with Israel. Most Egyptians are resigned to the status quo generated by Sadat's initiatives. A few justify it, a few apologize for it, and a significant but growing minority are actively working against it.

Camp David has become a code word, not just for the two agreements signed in September 1978 but also for the entire spirit and process of Sadat's "historic reconciliation" between the Arabs and Israel. The process began in earnest immediately after the October 1973 war and has had ebbs and flows since.

From a domestic Egyptian perspective, Camp David was an integral part of Sadat's vision for Egypt, and significant policies were generated by that vision. Egyptians have been disposed to judge Camp David in the overall context of Sadat's vision for Egypt and how it affected them, fellow Arabs, and others.

This chapter attempts to describe and account for the evolution of the public attitudes of major domestic sociopolitical forces toward Camp David. How Sadat's vision and its resulting policies affected the Arab-Israeli reconciliation process is an essential part of this analysis. Sadat's open door economic policy (*infitah*), controlled democratization, alliance with the West—especially the United States—and reconciliation with Israel were interlinked policies. Hence the success or failure of any one of them would affect not only other policies but also the public perception of Sadat's entire vision. There were moments of public enthusiasm for Sadat's vision following the October war in the mid-1970s. There were moments of despair at the end of Sadat's political career in the early 1980s. Under Husni Mubarak, the legacy of Sadat's vision is increasingly viewed with sober realism.

Some important caveats are in order before my analysis proceeds. Egypt's democratization is still in its embryonic stage. The freedom of various socioeconomic forces to establish legally their own political parties remains limited. Sizable forces, namely, the Islamists and the Nasserites, often have to express themselves through other legal parties. Nor does Egypt have a tradition of regular public opinion polls. The fairness of parliamentary elections is invariably called into question by the opposition parties. In several cases, Egyptian courts have substantiated charges of irregularities—if not outright fraud. Finally, Camp David and the entire Arab-Israeli conflict are difficult to dislodge or separate from other domestic and external issues for independent assessment in Egyptian political discourse. For most of the decade following Camp David, other issues have competed for primacy of attention by state and society alike.

These considerations leave analysts with a limited and very soft data base. Partially reliable information has to be supplemented by substantial indirect inferences. Making generalizations or drawing firm conclusions is difficult.

With these caveats in mind, this analysis starts with an overview of the Egyptian scene and how it evolved in relation to the Arab-Israeli conflict. The salient domestic and external conditions underlying the evolution are discussed. An account of the various sociopolitical formations, their relative weights, and the evolution of public opinion toward Camp David follows. Finally I assess the Egyptian public's mood ten years after Camp David.

EGYPT AND THE ARAB-ISRAELI CONFLICT

During the last two decades, Egypt has gone through two marked transformations with respect to the Arab-Israeli conflict. The death of Gamal Abd al-Nasser, Sadat's ascendance to power, the October 1973 war, the oil price revolution, and the mounting internal problems have been decisive in setting the stage for the first transformation. The apex of this transformation was the signing of the Egyptian-Israeli peace treaty. Israeli behavior since the treaty, the Egyptian regime's record in dealing with domestic problems, U.S. policies toward Egypt and the Middle East, the assassination of Sadat, Mubarak's presidency, the invasion of Lebanon, the escalation of the Gulf war, and the most recent Palestinian uprisings in the occupied territories, beginning in December 1987 and continuing into 1988, have set the stage for a second transformation.

In the last days of Nasser, Egyptians had resigned themselves to the inevitability of a war to liberate the Arab territories occupied by Israel in 1967. The 1967 defeat had confirmed certain beliefs previously held about Israel. But it had also questioned and challenged other beliefs. Israel's expansionism, disposition to use force to impose its will in the region, and the unwavering U.S. support for the Zionist state were confirmed. Belief in the Arabs' ability to liquidate Israel, their power to restore Arab preeminence in all of Palestine, and in unwavering Soviet support, previously upheld by most Egyptians, was strongly shaken. New appreciation of the power of the self and the enemy, and what to expect from the Soviets were the hard lessons of the 1967 defeat. A new rationality began to emerge. A limited war, with the modest objective of "erasing the consequences of the Israeli aggression" of 1967, became the slogan and the policy of the Nasser regime. Plans and arrangements to that effect were formulated and implemented. Domestically, they were accompanied by some measures to relax the economy and encourage popular political participation. The March 1968 declaration by Nasser in which he declared that Egypt was prepared to support the Palestinian resistance against Israel formalized this new Egyptian consensus. Regionally, Egypt had already embarked on a policy of accommodation and solidarity with all Arab regimes. The Khartoum Arab summit had officially blessed Egypt's strategy, and United Nations Security Council Resolution 242 had given it global acceptability. Internally, Egypt was united behind Nasser's modest strategy. Some accepted it as final, others thought of it in provisional and pragmatic terms. Egyptians silently bore the ravages of the "war of attrition" along the Suez Canal (1969–70), accepted their leader's diplomatic maneuvers (for example, the Rogers plan that ended the war of attrition), and continued to prepare for possible limited military confrontation with Israel.

In the midst of all this, a civil war broke out in Jordan between King Hussein's army and the Palestine Liberation Organization (PLO) forces, Nasser died in September 1970, and Sadat took over as Egypt's new president. Despite a feeling of demoralization within Egypt, the internal front remained intact. Sadat continued to hold on to the same limited war objective and to the domestic and regional policies of his predecessor. Indications that he favored some of these policies over others were perceived by most Egyptians as mere maneuvering or as functions of a difference in style.

The decent performance of the Egyptian army in the October 1973 war gave Sadat immense popularity. His legitimacy was no longer derived solely from being Nasser's former comrade and successor. Shortly after the war, Sadat began to act in his own right. Between 1974 and 1977, his major choices crystallized. They added up to nothing less than a total, though gradual, reversal of Nasserism. An open door economic policy, controlled "paternalistic democracy," alliance with the West, and reconciliation with Israel were the four cornerstones of Sadatism.[1] To be sure, each policy was initiated somewhat separately, couched in the mildest of tones, and

1. For a recent account of the outcome of Sadat's four policies, see Lillian Craig Harris, ed., *Egypt: Internal Challenges and Regional Stability,* Chatham House Papers 39 (London: Routledge and Kegan Paul for the Royal Institute of International Affairs, 1988).

often with ritualistic tribute to Nasser and the July 1952 revolution. Sadat and his mass media would say, for example, that this or that policy "was actually initiated by the late President"; "if he were alive, he would have done the same"; or "that it was merely a tactical correction of a policy and not a change of principles." Because of their bearing on one another, Sadat's four policy orientations are briefly outlined as follows.

The Open Door Economic Policy

Symbolized by Law 43 of 1974, the open door economic policy was launched less than six months after the October war. It aimed at liberalizing the Egyptian economy by ending the near monopoly of the public sector and encouraging the private sector (Egyptian, Arab, and foreign investments). *Infitah,* the word in Arabic for "opening," seemed well-intentioned, and in fact it made good sense in view of current developments. Egypt's economic expansion and industrialization, in full swing between 1955 and 1965, had come to a halt by the late 1960s. The chief, but by no means only, factor in the halt was the 1967 defeat in the third Arab-Israeli war. Preparation for another war "to erase the defeat" appropriated most of what would have otherwise gone to economic development. Egypt's rate of economic growth dropped from the previous 6.9 percent (in 1963) to 2.9 percent (in 1974).[2] New employment opportunities nearly disappeared, and an increasing number of would-be new entrants into the labor force were drafted into the army.

Thus Sadat's new economic policy was initially welcomed by nearly all Egyptians. Few at the time thought Law 43 of 1974 would mean a gradual retreat from Nasser's socialist policy. When another law (Law 32 of 1977), and numerous other decrees were issued, however, it became clear that the new open door economic policy was nothing less than a total retreat from Nasser's socialism and a wholehearted endorsement of a new capitalist orientation. Though not immediately or blatantly attacked, Nasser's focus on the public sector, central planning, and state intervention in the economy were subjected to benign neglect.

Along with other policies, Sadat's open door generated an ideological polarization in Egypt. Supporters of the new policy were

2. Saad Eddin Ibrahim, "Social Mobility and Income Distribution in Egypt, 1952–1977," in Gouda Abdel-Khalek and Robert Tignor, eds., *The Political Economy of Income Distribution in Egypt* (Holmes and Meier, 1982), p. 383.

disproportionately from the upper strata of society—for example, the wealthy returnees from the oil-rich Arab countries with substantial savings, contractors, and the like. Detractors of *infitah* were generally the less well-to-do—for example, public sector workers, the lower middle classes, Nasserites, and other leftists. The detractors would have been easily muffled had *infitah* produced positive results. But early yields were either meager or outright negative. Thus by January 1977, that is, three years after the introduction of the new policy, there were massive urban food riots, the like of which had not been witnessed since Black Saturday twenty-five years earlier in prerevolutionary Egypt, when downtown Cairo went up in flames.

Sadat's reaction to this early warning signal was typical—massive arrests of opposition elements who were blamed for instigating what he termed "the uprising of thieves" and more of the same open door approach (for example, Law 32 of 1977). In July 1977, the regime experienced another bloody confrontation with an Islamic militant group, *Al-Takfir wa al-Hijra*. In November of the same year Sadat undertook his historic visit to Israel.

Paternalistic Democratization

In the showdown with his Nasserite challengers in May 1971, Sadat presented his case to the Egyptian public as a quest for democratization and as an end to autocratic "centers of power" and the "police state." Some nominal measures were declared to substantiate his claim, with the promise of more such steps as soon as Egypt liberated its territories from Israeli occupation. Members of the Muslim Brotherhood and other political prisoners were released between 1971 and 1975. Politicians and journalists in exile were given clemency and encouraged to come home.

It was not until 1976, however, that Sadat reinstated a multiparty system, though with some controls. He decided to restrict the number of parties to three—his own (Egypt's Arab Socialist party) being the centrist party, one to his right (the Liberal party), and one to his left (the Unionist Progressive party). The two chairmen of what were to be opposition parties were former Free Officers whom Sadat had known for more than twenty years—Mustafa Kamil Murad and Khalid Mohieddin. Requests to form additional parties—for example, from the Muslim Brotherhood and Nasserites—were denied.

Modest and restricted as it was, this step toward democracy was welcomed by most Egyptians. A growing freedom of the press and expression was enjoyed for the next two years. The step was most applauded by the upper and middle classes, primarily intellectuals and professionals. Freedoms began to narrow, however, as Sadat's difficulties began to mount. The food riots of 1977 were the start of this gradual retreat from democratization. Sadat was outraged at his party for failing to stand up to the opposition, and in 1978 he established a new party—the National Democratic party (NDP).

By 1981 Sadat had grown impatient with rising criticism. Opposition newspapers were frequently confiscated. In September 1981 he banned several of their publications. More ominously, he threw more than 1,500 political activists in jail, including some prominent and highly respected figures such as Fouad Serageddin, Muhammad Heikal, Hilmi Murad, and Fathy Radwan. This drastic measure was quite indiscriminate. It included the entire sociopolitical spectrum—right, left, and center. The Coptic pope was removed from his office, something that had not been done in fourteen centuries of Islam. The Supreme Guide of the Muslim Brotherhood was also jailed. A month later Sadat was assassinated.

The American Connection

The third serious policy change initiated by Sadat was a steady shift in Egypt's global alignment, away from the Soviets and toward the Americans. The cooling of Egyptian-Soviet relations reached a dramatic point when Sadat expelled some 20,000 Soviet military experts in mid-1972. Despite the courteous way in which he did it, Sadat's move confirmed earlier signs of a mutual loss of confidence. Such signs included his showdown with Nasserite elements, who had been perceived as friends of Moscow, in May 1971; his support of Sudan's Jafaar al-Numeiry in crushing the Sudanese Communist party in July 1971; and his continuous suggestions that the Soviets were dragging their feet in arms delivery to Egypt. The fact that they stood by Egypt in the October war and countered the American arms airlift to Israel by an airlift of their own to Egypt and Syria warmed Sadat's relations with the Soviets momentarily but did not reverse the trend. Most Egyptians had grown weary of Nasser's Soviet connection after the 1967 defeat. Thus Sadat's unfriendly actions toward the Soviets were regretted by few Egyptians.

However, cautious rapprochement with the United States, through Saudi and other channels, began in the early years of Sadat's presidency. Within weeks of the October war, Sadat's drive for "a special relationship" with the United States had become relentless. By early 1974, full diplomatic relations between the two countries (severed since the June 1967 war) had been restored; Henry A. Kissinger's famous shuttle diplomacy dominated the Middle Eastern scene with Sadat's explicit blessing and appreciation. Equally significant was President Richard M. Nixon's visit and the resumption of U.S. aid to Egypt in 1974. American mediation and help resulted in two disengagement agreements of Egyptian and Israeli forces along the Suez Canal and in Sinai, and a similar one on the Syrian front. American and European help was also instrumental in clearing and reopening the Suez Canal for international navigation.

The open door economic policy and Sadat's anticipation of vast investments and advanced technology (for example, a new Marshall Plan, as he called it) fueled Egyptian dreams of an imminent economic breakthrough. America was to become, in Sadat's words, a "full partner" in Egypt's drive for peace and prosperity. The years 1974–77 witnessed what may be called a honeymoon in Egyptian-American relations, and most Egyptians welcomed it.

However, the sluggish efforts between 1975 and 1977 at settling the Middle East conflict and the food riots of 1977 were early signs of Egypt's disillusionment with Sadat's American connection. To be sure, U.S. economic aid to Egypt continued to rise steadily during those years, but concrete results were not directly felt by most Egyptians. Tales of waste and corruption were associated by the opposition with American aid. Sadat's historic visit to Israel in 1977, which had the full backing of the United States, halted Egypt's growing weariness with the American connection for a while.

President Jimmy Carter's efforts in mediating the Camp David Accords and the peace treaty were definitely appreciated by most Egyptians and indeed revived their hopes that peace and prosperity might after all be possible through the American connection. But by 1980, hopes were fading. After his 1981 visit to the United States, even President Sadat seemed less optimistic about the prospects for the American role in delivering comprehensive peace and prosperity.

Peace with Israel

The most dramatic change in Egypt's policies under Sadat was that toward Israel. Egyptian public opinion was to undergo an intense and sustained media campaign to prepare it for the change. Egyptians were told that they had done all that was humanly possible in their fight against Israel.

Their sacrifices in war casualties stood at 100,000 and in

> money at $30 billion. . . . No other Arab country matched their sacrifices. . . . The United States will never allow Israel to be defeated and the Soviets will never give Egypt enough arms to decisively win in war. . . . Egypt's severe economic problems are due to the continuous state of war with Israel. . . . Egypt is heavily indebted while the rich Arabs are depositing billions of dollars in foreign banks. . . . The Syrians and Palestinians are not interested in resolving the Arab-Israeli conflict because they are benefiting from it along with their Soviet patron.[3]

A debate even raged in the Egyptian media on whether "the Egyptians were truly Arabs."[4] The thirty-year national consensus on armed struggle against Israeli usurpation of Arab Palestine was steadily cracking.

Some small-scale public opinion surveys of Egyptians demonstrate this erosion. In 1974 as many as 55 percent of one Egyptian sample solidly supported the PLO strategy of continuing the struggle until the creation of a "secular, democratic state in Palestine," and 43 percent opted for a solution along the lines of United Nations Security Council Resolution 242. By 1978 only 18 percent of a similar Egyptian sample still supported the PLO strategy, while as many as 77 percent supported Sadat's peace initiative, which was even more accommodating toward Israel than Resolution 242.[5] This dramatic swing was reinforced by the promise that peace with Israel would bring prosperity to the Egyptians and justice to the Palestinians.

Those Egyptians who felt otherwise, about 20 percent, consisted of leftists, Nasserites, and Islamic militants. For a while after Sadat's visit to Israel, they were isolated and muffled by his powerful media. With the signing of the Camp David Accords in 1978 and the peace treaty in 1979, Sadat was hailed by the state-controlled media as "the hero of war and peace." The rest of the Arab world stood in shock, disarray, and impotence. Sadat fueled Egyptians' sense of patriotism and depressed their sense of Arab nationalism. A new spirit of "Egypt first" was drummed up, and expectations of instant

3. See Saad Eddin Ibrahim, ed., *Egypt's Arabism: The Dialogue of the Seventies* (in Arabic) (Cairo: Al-Ahram Center for Political and Strategic Studies, 1978) for an analysis of official statements and state-controlled newspaper editorials during the 1974–78 period.

4. Ibid. The entire book is an analytical documentation of this debate, which was triggered by the prominent Egyptian author Tawfik al-Hakim in 1978.

5. Saad Eddin Ibrahim, *Trends of Arab Public Opinion toward the Question of Unity* (in Arabic) (Beirut: Center for Arab Unity Studies, 1980), p. 319.

prosperity skyrocketed. The promise that the Palestinians would get self-rule in preparation for a state of their own cleared the conscience of most Egyptians.

The years that followed the signing of the peace treaty were to witness another transformation of Egyptian public opinion. For some Egyptians the terms of the treaty seemed unfair. Even among organized groups who supported Sadat's peace initiative, apprehension existed. The major opposition, the Socialist Labor party (SLP), while voting for the treaty in the People's Assembly, recorded ten reservations. As Israel continued to build new settlements in the West Bank, Gaza, and the Golan Heights, despite Egyptian protestations, apprehension grew. When the deadline for completing the Palestinian autonomy talks came and went with no agreement, popular Egyptian misgivings intensified.

The constituency for peace in Egypt was steadily eroding. A tacit popular unwillingness to normalize relations with Israel grew. The continued deadlock of the autonomy talks and the unilateral Israeli annexation of Arab Jerusalem led the SLP to join the leftists and Islamic militants in their criticism of the whole process. On the second anniversary of its signing, the SLP publicly repudiated the treaty and withdrew its support. By the summer of 1981, the organized opposition to the treaty had been reinforced by massive popular sentiment of anger toward Israel. The bombing of the Iraqi nuclear reactor in June, only two days after a meeting between Begin and Sadat in Sharm al-Sheikh, destroyed much of the faith some Egyptians still had in Israel's genuine desire for peace. Worse still, many Egyptians perceived their president either as a fool or as a traitor. Israeli bombing of the Fakahany civilian district of Beirut a few weeks later added injury to humiliation. Despite Sadat's public verbal denunciation of these Israeli actions, he did nothing concrete to appease the growing number of his domestic critics.

A host of other internal problems magnified Egypt's discontent. The promised prosperity had not only failed to materialize but inflationary pressures continued to build up in the economy. Equity was less than it had been since the early 1950s—despite substantial economic growth of about 8 percent in 1977.[6] Rumors of corruption in high circles became rampant. Incidents of sectarian conflict

6. See Ibrahim Hassan El-Issawy, "Interconnections between Income Distribution and Economic Growth in the Context of Egypt's Economic Development," in Abdel-Khalek and Tignor, *Political Economy of Income Distribution*, p. 104.

increased in frequency and scale.[7] Sadat's last visit to the United States in the summer of 1981 was rumored to be a big disappointment, as he failed to get enough weapons for his underequipped army or to get the Reagan administration to put enough pressure on Israel to make concessions on the Palestinian autonomy question.[8]

By the early fall of 1981, Sadat's regime was under increasing pressure, both from within and without. Israel was embarrassing him, the United States was failing him, Arab moderates had long turned their backs on him, and domestic opposition was growing and becoming more daring. Militant Muslims and Copts alike were challenging his authority. True to his favorite style of shock treatment, he had to strike big somewhere to break the siege. He chose the domestic front. In the process he was struck down by a domestic enemy.

It would be an oversimplification to contend that Sadat's policy toward the Arab-Israeli conflict was the sole or even the most important cause of his demise. Had he scored some dramatic successes on any of his other three policies, he could have survived what many Egyptians saw as failure on the peace-with-Israel front, at least for a while. But the convergence of difficulties in all four important policies made Sadat's survival a near impossibility. When he ordered the arrest of many in Egypt's political community in early September 1981, he had in fact written his own political death certificate. His actual death took place a month later. The regime was in an acute crisis.

HUSNI MUBARAK AND EGYPTIAN-ISRAELI RELATIONS

Domestic alignments and political attitudes toward Camp David have not changed much in quality or direction from what they were in the fall of 1981. However, there have been marked changes in the relative size of various political forces, the primacy of Egyptian-Israeli relations in the popular consciousness, and the intensity of

7. The major one of a series of such conflicts erupted in June 1981 between Muslims and Copts in a crowded slum of Cairo, Al-Zawiya al-Hamara. More than ten people were killed, and twice as many were wounded because of an initial quarrel between two individuals on property rights. This kind of incident happens often but without similar repercussions in more normal times.

8. Author's impressions from a conversation with President Anwar Sadat in Alexandria on August 29, 1981, a few days after his return from the United States.

expressed feelings and manifest behavior. Islamic groups have attracted a larger following and are increasingly leading the opposition in an anti-Israeli campaign.

In general, there has been less polarization on Israel between President Husni Mubarak and his National Democratic party on the one hand, and the opposition parties on the other hand. In times of highly strained Egyptian-Israeli relations, the two sides generally express the same public sentiments, with the opposition asking for more concrete action than Mubarak and his party are willing or able to take.

Under Mubarak, three critical moments have occurred in Egyptian-Israeli relations: the invasion of Lebanon in 1982; the bombing of the PLO headquarters in Tunisia in 1985 and its aftermath; and the 1987–88 uprising in the occupied territories, which coincided with Egypt's return to the Arab fold after the Amman summit in November 1987. At all three moments, the issue of Israel and Camp David came to the fore, and popular anger flared up. In between crises the issue has remained dormant, but not marginal, in the Egyptian consciousness. Other domestic and regional issues have assumed greater saliency, for example, economic policies, emergency laws and the constitution, and the Gulf war.

In the remainder of this section, I will review the handling of Egyptian-Israeli relations and the Middle East conflict by President Mubarak and his NDP. The NDP was established by President Sadat in 1978 to replace Egypt's Arab Socialist party as "the majority party" of his government. The leadership and most of the membership of the two parties have remained nearly the same. There was no apparent reason for Sadat to make this ritualistic change in name, except possibly to drop the word "socialist" from the title.

The social base of the NDP is amorphous. Its top and mid-level leaders encompass elements of the Arab Socialist Union, which was active in the Nasser regime and in his single party. The NDP also includes many of those who served under Sadat and were vocal supporters of his policies—state and public sector technocrats, professionals, old and new bourgeois elements. Leaders of most trade unions and rural notables are also members of the NDP. This broad range gives the NDP a superficial strength but leaves it without much internal cohesion. In many ways, the NDP still behaves like, and performs the functions of, the Arab Socialist Union. The NDP takes its lead from the president and is a vehicle of political mobilization, especially during election times. Members seem to be mostly interested in patronage and occupancy of public office, and many of the top leaders discard the NDP or join opposition parties as soon as they leave their public offices. Political appointees such as cabinet members, governors, and public corporate executives, if not already NDP members, almost automatically join the party.

The position of the NDP on the issue of peace with Israel, as with other issues, is indistinguishable from that of the Egyptian government or, specifically, that of the president (Sadat or Mubarak). Mubarak automatically took over the chairmanship of the NDP after Sadat's assassination in 1981.

The NDP was as vocal and combative as President Sadat in defense of Camp David and the treaty. It is now as low key on the same issue as its new chairman, President Mubarak. Mubarak's manner of handling Egyptian-Israeli relations is echoed by the NDP's congresses, specialized committees, and its newspaper *Misr*.

While Sadat considered Camp David a great achievement, not only something to be defended but also an accomplishment to be proud of, Mubarak considers Camp David a "legal obligation to be observed and respected." He is neither proud nor ashamed of it. He neither brags about nor apologizes for it. This attitude is in keeping with his overall style toward the policies of his two predecessors in the presidency. He either has something good to say about them or says nothing at all.

Mubarak has never visited Israel nor does he seem keen to do so. He has always found good reasons or excuses to decline Israeli invitations, and Israeli actions never cease to provide him with them. He has been critical of Israel on numerous occasions. But he has been equally restrained and measured in his reactions. He has tried to avoid receiving Israeli leaders. However, if pressed to do so, he does—as was the case during the visit of Shimon Peres who was then the Israeli prime minister, in September 1986. But Mubarak would not visit with Yitzhak Shamir so long as the Israeli prime minister objected to the holding of an international peace conference. Mubarak never goes out of his way to encourage or discourage the process of normalization. On a few occasions, however, he has responded positively to reasonable Israeli conduct. Thus, when Israel withdrew from most of Lebanon and agreed to accept international arbitration on the contested Taba strip, he returned the Egyptian ambassador to Tel Aviv.

Former Prime Minister Mustafa Khalil is the NDP's vice chairman for foreign relations. He has been an active proponent of Camp David, frequently visits Israel, and is visited by Israeli political figures. However, his daily role in NDP activities has been marginal during Mubarak's presidency. Other prominent NDP members who occasionally visit Israel include Boutros Boutros-Ghali, the minister of state for foreign affairs, and Yusif Wali, the secretary general of the party and deputy prime minister. Such visits are often kept low key in the state-controlled media, which consists of three major dailies (*Al-Ahram, Al-Akhbar, Al-Goumhuriyya*), weekly magazines, radio and television, as well as the NDP's own daily, *Misr*.

In the 1984 and 1987 elections, not a single word was mentioned either for or against Camp David or the treaty in the NDP platform. The party continued, however, to reiterate commitment to the cause of a "just and comprehensive peace which observes the legitimate rights of the Palestinian people."

The NDP managed to score a landslide (two-thirds majority or more of the seats) in the two parliamentary elections held under President Mubarak, as it had done under Sadat. These results have always been contested by the opposition, and charges of election rigging are often loud. The opposition, however, conceded that though the NDP might not have won as large a majority had the election been conducted "fairly," it would still have won a majority because of Mubarak's popularity as president and not because of the NDP. All the opposition parties have repeatedly appealed to Mubarak to leave the chairmanship of the NDP and be above partisan politics altogether, especially as he was elected through a plebiscite and not as a party candidate. But he has not responded to such appeals.

The centrality of the presidency in the Egyptian political system is rooted in the country's economic conditions in which control of the waters of the Nile gives the government immense power. This tradition dates back several millennia. It is thus crucial to examine Mubarak's handling of the issue at hand, Camp David, and the Arab-Israeli conflict in general.

After Sadat's assassination there was a national consensus to support Mubarak and to give him ample time to deal with the regime's crisis. A tacit silence over Israel was in place until it had completed its withdrawal from Sinai in April 1982. Except for a few scattered voices who still argued the merits of Sadat's policy, the active peace constituency had nearly vanished. Most Egyptians, including the organized opposition, felt nevertheless that their country had already paid a high price for Sinai by signing the peace treaty. They might as well wait silently for the only concrete payoff. Egyptians had no desire, and sensed that they had no ability, to return to a war footing with Israel. But there was no more willingness for further concessions or accommodations with Israel.

The 1982 Israeli invasion of Lebanon produced Egyptian sentiments of active hatred and total distrust of the Jewish state. The few scattered voices that had persisted in celebrating the peace treaty had now fallen silent. One prominent intellectual, Tawfik al-Hakim, had, a few years earlier, initiated the debate over the Arabism of Egypt, repudiated Egypt's involvement in the Arab-Israeli conflict, supported the peace treaty, and called for Egypt's neutrality between Arabs and Jews.[9] He shifted his position nearly 180 degrees after the Israeli invasion of Lebanon. In a Cairo daily, al-Hakim published a short play featuring a heart-to-heart dialogue between Israel's Prime Minister Begin and himself. The play was a touching if agonizing piece of soul searching by Egypt's foremost literary figure of the twentieth century. Al-Hakim, whose name literally means "wise man," concludes the play with a line to the effect that he "has been deceived in his search for peace with Israel," and Begin concurs with a smiling nod.[10]

What Tawfik al-Hakim and Anis Mansour expressed was a typical reaction of the most moderate Egyptians. Others who had been in doubt or in outright opposition to Sadat's initiatives were naturally more outraged. In daily television news during the summer of 1982, Egyptians saw for the first time the awesome power of the Israeli Air Force brutally administered against Lebanese and Palestinian civilian and military targets. In their previous rounds of armed conflict with Israel, they had never seen as vivid a portrayal of the savagery and ravages of war as they had during the siege of Beirut. In many ways, the experience was not unlike that of the American public with the televised war in Vietnam, with the important difference that victims in this case were fellow Arabs, Lebanese, and Palestinians. The victimizer was a "former enemy" with whom they had just signed a peace treaty. Anis Mansour's phrase, "We had reconciled with Israel, looking forward to a comprehensive peace. . . . It turned out to be a mistake," was echoed by most Egyptians during the summer and fall of 1982.

Domestic pressure mounted on Mubarak to correct the mistake. Moderate voices called for a freeze of the normalization process, sending the Israeli ambassador home, recalling the Egyptian ambassador from Tel Aviv, stopping the shipping of Sinai oil to Israel, and returning quickly to the Arab fold. The more outraged Egyptians called for the abrogation of the peace treaty and sending Egyptian

9. See Ibrahim, *Egypt's Arabism*.
10. *Akhbar al-Yawm*, September 25, 1982.

volunteers to fight alongside the PLO in Lebanon.[11] The United States was perceived by most Egyptians as a silent partner in the Israeli invasion of Lebanon and the siege of Beirut.

Mubarak's response to the mounting anti-Israeli and anti-American feeling was restrained. The government publicly condemned the Israeli invasion and allowed Egyptian medical and relief supply ships, but not volunteers, to leave Egyptian ports for Beirut during the siege. The government also highlighted its frantic diplomatic activities to contain the Lebanese crisis. By the third week of the Israeli invasion, the Mubarak regime began to express public misgivings about the United States as well. By the sixth week, July 15, 1982, Mubarak called publicly for an Arab summit to coordinate efforts to cope with the crisis. He was willing to go to any Arab capital for such a meeting.[12] In August, as the bombing of Beirut reached an all-time high, Egyptian public opinion became not only angry at Israel and the United States but also resentful of its own government. A mass demonstration, which was to march from Al-Azhar Mosque to the Abdeen Republican Palace after Friday prayer on August 12, was blocked by thousands of armed Central Security forces (Egypt's riot police). To avoid bloodshed, a small delegation led by Ibrahim Shukry and Fathy Radwan, two prominent opposition figures, was allowed to reach the palace and present its demands. The Mubarak regime looked morally isolated for the first time since coming into office.

The day the PLO fighters began to leave Beirut was a moment of profound sadness all over Egypt. The sadness was mixed with an amorphous collective sense of guilt and impotence. A few days later, when the news of the massacre in the Sabra and Shatila Palestinian refugee camps of Beirut broke out, the Egyptian government felt compelled to do something to restore some semblance of self-respect before its own people. It recalled its ambassador in Tel Aviv. Mubarak's decision to receive Yasir Arafat a year later in Cairo was another symbolic gesture aimed at restoring that respect.

The erosion of the faith of the Egyptian public in the peace enterprise with Israel intensified again three years after Sabra and Shatila. This time, October 1985, it was triggered by the Israeli bombing of the PLO headquarters in Tunisia. The Egyptian government could not prevent anti-Israeli demonstrations protesting the

11. For detailed accounts of the news and views of this period, as reflected in the Egyptian media, see Muhsin Awad, *Egypt and Israel: Five Years of Normalization* (in Arabic) (Cairo: Dar al-Mustaqbal al-Arabi, 1984).

12. *Al-Ahram*, July 16, 1982.

air raid. The proximity of the Israeli embassy to Cairo University made it more difficult for the government to preempt demonstrations. In fact, through the fall of 1985, these angry protests and confrontations with the Central Security forces never stopped. For in the three months following the raid, a chain of events was fueling tidal waves of popular anger. The relevant events unfolded as follows: the hijacking by four Palestinians of an Italian cruise ship, the *Achille Lauro,* with American tourists on board; mediation by the Egyptian government to free the hostages; the surrender of the gunmen to Egyptian authorities at Port Said in return for a promise of safe passage to Tunisia; the discovery that an American passenger had been killed and thrown overboard by the hijackers; the interception of the Palestinian gunmen on their way to Tunisia by U.S. Navy F-14 fighters over the Mediterranean, forcing an Egyptair plane to land at a NATO base in Sicily; and the subsequent abduction of the Palestinians by Italian authorities.

Meanwhile, as these events were unfolding at sea and in the sky, an Egyptian border guard stationed in Sinai, Suleiman Khater, opened fire on an Israeli tourist group visiting Egypt, killing seven tourists. His arrest and trial became a cause célèbre. Khater became an instant folk hero for many Egyptians. His action was perceived as a fair revenge for the raid on the PLO in Tunis. Egypt's most prominent lawyers stood in line to passionately defend Khater. When he was sentenced to death by a martial court, a wave of popular protest broke out. When, a few days later, the government announced that Khater had committed suicide in his prison cell, a bigger wave of protest broke out. Many Egyptians cast doubt on the government's version of the death.

The diametrically opposed reactions to these events by Egyptians and other Arabs on one side and by Americans and Israelis on the other side testified once more to the thin veneer of reconciliation that covers an otherwise deep gulf separating the three peoples and their respective leaders. Mubarak's expressed indignation was indeed restrained compared with that of the Egyptian media and public opinion. Both Israeli and American actions during October 1985 were described by an angry media and various demonstrators as terrorism, arrogance, piracy, cowardice, and ingratitude. Demonstrations and opposition papers again called for the abrogation of the Camp David Accords and the peace treaty. But Mubarak resisted the pressures and rode the storm until other ominous troubles at home dominated Egyptians' concern.

For on February 25, 1986, major units of the Central Security forces stationed in Giza across the Nile from Cairo, which had been quelling riots and demonstrations in the previous six months, mutinied against the state. Their mutiny spread quickly to other units in Cairo and upper Egypt. Several thousand looted, burned, and destroyed hotels, stores, cars, and nightclubs in the Pyramid district—Egypt's main tourist district. The mutiny of the Central Security forces was triggered by a rumor that their tour of duty was going to be extended for one year.

To their credit, all of Egypt's opposition parties as well as public opinion at large lined up firmly in support of President Mubarak. Ultimately the army was called in, successfully quelled the mutiny, and restored law and order. This was the first time in recent Egyptian history that an arm of the state, especially one whose sole function is to deal with riots, had challenged the authority of the regime (the last time was the 1952 army coup d'état).

Adverse living conditions, low pay, and unpleasant duties were often cited as underlying causes of the mutiny. Almost daily interaction with anti-Israeli and anti-American demonstrations in the previous four months may also have radicalized the men in the Central Security forces. Suleiman Khater, a folk hero to many, was one of their comrades. This proposition is reinforced by the fact that the mutineers were from units stationed near Cairo University in Giza and had to deal with student demonstrations, including those in support of Khater.

For nearly two years the issue of Egyptian-Israeli relations was pushed to the back of the mind of most Egyptians. The opposition parties continued to invoke it, especially during election campaigns, but with no active popular involvement. It was not until the most recent Palestinian uprising, which began in December 1987, that the issue came to the fore of Egyptian politics again. The fact that the uprising was civilian, large scale, and sustained has rekindled Egyptian popular interest in, and sympathy for, the Palestinians. The fact that Israeli occupation forces used brutal methods in dealing with the uprising has revived active popular dislike and distrust of the Jewish state. Finally, the fact that the uprising came shortly after the Amman summit and Egypt's nearly complete return to the Arab fold added to Egyptians' renewed sense of pan-Arab responsibilities in general and toward the Palestinians in particular. The Egyptian return and the Palestinian uprising coincided with, and overshadowed, the tenth anniversary of Sadat's visit to Israel. These events also nearly coincided with other sad remembrances for the Arabs—the fortieth anniversary of the UN partition resolution and the seventieth anniversary of the Balfour Declaration.

As in the two previous critical situations in Egyptian-Israeli relations, Mubarak echoed popular sentiments in support of the Palestinians and condemnation of Israeli policies. The Egyptian government filed several protests, whose tone was increasingly harsh. As the uprising entered its seventh week with no sign of abating, Mubarak declared a new initiative to deal with the uprising and the Palestinian question in general. He called for a cessation of violence in the occupied territories for six months, during which Israel would stop all settlement activities; respect for the basic rights of Palestinians under occupation; the acceptance of suitable international mechanisms to guarantee the protection of the Palestinian people; and the convening of the international peace conference to work out a comprehensive settlement of the Arab-Israeli conflict.[13] Mubarak indicated that he intended to discuss his initiative with President Ronald Reagan and other West European leaders in his forthcoming visit to their respective countries set for the last week of January 1988.

The opposition parties behaved during this new crisis in much the same manner as in previous ones. They condemned Israel, declared solidarity with the Palestinians, and called for the expulsion of the Israeli ambassador in Cairo and the recall of his Egyptian counterpart in Tel Aviv. They organized a big demonstration from Al-Azhar Mosque after the Friday prayer of January 1, 1988, which was forcefully dispersed by the security forces. Students staged similar demonstrations on several university campuses and clashed with these forces in the streets nearby. The ones at Ain Shams University in Cairo were particularly violent, especially on December 23, 1987. Syndicates of lawyers, doctors, journalists, artists, and trade unionists held peaceful rallies in support of the Palestinian uprising.

One novel element in this wave of popular protestation was the overt leadership assumed by Islamic activists, namely, the Muslim Brotherhood. The government tolerated the peaceful rallies but dealt firmly with street demonstrations, including those staged by Palestinians in the Egyptian-controlled sector of Rafah across the barbed wire from the Israeli-controlled sector. All signs indicated that Mubarak would ride this new storm with his usual restraint.

13. See details in "A New Egyptian Initiative Calls for an End to Violence in the Occupied Territories and a Resumption of the Peace Process" (in Arabic), *Al-Ahram*, January 23, 1988.

OPPOSITION PARTIES AND THEIR POLITICAL STANDS

Beneath the periodic flare-ups of Egyptian public opinion against Camp David is the relentless process of political socialization and mobilization undertaken by opposition parties, major trade unions, professional associations, and other ad hoc groups.

It may be argued that the Israeli raid on the Iraqi nuclear reactor in June 1981, the Israeli invasion of Lebanon and the massacres at Sabra and Shatila in September 1982, the Israeli raid on PLO headquarters in Tunisia in October 1985, and the recent Palestinian uprising are too dramatic to use as evidence in a sober analysis of the Egyptian domestic scene in relation to Camp David. But it is precisely these dramatic moments that reveal the structure behind the feelings and attitudes of most Egyptians. This structure is as much a product of psycho-political conditioning, as it is a response to objective realities and events—both historical and contemporary. To be sure, Egyptian public opinion has been subject to a fierce battle of conditioning and counterconditioning by the ruling regime on the one hand and the opposition on the other hand.

Immediately after the 1973 war, President Sadat and the state-controlled media launched a sustained campaign to rehabilitate the U.S. and later the Israeli images. Between 1974 and 1980, it looked as if the rehabilitation process was succeeding. A large sector of Egypt's public opinion was positively impressed by the U.S. role in negotiating a peaceful settlement of the Middle East conflict and its generous aid of Egypt's development. Two American presidents, Richard M. Nixon and Jimmy Carter, visited Egypt during those six years—something unprecedented since President Franklin D. Roosevelt's visit thirty years earlier. U.S. aid grew steadily over those years.

However, by early 1981, most Egyptians had become disillusioned with the American link and its results. For reasons already mentioned, Israel and its actions disillusioned them even more. This response gave the opposition a growing edge in the battle for Egyptian public opinion.

Before describing the evolution of the public stands of major opposition polities and organized groups in relation to Camp David, I must reiterate a word of caution about their representativeness. Currently, there are six legally recognized parties—the NDP in power and five in the opposition: the Wafd, Socialist Labor, Progressive Unionist, Liberal, and Umma. On an ideological spectrum, the Wafd, the Liberal, and the Umma parties are right of center. They are committed to the private sector, would scale down or liquidate the public sector, and are generally in favor of less state-subsidized food and fewer government services. The Socialist Labor and Progressive Unionist parties are left of center, that is, they favor a more streamlined and better-managed public sector, state subsidy of basic commodities and services, and greater equity in taxation and income distribution than exist under the NDP government. All opposition parties favor greater democratization, amending the constitution, and abolishing the emergency laws in existence since 1981.

On foreign policy, all the opposition parties favor nonalignment between the two superpowers, with a subtle pro-Western tilt among the rightist parties. On regional issues, all opposition parties espouse more vocal pro-Arab and anti-Israeli policies than those generally expressed by the NDP. This is particularly true of the Socialist Labor and Progressive Unionist parties.

Besides the legalized opposition parties, there are two major active political forces that exist and act as parties—the Muslim Brotherhood and the Nasserites, right and left of center, respectively. All of Egypt's legal and de facto parties claim to be representing the entire nation or at least the vast majority of the people. If given the chance in "a truly honest election," each would prove this claim. In fact, none of these parties, including the regime's NDP, has a solid social base, let alone a reliable knowledge of its relative size. The best approximation of whom these parties truly represent can only be indicated by looking at the background of their respective leaders. All opposition parties combined got no more than 30 percent to 35 percent of the votes in the last two parliamentary elections, 1984 and 1987.

Most of the Wafd party leaders and cadres are members or descendants of the 1952 pre-revolutionary upper and upper-middle classes. Several were subjected to the Agrarian Reform Laws of 1952, 1961, and 1968, and the Socialist Laws of 1960–61. Until recent court rulings in 1984, Wafd members were banned from active political life. The party also includes a disproportionate number of professionals, especially lawyers. The Wafd generally appeals to the more liberal minded in the urban areas and to the old landed gentry in rural areas. Its claim that it matches or surpasses the NDP is not without foundation, since it used to be the real majority party during Egypt's first liberal age, 1922–52.

The Liberal party (LP) is similar to the Wafd in most of its public stands but without the Wafd's credibility, seasoned leadership, or wide appeal. While its followers are generally well-to-do, they tend to represent "new money." The Umma (Nation) party is the smallest and least significant in Egyptian politics. It espouses an Islamic orientation but with no credibility—compared with other Islamic activists.

At the left of center, the Socialist Labor party (SLP) draws its leadership and cadres from the middle classes, with a combined commitment to social justice, Arabism, and Islam. Its chief base exists in middle-sized and small urban centers, with a disproportionate number of teachers, middle-level professionals, and civil servants. Further to its left is the Progressive Unionist party (PUP). It claims to represent the working classes and peasants. Most of its leaders and cadres are drawn from the old communist organizations, new Marxists, and a sprinkling of Nasserites. Some of these are indeed workers and peasants. But most are middle and lower-middle class intellectuals and professionals. Some even come from the old Egyptian aristocracy, for example, Muhammad Sid-Ahmed, Nabil al-Hilaly, Sherif Hitata.

The other de facto, though not legal, political forces are the Muslim Brotherhood and the Nasserites. They draw their following from nearly the same social base—the small middle class. They are both committed to social justice. One has a pan-Islamic and religious ideology, while the other, the Nasserites, espouses a pan-Arab and socialist ideology. Their supporters are generally urban based.

The Socialist Labor Party

The Socialist Labor party (SLP) was the major opposition party in Egypt's People's Assembly, that is, parliament, when the Camp David Accords were ratified. In fact, the SLP was established between the signing and the ratification of the accords, a significant fact in itself. As President Sadat felt that the other opposition parties in the assembly were going to vote against the accords, he encouraged a few independent members of the assembly from the pre-revolutionary Young Egypt's Socialist party, led by the highly respected statesman Ibrahim Shukry, to revive their old party under the new name, SLP. The law at the time required that a minimum of twenty assembly members be among the founders before a party became legal. Sadat persuaded several of his own National Democratic party (NDP) members to switch to the newly proposed SLP, including his brother-in-law Mahmoud Abu Wafia, to fulfill the required minimum. Thus the new "opposition" party was born in President Sadat's lap, a few weeks before the ratification of the accords.

Naturally this tailor-made opposition was obliged to go along with the "mid-wife," as Egyptians would joke. However the SLP went along only part of the way. It voted for the Camp David Accords and the Egyptian-Israeli peace treaty, but with major reservations. First the SLP objected to any normalization of relations with Israel, including exchange of ambassadors, while any part of Egyptian territory was still under Israeli occupation. Second, the SLP made its final approval of the accords and treaty contingent on an Israeli withdrawal from other Arab territories, including Arab East Jerusalem. In other words the SLP implicitly made its approval provisional or conditional.[14]

This cautious stand by the SLP was a perfect compromise. On the one hand, it tried to satisfy President Sadat, who exerted maximum pressure on the party leaders directly and indirectly (through his brother-in-law who was then the deputy chairman of the SLP). On the other hand, the SLP tried to be true to the patriotic past of its other leaders and cadres who harbored serious doubts about the true intentions of Israel and the United States. In the assembly's ratification session, the SLP chairman, Ibrahim Shukry, voiced the division in the party: "We held many meetings, discussed the Treaty and the condition which our country is going through. The majority of our members in the Assembly approve of the Treaty. There is a minority which has reservations. I, therefore, declare the SLP approval of the Treaty." He added, however, that "since the matter is of paramount national importance, the SLP had absolved its members from strict party discipline, leaving it up to each to vote as his conscience dictates."[15]

The SLP, in less than two years, gradually shifted its position. By February 1981, the party congress officially declared the nullification of its earlier approval of the accords and the treaty.[16] In a lengthy document, the SLP gave its reasons for doing so. It listed what the party considered "serious Israeli violations of the letter and spirit of the Treaty." Among these were Israeli intransigence, delaying tactics, and the narrow definition of Palestinian autonomy. The SLP also criticized Israel's continued denial of the rights of Palestinians to self-determination, building of settlements in the occupied Arab territories during the "transitional period" in which

14. See Ibrahim Shukry's speech in *People's Assembly Records* (in Arabic), 2d legislative season, meeting 3, session 61, April 10, 1979, pp. 209–13.

15. See ibid. for both quotations.

16. See a detailed account of the debate in the Socialist Labor party (SLP) weekly, *Al-Shaab,* "No to the Camp David Agreements since Israel Refuses to Implement Them" (in Arabic), March 3, 1981.

there was to be a freeze on building Israeli settlements, annexation of Arab Jerusalem, harassment of Palestinians and violations of their human rights, and encroachment and aggression toward Lebanon.

The SLP's nullification of the treaty in 1981 came as no surprise to observers of the Egyptian scene, for they had noted the party's reservations in 1979. Subsequently, the SLP increased attacks on Israel and escalated criticism of the government in 1980. Nevertheless, such a change in its official stand outraged Sadat. He opened fire on the SLP, reminding it that if it was not for him the SLP would not have seen the light of day. Sadat's brother-in-law resigned from the SLP and was replaced by a prominent figure, Muhammad Hilmi Murad, who had just joined the party. The following months, February-September 1981, witnessed the most vehement attacks by the SLP not only on the accords and treaty but also on Sadat's other domestic and foreign policies. Murad spearheaded those attacks. Especially painful to the president was Murad's exposure of rampant corruption in the country, with implicit accusations of Sadat's close associates, including his wife. It was little wonder, therefore, that when Sadat cracked down on the opposition in September 1981, he singled out Murad from the SLP's top leadership and another regular columnist, Fathy Radwan, to throw in jail.[17]

The SLP did not stop at the repudiation of Camp David and the treaty. It started an active campaign against all its ramifications. On the first anniversary of the exchange of ambassadors between Egypt and Israel, February 26, 1981, the SLP raised the Palestinian flag on its headquarters. Two months later, Shukry led a party delegation to the Palestine National Council in Damascus in April 1981 and declared his full backing of the Arab Rejectionist Front. During the siege of Beirut, the SLP raised funds, collected blood, and urged its youngsters to volunteer in support of the PLO.[18] The SLP renewed its call for the abrogation of the treaty and escalated its attacks on the United States for its continued support of Israel and its collusion in the invasion of Lebanon. It is noteworthy, however, that unlike the year before when Sadat was in power, the SLP spared President Mubarak from its biting attacks.

By the time of the parliamentary elections of 1984, the SLP did not demand the abrogation of Camp David and the treaty, simply

17. See, for example, H. Murad's and F. Radwan's weekly articles in *Al-Shaab*, June 2, 9, 16, and 23, 1981, and especially F. Radwan's article on June 23, entitled "Reagan Destroys the Nuclear Reactor" (in Arabic).

18. See an account of these appeals in various issues of *Al-Shaab*, June–August 1982.

their "freezing." This is quite moderate by Arab and Egyptian standards. It implicitly recognized Israel, and whatever rebuke this posture contained was because of Israel's "unstately manners."[19] This moderate tone is in contrast with the SLP's harsher stand on Israel during the 1980–82 period. Part of this moderation is because of the party's overall attitude toward President Mubarak, which was markedly more positive than that exhibited toward Sadat in his last two years in office. There has also been an attempt to spare Mubarak unnecessary embarrassment. In the 1987 parliamentary election the SLP did not have a detailed or separate platform. It joined in a coalition with the Muslim Brotherhood and the Liberal party (LP) under the name of the Islamic Alliance.

The Islamic Alliance platform contained a ten-point program, with two points having a bearing on the peace with Israel. The first stated that "Egyptian security requires Arab integration, support of the Palestinian struggle, and cooperation with the Islamic countries in all spheres. This definitely calls for the freezing of Camp David in preparation for its abrogation." The second point in the program simply stated that "nonalignment with respect to both East and West is an imperative for Islamic renaissance. Zionism is our most dangerous enemy. We refuse any special relations with the United States economically or militarily."[20]

Since the Muslim Brotherhood is not a legalized political party in its own right and has no newspaper of its own, the SLP newspaper, *Al-Shaab,* has opened its pages to the leaders and writers of the Muslim Brotherhood. The latter have continued to echo the SLP's anti-Israeli and anti-American statements, except that theirs are more couched in Islamic religious terms.[21]

The Islamic Alliance was even more vocal and assertive in response to the recent Palestinian uprising. It took the lead in organizing the mass demonstrations from Al-Azhar Mosque on January 1, 1988. Ibrahim Shukry, the SLP chairman, demanded "immediate severing of diplomatic relations and stopping all normalization with Israel."[22] Mustafa Mashour, the Muslim Brotherhood leader, declared in the same mass rally the brotherhood's continued "rejection of Camp David and the treaty, its insistence that there is no choice but to liberate Palestine through military

19. See the full text of the SLP platform in a special supplement of *Al-Siyasa al-Duwaliyya,* no. 77 (July 1984), pp. 95–96.

20. See the program of the Islamic Alliance in *Al-Shaab,* March 24, 1987.

21. See, for example, the regular weekly columns by Hamed Abu Nasr, Mustafa Mashour, and Muhammad Abd al-Quddus in *Al-Shaab,* starting March 17, 1987.

22. See details in *Al-Shaab,* January 5, 1988.

struggle (jihad), and its demand that Arab governments open their borders for the 'mujahideen' from other countries to fight alongside their Palestinian brothers.'"[23] The same rally had speakers from other opposition parties who echoed similar, though less extreme, sentiments.

The New Wafd Party

Like the SLP, the New Wafd party (NWP) has its roots in pre-1952 revolutionary Egypt. It was born during the 1919 revolution against British occupation and was the mass party that dominated the Egyptian political landscape between 1920 and 1952. Its orientation and programs at the time revolved around Egypt's independence from the British and the defense of the 1923 constitution that the monarch and the British frequently violated. The Wafd party, along with all others, was liquidated by a law banning political parties in 1953. When a multiparty system was reinstated by Sadat in 1976, some of the surviving leaders, namely Fouad Serageddin of the old Wafd, attempted to revive it. In 1978 the New Wafd was declared with the tacit approval of Sadat but not with his help. The relative ease of reestablishing the party, together with other signs of rapidly growing support, and the appeal of Serageddin (despite having been out of the political limelight for more than twenty-five years) seem to have shaken Sadat. A hurriedly prepared law (Law 33 of 1978) was passed by the assembly to ban pre-1952 figures who had "corrupted political life" from participating in politics.[24] Law 33 was blatantly tailormade to obstruct the Wafd party generally and specifically to remove Serageddin from the arena. The party's political bureau, in light of this, met and announced the dissolution of the New Wafd.

Five years later, in 1983, with Sadat gone, the Wafd revived its bid for legality and contested Law 33 in court against the government's objection. Egypt's Supreme Constitutional Court ruled in favor of the Wafd in February 1984, only three months before a new parliamentary election. Despite this late start, the Wafd, in a curious

23. Ibid.

24. Hassan Nafaa, *Egypt and the Arab-Israeli Conflict: From an Inevitable Struggle to an Impossible Settlement* (in Arabic) (Beirut: Center for Arab Unity Studies, 1984), p. 99.

alliance with the Muslim Brotherhood,[25] entered the 1984 election, obtained some 58 seats (out of 448), and emerged as the second largest bloc (next to the government's NDP). Hence the Wafd became the major opposition party in the following three years.

In its first reentry into public life in 1978, the Wafd had not taken a stand on Camp David. It had dissolved itself before the accords and the treaty came up for ratification in the assembly.[26] Thus, unlike the SLP, it did not have the stigma of having approved and then denounced these agreements. However, the Wafd took a very judicious approach to the accords and the treaty. In its 1984 platform, the party stated general principles of foreign policy, then devoted five out of ten headings to various aspects of the Middle East conflict.[27]

Under a general heading, "Permanent and Just Peace," the Wafd stated that such a peace "cannot be brought about in a vacuum, nor as a result of an imposed imbalance of power. . . . The Arab-Israeli conflict has been imposed on the area and it is continuing because of Israel's reliance on force to realize its expansionist policies. . . . Egypt and the Arab world must confront this reality through a counter deterrent military power . . . based on legality and justice."[28] The NWP's platform then addressed Camp David under a second heading. It stated,

> Israel has violated the Camp David Accords in letter and in spirit by its aggression on the Iraqi nuclear reactor, its invasion of Lebanon, the occupation of Lebanese territory, the killing of Arab citizens in Lebanon and the West Bank, the expansion in the building of Israeli settlements in the occupied Palestinian territories, the expulsion of Palestinian residents from their rightful land . . . and its annexation of Arab Jerusalem and the

25. The Wafd party has acquired the reputation of being the most secular of all pre-1952 Egyptian political parties and has had a disproportionate number of Christian Copts at both the leadership and rank-and-file levels. Its alliance with the Muslim Brotherhood in 1984 was a significant turning point in what was seen by some observers as the party's new pragmatism and by others as opportunism.

26. Some of the New Wafd party (NWP) assembly members did speak and vote against the treaty, including H. Murad, the deputy chairman of the NWP until June 5, 1978, when the party dissolved itself. See his speech in *People's Assembly Records* (in Arabic), 2d legislative season, meeting 3, session 61, April 10, 1979, pp. 219–24. Later on H. Murad joined the Socialist Labor party (SLP) and became its deputy chairman.

27. See the full text of the NWP platform in *Al-Siyasa al-Duwaliyya*, no. 77 (July 1984), pp. 92–93.

28. Ibid., p. 92.

> Syrian Golan Heights . . . in defiance of all Security Council, General Assembly, and UN resolutions. Therefore the NWP considers the Camp David Agreement null from its foundation and of no binding consequence.[29]

On the Egyptian-Israeli treaty, the NWP was careful enough not to call for nullification but continued to denounce Israel for violating the spirit of the treaty. The NWP absolved Egypt from observing it.[30]

The Wafd offered its interpretation of the supremacy of Egypt's competing contractual obligations as part of various international agreements. It made clear that the treaty with Israel does not supersede Egypt's rights and obligations toward the Arab League and the Arab Defense Pact. The latter, especially, rests on Article 51 of the UN Charter, which gives member states the right of unilateral and collective self-defense. Article 51 takes precedence over any obligation in any other treaty that may be contrary to it.[31] The Wafd also called for modification of the treaty to restore full Egyptian sovereignty over all of Sinai and to end the presence of the multinational force stationed there.

The NWP devoted a special section of its 1984 platform to the Palestinian question, that is, separate from Camp David and the treaty. There it states general principles about the Palestinians' "inalienable right of self-determination" and about the "sacred obligation to liberate Jerusalem as a collective Arab responsibility."[32] The party reiterated what all other Egyptian parties maintain regarding the PLO as "the sole legitimate representative of the Palestinian people" and gave the PLO full support.

As the leader of the opposition in Egypt's People's Assembly, from 1984 to 1987, the NWP was supportive of governmental policies and measures to pressure Israel and the United States about Taba, Lebanon, and the convening of an international peace conference. Its deputy chairman, Wahid Raafat, a well-known international lawyer, was chosen by Mubarak to advise the Egyptian side on the Taba legal arbitration that started in 1986. So, for all practical purposes, the NWP, like the SLP, implicitly recognized Israel but continued to be critical of its conduct. Unlike the SLP, however,

29. Ibid., p. 92.
30. Ibid., p. 92.
31. Ibid., p. 92.
32. Ibid., p. 93.

the NWP is not as critical and is often more supportive of Mubarak's foreign policies, including that toward Israel.

The NWP newspaper, *Al-Wafd,* reflected this orientation in editorials and news analysis in subsequent years. In the 1987 election the party did not issue a new platform. Instead it reprinted relevant sections of its 1984 one. The party also made a point of highlighting Yasir Arafat's visits to its headquarters whenever he came to Egypt during the last four years. The party sent a large delegation to the 1987 PNC meeting in Algiers.

The NWP did not do well in the 1987 parliamentary election, winning thirty- six seats compared with fifty-eight in 1984. It came in third place and thus lost the opposition leadership to the Islamic Alliance. As indicated earlier, the Muslim Brotherhood had dissolved its coalition with the NWP before the 1987 election and joined the SLP.

The Progressive Unionist Party (PUP)

The Progressive Unionist party (PUP) is the most leftist of the existing legal parties of Egypt. Its leadership and membership are mostly composed of well-known Egyptian Marxists, with some Nasserites and other socialists. The PUP chairman is Khalid Mohieddin, one of the leaders of the 1952 revolution, who disagreed with Nasser as early as 1954 and resigned from the Revolutionary Command Council. He has not assumed any executive office. His public image is one of integrity and idealism.

The PUP has been the clearest and most consistent of all Egyptian parties on the issue of Camp David. Its socialist ideology accounts for much of this clarity and consistency. It viewed Sadat's "peace initiative" in the context of his socioeconomic choices and class alliances at home and his global alliances abroad. For the PUP, Sadat's adoption of the open door policy meant an alliance with the sprouting new bourgeoisie at home and the U.S.-led international capitalist system abroad. It was therefore natural for Sadat to consolidate these choices by pushing for "peace with Israel at any price." For the PUP the totality of Sadat's policies after the October 1973 war amounted to a counter-revolution, that is, "de-Nasserization" of Egypt, which the party steadfastly opposed.[33]

The PUP has been vehement and loud in its opposition to Sadat's visit to Israel, Camp David, and the Egyptian-Israeli treaty. More than any other opposition newspaper, the PUP newspaper *Al-Ahali*

33. See a penetrating analysis of the PUP's position in Nafaa, *Egypt and the Arab-Israeli Conflict,* pp. 97–99.

(circulation of about 100,000) spearheaded those frontal attacks. More frequently than any other newspaper in Sadat's time, *Al-Ahali* was confiscated, its offices raided by state security forces, and its editors arrested.

The last assembly in which PUP members served was that whose term ended in 1979, immediately after the ratification of the treaty. Sadat and his successors have made sure ever since that the PUP stays out of the People's Assembly. In the ratification sessions of the assembly, Khalid Mohieddin, the party leader, made an eloquent speech rejecting the Egyptian-Israeli treaty. He said the treaty undermined Egyptian sovereignty because it only allowed for a conditional Israeli withdrawal from Sinai. It also undermined Egypt's Arab commitments and leadership role. Mohieddin also said that the treaty transcended normal codes of international relations by requiring the establishment of "complete normal relations between Egypt and Israel." Finally, Mohieddin criticized the treaty for being a bilateral and not a comprehensive agreement.[34]

Since then, the PUP has added other reasons for objecting to Camp David and the treaty. Egypt's leadership role in the Islamic world and the Non-Aligned Movement would also decline. This result would make Egypt more vulnerable to American and Israeli pressures in the future.[35]

In the years following Camp David, the PUP has taken the lead in resisting normalization. It has formed various bipartisan and popular committees for that purpose. The Committee for the Defense of National Culture is one noteworthy group. Its objective is to alert intellectuals to Israeli attempts to penetrate the "Egyptian mind," culture, and mass media. In the few times that Israel was allowed by Egyptian authorities to participate in the Cairo book fair, the committee staged demonstrations and sit-ins blocking the Israeli wing, thus provoking violent confrontations with Egyptian security forces. It also discourages Egyptian and other Arab publishers from participating in such fairs whenever Israel is allowed. The Egyptian Ministry of Culture finally gave in to the committee's pressure and was forced to come up with a new formula for Israeli participation in the Cairo Book Fair after 1983.[36]

34. See the full text of Khalid Mohieddin's speech in *People's Assembly Records* (in Arabic), 2d legislative season, meeting 3, session 60, April 9, 1979, pp. 195–201.

35. Nafaa, *Egypt and the Arab-Israeli Conflict*, p. 99.

36. See a detailed account of the activities of the Committee for the Defense of National Culture in Hazem Hashim, *The Israeli Conspiracy against the Egyptian Mind—Secrets and Documents* (in Arabic) (Cairo: Dar al-Mustaqbal al-Arabi, 1986), pp. 269–88.

In its 1984 and 1987 election platforms, the PUP echoed the same objections to Camp David. All of the party's foreign policy statements revolved around this issue. The preface to that section in the platform divides recent Egyptian foreign policy into two phases—before and after Camp David. To the PUP,

> Egypt had remained, until Nasser's departure, a shining model of liberation and national independence. . . . But in the seventies, under Sadat's rule, Egypt was made vulnerable to a fierce imperialist attack led by the United States of America in a quest to impose its sovereignty on Egypt and to complete its control over the Arab homeland. . . . Camp David was a turning point in the history of the area. It led to a detrimental strategic imbalance. . . . It isolated Egypt officially from the Arab-Israeli battlefield.[37]

The PUP platform states priorities in foreign policy as follows: putting an end to Camp David in a series of escalating steps; terminating normalization of relations with Israel; and removing the restrictions imposed by Camp David and the treaty on national sovereignty, including the shameful restriction that forbids the formation of new Egyptian political parties opposed to Camp David and the treaty. The PUP platform also favors correcting the present strategic imbalance by strengthening the Egyptian armed forces and restoring normal relations with the Soviet Union, committing Egypt to Palestinian rights of self-determination, and resisting any attempt by any other Arab country to enter into a Camp David-like unilateral agreement.[38]

The PUP did not win a single assembly seat in either the 1984 or 1987 elections, partly because of the way the government structured the electoral system and partly because of the alleged intervention of the government—the NDP—a complaint shared by

37. See the full text of the PUP platform in *Al-Siyasa al-Duwaliyya,* no. 77 (July 1984), pp. 94–95.

38. Ibid., p. 94. The restriction on political parties refers to a law passed under President Anwar Sadat after a referendum in 1979, which prohibits "the licensing of new political parties whose founders are known to have publicly opposed the Egyptian-Israeli Treaty." See *Sawt al-Arab,* November 8, 1987. On these grounds, the Nasserists' application to form their own party was turned down by the government in 1983. The case is still pending in Egypt's Supreme Constitutional Court.

opposition parties and occasionally validated by the courts.[39] But it is also true that the PUP is a small minority party. Its extreme positions, combined with the stigma of "atheist Marxism," limit its appeal. The PUP's chief role in Egyptian political life has been its ability to set up national debates on important issues. Its disproportionate number of high-caliber intellectuals and scholars enables the PUP to perform this role effectively.

The most recent debate in which the PUP has engaged is whether or not the Egyptian left should enter into a dialogue with its Israeli counterpart. The pros and cons are hotly debated—with Nasserite leftists adamantly opposed, and some Marxists just as adamantly in favor. The Marxists have made it clear that they would talk with Israeli leftists who are publicly committed to the Palestinians' right of self-determination and are opposed to the Israeli occupation of Arab territories. Egyptian Marxists do not believe that such a dialogue is part of the normalization called for at Camp David. They further argue that the PLO and Yasir Arafat have engaged in similar dialogues, the most recent ones in Moscow and Budapest in October 1987. Opponents counterargue that there is no "real Israeli left." A true leftist would not have come to, or stayed in, Israel; and if Egyptian leftists talked to Israeli leftists, how could the Egyptian leftists then morally condemn Egyptian centrists and rightists for doing the same with their Israeli counterparts? And if all forces of the ideological spectrum on both sides engaged in such dialogues, would that not be total "normalization"?[40] This kind of debate would have been unthinkable ten years ago, that is, before Camp David.

The Islamic Movements

Like the PUP, the politicized Islamic movements, epitomized by the Muslim Brotherhood, have consistently and adamantly opposed Camp David and the entire process initiated by President Sadat.

39. Shortly before the 1984 election the government passed a new law changing the electoral system to one of proportional representation. However, for a party to win any district seat in the assembly, it must first win a minimum of 8 percent of total national votes cast in the election. Thus, theoretically, a party list may win as much as 90 percent of the vote in a given district but would not get any assembly seats because the party does not have the 8 percent needed nationwide. In fact this was the case with the PUP, SLP, and Liberal party (LP) in the 1984 election—in which only the government's NDP and the NWP made it. In the 1987 election, the PUP did not obtain the 8 percent nationwide.

40. For details of this debate, see Abd al-Halim Kandel, "We and the Dialogue with the Israeli Left" (in Arabic), *Al-Mawqif al-Arabi*, November 1987, pp. 29–61.

Politicized groups, subsumed under the term "Islamic movements," are to be clearly distinguished from "establishment Islam" and Sufi Islamic groups (*tarikas*). Although all three types of Islam have substantially grown in the last two decades, only the politicized groups have taken a clear stand on Camp David as they have on other public issues of Egyptian life.[41] After all, members of one of these groups shot President Sadat on October 6, 1981, because of fierce opposition to his policies, including those toward Israel.

Establishment Islam, embodied in Al-Azhar and the Ministry of Religious Endowments, is for all practical purposes, merely an arm of the Egyptian government. It is often willing to issue religious pronouncements (*fatwas*) to justify governmental policies. On issues such as Sadat's visit to Israel, Camp David, and the treaty, such a *fatwa* was readily issued. "If your enemy opted for peace so must you" is the Quranic verse on which the *fatwa* was based. Sufi Islam is apolitical and retreatist in nature, and Sufi groups are often silent on public issues.

But politicized Islamic movements are socially involved, activist, and disposed to pursue their objectives in militant ways.[42] Their ultimate aim is to establish an Islamic social order, that is, a pious, just, prosperous, and strong society, modeled after the "Islamic Umma" under the Prophet Muhammad and the four rightly guided caliphs of the seventh century in Medina. The main group in the movement is the Muslim Brotherhood, which clashed with Nasser in the 1950s and was then suppressed and marginalized in Egyptian life for nearly two decades. Curiously enough, President Sadat released its leaders from prison and allowed them a measure of freedom unprecedented since their heyday in the 1940s. Sadat's motives were not all unselfish. He thought that the Muslim Brotherhood would help him in countering his Nasserite and leftist detractors. In the first four years of Sadat's presidency the Muslim Brotherhood and other Islamic groups kept their side of the bargain.

As Sadat's new orientation began to crystallize in 1974, the Islamic groups began to part ways with him. Three of these groups entered into bloody confrontations with the regime—the Technical Military Academy Group (April 1974), Repentance and Holy Flight

41. For mapping these types of Islamic groups, see Saad Eddin Ibrahim, "An Islamic Alternative in Egypt: The Muslim Brotherhood and Sadat," *Arab Studies Quarterly*, vol. 4 (Spring 1982), pp. 75–93.

42. For case studies of these groups, see Saad Eddin Ibrahim, "Anatomy of Egypt's Militant Islamic Groups: Methodological Note and Preliminary Findings," *International Journal of Middle East Studies*, vol. 12 (December 1980), pp. 423–53.

(*Al-Takfir wa al-Hijra,* July 1977),[43] and *Al-Jihad* (September-October 1981).[44] Although it did not resort to violence, starting in 1974, the Muslim Brotherhood vehemently opposed Sadat's policies in general and his peace initiatives toward Israel in particular.

The antagonism of the Muslim Brotherhood toward Israel long predates Sadat's reconciliation policies with the Jewish state. The Muslim Brotherhood was the first organized political group in Egypt to draw attention to the "creeping dangers of Zionist designs in Palestine" in the 1930s. It was also the first Egyptian organization to send volunteers and military assistance to the Palestinian resistance in the 1940s, long before Arab armies were dispatched in May 1948 to fight the newly created state of Israel.

Fighting Israel was not one of the many issues of contention between the Muslim Brotherhood and Nasser. The Muslim Brotherhood was critical, however, of his mismanagement of the fight. An elaboration of the Islamic group's stand on Israel and Sadat's peace initiatives can be found primarily in their periodicals, *Al-Dawa* (the Call), and *Al-Itisam* (Steadfastness) in the four years following Sadat's visit to Jerusalem. Sadat banned the publications in 1981, shortly before his assassination.

To the Muslim Brotherhood, Israel is one of the three archenemies of Islam, the other two being the never-ending crusade of the West (*al-salibiyya al-gharbiyya*) and communism. In most of its literature, the Muslim Brotherhood alleges that the Jews are behind both Western imperialism and international communism. There is, they argue, a tacit alliance among all three to usurp or weaken the homeland of Islam (*dar al-Islam*).[45] A content analysis of *Al-Dawa* and *Al-Itisam* between 1977 and 1981 shows the persistence of this line. In no single issue of both periodicals would the reader fail to encounter two or three articles about the Jewish danger or the atrocities of Israel.

Understandably, therefore, President Sadat's peace initiative came under bitter attack from the Muslim Brotherhood right from the

43. Ibid.

44. Members of *Al-Jihad* assassinated President Sadat on October 6, 1981. For details see Nemat Genena, *The Jihad: An Islamic Alternative in Egypt,* Cairo Papers in Social Science, vol. 9, monograph 2 (Cairo: American University in Cairo Press, 1986).

45. See Muhammad Rishad Khalil, "To Avoid Turning the Islamic World into Another Andalus," *Al-Dawa,* October 1976, pp. 14–15; and Muhammad Shams al-Din al-Shinawi, "The Real Reasons Behind Liquidating the Muslim Brotherhood," ibid., pp. 5, 57. In "Real Reasons," the author contends that the 1948 and 1954 liquidations were based on orders of the West and Israel to lackey Egyptian governments. The third liquidation, which occurred in 1965, was based on orders from Moscow.

start. It is safe to say that the Muslim Brotherhood was the only credible political force in Egypt that dared to take him on, at least in the first year following his trip to Jerusalem. This frontal attack emboldened other opposition groups to come out gradually against Sadat's policy of reconciliation with Israel.[46]

The Muslim Brotherhood arguments revolve around the impossibility of peaceful coexistence with the Jewish state. It is an aggressor on *dar al-Islam*. Israel is directly or indirectly behind the major calamities befalling Muslims everywhere, especially in Palestine. It has desecrated Muslim shrines in the Holy Land. As an evil, it must be eradicated. These assertions were echoed in nearly every issue of *Al-Dawa* and *Al-Itisam*.

The Muslim Brotherhood often prefaced its attack with the assertion that it is speaking for Islam and that it fears no one but God. The following is a typical example. Under the heading, "Treaties Based on Usurpation Are Illegitimate," *Al-Itisam* said,

> Whatever Islam does not allow we must reject and struggle to eradicate. We fear no one but God. Prisons and hanging do not frighten us. Dying for the sake of God is our dearest aspiration. From this vantage point we consider the shameful peace produced at Camp David and the Treaty with the enemy of God, the Prophet, the believers, humanity and justice to be an illusion. We believe from the depths of our hearts that it is a false peace. The Zionist existence on the land of Muslim Palestine at the expense of the Palestinian people is totally illegitimate. . . . As the treaty [with Israel] is false, so are all its consequences. . . . It is a disguised Jewish invasion of Egyptian society which hitherto was the fortress of Islam. Egypt has been the last line of defense against the three enemies of Islam: Western crusaders, Communists, and Jewish Zionists.[47]

What alternative does the Muslim Brotherhood provide to Sadat's policy toward Israel? In a four-article series, *Al-Dawa* concludes that war is the way to liberate Palestine.[48] After a detailed analysis of the Arab-Israeli conflict and more than three years of Sadat's

46. The leftist Progressive Unionist party (PUP) has been equally vehement in attacking Sadat's peace initiative. But the regime easily dismissed the PUP as being a communist group following Moscow's orders.
47. *Al-Itisam*, April–May 1981, pp. 28–29.
48. *Al-Dawa*, February through May 1981.

quest for a "just peace," *Al-Dawa* reminds its readers that the whole exercise is futile as it had predicted all along. It says,

> War is the authentic means stipulated by God in his Holy Book for those whose rights, honor or wealth have been encroached upon by an aggressor. . . . Muslims do not seek fighting if they can protect or restore their rights through other means. If the aggressor ceased his aggression and "opted for peace, then [Muslims should] opt for peace and reliance on God." Thus, when we assert that war is the authentic means for liberating Palestine, it is because for more than half a century Israel and its western supporters have neither ceased their aggression nor showed any real inclination for peace. . . . The Arabs have tried to get the West to help them restore their rights but to no avail. If anything, the West has persistently supported Israel with money and weapons and thus encouraged further aggression and expansion. There is no way out for the Arabs in this predicament except through fighting.[49]

The Muslim Brotherhood outlined the necessary measures for the war preparations. They include strengthening the internal front through the institution of justice and eradication of social and moral ills; the formation of a broad Arab-Islamic front with plans for serious contribution to the battle with volunteers, arms, money, and diplomatic pressure; severing ties with, and terminating the interests of, those who support Israel with money, arms, and diplomacy; sustained military, economic, and spiritual mobilization of Arab material and human resources for a protracted war until victory.[50]

Finally, the Muslim Brotherhood has vehemently criticized Sadat's global alliance with the West. Initially, Sadat's break with the Soviets was warmly endorsed. But as he began tilting toward the West, the brunt of the Muslim Brotherhood's attack shifted from communism and the Soviet Union to the West and the United States.

In his September 1981 crackdown on the opposition, Sadat spared one or two top leaders of each party, for example, Khalid Mohieddin of the PUP and Ibrahim Shukry of the SLP. However, Sadat spared no one in the Muslim Brotherhood. The top leadership, including

49. Fathy Radwan, "War Is the Solution, It Is the Way to Liberate Palestine" (in Arabic), *Al-Dawa,* May 1981, pp. 62–64.
50. Ibid., p. 62.

the seventy-year-old Supreme Guide of the Muslim Brotherhood, Omar al-Telmissany, was thrown in jail. Of the more than 1,500 arrested and detained September 3–5, 1981, about two-thirds were from Islamic groups. The main periodicals, *Al Dawa, Al-Itisam,* and *Al-Mukhtar al-Islami* (Islamic Digest), were banned by Sadat.

Shortly after Sadat's assassination, the Muslim Brotherhood leaders, and other opposition figures, were released from jail. The more militant members of other Islamic groups who had been implicated in the 1981 violence were tried and received varying sentences, including the death penalty for the five who were accused of assassinating President Sadat. With President Mubarak, there was a four-year lull in militant and overt Islamic activities. But this came to an end in mid-1985, when one Islamic group led by Sheikh Hafez Salama attempted to stage a march in the streets of Cairo demanding an immediate application of Islamic law (*sharia*). Following that incident, a series of violent acts by militant Islamic groups directed at public figures, video shops, and taverns has occurred.[51]

While all other opposition newspapers have been allowed to resume publication under the Mubarak regime, those of the Muslim Brotherhood have not. Technically, the Muslim Brotherhood is not a legalized political party. Therefore it is not entitled to issue its own newspaper. Nevertheless, the Muslim Brotherhood has managed to keep its voice heard through other opposition newspapers, including the leftist *Al-Ahali,* that have granted the Muslim Brotherhood leaders ample space.

When the Muslim Brotherhood decided to run candidates in the 1984 elections on the Wafd lists, its newspaper regularly granted them space to express their views. The same thing happened in the 1987 election, this time with the Socialist Labor and the Liberal parties' newspapers *Al-Shaab* and *Al-Ahrar,* respectively. Hamed Abu Nasr, the new Supreme Guide of the Muslim Brotherhood (following Omar al-Telmissany who died in 1986) and Mustafa Mashour (a ranking Muslim Brotherhood member) have written regular weekly columns in *Al-Shaab* since early 1987. Both leaders continue to express the same views and sentiments as those described earlier on Camp David, Israel, and the United States.

51. These included firing on and wounding General Hassan Abu Basha (a former minister of the interior), Makram Muhammad Ahmed (editor-in-chief of the weekly *Al-Musawwar*), and General Nabawi Ismael (a former minister of the interior). The two ministers were accused by Islamic groups of having ordered the detention and torture of fellow members between 1981 and 1984. Ahmed had been especially outspoken in criticizing Islamic militants.

However, one senses less passion in these writings compared with those of ten years ago. This moderate tone may be attributed to the overall cooling of political discourse under Mubarak—compared with the atmosphere of his two predecessors, Nasser and Sadat. The Muslim Brotherhood has also opted to play politics as usual. Its candidates have entered parliamentary elections and hence must appear "moderate" and "respectable." But during the recent Palestinian uprising, Muslim Brotherhood leaders resumed their extremist stand on Israel and called for jihad.

The Nasserites

Like the PUP and the Muslim Brotherhood, Nasserites have consistently opposed Sadat's policies in general and those toward Israel and the United States in particular.[52] Until 1985 Nasserites had no legally recognized party or newspaper. They used to express their political stands through other opposition parties and newspapers—especially the PUP's and SLP's. However, after declaring their intention to form a party and filing applications in 1983, they were entitled to limited public activities under the law.[53] One of their prominent figures, Muhammad Fayek, established a publishing house, Dar al-Mustaqbal al-Arabi. Its publications have gained instant popularity, as they combine high scholarly quality and clear ideological commitment to the spirit and principles of the 1952 revolution. In its four years, Fayek's outlet published more than 150 titles, and several are in their second or third editions. A disproportionate number are devoted to the Arab-Israeli conflict, national security, and Camp David. The first documentary-analytical book ever written on the impact of Camp David and the treaty was published by Dar al-Mustaqbal al-Arabi in 1984, Muhsin Awad's *Egypt and Israel: Five Years of Normalization.*[54]

Another Nasserite figure, Abdul Azim Munaf, managed to obtain a license for a weekly newspaper, *Sawt al-Arab* (*Voice of the Arabs*). Since its appearance, *Sawt al-Arab* has sustained a relentless attack

52. The few members of the assembly who called themselves Nasserites opposed the Camp David Accords and the treaty and were among the 15 members who voted against it—compared with 329 who voted for and 1 who abstained. The member who spoke on behalf of the Nasserites was Ahmed Hussain Nasser. His views were similar to those of the PUP, mentioned earlier. See *People's Assembly Records* (in Arabic), 2d legislative season, meeting 3, session 60, April 9, 1979, pp. 202–03.

53. These include public meetings but with prior notification of the police, issuing limited-circulation newsletters, and placing ads in the media in their names.

54. Another book directly related to post-Camp David Egyptian-Israeli relations, also published by Dar al-Mustaqbal al-Arabi, is Hashim, *Israeli Conspiracy.*

on Camp David and the normalization process. At least one full page of every twelve-page issue is devoted to one aspect or another of the Arab-Israeli conflict. It regularly monitors the normalization process and Israeli activities in Egypt. Thus, in its November 1, 1987, issue, the reader learns that 15,533 Israelis came to Egypt in October 1987, compared with 4,515 in September and 3,435 in August of the same year. The number of Egyptians visiting Israel was 714 in October, 870 in September, and 1,000 in August. *Sawt al-Arab* never fails to point out that most Egyptians traveling to Israel are of Palestinian descent and are visiting their relatives in the occupied territories, especially during the summer months. The message conveyed is clear—"The mass of Egyptians refuses normalization." Other titles of the same issue of *Sawt al-Arab* include "No to Zionist Films" and "The Star of David Burns at Ain Shams University."[55] In successive issues, *Sawt al-Arab* launched a campaign against Egyptian leftists who had entertained a dialogue with Israeli counterparts, a debate then raging among PUP members and Nasserites, as mentioned earlier.[56]

Although there has been a slight lull or a moderation of tone among other opposition parties on Camp David in the last two years, the opposite has occurred among the Nasserites. Part of this sustained vehemence occurs because Arabism figures more prominently in Nasserism than in any other ideology now current in Egypt's political discourse. However, Nasserites do not yet have their own legal political party. Once they do and hence have to play politics as usual and run for election, they may moderate their tone, which other opposition parties already have done.

The Liberal Party

The last opposition party to change its public stand on Camp David and the treaty was the Liberal party (LP). It was one of the earliest parties to be established after President Sadat reinstated the multiparty system in Egypt in 1976. The founder and leader of the Liberal party is Mustafa Murad, a former Free Officer who participated in the 1952 revolution. He later left the army and went into

55. The reference is respectively to an Israeli-produced film (*On Top*), being shown in one of Cairo's downtown theaters at the time, and to the second anniversary of the clashes between university students and Central Security forces on the occasion of the trial of Suleiman Khater. Khater is the soldier who shot the Israeli tourists in Sinai two years earlier in the aftermath of the Israeli air raid on the PLO headquarters in Tunisia.

56. See *Sawt al-Arab*, November 1 and 8, 1987.

business. The Liberal party espouses liberal ideas in politics and economics and is an ardent supporter of the private sector. Since its establishment, the Liberal party has remained one of the smallest minority parties. Its weight in Egyptian political and intellectual life is minimal.

Like the SLP, the Liberal party initially supported President Sadat's peace initiatives. As early as November 16, 1977, that is, shortly after Sadat's speech in the assembly declaring his willingness to go to Israel for the sake of peace, the Liberal party declared "its support for the courageous political move of President Anwar Sadat which puts Israel in a critical position and exposes its intentions."[57] The Liberal party chairman was the only opposition figure who agreed to accompany President Sadat on his historic visit to Israel in November 1977. The party stuck to its position until 1986, though it did not fail to condemn Israeli actions and violations of Camp David and the treaty. Beginning in mid-1981, the time of the raid on the Iraqi nuclear reactor, the Liberal party took a harsher line toward Israel, as did other parties. Its criticism became even more vehement after the 1982 Israeli invasion of Lebanon.

In 1986 several Islamic public figures, especially Sheikh Salah Abu-Ismael who had voted in the assembly against Camp David and the treaty in 1979, joined the Liberal party. Under their influence, and partly because of its growing insignificance, the LP declared, in April 1986, its "rejection of Camp David and the Egyptian-Israeli Peace Treaty."[58] In the press conference that followed, the LP chairman, Mustafa Murad, gave a long list of reasons, not dissimilar to those given by the SLP, for changing the party's position of seven years earlier. With the LP's withdrawal of support, all legalized opposition parties are now publicly against Camp David.

Other Domestic Forces

Other than partisan forces, one finds professional associations and trade unions that have been equally vocal on Camp David and the treaty. Lawyers, journalists, syndicates of medical professionals and artists, the writers' unions, clubs of university professors, and the Federation of Trade Unions have been the most active. All of

57. "The Liberal Party Supports Sadat's Courageous Act" (in Arabic), *Al-Ahram*, November 17, 1977.

58. "Wide-Ranging Reactions to the Decisions of the Liberal [Party] to Withdraw Its Support for Camp David" (in Arabic), *Al-Ahrar*, April 14, 1986.

these organizations have boycotted the normalization process with their Israeli counterparts.[59]

The lawyers' syndicate has had the highest profile in resisting normalization. On the day in February 1980 that the first Israeli ambassador was to arrive in Cairo, the syndicate organized a mass rally, burned an Israeli flag, and raised the Palestinian flag permanently on its headquarters in the center of Cairo. Sadat was especially disturbed by the syndicate's continuous challenge to his policies in general and to his peace initiatives in particular. Shortly after the flag incident, the government hurriedly passed a new law dissolving the syndicate's board and reorganizing the legal profession in such a way as to ensure government control over it. The dissolved board challenged the new law as unconstitutional, engaged the government in protracted court litigation, and finally won the case. With that victory, the lawyers' syndicate has become even more aggressive in challenging governmental policies on Israel. Hardly a month passes without some anti-Israeli or pro-Palestinian activity in the syndicate's headquarters, often in cooperation with other syndicates and associations. The journalists' syndicate, which is physically adjacent, has been particularly active.

During the first months of the recent Palestinian uprising in the occupied territories, which began in December 1987, these syndicates and professional associations held several solidarity rallies. Again, demands were expressed to sever diplomatic relations and freeze all other normalization processes with Israel. Members of these syndicates and associations who are partisans usually echo the stands of their respective parties.

CONCLUSION

President Sadat's daring initiatives of more than ten years ago may not have produced all the intended results. But his quest for a historic compromise and peace with Israel triggered processes, some of which seem to have had lasting effects, while others may be limited in their impact or even reversible.

Neither government seems intent on tampering with concrete gains such as Israeli withdrawal from Sinai, recognition and full diplomatic relations, and binding agreements. These actions have

59. Detailed documentation and analyses of the positions and activities of these associations as they relate to Camp David, the treaty, and normalization are to be found in Muhsen Awad, *Egypt and Israel*, pp. 220–34; and Hashim, *Israeli Conspiracy*, pp. 269–93.

withstood several severe tests during the last decade. The passionate negation of Israel or its right to exist has vanished from Egyptian political discourse. Even the political forces most ardent in their hostility toward Israel and Camp David no longer use such language. Egyptians have grown accustomed to accepting Israel as a neighboring state. Most Egyptians may be disenchanted, disillusioned, or outraged at Israeli behavior. Some organized political forces have continuously called for the abrogation of Camp David and the treaty, and several have called for the severing of relations and an end to normalization. But none has reiterated the pre-1977 language of existential negation. None has suggested a declaration of war or a return to the state of war with the Jewish state. Camp David "normalized the feelings" of most Egyptians toward Israel across the spectrum—hate, anger, disapproval, acceptance, accommodation, and even disposition for cooperation—but no negation.

To a lesser extent, Camp David accomplished something similar on the pan-Arab level. The 1982 Fez summit and subsequent Arab summits have shown a willingness for de facto recognition of Israel and a disposition toward peaceful coexistence with Israel. The idea of an Arab leader meeting with an Israeli counterpart may still dismay many Arabs but no longer shocks anyone. Eleven years ago Sadat stunned the Arab world with his visit to Israel. Nine years later when King Hassan II of Morocco invited Israel's Shimon Peres to visit his country, many Arabs were dismayed but few were shocked. No emergency summit was held to penalize him (such as the Baghdad summit of November 1978, which called for a break in Arab relations with Sadat and the suspension of Egypt's membership in the Arab League should Egypt sign a peace treaty with Israel).

Mubarak has successfully, if slowly, inched his way back into the Arab fold. He is doing so without succumbing to the standard Arab precondition of discarding Camp David. Even before the Arab summit in Amman in November 1987, Egypt had full diplomatic ties with the PLO and with five out of twenty-one Arab countries. The Amman summit resolved, "after a detailed and brotherly discussion, that diplomatic relations between any member of the Arab League and Egypt is an act of sovereignty to be decided by each state in accordance with its constitution and laws; and is not within the jurisdiction of the Arab League."[60] This historic resolu-

60. "INA Carries Summit Resolutions," Baghdad INA, November 12, 1987, in Foreign Broadcast Information Service, *Daily Report: Near East and South Asia*, November 13, 1987, pp. 23–25.

tion, while falling short of restoring Egypt's membership in the Arab League, was hailed as a great victory both for Mubarak's Egypt and the skillful diplomacy of Jordan's King Hussein who convened and presided over the Amman summit. Almost instantly, nine Arab states restored full diplomatic relations with Egypt—the United Arab Emirates, Kuwait, Iraq, Bahrain, Qatar, the Arab Republic of Yemen, Saudi Arabia, Morocco, and Mauritania. Tunisia and South Yemen followed suit several weeks later. At this writing only four Arab countries, Libya, Syria, Lebanon, and Algeria, have not done so. The gains at the Amman summit consolidated an earlier one on the Islamic front. Egypt's membership in the Organization of the Islamic Conference was restored in 1984, and Mubarak attended its summit in Kuwait in January 1987.

This relative success results partly from Mubarak's style, which is perceived by most of the Arab world as reasonable and rational. But success also comes from the recent trend of regional events. The growing power of Israel, the preoccupation with the Gulf war, the mounting Iranian threat to Kuwait and other Gulf countries, and the relative decline of the financial power of the oil-producing Arab countries are circumstances that have caused other Arabs to gain a new appreciation of Egypt's regional role.

Mubarak and his aides have recently dramatized, in word and deed, Egypt's commitments to Arab national security in general and to that of the Arab Gulf countries in particular. On October 12, 1987, in the inaugural speech of his second presidency, Mubarak made his strongest bid ever to this effect. Field Marshal Abu Ghazalah, in a series of statements in the ten days preceding the Amman Arab summit, reiterated the same commitment. In December 1987 Abu Ghazalah made an important visit to Kuwait. A month later Mubarak made a highly publicized tour of all six countries of the Gulf Cooperation Council. In February 1988 he visited Morocco and received a warm official and popular reception, which Egyptians saw live on television.

Egyptian opposition parties seem heartened by these aspects of Mubarak's policy at present. It is, of course, difficult to know the exact public assessment of Mubarak's performance on the Arab-Israeli issue. But it is safe to say that his Arab policy is generally well received by most Egyptians.

Ten years after Camp David, most Egyptians, and probably most Arabs, have grown accustomed to it. For the Egyptians the past fifteen years have been the longest stretch of time without a war with Israel since 1948. This does not displease them. The spirit of Camp David and the promise of peace would have been more widespread and deeper had it not been for Israeli provocations. The phrase once used by Boutros-Ghali describing the current Egyptian-Israeli relationship as a cold peace is accurate. It could equally be described as a cold war. Or, more accurately, it oscillates between the two. There are, however, no ominous signs that this state of affairs may dissolve into an open conflict in the foreseeable future.

A treaty may succeed in containing the Arab-Israeli conflict for a long time to come (it has in chronic regional disputes elsewhere in the world, for example, Korea, Cyprus, and Germany). But if greater peace, stability, and prosperity are to prevail in the Middle East, Mubarak's moderation, more than Camp David and the treaty, will be required. The success of his Arab policy, and hence Egypt's gradual reintegration into the Arab fold despite Camp David, leaves Mubarak with more regional options than Egypt has had since 1977. He can lead the Arab world into a comprehensive settlement with Israel. He can, equally, lead the Arab world into a new round of conflict and escalation with the Jewish state. Much will depend on Israeli and U.S. behavior, the course of the recent Palestinian uprising, and the willingness of the richer Arab countries to bail Egypt out of its economic difficulties.

ABDEL MONEM SAID ALY

Egypt: A Decade after Camp David

FROM AN EGYPTIAN historical perspective, ten years fills less time than the blink of an eye. Yet ten years after the Camp David Accords and the subsequent signing of the Egyptian-Israeli peace treaty, historians are coming to terms with the importance of these events in the modern history of Egypt. Only a decade after Camp David, Egypt has changed considerably, though elements of continuity with the past remain. To understand the reality of continuity and change, one has to ask, how was Egypt's future perceived ten years ago?

Not too long after Camp David, Malcolm H. Kerr speculated about Egypt in the 1980s.[1] He offered three scenarios. First, he envisaged the continuation of the Sadat regime "under President Sadat himself or under a constitutional successor." In such a scenario, Sadat's peace with Israel and his policy of *infitah* or open door, which calls for the participation of private domestic and foreign investment in the national economy, would reach its zenith, leading to growth and prosperity. Kerr, however, predicted that this scenario was not likely to survive until the year 2000 because of the increasing gap between the rich and the poor and the alienation that generally accompanies Westernization.[2]

In the second scenario, Sadat was replaced by a Nasserist regime. A leader—either one of the Nasserist old guard or a new leader—would invoke the Nasserist legacy, accuse Sadat of betrayal of the Palestinian cause, criticize his policy of *infitah,* and condemn him for breaking with the Arab fold and changing alliances from the

1. Malcolm H. Kerr, "Egypt and the Arabs in the Future: Some Scenarios," in Malcolm H. Kerr and El Sayed Yassin, eds., *Rich and Poor States in the Middle East: Egypt and the New Arab Order* (Boulder, Colo.: Westview Press, 1982), pp. 449–72.

2. Ibid., pp. 451–57.

Soviet Union to the United States. Central economic planning would be reinstated, the public sector would regain supremacy in the national economy, and foreign trade and currency exchange would be controlled. Income distribution would be emphasized while growth in the gross national product (GNP) would be deemphasized. Although the new regime might try to be cautious and implement its policies slowly to deal with the external as well as the internal constraints on the system, it "would eventually accumulate the same errors of inefficiency and wastefulness" of the old Nasserist regime.[3]

In the third scenario Kerr sees Sadat replaced by a Muslim fundamentalist regime similar to the one in Iran. In a Khomeinist Egypt, austerity, self-reliance, rural development, and egalitarianism would be imposed under the leadership of a devoted and authoritarian Islamic party. In Kerr's opinion, Egypt would resemble Maoist China with "Islam rather than Marxism-Leninism suppl[ying] the ideological symbols." Yet this regime would most likely lead to a confrontation with Israel, Saudi Arabia, and the United States. The most likely ally would be Muammar Qadhafi's Libya.[4]

A look at Egypt in 1988 shows that none of these scenarios accurately describes reality. Sadat was assassinated even before Kerr's speculations appeared in print. Mubarak's regime is neither a Nasserist regime nor an Islamic one. A deeper look at the present regime, however, shows that the three scenarios are coexisting.

Sadat's National Democratic party (NDP) is the ruling party with a large majority in the People's Assembly that it has achieved in two elections (1984 and 1987) since the death of Sadat. *Infitah* is still the official economic policy of the state. The government persistently calls for domestic and foreign private investment. President Husni Mubarak has consolidated the pluralization and democratization of the Egyptian political system that started under Sadat. Peace with Israel, the hallmark of Sadat's era, has continued despite the challenges to it presented by the 1981 bombing of the Iraqi nuclear reactor, the 1982 Israeli invasion of Lebanon, the 1985 bombing of the headquarters of the Palestine Liberation Organization (PLO) in Tunisia, the 1987–88 Palestinian uprising, and a host of differences on the autonomy talks, the Middle East peace process, and the territorial dispute over Taba.

Egypt's "alliance" with the United States, initiated by Sadat following the October 1973 war, has survived serious differences

3. Ibid., pp. 457–61.
4. Ibid., pp. 461–63.

over Israel, the settlement of the Arab-Israeli conflict, disagreements over aid to Egypt, Egypt's growing indebtedness to the United States, the *Achille Lauro* incident, and the subsequent "skyjacking" of an Egyptian civilian plane. Furthermore, Egypt, during the past decade, has become one of the largest recipients of American aid and assistance, second only to Israel on the American list of priorities. The process started in 1974 when President Richard M. Nixon appropriated $250 million in economic aid to Egypt. In 1979, as a result of the signing of the Egyptian-Israeli peace treaty, American aid to Egypt reached $1 billion. By 1984 aid had reached $2.3 billion a year, which remained the level of American aid through 1988.[5]

The conditions of American aid have improved substantially. In 1975, 78.7 percent of American aid was in the form of loans and 21.3 percent in grants. By 1983 the ratio of loans to grants had been reversed. Loans were now 21.2 percent, and grants were 78.8 percent of aid. By 1985 grants constituted all American aid to Egypt. Perhaps of greater importance is the fact that American aid to Egypt since 1979 has included military assistance. Initial military aid levels of approximately $300 million reached $1.3 billion by 1983. Military aid has continued at that level since 1983, and since 1985, it has been entirely on a grant basis.[6]

While levels of military aid remain at approximately the same level, military cooperation between the two countries has increased over time. Egypt has granted the United States the right to use its military facilities in times of crisis in the Middle East. During the American-Iranian hostage crisis, for example, Egyptian facilities were used in President Jimmy Carter's aborted rescue mission in the spring of 1980. In 1987 the two countries worked closely in strengthening the defenses of the small Gulf countries against Iranian threats. Egypt and the United States conducted military maneuvers under the code names Bright Star and Sea Wind on several occasions during the mid-1980s. By 1988 Egypt and the United States had negotiated and signed an agreement under which Washington granted Cairo a non-NATO ally status, elevating the relationship between the two countries to a new level of closeness. Egyptian-American relations have remained very special indeed.

If Sadat's legacy is still alive and well, the Nasserist legacy also remains resilient and vibrant. The Egyptian army as the prime mover behind Nasser's July 1952 revolution continues to be the

5. U.S. Embassy, Cairo, Office of Programs and Planning.
6. Ibid.

final arbiter in Egyptian politics. When 17,000 troops of the Central Security forces mutinied and rioted on February 25, 1986, the government called on the army, with the approval and support of the opposition parties, to restore law and order.[7] The president's constitutional powers, part of Nasser's legacy, are still in place as they were during the times of Nasser and Sadat. In the words of Tarek al-Bishry, a prominent Egyptian judge and intellectual, the powers invested in the president by the constitution are similar to those given to the caliphs and the Shiite imams.[8] The public sector, which was dominant in Nasser's times, continues to be the backbone of the economy. The state is still the largest employer and enjoys a monopoly on information through the government-controlled broadcasting and television networks. In addition, Mubarak reinstated economic planning with the introduction of two Five-Year Plans, 1982–87 and 1987–92.

In foreign policy, Egypt has not departed from the Nasserist position on the necessity of Israeli withdrawal from all Arab territories occupied by Israel since 1967. Mubarak, through patience and persistence, has succeeded in revalidating Egypt's Arab credentials. In November 1987 the Amman Arab summit endorsed the resumption of diplomatic relations with Egypt, thus reversing the Baghdad summit resolution in 1978 that had called for the breaking of diplomatic relations, the implementation of economic sanctions, and the isolation of Egypt in international forums. By early 1988, fourteen of twenty-one Arab League members had restored diplomatic relations with Egypt. Egypt's isolation and ostracism had ended. Furthermore, Mubarak had embarked on improving relations with the Soviet Union. Not only was the Egyptian ambassador returned to Moscow, but political, economic, trade, and cultural relations were improved greatly as well.

Not least in importance, Nasser's reputation has been resurrected in the Egyptian body politic. He is once again hailed as the leader of the 1952 revolution, his death has been commemorated, and his pictures are being displayed along with those of other Egyptian heroes. Furthermore, the NDP, which was established by Sadat, found that it was prudent election strategy to demonstrate allegiance to Nasser and his principles. The NDP has also tried to persuade,

7. Ann M. Lesch, "Mutiny in Cairo," *Middle East Report* (*MERIP*), vol. 16 (March-April, 1986), pp. 43–44 (hereafter *MERIP*).

8. Tarek al-Bishry, *Democracy and Nasserism* (in Arabic) (Cairo: Dar al-Thaqafa al-Jadida, 1975), p. 24.

with limited success, some of the Nasserist figures to join the party. Nasserist groups, however, have joined the Socialist Labor party (SLP) and the Progressive Unionist party (PUP). Other Nasserists are grouped into two parties: the Alliance of the People's Working Forces party and the Nasserist Arab Socialist party. Both parties have begun the legal process that, when completed, will allow them to compete in elections.

Islamic fundamentalism is just as visible in Egypt today as Sadatism or Nasserism. Defined as social, economic, and political forces that seek to establish an Islamic polity in Egypt, Islamic fundamentalism is pervasive. Egyptians in general are observing more Islamic traditions than at any other time in Egypt's recent history. The Egyptian constitution names Islamic law (*sharia*) as the major source for legislation. Most political parties, in government and in the opposition, claim that they accept the principle of applying the *sharia*. In the 1984 parliamentary elections the Muslim Brotherhood—the most important, and mainstream, Egyptian fundamentalist group—gained eight seats in Parliament.[9] By the time of the 1987 elections, it had become the largest opposition group in the People's Assembly with forty seats. Although the group is not one of Egypt's legal parties, it has enjoyed some success by joining coalitions first with the New Wafd party (NWP) in 1984, and later with the SLP and the Liberal party (LP), and by running independent candidates in 1987.[10] Throughout the past decade, Egypt has witnessed the rapid growth of an "Islamic economy" with total assets of between $4 billion and $6 billion. Islamic corporations are created on the basis of Islamic codes of conduct. Islamic banks have become the largest recipient of Egyptian savings.[11]

Thus Egypt today is more complex than any of Kerr's scenarios. It has all the elements of liberalism embodied by Sadat, Arab nationalism embodied by Nasser, and Islam. This phenomenon is not new in modern Egyptian history, which dates, according to most scholars of the subject, from 1798, the year of the invasion of Egypt by the army of Napoleon. During their brief stay in the country, the French contributed not only some of their revolutionary

9. See Abd al-Monein Said Aly and Manfred W. Wenner, "Modern Islamic Reform Movements: The Muslim Brotherhood in Contemporary Egypt," *Middle East Journal*, vol. 36 (Summer 1982), pp. 336–61.

10. See Abdel Monem Said Aly, "Democratization in Egypt," *American-Arab Affairs*, no. 22 (Fall 1987), p. 20.

11. See Louise Lief, "Egypt's Islamic Challenge," September 1987, pp. 6–8; and Martin French, "Clobbered by Cairo Irregulars," *Euromoney*, June 1987, pp. 81–87.

liberal ideals, but also gave one of the few important "gifts" of the West to Egyptian society: the printing press (in Arabic) and the consequent opportunity for the widespread dissemination of Arabic works on both Islamic subjects and Western thought and history. It may well be argued that this development contributed the most to the eventual renaissance of Arabism, as well as Islam, as political ideologies. Since educational establishments could accept and educate a greater number of students than ever before, more and more of them became concerned with issues that had either been nonexistent or ignored up to this point. Arab nationalism, Islam, and liberalism were among these issues, and these three trends came to dominate the political debate in Egypt for years to come.

In 1803 Muhammad Ali was the first ruler of Egypt who came to power on the basis of semipopular consent. He, in turn, was instrumental in accelerating modernization with distinctly Egyptian characteristics. Muhammad Ali's modernization efforts were based on the technique of creating new structures and institutions without destroying the older ones. So rather than confronting "head on" the two major influences on traditional society, that is, the norms prescribed by the *sharia* and the religious establishment that administered this code (Al-Azhar), Muhammad Ali elected to establish secular schools and begin a separate, secular legal and administrative framework that could accommodate the reforms he sought.[12] This technique was successful enough to become widely employed by most of Egypt's rulers since, including Nasser, Sadat, and Mubarak.

One hundred and eighty-five years after Muhammad Ali, Egypt continued to embrace all three trends—liberalism, nationalism, and Islam—as the basic ingredients of political life. One trend has never succeeded in completely excluding the other two. During the liberal era, 1922–52, Egypt led the way for the creation of the Arab League and was in the forefront of the Arab attempt to prevent the creation of Israel in 1948. In the same period, in 1928 the Muslim Brotherhood (*al-Ikhwan al-Muslimun*) came into existence for the purpose of

12. For more discussion of Egypt's nineteenth-century modernization, see Said Aly, "Democratization in Egypt," p. 12; Kenneth Cragg, "The Modernist Movement in Egypt," in Richard N. Frye, ed., *Islam and the West,* Proceedings of the Harvard Summer School Conference on the Middle East, July 25–27, 1955 (The Hague: Mouton and Co., 1957), pp. 149–64; Christina P. Harris, *Nationalism and Revolution in Egypt* (The Hague: Mouton and Co., 1954); Zaheer Mas`ud Quraishi, "Heritage of Egyptian Nationalism, 1798–1914," *Islamic Culture,* vol. 40 (April 1966), pp. 57–77; and Nadav Safran, *Egypt in Search of Political Community: An Analysis of the Intellectual and Political Evolution of Egypt, 1804–1952,* Harvard Middle Eastern Studies 5 (Harvard University Press, 1961).

transforming Islamic intellectual ideas into political action.[13] Nasser led the largest modernization and secularization drive in Egyptian history. He put Al-Azhar and *awqaf* (religious endowments) under the control of the state, and, in 1955, he announced the abolition of all communal judicial systems and the transfer of their jurisdiction to the national courts.[14] At the same time Nasser spoke often of "Islamic socialism." In 1954 he wrote in *The Philosophy of the Revolution* that the "Islamic circle" (in addition to the Arab and African circles) was a main focus of Egypt's foreign policy.[15]

Sadat was no less ambivalent than his predecessors. He signed a treaty of unity with Libya and Syria in 1971, despite the opposition of his presumably Nasserist colleagues led by Ali Sabri. Sadat led the largest Arab coalition to fight Israel in 1973 and died while attempting to achieve a complete Israeli withdrawal from the occupied Arab territories. At the same time, he declared Egypt a state of "science and faith," released the Muslim Brotherhood from jail, and amended the Egyptian constitution in 1979 to make the *sharia* the chief source of legislation.

Even the Muslim Brotherhood has borrowed from the ideas of liberalism and nationalism. The Muslim Brotherhood believed in the importance of Arab nationalism, even though its understanding of the term Arabism was quite different from the secular concept of pan-Arabism. The Muslim Brotherhood considered Arab unification an essential prerequisite for the revival of Islam, since the Prophet Muhammad said, "Arabs are the first Muslims: if the Arabs are humiliated, so is Islam." The Muslim Brotherhood found it easy to accept the unity of faith and language represented by the term "the Arab world" and believed that a liberation of all Muslim lands, especially Arab lands, had to precede a truly Islamic renaissance. In serving the cause of Arabism, the Muslim Brotherhood was "serving Islam and the welfare of the entire world."[16] Recently, the Muslim Brotherhood has also pronounced its adherence to the democratic process in Egypt.

In sum, since the time of Muhammad Ali none of the three chief

13. The literature on the Muslim Brotherhood is extensive. See Ishak Musa Husaini, *The Moslem Brethren: The Greatest of Modern Islamic Movements* (Beirut: Khayat's College Book Cooperative, 1956); and Richard P. Mitchell, *The Society of the Muslim Brothers* (Oxford University Press, 1969).

14. See Donald N. Wilber, *United Arab Republic—Egypt* (New Haven: Human Relations Area Files, 1969); and Daniel Crecelius, "Al-Azhar in the Revolution," *Middle East Journal*, vol. 20 (Winter 1966), pp. 31–49.

15. Gamal Abdel Nasser, *The Philosophy of the Revolution* (Buffalo, N.Y.: Smith, Keynes, and Marshall, 1959).

16. Mitchell, *Society*, p. 267.

political trends, liberalism, Arabism, and Islam, has dominated Egypt to the exclusion of the others. Rather, at any given moment, there has been a blend and an equilibrium among them. None of the three trends has been pure or has completely broken with the others. Throughout its recent history, Egypt has not been led by an Ataturk, a Khomeini, or a Qadhafi.

Egyptian political life is indeed dialectical. Scholars cannot look at it as successive stages or as regimes replacing one another. Rather, historians should see Egypt in light of the important trends that are always interacting. The relative strength and power of the trends constantly change, but the main elements remain the same. In each historical period one must observe the relative power of each trend, the ever-new synthesis among trends, and the new problems and dilemmas that grow out of each new complex equilibrium.

With that perspective in mind, this chapter analyzes Egyptian politics from 1978 to 1988. To identify the changes that Egypt witnessed in the past ten years, one must understand how Egypt, as a polity, has perceived itself and its direction. In essence, Egypt under Sadat's leadership perceived itself as capable of achieving security, economic, and developmental goals without the help or the endorsement of the other Arab countries. Peace with Israel, alliance with the West, particularly the United States, *infitah,* and a degree of pluralism were the four pillars of Sadat's politics. Egyptianism, or *al-wataniyya al-misriyya,* was the ideological cover. However, these views did not last long. During the decade since Sadat's trip to Jerusalem, a steady transformation in Egyptian politics took four interrelated forms: reidentification, relegitimization, restructuring, and reorientation.

REIDENTIFICATION

As soon as Sadat returned from Jerusalem on November 21, 1977, a great debate arose in Egyptian intellectual circles.[17] The debate was launched by Tawfik al-Hakim who in 1973 had created a storm with the publication of his short book, *The Return of Consciousness,* in which he questioned the Nasserist legacy. At the end of the 1970s, al-Hakim extended his earlier work to question the Arab identity of Egypt. He was soon followed by other prominent Egyptian intellectuals such as Hussain Fawzi, Lewis Awad, Anis Mansour,

17. For a full account of the arguments presented in this debate, see Saad Eddin Ibrahim, ed., *Egypt's Arabism: The Dialogue of the Seventies* (in Arabic) (Cairo: Al-Ahram Center for Political and Strategic Studies, 1978).

Nagib Mahfouz, Mustafa Amin, and others.[18] They varied in their analyses and points of departure, but they agreed on the following themes: Egypt has an older civilization than the Arab one. Its civilization is part of the Mediterranean culture, hence, it is more attached to the Greco-Roman traditions than the Arab-Islamic values. In short, Egypt is part of European and Western civilization. The Arabs are still nomadic barbarians who cannot understand that peace with Israel is an expression of the civilized conduct of world politics on the one hand, and a meeting between two great, ancient civilizations on the other. Egypt, therefore, should conclude peace with Israel and be neutral, like Switzerland, in world politics in general and in Arab-Israeli politics in particular. Egypt should reduce defense spending and its army, pursue its aims in foreign policy peacefully, and concentrate on economic and social development as all civilized people do.

These ideas were not new to the Egyptian intelligentsia. They can be traced back to Khedeve Ismail's vision of Egypt as a part of Europe in the 1860s. In fact they were the resurrection of Egyptian liberalism pioneered by Taha Hussain, Salama Musa, and others who stressed Egypt's identification with the Mediterranean civilization. The time, circumstances, and the resurrection itself were new, coming long after it was thought that the Arab and Islamic ideologues had carried the day once and for all. These ideas had the blessings of Sadat, his party, and the government propaganda machinery. They had the full support of the state.

However, Egypt was not short of Arab nationalists who attacked these ideas. Intellectuals such as Sayed Yassin, Saad Eddin Ibrahim, the "Tagammu" brigade of Nasserists and Marxists, and some of the Islamists such as Aisha Abdul Rahman used all the arguments of Arabism: the common culture, language, and values; the economic advantages of large international units; and the Israeli threat to Egyptian national security with or without the Arabs.

This intense debate seriously affected the Egyptian public. Its results were evident in roughly two periods. In the first period, from 1977 until mid-1982, Egypt's rejection of identification with the Arab world triumphed. In the second period, from mid-1982 until the present, an emphasis on the commonality of Egypt's interest with the Arab world prevailed. During the first period, Egypt witnessed, for the first time in its history, anti-Arab and anti-Palestinian demonstrations after the events in Cyprus in February

18. Ibid.

1978.[19] Egyptians, both privately and publicly, denounced the Arabs who had become rich while Egypt lost 100,000 men on the Arab-Israeli battlefield and spent $40 billion in the war with Israel. The Arabs were harshly criticized for their opulent lifestyle and investments in Europe and the United States. The Syrians and the Palestinians, it was argued, were not interested in a solution to the Arab-Israeli conflict because they got richer with the continuation of the conflict, while, of course, the Egyptians became poorer. The Egyptian media echoed these sentiments. The Arabs were portrayed as divided, incapable of action, vicious, irresponsible, corrupt, and ungrateful partners who wanted to humiliate Egypt.[20]

To be sure, many of these themes simply echoed what Sadat had been saying. However, the available public surveys seem to indicate a great change in Egyptian attitudes toward Arabism and the Arab-Israeli conflict. In early 1977, Saad Eddin Ibrahim conducted a survey of Arab attitudes toward Arab unity in ten Arab countries. In his Egyptian sample he found 72.6 percent wanted to have a single federated Arab state.[21]

By 1978, after Sadat's trip to Jerusalem, however, it seemed that the trend had reversed. In a survey conducted by Raymond A. Hinnebusch in late 1977 and early 1978, only 34.4 percent considered Egypt part of the Arab nation, while 53.9 percent considered Egypt the land of the Pharaohs and the oldest nation in the world.[22] Abd al-Monem al-Mashat found in March 1982 that only 44 percent of the sample identified themselves as Arabs.[23]

Between 1974 and 1978 Egyptian support for the strategy of the Palestine Liberation Organization dropped from 55 percent to 18

19. The events started when a group of Palestinians hijacked an Egyptian plane on its way to Larnaka, Cyprus. On February 19 Egyptian troops stormed the Larnaka airport and fought with the hijackers. Fifteen Egyptians were killed and others were wounded. Among those killed was Yussuf al-Sibai, Egypt's minister of culture and a noted writer.

20. For an analysis of the Egyptian press, see Abdul-Monem al-Mashat, "The Egyptian-Israeli Settlement," *Journal of Arab Affairs*, vol. 5 (January 1986), pp. 81–110; and Karem Yehia, "The Image of the Palestinians in Egypt, 1982–85," *Journal of Palestine Studies*, vol. 16 (Winter 1987), pp. 45–63.

21. Saad Eddin Ibrahim, *Trends of Arab Public Opinion toward the Question of Unity* (in Arabic) (Beirut: Center for Arab Unity Studies, 1980). See Saad Eddin Ibrahim, "Domestic Developments in Egypt," in this volume.

22. Raymond A. Hinnebusch, "Children of the Elite: Political Attitudes of the Westernized Bourgeoisie in Contemporary Egypt," *Middle East Journal*, vol. 36 (Autumn 1982), p. 543.

23. Abdul-Monem al-Mashat, "Egyptian Attitudes toward the Peace Process: Views of An 'Alert Elite'," *Middle East Journal*, vol. 37 (Summer 1983), p. 402.

percent. By 1978, 77 percent of Egyptians supported President Sadat.[24]

Ali Layla's survey of Egyptians working in the Gulf showed a prevailing negative attitude toward Palestinians. Of these Egyptians, 49 percent believed that the Palestinians were the source of hostile feelings toward them, while only 19.1 percent believed the Syrians were hostile, and 12.5 percent felt the Iraqis were hostile. Salwa al-Amri's survey of Egyptian perceptions of thirteen national groups showed that Palestinians ranked tenth in terms of how much affinity the Egyptians felt toward them, followed only by Libyans, Russians, and Israelis.[25] The results of these surveys should be viewed with caution and their comparability questioned. However, they are the only available indicators of Egyptian perceptions. They all show that Egypt was witnessing, if not a complete reversal of attitudes, at least a severe identity crisis as a result of Sadat's break with the Arab world.

This identity crisis, however, was not to last long. The Israeli invasion of Lebanon in June 1982 was a watershed in the process of Egyptian reidentification with the Arab world and Arab issues. Previously, Israeli actions such as the invasion of Lebanon in 1978 and the attack on the Iraqi nuclear reactor in 1981 had frustrated some Egyptians. However, they continued to hope for the best. Some in the media even hinted at Arab intransigence. The invasion of 1982 was different. As the events unfolded that led to the lonely stand of the PLO in Beirut, Egyptians began to feel guilt and shame. Suddenly all the claims of Tawfik al-Hakim and others disappeared from the Egyptian media. Many even reversed their positions.[26]

Egyptian demonstrations in this period were different. They were not anti-Arab or anti-Palestinian, but anti-Israeli and anti-American. The Israeli invasion of Lebanon and the Sabra and Shatila massacres fueled anger and resentment among the Egyptian youth. Moreover, the invasion put the comprehensiveness of the peace process—an aspect stressed by the Egyptian government—into question. The

24. Ibrahim, *Trends of Arab Public Opinion,* p. 308.

25. In Ali Layla's survey about 80 percent of the Egyptians perceived hostility from other nationalities as noted above; the remaining 20 percent did not perceive hostility from any other nationality in numbers significant enough to be cited. See Ali Layla, "Emigration and the Question of Arab Unity: A Study on Egyptian Emigration Trends to the Oil Countries" (in Arabic), *Al-Siyasa al-Duwaliyya,* no. 73 (July 1983), p. 81; and Salwa al-Amri, "Opinions and Attitudes of Egyptian Intellectuals concerning Certain Nationality Groups" (in Arabic) (Ph.D. dissertation, Ain Shams University, Cairo, 1983).

26. See Ibrahim, "Domestic Developments in Egypt," p. 33.

anger increased sharply after the Israeli bombing of Tunisia, the *Achille Lauro* incident, and the subsequent American skyjacking of an Egyptian civilian plane on the night of October 10, 1985. Furor escalated after the death of Suleiman Khater, a conscript in the Central Security forces who shot seven Israeli tourists who approached his military post in the Sinai. Although the Egyptian government claimed that he committed suicide, the prevailing belief in Egypt was that he was murdered by the Israeli intelligence service, the Mossad. The events in the West Bank and Gaza starting in December 1987 and continuing through 1988 fueled another wave of demonstrations in Egypt. In all these events, the demonstrators have expressed their solidarity with other Arabs and used slogans with unmistakable pan-Arab tones. Public surveys conducted during this period indicate that Egyptians had once again reversed their attitudes toward the Arab world. In a survey conducted by Nader Fergani in 1985, 73.7 percent of the Egyptian work force favored unity with another Arab country.[27]

RELEGITIMIZATION

One of the main sources of legitimacy for the Egyptian regime of July 1952 was its anti-West, defined as anti-imperialist and anti-Israeli, stand. The centralization of authority was always justified on the basis of resisting outside enemies. The defeat of 1967 put this source of legitimacy into question. The peace with Israel and the relocation of Egypt to the Western camp made it irrelevant. The decentralization of authority and the democratization of Egypt became imperative. Sadat understood this reality. Parallel with his steps toward peace with Israel and alliance with the United States, Sadat embarked on a process of pluralizing Egyptian politics. When this process suffered a setback, Sadat was assassinated and Mubarak resumed the process.

The pluralization and democratization of the political system has been the most distinctive aspect of the last decade. By 1988 Egypt had six legal political parties, in addition to the semilegal Muslim Brotherhood. The dominance of the NDP, which continues to enjoy the legacy and legitimacy of the Nasserist Arab Socialist Union of the 1960s, has waned somewhat. The 1987 elections led to one of the largest representations of the opposition in the People's

27. Nader Fergani, "Egyptian Arab Attitudes in the Mid-1980s and Their Relationship to Work in the Arab Gulf Countries" (in Arabic), *Al-Mustaqbal al-Arabi*, no. 99 (May 1987), p. 36.

Assembly in the history of Egypt. The opposition share of the elected seats in the People's Assembly rose from 8.6 percent in the 1979 election and 15.0 percent in the 1984 election to 22.3 percent in the 1987 election. The ruling NDP share decreased from 88.7 percent and 87.0 percent in the first two elections to 77.8 percent in the 1987 election.[28]

A full description and an evaluation of the democratization process in Egypt are beyond the scope of this discussion.[29] Instead, my focus is on the effect of this process on the Egyptian posture toward the Arab world. The process of democratization accelerated the re-Arabization of Egyptian politics. First, Egyptian political parties have increasingly affirmed their Arab stands. The Socialist Labor party (SLP), which had accepted the Camp David Accords with some reservations, soon announced its total opposition. The Liberal party (LP), which had accepted the accords without reservations, declared that it was withdrawing support. Since its return to politics in 1984 the New Wafd party (NWP) has declared the nonexistence of the accords because of the Israeli violations. Of course, the Progressive Unionist Party (PUP) opposed the accords from the beginning. The Muslim Brotherhood, which has reservations about the idea of pan-Arab nationalism, preferring instead a pan-Islamic nationalism, has in practice supported the opposition to Camp David and the call for Egypt to shoulder its Arab responsibilities. The National Democratic party, the majority ruling party, was not to be outbid by the opposition parties. Although it continued to support the accords, it increasingly adopted pan-Arab stands in the People's Assembly, in consultative assemblies, and in its newspapers.[30]

Second, the decentralization process has led to a proliferation and an increase in the assertiveness of social, intellectual, professional, and business syndicates and associations. These groups have usually followed the government line. Under Sadat, they were split

28. Even in comparison with the liberal era before the 1952 revolution, the opposition representation in 1987 was striking. The opposition won 15.1 percent of the seats in the 1924 election, 18.9 percent in 1926, 6.9 percent in 1929, 18.1 percent in 1936, and 12.1 percent in 1942. The 1950 elections were the only exception, with the opposition's share being 29.2 percent. See Ali E. Hilal, "Mubarak and the Completion of the Democratic March" (in Arabic), *Al-Ahram al-Iktisadi*, no. 953 (April 20, 1987), p. 92.

29. For additional information, see Said Aly, "Democratization in Egypt," pp. 11–27.

30. For more details on the changing attitudes of political parties in Egypt, see Yehia, "Image of the Palestinians in Egypt," pp. 50–52; and Ibrahim, "Domestic Developments in Egypt," in this volume.

between those who supported the president, such as business associations and the medical profession's syndicates, and those who opposed him, such as the press and lawyers' syndicates. Lawyers and the press were targets of Sadat's repressive policies in his last years in office.[31]

The democratization under Mubarak has made the government less influential in these associations, and Mubarak has consistently followed a hands-off policy toward them. The members of these associations now have the opportunity to promote their economic interests. In regard to work opportunities and income, these interests are largely connected with the Arab world. These groups, therefore, have become vocal in supporting Arab causes, particularly the Palestinian cause, and pressuring the government to take the same position. They headed the pro-Arab and pro-Palestinian demonstrations and did their best to disrupt the normalization process with Israel. Even business associations that were always suspicious of the linkage between pan-Arabism and socialism in the Nasserist ideology were soon to discover that they were tied to Arab capital and Arab markets more than they previously realized. They therefore lobbied for increasing interactions with the Arab world.

Third, traditionally, the Egyptian bureaucracy has significantly influenced Egyptian politics. However, under Nasser and Sadat, the area of "high politics" was kept as the prerogative of the presidency. Sadat frequently excluded the bureaucracies of the Foreign Ministry and the army from the peace process.[32] Under Mubarak, the process of decentralization has loosened the presidential grip on the Egyptian bureaucracy. Consequently, Egyptian bureaucracies have participated in decisionmaking to a greater extent than at any time before, even on the issues of high politics.

The Israeli invasion of Lebanon was one event among others that raised grave concerns among those in the bureaucracies of the Foreign Ministry and the army about Egypt's national security, which they increasingly saw as linked to Arab security. Arab nationalism has always been important to the Foreign Ministry and the army. The rest of Egypt's bureaucracy has been interested, more

31. The lawyers' union was in the forefront of Egyptian professional associations opposing the Camp David Accords. On the day of the opening of the Israeli embassy in Cairo, the union staged a large demonstration in which the Israeli flag was burned and Palestinian flags were raised. Sadat responded by forming a new leadership for the union. Under Mubarak, the legal and elected leadership of the union won a court ruling that nullified Sadat's decision.

32. See the testimony of the former Egyptian foreign minister Mohamed Ibrahim Kamel, *The Camp David Accords: A Testimony* (London: KPI, 1986).

so than other Egyptians, in Arab jobs and money. Workers in such government organizations were the hardest hit by inflation and the deterioration in Egypt's economic fortunes. They had been looking forward to the four years that they would be able to live and work in one of the oil-producing states as the way to secure the future of their children. This opportunity would not exist without the consolidation of Egyptian-Arab relations, and, therefore, a cooling of Egyptian-Israeli relations.[33] Consequently, the normalization of relations between Egypt and Israel was doomed.

RESTRUCTURING

For most of its modern history, the development of Egypt has occurred under the shadow of conflict with external powers. First, there was Muhammad Ali's conflict with Turkey to gain independence for Egypt from the Ottoman Empire. Then came the protracted conflict for independence from Great Britain that continued from 1881 to 1952. The conflict with Great Britain overlapped the Arab-Israeli one that started in 1948, accelerated in the mid-1950s, and became particularly significant for Egypt in 1967 when Egyptian territories came under direct Israeli occupation. The question of a national identity has thus dominated the evolution of Egyptian society and politics.

The Camp David Accords and the subsequent Egyptian-Israeli peace treaty have allowed Egypt to live under a new promise of peace. Political and socioeconomic restructuring of the country, formerly suppressed for the sake of unity needed to combat the external threat, was given a chance to evolve. Consequently, as noted, relegitimization and democratization have been the outcome in the political sphere. In the socioeconomic field, three processes have taken place: the growth of civil society, the rise of Islam, and the intensification of Egyptian-Arab interdependence.

Egyptian Civil Society

The mark of Egyptian history is the dominance of the state over society. Geography and demography have made centralism and authoritarianism an Egyptian tradition. Modern times, however, have modified and moderated this tendency since the middle of the

33. Traditionally, Egypt has allowed government and public sector employees to have a leave of absence from their work for a period of up to four years, after which they have to return to their jobs.

nineteenth century and certainly during the 1923–52 liberal era in Egyptian politics. Gamal Abd al-Nasser's July revolution of 1952 reversed the trend toward declining state power. Over the years, Nasser brought the political system, banking, most of industry, much of the commercial activity, most education, most of the information agencies (press, broadcasting, and television), professional and labor unions, and even the religious institutions under state control. The government imposed controls on virtually all private economic, political, and social activities. It also undertook a series of broad obligations to the Egyptian people: provision of basic human needs—food, health, and housing—at subsidized prices, free education through the university level, and guaranteed employment. The need to mobilize for war against Israel was a sufficient reason for this kind of social contract.

After the October 1973 war, and certainly since Camp David, the development of the Egyptian civil society has been resumed. The legacy of the 1960s has lost some of its luster and logic. The firm grip of the state has loosened in politics as well as economics. As noted, Egypt was transformed from a one-party system into a multiparty system. In economics, different indicators show the erosion of state dominance and the reemergence of independent or private sector socioeconomic initiatives.

A profile of the growth of the private sector in Egypt since 1978 reveals steady gains in its size and level of activity.[34] From 1974 to 1986, the private sector share of industrial output rose from 23 percent to 33 percent.[35] Joint venture banks, Islamic investment companies, and private Egyptian banks have emerged and are now beginning to compete with government banks for investment savings and foreign exchange. The economic situation in Egypt, though not ideal, is nonetheless attracting business initiatives. Invested capital in Egypt as of March 1987 stood at slightly more than $16 billion: 65 percent of which was Egyptian, 18 percent Arab, and 17 percent foreign.[36] The private sector has extended its activities to new areas

34. Private sector regeneration and the accompanying economic trends can also be evaluated from the inception of *infitah* in 1974.

35. U. S. Embassy, Cairo, *Foreign Economic Trends and Their Implications for the United States,* prepared for the U.S. Department of Commerce, International Trade Administration (Government Printing Office, 1986), p. 7.

36. This figure reflects approved projects as of March 31, 1987, according to Egypt's General Authority for Investment and Free Zones. Cited in "Foreign Investment: Making Participation Pay," *Business Monthly,* vol. 3 (October 1987), p. 6.

such as insurance and external trade and increased its share in agriculture, land reclamation, education, housing, and tourism.

Indigenous private sector initiatives are on the rise, and the government has taken steps to deregulate private sector activities and stimulate domestic and foreign capital formation. Actual percentages of gross fixed investment in the public sector have been reduced from 79 percent in fiscal year 1983 to 70 percent in fiscal year 1986. Although the Nasserist concept of economic planning in the form of five-year plans has been resurrected, these plans in no way seek exclusively to reestablish a state-run public sector as the chief socioeconomic force in Egypt. Between the 1982–87 Five-Year Plan and the 1987–92 plan, the percentage of investment of the gross domestic product (GDP) in the public sector dropped from 77 percent (with 23 percent going to the private sector) to approximately 50 percent in both the private and public sectors.[37]

The state share of GDP investment remains high because of government involvement in oil production and the Suez Canal enterprises; however, government sales of other characteristically public sector enterprises such as hotels and tourism services to private buyers reflect the expanding private sector. In summary, not only are government programs espousing privatization policies in historically public sector enterprises, but the private sector is assuming a substantial share of the economic activity in Egypt. The trend has been toward privatization since 1978. In other words, deregulation and decentralization have resulted in the liberalization of Egypt's economy.

If the growth of civil society is measured by the evolution of various organizations and associations, both professional and social, and business groupings, Egypt has witnessed remarkable progress.[38] The timid labor unions, professional syndicates, and business associations under Nasser have gained strength and influence within the society and the government. Their membership has increased, particularly among the younger people who constitute a large proportion of the politically active population. Increasing youth membership has prompted these interest groups to focus on the problems of young people, particularly with salaries, education, and housing. This, in turn, has led these groups to seek influence in both education and training. The medical profession's syndicate,

37. Ibid.

38. Osama al-Ghazaly Harb, "The Recovery of the Civil Society in Egypt" (in Arabic), *Al-Ahram*, April 8, 1988.

for example, in which about 50 percent of the members are less than thirty-five years old, is pressuring the government for a 10 percent annual reduction in the number of medical students. The same demands are being made by the lawyers' and engineering syndicates. The labor unions are opposed to these restrictions on education, especially higher education, and they defend each citizen's right to a free education through the university level. At the same time, these organizations are formulating opinions and demands on most of the national issues: the role of the private and public sectors in the economy, subsidies, environment, and most important of all, politics.[39] These groups use propaganda, meetings, strikes, and demonstrations to inform the public and pressure the government.

The experience of the past decade shows that the business associations are the most influential of all the interest groups. Although Egypt has had organizations such as the Egyptian Chamber of Commerce and the Egyptian Federation of Industries to defend the interests of the private sector, they have historically been highly controlled by the government. Recently, however, the Egyptian Businessmen's Association has gained increasing influence over the government's economic decisions. Financially independent and representing the steadily growing private sector, the association has established institutional links with government that allow for consultations over policy decisions. The Egyptian Businessmen's Association makes propositions concerning the national economy and airs them in the press to rally public support.[40] All in all, the civil society in Egypt is not only growing but is influencing state behavior.

The Rise of Islam

Observers of Egyptian society and politics have often noted the rise of Islamic fundamentalism. The term "Islamic fundamentalism" is usually used to describe the violent way in which political groups apply the *sharia* laws. The Islamic government in Iran is invoked to show the typical or the ideal form of Islamic fundamentalism.

39. See "Interest Groups," in El Sayed Yassin, ed., *The Arab Strategic Report, 1986* (in Arabic) (Cairo: Al-Ahram Center for Political and Strategic Studies, 1987), pp. 380–89; and Amani Kandil, "Political Evolution in Egypt and the Making of Public Policies," in Ali Eddin Hillal, ed., *The Democratic Evolution in Egypt: Issues and Discussions* (in Arabic) (Cairo: Maktabat Nahdat al-Sharq, 1986), pp. 87–113.

40. Amani Kandil; "Interest Groups in Egypt . . . Where Are They Going?" (in Arabic), *Al-Ahram*, April 15, 1988.

In Egypt, however, the term must be examined carefully to understand its complexity and unique meaning. As noted earlier, Islam is one of the principal ideological trends in Egypt, besides liberalism and nationalism. It has also been noted that the existence of Islam as a political force is not completely divorced from the other two political trends. However, the last decade has witnessed the rise of Islam as an ideology, as a political force, and as part of civil society in Egypt. To understand the Islamic phenomenon, it is important to separate it into five layers of political and social behavior all linked by the very loose term Islam.

First, the Egyptian people as a whole, both Muslims and Christians, have become more religious and conservative. The Westernization drive, which continued from the beginning of the century until the mid-1970s, has begun to decline. Egyptians have become more observant of religious rituals, such as praying, fasting, and the pilgrimage to Mecca. Islamic dress is more often worn by both men and women. All Egyptian institutions—be they government, unions, opposition parties (including the leftist PUP), or public and private companies—organize religious events, encourage religious behavior, and sometimes subsidize the pilgrimage trips. Surveys show that the Egyptian public is in favor of the application of the *sharia* laws.[41] This could be interpreted in part as an intensification of the religion-oriented culture of the Egyptian people and in part as a reaction to the deterioration in the moral standards of the country and the increased corruption that accompanied the *infitah* policy of Sadat. Most observers, however, consider the 1967 defeat as the main reason for the religious awakening in Egypt.

Second, the traditional Al-Azhar religious institution is gaining strength within the society. Radio, television, and other means of modern communication have resurrected the traditional role of Al-Azhar. This role, however, is guided by the government since the *ulama*—contrary to the case in Iran—are employees of the religious public sector. The government, therefore, is using this prestigious religious institution both to promote the more moderate and modern Islamic ideas and to fight the more radical and violent religious groups.

Third, the Muslim Brotherhood, the main Islamic movement in

41. In a 1980 survey of 3,425 Egyptians, it was found that 98 percent of Muslims and 63 percent of Christians agreed or agreed strongly with the application of the *sharia*. See National Center for Social and Criminological Research, *A Study of Egyptian Public Opinion concerning the Application of the Sharia for Certain Crimes* (in Arabic) (Cairo: National Center for Social and Criminological Research, 1985), p. 84.

Egypt since the 1920s, has achieved a prominent standing in Egyptian politics. Although the Muslim Brotherhood has no officially recognized status as a party, it has tried to work within the legal political system of the country. Following its resurrection under Sadat, it has become more willing to accept liberal democracy as a way to achieve political legitimacy.[42] In the 1984 elections to the People's Assembly, the Muslim Brotherhood allied with the NWP and gained eight of its fifty-eight seats. In the 1987 elections, it allied itself with the SLP and the LP and gained forty of the sixty seats won by the alliance. It became the largest single opposition group in the People's Assembly. Furthermore, the Muslim Brotherhood has become influential in most professional organizations. In some organizations, particularly in the syndicates of the medical profession, it has become the dominant force.[43]

The chief characteristic of the Muslim Brotherhood is increasing moderation and acceptance of democracy. Its election platform of 1987 was more moderate than had been expected. Not only did the platform call for establishing a Western-style democratic system, it also maintained that the application of the *sharia* should be gradual through the step-by-step amendment of the existing laws. This view stands in sharp contrast to the idea of completely changing these laws. Further, the platform stated that the application of the *sharia* should be based on *ijtihad* (interpretation), which considers the new needs and interests of society and calls on experts in law, economics, commerce, and industry to participate in this process.[44] This approach allows greater flexibility and compromise in the political process, particularly when it is applied to more concrete issues. Furthermore, the Muslim Brotherhood is increasingly distancing itself from the radical and violent Islamic groups. In the 1987 election campaign, the radical groups distributed leaflets denouncing the Muslim Brotherhood for participation in the election, accusing it of selling out the Islamic cause.[45] The Muslim Brotherhood denounced the acts of violence and terrorism committed by these groups.

42. Said Aly and Wenner, "Modern Islamic Reform Movements," pp. 352–53.

43. "Interest Groups," in Yassin, *The Arab Strategic Report, 1987* (in Arabic).

44. These aims of the Muslim Brotherhood are expressed in the election platform of the Socialist Labor party.

45. Interview with Maamoon H. al-Hudaibi, a leading figure of the Muslim Brotherhood in the People's Assembly, *Al-Majalla*, no. 375 (April 15–21, 1987), p. 11; Adel Darwish, "Mubarak's Electoral Triumph," *Middle East*, no. 151 (May 1987), pp. 11–14; and Bertus Hendriks, "Egypt's New Political Map," *MERIP*, vol. 17 (July-August, 1987), p. 27.

Fourth, the growing strength of the Muslim Brotherhood could not have taken place had it not already been significant in the fast growing "Islamic economy." During the 1960s many of the leaders and followers of the Muslim Brotherhood went to Saudi Arabia and the Gulf region, where they prospered. In the late 1970s, as part of Sadat's open door policy, they returned to Egypt to invest their newly acquired wealth. They first called for the establishment of Islamic banks. Faisal's Islamic Bank, with $1.7 billion in deposits in 1986, has become one of Egypt's largest banks.[46] They also established Islamic investment companies or *sharikat tawzif al-amwal,* which use deposits from Egyptians to reinvest in Egypt and in the world financial and commodity markets. By 1988 there were 154 of these companies.[47] The exact value of these deposits is not known, but estimates go as high as $20 billion.[48] These companies are "capitalist" oriented and are highly connected with the world's capitalist economy. They call for a free market economy in Egypt, and they invest heavily in the world money and commodity markets.[49] The Faisal Islamic Bank has invested $500 million (about one-third of total deposits) outside Egypt, while the Islamic companies have invested no less than 80 percent of their total deposits outside.[50] This new brand of "Islamists" in Egypt is not like the bazari merchant class in Iran that called for disengagement from the world economy; instead these Islamic companies recognize their role in the world economy. Their support for the Muslim Brotherhood as a political group is an expression of support for the liberalization of the Egyptian economy in an Islamic garb.

Fifth, relatively radical and more violent Islamic groups have appeared in Egypt since the mid-1970s. They made a mark on Egyptian history when the *Jihad* assassinated Sadat. Since then they have continued to attract members, especially among students where they found a loyal following. These groups, generally called *jamiat islamiyya,* have continued to carry out violent acts not only against politicians but against society as a whole. In 1987 they tried to assassinate the former interior ministers, Hassan Abu Basha and

46. Interview with Mahmoud al-Helw, chairman of the board, Faisal Islamic Bank, "The Islamic Organizations . . . and the Egyptian Economy," *Al-Ahram al-Iktisadi,* no. 903 (May 5, 1986), p. 27.

47. *Al-Wafd,* March 3, 1988.

48. Abd al-Wahaab Saad Ali, "Reforming the Money Companies" (in Arabic), *Al-Ahram al-Iktisadi,* no. 995 (February 8, 1988), p. 26.

49. Interview with Abd al-Latif al-Sharif, the head of Al-Sharif, a leading Islamic investment company, *Al-Shaab,* March 8, 1988.

50. Interview with Mahmoud al-Helw; and interview with Atif Sedky, Egyptian prime minister, *Al-Musawwar,* April 22, 1988, p. 32.

Muhammad Nabawi Ismail, and the chief editor of *Al-Musawwar,* Makram Muhammad Ahmed. They also attacked everything that they considered immoral in music and art. By 1988 the group had begun to attack parties in the universities and even wedding parties in Egyptian villages, particularly in the Minya and Asyut governorates in Upper Egypt.[51]

The picture that emerges from this five-layered description of Islamic fundamentalism in Egypt is one of complexity and contradiction. Although an element of violence appears in the fifth layer, the other four remain within the Egyptian tradition and are trying to merge liberalism and nationalism. In the 1980s Islam is Egypt's leading force, in contrast to nationalism in the 1950s and 1960s and liberalism in the 1970s.

Egyptian-Arab Interdependence

Scholars of inter-Arab relations in general and Egyptian-Arab relations in particular have tended to minimize the value of Arab interdependence on the basis of trade statistics. Influenced by studies on European integration and interdependence among advanced industrial states, the argument has been that since inter-Arab trade never exceeded 8 percent of overall Arab trade, interdependence among Arab countries has been very low indeed. The conclusion then is that for Egypt, with only about 6 percent of its trade with Arab countries, interdependence will be almost nonexistent.[52]

In the Arab context, however, trade statistics give, at best, a small part of the overall picture. The experience since the late seventies shows that Egyptian interdependence with the Arab world is more intense and structural than previously estimated for the following reasons.

First, the well-known phenomenon of labor migration in the Arab world has profoundly influenced Egyptian society, economy, and politics. More than 3.3 million Egyptians have, at some time, migrated to work in the Arab oil-producing countries, with the result that in almost every Egyptian family at least one member has worked or is working abroad. This situation has been at least partially responsible for the changes in Egyptian attitudes toward the Arab world mentioned earlier. Nader Fergani's survey on the

51. The Egyptian press in the fall of 1987 and the winter of 1988 holds full accounts of these events.

52. Muhammad Labib Shukair, *Arab Economic Unity: Experience and Expectations,* part 2 (in Arabic) (Beirut: Center for Arab Unity Studies, 1986), p. 1207.

attitudes of the Egyptian work force toward Arab unity found that the greatest support for the idea came from the migrant work force (78.1 percent). The least support was found among those outside the work force (68.8 percent), while 74.2 percent of the nonmigrant work force supported the idea. The survey also showed that most of the migrant workers had positive attitudes toward the host countries.[53] These findings run contrary to the propositions previously expressed by some scholars, including Nader Fergani, that the more Egyptians work in Arab countries, the less likely they will be to support unity with Arab countries.[54] They also showed that Egyptians interested in working in an Arab country were likely to support Arab unity.

Second, remittances have represented a significant share of the hard currency flows to Egypt, reaching slightly more than $3.2 billion in 1985, surpassing such other sources as oil, tourism, and the Suez Canal.[55] That figure declined sharply to about $600 million in 1986. The sudden decline was not primarily because of the decline in oil prices or the return of large numbers of migrant workers; it occurred because of the overvaluation of the Egyptian pound. When the government went some way toward reforming the value of the pound in May 1987, remittances transferred through official banks reached $2 billion by the end of the year, more than a threefold increase in eight months.[56]

Third, the impact of remittances is not only on the government's foreign currency resources but also on investment in Egypt. Fifty-seven percent of total direct investment under Law 43 of 1974 was Egyptian money generated by Egyptians working in Arab countries. If this figure is added to the 25 percent of direct Arab investment under the same law, one finds that 82 percent of the investment was derived from Arab money.[57] Further, most of the Islamic companies, with assets estimated between $4 billion and $8 billion, have been dependent on the savings of Egyptians who worked or are working in Arab countries.[58] Furthermore, a recent study about

53. Fergani, "Egyptian Arab Attitudes in the Mid-1980s," pp. 33–38.

54. Nader Fergani, *Migration to Oil: Dimensions of the Migration to the Oil States for Work and Its Effect on Development in the Arab World* (in Arabic) (Beirut: Center for Arab Unity Studies, 1983), pp. 193–94.

55. World Bank, *World Development Report 1987* (Oxford University Press, 1987), p. 230.

56. Osama Saraya, "How Egypt Faced Its Debts Problem" (in Arabic), *Al-Ahram al-Iktisadi*, no. 990 (January 4, 1988).

57. Saad Eddin Ibrahim, "Oil, Migration and the New Arab Social Order," in Kerr and Yassin, *Rich and Poor States in the Middle East*, p. 40.

58. Lief, "Egypt's Islamic Challenge," pp. 6–8.

small-scale manufacturing in Egypt found that remittances have a significant effect. Günter Meyer of the University of Erlangen-Nürnberg in West Germany surveyed two popular quarters (Bab al-Sharqiyya and Al-Gamaliyya) in Cairo between September 1985 and and April 1986, interviewing 2,432 owners and employees of 531 manufacturing enterprises. He found that 12 percent of the employees had worked abroad at least once. One of four owners of the enterprises studied had worked abroad, with a record 37 percent in the shoe-producing firms. The results of the survey show that 35 percent of the proprietors of manufacturing enterprises who were former labor emigrants had used their remittances as a principal source of capital to establish new workshops of their own. A large number of the workshops, which were equipped with the most advanced machinery, belonged to returning migrants.[59] Thus remittances not only fuel the demand for consumer goods, as Saad Eddin Ibrahim has argued,[60] but they also provide the means for the creation of new enterprises that produce consumer goods.

Fourth, the future prospects of labor migration and remittances, because of the decline in oil prices, are not as gloomy as some might predict. In two recent articles by Bakr Suliman al-Naggar and Muhammad al-Awady Galal al-Din, it was found that despite the decline in oil prices, the number of migrant workers has been increasing slightly in the countries of the Gulf Cooperation Council (GCC). They also conclude that the local GCC population employed in many areas and professions is going to decline.[61] Between 1979 and 1982 the share of Saudi medical doctors in Saudi Arabia had declined from 6.5 percent to 4.6 percent. Between 1981 and 1984, the share of Saudi pharmacologists had dropped from 20.0 percent to 13.0 percent. In 1983 Saudis were only 8.7 percent of all engineers and only 5.3 percent of dentists in the country.[62] In Kuwait, in 1985, only 22.6 percent of all professionals (doctors, engineers, lawyers, and others) were Kuwaitis.[63]

In the area of unskilled labor in construction, the number of

59. Günter Meyer, "Socioeconomic Structure and Development of Small-Scale Manufacturing in Old Quarters of Cairo," paper presented at the annual meeting of the Middle East Studies Association, Baltimore, November 15–17, 1987, pp. 4–5.

60. Ibrahim, "Oil, Migration and the New Arab Social Order," pp. 47–50.

61. Bakr Suliman al-Naggar, "The Returning Arab Workers in the Arab Gulf Countries: Problems before the Return" (in Arabic), *Al-Mustaqbal al-Arabi*, no. 105 (November 1987), pp. 52–74; and Muhammad al-Awady Galal al-Din, "Labor Markets in the Gulf with Special Reference to the Health and Construction Sectors" (in Arabic), ibid., pp. 75–95.

62. Galal al-Din, "Labor Markets in the Gulf," pp. 78, 92.

63. Ibid., p. 93.

foreign workers is not likely to decline as sharply as the countries in the Gulf might have hoped. The local population continues to avoid this field, and the governments rely increasingly on the private sector, which prefers cheap foreign labor. Although Bakr Suliman al-Naggar and Muhammad al-Awady Galal al-Din realize that the income of the labor migrants will decline relatively, the decline is partially compensated for by the decline in the rate of inflation. Inflation had reached 50 percent in housing, which accounts for the largest part of migrant spending in the host country.[64] Only one-third of Egyptian migrant workers are unskilled, and this group will be the hardest hit by the decline in oil prices and the competition from much cheaper Asian labor. Their transfer of money back home is limited and rarely goes to investment. The other two-thirds of the migrant work force, however, will continue to make a significant contribution to the Egyptian economy well into the future.

Fifth, remittances are not the only source of income transferred to Egypt because of its Arab connection. Egypt received a little more than $6.1 billion of bilateral OPEC aid between 1973 and 1981, 19.5 percent of what was awarded to twenty different countries by OPEC.[65] Moreover, more than one-third of the tourists going to Egypt in 1985—an estimated 1.5 million—were Arabs. In 1987 the Arab share of tourism—an estimated 2.0 million people—reached 40 percent.[66] Their contribution to Egypt's income from tourism is much larger because they stay longer and spend more than European and American tourists. Arab journalism, broadcasting, and television are dependent on Egyptians working in Egypt. Egyptian private sector hospitals are preferred by the middle income groups in the Arab oil-producing states. Consequently, it is not surprising that many Egyptians, even if they stay at home, have a source of income related to the Arab countries.

REORIENTATION

Sadat's peace with Israel and his de facto alliance with the United States represented a new strategy in Egyptian foreign affairs. In

64. Al-Naggar, "Returning Arab Workers," p. 56.

65. Richard P. Mattione, *OPEC's Investments and the International Financial System* (Brookings, 1985), p. 148.

66. Osama Saraya, "How to Keep Tourists Flowing to Egypt" (in Arabic), *Al-Ahram al-Iktisadi*, no. 991 (January 11, 1988), p. 11.

general states pursue one of three strategies: joining or bandwagoning, balancing, and self-reliance.[67]

Egypt, with its meager economic resources, could not follow the strategy of self-reliance, although some attempts were made. Nasser's strategy was basically one of balancing Israeli might by trying to build an Arab alliance and of balancing the Israeli-American de facto alliance with an Egyptian-Soviet one. Sadat's strategy between 1970 and 1973 was virtually the same. Immediately after the 1973 war Sadat changed his strategy to one of joining the Israeli-American alliance to appease and contain Israel and to compete with it for American favors and assistance.

Although Sadat succeeded in regaining Sinai—though with various constraints on Egyptian sovereignty—and in extracting considerable aid from the United States, his strategy did not succeed in achieving a comprehensive Arab-Israeli peace. Further, and more important, his strategy failed to appease or contain Israel. In fact, the opposite occurred. With its southern flank secured, Israel went after its northern flank in Lebanon. Israel increased its national security domain to cover an area that stretched from Tunisia to Iraq. Former Israeli defense minister Ariel Sharon's boast that he hoped to extend the Israeli security concept to areas even farther away was certainly disconcerting to Egypt.

The limited extent of American influence on Israel was even more discomforting to Egypt. As Egyptians were soon to learn, the Israeli hold on American politics was beyond their imagination. The lesson began immediately after the Camp David Accords when Menachem Begin overruled Carter on the issue of Israeli settlements in the West Bank. Despite the American-Egyptian agreement on "full autonomy" for the Palestinians, Israel prevailed and the process ended. American anger over the Israeli bombing of the Iraqi nuclear reactor was soon to vanish. While the United States looked the other way on matters regarding Israel's nuclear capability, it pressured Egypt to sign the nonproliferation treaty. Moreover, Egyptians believed the Israeli invasion of Lebanon could not have happened without American collusion, if not outright collaboration. In addition, American aid to Egypt never matched that given to Israel. Egypt was kept militarily inferior to Israel, and Sinai became a hostage to any Israeli change of mind. Even when Egypt agreed with the United States on the importance of fighting terrorism, the

67. For more details about joining and balancing, see Stephen M. Walt, "Alliance Formation and the Balance of World Power," *International Security*, vol. 9 (Spring 1985), pp. 6–8.

United States did not hesitate to humiliate Egypt during the *Achille Lauro* incident.[68]

In sum, Egyptian national security since Camp David has become increasingly threatened. Depending on Israeli good intentions has not been reassuring. No country can afford to rely on goodwill for its security.

Egypt's economic security has not improved. American aid to Egypt has increasingly been used to pressure Egypt in matters of interest to Israel, such as the case of returning the Egyptian ambassador to Tel Aviv (he had been recalled after the Israeli invasion of Lebanon), the dispute between Israel and Egypt over the territory of Taba, and the normalization of relations with Israel. The Egyptian-American connection, which it was thought could develop into a vehicle of Egyptian influence over Israel, has become precisely the opposite.

Ten years after Sadat's trip to Jerusalem, Egypt has regained Sinai but continues to be insecure and vulnerable. Mubarak has realized the dark side of the joining strategy. As a result, he has begun to add to it some elements of the balancing strategy in order to increase his options.

Improving Soviet-Egyptian relations, therefore, has become a goal of Egyptian foreign policy. These relations deteriorated rapidly during the 1970s. In 1972 Egypt expelled Soviet military advisers. In 1976 Egypt canceled the Egyptian-Soviet Friendship and Cooperation Treaty. In September 1981 Egypt expelled the Soviet ambassador to Cairo. However, after the Israeli invasion of Lebanon, Egypt started to reverse this process. In 1983 Egyptian-Soviet trade, cultural, and technical relations were resumed. In 1984 the two countries exchanged ambassadors once again and Soviet industrial advisers returned to Egypt. By 1986 Egypt had become the largest trading partner of the Soviet Union in the Arab world—second only to India in the third world. Trade between the two countries has approached $850 million, making the Soviet Union Egypt's second largest trading partner after the United States.[69]

68. On October 7, 1985, four Palestinian guerrillas hijacked the Italian luxury liner *Achille Lauro.* Egypt negotiated with the hijackers and convinced them to surrender on October 9 after one American hostage, Leon Klinghoffer, was killed. Egypt decided to send the four Palestinians to Tunisia to face trial by the Palestine Liberation Organization. On October 12, a squadron of U.S. Navy F-14 jet fighters intercepted the Egyptair passenger plane that was carrying the Palestinians to Tunis. The plane was forced to land at a naval base in Sicily where the Palestinians were arrested.

69. "Egypt Is in the Forefront of Arab Trade with the Soviets" (in Arabic), *Al-Ahram,* April 27, 1986.

In 1987 Egyptian-Soviet relations improved dramatically. In March the Soviet Union agreed to reschedule Egypt's debt to Moscow, estimated at $3 billion, with a twenty-five-year-repayment schedule, including a ten-year grace period.[70] In April Moscow agreed to resupply Egypt with spare parts for Soviet-made weapons.[71] Finally in February 1988, the Soviet Union agreed to give Egypt a six-year grace period for the repayment of its military debt to Moscow, estimated at $1.5 billion. These debts are to be paid over a nineteen-year period in the form of Egyptian products.[72] In return, it has become official Egyptian policy to call for the convening of an Arab-Israeli international conference with Soviet participation.

However, since there are limits to American tolerance of Egyptian-Soviet rapprochement and because of Egyptian domestic opposition to such a move, a return to the Arab fold became imperative. Slowly but steadily Mubarak started to mend fences with the rest of the Arab world. By early 1988, Egypt had restored relations with seventeen of the twenty-one Arab League members. The remaining four—Syria, Libya, Lebanon, and Algeria—still boycott Egypt diplomatically.

Of these four countries, Syria will continue to be an important target of Egyptian diplomacy because of its special position in the Arab-Israeli conflict and the fact that it remains the chief obstacle to Egypt's return to the Arab League. Contacts between the two countries intensified throughout 1987. In January Asad and Mubarak met for the first time in more than a decade at the Islamic conference in Kuwait. Art, theater, and sport groups have been exchanged. Egyptian teams participated in the Mediterranean Olympics in Latakia. Emissaries and messages have been exchanged between the two sides both directly and indirectly. It was even reported that Osama al-Baz, Mubarak's senior political adviser, met with Faruq al-Sharaa, the Syrian foreign minister, more than once. Furthermore, Mubarak and Asad have gone to great lengths to distinguish between the personality, character, and integrity of the other leader and the foreign policy of his country. While policies continued to be condemned, leaders are praised.

Most important of all, when Syria objected during the Amman summit to the decision to resume diplomatic relations with Egypt because it felt that Egypt had given Camp David priority over its other commitments, Mubarak announced that Egypt's commitment

70. Ibid., April 24, 1987.
71. "The Soviet Ambassador to Cairo" (in Arabic), ibid., April 16, 1987.
72. "A Period of Forgiveness" (in Arabic), ibid., February 23, 1988.

to the Arab Defense Pact had priority over any of Egypt's other commitments. None of these steps has led to a breakthrough, much less a takeoff in Egyptian-Syrian relations, but a dialogue has begun. The deterioration in their relations has been stopped. Ten years after Camp David, Egypt's isolation and ostracism from the Arab fold has effectively ended because of the imperatives of Egyptian national security.

DILEMMAS OF THE COMING DECADE

This discussion has painted a complex picture of Egypt. As demonstrated, the forces of economic and political liberalism, Arabism, and Islam are on the rise in Egyptian politics. Although contradictions among them persist, Mubarak has so far managed to maintain a balance that is true to the tradition of his predecessors. Democratization has given the political system the ability to adapt to changing circumstances. Political and socioeconomic differentiation has allowed coalitions to be built without sharp polarization. Moderation in foreign policy has made it possible for Egypt to deal with competing powers: the Soviet Union and the United States, Israel and the Arab states.

Egypt, however, will face serious dilemmas arising from this seemingly satisfactory position. In the coming decade, Egypt will have to confront what it has so far avoided through either the wisdom of its leaders or sheer luck. Domestically, Egypt has to deal with the task of solving the contradiction between the continuation of democratization and the demand and expectations associated with it. Democracy is a political system that gives sociopolitical forces the opportunity to lobby not only for power, but also for a larger share of the existing limited national wealth. Democracy also thrives on competition and a degree of political tension. This could be moderated through consensus building, which can be achieved only through an extensive dialogue in which different political forces have equal opportunity. The Egyptian regime, while it is allowing these forces to emerge and consolidate, cannot at present grant them a wide-open playing field. The gap between the sociopolitical differentiation in the country and the rigid institutions that should channel and moderate the demands of various groups is still wide.

While civil society has grown, state power has remained overwhelming. The Egyptian constitution of 1971—along with the historical legacy—gave the institution of the presidency enough power to overshadow and overrule all other political institutions in the country. State bureaucracy has continued to interfere in every facet of Egyptian political, social, and economic life. The current National Democratic party continues to carry the legacy and legitimacy of the 1960s Arab Socialist Union. The NDP's dominance over the bureaucracy and the security forces means that the government can never be neutral toward the political parties. In short, the balance between the state and the society is tilted in favor of the state, which at any moment can narrow the range of free political expression of various social forces.

The Egyptian economy, which has been kept afloat so far by massive amounts of external money transferred from the West and the Arab countries, is continuing to suffer. At best, Egypt can hope to sustain the present levels of these transfers while its economic problems continue to mount. Egypt can no longer avoid a serious mobilization of its limited resources that are largely in the hands of the private sector. Since the early 1980s, Egyptian capitalists have been acquiring a larger share in the national economy than they did under Sadat and certainly under Nasser. However, a real takeoff for capitalism in Egypt will be possible only through a fundamental restructuring of the economy and society. Capitalism produces a growing national economy, but it may also work against the interests of the less fortunate—of which Egypt has an abundance. The dilemma of achieving growth while not ignoring equity and justice is not only an Egyptian problem. However, it is especially acute in Egypt because it coincides with a volatile political and economic environment.

Externally, Egypt is faced with serious dilemmas. First, Egypt has large stakes in close relations with the United States. The United States is important not only because of aid and assistance, but also because Washington is essential for any comprehensive Arab-Israeli peace. However, as previously illustrated, the limited ability of the United States, because of domestic conditions, to force Israel to withdraw from the occupied territories or to curtail the ambitions of the Israeli right, makes it imperative for Egypt to balance the Israeli-American connection with better relations with the Soviet Union and stronger ties with the Arab world. This objective will not go unnoticed in the United States and will probably lead to several tests in which Egypt will be asked to prove its loyalty to the Western alliance. So far, Egypt has succeeded in avoiding this moment. The situation will be different if difficult choices are forced upon it.

The dilemma is compounded by a second one related to Egypt's relations with the Arab world. Certainly Egypt needs the Arab world for the reasons already mentioned. Returning to the Arab fold, however, is not without its price. Although Egypt has no grand vision for the Arab world, as it did in the 1950s and 1960s, it cannot be an effective player, not to mention a leader, in the Arab system without shouldering certain responsibilities in the Gulf and the Arab-Israeli arenas. Although there is no serious disagreement between Egypt and the United States over the Gulf, there are serious differences related to the Arab-Israeli conflict. During the Palestinian uprising in 1987–88, the Arab states and the Palestine Liberation Organization pressured Egypt to break diplomatic relations with Israel or at least to withdraw its ambassador as it did after the Israeli invasion of Lebanon. This pressure is strengthened by the growing domestic opposition in Egypt to the Israeli actions in the occupied territories. As the uprising continues and the level of Israeli violence mounts, the Egyptian government will have to choose between conceding to domestic and Arab pressure, thus endangering the Egyptian-American link and the Egyptian-Israeli relationship, or doing nothing and thus relying on suppression at home and losing credibility in the Arab world.

The third dilemma is related to Egypt's relations with the United States and with the Arab world. Egypt has a stake in the continuation of peace with Israel. Peace is essential for Egypt to solve its mounting domestic and economic difficulties. However, the continuation of peace is largely dependent on resolving the Palestinian issue. Since Israel is not yet ready to accept the Palestinians' right of self-determination and the Israeli right wing will not accept the exchange of land for peace formula or negotiations with the Palestine Liberation Organization, Egypt will be left with hard choices. The Palestinian uprising of 1987–88 and resistance to the occupation will make this dilemma more pressing with every passing day.

These internal and external dilemmas are hardly new to Egypt. They grow out of interactions that occurred in the past decade. The coming decade will be no less difficult for Egypt. Forecasting is the nightmare of scholars. However, if Egyptian history is any guide, Egypt will try to muddle through these formidable dilemmas. Avoiding disasters and catastrophes will be the equivalent of achieving victories. Minimizing losses will be more like maximizing gains. Success, like beauty, will be in the eye of the beholder.

ALI E. HILLAL DESSOUKI

Egyptian Foreign Policy since Camp David

THE SIGNING of the Camp David Accords on September 17, 1978, symbolized a new era in Egyptian foreign policy. President Anwar Sadat's decision "to go it alone" caused a rupture in the Arab system of relations and was a destabilizing element in the region. The decision confirmed the change in Egypt's strategic position and in its relations with the two superpowers that had begun after the October 1973 war. Sadat was committed to a special relationship with the United States, which entailed a further deterioration of Egypt's relations with the Soviet Union. For the following decade, the Camp David Accords and their consequences remained a contentious domestic political issue.

Political and ideological perspectives on these issues abound, but several serious historical and analytical issues remain unsettled independent of these perspectives. For instance, were the Camp David Accords and the ensuing Egyptian-Israeli peace treaty of March 26, 1979, the product of a process that started a number of years earlier and was subsequently given new life and strength? Or were they really a watershed and a turning point, with Sadat alone carrying the burden of failure or enjoying the fruits of success?[1] It seems to me that the treaty was part of a process that preceded

1. A good analysis of the debate over person versus process is in Salua Nour and Carl F. Pinkele, "Camp David and After: Foreign Policy in an Interdependent Environment," in Carl F. Pinkele and Adamantia Pollis, eds., *The Contemporary Mediterranean World* (Praeger, 1983), pp. 257–75. Bahgat Korany writes, "Contrary to accepted wisdom, the Egyptian-Israeli peace process did not start with Sadat's arrival in Jerusalem in November 1977. Four years earlier, the immediate reestablishment of diplomatic relations with Washington following Kissinger's 1973 visit to Cairo was tantamount to a commitment to seek peace with Israel through American mediation." See Korany, "The Cold Peace, the Sixth Arab-Israeli War, and Egypt's Public," *International Journal*, vol. 38 (Autumn 1985), p. 659.

Sadat's visit to Jerusalem in November 1977, a process in which Arab, regional, and global actors participated, and to which economic, political, and military strategic factors contributed.[2]

In the context of the volatile and changing Middle East, ten years is not a short period of time. In assessing the Camp David Accords ten years later, one has to look at their achievements and shortcomings, from within and from without, what they brought to realization, and what they prevented from taking place.

At first glance, Camp David precluded an Arab-Israeli war on the magnitude of the one in 1973. It ensured the removal of Egypt from a position of military confrontation and the establishment of "delinking" as a principle in the resolution of the Arab-Israeli conflict. It reinforced the Israeli view that the problem was a series of interstate conflicts, a view that put the Palestinians in jeopardy. Further, the accords supposedly set a ceiling on what other Arab states could aspire to, since it is neither conceivable nor realistic for them to expect to get more than what Egypt settled for.

The most striking achievement of the accords is their endurance and stability. Despite many uncertainties in the bilateral Egyptian-Israeli relationship and many difficult tests, including among other things, the Israeli invasion of Lebanon, the border dispute on Taba, and the Palestinian uprising of 1987–88, the treaty has not been questioned by the two governments. The main failure of the accords was in the collapse of negotiations concerning Palestinian autonomy in the West Bank and Gaza. Eventually, the accords ended up not as the beginning of a comprehensive settlement but rather as a separate Egyptian-Israeli peace treaty.

In foreign policy there is no free ride. In almost all relations each party calculates costs and benefits, assets and liabilities. In a system based on nation-states, relations among states are usually a function of the balance of power and capabilities among them. A peace treaty or an alliance is maintained as long as its partners perceive it as fulfilling their national interests, as preserving their national security, and as long as the benefits outweigh the costs. The Camp David Accords are no exception. They are the outcome of a political environment in which the Egyptian leadership, primarily but not exclusively President Sadat, perceived the continuation of a state

2. On this process see Indar Jit Rikhye and John Volkmar, *The Middle East and the New Realism* (New York: International Peace Academy, 1975); and Lester A. Sober, ed., *Peace-Making in the Middle East* (New York: Facts on File, 1980).

of war with Israel as harmful to Egypt's national interests. This chapter underlines three patterns of Egypt's relations resulting from the implementation of the Camp David Accords—relations with Israel, with the Arab states, and with the United States.

THE PROBLEM OF NORMALIZATION

The early 1970s witnessed a great deal of literature on war termination and conflict resolution. Notwithstanding the empty moralizing, one important conclusion that emerges from this literature is that a war will end when the adversaries no longer have the means of continuing it or when they no longer perceive it as useful. A war will end, therefore, when there is no longer the capability or the will to continue it.

It is in this context that Egypt's foreign policy toward Israel since 1975 can be understood. The Egyptian ruling elite shared three perceptions: first, the 1973 war had taken place in ideal circumstances that would be impossible to replicate (Egyptian-Syrian military coordination, a unified Arab front, and taking Israel by surprise); second, the results of the October war were the most the Arabs could hope to achieve by military means; and third, Egypt's economic resources were no longer capable of shouldering the burdens of war.

Of particular interest is the economic background for decisions about war and peace. One of Sadat's favorite themes was that war had exhausted Egyptian resources and made Egypt—once among the richest—the poorest Arab country. The link between the food riots of January 1977 and Sadat's visit to Jerusalem of November of the same year, though not linear, should not be underestimated. Gradually the Egyptian president embraced a notion of national interest whose primary concerns were domestic and economic. A series of cabinets was formed with the objective of economic reform. Ending war with Israel was, therefore, perceived as a necessary condition for such a reform.

There is no evidence to conclude that Sadat had a view of Israel, Jews, and Zionism that differed radically from that held by others of his generation. On the contrary, his admiration for German military discipline, his war connections with pro-Nazi agents, and some of his public statements on Jews in the early 1950s suggest the opposite. Thus it is more reasonable to assume that his statements on Israel after 1977 were acts of necessity rather than a reflection of his state of mind. Ahmed Baha al-Din, Sadat's confidant at the time, relates how Sadat, in moments of strain in negotiation with Israel, would refer to Israelis in harsh terms.[3]

President Husni Mubarak inherited and promoted the main legacy of Sadat's notion of peace with Israel. Peace means the end of military hostilities and the establishment and maintenance of proper relations with a neighbor state. Both Sadat and Mubarak stated that Israel had no privileged position in Egypt; its embassy is just one of some 120 embassies in Cairo, no more and no less. In 1988 the Egyptian leadership asserted the continued validity of the Arab collective defense treaty and stated that the Egyptian-Israeli treaty would not be given priority over Egypt's other Arab commitments.

Thus the Egyptian notion of peace is a pragmatic solution to fundamental problems faced by the Egyptian society and economy and compounded by a population explosion that increases the population by more than 1 million every ten months. Peace was a means to divert resources to developmental objectives and to create an atmosphere of stability.[4]

Egypt resisted the Israeli notion of peace that was laden with ideological and symbolic meanings. Peace with the largest Arab state was the fulfillment of the Zionist dream. A concrete problem that emerged from this idea was that of peace as normalization—in other words, the establishment of a complex web of relations in economic, social, athletic, touristic, academic, and other fields. Many protocols of cooperation between the two countries were signed. However, most of them were later frozen. In this context one has to look at the record of Egyptian-Israeli relations, which were characterized by lingering suspicion and doubts on both sides.

From the outset, Israeli policy put a strain on Egypt and the Egyptian-Israeli relationship. Indeed, it exposed the Egyptian government and made it vulnerable to criticism from domestic opposition forces and other Arab states. The autonomy talks came to a halt because of Israel's limited interpretation of Palestinian auton-

3. Ahmad Baha al-Din, *Dialogues with Sadat* (in Arabic) (Cairo: Dar al-Hilal, 1987), p. 166.

4. For an Israeli perspective see Rivka Yadlin, "Egyptian Perceptions of the Camp David Process," *Middle East Review*, vol. 18 (Fall 1985), pp. 45–50. For an Egyptian perspective see Abdul-Monem al-Mashat, "Egyptian Attitudes toward the Peace Process: Views of an 'Alert Elite,' " *Middle East Journal*, vol. 37 (Summer 1983), pp. 394–411. See also Ann Mosely Lesch, *Egyptian-Israeli Relations: Normalization or Special Ties?* Universities Field Staff International, no. 35 (Indianapolis: UFSI, 1986). Another view is Marie-Christine Aulas, "The Normalization of Egyptian-Israeli Relations," *Arab Studies Quarterly*, vol. 5 (Summer 1983), pp. 220–36.

omy.[5] Another issue was Israel's settlement policy in the West Bank. Prime Minister Menachem Begin indicated that the peace treaty called for only a three-month freeze, and the Israeli cabinet soon authorized new settlements, a policy not conducive to the introduction of Palestinian autonomy. In 1980 the Knesset resolved to make unified Jerusalem the "eternal capital of Israel." Three days after the Sadat-Begin meeting in Sharm al-Sheikh on June 4, 1981, Israeli planes bombed Iraq's Osirak nuclear reactor. Then, in December 1981, Israel declared that the Golan Heights would be subject to Israeli civil law, in effect annexing it.

A turning point came in June 1982 when Israel invaded Lebanon, just six weeks after its withdrawal from Sinai. Most Egyptians perceived the invasion as "a slap in the face," and the government position was severely undermined.[6] The week before the invasion witnessed active political exchanges between the two countries; a National Democratic party delegation headed by Mustafa Khalil, deputy prime minister, visited Israel; the Israeli minister of industry was in Egypt; and Egypt's foreign minister, Kamal Hassan Ali, had talks with his counterpart in Tel Aviv.[7]

The invasion was seen in Egypt as proof that by neutralizing Egypt militarily Israel had gained a free hand in the Arab East. The invasion, however, also offered Egypt's government an opportunity to boost its position in the Arab world. This was made possible by the fact that almost all Arab governments took no action other than condemning the invasion. Thus, as Louis J. Cantori concludes, "Egypt's constraints under the peace treaty with Israel . . . did not look all that damning by way of comparison."[8]

In response to mounting popular anger, the Egyptian government froze the normalization process, and planned official visits to Israel were canceled. Contractual commitments, however, were respected. Egyptian oil continued to flow to Israel, and Mubarak refused to recall his ambassador from Tel Aviv. When the Phalangist forces murdered Palestinians in the Sabra and Shatila refugee camps in September with the knowledge and protection of the Israeli army, however, Egypt was forced to recall its ambassador to Cairo in response to public outrage.

5. Louis J. Cantori, "Egyptian Policy," in Robert O. Freedman, ed., *The Middle East since Camp David* (Boulder, Colo.: Westview Press, 1984), pp. 176–77, 182.

6. Lesch, "Egyptian-Israeli relations," p. 2.

7. Louis J. Cantori, "Egyptian Policy under Mubarak: The Politics of Continuity and Change," in Robert O. Freedman, ed., *The Middle East after the Israeli Invasion of Lebanon* (Syracuse University Press, 1986), pp. 330–31.

8. Ibid., p. 320.

For the following years a cold peace reigned. A number of problems surfaced in Egyptian-Israeli relations. Chief among them were the assassination of Israeli diplomats in Egypt, the shooting of Israeli tourists in Sinai by an Egyptian draftee, the status of Coptic properties in Jerusalem, and the border dispute over Taba.[9]

As to the attacks on Israeli diplomats in Egypt, three cases (and a fourth incident involving U.S. diplomats in 1987) were engineered by a group called the "Revolution of Egypt Organization." The first attack was on June 4, 1984, when an Israeli administrative attaché, Zvi Kedar, was shot and wounded. Fourteen months later, on August 20, 1985, Albert Atrakchi, also an administrative attaché, was shot and killed. Atrakchi, who had just joined the embassy, served for a decade in military intelligence. Both Kedar and Atrakchi had no Egyptian security protection, since the Israeli embassy had declined to request it. On March 19, 1986, an embassy car carrying four Israelis was ambushed in front of the International Trade Fair in Cairo. The wife of an Israeli diplomat, Eti Tal-or, was killed, and the rest were wounded.

The group behind the three events was arrested in 1987 and brought to trial in 1988. The accused involved some twenty civilian and military men, most important of whom was Khaled Gamal Abd al-Nasser (son of former President Gamal Abd al-Nasser). Ann M. Lesch was prophetically correct when she wrote in December 1986, "If the persons responsible are caught and brought to trial, and if they are Egyptian citizens without ties to a hostile foreign power such as Libya, their imprisonment could result in a wave of sympathy among elements of the public that are critical of the rapprochement with Israel."[10] This is exactly what happened in 1988 when opposition papers competed in explaining the patriotic motives of the accused, and some commentators compared their actions to anti-British resistance during the occupation.[11]

Another public outcry in Egypt and Israel took place on October 5, 1985, when, at dusk, Suleiman Khater, a military conscript serving in Ras Burka (Sinai) shot a group of Israeli tourists who were climbing toward his position. He killed seven of them. Khater maintained that he was following orders to prevent anyone from

9. A detailed treatment is found in Ann Mosely Lesch, *Irritants in the Egyptian-Israeli Relationship*, Universities Field Staff International, no. 34 (Indianapolis: UFSI, 1986).

10. Ibid., p. 3.

11. See in particular *Al-Ahali* and *Sawt al-Arab* weeklies during February and March 1988.

approaching the post at night. He said that he asked them to stop more than once and that he was unaware of their nationality.

Egypt claimed that Khater had gone berserk and that it had taken his colleagues two hours to disarm him. Opposition parties seized the opportunity to explain that Khater was avenging the Israeli bombardment of the headquarters of the Palestine Liberation Organization (PLO) in Tunis and that his act was motivated by anti-Camp David feelings. The Israeli government protested Egypt's refusal to allow the wounded to be hospitalized in Israel or to permit Israeli doctors to treat them. Eventually, Khater was tried, sentenced to life imprisonment, and found dead in his cell ten days later. Whether Khater committed suicide, as a government statement explained, or was killed, as most opposition parties alleged, became a subject of heated debate for months.

A third issue in Egyptian-Israeli relations concerned Deir al-Sultan, a Coptic monastery in Jerusalem. The Deir had been owned for generations by the Egyptian Coptic Orthodox Church. In 1970, however, Israeli military authorities ordered Egyptian monks to evacuate the premises and turn them over to Ethiopian Coptic monks. In response to the Israeli government's failure to intervene, Egyptian monks went to court. The Israeli high court ruled, in 1971, that the Israeli government should restore the Deir to the Egyptian monks within one year, but nothing happened. In 1979 Egypt raised the issue diplomatically with Israel and in 1982 the Egyptian church prevented Copts from making pilgrimages until Deir al-Sultan was returned. Israel responded by establishing a ministerial committee to resolve the problem in a way satisfactory to Egypt. No progress has been achieved yet.

Last but not least was the issue of Taba. Taba is a 250-acre triangle of land located twelve miles southwest of Eilat. The area includes a hill, a valley, and a natural harbor. Israel had not previously claimed the area, either in the armistice accord signed with Egypt in February 1949 or during the Israeli withdrawal from Sinai after the Suez war in 1956. But in December 1981, four months before the date of the final Israeli withdrawal from Sinai, the Israeli government raised doubts about the exact demarcation of the border at several points, including Taba. That was a most difficult time for Cairo, which had witnessed the assassination of its president two months earlier. The new president was keen to see the withdrawal completed as scheduled and did not want to cause delay. Any delay would have made the Mubarak regime vulnerable to criticism from opposition parties and other Arab states.

The two countries agreed to have multinational forces and

observers stationed in the disputed area and to start negotiations on how to handle the issue on the basis of Article 7 of the peace treaty, which calls for conciliation or arbitration if negotiations fail. The Egyptian government understood that Israel would not construct new installations in the area. Thus Israel made a point of granting two leases before the date of final withdrawal in April: one to Rafi Nelson's tourist village and the other to Aviya Sonesta Hotel. Egypt complained of continued construction after April 1982.

Without reviewing the legal dimension of the dispute, it nonetheless seems that the Egyptian position rests on solid ground.[12] Recognizing the strength of its position, Egypt sought arbitration while Israel preferred conciliation. The first technical meeting between the two countries took place in Eilat in May 1982, and the next one in March 1983 in Ismailiya. The meetings dragged on for a year and a half. Egypt insisted that no progress in relations was possible before agreement was reached on Taba. Toward the end of 1984 President Mubarak set three conditions for improving relations with Israel: resolution of the Taba dispute, withdrawal of Israeli troops from Lebanon, and amelioration of the conditions of the Palestinians in the occupied territories.

New political developments occurred in 1985 that affected Egyptian-Israeli relations. The Israeli elections of July 1984 brought a national unity government to power, and Shimon Peres became the prime minister for two years. Peres wanted to withdraw Israeli forces from Lebanon before June 1985. In February, Jordan and the PLO concluded an agreement on a framework for peace, which allowed Palestinian participation in a joint delegation to negotiate the future of the West Bank and Gaza in an international conference (see appendix F). Egypt played an important role in the agreement and applauded it. The Egyptian government allowed some improvement in relations with Israel and some ministerial exchanges took place. In March, President Mubarak made an important concession when he indicated that if Israel would accept a timetable for arbitration, relations would improve. Relations were strained later in the year, however, because of the Israeli bombing of the PLO headquarters in Tunis, the Khater affair, and the turmoil over the *Achille Lauro* hijacking and Egypt's refusal to detain the hijackers.

Finally, in January 1986 the Israeli cabinet accepted arbitration on Taba. Negotiations between the two technical teams resumed

12. Ann Mosely Lesch, *The Egyptian-Israeli Summit: Protracted Negotiations and Reduced Expectations*, Universities Field Staff International, no. 33 (Indianapolis: UFSI, 1986), pp. 2–3.

and on September 10 an agreement on principles was reached. Shimon Peres wanted to have a meeting with Mubarak before the end of his tenure as prime minister and he got it. The Taba agreement was signed on September 11, at 1:30 a.m., and Peres arrived in Egypt fourteen hours later. Muhammad Bassiouni who had served as the Egyptian chargé d'affaires in Tel Aviv was designated ambassador. The communiqué of the Mubarak-Peres meeting referred to the search for a just and comprehensive peace (one that would resolve the Palestinian question in all its dimensions) in the Middle East and their shared commitment to proceed jointly toward that goal. Egypt and Israel differed on their understanding of how to achieve the much-sought "just and comprehensive peace." Egypt supported the idea of an international conference under the auspices of the United Nations, though it was flexible on the functioning of the conference. Mubarak proposed that bilateral committees should negotiate concrete issues within the framework of the conference. The two countries also differed on Palestinian representation. Egypt endorsed the PLO and supports the right of Palestinian self-determination.

The analysis of these issues shows "the degree of routinization that has evolved in official contacts."[13] But more fundamental is the Israeli position on the PLO, Israeli policy and practices in the occupied territories and Lebanon, and the means for settling the Arab-Israeli conflict.[14] These issues will eventually determine the course of Israeli-Egyptian relations and whether they will continue as a cold peace involving suspicion and doubts or will develop positively as part of a comprehensive settlement in the Middle East.

THE EGYPTIAN-ARAB SYMBIOSIS: LEGAL VERSUS FUNCTIONAL APPROACHES

In the post-1967 era, Egypt's Arab policy has been primarily motivated by two objectives: the need for a solid Arab consensus to reach a comprehensive solution of the Arab-Israeli conflict and the need to generate massive economic and financial aid. Egyptian tactics and positions have changed over time in pursuing these two objectives.

In the early 1970s, Sadat ridiculed the distinction between

13. Lesch, "Irritants in the Egyptian-Israeli Relationship," p. 6.

14. Cantori, "Egyptian Policy under Mubarak," pp. 323–44. See analysis of Egyptian press reactions to the Israeli invasion of Lebanon in Korany, "Cold Peace," pp. 662–72.

revolutionary and conservative Arab states. The real criterion, he argued, should be a country's position toward the Arab effort against Israel. He started to build a broad Arab front by reconciling differences among Arab regimes, advocating the principle of nonintervention in one another's internal affairs, and emphasizing the need for Arab solidarity. To achieve these goals, Sadat paid many visits to various Arab countries. He was the first Egyptian head of state to visit Iraq and Kuwait.

Sadat demonstrated his ability for swift action. In most cases, he could outbid and outmaneuver his critics. The ups and downs of Egypt's relations with other Arab countries must be seen in the context of its search for an end to the Arab-Israeli conflict. Thus, for instance, the first public rift between Egypt and Syria centered around Egypt's second disengagement treaty and the acceptance of Henry A. Kissinger's step-by-step approach. The major developments, however, took place after Sadat's visit to Israel in November 1977. The decision to go to Israel was motivated by several factors: Sadat's frustration with Arab disunity, the feeling that Syria was not enthusiastic about an early resumption of the Geneva conference, increasing economic problems at home, and U.S. impatience with the push and pull of Arab politics.

The reactions of Arab states to the Jerusalem visit differed markedly. Morocco, Sudan, Somalia, and Oman supported the move. Algeria, Libya, Syria, Iraq, South Yemen, as well as the PLO, condemned it in a meeting they held in Tripoli in December 1977. Sadat responded by severing diplomatic relations with these five Arab states. In the middle, Saudi Arabia, Jordan, and the Gulf states were neutral, giving Sadat the benefit of the doubt.

The Camp David Accords were met by almost universal Arab rejection. In an Arab summit meeting in Baghdad in November 1978 Arab states decided that they would break diplomatic relations with Cairo, suspend Egypt's membership in the League of Arab States, transfer the headquarters of the Arab League from Cairo to Tunis, and boycott any Egyptian company that would do business with Israel if Egypt went further and signed a treaty with Israel.

Peace with Israel violated a basic tenet of Arab consensus and challenged one of the core values in Arab political culture. Thus it is not surprising that Arab governments initiated a harsh propaganda campaign against Sadat and his policy to which Sadat responded in a similar vein. He described Arab leaders as ignorant and dwarfs and did not shy away from reminding Arab countries of the help they received from Egypt. Sadat described the Arab League as dead and established a League of Arab and Islamic Peoples to replace it.

Under Mubarak things changed radically. Propaganda campaigns against Arab governments, with the exception of Libya, were halted. Mubarak seized every opportunity to demonstrate that Camp David did not really tie Egypt's hands. For example, he decided to withdraw Egypt's ambassador from Tel Aviv in September 1982, following the Israeli invasion of Lebanon. He condemned Israeli policy in the occupied territories in the UN and other international meetings, and he refused to visit Jerusalem.

By 1987 the Egyptian president had visited Morocco, Iraq, Saudi Arabia, Kuwait, and the United Arab Emirates on different occasions. In addition he traveled to Sudan, Somalia, Jordan, and Oman with which Egypt already had full diplomatic relations. Presidential aides and emissaries carried messages to almost all Arab capitals, with the possible exceptions of Tripoli and Aden.

There were three positions held by Egyptians concerned with Egypt's Arab relations. One position held that the Arabs broke relations with Egypt, and that they must reestablish them. Another viewpoint was more cognizant of the importance of Arab links to Egypt through identity, tourism, remittances, potential economic aid, and international prestige. Its advocates believed in the necessity of bringing Egypt back into the Arab fold. A third position emphasized functional relations (such as labor migration, remittances, and economic cooperation) between Egypt and other Arab countries, rather than the legal and diplomatic ones. Egypt's reintegration into the institutions of the Arab system might drag it into the never-ending Arab quarrels and disputes, they warned. Despite the importance of this last argument, Egyptian decisionmakers perceived Egypt's official isolation as unacceptable. Its rehabilitation required the undoing of the Baghdad summit resolutions.

In September 1984, Jordan resumed diplomatic relations with Egypt, and the leaders of the two countries later began to exchange visits on a regular basis. Relations with Iraq continued to grow as did support of the Iraqi war effort. With the intensification of the Gulf war and its potential geographic spillover, Arab countries were increasingly in need of Egypt's influence and power. That became evident in the Arab summit meeting held in Amman in November 1987. The conference resolved that the Arab League had no jurisdiction over bilateral relations between Arab states, which opened the door for those who wanted to resume their diplomatic relations with Cairo. In the span of three months, relations were resumed with all Arab states except Algeria, Lebanon, Libya, and Syria. In January 1988, President Mubarak paid a goodwill visit to Bahrain, the United Arab Emirates, Kuwait, Oman, Qatar, Saudi Arabia, and Morocco. Arab ministers and dignitaries became familiar faces again in Cairo.

The resumption of Egyptian-Arab diplomatic relations raises three issues for Egypt's foreign policy. The first relates to the potential contradictions between its Arab and Israeli commitments. For instance, in March 1988 the Egyptian leadership called for the rejuvenation of the Arab collective defense treaty and for the establishment of an indigenous Arab military industry. The second issue relates to the intricacy of Egypt's Arab position. Egypt restored relations on a bilateral basis with most Arab states but not collectively with the Arab League. The third issue is the change in the Arab system during the last decade. When Sadat signed the Camp David Accords, he thought that other Arab governments would follow suit. This did not take place. The Arab governments, in imposing economic sanctions on Egypt, thought that Egypt could not do without their aid. This did not prove to be the case. Ten years of Arab politics without Egypt created new roles and vested interests.[15] The resistance of some Arab governments, such as Syria, to Egypt's reintegration into the system is in part related to their doubt over the future of their own roles in the new configuration of inter-Arab relations if Egypt were reintegrated.

THE EGYPTIAN-ISRAELI-AMERICAN TRIANGLE

In the 1970s, the United States made a dramatic return to Egypt and the Arab world. U.S. diplomacy was able to contain, outmaneuver, and sometimes expel Soviet influence from most of the area. Even with "radical" Arab states such as Algeria, the United States maintained flourishing commercial and economic relations. The big success story, however, was that of U.S.-Egyptian relations. In 1970 there were no formal diplomatic relations between the two countries; they were resumed in February 1974. Within four to five years, Egypt had developed special relations with the United States. Since 1978 the United States has become a partner in Egyptian-

15. See Ali E. Hillal Dessouki, "The New Arab Political Order: Implications for the 1980s," in Malcolm H. Kerr and El Sayed Yassin, eds., *Rich and Poor States in the Middle East: Egypt and the New Arab Order* (Boulder, Colo.: Westview Press, 1982), pp. 319–47.

Israeli relations, the major supplier of arms, and the primary donor of economic assistance to Egypt.[16]

Through his famous shuttle diplomacy, Kissinger monopolized the indirect negotiation process that took place after the war, resulting in the first disengagement agreements between Egypt and Israel, and between Syria and Israel in 1974. Egypt signed the second Sinai agreement in September 1975, a step that created a rift in the Arab world because of the failure of Syria and Israel to achieve a similar agreement.

In 1977–78 Sadat became more emphatic about the importance of the U.S. role. The United States was seen not just as a mediator but as a full partner in the peace process. Thus Sadat concentrated on American public opinion. He spent endless hours with media people, senators and representatives, and leaders of the American Jewish community. And he did make an impact on them. One is tempted to argue that the target of his visit to Jerusalem was not only the Israeli but equally the American people. He made the visit in front of television cameras, and well-established news stars such as Walter Cronkite and Barbara Walters accompanied him. The visit was a media event, an exercise in television diplomacy, and Sadat captured the imagination of millions in the United States. He definitely improved Egypt's image, but his other more subtle objective—political disengagement between Israel and the United States—did not materialize, and strong U.S. pressure on Israel was not forthcoming.

In this effort to befriend and entice the United States, Sadat was ready to forge strategic-military links between the two countries. He projected the image of a stable Egypt, which could become an asset for Western strategy in the Middle East, and possibly in Africa. In 1977 Egypt intervened in support of the pro-Western Mobutu regime in Zaire against his political opposition. In 1979 Sadat offered to help Morocco in its war with Algeria, and Egypt actively supported Iraq against Iran.

Sadat's military connection with the United States was designed to achieve three objectives. The first was to demonstrate to pro-

16. Ibrahim Karawan, "Egypt and the Western Alliance: The Politics of Westomania?" in Steven L. Spiegel, ed., *The Middle East and the Western Alliance* (London: George Allen and Unwin, 1982), pp. 164–75; and Ali E. Hillal Dessouki, "The Primacy of Economics: The Foreign Policy of Egypt," in Bahgat Korany and Ali E. Hillal Dessouki, *The Foreign Policies of Arab States* (Boulder, Colo.: Westview Press, 1984), pp. 140–42. See also Robert Springborg, "U.S. Policy toward Egypt: Problems and Prospects," *Orbis*, vol. 24 (Winter 1981), pp. 805–18; and Mohamed I. Hakki, "U.S.-Egyptian Relations," *American-Arab Affairs*, no. 6 (Fall 1983), pp. 28–33.

Western Arab regimes, which disagreed with his policy, the centrality of Egypt in American strategy. The second was to satisfy the army, which suffered from "arms starvation," and enhance its prestige. The third was to prove that Egypt was a strategic asset to the United States.

The signing of the Camp David Accords and the Egyptian-Israeli peace treaty opened the door for much closer military and economic relations. Military cooperation between the two countries has taken various forms: arms supplies, transfer of military technology and coproduction of arms, provision of military facilities, and joint training and maneuvers. In April 1988, American and Egyptian ministers of defense signed a memorandum of understanding that established the principles of cooperation between the two countries and enhanced their military-strategic relations.

As another form of cooperation, Egypt offered the United States "temporary limited access" to airfields near Cairo (Cairo West) and discussed the possibility of such arrangements at Ras Banas on the Red Sea as well. Though separated from the Gulf by Saudi Arabia, Ras Banas is still a strategic point in relation to the Suez Canal and the Mediterranean. It becomes more important as more oil is shipped through Saudi Arabia by pipeline and up to the Red Sea, through the Suez Canal to the Mediterranean.

The United States hoped to convince Sadat to sign an agreement making the Ras Banas base available to the U.S. military. Secretary Alexander Haig discussed this issue during his visit to the region in April 1981 but with no success. Egypt resisted the idea of signing a formal agreement that guaranteed access to military facilities. Sadat's formal position was that Egypt would consider making the facilities available to the United States in response to a request by any member of the Arab League. This commitment was reiterated by Mubarak. Eventually talks between the two countries broke down and the whole issue was shelved.

The United States and Egypt also collaborated in joint training and maneuvers. On January 1, 1980, two U.S. AWACS (airborne warning and control system) planes flew to Qena air base in Upper Egypt with 250 U.S. Air Force personnel to practice contingencies such as directing fighter-bombers to targets. In November, the U.S. Rapid Deployment Force participated in a two-week exercise in Egypt. The exercises, called Bright Star, gave the Rapid Deployment Force its first experience in Middle Eastern deserts and brought to attention a number of problems in both operations and equipment. Similar exercises were conducted in 1982, 1983, 1984, and 1986. They were not held in 1981 because of Sadat's assassination, and in 1985 as a reflection of Egypt's unhappiness with American actions in the *Achille Lauro* affair when American fighters forced an Egyptair plane carrying four Palestinian guerrillas to land.

As to economic relations, Egypt was second only to Israel in receiving U.S. aid. The increase in economic aid coincided with the shift in Egypt's domestic and foreign policies. The political underpinnings of the aid were articulated in a 1981 document issued by the Agency for International Development as follows: "Our high level of aid to Egypt is premised on the belief that President Sadat's peace initiatives are crucial to that objective [stability] and that these efforts will be supported and enhanced by a vigorous and growing economy."[17]

One important conclusion that emerges from this brief presentation of Egyptian-American relations is the primacy of the Israeli factor. In fact, no bilateral Egyptian-American relationship exists. Rather the relationship is triangular. As perceived by many Egyptians, their country is measured not only by what it does or fails to do toward the United States but also by its policy toward Israel. This uneasy situation gives Israel added leverage over Egypt, given its close alliance with the United States.

Egyptian-American relations have their own strains as well. Egypt's debts represent a heavy burden on its troubled economy. Egyptian officials argue that these debts are of a political nature, linked with the opening to Israel, and that the issue should be resolved politically. Another strain, alluded to earlier, stems from Egypt's weak position in the Israeli-American-Egyptian triangle and the recognition that Israel has more influence in Washington, which makes Washington more sensitive to Israeli demands. A third issue is the means of achieving a comprehensive peace in the region. Egypt prefers an international conference, but the United States is closer to the Israeli position. Mubarak's ideas of February 1988 concerning the situation in the occupied territories were quietly put aside by Washington. But the fundamental strain came from Egypt's recognition that its relations with Arab and nonaligned countries were adversely affected because of Egypt's special relations with the United States. Thus Mubarak has had to distance himself from American views on a number of issues.

However, the ability of Egypt and the United States to institutionalize and routinize their relations during the last decade is striking. The death of Sadat removed the element of drama from

17. Quoted in Saad Eddin Ibrahim, "Superpowers in the Arab World," *Washington Quarterly*, vol. 4 (Summer 1981), pp. 88–89.

the relationship. Sadat was able to conduct the relationship in the prime time of American politics and media, at the level of presidents and foreign ministers and with a high degree of visibility. To maintain it, Sadat had to keep media attention on Egypt and demonstrate that he was a close ally of the United States, a policy that had risks and dangers. Egyptians grew wary of the increasing dependence of their country on the United States and the decline of Egypt's image as a nonaligned state.

Under Mubarak, relations with the United States became more regularized and institutionalized. The day-to-day relationship is no longer a visible political matter. Even crises that erupt in the process are quietly contained and diplomatically managed.

The main thrust of Mubarak's foreign policy is an attempt to rehabilitate the country's position in Arab, African, Islamic, and nonaligned councils, without introducing a sudden or major shift in its foreign policy orientation. On the one hand, Mubarak has emphasized the continuity of Sadat's basic policies: peace with Israel and close relations with the United States. On the other hand, he has stressed Egypt's nonaligned position. Mubarak attended the 1983 nonaligned summit meeting in New Delhi and the 1987 Islamic summit in Kuwait. The Egyptian press criticizes U.S. policy on a great number of issues, including its support of Israel. Vehement anti-Soviet attacks are no longer pronounced in Cairo, and relations with the Soviet Union have gradually become normal.

CONCLUSION

Where does Egypt stand today ten years after signing the Camp David Accords? Mubarak perceives the accords as a phase in the resolution of the Arab-Israeli conflict. In part the accords have fulfilled their objectives, and in other ways they have to be transcended in view of new circumstances. He makes a clear distinction between the framework for peace in the Middle East, which deals with the future of the West Bank and Gaza, and the framework for the conclusion of a peace treaty between Egypt and Israel. After being rejected by both Jordan and the Palestinians and the collapse of autonomy talks in 1982, the plan for peace in the occupied territories became obsolete. In 1988 Mubarak resisted all ideas to revive the Camp David solution for the West Bank and Gaza.

The second part of Camp David has been implemented and has been in force for a decade. While upholding a minimalist interpretation of the peace treaty, Mubarak does not shy away from declaring Egypt's commitment to its contractual agreements. How far the resumption of diplomatic relations with Arab states will affect the Egyptian position remains an open question.

Ten years ago Sadat sought an Egyptian-Israeli peace that was to be the centerpiece of a comprehensive settlement of the conflict. Peace between Egypt and Israel has become a reality, though strained by domestic political opposition and Israeli policy in Lebanon and the occupied territories. The cold peace is likely to continue in the absence of a broader settlement. Sadat's second objective remains a remote possibility.

HERMANN FREDERICK EILTS

The United States and Egypt

TEN YEARS AGO, on September 17, 1978, the Camp David Accords were signed. Two in number, they were qualitatively asymmetrical. One offered fairly specific guidelines for an Egyptian-Israeli peace; the other envisioned negotiated Palestinian autonomy, whatever that might mean, for the West Bank and Gaza as a kind of halfway house to an ultimate final disposition of those Israeli-occupied areas. The accords followed two weeks of arduous negotiations, catalyzed by President Jimmy Carter, between President Anwar Sadat of Egypt and Prime Minister Menachem Begin of Israel. Hard compromises were forged, often through ambiguous language, susceptible to divergent interpretations. Some crucial issues were perforce deferred, presaging future problems.

It is difficult today to recapture the euphoria of the White House signing ceremony. For most of the invited guests, the Egyptian delegation members and press excepted, an American president had finally achieved a partial, but significant, breakthrough in the long, unresolved Arab-Israeli conflict.[1] The event was momentous and portentous. A new Camp David "spirit," that participants hoped would be infectious, was hailed.[2] It emanated from a belief that, however contentious the talks had been, determination, patience, flexibility, and effective American mediation had overcome obstacles long deemed insurmountable. In this residual heady atmosphere,

1. The Egyptian delegation and press were painfully aware that Sadat's foreign minister had resigned at Camp David in protest over the accords that were to be signed. For the minister's account of his resignation, see Mohamed Ibrahim Kamel, *The Camp David Accords: A Testimony* (London: KPI, 1986), pp. 326–82.

2. The Camp David spirit, if it ever existed, was ephemeral. It virtually vanished on the day after the signing ceremony, when Begin publicly stated his view of the narrow limits of West Bank and Gaza autonomy, which seemed to make fatuous the U.S. and Egyptian explanations of what was intended.

the signing six months later of an Egyptian-Israeli peace treaty, formalizing one of the two Camp David agreements, almost verged on the anticlimactic.

To be sure, many saw the accords and the derivative peace treaty, which collectively constitute the Camp David package, as a bilateral accommodation between Egypt and Israel. Egypt was charged with having been persuaded by the United States to break Arab ranks. Arab and Soviet critics, along with European skeptics, derided public assertions of Sadat and Carter that the agreements would be the "cornerstone" of a comprehensive settlement. But the Camp David package also portended a new, closer bilateral U.S.-Egyptian association.

Such had been foreshadowed by Carter in his first meeting with Sadat on April 4, 1977, at the White House. There, the American president had opined that, should peace talks succeed, the overall U.S. association with Egypt could in ten years time become as strong as that with Israel.[3] This presidential prognosis of parity with Israel significantly encouraged Sadat to concede what he did at Camp David the following year, largely at Carter's behest and against the unanimous counsel of the Egyptian president's advisers. Egypt's leadership would interpret Carter's observation literally. Following the peace treaty in March 1979, it would repeatedly contend that a U.S. commitment existed to give Egypt parity with Israel in economic and military aid.

Although Sadat was disappointed when Gerald R. Ford lost the presidential election, he soon developed a warm regard for and trust in Carter. That confidence and candor was reciprocated. Sadat had repeatedly assured Carter, "I will not let you down." It was an extraordinary personal relationship.[4]

The high point of the U.S.-Egyptian bilateral relationship was the seven-month period between the signing of the Camp David Accords and the exchange of the instruments of ratification in late April 1979 of the Egyptian-Israeli peace treaty. In the ensuing decade, that bond, so artfully crafted by Nixon, Ford, Carter, and their secretaries of state, showed intermittent signs of dysfunction.

In truth, both the United States and Egypt held inflated ideas of the other's will and capability on the Middle East scene. Americans

3. See William B. Quandt, *Camp David: Peacemaking and Politics* (Brookings, 1986), p. 52, for President Jimmy Carter's statement.

4. For Carter's feelings toward Sadat, see Jimmy Carter, *Keeping Faith: Memoirs of a President* (Bantam Books, 1982), pp. 282–84. Anwar Sadat recounts his close working relationship with Carter in Anwar el-Sadat, *In Search of Identity: An Autobiography* (Harper and Row, 1977), pp. 297–302.

had come to equate Egypt with Sadat, as he did, discounting the continued prevalence of Egyptian dissentient views, which would sooner or later reassert themselves. As the great signing events of the Camp David Accords and the peace treaty receded in time, and the enduring realities of American and Arab politics again intruded, each party was disappointed with what it came to regard as the other's vacillation and uncertain dependability. The "full partnership," heralded at Camp David, frayed and became a vacuous phrase. While the essential relationship remains close and positive, it is also often querulous and suffused with some subliminal mistrust. Perceived uncritical U.S. acquiescence in Israeli policies has raised misgivings in Egypt about professed American evenhandedness. By the same token, Egypt's seeming equivocation on matters of concern to the United States has troubled American leaders. Not surprisingly, the reality of sometimes divergent, even conflicting, American and Egyptian political agendas has recurrently manifested itself.

Other reasons also account for the mutual attitudinal change. Soon after Camp David, the American and Egyptian principals who negotiated the agreements left the political scene: Carter lost the presidential election in 1980; Sadat was assassinated on October 6, 1981.[5] The incoming American president, Ronald Reagan, had a variant *Weltanschauung* from that of his predecessor. In consequence, to Egypt's disappointment, the new American administration, which had not shared in the arduous Camp David talks but received the package gratis, appeared to show but passing interest in maintaining the momentum of the peace process. Lip service was rendered, but little more. The most pressing outstanding issue was negotiating West Bank and Gaza autonomy.

Egypt's new president, Husni Mubarak, who assumed office in October 1981, had as vice president endorsed Sadat's peace policies, but as chief of state seemed equally concerned with restoring Egypt's role in Arab ranks. Moreover, he was no media personality. Lacking the dramatic flair of Sadat, he found it difficult to create the positive personal impact that his predecessor had made on successive American administrations, Congress, and the public. The immediate post-Camp David period had also demonstrated that Egypt, though the largest and strongest Arab state, did not on that account command the unquestioned obedience of Arab confreres. Indeed, to the surprise of some Americans, Egypt was summarily suspended from the organization it had so long dominated, the Arab League,

5. Israeli Prime Minister Menachem Begin resigned in September 1983. He was succeeded by Yitzhak Shamir, who had opposed the Camp David agreements.

and from the Islamic Conference Organization, of which it had been a founding member.

The Camp David package, seminal though it was, deepened existing divisions in the Arab world. American inability to obtain at least Saudi Arabian endorsement for the accords, something Sadat had counted on, spelled a lengthy period of isolation for Egypt among Arab and Islamic polities. To some extent that cleavage persists, though most Arab states, each for its own reasons, and especially after the Arab summit in Amman in November 1987, have opted to restore diplomatic relations with what they earlier condemned as an errant Egypt. The protracted Iraq-Iran war has accelerated that process.

Separately but concurrently, the advent of the Ayatollah Ruhollah Khomeini and the Iranian Islamic Republic in 1979, and their humbling of the United States in the ensuing hostage crisis, encouraged Islamic fundamentalism elsewhere in the Middle East as well. Egyptian Islamic militants, who were responsible for the assassination of Sadat, are anti-American, anti-Israeli, and anti-Camp David in outlook. To them, the Camp David package is anathema. In fact, as the decade progressed, the imprimatur Camp David, except in Israel and the United States, came increasingly to be a political liability for reviving broader peace talks.

The Camp David package needs to be seen in historical perspective. Its components were steps, albeit major ones, in an ongoing process. For the United States, Sadat's decision after the October 1973 Arab-Israeli war, to work with Washington to achieve a settlement with Israel, was an exceptional opportunity. Soon after his assumption of the presidency in late September 1970, Sadat took various initiatives to intimate his desire for improved relations with the United States. Until conflict erupted, which threatened a superpower confrontation, Washington responded passively. Yet whatever initial American doubts existed about Sadat, he came to be recognized by the Nixon administration as a "moderate," measured in normally intransigent Arab terms. Since Egypt was the largest and strongest Arab state, and had contributed most of the Arab military manpower in recurrent Arab-Israeli hostilities, Washington nurtured the perception that an Egypt, headed by Sadat, should also be able to lead its fellow Arab states into a peace dialogue with Israel.

True, not all took Egypt's leadership role among Arab states for granted. Since the heyday of Gamal Abd al-Nasser's pan-Arabism mystique, and especially after Egypt's disastrous defeat by Israel in June 1967, competitive centers of Arab power had emerged. Syria,

Algeria, and Iraq were but three such challengers. Nor, as some American observers foresaw, could one be confident that Egypt would be able to bring the fractured Palestine Liberation Organization (PLO) to accept its fiat. Since Palestinian nationalism had always figured negatively in U.S. thinking on Middle East politics, and Sadat often spoke contemptuously of it, assuring American interlocutors that Yasir Arafat would ultimately do his bidding, that potential Egyptian vulnerability was dismissed. Sadat, it was believed, whatever lip service he might give to Palestinian aspirations, did so for Arab postural reasons rather than from conviction. His nationalism was primarily Egyptian rather than Arab oriented. If Egypt's national interests could be made to prosper, he would be prepared to compromise on overall Arab issues. Once Egypt did so, other Arab states might protest, but eventually they would have no choice but to acquiesce. While plausible, this widely held American estimate was overdrawn.

A second American perception existed in 1973 to make Sadat's Egypt a promising negotiating partner. This was the belief that Egypt, after several disastrous wars with Israel, and the deleterious effects of Nasser's inefficient statist system of Arab socialism, was economically prostrate. Peace, it was argued, was mandatory for Egypt. It was only a matter of time and of cosmetically assembling the right pieces. The Egyptian leadership might, for domestic political reasons, proclaim its military successes against Israel during the October 1973 war, but both Richard M. Nixon and Henry A. Kissinger knew that, had it not been for timely U.S. intervention, Israel—with substantial U.S. military aid—would again have bested Egypt. Conversely, the realization of how close Egypt had again come to military defeat, coupled with economic imperatives, would compel Sadat to work with the U.S. government and, through a negotiating process, try to undo the adverse consequences of past defeats.

This view was strengthened by Sadat's ready acquiescence in Kissinger's first disengagement proposals, despite their modest nature and the vehement opposition of his senior advisers, and by the Egyptian president's immediate and urgent requests for U.S. economic and military aid. If such aid could be provided to Egypt, Washington postulated, it should be possible to mediate sufficient mutual compromise between Egypt and Israel to move toward Middle East peace. Sadat was viewed by Washington as the more compliant party. At the same time, U.S. aid, whatever it might be, offered prospects of eliminating—or, at least, reducing—the hitherto preeminent Soviet influence in Egypt. Sadat's frequent vitriolic public outbursts against the Soviets, and his subsequent sharp constriction of the Soviet presence in Egypt, though not directly inspired by the United States, earned American plaudits. Although Sadat personally distrusted the Soviets' purposes in Egypt, his actions against them were also intended to impress the United States favorably.

As early as November 1973, on his first visit to Egypt, Kissinger had promised U.S. economic and military aid. Despite Nixon administration efforts to expedite economic aid, a balky Congress failed to appropriate funds until late December 1974. Because of anticipated congressional objections, consideration was given to channeling some military aid, indirectly, through Saudi Arabia. Kissinger eventually discarded that idea because of opposition from some of his advisers. Much to Sadat's disappointment, Nixon's resignation as president, as a result of Watergate, brought the idea of military assistance to a standstill. Small amounts of nonlethal equipment were provided to Egypt after the Sinai II disengagement agreement of 1975, in the face of vigorous Israeli objection, but it was impressed on Sadat that requisite congressional acquiescence in substantial military aid would not be forthcoming until there was meaningful progress toward peace. In the process that began with Sinai I and terminated with the Camp David package, the United States consistently used ongoing economic aid and possible future military assistance as a lubricant to induce Egyptian political flexibility.

In the post-Camp David decade, U.S. policy toward Egypt embraced general and complementary specific objectives. It was generally expected that the peace treaty, by sidelining Egypt, would reduce the risk of wider Arab-Israeli hostilities or, if conflict occurred, would localize it. Israel would be given a greater sense of security, which, it was hoped, might make it more amenable to compromise with other neighboring Arab states. Finally, Soviet influence in the area would be further reduced.

Specific policy objectives, which came increasingly to figure in the bilateral dialogue between the two countries, included U.S.-Egyptian security cooperation in the Middle East and Africa, U.S. access to Egyptian military facilities for staging or other contingency purposes, and even vague hopes for some kind of areawide tripartite security cooperation with Israel. On the economic front, with the termination of the state of war, Egypt could be urged to shift resources to badly lagging economic development, undertake long-needed economic structural reform, and forge mutually beneficial

Egyptian-Israeli commercial ties, which might help to reinforce the peace treaty.

Two periods of uneven length mark the decade: the first, 1979–81, saw the final year and a half of Carter's presidency, Reagan's first months in office, and ended with Sadat's assassination in October 1981; the second spans the bulk of the roughly coterminous Reagan and Mubarak presidencies. Basic outlines of the bilateral relationship, and some of its difficulties, took shape during the first period. Since 1981, periodic mutual misgivings about respective Middle East policies and issues in U.S. aid have marred the relationship, but never to a point at which it became fundamentally endangered.

The quality of any bilateral relationship, that with Egypt included, depends in large measure on the permanence of mutual interests, the interaction of respective leadership elites on specific issues, and sustained domestic support in each country for close cooperation. These factors were stronger before Camp David than they have been since. Put differently, areas of disagreement, consciously muted before the Egyptian-Israeli peace, have since loomed larger. An analysis of the bilateral relationship in the past decade reveals significant but generally manageable political, economic, and military differences.

THE POLITICAL DIMENSION

The Camp David package was unquestionably seminal in the political association between the United States and Egypt. Yet, paradoxically, it spawned both expanded cooperation and more visible discord. For the United States and Egypt alike, the political dimension of the relationship dominates their dialogue. Even aid, economic or military, carries political overtones. In the political context, several factors have contributed to dissonance: a faltering Middle East peace process, the growing influence of Israel on U.S. policies in the area, the Palestinian issue, ambivalent Egyptian policies on matters affecting the United States, diminished mutual candor, disparate power status, growing Egyptian restiveness over perceived economic dependency on the United States, and persistent American concerns about internal political and economic structural weaknesses in the Egyptian regime. U.S. failures, such as the Lebanese debacle of 1982–83, have also eroded Egyptian belief in American fairness, wisdom, or capability. None is of itself decisive, but their cumulative effect clouds relationships.

A Faltering Peace Process

The West Bank and Gaza autonomy talks mandated by Camp David began in August 1979. To Sadat's disappointment, Carter could not play an active role. Not only was the American president embroiled in the agonizing Iranian hostage crisis from November 1979 onward, but he was concurrently running for a second term. His closest advisers warned against presidential participation in what they foresaw would be protracted negotiations dealing with controversial West Bank and Gaza issues. Carter had incurred criticism from members of the American Jewish community for demanding that Israel relinquish its settlements in Sinai. Any renewed effort on his part to mediate between Egypt and Israel on the occupied territories could further impair his prospects for reelection. Instead, Carter designated special presidential representatives—first, Robert S. Strauss and, subsequently, Sol M. Linowitz—to represent him in those talks. They were able men, but the Camp David precedent had virtually mandated a high degree of presidential involvement as a condition of success. Moreover, West Bank and Gaza issues were patently more complex than those of Sinai and thus more difficult to resolve.

Despite the efforts of these presidential envoys, especially Linowitz, to define West Bank and Gaza autonomy in mutually acceptable terms, only peripheral progress was made.[6] The gap between the Egyptian and Israeli sides remained wide. At Camp David, Israel, Egypt, and the United States had been unable to define what autonomy might mean; hence the nettlesome issues of practical delineation of that amorphous concept reemerged in full force during the negotiations. Dissatisfied with the lack of progress, Sadat suspended autonomy talks three times in 1980 to gain time so that Carter, once reelected, as Sadat hoped would be the case, would be able to participate. To Sadat's disappointment, official and personal, Carter lost the election.

The new American president, Ronald Reagan, it soon became apparent, had different priorities from those of his predecessor. West Bank and Gaza autonomy talks ranked low on his agenda. Rather, strategic consensus, aimed at meeting a putative Soviet threat to the Middle East, was Reagan's prime foreign policy objective. The new president envisioned that Egypt, Israel, Jordan, and perhaps

6. Sol M. Linowitz believes some progress was made in the autonomy talks. See Sol M. Linowitz, "The Prospects for the Camp David Peace Process," *SAIS Review*, no. 2 (Summer 1981), pp. 93–100.

Saudi Arabia would somehow subordinate their differences over unresolved Arab-Israeli issues and, instead, cooperate with one another and with the United States to counter the Soviets in the area. Though Sadat was strongly anti-Soviet, and indeed expelled the Soviet ambassador in September 1981, this shift of emphasis disturbed him. His nagging concern that it portended downgrading of the peace process seemed confirmed when, in February 1982, after Sadat's death, a mid-level State Department functionary, with no Middle East experience, was named not as presidential, but as Secretary of State Alexander M. Haig, Jr.'s, representative to already languishing autonomy negotiations. Talks continued, sporadically, until the Israeli invasion of Lebanon in June 1982, but without progress. Since then they have been in limbo.

Equally disturbing, from Sadat's viewpoint, was Reagan's delay in inviting him to visit the United States. Although Sadat had expected to be invited in March of 1981, such a visit did not take place until early August of that year. No slight was intended, but Sadat saw the delayed invitation as the new administration's failure to appreciate adequately the political risks he had taken. Some Egyptians contend it contributed to the "nervousness," as they describe it, that characterized his final year in office.

To the Reagan administration's surprise, Sadat, while traveling through London in August 1981, en route to the United States, publicly proposed the establishment of a Palestinian government-in-exile. This idea was an unwelcome shock to an administration still fumbling for a Middle East policy. His action seemed to belie past assumptions that Sadat had no real interest in the Palestinian problem. Washington failed to appreciate that, whatever criticisms Sadat might regularly level at the Palestinian leadership, Egypt required some kind of satisfactory resolution of the Palestinian issue if it was to reestablish its tarnished credentials in the Arab world. Although Sadat personally liked Reagan, he left Washington depressed. The new American president, he told friends, was well-intentioned but knew little about the Middle East and was heavily influenced by Israel.

In early September 1981, Sadat took the unprecedented step of jailing some fifteen hundred perceived opponents of all political shades. He did so out of concern, perhaps exaggerated, that such elements might in the next few months mount demonstrations, which could be used by the Israeli leadership to delay final withdrawal from Sinai, as it seemed to be intimating. Sadat's clampdown, coming on the heels of his visit to Washington, was interpreted by many Egyptians as American inspired. The new administration, still seeking to orient itself, saw these mass arrests as suggestive of internal instability in Egypt. Sadat's assassination one month later heightened such worries.

With Sadat's untimely death, Egypt's influence in Washington, which had been largely based on the courage and personality of the Egyptian chief of state, declined. His successor, Husni Mubarak, was not well known to American leaders, and his leadership qualities were unappreciated. The long, successful effort that Sadat had made to cultivate Congress quickly dissipated but has of late been revived. On his several visits to Washington before Sadat's demise, Mubarak had made an indifferent impression. In contrast to Sadat's geniality and general willingness to acquiesce in American proposals, which had come to be expected by U.S. leaders, Mubarak was seen as demanding, somewhat abrasive, and unbending. His critical candor in speaking to U.S. leaders sometimes grated. His accession to the Egyptian presidency also revived in some American (and Israeli) official minds the nagging question of whether Egypt would continue to honor the peace treaty. That concern was unjustified, although Mubarak—influenced by advisers more Arab than Egyptian nationalist in orientation—seemed to give the perennially obstructive Egyptian governmental bureaucracy greater scope to decelerate the already snail-like pace of normalization of relations with Israel. There were, for example, reports that the Ministry of Interior was actively discouraging Egyptians who might want to visit Israel. Israel's concern was quick, negative, and soon communicated to Washington. In senior U.S. government circles, scantily knowledgeable of Middle East political dynamics, Egypt's actions aroused further uneasiness.

By then, Washington had belatedly recognized another salient fact. Whatever Sadat might have said, Egypt, contrary to earlier American hopes, could not speak for Palestinian national aspirations. Since the PLO leadership was unacceptable to Israel as a negotiating partner, a new spokesman for the Palestinian cause had to be found. In the eyes of the Reagan administration (and Israel), the logical choice was King Hussein of Jordan. Hussein had earlier refused to participate in autonomy talks on the grounds that the Rabat Arab League summit of October 1974 had replaced Jordan with the PLO as spokesman for the Palestinians and, separately, that he had not been consulted about the Camp David Accords. Nevertheless, discrete, though coordinated, American and Israeli efforts were made throughout 1981 and 1982 to persuade the Jordanian monarch to reconsider. Jordan's primary role in resumed peace talks was also implicit in Reagan's September 1, 1982, peace proposal, rejecting an independent Palestinian state or incorporation of the West Bank and Gaza into Israel, and calling instead for the occupied territories to be associated with Jordan (see appendix D).

Gradually but inexorably, in the eyes of the Reagan administration, Egypt's role in any resumed future peace talks came to be seen as secondary and at best supportive of Hussein, if Jordan could be persuaded to engage itself. This was the indirect message carried by Reagan's peripatetic special Middle East envoys, among them Philip C. Habib and Donald H. Rumsfeld, from 1981 to 1983. It created mixed Egyptian reactions. On the one hand, the Egyptian leadership was relieved to be divested of Palestinian responsibility; on the other, there was concern that Egypt's importance in U.S. eyes might be reduced. Despite limited influence on the Palestinians, Egypt saw its future political role in the Arab world linked to achieving an acceptable Palestinian settlement and to active participation in the process.

A related disappointment flowed from what was perceived as U.S. failure to follow through on Camp David commitments. Egypt's leaders, mindful that Sadat had placed a large part of their nation's destiny in American hands, had expected the United States, regardless of the change in administration, to continue to act as an "honest broker" on unresolved aspects of the accords. Experience with the Nixon, Ford, and Carter presidencies suggested a basic consistency in U.S. foreign policy. To their distress, they soon found Washington had, with rare exceptions, become a rigid advocate of Israeli procedural and even some substantive ideas. Their views, Egyptians observed, were often ignored or given short shrift. A few spoke bitterly of U.S. betrayal; most resignedly ascribed the situation to "American politics." Erstwhile Nasserists exulted that they had foretold this would happen. But what troubled Egyptians most was U.S. insistence on direct talks between Jordan and Israel, as Israel demanded, with no clear indication what mediatory role the United States might play. Egypt has come to support Jordanian insistence on an international peace conference and remains uneasy about seeming U.S. vacillation on such a forum.

On another level, in the immediate wake of Sadat's assassination, Mubarak feared that Israel would seize on local disturbances in Egypt and refuse to withdraw from Sinai in accordance with the peace treaty. That concern was aggravated when Israel insisted that a tiny enclave on the Gulf of Aqaba, Taba, was neither historically nor geographically part of Sinai and that Israel would remain there. Taba, despite its strategic and economic insignificance, came to assume inordinate symbolic importance for Egypt. Through the efforts of the then-undersecretary of state, Walter J. Stoessel, Jr., who was sent to the area in April 1982 to reassure the parties, a protocol was concluded between Egypt and Israel. Israel reaffirmed its intention to withdraw from Sinai on April 25, 1982, and did so. On the Taba issue, direct negotiations would be conducted between the parties to try to resolve the matter. Should these fail, sequential fall-back procedures of mediation and arbitration were envisioned.

The United States, always caught between Israel and Egypt and impatient that Egypt should attach such importance to Taba when virtually all of Sinai would be recovered, saw the Stoessel protocol as constructive engagement; Egypt's leadership was only tepidly satisfied. In its view, Israel's claim to Taba was tendentious, the United States should have strongly supported Egypt's position, and direct negotiations would come to nothing. They would only enable Israel to entrench itself in the disputed fleck of territory. Four years of desultory but fruitless direct negotiations followed before the issue was eventually submitted to binding arbitration.

The Lebanese Factor

By early 1982, Washington was persuaded that, as long as Jordan refused to participate and Egypt was unable to recatalyze peace talks, a broader Middle East peace negotiation might be revived through American intervention in Lebanon in order to resolve that country's anarchic internal situation and, simultaneously, to conclude a Lebanese-Israeli peace. There was strong U.S. interest in supporting the Maronite Christian leadership, which already had informal, though ambivalent, ties with Israel.

Egypt sympathized with Lebanon's internal dilemma, but saw such U.S. notions as naive and a digression from the nodal dilemma. Egyptians were convinced that the Lebanese settlement envisaged by the United States would not satisfactorily resolve the Palestinian problem. Echoing Israeli views, the Reagan administration deemphasized the centrality of the Palestinian problem; in contrast, Egypt saw it as the core issue.

In June 1982, Israel invaded Lebanon, ostensibly to remove the Palestinian military presence in the south. That such an assault would sooner or later occur had long been an open secret. Egypt had earlier expressed concern to Washington about Israeli intentions. The failure of the United States to stop Israel from doing so, despite much advance warning, and the suspicion that Israel's action was undertaken with high-level American acquiescence, significantly strained Egypt's relations with the United States.[7] Mubarak found himself in an acutely politically embarrassing situation. Rejectionist Arab states accused Egypt of culpability. His treaty partner, Israel, had again acted against Arab interests, rebuffing all Egyptian appeals not to do so; his alleged friend, the United States, whatever it might publicly say, appeared to condone the action. Israel seemed to regard the Camp David package as giving it carte blanche in the Levant area, and the United States appeared essentially indifferent to the Israeli attitude. Anti-American sentiment swept the country. Many young Egyptians flocked to Islamic fundamentalist rallies as the only feasible means of protest—not only against Israel, but also against the United States.

Mubarak faced mounting domestic pressure to respond to what Egyptians saw as Israeli aggression against Arabs. He had long resisted doing so, warning critics that retaliation would risk reduction or even elimination of U.S. military and economic aid. Egypt had no alternative source for such assistance. The oil-rich Arab states might have been asked to resume economic help, but their condition would have been jettisoning the peace treaty. Doing so would have alienated the United States and in all probability caused Israel to retake a large part of Sinai. The Sabra and Shatila massacres of September 16, 1982, forced Mubarak's hand. While the Reagan administration also deplored the massacres, and found itself momentarily embarrassed since Habib had assured the PLO leadership in writing that Palestinian families would be protected if their fighters left, Washington's public posture generally seemed indulgent of Israeli complicity. Responding to domestic outrage, Mubarak withdrew his ambassador from Tel Aviv and froze further normalization of Egyptian-Israeli relations. To the U.S. leadership these actions were unhelpful and only complicated the issue.

For the next four years, despite incessant American pressure, especially from Congress, for Mubarak to return the Egyptian ambassador and resume normalization of relations, the Egyptian president refused to do so. To American (and Israeli) annoyance, the Egyptian press was permitted to resume attacks on Israel and did so with gusto. The Lebanese-Israeli accord of May 17, 1983, negotiated by Secretary of State George P. Shultz, was seen by

7. For the former secretary of state's exculpatory account, see Alexander M. Haig, Jr., *Caveat: Realism, Reagan, and Foreign Policy* (Macmillan, 1984), pp. 306, 332–35. For two Israeli journalists' view of a perceived American "green light," see Ze'ev Schiff and Ehud Ya'ari, *Israel's Lebanon War,* ed. and trans. Ina Friedman (Simon and Schuster, 1984), pp. 62–77.

Egyptians as favoring Israel and injurious to the Palestinians. Egyptian officials expressed puzzlement that the United States should predicate such an agreement on Syria's withdrawal from Lebanon when Israel retained security rights in the southern areas of that country. In contrast to Washington's disappointment, there was scant regret in Egypt when the Lebanese president unilaterally abrogated it in March of the following year.

Even after Israeli withdrawal from most of Lebanon in late 1983, except for a security zone in the south, Mubarak maintained his rigid posture. It enabled him to parry domestic charges of inaction in the face of perceived Israeli provocation. A "cold peace" set in and persisted. The situation became associated with Egyptian insistence that Israel must first also agree to submit the unresolved Taba issue to arbitration before an Egyptian ambassador would be returned to Tel Aviv. Egypt saw direct talks on the issue as failed and considered mediation unpromising and a waste of time. The Reagan administration, and many in Congress, ignorant of the negotiating history of the ambassadorial-level diplomatic relationship, shared the Israeli view that Egypt's stance was inconsistent with the letter and spirit of the Camp David package.[8]

Worse still, Shultz considered that Mubarak had broken a commitment, allegedly made to the United States, that an ambassador would be returned to Tel Aviv once Israel had withdrawn from Lebanon. Egypt denied any such commitment had ever been made. It insisted, moreover, that Israeli forces had never entirely withdrawn. In one guise or another, some remained in south Lebanon. Not until September 1986, through a combination of U.S. suasion and mediation, did Egypt and Israel agree on a *compromis,* outlining terms on which the Taba issue would be arbitrated. Thereafter, the Egyptian chargé d'affaires in Tel Aviv was upgraded to ambassadorial status and symbolic diplomatic symmetry was restored.

As already indicated, on September 1, 1982, in the wake of the Israeli invasion of Lebanon, Reagan had for the first time set forth his ideas for a Middle East peace settlement. Israel rejected the proposal, contending it was inconsistent with Camp David. Jordan,

8. Although Egypt's action did not violate the letter of the Camp David package, arguably it may have violated the spirit of the agreements. When Sadat was persuaded to agree to ambassadorial-level diplomatic relations with Israel, he was told by the United States that this agreement would not preclude either party from withdrawing its ambassador if one country was deemed to have acted in a manner deleterious to the other's interests. Egypt saw the Israeli attack in Lebanon as harmful to its broader Arab interests. Israel contended its actions in Lebanon were not directed against Egypt and should in no way be linked to Egyptian-Israeli relations.

which had remained wary of participating in peace negotiations, showed interest if talks could be conducted in the context of an international peace conference and a joint Jordanian-Palestinian delegation could be formed. Among other things, this step required an arrangement with the PLO leadership. After protracted negotiations, an ambiguous Jordanian-PLO agreement was finally concluded in February 1985 (see appendix F).

Egypt supported the Reagan proposal as the only means of reviving the peace process, insisting it was consistent with Camp David concepts, but Cairo was disappointed when the administration failed to follow up vigorously on it. To U.S. gratification, and Egyptian disappointment, the Jordanian-PLO agreement aborted in early 1986 over differences of interpretation. Henceforth, Washington (and Israel) hoped West Bank and Gaza Palestinians would replace the PLO as negotiating partners with Jordan. Egypt continued to insist on the necessity for PLO participation in any peace negotiations and to urge Jordan to reestablish ties with Arafat. Hussein and Arafat, both nominal friends of Egypt, remain at odds and the Egyptian leadership continues to urge reconciliation on both, thus far without success.

While recognizing the difficulties of reviving the peace process, Egypt's leaders were disappointed with the U.S. position that no further initiatives be taken unless Israel and the Arab parties indicated a clear desire for resumed talks. The United States, in the Egyptian view, should continue to try to catalyze new talks. They noted that previous administrations had done so against considerable odds. The Palestinian uprising in the West Bank and Gaza, which began in December 1987, belatedly brought home to Washington the need for urgent U.S. intervention if further political deterioration in the Middle East area was to be prevented. Mubarak, during his visit to Washington in January 1988, pressed for immediate U.S. reinvolvement. Shultz's four visits to the Middle East in the ensuing six months, during which he proposed a telescoped version of the Camp David autonomy plan for the West Bank and Gaza, were at least partially attributable to the Egyptian president's urgings (see appendix K). Although Shultz made no tangible progress, Egypt's leaders sought to be helpful to the secretary of state's mission by urging Hussein and PLO leaders to be receptive to the U.S. proposal. Egypt also tried to arrange a meeting in Cairo with Palestinian leaders, which Shultz declined. The Egyptian leadership was unsuccessful, but its overall efforts were appreciated in Washington. Mubarak's helpfulness unquestionably raised his stock with the administration. Moreover, his meetings with members of Congress, while in Washington, enhanced his image as a friend, even if sometimes critical, of the United States.

The Israeli Factor

To Egypt's disquiet, the advent of the Reagan administration heralded an increasingly intimate relationship between the United States and Israel. Whatever vexation Washington might occasionally profess about Israeli actions that damaged U.S. regional interests, such as the bombing of the Iraqi Osirak nuclear reactor on June 7, 1981, or the Israeli invasion of Lebanon in the summer of 1982, such displeasure rarely translated into anything more than what Egypt saw as token opposition. True, the administration suspended delivery of promised military equipment to Israel twice: once for two months after the Israeli bombing of the Osirak nuclear reactor in 1981 and again for six months after the Israeli invasion of Lebanon in June 1982. Egypt's leadership, while publicly applauding these actions, privately considered them inadequate, selective, and essentially ineffective. It observed that they were never sustained for any length of time.

In contrast, the administration deemed its actions appropriately hortatory, given likely negative domestic reaction to any such cutoffs, and found persistent Egyptian suggestions of inadequacy grating. Congress, too, might criticize Israel for casualties inflicted in indiscriminate shelling of Beirut, but regularly refused to take punitive measures. Instead, in 1985, Congress seemed to reward Israel by appropriating additional economic aid in an amount even exceeding the administration's recommendations.

In the United States, Israel's militant actions could readily be rationalized. No formal diplomatic relations existed at the time between the United States and Iraq, and Iraq had consistently sought to frustrate American efforts to achieve an Arab-Israeli peace. Although the bombing of the Osirak nuclear reactor was publicly disapproved by Washington, many Americans believed the action would stop Iraq from obtaining a nuclear capability. The invasion of Lebanon, some highly placed administration officials expected, would eliminate the militant Palestinian "state within a state" in that country. Moreover, however difficult Israel might sometimes be, many senior U.S. leaders saw it as the only dependable ally in the area. Its military leaders were professionally competent, its soldiers dedicated and combat wise. Beginning in 1981, strategic cooperation with Israel became a keystone of U.S. Middle East policy and was codified into a signed agreement. Though briefly frozen after unilateral extension of Israeli law to the occupied Golan Heights in December 1981, it was soon resumed and remains a cardinal element in the U.S.-Israeli tie.

In contrast, Egypt's policies often seemed ambivalent and, in some American eyes, ungrateful. Since Camp David, Egypt had become heavily dependent on generous American economic and military aid, yet Cairo seemed incessantly to cavil and to qualify its cooperation. The different U.S. attitude toward the two countries was patently evident to Egypt's leadership. Egypt could not object to a close U.S. association with Israel, but resented what it interpreted as the subordinate role assigned to it in the trilateral Washington-Jerusalem-Cairo equation.

Since diplomatic relations were resumed in February 1974, Egypt had sought a free-standing, bilateral tie with the United States. Instead, following the Camp David package, Egypt found itself enmeshed in a superimposed, asymmetrical trilateral relationship. This meant, in effect, that Egypt was in part judged by Washington on how it conducted itself toward Israel. Whenever the Egyptian-Israeli link deteriorated for whatever reasons, U.S.-Egyptian ties were reflexively strained. Israel could always influence U.S. policy toward Egypt; Cairo lacked any comparable capability. Israel had powerful public and congressional constituencies in the United States; Egypt had no such assets, simply a certain amount of goodwill as long as it adhered to the peace treaty. Egypt's leaders understand the dynamics of this situation, but it rankles and repeatedly poses domestic problems for the Egyptian regime.

The Palestinian Factor

Disagreement also persisted over the Palestinian issue. When, in 1982, U.S. special Middle East envoy Philip C. Habib negotiated arrangements for the departure of Palestinian fighters from Lebanon, Egypt declined to receive four thousand such combatants, as Habib had requested. Washington considered this response unhelpful. It ruefully noted that, subsequently, in 1983, Egypt sent naval vessels to escort the ship on which Yasir Arafat left Tripoli, and Mubarak publicly met with Arafat in Cairo as the Fatah leader's vessel transited the Suez Canal. The Egyptian media hailed the Mubarak-Arafat rapprochement as Mubarak again vainly urged the United States and Israel to accept the PLO as a negotiating partner. In Washington's eyes, this Egyptian policy ran counter to the U.S. (and Israeli) view that the PLO in general and Arafat in particular were international terrorists.

Conflicting U.S. and Egyptian views on the Palestinians came to a head in October 1985 with the *Achille Lauro* incident. By persuading the Palestinian terrorists who had seized the Italian liner and murdered an American invalid aboard, Leon Klinghoffer, to submit, the Egyptian government contended it had saved the lives of other passengers. Yet Egypt's refusal to extradite the detained Palestinian terrorists to the United States, as Washington demanded, and Mubarak's attempt secretly to send them to Tunis, nominally for trial by the PLO leadership, which no one believed would take place, disturbed the Reagan administration. Thinly veiled U.S. charges of dissembling were leveled at Mubarak.[9] In turn, the subsequent forcing down over Italy of an Egyptian airliner carrying the Palestinian terrorists and their leader, Muhammad Abbas (Abul Abbas), by American naval aircraft was seen by Mubarak and the Egyptian people as a national affront. That American action, most Egyptians contended, was hostile and inconsistent with professed American friendship.

Clearly, neither side understood the legitimate concerns of the other. The Egyptian leadership dismissed American outrage over the Klinghoffer killing as exaggerated; the American leadership could not comprehend why Egypt should be indignant over U.S. military action taken to down a plane carrying acknowledged terrorists. That it was an Egyptian plane almost seemed incidental to the U.S. administration. A renewed wave of anti-American public feeling crescendoed in Egypt. While the Egyptian leadership sought to mute official reaction, and American help a few months later in enabling Egypt to recover a hijacked Egyptair aircraft in Malta acted as a counterbalancing factor of sorts, a measure of mutual resentment over the handling of the *Achille Lauro* affair lingers, perhaps more so today among Egyptians than among most Americans. Fortunately, the diplomatic mechanisms in place between the two countries and Egypt's overriding need for ongoing American aid ameliorated the disruptive potential of the incident.

The Reagan administration, which has made combating international terrorism an autonomous foreign policy objective, interpreted Mubarak's action as defaulting on Egypt's moral responsibility to the international community and prevaricating on an inferred obligation to the United States, whose citizen had been brutally murdered. To Egypt, the administration's categoric contention that

9. Washington's reaction to Husni Mubarak's handling of the *Achille Lauro* terrorists is reflected in Bob Woodward, *Veil: The Secret Wars of the CIA, 1981–1987* (Simon and Schuster, 1987), pp. 414–16.

terrorism could only be confronted by force, with no consideration of its root causes, was politically myopic. Egypt pointed to similar European misgivings about American antiterrorist policy.

Following the Soviet-encouraged Algiers Palestine National Council conference of April 1987, and the apparent reunification of the ranks of some PLO components, Egypt closed various Fatah offices in its cities. It did so because of criticisms emanating from the conference against Egypt, the Camp David Accords and the peace treaty, and the praise seemingly given to Syria. To the Reagan administration, Arafat's conduct at the Algiers conference should have demonstrated to Egypt that flirtation with the PLO was shortsighted. Washington, like Israel, would have liked Mubarak to wash his hands of Palestinian nationalist aspirations. Any such hope was illusory. By the end of 1987, PLO offices had been permitted to reopen in Cairo. Egypt may publicly denounce international terrorism, but it is unlikely in the foreseeable future to take action against Palestinian terrorists unless they act directly against Egyptian interests.

The perennial Palestinian irritant in the trilateral U.S.-Egyptian-Israeli equation forcefully resurfaced with the ongoing Palestinian uprising in the West Bank and Gaza. Stringent Israeli suppressive measures, resulting by mid-1988 in more than two hundred Palestinian dead, several thousand injured, more than five thousand arrests, and a score or more deportations, evoked immediate strong Egyptian protests and once again exacerbated the tenuous Egyptian-Israeli tie. A senior Egyptian minister publicly charged that Israel's conduct violated the Camp David Accords, which had called for negotiations on the occupied territories.[10] Not since the invasion of Lebanon six years earlier had Israeli actions spawned such spontaneous Egyptian public outcry. Islamic fundamentalist demonstrations have sporadically been staged in Cairo, denouncing Israeli mistreatment of the Palestinians and demanding severance of diplomatic relations with Israel. They were controlled through police action but symbolize continued strong Egyptian public support for Palestinian aspirations. The Israeli actions, coming on the heels of the Amman summit at which Egypt had been largely politically rehabilitated, embarrassed Mubarak, particularly in the Arab world.

Egyptians could initially be gratified that there was some commonality in U.S. objections to Israeli actions. Washington urged

10. Alan Cowell, "Israel Crackdown Frustrates Egypt," *New York Times*, December 27, 1987; and "Egyptian Says Israel Violates Peace Pact," *Boston Sunday Globe*, December 27, 1987.

moderation on Israel and on two separate occasions, in late 1987 and early 1988, took the unusual step of abstaining on United Nations resolutions deploring Israeli actions. It also pressed Israel not to resort to punitive deportations and, to the surprise of many, it voted in early January 1988 for a UN resolution calling Israel's plan to deport nine Palestinians a violation of their human rights. Since that time, to Egypt's bitter disappointment, the United States has reverted to its traditional position of vetoing any United Nations resolution criticizing Israeli actions in the West Bank and Gaza. To be sure, Department of State spokesmen have publicly deplored continued Israeli deportation of Palestinians, but Egyptians ruefully observe that there seems to be no desire on the part of the administration to press Israel to desist.

Other Middle East Issues

The Reagan administration, as the Carter administration before it, has welcomed political consultations with Egypt, especially those aimed at some measure of cooperation on Middle East and North African issues of common concern to both states. A consultative process has existed for years between the two states at various levels. The scope and candor of their analytical and operational dialogues are extensive, but are circumscribed for several reasons. In Washington's view, Egyptian cooperation on substantive issues has sometimes been erratic. To Cairo, the United States often lacks subtlety and tends to heavyhandedness. As a rule, neither side persuades the other of its political acumen. Each regards the other's estimates as skewed: those of the United States by Israel, those of Egypt by Arab considerations. The Egyptian leadership is also concerned about what it regards as an American proclivity to "leak" highly sensitive information to Israel or to the world at large.

Both Syria and Libya have since 1974 been inimical to Egypt's political interests in the area. Egypt's leadership nonetheless deplored what it saw as U.S.-Israeli collusion against Syria in Lebanon in 1982–83. It did so not because of sympathy for Syria, but because such collusion, as perceived in the broader Arab world, was politically detrimental to Egypt's efforts to restore its standing among Arab states. Asad, Egyptians argued, should be politically isolated, but Syria should not be physically attacked. For the United States to appear to be acting in concert with Israel in military action against Syria, even indirectly, would enhance Asad's claim to Arab leadership. It would also make it more difficult for any Egyptian-Syrian rapprochement eventually to take place. The Egyptian leadership believes that Syria has in the past three years slightly assuaged its enmity toward Egypt. Thus, it notes, when Egypt was readmitted to the Islamic Conference Organization in 1984, the articulated Syrian objections were relatively restrained. Mubarak and Asad also met at the Islamic summit conference in Kuwait in January 1987. Egyptians observe that, beginning in the summer of 1987, the Reagan administration itself began to seek a new opening with Syria. While they commend this development in principle, there is nagging concern that any new U.S.-Syrian dialogue not evolve to a point at which Syria supersedes Egypt in U.S. eyes as the primary Arab polity. This is an unlikely contingency.

Libya represents a much more complex issue. During Sadat's period, Egyptian-Libyan tensions were high, and Egyptian public media attacks on Muammar Qadhafi reached unprecedented levels. After assuming office in October 1981, Mubarak ordered a cessation of such attacks on Qadhafi, but there has been little substantive change in the relations between the two North African neighbors. Qadhafi's excoriations of the Egyptian leadership and the Egyptian-Israeli peace treaty have continued unabated. Libyan actions in Chad, the Sudan, and threats against Tunisia also concern Egypt.

The United States and Egypt have regularly exchanged views about the danger that Qadhafi poses to their respective interests. In both Washington and Cairo, however, there are complaints that the other has been ambivalent on appropriate responses to contain Qadhafi. Senior Egyptian leaders recall, for example, that Carter withdrew an earlier commitment to Sadat by President Ford to provide certain military assistance, if needed, for a possible Egyptian military intervention in Libya.

Egyptian leaders acknowledge that, during the Reagan administration, there has been renewed American interest in cooperating with Egypt in contingency planning to deal with Qadhafi, forcibly if necessary. Nevertheless, they are critical of chronic American media leaks that have often compromised joint planning. Thus, they aver, in February 1983, because of such leaks, the Egyptian air force was forced to abort an entrapment operation against the Libyan air force in connection with an expected attack by Libya on Khartoum.[11] Later in that same year, following joint U.S.-Egyptian planning in connection with the Libyan invasion of Chad, the Egyptian leadership imposed a news blackout on all pertinent planning, lest it leak in the American media.

11. Patrick E. Tyler, "U.S. Aborted 1983 Trap Set for Libyan Forces," *Washington Post*, July 12, 1987.

In September 1985, the then-deputy national security adviser, Vice Admiral John M. Poindexter, visited Cairo to propose to Mubarak that the United States and Egypt jointly undertake military action against Qadhafi in order to depose him. Egypt was to spearhead an overland assault with American air support. Mubarak, annoyed at the U.S. pressure, reportedly responded that Egypt would act appropriately at a time and in a manner of its choosing. Further joint U.S.-Egyptian military planning against Libya, for both defensive and preemptive contingencies, was discussed in Cairo in February 1986.[12] In early 1986, Reagan reportedly approved a presidential finding that would enable the United States to support Egypt, militarily, in the event of a preemptive attack by Egypt on Libya.

Despite such joint planning, Egypt publicly criticized the U.S. bombing of Tripoli and Benghazi in April 1986 as politically shortsighted and joined with other Arab and Islamic states in condemning it. Privately, its leaders contended, such U.S. action mobilized Arab and Islamic support for Qadhafi. To an American administration faced with Libyan- (and Syrian-) inspired terrorism, Egyptian counsel to allow the Arabs to deal with maverick leaders like Qadhafi seldom produced any salutary results. Egypt's leaders view the United States as frequently wavering in its advice on what to do about Qadhafi. Egypt criticizes the often sharply divided views in the Reagan administration, especially between the National Security Adviser's office and the Department of State, on dealing with Libya and is skeptical of U.S. reliability in a crunch. In support of its view, Egypt points to the covert visit to Libya of the former U.S. ambassador to the Vatican, William A. Wilson, in early January 1986,[13] and the planned visit to Tripoli of a U.S. delegation one month after the American bombing of that city. The visit was aborted at the last minute.[14]

There have, however, been instances of congruent and coordinated Egyptian and U.S. cooperation. In September 1985, for example, Mubarak, with U.S. support, publicly warned Qadhafi not to attempt an armed invasion of Tunisia. In 1986 there were joint U.S.-Egyptian naval maneuvers off the coast of Libya. These actions may have had a deterrent effect. There has also been U.S.-Egyptian collabo-

12. Woodward, *Veil*, p. 414; Bob Woodward, "U.S. Decided to Give Libya Firm Message," *Washington Post*, March 26, 1986, and "U.S. Unable to Persuade Egypt to Back Plan for Joint Anti-Qaddafi Move," *Washington Post*, April 2, 1986.

13. Leslie H. Gelb, "U.S. Diplomat Reportedly Held Talks in Libya," *New York Times*, March 23, 1986.

14. Stephen Engelberg, "U.S., a Month after Tripoli Raid, Reportedly Planned to Meet with Libyan," *New York Times*, August 16, 1987.

ration in 1986–87 in supporting the Chadian government of Hissein Habré to contain and repel the Libyan military intervention in northern Chad.[15] In still another area, the United States and Egypt have over the years cooperated, with Saudi Arabia and Pakistan, in providing military equipment to the Islamic insurgents in Afghanistan to enable them to combat the Soviet-supported Afghan government and Soviet military forces in that country.

U.S. Saudi Arabian relations are likewise viewed ambivalently by Egypt. Since Sadat's days, many Egyptian leaders have conceived of the kingdom as virtually an American client state. If the United States wished Saudi Arabia to undertake certain actions, Washington was assumed to have the capability to press the Saudi leadership to do so. Inevitably, therefore, the failure of the Carter administration to obtain Saudi Arabian endorsement of the Camp David Accords was seen not as an assertion of Saudi sovereign rights, but as a contrived U.S. effort to keep its options open. Some Egyptian leaders, with a concern similar to the apprehension about U.S.-Syrian relations, suspected that Washington might be deliberately seeking to make Riyadh rather than Cairo the primary focus of American policy in the Arab world. The intensity of concern is often related to the prevailing state of Egyptian-Saudi Arabian relations. As these have improved after the Amman summit, pertinent Egyptian fears are for the time being eased.

In the Gulf region, Egypt supported Iraq in its conflict with Iran and believed the United States was doing the same. Egypt considers Iranian-exported Islamic fundamentalism a threat to the entire Middle East and thought the United States shared this view. The disclosure in November 1986 of covert U.S. arms shipments to Iran, in collusion with Israel and at the same time when Washington was nominally seeking a global arms ban on Iran, came as a shock. In Egypt, as elsewhere, it was seen as U.S. perfidy and suggested an administration in disarray. Conspiracy theories, perennially spun by Egyptians to explain the vagaries of U.S. Middle East policy, seemed confirmed. The subsequent protracted congressional Iran-Contra hearings projected the image of an enfeebled American presidency.

More recent U.S. resolve in the Persian Gulf has heartened the Egyptian leadership. Cairo is gratified that the United States, by augmenting its naval forces in the Gulf and successfully soliciting broader European security interest in that area, has shown deter-

15. Tyler, "U.S. Aborted 1983 Trap."

mination to stand up to Iran. Egypt is concerned about Iraq's survivability in the face of superior Iranian manpower and has provided Baghdad with some military equipment. Numerous expatriate Egyptians are performing auxiliary services for the military. Egypt, like the United States, has also publicly expressed support for Kuwait and Saudi Arabia. Following a visit by Mubarak to the Arab states of the Gulf in January 1988, Egypt pledged security assistance to those countries. In the Gulf area, the current efforts of Washington and Cairo complement each other. The U.S. Navy's success in the Gulf is welcome. The Egyptian leadership shares the current view of the Reagan administration that an international arms ban should be imposed on Iran in order to press Tehran to agree to a cease-fire.

The Soviet Factor

In contrast to Sadat's effusive cooperation with the U.S. policy of reducing Soviet influence in the Middle East, Mubarak seemed to want normalization of relations with the Soviet Union. Having publicly analogized U.S.-Egyptian relations with Indian-Soviet ties, he observed that neither precluded normal diplomatic discourse with the other superpower. While limited, his actions were worrisome to an administration that conceived global politics largely in terms of a Soviet menace.

In January 1982, Egypt requested the return of sixty-six Soviet technicians. The ostensible purpose was to ensure maintenance of Soviet-manufactured equipment in Egypt. In March 1983, Egypt and the Soviet Union agreed in principle to restore diplomatic relations and the following year a Soviet ambassador again appeared in Cairo. In May 1983, a new Egyptian-Soviet trade agreement, calling for an increase in trade between the two countries, was concluded. Annual trade agreements followed. Trade between Egypt and the Soviet Union is expected to double in the period 1988–90, perhaps reaching the equivalent of $1.8 billion a year, as Egypt barters textiles, leather, and spirits in return for Soviet-manufactured industrial and agricultural machinery.

In mid-March 1987, an Egyptian ministerial delegation was sent to Moscow to discuss debt problems, trade, and possible greater Soviet assistance in upgrading Egyptian industrial plants. It returned with a new—and, from an Egyptian point of view, advantageous—agreement, deferring for twenty-five years repayment of the military debt to the Soviets. The agreement was substantively cosmetic, but it was hailed in Egypt as indicating Soviet goodwill and was seen by many Egyptians as tantamount to canceling that debt. The agreement came when U.S.-Egyptian relations were roiled because of what Egyptians saw as an unsatisfactory American debt relief proposal. Unfavorable official and public comparisons were drawn between the Soviet and American offers.

Shortly afterward there were reports in Cairo that Egypt had requested Soviet antiaircraft missiles and artillery. Early in 1987, the Soviets also invited Mubarak to visit Moscow. He reportedly accepted in principle, but no firm date has been set for such a visit.

If Egypt should acquire Soviet military equipment, this would pose problems for the United States in terms of traditional American objections to the commingling of American and Soviet weaponry. Egypt's explanations that its dealings with Moscow are only part of its nonalignment policy and limited in scope fail to reassure suspicious administration officials or Congress. They are closely scrutinizing how far the Egyptian opening to the Soviet Union will proceed. For Egypt, excessive dependency on the United States is at times galling, and forging reasonable relations with the Soviet Union assumes almost a politically therapeutic quality. Egypt insists, moreover, that since the Reagan administration seems to be taking steps to improve the dialogue with Moscow, Egypt has that same right.

Islamic Fundamentalism and Neo-Nasserism

The U.S. leadership perceived Mubarak's handling of the attack on Israeli diplomats in Cairo in August 1985 as cavalier. The killing soon afterward of seven Israeli tourists in Sinai by an allegedly berserk Egyptian military conscript further dismayed Washington. Although Egypt tendered apologies, Mubarak seemed to discount the seriousness of the incidents. Since the incidents were suspected of being the work of Islamic militants, Mubarak's failure to react more vigorously suggested that he might be seeking to propitiate such elements. Other examples of tolerance for Muslim fundamentalists were cited. To some Americans, Mubarak consciously or otherwise seemed to be inadequately aware of the threat of the Islamic radical right. There is little U.S. comprehension of the great skill and flexibility Mubarak has shown in dealing with Egypt's complex Muslim fundamentalist problem.

Mubarak insists Egypt's Islamic militants are under control. Many Americans are not so sure. The serious wounding in May 1987 of Mubarak's former minister of interior, an attack on a prominent Egyptian magazine editor in early June 1987, and an abortive attack on a second former minister of interior in August 1987 heightened U.S. concerns about political and security instability in Egypt, possibly inspired by Islamic fundamentalists.[16]

Alongside the putative Islamic fundamentalist threat, the United States became concerned in mid-1987 about incipient neo-Nasserist terrorism directed against Americans in Egypt. The shooting attack on three American diplomats in Maadi in May 1987, investigations showed, was the work of a Nasserist-oriented group, professing patriotic loyalty to Mubarak, but violently denouncing what its adherents depicted as an Egypt in the political and economic thrall of the United States. The eldest son of the late president, Gamal Abd al-Nasser, was allegedly implicated in the incident.[17] His possible participation posed political problems for both Mubarak and the United States. The Egyptian government wanted prosecution of the arrested perpetrators and accomplices to focus on the criminal aspects of the deed. Defense attorneys, however, were expected to introduce nationalist coloration into the judicial proceedings. The involvement of the late president's progeny was used to evoke the image of Nasser's challenge to what he termed the neo-imperialist United States. The opposition press drew invidious comparisons. At a time when charges of Egyptian tutelage to the United States were being leveled, and Egyptian public opinion was inflamed over Israeli actions against Palestinians, the appeal to secular nationalist sentiment had political potency. The trial was postponed until the fall of 1988.

Granted, the neo-Nasserist lodestone is currently less powerful than that of Islamic fundamentalism, but it is not without support in both the older and younger generations. Whatever ideological differences divide the two movements, they identify the same antagonists, the United States and Israel, and thus complement each others' anti-American attitudes.

THE ECONOMIC DIMENSION

Two main elements constitute the economic dimension of the U.S. relationship with Egypt: economic aid and U.S. efforts to persuade Mubarak to undertake needed economic reform.

At the time of Camp David, Egypt was already receiving roughly

16. Patrick E. Tyler, "Recent Cairo Shootings Alarm U.S., Egyptian Officials," *Washington Post,* June 5, 1987.

17. John Kifner, "Cairo Embarrassed by Report on Nasser's Son," *New York Times,* December 10, 1987.

the equivalent of $1 billion in economic aid each year, partly through appropriated funds and partly in the form of Public Law 480 wheat and wheat flour.[18] During the final negotiations for a peace treaty, Sadat raised with Carter the need for additional economic aid and urged an American-organized "Marshall Plan" for the development of Egypt. He was disappointed in his hopes. Although Carter agreed to a modest additional $300 million in economic aid over a three-year period, there was no American commitment to increase such help substantially. Nor did Carter endorse the idea of a Marshall Plan for Egypt. Concerned about what was widely regarded as Egypt's persistent failure to address structural deficiencies in its economic system, the administration believed additional economic aid would simply cause Egypt to procrastinate further in coming to grips with its diverse economic difficulties.

The American reappearance on the Egyptian scene in late 1973 induced a visceral public reaction, encouraged to some extent by government officials, that the nation's ailing economy would now be set right through limitless assistance. This was an unrealistic expectation. U.S. economic aid has been generous and represents the largest such program (after Israel) that Washington conducts anywhere. Since it began thirteen years ago, close to $13 billion in economic assistance has been provided. Accomplishments, while sometimes slow, have been laudable—a power-generating capacity equal to that of the High Dam complex; cement plants; granaries; improved sewage systems in Cairo and Alexandria; agricultural improvement through drainage systems, better seeds and more efficient use of water resources; commodity imports in the form of raw materials and spare parts; and annual substantial quantities of wheat and wheat flour, to mention but a few. About half of Egypt's daily unleavened bread consumption is from American-provided flour offered on concessionary terms.

Regrettably, there is little appreciation of the American economic assistance program among the Egyptian public at large and even among some officials. So sizable and diffuse a program inevitably suffers from endemic problems, and although the program is massive, visible results are often slow to appear. The implementation of important projects requires long lead times, including feasibility studies, design work, and eventually what is often excruciatingly delayed construction. Consumables and cash, moreover, are by definition ephemeral and produce scant residual gratitude or lasting

18. Public Law 480 provides for the sale of surplus U.S. agricultural products to countries such as Egypt on concessionary terms.

effects. While government officials are keenly aware of the need for such help, the Egyptian public is largely disenchanted with it. To the impoverished masses, American economic aid has not appreciably improved the quality of their lives. There is much public scoffing at periodic U.S. and Egyptian press releases of newly signed American aid increments. Predictably, too, partly because of heavy Egyptian dependence on American economic assistance, it has introduced its own set of frictions into the picture.

Besides regular complaints that American economic aid is insufficient, Egyptian officials, mindful of the country's enormous needs, often criticize the selection process and slow implementation of American-funded projects sponsored by the Agency for International Development (AID). Substantial amounts of appropriated funds, they observe, remain in the pipeline, while American-demanded feasibility studies and AID bureaucratic red tape are tortuously being worked out, even though in recent years such clogging of disbursements has been greatly reduced. Moreover, Washington has rejected various high-priority Egyptian project proposals, especially those having to do with horizontal land reclamation and low-cost housing, as uneconomic. Some concomitant dissatisfaction exists with the high American official profile in Cairo, mostly AID (and military) personnel. Egyptians are also dissatisfied with the "buy American" provisions of U.S. aid, which they rightly assert make goods and services more expensive than if they were procured in Europe or elsewhere.

Egyptian leaders have occasionally urged that the United States do for Egypt what it does for Israel, namely, turn over appropriated funds and allow Egyptians to decide on projects and to spend funds as they see fit. Once again the argument for parity, this time in procedural terms, is advanced. In American eyes, the Egyptian government is inadequately organized or disciplined to enable a single purchasing mission, such as that of Israel, to buy for all government ministries. There is related concern that AID funds might be siphoned off by private individuals.

In 1985, as a result of Israel's economic crisis and congressional action to increase economic aid for Israel and to convert most of it into grant aid, Egypt demanded similar treatment. Alluding to the Carter administration's alleged commitment to parity, Egypt sought a comparable increase in aid in the form of grant aid. Eventually, the Reagan administration obtained congressional approval for an additional $500 million in appropriated economic aid and agreed that henceforth most of the aid would be on a grant basis. Since 1985, some aid has also been provided on a cash basis for Egypt's balance of payments. This, too, had long been sought by Egypt but was generally uncongenial to Washington. However reluctantly, the United States may in future years have to give more cash payments to Egypt to bolster the country's faltering economy.

If there are Egyptian complaints about American economic aid, there are corresponding U.S. criticisms of Egyptian procedures. Egypt's economic planning is seen as inefficient and drifting. Priorities are difficult to determine, and little cooperation exists between and among economic ministries. Each goes its own way with little coordination with others. The bureaucracy can be stifling and frequently delays project agreements. Above all, many American officials believe that Egypt's leadership fails to address seriously its manifold economic structural problems. Unless Egyptian leaders do so, Washington contends, no amount of foreign aid will lead to meaningful development. Lately, there has been some improvement, but more reform is felt to be needed.

The huge Egyptian subsidy payments have long been especially disturbing to the United States. In the years between 1978 and 1986, direct and indirect subsidies disbursed by the Egyptian government totaled about $6 billion a year. Direct subsidies are now said to be stabilized at about $3 billion a year, but this figure is suspected by some to be concealingly low. For years, the International Monetary Fund (IMF), strongly supported by the United States, has urged the gradual elimination of most subsidies and attendant price rationalization. Aware of the potential domestic political danger at home of increased prices for staples, housing, and other things, successive Egyptian governments have been careful not to press too rapidly for the removal of subsidies. The memory of the January 1977 price riots is indelibly engraved on the minds of Egypt's political leaders. The United States has sought to make additional economic aid to Egypt conditional on more vigorous Egyptian action to address price rationalization. After years of difficult discussions, frustrating for both sides, Egypt finally concluded in May 1987 a standby agreement with the IMF for gradual but more significant subsidy reductions and for a limited float of the Egyptian pound.[19] U.S. efforts to induce a measure of IMF flexibility in its demands on Egypt facilitated the agreement. Since that agreement, the Egyptian pound has twice been devalued, although the Central Bank conversion rate—on

19. "Egypt Reaches an Agreement with the IMF," *Wall Street Journal*, May 18, 1987; and John Kifner, "Egypt Wins Pact on Debt Payment," *New York Times*, May 24, 1987.

which subsidy payments are calculated—remains unchanged. Desirable though broader price rationalization may be, it is fraught with domestic political dangers in Egypt and requires deft handling.

During the boom years of oil prices, up to and including 1985, Egypt's foreign exchange earnings were considerable. They flowed largely from petroleum sales, remittances from Egyptians working abroad, Suez Canal tolls, and tourism receipts. Some American officials criticize Egypt for failing to use this windfall income, when it was available, to redress internal economic problems. In the past two years, as a result of the oil glut and reduced oil prices, Egypt's balance of payments has suffered sharp reversals. Expatriate remittances dropped sharply, tourist earnings fell as a result of foreigners' (especially American) fear of terrorism and police riots in Cairo in March 1987, and oil income dropped in 1985 because of the global depression of petroleum markets. As a result, the United States has become increasingly concerned that Egypt could be approaching a state of economic collapse, whatever that might mean in political terms. For the United States, this situation underscores the urgency of drastic economic reform in the country. There is also a widespread U.S. view that Egypt could obtain more hard currency assets from expatriate remittances if greater incentives were offered.

Egypt's foreign debt was estimated as of mid-1987 to be in the neighborhood of $44 billion, of which about $10 billion is owed to the United States. Each year Egypt's repayment of interest alone consumes approximately $2.5 billion of its reduced foreign exchange revenues. Egypt's first repayment on its initially deferred military debt to the United States came due in 1986. Annual payments due amounted to about $0.5 billion principal and interest. Predictably, Egypt sought debt relief. Initially, the United States proposed spreading out repayment over a longer period of time, but with exceptionally bulbous final installments and with no reduction of the interest requirement. It was harshly received by the Egyptian leadership and, as already indicated, unfavorably compared with the Soviet arrangement. There are legal constraints on what any administration can do to accommodate debtor nations, and the United States is reluctant to seek any increase of annual economic aid appropriations for Egypt.

Nevertheless, on November 14, 1987, following protracted diplomatic negotiations, a bilateral agreement was signed, rescheduling a significant part of Egypt's civilian and military debts to the United States. Covering all arrears due by December 31, 1986, and amounts falling due between January 1987 and June 1988, the agreement stipulated a ten-year repayment period, including a five-year grace period during which only interest payments of between 2 percent and 7 percent will be made. The agreement represented a serious effort by the administration to assist Egypt in its financial quandary, although many Egyptians consider it less favorable than similar rescheduling arrangements worked out with the West German, French, and Spanish governments. This reaction is inevitable since more is expected of the United States than from lesser creditor states. For the moment, however, the agreement obviates what seemed to loom as a potential problem, namely, legislatively mandated suspension of aid if Egypt were to default on debt repayment.

Another element needs to be cited. By the time the Camp David package was concluded, Sadat's *infitah,* or open door economic policy, had been in effect for about five years, but only modest amounts of foreign, including American, capital investment had been attracted into Egypt. In September 1982, an agreement was signed with Egypt in which the U.S. government undertook to encourage American capital investment in Egypt. Success has been limited. About $1.6 billion in private American capital is currently estimated to be invested in Egypt. Putative American investors still point to Egypt's protracted bureaucratic delays in approving joint venture projects. Egyptians complain that many would-be American investors seek to capitalize on their know-how and management but are reluctant to provide equity capital. Both charges have substance. With the limited inflow of private American capital investment, many Egyptians came to associate the open door policy with what many condemned as conspicuous consumerism and increasingly castigated it as a device enabling a new wealthy elite to emerge. Inevitably, the United States came to be associated in the Egyptian public mind with the new, much pilloried "fat cats." Among some Egyptians, especially Islamic fundamentalists, the open door policy is denounced as a Western (read American) means of keeping Egypt weak and economically dependent.

Throughout the eighties, the Reagan administration emphasized its desire that the Egyptian private sector be broadened. By mandating an apportionment of annual U.S. aid for this purpose, it pressed the Egyptian authorities to unleash the long-constrained private sector. Egyptian economic planning generally postulates that about 15 percent of the nonagricultural economy can appropriately be conducted by the private sector, but that for sociopolitical reasons most of it will have to remain with the public sector in the context of a mixed economy. Although American AID officials have avoided proposing a percentage target for the private sector, their persistent efforts to reorient the Egyptian economy in favor of that sector inevitably arouse governmental, media, and public ire. U.S. interference in the Egyptian economy is imputed.

In sum, American leaders regard Egypt as only casually responsive to sound economic advice. Hence, they conclude, U.S. economic aid must sometimes be used as leverage to require Egypt to correct structural deficiencies if the state is to survive as an economic entity. Egyptians react negatively to American pressure and see it as patronizing and even bludgeoning. Their economic dependency, and resultant vulnerability to U.S. pressure, rankles and is a running sore in the relationship. By early 1988, however, there was cautious U.S. optimism that Egypt might risk more significant, even if gradual, economic reform. That remains to be seen.

THE MILITARY DIMENSION

Since the signing of the Egyptian-Israeli peace treaty, the military dimension has loomed large in the bilateral relationship between the United States and Egypt. As early as 1974, Sadat had sought American weaponry and equipment. He had repeatedly assured senior officers, desperate for spare parts and supplies after the costly October 1973 war, that such U.S. military equipment would soon be forthcoming. He did so to gain their support for his new and still untested policy of cooperation with the United States. Despite initial U.S. promises, no American military support went to Egypt until after Sinai II and then only in sales of token amounts of logistical support equipment and air transport.

On another level of military cooperation, and to show a willingness to cooperate, Sadat had agreed as early as 1974 that combat vessels of the Sixth Fleet could make four goodwill and liberty visits to Egyptian ports each year. The U.S. Navy sought to make Alexandria a regular port of call, and the Egyptian minister of defense eventually raised the permitted number of such visits to eight each year. This was a significant boon to the U.S. Navy, short as it was of liberty ports in the eastern Mediterranean. For a time, the navy also entertained hopes of broader use of Alexandria's port and drydock facilities, but Egypt's offer—when finally made in 1979—was economically unattractive.

With the signing of the peace treaty, the way was cleared for the Carter administration to seek congressional concurrence in a substantial arms program to Egypt. Indeed, the renewed promise of such a military aid program to reequip the Egyptian armed forces was significant in persuading Sadat to accept the Camp David Accords and the peace treaty, even though he knew these documents were deficient in expressing Egypt's political commitment to the overall Arab cause. Immediately after the signing of the peace treaty, high-level talks commenced between U.S. and Egyptian defense officials in an effort to delineate the arms program.

To Sadat, keeping the potentially important military sector supportive of his peace policies was essential. Not all senior Egyptian officers, let alone the military rank and file, were enamored of the peace treaty. It was not peace they opposed but the terms of the treaty. This was especially true of what were perceived as prescribed servitudes on Egyptian military garrisoning of Sinai. There might now be formal peace, but most senior Egyptian military defense planners remained deeply conscious of thirty years of war with Israel. Although they might henceforth mute public identification of Israel as the threat, they continued to see their new peace treaty partner as the major putative military opponent. Israel, they recognized, could again seize Sinai at will.

The United States was concerned about a different set of conditions. Israel was tepid on any substantial post-treaty U.S. military aid program for Egypt but reluctantly accepted the idea so long as careful limits were placed on types and volumes of American military equipment that might be provided. For the administration, any American military aid program to Egypt had to be sufficient in types and volumes of equipment to be at least passably satisfactory to Egyptian military leaders, yet not seem to give Egypt a revived military capability that some future Egyptian leader might use against Israel. There could be no absolute Egyptian military parity with Israel if continued congressional support was to be obtained.

In seeking legislative approval for a substantial military aid program to Egypt, successive administrations also had to respond credibly to congressional inquiries about the nature of the external threat to Egypt in the period after the peace treaty. The resultant analysis, as explained to Congress, was convoluted. A chronic threat from Soviet-supplied Libya was cited, but few really believed Qadhafi posed a serious military danger to a stronger and more populous Egypt. A possible need to deploy Egyptian troops to the Sudan, the critical source of Nile waters for the Egyptian economy and a country with which Egypt then had a security agreement, was postulated in the event of Qadhafi-inspired subversion of the Sudanese regime. Contingency deployment of Egyptian military forces to the Persian Gulf, should the oil-rich Arab states of the Gulf be threatened by the Iranian Islamic Republic, was also adduced to justify a continuing need for an effective Egyptian military force structure. So was possible future Egyptian military deployment to parts of sub-Saharan Africa to assist moderate regimes faced with aggression by neighboring communist proxy states. Despite the sogginess of the threat estimates, Congress, not without reservations, sanctioned a significant military aid program. Legislators reluctantly recognized that the price of Egypt's continued support for peace with Israel was not only economic aid but also military assistance.

Since the beginning of the military aid program for Egypt through 1987, almost $9.5 billion has been appropriated for new equipment and training. Weaponry began to arrive in mid-1980 and continues to do so. This has included F-4 and later F-16 aircraft, tanks, armored personnel carriers, air defense missiles, artillery, and much other equipment and training. The military aid program is administered through a U.S. Office of Military Cooperation in Cairo, a designation that is meant to avoid Egyptian political sensitivity about foreign "advisers."

Predictably, the U.S. military assistance program to Egypt has engendered some problems. There are Egyptian complaints of inadequate volumes, less sophistication of equipment than that provided to Israel, slow deliveries, and alleged cultural insensitivity by some American military instructors in dealing with Egyptian trainees. Fortunately, Field Marshal Muhammad Abd al-Halim Abu Ghazalah, former Egyptian military attaché in Washington, has been designated deputy prime minister and minister of defense. He enjoys numerous, cordial relations with senior Department of Defense officials, which is helpful in keeping problems tractable. But problems periodically recur and must be carefully monitored lest they get out of hand.

The question of broader defense cooperation also had to be addressed. As early as February 1979, Sadat proposed to visiting Secretary of Defense Harold Brown that the United States rehabilitate and utilize Ras Banas, on the Egyptian Red Sea coast, as a possible naval and air facility. Despite the administration's initial disinterest, Egypt's offer became increasingly attractive. This was particularly true because of Soviet bases, first at Massawa, Ethiopia, and, subsequently, on the Dahlak Islands.

To obtain a congressional appropriation for rehabilitating the Ras Banas military facilities, the administration needed a written agreement from Egypt permitting U.S. use of those facilities. Sadat was reluctant to give written permission. As usual, he initially insisted his oral commitment should suffice. Eventually, on his last visit to Washington in 1981, Sadat proffered a somewhat vague letter inviting the United States to make use of the Ras Banas facilities.

By then, there was great interest by the Department of Defense in doing so, and Congress appropriated funds for this purpose. To U.S. chagrin, with Sadat's assassination a month later and Mubarak's assumption of the presidency, the new Egyptian leadership withdrew the offer of Ras Banas. On Egypt's initiative, talks for possible basing of the Rapid Deployment Force (RDF) were also suspended in May 1983. Some American leaders saw these reversals as whimsical and as evidence of Egypt's limited reliability. To Egypt, the permanent presence of U.S. military facilities in Egypt would impugn the nation's long-proclaimed nonalignment.

In Sadat's last two years, he also offered the United States use of various Egyptian military airfields on a case-by-case, individually approved basis. The facilities have occasionally been used by U.S. Air Force aircraft, including aerial tanker staging in the abortive 1980 Tabas hostage rescue operation in Iran. These arrangements have been continued under Mubarak. The United States would prefer more extensive and automatic U.S. Air Force usage rights at Egyptian military air bases, but these have not been granted. Egypt is concerned about the possible use of its facilities for operations that may be politically unacceptable. Hence it insists on exercising advance approval. Nevertheless, to the United States the existing arrangement has been generally satisfactory.

Since the establishment of the U.S. Central Command (CENTCOM), the specified command that grew from the original RDF, Egyptian and U.S. military planners have done limited joint defense planning for possible contingencies in the Middle East and African areas. Beginning in 1981, biennial joint military exercises between Egyptian and CENTCOM-assigned U.S. troops, dubbed Bright Star, have been conducted in the Western Desert. American commanders have lauded the performance of Egyptian troops in these exercises. There have also been occasional joint naval exercises between the Egyptian navy and units of the Sixth Fleet. The Egyptian authorities insist on minimal publicity for joint military exercises. For a Pentagon conscious of public relations, this Egyptian restriction is sometimes chafing, but bearable.

Although the United States has not acceded to the 1888 Suez Canal treaty, despite Sadat's frequent urgings that it do so, the U.S. Navy attaches much importance to free and unhindered passage through that strategic artery of its combat and other vessels. With one exception, there have been no difficulties on this score. The exception is nuclear-powered warships (NPW). Despite years of persistent effort by American officials to persuade the Egyptian leadership that U.S. Navy NPWs have an extraordinary safety record, and a stipulated willingness to compensate for any damage resulting from unexpected malfunction, the Egyptian authorities remain chary of allowing NPW passages. There is inconsistency in the Egyptian position. Sixth Fleet NPWs have for years been permitted to make port visits to Alexandria, yet passage of this type of vessel through the Suez Canal was long refused. The objection came largely from officials in charge of the autonomous Suez Canal administration, who worry about a possible nuclear accident in that vital waterway.

Not until 1986 was the first NPW, the *USS Arkansas,* allowed to pass through the canal. Even then the Suez Canal authorities insisted it transit southward alone and suspended regular north and southbound convoys until the vessel had exited. To American surprise, Egypt charged an exceptionally high transit levy, contending it represented revenue lost by suspending regular convoys during the vessel's passage. Considering the substantial U.S. aid given to Egypt, American officials saw this demand as extortionist. Since that time, only one other U.S. Navy NPW, with escorts, has been allowed to pass through the canal with the same high fee. American efforts continue to be made to obtain unrestricted NPW transit rights, with standard transit tolls, but Egyptian authorities will probably continue to insist that any such transits be on an individually approved basis and under restricted conditions.

In sum, although a considerable measure of military cooperation has developed in the past ten years between the two countries, it is less than the United States would like and has been subject to sporadic Egyptian vacillation. It goes as far as the Egyptian authorities, for political reasons, consider necessary and politic to ensure continued American military aid. Should U.S. military aid at any time be terminated or sharply reduced by congressional or executive action, such military cooperation as exists between the two countries is likely to come to a quick halt.

CONCLUSION

In the ten years since the Camp David package, U.S. relations with Egypt have generally remained good, but the two countries have also sometimes been at cross purposes. Each party blames the other for occasional actions deemed inimical to its interests. Relations have ebbed since Sadat's day, but have in the process attained a more pragmatic level of realism. This was desirable and is politically healthy. Mubarak continues to honor the peace treaty with Israel and to support efforts to resume a broader Middle East peace process, but erstwhile American hopes that a close Egyptian-

Israeli political, strategic, and economic link would flow from the peace treaty have eroded. They were illusory from the outset. Egypt goes through minimal forms of maintaining and normalizing relations with Israel but little more. This is unlikely to change unless a broader Middle East peace evolves, including an acceptable Palestinian settlement. It is gratifying to Washington, nevertheless, that a reasonable dialogue has developed between Mubarak and Israeli Foreign Minister Shimon Peres on an international peace conference, for whatever that may prove to be worth. Both Washington and Cairo see Prime Minister Yitzhak Shamir as an obstacle to negotiations.

For years, Americans in both government and the private sector have expressed foreboding about the future of Egypt. Its seemingly uncontrollable population explosion, array of staggering internal economic problems, bureaucratic sluggishness, huge external debt, and other problems have contributed to the prevailing state of despondency about what the future holds. The increasing strength of Islamic fundamentalism in Egypt and perhaps of neo-Nasserism, and their likely portents for the future, adds to the worries of American leaders. Americans often fail to understand Mubarak's innately cautious approach to decisionmaking. He is also seen as lacking the economic expertise needed to come to grips with the country's formidable economic dilemmas. Washington regards the existing relationship as valuable and viable, but uncertainty exists whether, in the event of renewed crisis in the Middle East involving Israel, Egypt can be counted on. Egypt's recent flirtations with the Soviets also trouble the administration. On broader international issues, the U.S. representative to the United Nations has complained that Egypt voted against the United States 80 percent of the time. From Egypt's point of view, the exact reverse is, of course, the case.

At the same time, in the United States there is a tendency among officials to take Egypt for granted. Because of massive U.S. economic and military aid programs, some American leaders, consciously or unconsciously, conceive of Egypt as a client state and expect it to conduct itself as such when asked by Washington to cooperate in whatever international endeavors Washington pursues. U.S. officials sometimes give the impression of seeking to remold Egyptian policy. This is especially true of some members of Congress and senior AID officials. There is little comprehension of Egyptian cultural sensitivities and Mubarak's separate political agendas in the Arab and Islamic worlds. In actuality, there is no extensive commonality of interests between the United States and Egypt, only an overlap of some and a discordancy in others. The peace treaty notwithstanding, Israel stands between Cairo and Washington and will continue to do so. So does the negative official U.S. attitude toward Palestinian national aspirations. These two obstacles to close U.S.-Egyptian relations are intimately linked.

The publication in 1987 of Bob Woodward's exposé, *Veil*, with its damaging revelations of the Central Intelligence Agency's covert activities against Egypt these past five years or more, has not endeared the United States to Egyptians at large. Mubarak is not only personally irked, but he is domestically politically embarrassed by the revelations, which are widely known in Egypt. They are grist for the mill of anti-American elements. Egypt is, of course, no stranger to intelligence operations of its own, and American officials in Egypt may be expected to be more closely monitored in the future. Mubarak's visit to Washington in January 1988, his first since 1985, offered opportunities to clear the air. But that positive spirit has at least been partially undermined by the news, in June 1988, of an abortive attempt by an Egyptian military procurement officer in Washington to smuggle highly sensitive carbon compound matériel out of the United States for use in developing surface-to-surface missiles.[20]

As long as substantial American economic and military aid for Egypt continues, the bilateral dialogue between the two countries should remain positive, even if sometimes disputatious. On some issues, the two countries have agreed to disagree. With effort by both sides, it should be possible to keep residual disagreements within manageable limits. Unlike Israel, which is considered a non-NATO ally, no alliance exists between the United States and Egypt. Nor do most Egyptians, public or private, show any desire for an alliance. Nonalignment has long been ingrained in Egyptian political thinking, even if its implementation is at times somewhat tilted. Egypt refused a limited U.S. security agreement, such as that given to Israel, when the peace treaty was signed. Friendship and cooperation within mutually prescribed parameters, coupled with Egyptian wariness over any real or imagined U.S. encroachment on its sovereign prerogatives, is likely to be the pattern of the foreseeable future bilateral relationship. For both countries, this is a tolerable modus operandi.

But a final cautionary note is in order. Some Americans are persuaded that Egypt's ties with the United States are virtually irreversible. They point to the present elite leadership's orientation,

20. Philip Shenon, "U.S. Accuses Two Egyptian Colonels in Plot to Smuggle Missile Material," *New York Times*, June 25, 1988.

its economic planning, and its military dependence to support their contention. Though not without some substance, such hubris reflects excessive complacency and ignores historical experience. Egypt has dramatically altered its superpower relationship in the past and, depending on leadership and circumstances, can do so again. Unquestionably, Mubarak, like Sadat before him, wants continued close links with the United States. The Mubarak regime may be expected to do what it can to preserve that association, despite occasional differences between the two countries. One assumes future U.S. administrations will share this desire.

Much will depend on variables outside the control of either leadership: for example, future congressional action on economic and military aid, a putative serious Israeli-Syrian clash, Israeli treatment of Palestinians and U.S. reaction, future domestic political determinants of Egyptian policy, and so on. For the leaders of both countries, one salient reality must be borne in mind: the relationship is primarily an elite leadership tie, as yet only shallowly rooted in Egyptian society as a whole. The United States, therefore, either through politically insensitive executive policies or legislative actions, can gravely damage a moderate Egyptian leadership in the eyes of its domestic constituency and, conversely, can fuel demagogic opposition elements.

Despite such uncertainties, the present bilateral relationship is optimally cooperative and benefits both sides. American officials and legislators would nevertheless be well advised not to imply that substantial U.S. aid to Egypt somehow creates political bondage. Any such suggestion is galling to the Egyptian government and people and will certainly be counterproductive. The relationship must remain between sovereign equals, and continued U.S. empathy for Egypt's array of problems and sensitivities is requisite if the relationship is to prosper.

NAOMI CHAZAN

Domestic Developments in Israel

THE ISRAELI political scene changed in significant ways in the decade following the signing of the Camp David Accords on September 17, 1978. Four distinct phases are discernible: an initial period of diplomatic achievement and growing internal polarization, roughly coinciding with the first administration of Menachem Begin's Likud bloc (1977–81); a second stage of political turmoil and diplomatic stagnation, punctuated by the Israeli invasion of Lebanon in June 1982, intense domestic strife, and rapid economic deterioration (1981–84); a third phase characterized by gradual domestic stabilization coupled with political indeterminacy under the joint Labor-Likud national unity government (1984–87); and a fourth set in motion by the civilian uprising in the West Bank and Gaza that began in December 1987.

During these years the founding fathers of Israel disappeared completely, replaced by a new generation of political leaders. Social cleavages intensified, the balance of political power shifted, and political priorities were transformed. The heady atmosphere generated by President Anwar Sadat's visit to Jerusalem in November 1977 gave way to a mixture of extremism on the one hand and, on the other, to introspection and then inertia. By the end of the decade, the country's political parameters had changed substantially.

What is the relationship between the ratification of the Camp David Accords and these domestic political trends? To what extent and in what ways did the broader Egyptian-Israeli peace process

This paper benefited from insights provided by many people. Special thanks are due to Akiva Eldar, Yaron Ezrahi, and Avraham Harman for their many suggestions and ideas, and to Sidra Dekoven Ezrahi for her painstaking review of an earlier draft. The Harry S Truman Research Institute for the Advancement of Peace at the Hebrew University of Jerusalem provided research facilities.

affect the currents of Israeli political life? With the benefit of some hindsight, where should one situate the negotiations of the late 1970s within the broader context of Israel's recent political history? This paper looks at the consequences of the Camp David Accords specifically and of the Egyptian-Israeli peace initiative more generally for Israeli politics, a topic largely ignored in the now voluminous literature on the subject.

The Camp David Accords and the processes associated with them had an effect on the terms of political discourse in Israel, on attitudes toward the Arab-Israeli conflict, on political alignments, on the public agenda and modes of political behavior, and on foreign relations. In the following pages the immediate influence of the peace treaty in each of these five major spheres is examined and the political processes that were set in motion are analyzed. An attempt is then made to evaluate their significance for Israeli political life during the ensuing decade and to pinpoint their implications for the resumption of the peace momentum.

The rapprochement between Israel and Egypt triggered a series of political adjustments that assumed a trajectory of their own in the course of the 1980s. As the form and substance of political action changed, it became increasingly difficult to distinguish the direct effects of the talks from the processes with which they merged.

The symbolism of the Egyptian-Israeli accords still carries significant weight and evokes diverse reactions within Israel. The peace treaty has become one of many political resources employed by politicians and social groups to promote their interests, mobilize support, and justify policies. Camp David, in all its complexity, has been absorbed into the Israeli political experience.

THE CAMP DAVID ACCORDS AND ISRAELI POLITICS

Israel on the eve of President Sadat's dramatic initiative was at a political crossroads. In 1977 the country marked the tenth anniversary of the Six-Day war and the occupation of the Golan Heights, the West Bank, Sinai, and Gaza. No consensus existed on the implications of the ongoing Israeli presence in these areas for the physical shape, the demographic composition, and the political fabric of the state.[1]

1. Sinai was something of an exception. Two disengagement agreements were negotiated in the mid-1970s, and a consensus emerged on withdrawal to a Yamit to Sharm al-Sheikh line in exchange for nonbelligerency.

The October 1973 war had isolated Israel internationally. The Israeli near-defeat had a demoralizing effect on many citizens: the commanders of the Israel Defense Forces and the responsible ministers had been exposed as all too human, the reigning myth of military invincibility had been shattered, and a measure of fatigue had set in. As economic conditions worsened and domestic strife grew, the integrity and efficiency of the existing leadership was increasingly challenged. Finally, in May of 1977 elections ended the twenty-nine-year hegemony of the Labor party, ushering in an inexperienced and untested Likud government. The peace negotiations with Egypt began in this atmosphere of fluidity and uncertainty. Their outcome could not but touch upon key facets of the domestic political debate.

The Ideological Dimension

Zionism is the core ideology of modern Israel. It is based on the assumption that there is an integral relationship between the land of Israel, the Jewish people, and the creation of sovereign political institutions.[2] The main contours of the Zionist enterprise have always been subject to multiple interpretations. Before the establishment of the state, several ideological strains competed. Labor-Zionists elaborated an outward-oriented and humanistic conception based on universal values of equality and justice; revisionists stressed sovereignty, nationhood, and the historic rights of the Jewish people in the Holy Land; and religious Zionists saw political independence as a precondition for creating an environment conducive to the pursuit of Jewish law and custom.

Until 1967 these viewpoints coexisted with cultural and Marxist approaches to Zionism in what was a delicate and tenuous balance. The occupation of territories in the 1967 war, however, required the reexamination of the relationship between the geographic, human, and political foundations of the state. The subsequent ideological conflict pitted security and territorial concerns, articulated primarily by the Likud, against democratic and social considerations, voiced by Labor circles.[3] Each party attempted to appropriate the national symbols of Jewish history, security, peace,

2. Arthur Hertzberg, ed., *The Zionist Idea: A Historical Analysis and Reader* (Atheneum, 1977); and Shlomo Avineri, *The Making of Modern Zionism: The Intellectual Origins of the Jewish State* (Basic Books, 1981), provide excellent background analyses of the development of Zionist thought.

3. Charles S. Liebman and Eliezer Don-Yehiya, "The Dilemma of Reconciling Traditional Culture and Political Needs: Civil Religion in Israel," *Comparative Politics*, vol. 16 (October 1983), pp. 53–66.

settlement, and equity to advance its own vision of Israel's destiny. The incompatibility between these contradictory approaches was pronounced when Israel entered the peace negotiations with Egypt.

Menachem Begin sought to justify the two accords emanating from Camp David by separating the issue of peace from the question of territory. During the debate in the Knesset on the provisions for peace with Egypt, he declared unequivocally: "Israel will never return to the June 4, 1967, borders; united Jerusalem is the eternal capital of Israel and will never be divided again. A Palestinian state will not be established in Judea, Samaria, and Gaza."[4] In this way he hoped to rationalize the return of Sinai to Egypt, lay the groundwork for the indefinite retention of the West Bank by Israel, and mollify ultranationalist factions within his own camp.[5]

Inevitably, therefore, the Camp David negotiations directly affected the matrix of the political debate in Israel. The participants in the discussion multiplied. Doves of various hues continued to assert the connection between withdrawal from territories and peace.[6] At the same time, both moderate doves and moderate hawks found in the Begin formulation a means of allaying their security concerns while continuing to uphold their professed commitment to peace.

The greatest confusion was felt in revisionist circles. Within the Likud's own political aviary, both the unconditional hawks, who insisted that only Israel's own strength could guarantee its survival, and some of the militant hawks, who believed in the assertion of Jewish control throughout the land of Israel, loudly opposed any territorial concessions. The nationalist persuasion, represented by the dominant Herut faction in the Likud, could not carry the ultra-right. The peace accords thus led to the beginning of the ideological fragmentation of the Likud's support base. The path of religious and ultranationalist extremism (expressed by the creation of the Tehiya party by Herut renegades Geula Cohen and Yuval Neeman in 1979) was charted at this juncture.

The terms of political discourse also changed. The Egyptian-Israeli peace process introduced the possibility of distinguishing between sovereignty over people and sovereignty over territory, between administrative and legislative autonomy, and between

4. Shiloah Institute, *The Peace Treaty between Israel and Egypt: Selected Documents* (in Hebrew) (Tel Aviv: Shiloah Institute, 1981).

5. Shlomo Avineri, "Beyond Camp David," *Foreign Policy*, no. 46 (Spring 1982), pp. 22–23.

6. Avi Shlaim and Avner Yaniv, "Domestic Politics and Foreign Policy in Israel," *International Affairs*, vol. 56 (Spring 1980), pp. 242–62.

political supervision and military control. More significantly, it demanded, for the first time since 1967, that arguments in favor of continued occupation be cast in domestic terms, since externally derived defensive rationales could no longer be sustained on their own. This change opened the door for greater introspection revolving around approaches to the territories and for a more fundamental clash of worldviews. Debate intensified on the nature and direction of Israeli social change, as well as on whether force or compromise was the best means to bring about desired changes.

Yet ironically the peace treaty between Egypt and Israel also reduced the urgency previously attached to the quest for a solution to the broader Arab-Israeli conflict. By granting the Israeli government some breathing space, and by tying further movement in the peace process to the improvement of relations with Egypt, the accords of September 17, 1978, delayed, at least temporarily, a more serious confrontation with the question of Israel's future relations with its other neighbors. In these circumstances subjective feelings toward the viability of relations with Egypt acted as a substitute for analysis and careful policy designs.

The effect of the Egyptian-Israeli accords on the ideological dimension of Israeli political life related to three quite distinct processes. The first, and by far the most important, concerned Israeli approaches to the other territories taken over in 1967. The breakdown in the autonomy talks (unilaterally suspended by Sadat in May 1980 after long and fruitless discussions), together with the Likud's dissociation of the peace process from the continued Israeli presence on the West Bank, paved the way for the legal change of the status of Jerusalem and for accelerating the pace of Israeli settlement in the territories.[7]

During the first Likud administration, under the aegis of the then-minister of agriculture, Ariel Sharon, substantial tracts of land were expropriated and plans were made for constructing a variety of rural and suburban settlements.[8] These plans were carried out despite the fact that the final withdrawal from the Sinai in April 1982, and with it the razing of the Israeli town of Yamit in the Rafiah quadrant, might have served as something of a disincentive to relocating outside the confines of the 1967 boundaries (the green line). Between

7. Mark Tessler, *Israeli Politics and the Palestinian Problem in the Wake of Camp David,* part 1: *The Camp David Accords and the Palestinian Problem,* American Universities Field Staff Reports, no. 33 (Hanover, N.H.: AUFS, 1980).

8. Meron Benvenisti, *The West Bank Data Project: A Survey of Israel's Policies* (American Enterprise Institute, 1984).

1977 and 1984, ninety new Jewish communities were established.[9] Cheap housing, tax relief, and attractive mortgage conditions were offered to citizens willing to move to these settlements. Resources were poured into constructing new units and supplying social amenities. To ensure control, a grid of roads was built throughout the West Bank. In word and in deed, the government gave every sign that it had no intention of relinquishing its hold in the area.

The Lebanon war, too, was connected to the future of the territories. A subsidiary goal of the June 1982 invasion was to perpetuate Israeli rule by imposing the government's narrow version of autonomy on the West Bank, by weakening Palestinian nationalism and especially the Palestine Liberation Organization (PLO), and by encouraging the creation of a Palestinian state on the east bank of the Jordan.[10] The consensus on three negative policy principles (no withdrawal to the 1967 lines, no Palestinian state on the West Bank, and no recognition of the PLO), which made possible the formation of a national unity government in 1984, precluded changes in official positions regarding the territories. Although some efforts were made to institute a variant of local autonomy between 1984 and 1986, the status of the West Bank and Gaza was less subject to debate within Israel in 1987 than it had been at the time of the ratification of the Egyptian-Israeli agreements.

The outbreak of widespread resistance to Israeli rule in December 1987 in Gaza and the West Bank reopened the dormant domestic debate. The public as well as decisionmakers were galvanized into a reconsideration of the status quo. If the Camp David Accords furnished an incentive to Israeli retrenchment, the events of late 1987 reawakened the territorial issue in circumstances far less conducive to political and diplomatic resolution.

Thus in retrospect the Camp David Accords indirectly curtailed for a time the prospects of territorial compromise in the West Bank and Gaza. By decoupling peace from territories they actually encouraged Israeli settlement. By leaving the notion of Palestinian autonomy purposely vague, they permitted the gradual elaboration by various Israeli leaders of functional autonomy as a palliative to the demand for self-determination. By giving successive governments a false sense of security, they blinded Israeli leaders to

9. E. Efrat, "Where and How Many Are Settled in Judea and Samaria?" (in Hebrew), *Ha'aretz,* May 24, 1984.

10. Ze'ev Schiff and Ehud Ya'ari, *Israel's Lebanon War,* ed. and trans. Ina Friedman (Simon and Schuster, 1984), and in Hebrew, *Milhemet Sholal* (The War of Deception) (Jerusalem: Schocken, 1984).

Palestinian responses to the consequences of Israeli rule. And by minimizing the sense of urgency previously associated with the occupation, they deferred negotiations on alternative solutions.

A second, related, process focused more squarely on the development of domestic attitudes toward peace. From the outset, as Shimon Shamir's contribution to this volume elaborates, public notions of the meaning of peace were rarified and idealized. Many Israelis expected Egypt to move promptly from enmity to friendship. The transition from animosity to nonbelligerence was depicted by the press and in public opinion in the psychological terms of personal relationships. This outlook meant that every Egyptian hesitation, equivocation, or procrastination was seen as a sign of betrayal. Throughout the 1978–88 period Egyptian actions were monitored diligently in these terms. The normalization process preparatory to the final Israeli withdrawal from Sinai was scrutinized for signs of warmth, not analyzed for difficulties. The recall of the Egyptian ambassador after the invasion of Lebanon was generally seen as a sign of Egyptian disengagement. The terms "hot" and "cold" abounded in popular discussions of relations with Egypt. The tepid response of Egyptian authorities to the killing of seven Israeli tourists by a fanatic guard at Ras Burka in October 1985 was widely considered the nadir in the interactions between the two countries. Even the September 1986 agreement to refer the outstanding dispute over Taba (a tiny piece of land near Eilat claimed by both Egypt and Israel) to arbitration and the later return of the Egyptian ambassador did little to alter these perceptions. The reality of the peace with Egypt sometimes failed to measure up to the heady expectations implanted in Israeli minds by the drama of Camp David.

During the first decade of Egyptian-Israeli rapprochement, the question of the workability of the peace treaty became part of the political debate within Israel. Those unwilling to explore new avenues to peace pointed to the obstacles between the two countries and the heavy toll they exacted from Israel; those who sought to promote further initiatives highlighted the quiet on Israel's southern front. While the rhetoric flowed, little effort was spent on working out an orderly transition from hostility to nonaggression or acknowledging how long such a process might take. The aftermath of the Camp David process, while launching a new era in Israeli-Egyptian relations, nonetheless had a sobering effect on Israeli perceptions of peace.[11]

11. Mark A. Heller, "Israeli Politics and the Arab-Israeli Peace Process," *Washington Quarterly*, vol. 10 (Spring 1987), pp. 129–36.

The third process accentuated following the Egyptian-Israeli negotiations was the symbolic one. The phrases and images emanating from Camp David exacerbated domestic disagreements, sharpening the differences between proponents of alternative approaches to the Israeli experience. Although the substance of the discussion did not alter significantly, certain arguments were amplified to buttress opposing views and tactics. Of special note was a growing concern with the demographics of the territories. Those favoring compromise claimed that Israel could maintain itself as a Jewish state only through withdrawal from territories with large concentrations of Arabs. Those striving to fulfill their vision of a greater Israel wanted to maintain the occupation (by force, if necessary), and some went so far as to propound schemes of population transfer. Inevitably, demographic considerations were cited in arguments for increasing the number of Jews, either through higher birthrates or through stepped-up immigration (*aliyah*), mostly from the Soviet Union.

Many of these debates deflected attention from the contemporary Zionist predicament. "What is really at issue," Michael Walzer wrote, "is not the future negotiating posture of the government, but the internal character of the state, its democratic values, the quality of its public and private life."[12] The breakdown, in the 1970s, of the terms of coexistence that had prevailed in the early years of the state was made worse by the ideological fragmentation that accompanied the signing of the peace treaty with Egypt.

For most of the ten years after Camp David political discussions in Israel stayed within the territorial-based frame of reference set down in the 1970s. The Palestinian revolt of 1987–88 forced Israelis to ask new questions. For the first time since 1967 the possibility that continued occupation could be an impediment to survival was raised in official circles. Issues on the ideological agenda began to shift, and the language of discourse changed. More significantly, upholders of conflicting viewpoints were forced to reevaluate their positions. An ideological fluidity, so lacking in the preceding decade, became apparent.

In 1988 Israel was at a paradigmatic conjuncture. Minor adjustments were no longer adequate to the challenge of facing some of the basic tenets of the Zionist ethos. The issue of the preservation of the democratic foundations of the state and its Jewish character could not be neatly divorced from the question of the occupation.

12. Michael Walzer, "Notes from an Israel Journal," *New Republic*, September 5, 1983, p. 17.

The protracted retention of the West Bank had already altered the human composition of the state and its political structures. Adherence to democratic principles and Jewish considerations could hardly be preserved without an adjustment in the post-1967 boundaries.

The philosophical justifications presented by Menachem Begin to support the Camp David Accords created a fallacy of "peace with territories" that was sustained for almost ten years. By the latter part of the 1980s, Israel and Israeli policymakers were trapped in its contradictions. They sought to achieve consensus without being willing to redefine the terms of the political debate or to reconsider some of its underlying presumptions. This reluctance bred ideological ambiguity, fostered a growing cynicism within the country, and impeded creative approaches to conflict management and resolution. The Egyptian-Israeli peace treaty, which seemed initially to signal greater pragmatism, has become at least in the short run a deterrent to further compromise because of its influence on the domestic ideological debate.

The Security Dimension

The Arab-Israeli conflict has always been at the center of the Israeli political experience. Since before the establishment of the state in 1948, security considerations have been paramount in the eyes of policymakers and the population at large. The four wars fought by Israel during its first thirty years reinforced the view that Arab countries were bent on destroying the Jewish state and that its survival depended on developing its defenses.[13] Before 1977 Egypt, the largest and most powerful of Israel's inimical neighbors, was seen as the primary threat to the existence of the country. Unlike Syria, Jordan, or Lebanon, Egypt had taken an active part in all four wars. It had been a leader in the diplomatic offensive against Israel in international forums. And in launching the 1973 Yom Kippur war, it had been directly responsible for undermining Israel's sense of military invincibility. The Sadat initiative enhanced the prospects of removing Egypt from the confrontational circle surrounding Israel, of neutralizing the threat to the country's long and sparsely populated southwestern frontier, and not insignificantly, of bringing about a split in the Arab ranks.[14] From the perspective of Menachem Begin and his government, the opportunity offered

13. Michael Brecher, *The Foreign Policy System of Israel: Setting, Images, Process* (Yale University Press, 1972).

14. Shlaim and Yaniv, "Domestic Politics and Foreign Policy."

by Camp David was as significant strategically as it was diplomatically, politically, and historically. The slogan "Peace and Security" propounded by the Likud conveyed the integral connection its leaders made between the Camp David Accords and the improvement of Israel's military posture.

The accords addressed the security concerns of virtually all of Israel's political factions. Moderates (in Likud as well as Labor) could point to the treaty as evidence against the conventional wisdom that all Arabs were determined to eradicate Israel and hence that no one could be found in the Arab camp with whom reasonable discussions could be held. Hard-liners were appeased because the treaty actually increased Israel's ability to pursue its military goals elsewhere. And war-weary citizens saw in the accords at least a measure of relief.

The Camp David Accords did not, however, allay Israel's security suspicions so much as redirect them. If certain strategic considerations no longer applied to Egypt, they were still valid on other fronts. In the aftermath of the peace negotiations a reorientation of strategic objectives, rather than premises, occurred. By the early 1980s, Syria had become Israel's major external antagonist. And more attention was given to "the enemy within," as the Palestinians—and especially the PLO—became a prime focus of Israel's security concerns. Camp David thus brought about the redefinition and partial internalization of the enemy.

These perceptual changes influenced the course of the Arab-Israeli conflict over the next decade. On the regional level, attention was drawn to the northern front. The bombing of the Iraqi nuclear reactor in June 1981 was a preliminary sign of this reorientation and the imposition of Israeli law on the Golan a more serious expression of it.[15] The Lebanon war was its culmination.

The planning and execution of the Israeli invasion of Lebanon in June 1982 was undertaken by certain leaders (notably Ariel Sharon, who was then minister of defense, and Chief of Staff Rafael Eitan) who took advantage of the fact that Israel did not have to fear an Egyptian attack to test their strategic ideas. The Lebanese campaign was launched with five main goals: the creation of a forty-kilometer security belt along Israel's northern border; the expulsion of Syria from Lebanon; the elimination of the PLO military infrastructure in southern Lebanon and the delegitimation of its leadership; the replacement of the Lebanese government with a Christian coalition

15. Moshe Ma'oz, *Asad: The Sphinx of Damascus, A Political Biography* (London: Weidenfeld and Nicolson, 1988).

willing to sign a peace treaty with Israel; and the entrenchment of Israeli hegemony over the West Bank.[16]

At first domestic reactions to the war followed partisan lines, with supporters accepting government assurances about the necessity of the operation and skeptics questioning those assertions. Gradually, however, discontent with the war became more widespread. Reservations focused, first, on the futility of using military means to achieve political goals. Next, doubts were expressed about the soundness of the strategic thinking behind the Lebanese initiative. The overtly offensive character of "Operation Peace for the Galilee" was a departure from the defense-rooted concepts that had guided previous military engagements.[17] The bombing of Beirut in August 1982 and the Sabra and Shatila massacres of September precipitated, for the first time in Israel's history, a serious debate on the morality of war. There was a widespread sense that the public (and portions of the cabinet) had been duped. And, in a more pragmatic vein, questions were raised about the conduct and effectiveness of the Israel Defense Forces. Many experts claimed that security priorities had been distorted and that the Lebanese escapade adversely affected Israel's defensive capacity.[18]

By the time of the 1984 elections it was clear that the ostensible objectives of the war had not been achieved. The PLO had been dispersed but not discredited; Syria had been engaged but neither weakened nor isolated; the issue of the West Bank and Gaza had been sidestepped but hardly subsumed; and the political map in Lebanon had been altered, but in ways unconducive to Israeli interests. The Lebanese invasion had cost more than 600 Israeli lives and more than $5 billion.[19] After the publication of the Kahan Commission investigation of the Israeli role in the Sabra and Shatila killings, the condemnation of Ariel Sharon and senior military personnel, and Menachem Begin's resignation, even Likud leaders were hard put to defend the operation.

Disengagement from Lebanon was high on the list of priorities

16. Shai Feldman and Heda Rechnitz-Kijner, *Deception, Consensus and War: Israel in Lebanon,* paper 27 (Tel Aviv University, Jaffee Center for Strategic Studies, 1984).

17. Dan Horowitz, "Israel's War in Lebanon: New Patterns of Strategic Thinking and Civilian-Military Relations," *Journal of Strategic Studies,* vol. 6 (September 1983), pp. 83–102.

18. Schiff and Ya'ari, *Israel's Lebanon War.*

19. Haim Barkai, "Reflections on the Economic Cost of the Lebanon War," *Jerusalem Quarterly,* no. 37 (1986), pp. 95–106.

of the national unity government when it assumed office in September 1984. Barely nine months later Prime Minister Shimon Peres and Defense Minister Yitzhak Rabin had effected a unilateral withdrawal of Israeli forces from most of Lebanon. The rapid Israeli pullback satisfied domestic demands without eliminating Israel's military presence in the security belt in southern Lebanon and without affecting Israel's strike capacity farther north. By mid-1985 the Lebanese dilemma had been externalized, thus removing it from the domestic political agenda.

If Camp David indirectly fueled Israeli militarism and the Lebanon invasion, the war and its aftermath, in turn, significantly narrowed the likelihood of additional acts of Israeli military adventurism in the foreseeable future. Ten years after the signing of the accords, Syria was still viewed as Israel's indisputable adversary. Although Israel's strategic strength was reinforced by a series of agreements with the United States, the inclination to engage in an open military confrontation was substantially reduced.

In fact, over the decade the Palestinian issue came to dominate Israel's strategic thinking, though Israeli officials failed to acknowledge the change. In the early 1980s the various Palestinian movements came to be viewed as distinct military threats to Israel. The tacit 1981 cease-fire along the Lebanese border and the 1982 invasion reflected this reassessment upward of Palestinian military activities. During the mid-1980s strikes by Palestinian terrorist groups, both outside of and within Israel, occupied center stage. These actions were portrayed as well planned, well funded, and well executed; in other words, as perhaps the most serious ongoing danger to the physical well-being of the population of Israel. This outlook lay behind the employment of strong-arm tactics in the territories; it was also used before 1987 to explain administrative detentions, communal punishment, and the periodic mistreatment of political detainees.

The spontaneous acts of violence that erupted at the close of the first post-Camp David decade reinforced the perception that Palestinian actions constituted the major source of aggression against Israel. The severity, at times brutality, with which the Israelis handled the uprising accentuated the view of Palestinians as a formidable, and heretofore underestimated, security threat. More significantly, these events exemplified the shifting nature of the Arab-Israeli conflict during this ten-year span. Between 1978 and 1982 the conflict was acted out in conventional military terms; the 1982–87 period was one in which guerrilla tactics were increasingly employed; and December 1987 created the conditions for the re-Palestinianization of the Arab-Israeli conflict and with it a new phase of civilian resistance and mass confrontation.

Another facet of the altered significance of the Palestinian question in the Israeli view of the Arab-Israel equation was expressed in diplomatic and political terms. Israel's representatives abroad, and especially its delegates to the United Nations, sought to undermine the legitimacy of Palestinian claims to self-determination and to impugn the credentials of their spokespersons. At the same time, particular attention was paid to removing leaders identified with the PLO from positions of influence on the West Bank. The dismantling of the National Guidance Committee, an informal group of nationalist leaders, and the dismissal of the mayors who had served at its helm is one case in point.[20] The feeble effort to nurture a West Bank leadership more sympathetic to Israel through the creation of "village leagues" is another. The attempt to elevate pro-Jordanian forces to positions of influence was an additional step in this process. The Knesset decision to declare illegal all contacts with people openly associated with the PLO further demonstrated the extent to which Palestinian organizations were transformed into the predominant enemy.

This campaign to denigrate Palestinian aspirations was taken perhaps most seriously by Israeli officials themselves. It left Israel's political and military leadership ill-equipped to monitor trends in the territories and unprepared for the outbreak of widespread resistance. It also served, to a large extent, as a self-fulfilling prophecy: the removal of Palestinian leadership not only bolstered the claim that Israel could not find responsible partners for negotiation, it also opened the door for mass Palestinian action against the occupation.

The problem of Palestinian representation has become a significant stumbling block in attempts to resume the peace process. There are many reasons for the Israeli reluctance to negotiate with members of Palestinian nationalist groups. Many of these hesitations are political, symbolic, ideological, and emotional. But increasingly they also mirror the changed position of Palestinian organizations in Israeli strategic orientations. For this reason, too, recognition of

20. Moshe Ma'oz, "Israeli Positions Regarding the Palestinian Question," *Vierteljahresberichte*, no. 99 (March 1985), pp. 21–28. For an in-depth analysis of the effect of the creation of a Palestinian state on Israel see Mark A. Heller, *A Palestinian State: The Implications for Israel* (Harvard University Press, 1983).

Palestinian claims might be the main alternative to rule by force. In effect the Israeli campaign to delegitimize Palestinian aspirations focused attention precisely on this aspect of the Arab-Israeli conflict.

Consequently, attitudes toward Palestinians, who live in such close proximity to Israelis, became a central moral issue. After the signing of the Camp David Accords Israeli attitudes toward Palestinian Arabs were more clearly articulated. They covered the spectrum. At one end were the racist proclamations of Rabbi Meir Kahane and his cohorts, who viewed Palestinians as subhuman, and the stereotypical views of the nationalist right, who insisted on the inferiority of the Palestinians and rejected their separate claims to recognition. In the center were the more detached views of many Israelis who avoided coming to terms with Palestinians as individuals yet attempted to forge a distinction between the PLO and the Palestinian people, and the more sophisticated positions of many supporters of Labor-Zionism, who acknowledged the notion of a Palestinian people and differentiated among the many factions of the Palestinian movement. Finally, there were the pronouncements of a small group on the left who identified with the plight of the Palestinians and demanded that Israel work toward their human and political liberation. The self-identity of Israelis thus became intertwined with their image of the Palestinians. And insofar as the events of late 1987 compelled a reconsideration of these attitudes, the self-perceptions of Israelis were also affected.

After 1978 there was a growing awareness that for Israelis to come to terms with themselves they had to confront the Palestinian question. This realization helps to explain the expansion of informal contacts between some residents of Israel and their counterparts in the West Bank, and between Israelis and Palestinians (including PLO officials) abroad. If in the early 1980s such encounters were rare, by the mid-1980s such meetings were held regularly. The ambiguities evident in many of these overtures reflected the difficulties inherent in relocating the focus of Israeli strategic concerns after the initiation of the peace talks in the late 1970s.

The Camp David process did alleviate some of Israel's most pressing security concerns. For one thing, it reduced the military tension in the area, and hence the centrality of the Arab-Israel conflict in the international arena. It also, somewhat counterintuitively, bolstered the militarization of Israel and Israeli society. The terms of the Arab-Israel confrontation consequently changed. Within domestic politics, the threat posed by various Arab countries and organizations was no longer considered either uniform or inexorable.

The new foci of military concern were not only fewer, they were also, as the Lebanon fiasco demonstrated, less suited to conventional military treatment. Terror rather than war, rocks rather than guns, guerrillas and children rather than armies, civilians rather than states or armed movements came to define the Israeli view of the nature of the danger it faced. Thus, while the peace treaty with Egypt eased Israel's strategic posture, it also confounded its military options and set in motion processes distinctly unamenable to military solutions. Ten years after Camp David, security issues still plagued the country and preoccupied its leadership; less agreement existed, however, on how to deal with the new parameters of the conflict.

The Political Dimension

The Camp David meetings took place at a critical turning point in the evolution of Israel's political system. Israel's parliamentary democracy is based on the sovereignty of its national assembly, the Knesset. Its proportional representation system, originally shaped to give divergent groups a voice in policymaking, has discouraged individual competition while spawning a multiplicity of parties. Because garnering 1 percent of the vote is enough to obtain a Knesset seat, the party scene has traditionally been highly fragmented. Access to power, however, has been mediated through these parties, whose leaders invariably wield inordinate power. Smaller parties, representing very specific constituencies, have generally been homogeneous; the larger alignments, by definition, have incorporated a variety of often discordant interests. They have constantly been wracked by internal schisms rooted in personal as well as ideological and tactical divisions. It is hardly surprising that under these circumstances no single party has ever received a majority, and that governments have had to rely on delicate coalitions to remain in office. Political life in such an unwieldy system veers toward the tendentious and the precarious. Despite the dominance of the Labor party during the first three decades of Israel's independence, these traits were abundantly in evidence; some of their more extreme manifestations, however, had been held in check.

The May 1977 elections dramatically shifted the balance of power in the country. The Likud (consisting of Herut, the Liberal party, and a small Laam faction), with forty-three seats, became the largest party in the Knesset, galvanizing the discontent of disadvantaged, mostly Sephardi, voters in the development towns and poorer neighborhoods.[21] Labor's representation dropped precipitously, from fifty-one mandates in 1973 to thirty-two in 1977 (see table 1). The enfeeblement of the Labor establishment (also composed of several factions) had been apparent for some time: immobility, lack of responsiveness, inefficiency, and policy indeterminacy combined to dim the party's appeal. Labor's voters defected, mostly to the new Democratic Movement for Change, a centrist formation running on a platform of electoral reform. The election results constituted a critical challenge to Israel's fledgling democracy: for the first time since the creation of the state, the system had to adjust to a change in its ruling alliance.

Sadat came to Jerusalem at a time when many politicians, parties, and citizens were still attempting to come to terms with the new political reality. The peace negotiations further exacerbated an already highly charged political climate. Within the two major alignments, arguments raged over the substance and the political ramifications of the accords. Labor activists were caught between their basic support for the treaties and their concern over the implications of a successful agreement for their own political standing. The Likud was divided between militant nationalists, who saw in the return of Sinai an unacceptable concession with dubious returns, and those who favored the ratification of the peace settlement and welcomed it as an opportunity to consolidate their party's hold on power—a tension also used by the negotiation team to justify stances during the talks.[22] Each of the major alignments felt additional pressure from grassroots organizations that took hold at this time.

Gush Emunim (the Bloc of the Faithful), established in 1974, had acted as the main impetus for the acceleration of Jewish settlement in the West Bank and Gaza. Its members, together with allied groups (the Committee against the Withdrawal from Sinai, Rabbi Meir Kahane's Kach movement) lobbied against the accords. Peace Now, a movement that developed spontaneously after 350 reserve officers wrote a letter to Menachem Begin on the eve of his departure for Camp David pleading with him to put the cause of peace at the forefront of his agenda, became one of the main proponents of the agreements. Other parties, associations, and individuals added their

21. Howard R. Penniman, ed., *Israel at the Polls: The Knesset Elections of 1977* (American Enterprise Institute, 1979), contains a series of excellent analyses of various facets of the 1977 elections.

22. Dan Jacobson, "Intraparty Dissensus and Interparty Conflict Resolution: A Laboratory Experiment in the Context of the Middle East Conflict," *Journal of Conflict Resolution*, vol. 25 (September 1981), pp. 471–94.

TABLE I. *Distribution of Seats, First through the Ninth Knessets, 1949–1977*

PARTY	1949	1951	1955	1959	1961	1965	1969	1973	1977
Mapai	46	45	40	47	42 }	45 }			
Achdut Ha'avoda	...	...	10	7	8 }		*Labor alignment*		
Mapam	19	15	9	9	9	8 }	56	51	32
Rafi[a]	...	...	...	...	...	10 }			
Democratic Movement for Change	...	...	...	...	...	...	...	...	15
Herut	14	8	15	17	17 }	*Gahal*		*Likud*	
Liberal[c]	7	20	13	8 }	17 }	26	26	39	43[b]
Independent Liberal[d]	5	4	5	6 }		5	4	4	1
United Religious	16	...	...	...	...	...	...	...	...
National Religious	...	10	11	12	12	11	12	10	12
Agudat Israel	...	} 5	6	6	6 {	4	4 }	5 {	4
Poalei Agudat Israel	...					2	2 }		1
Communist[e]	4	5	6	3	5	4	4	4	5
Citizens' Rights	...	...	...	...	...	...	...	3	1
Arab lists	2	5	5	5	4	4	4	3	1
Others	7	3	...	...	...	1	8	1	5

SOURCE: Through 1973, Central Bureau of Statistics, *Results of Elections to the Eighth Knesset and Local Authorities*, Special Series no. 461 (Jerusalem, 1974); for 1977, final official returns as released May 26, 1977. Cited in Howard R. Penniman, ed., *Israel at the Polls* (American Enterprise Institute, 1979), pp. 310–11.

a. Rafi was formed by David Ben-Gurion after he broke with Mapai in 1965. In 1968 the majority of its members joined the Labor alignment.

b. This figure rose to 45 shortly after the election, when Shlomzion (here included under "Others") joined the Likud.

c. General Zionist through 1959.

d. Progressive through 1959.

e. The communist figure represents Communist party seats in the first through the fifth Knessets. In 1965 and 1969 the figure includes one seat for the "old" Jewish-oriented party (Maki) and three for the "new" Arab-oriented group (Rakah). In 1973 and 1977 the figure is for the latter only, in 1977 under the name Democratic Front for Peace and Equality. The left-wing parties Moked (1973) and Shelli (1977) are listed among "Others."

voices to the most important national debate to take place in Israel's history up to that time.

The Knesset gave the Camp David Accords an overwhelming vote of confidence, with the majority of dissenting ballots coming from within the ranks of the coalition (the Likud and the National Religious party accounted for two abstentions and for eleven of the nineteen negative votes). The ease with which the treaties were ratified is not difficult to explain: in the political constellation that existed at the time, Begin did not have to pay a serious political price for his policies. To his credit, he doggedly pursued the cause of the Egyptian peace domestically, devoting 117 of 162 cabinet meetings during his first two years in office to the topic,[23] and putting his standing within his own Herut faction on the line in the face of heavy attacks from the party's right wing, including Yitzhak Shamir, Moshe Arens, Geula Cohen, and after the merger of Shlomzion with Herut, Ariel Sharon. But he could afford to hold firm because he had no formal opposition from outside his own party on the subject. By skillfully co-opting Labor's own precepts, he placed his rivals in a position where they had no alternative but to support the agreements. It is doubtful whether at that juncture any government other than one headed by the Likud could have amassed the necessary parliamentary support for the treaties.

The domestic politics of the Israeli-Egyptian peace treaty, however, further unsettled an already shaky status quo. In the first place, the Labor opposition was effectively neutralized. Not only had the myth that the revisionists would, once at the helm, draw the country into another war been abruptly dispelled, but the Likud had achieved during its short term in office what no Labor government had succeeded in doing during its many years in power: breaking through the barrier of Arab intransigence. Labor politicians could berate the cabinet for its style of negotiation and warn about the consequences of some of its thinking, but their pronouncements seemed hollow and self-serving.

Second, the composition of political parties was affected by the signing of the Camp David Accords. The pivotal Democratic Movement for Change split, bringing about the collapse of the center of the political spectrum. Within months of the ratification of the peace treaty in 1979 the key negotiators, Foreign Minister Moshe Dayan and Defense Minister Ezer Weizman, had broken with the government over the conduct of the autonomy talks, removing two

23. Shlaim and Yaniv, "Domestic Politics and Foreign Policy," p. 258.

major voices of moderation. Right-wing militants in Herut, angered by the return of Sinai, broke away to form the Tehiya, and within Begin's party supporters and detractors of Camp David vied with each other for dominance in the party's central institutions. The National Religious party, too, was rocked by internal cleavages and by the defection of religious nationalists to splinter groups. Virtually every political grouping was severely factionalized and weakened in the aftermath of the Camp David negotiations.

Third, in this situation, extraparliamentary movements came to play a more prominent political role. Gush Emunim and Peace Now, together with a variety of movements on the left and the right, forged the organizational networks for a new form of political confrontation. Relieved of the obligations of party discipline, they transformed the arena of political action from the corridors of the Knesset and government offices to the streets of the major cities and the sites of proposed settlements. Because of their close institutional and personal connections with the parties, their activities affected factional alignments, thereby contributing to the growing confusion between national interest and partisan concerns. The political scene became further polarized, and its style of discourse more combative.

The last, and perhaps the most problematic, effect of the political adjustments of the late 1970s related to the reduction of checks on the centers of power. With the opposition party in retreat, the Knesset emasculated, the parties strife-ridden, the extraparliamentary groups becoming more militant, and Menachem Begin's personal position well-nigh unassailable, very few mechanisms were available to monitor government actions. The position of the Likud solidified at this juncture. The centrality of power and power considerations was underlined.

The 1981 elections aggravated domestic political tensions, already exacerbated by the Egyptian-Israeli Camp David process. Although the first Likud administration had proven itself ill-equipped to deal with the country's mounting economic malaise and social discontent was on the rise, the Labor alignment was unable to capitalize on the government's glaring frailties. Begin, once again, proved himself the consummate politician. He allowed his finance minister, Yoram Aridor, to lift import restrictions, reduce import taxes, and lower prices on luxury items on the eve of the elections. He stood aside as party cohorts engaged in what bordered on ethnic incitement to gain support among the numerically critical Oriental Jewish community. He approved of the attack on the Iraqi nuclear plant, Osirak, barely two days after a meeting

TABLE 2. *Israeli Election Results, 1981, 1984*

	1981		1984	
BLOC AND PARTY	VOTES	SEATS	VOTES	SEATS
Nationalist-Religious				
Likud (Nationalist)	718,762	48	661,302	41
Tehiya (Ultra-Nationalist)	44,559	3	83,037	5
N.R.P. (Religious-Zionist)	94,930	6	73,530	4
Shas (Orthodox-Sephardi)	...	...	63,605	4
Agudah (Orthodox-Non-Zionist)	71,682	4	36,079	2
Morasha (Orthodox-Nationalist)	...	...	33,287	2
Kach (Kahane-Religious-Ultra-Nationalist)	...	...	25,907	1
Labor-Liberal				
Labor alignment	709,075	47	724,074	44
Shinui (Rubinstein-Liberal)	29,060	2	54,747	3
Ratz (Aloni-Liberal)	27,123	1	49,698	3
Transient				
Yahad (Weizman)	...	...	46,302	3
Yigal Hurwitz	30,997	2	23,845	1
Tami (Abu Hatzera)	44,559	3	31,103	1
Predominantly Arab lists				
Communist	65,870	4	69,815	4
Progressive–Democratic Change (Arab-Nationalist)	...	...	38,012	2
Others	100,741	0	58,978	0
TOTAL	1,937,358	120	2,073,321	120

SOURCE: Gershom Schocken, "Israel in Election Year 1984," *Foreign Affairs*, vol. 63 (Fall 1984), p. 84.

with Sadat, thus suggesting, for domestic consumption, that the peace with Egypt had not weakened Israel's military strength or undermined its resolve. And, with unerring skill, he used the Camp David Accords to portray his image as one of peacemaker and national guardian.

The 1981 tally gave Likud forty-eight Knesset seats to Labor's forty-seven (see table 2). This ballot, in effect, sounded the death knell for the dominant party position of Labor in Israeli politics. It marked the demise of the country's founding elite and reflected the extent of the social, ethnic, psychological, and ideological schisms that had emerged in the preceding years.[24] Although Menachem

24. Shlomo Aronson, "Israel's Leaders, Domestic Order and Foreign Policy, June 1981-June 1983," *Jerusalem Journal of International Relations*, vol. 6, no. 4 (1982–83), pp. 1–29.

Begin received another electoral mandate, and with the support of the Tehiya, Tami (a National Religious party breakaway faction), and the other religious parties could form a narrow coalition, his power base was more parochial than in the past. The distance between those within and those outside the official apparatus was greater, and the channels of approach to decisionmakers more constricted.

The structural weaknesses of domestic politics in the late 1970s were accentuated and compounded during the stormy second tenure of the Likud (1981–84). The various formal and informal frameworks of political action—parties, movements, citizens' groups, grassroots organizations, underground cells—increased in number and diversity.

The Lebanese invasion in June 1982 revived the opposition that Camp David had rendered inert and gave it a substantive focus; it could not, however, generate any unifying organizational principles. Protest movements proliferated: alongside Peace Now, a number of antiwar groups sprang up, including Mothers against Silence, the Committee against the War in Lebanon, and There Is a Limit. Human rights activists strengthened the Committee for Solidarity with Bir Zeit University, the Association of Civil Rights in Israel, and the Civil Rights Movement of Shulamit Aloni.

In response, progovernment groups were formed (Israelis for Peace and Security) and extreme right-wing organizations gained momentum (Kach, the newly constituted Orthodox Morasha/Matzad, as well as clandestine vigilante groups). New religious movements developed, most notably the ultra-Orthodox Sephardi Torah Guardians (Shas). And key personalities in the large parties attempted to build up their factional strength through extraparliamentary support. The heterogeneity of these political institutions reflected both the extent of disagreement in the country and the structural limitations of formal parties in a period of extreme ideological polarization.

In such a confrontational context, the modes of political behavior were radicalized. Besides petitions, lobbying, strikes and demonstrations, certain organizations resorted to open confrontation and outright violence. Attempts by contending groups to delegitimize rivals through mutual accusations of treason and disloyalty fostered an intolerance that added to the acrimonious temper and the disjunctive rhythm of politics during these years.[25] The bombing of

25. Some of these manifestations are discussed in Myron J. Aronoff, ed., *Political Anthropology*, vol. 4: *Cross-Currents in Israeli Culture and Politics* (New Brunswick, N.J.: Transaction Books, 1984).

a Peace Now demonstration in February 1983, which resulted in the death of Emile Grunzweig, a peace movement activist, was perhaps the most unsettling instance of these trends. The rules of the political game had been defied but not fully reformulated.

The sudden, and still unexplained, resignation of Menachem Begin in September 1983 further undermined the precarious political balance.[26] Begin, to be sure, had unleashed populist emotions and orchestrated them for his own political purposes; he had, however, held extremists in check and been able to maintain some cohesion in the ruling coalition. His departure created a leadership vacuum only partially filled by his successor Yitzhak Shamir and the younger Likud members who had risen rapidly under his aegis.[27]

The growing tensions in the political system came to a head in the 1984 elections. Despite the prevailing climate of discontent, the rank ineffectiveness of the Likud government, and the clear advantage granted to Labor in the pre-ballot polls, the two main alliances finished virtually in a dead heat. Each major party lost votes to splinter groups of its own persuasion and fully fifteen parties won Knesset seats (see table 2). The leading blocs had underestimated the electorate's desire for a modicum of political predictability and the allure of parties that offered focused and lucid, albeit simplistic, solutions. They had overvalued the force of partisan loyalties, and they had mistakenly soft-pedaled issues during the campaign in the hope of attracting the elusive swing vote.[28] The results of the 1984 elections, far from indicating a further move to the right, confirmed the existence of a predominant two-party system and hinted at its structural inadequacy. The elections did not confer any clear political mandate.

The electoral deadlock yielded a pragmatic solution: a Labor-Likud national "unity" government was created with intricate provisions for the allocation of cabinet portfolios and a rotating premiership under Shimon Peres of Labor and Yitzhak Shamir of Likud. This arrangement represented compromise without consensus, the triumph of power considerations over ideology and principle. In the circumstances, it was also in all probability the only feasible escape from a total political stalemate.

The formation of the national unity government brought about

26. Ned Temko, *To Win or to Die: A Personal Portrait of Menachem Begin* (William Morrow, 1987).

27. Emanuel Gutmann, "Begin's Israel: The End of an Era?" *International Journal*, vol. 38, no. 4 (1983), pp. 690–99.

28. A good discussion of the election campaign may be found in Asher Arian and Michal Shamir, eds., *The Elections in Israel—1984* (Tel Aviv: Ramot, 1986).

several important changes in the contours of Israeli politics. First, by agreeing on a formula for joint rule, the structure of leadership was altered. The holders of the main offices of prime minister, foreign minister (alternately Yitzhak Shamir and Shimon Peres), and defense minister (Yitzhak Rabin) constituted a triumvirate in which Rabin was the key—albeit not always the most publicly prominent—actor. He not only balanced, politically and ideologically, the differences between Shamir and Peres, but he also accumulated considerable political capital because he continued in office throughout the four-year tenure of the government and hence was the chief beneficiary of the national unity arrangements.[29] What seemed to be a transition to collective modes of leadership turned into a way of sanctioning the division of power at the helm and of avoiding collective cabinet responsibility.

Second, by incorporating opposed forces within the ruling coalition, this construct seriously impeded governmental operations. Significant advances could be made on matters of common concern (the economy, withdrawal from Lebanon), but little movement was possible on fundamental issues on which either the larger cabinet of twenty-five or the inner cabinet of ten leading members was divided (territories, peace initiatives, certain aspects of foreign relations, and most notably, approaches to dealing with the civilian uprising in the West Bank and Gaza). This setting required moderation while fostering intractability.

Third, by reducing the dependence of the cabinet on the Knesset, the Peres-Shamir-Rabin government arrogated to itself an increased measure of autonomy. As a result, the principle of parliamentary accountability was severely weakened. Alternate mechanisms of supervision were not institutionalized, and as investigations into the activities of the security forces and the Pollard affair were to demonstrate, serious abuses of power could evolve unchecked.[30]

29. Thanks are due to Dr. Gabi Sheffer of the Leonard Davis Institute for International Affairs at the Hebrew University of Jerusalem for his ideas on this subject.

30. Jonathan Jay Pollard and his wife, Anne Henderson Pollard, both U.S. citizens, were convicted of spying for Israel in 1986. The Israeli investigation into the affair took the position that Israeli officials had established a spy operation without the knowledge of the formal Israeli spy agencies. At the same time, the activities of the security service within Israel (the *Sherut Bitahon Clali*, or *Shin Bet*) were scrutinized by a special commission chaired by Justice Landau after it became clear that two persons detained after the kidnapping of an Israeli bus were later beaten to death during interrogation. Those responsible, although forced to resign, were granted a presidential pardon. Both cases highlighted, within the prism of domestic politics, severe problems of accountability.

Fourth, by realigning political parties around a pragmatic core propped up by an overwhelming, if synthetic, numerical majority, some stability was reestablished and the stridency of political intercourse lessened. Ideological opposition through most of the period was confined to the fringes of the party spectrum (Kach and Tehiya on the right; Ratz, Mapam, the new Arab-Jewish Progressive List for Peace, and the Communists on the left). In the process, these groups may also have moved beyond the control of government authority.

Fifth, by encompassing a variety of political opinions, the national unity structure ultimately limited the effect of large extraparliamentary groups. Members of the key political movements of the early part of the decade, especially Peace Now and Gush Emunim, became either institutionalized or immobilized. Special interest groups with vastly divergent agendas surfaced, applying pressures on individual politicians who frequently represented these narrow concerns as the public interest.

Sixth, by ossifying political activity, the new arrangements sustained those already in power and prevented the regeneration of political leadership. And finally, by continually blocking avenues of political access and consequently limiting the impetus for change, the experience of the national unity government raised serious questions about the ability of Israel's democracy to sustain any momentum in its present form.

Some of these issues were magnified on the eve of the tenth anniversary of the Camp David meetings. Shimon Peres and Yitzhak Shamir disagreed on how to deal with the Palestinian defiance and how to move forward with the diplomatic process. During the critical months of December 1987 through February 1988 the government had no discernible policy, and measures were instituted largely by Yitzhak Rabin as the minister responsible for security. The Knesset, indeed, debated approaches to the events, but had little, if any, influence on decisionmakers. A variety of Israeli protest movements, many of them organized around professional associations—professors, writers, artists, psychologists, psychoanalysts—surfaced to give voice to deep dissatisfaction in important segments of the Israeli polity. Peace Now and Gush Emunim, together with some smaller groups, were reactivated but were unable to serve as umbrella organizations for extraparliamentary action as they had in the past. Throughout the critical period of heightened tensions, however, the government did not even acknowledge these activities, let alone address their demands.

In this atmosphere, the first stages of the 1988 election campaign proceeded apace. If prior to the end of 1987 it seemed as if the country were destined to experience an outcome not dissimilar to that of 1984, the events of the beginning of the election year made any forecasting of the results hazardous at best. The effects of the Palestinian upheavals on party politics could not be determined with any certainty. And although each of the main parties continued to make preparations for the electoral contest as if little were taking place beyond the partisan political scene, it was abundantly clear that not only had the focus of politics shifted elsewhere, but that the course of these events would directly affect the election results.

In sum, the domestic political scene of the late 1980s was quite different from that which prevailed on the eve of the Camp David meetings. The peace negotiations affected political alignments, procedures, rules, and practices. Although politics in Israel possess their own dynamic and many of the more recent political patterns cannot be traced directly to the events of this period, the Egyptian-Israeli peace treaty was negotiated at a particularly sensitive moment in Israel's political development. During the 1978–88 decade, in the absence of an agreement on the direction of national affairs, the place of power considerations in domestic politics was highlighted, while supervisory and participatory mechanisms withered. Barring a reordering of the electoral system, the drafting of a constitution, or massive internal unrest, institutional arrangements were likely to remain weak and rudderless. The foundations of Israel's regime—the principles, rules, and norms of political interaction—were less firmly in place in 1988 than they had been in 1978. The country's institutional structures became more and more incapable of supporting its politics. The terms of political action were severely constrained by these weaknesses.

The Socioeconomic Dimension

Israeli society, for all the outward cohesion it has projected at times, has always lacked internal coherence. In the course of the twentieth century, as immigration expanded and as a variety of social institutions were formed, cracks in the facade of unity became apparent even as the myth of "consensus" was vigorously fostered. Israeli society has been divided in recent years along six major axes: ethnic cleavages, broadly separating the country into Sephardi (Jews from Arabic-speaking countries) and Ashkenazi (Jews of European and Western extraction) camps and partially intersecting with growing class differences expressed in income and occupational disparities; geographical distinctions (largely between the veteran kibbutzim and the nearby development towns and among the various neighborhoods of the large cities); religious rivalries along an orthodox-secular continuum; ideological blocs that have provided a pivot for social communication and interaction; and national groups dividing the majority of Jews from the 600,000 Arab citizens of the country, who have remained largely outside the mainstream. Unlike the Jewish-Arab divide, the other distinctions have usually overlapped; individual Israelis have felt cross-cutting pressures. Social relations therefore contain a built-in fluidity, and the sources of domestic unrest are changeable.

Social cleavages among Jews in Israel became more pronounced in the early 1970s. The 1977 elections contributed to their politicization: the Likud played on the brewing discontent of lower-income groups, mostly of Sephardi origin, who had "developed a sense of grievance on socio-economic issues and . . . believed that their grievances would go unresolved unless the political status quo was radically altered."[31] The political awakening of young Sephardi leaders excluded from the Labor establishment, such as David Levy, Meir Shitrit, Moshe Katzav, and David Magen, was vital to the political turnabout. These men brought their constituencies into the Likud fold and with them a concern for issues of socioeconomic melioration and a distinctive political style.[32] Such groups, not part of the secular culture of Labor-Zionism, were more indulgent of religious interests and more parochial in outlook. The coalition with the political right of disaffected lower classes, Sephardim, and the religiously inclined was a formidable counterpoint to the Ashkenazi, secular, middle-class alliance that had held sway unchallenged for three decades.

The strain of the electoral confrontation was still apparent when Sadat visited Jerusalem. Nonetheless, his timing could not have been more opportune. Years of conflict had enhanced the appeal of peace. The psychological impact of the Egyptian president's grand gesture on a population schooled in suspicion and wariness cannot be exaggerated. That segment of the population seemingly most likely to resist a rapprochement with the Arabs, the Jews of Middle Eastern extraction, had been drawn into the nationalist camp and had a stake in its persistence in power. These factors, coupled with

31. Lee E. Dutter, "The Political Relevance of Ethnicity among Israeli Jews," *Plural Societies*, vol. 14, nos. 1–2 (1983), p. 18.

32. Efraim Ben-Zadok and Giora Goldberg, "A Sociopolitical Change in the Israeli Development Towns: An Analysis of Voting Patterns of Oriental Jews," ibid., pp. 49–65.

assurances that the economic cost of peace would be minimized, made for a social climate fairly amenable to a major shift in the terms of Israel's relations with its largest neighbor.

The Egyptian-Israeli peace process palpably relieved much of the anxiety felt by most Israelis. As the fear of war lessened, the public's attention and energy turned toward domestic issues, which had been held in abeyance for some time. Menachem Begin's skillful linkage of peace and social welfare in his argument for the ratification of the Camp David Accords reinforced this turn, with the added advantage of appeasing the demands of the Likud's newly consolidated support base. Thus the treaty indirectly sanctioned an extractive view of politics, one that highlighted the notion of the state as distributor of benefits, raising popular expectations of government and influencing the tempo, nature, and content of social exchanges.

These shifts were manifest first in the determination and gradual reorientation of domestic priorities. The mood of the post-Camp David period dovetailed neatly with the Likud's new economic program in 1978, based on the classical monetarist teachings of the American economist, Milton Friedman. The Liberal finance minister, Simcha Ehrlich, sought to replace the state-operated welfare socialism of the Labor era with an open, free-enterprise system responsive to market forces. The American aid package that accompanied the signing of the Camp David Accords supplied some of the wherewithal to carry out this plan (although Begin's inability to gain U.S. grant aid rather than credits to complete the construction of new airfields in the Negev raised the subsequent debt obligations of Israel in the 1980s).

In the late 1970s and early 1980s, many import tariffs were lowered, luxury goods became readily available, and the standard of living rose rapidly. The attempt by Yigal Hurwitz, Ehrlich's successor as finance minister, to restrain spending, increase investment, and devalue the currency was stymied by government leaders who supported the new materialism and hoped to reap political benefits from meeting the demands of *nouveau-arrivé* social groups.[33] On the eve of the 1981 elections, Hurwitz resigned and Yoram Aridor, an advocate of unharnessed spending in the name of economic liberalism, took over the Finance Ministry.

Aridor's self-proclaimed "Correct Economic Policy" was nothing short of a disaster. Government and personal spending bore little

33. Avi Gottlieb and Ephraim Yuchtman-Yaar, "Materialism, Postmaterialism, and Public Views on Socioeconomic Policy: The Case of Israel," *Comparative Political Studies*, vol. 16 (October 1983), pp. 307–35.

relation to productivity, credit was extended with few brakes, and Israelis embarked on a consumer binge that the country could ill afford. Massive construction schemes and prestige projects were launched (including the development of the Lavi fighter-bomber) but little thought was given to their financing.[34] By the fall of 1983, the national debt had risen to staggering proportions, inflation was out of control (reaching close to 200 percent a year), and the crash of bank stocks threatened the savings of many citizens. The second Likud government finally toppled on these issues. Clearly the economy needed a dose of predictability and responsibility.

The national unity government placed economic issues at the forefront of its agenda. These topics were uppermost in the minds of most Israelis, they were potentially solvable, and they did not arouse undue friction in the fragile coalition. A stringent stabilization program was designed and carefully implemented. Within two years a new Israeli shekel had been introduced, the exchange rate had been adjusted, and inflation had dropped dramatically for the first time in over two decades (below twenty-five percentage points a year). A more certain, if sober, reality replaced the economic fluctuations that had marred the daily routine of Israeli life in the first part of the eighties. The seeds for economic rejuvenation were not, however, necessarily in place.

The peace process with Egypt was one of many factors that licensed the pursuit of material goals and highlighted the pragmatic propensities of Israelis in their fourth decade of independence. During this period public attention came to focus more squarely on the immediate and the concrete, and priorities were increasingly defined in domestic terms. Even after core economic problems had been alleviated, local affairs were kept at the forefront of public concern by the deterioration of social services, ongoing wage demands and work slowdowns, persistent strikes, a spate of public scandals involving top businesspeople, government officials, and even judges, and growing tensions around issues of religious observance. While some pressures to address the issues of peace and the territories persisted, they were offset by a plethora of specific and narrow concerns that continued to preoccupy the government.

These shifts intruded on older patterns of social interaction. In the immediate post-Camp David phase, a measure of material comfort became correlated with heightened nationalism. Since ethnic and class interests had been refined and given organizational

34. Gerald M. Steinberg, "Large-scale National Projects as Political Symbols: The Case of Israel," *Comparative Politics*, vol. 19 (April 1987), pp. 331–46.

expression, the socioeconomic demands of previously disadvantaged groups fell on receptive ears; official disbursements were skewed accordingly. Those diverse Ashkenazi, white-collar, and politically liberal groups that had in earlier years pursued their own causes separately now banded together to protect their status and consolidate their gains. At the same time several other interest groups coalesced. Orthodox interests flourished in the comfortable ambience of Menachem Begin's traditionalism and his administration's parochialism. Intellectual and academic groups solidified, businesspeople and industrialists transformed themselves into a unified interest group, and the influence of the military-industrial complex grew.[35] Since many social interests contained strong political as well as economic dimensions, some demands were funneled through the large extraparliamentary movements.

By the beginning of the 1980s, a tripartite structure characterized the Jewish social scene. The two large social agglomerations that, roughly speaking, pitted Ashkenazi against Sephardi, dove against hawk, upwardly mobile against disadvantaged, and secular against traditional had been molded by this point. A third, largely amorphous and less ideological social force, containing groups concerned more with the exigencies of daily life than with the grand issues of war, peace, and security, had begun to develop around purely pragmatic issues. Each of these networks was largely self-contained and communication across lines was minimal and contentious. The Arab sector stood apart from these groups—its needs were being neglected, and its alienation grew.

The mode and manner of social exchanges were altered again during the second Likud incumbency. The administration's narrow political base compelled government leaders to be especially attentive to the demands of those groups on which it relied most heavily. In this opportunistic context, smaller, more distinct social networks and political factions vied with each other for a greater share of the national pie. The number of organizations and communities placing direct pressure on the government grew, and the partial success of some factions spurred further competition. The key beneficiaries were not only the political movements associated with the government, development towns, military industries, and poorer social groups, but also, significantly, religious segments of the population, whose number had been inflated by the influx of new Orthodox immigrants, high birthrates, and a rise of the phenomenon of born-

35. Alex Mintz, "The Military–Industrial Complex: The Israeli Case," *Journal of Strategic Studies*, vol. 6 (September 1983), pp. 103–27.

again Jews.[36] Their political centrality to the ruling coalition was translated into increased financial allocations to Orthodox institutions, the fortification of their hold over conversion and personal law, and numerous special concessions.[37] Those excluded from the circle of recipients (professionals, kibbutzim, secular groups) reacted stridently, organizing around a variety of social, economic, political, and ideological issues.[38] Social relations were tense and associational divisions more heterogeneous as the grand social coalitions gave way to more diverse groupings.

Indeed, appearances notwithstanding, the 1984 elections underlined the absence of societal cohesion. By limiting the opportunities for applying direct pressure on government, the national unity cabinet, with its seemingly broad social base, in effect prevented the reorganization of social alliances. Extraparliamentary movements could not continue to thrive under these conditions, broadly defined ethnic interests no longer served as rallying points for social action (in fact, ethnic protest gave way to a quest for incorporation and Sephardim underwent a process of political moderation), and even the influence of the Histadrut labor union and major business concerns waned. If in the past specific social interests had been able to exert an undue influence on the course of political events, after 1984 this situation may well have been reversed.

The growing ineffectiveness of direct political agitation generated a renewed interest in more specific, perhaps less state-directed, topics. A spate of new civic groups dealing with such varied concerns as social tolerance, urban beautification, women's issues, civil rights, Arab-Israeli dialogue, direct elections, and even the drafting of a constitution, were formed. Parallel groupings sprang up in the Arab sector. Organizationally, the social arena became even more fragmented and diffuse.

This move away from the great political issues of the decade was highlighted most dramatically by the intensification of religious cleavages. Ultra-Orthodox, Orthodox, traditional, secular, and antireligious groups all came to the fore. Religiously rooted conflicts proliferated and took on violent forms. Relations between groups of differing religious convictions became more acrimonious, and fundamentalism increased. Religious interests, unlike political and

36. Janet Aviad, *Return to Judaism: Religious Renewal in Israel* (University of Chicago Press, 1983), provides an in-depth study of this phenomenon.

37. Eliezer Don-Yehiya, "Religious Leaders in the Political Arena: The Case of Israel," *Middle Eastern Studies*, vol. 20 (April 1984), pp. 154–71.

38. For a case study see Lev Luis Grinberg, "Split Corporatism in Israel" (Tel Aviv University, 1987).

economic ones, were not subject to negotiation. Since these groups were less changeable and less amenable to pacts with those of other persuasions, they thrived in the absence of viable alternative frameworks for interest aggregation. The political repercussions of these trends were significant. By 1988 the old Labor-National Religious party coalition was apparently dead. The religious parties were more solidly in the Likud camp and could therefore have an important effect on the political balance after the 1988 elections. The rise of religious activism presented a challenge to the fundamental democratic values of tolerance and pluralism and thus touched upon the most essential norms of Israeli society.

In sum, after the signing of the peace treaty with Egypt, Israeli society first underwent a process of polarization, then of subdivision, and subsequently of fragmentation. While salient cleavages were accentuated, new coalitions did not take shape. The scope of activities shifted, then, from broad issues of national concern to more domestic matters, and finally to highly particularistic interests. Society may have become more politicized, but it lacked a coherent direction and hence political resonance.

These patterns were highlighted in the aftermath of the disturbances on the West Bank and Gaza in late 1987. The rise of Jewish movements protesting government actions took the by-then-familiar form of disparate, small groupings operating with little coordination. Unlike the mass coalitions formed in the wake of the Lebanese invasion, the response of most Israelis to the Palestinian uprising was highly fragmented.

Relations between Jews and Arabs within Israel were further polarized. The Arab sector, which had been systematically marginalized during the preceding decade, organized a general strike in support of the resistance, or *intifadah,* and sustained its opposition—at times violently—to Israeli policy. The divide between the Arab citizens of Israel and the Jewish majority grew. This separation was perhaps best exemplified by the decision of Abd al-Wahab Darousha, an Arab Labor member of Knesset, to leave the party. On the eve of the 1988 elections the non-Jewish voters had distanced themselves politically from the major alignments, and their potential fourteen Knesset seats, if mobilized electorally, could have a profound effect on the course of domestic politics in the ensuing years.

The national mood was of course expressive of many of these changes in the substance and rhythm of social life. The period of the negotiations with Egypt was one of engagement, involvement, concerted activity. Debates were heated and the atmosphere in the country was volatile precisely because individuals felt that they had a stake in the outcome of major decisions. The Lebanese invasion was accompanied by a growing sense of disillusionment, by a questioning of official values and policy norms. Participation was particularly intense as frustrations were aired and accusations exchanged. The modus operandi of normalizing conflict, of coping with uncertainty, was strained to its limits.[39] A certain cynicism ensued: a disaffection with leaders, a questioning of their motives, a growing estrangement from government. As complaints gave way to fatigue and a search for relief from the burdens of taxation and military service, the tendency to withdraw from public affairs grew.

Between 1985 and 1988 the dynamics of social life in the country fluctuated between extremism and inertia. On the one hand, fringe groups, frequently employing violent tactics, sought to impose their views on the country as a whole. Meir Kahane's Kach movement, the armed Jewish underground (exposed in the mid-1980s and held responsible for attacks on Palestinians on the West Bank), and small vigilante groups combined nationalism and Jewish messianism with racist outlooks to radicalize the right margin of Israeli society. On the other hand, indifference to the affairs of state became more widespread. The more settled conditions prevailing under the national unity government had a lulling effect: many individuals became absorbed in their private concerns, studiously separating themselves from the political arena. The will to engage diminished with the emergence of the *rosh katan* ("small mind") syndrome, a deliberate disinclination to understand and affect the political debate.[40]

Fundamentalism and inertia are both forms of escape. Before December 1987, every government leader and political party had to deal with the issue of how to combat indifference without conceding control to the fringes. The events of that month aroused many Israelis from their indifference, although there were signs that officials did not react so quickly. A mixture of uncertainty, disaffection, and fear came to replace the equanimity of the preceding years.

The peace negotiations, combined with the politicization of social schisms in the late 1970s, served as an impetus for socioeconomic change in Israel. The standard of living in Israel was radically

39. Baruch Kimmerling, "Making Conflict a Routine: Cumulative Effects of the Arab-Jewish Conflict upon Israeli Society," *Journal of Strategic Studies*, vol. 6 (September 1983), pp. 13–45.

40. David Grossman, *The Yellow Time* (in Hebrew) (Tel Aviv: Hakibbutz Hameuhad, 1987), and in English, *The Yellow Wind*, trans. Haim Watzman (Farrar, Straus and Giroux, 1988).

upgraded in the following ten years. Social relations, however, failed to stabilize during this period, and the desire to avoid many of these issues until compelled to do so grew. The public agenda was, if anything, more amorphous in 1988 than it was in 1978. In retrospect, the Israeli-Egyptian peace process was a catalyst of domestic transformation in Israel but not a guide to its future course.

The External Dimension

Since the 1947 United Nations' decision to endorse the creation of the state of Israel a year later, its survival and well-being have always depended, in some measure, on its position in the international arena. Foreign relations have thus played a major role in the politics of the country. The peace process with Egypt commenced when Israel's external standing was at a low point. The 1967 war had been accompanied by a rupture with the Eastern bloc, by the cutoff of French military support, and by a marginalization of Israel in international forums. In the wake of the 1973 war, the oil embargo, and the later global economic recession, diplomatic relations with most of Africa had been severed, and Israel shunted to the fringes of the international community.

The country's vulnerability was pronounced on the eve of the Camp David talks. The successful conclusion of the negotiations offered an opportunity for the renewal of maneuverability abroad. Yet just when diplomatic prospects improved, Israel's dependency on the United States increased. In domestic political terms, the active American involvement in the drafting of the accords raised two significant issues. First, to what extent should government leaders accede to external pressure, even if applied by Israel's major ally and supporter? And second, how did the nature and extent of foreign contacts affect the balance of power within Israel?

In the decade following the ratification of the peace treaty with Egypt, Israel's international posture improved perceptibly. The completion of the evacuation of the Sinai was accompanied by signs of a reassessment of attitudes toward Israel in many European and third world capitals. If not for the Lebanese invasion and the strong international reaction it evoked, these signals might have yielded tangible results earlier. In any event, by the end of 1983, with the renewal of diplomatic relations by Zaire and Liberia, the process of restoration of relations with Africa had commenced. Under the national unity government, Israel succeeded in making substantial inroads in both Asia and Africa (including the resumption of ties with Côte d'Ivoire, Cameroon, Togo, and the expansion of contacts with China), in renewing links with the Communist bloc, and in diversifying its transactions with Western countries and especially with the United States. The establishment of channels of communication with Arab leaders (King Hassan II of Morocco, King Hussein of Jordan, President Mubarak of Egypt) were symptomatic of a substantial turnabout in Israel's global fortunes.

To be sure, these shifts were as attributable to the changing nature of superpower rivalry, the altered content of the global agenda, the redirection of the foci of conflict, and the geopolitics of the Middle East as they were to the events of Camp David. The peace process, nonetheless, played a significant role in broadening the scope of Israel's foreign relations and reshaping the substance of its external links. The global reaction to the occurrences of late 1987 and 1988 reinforced the close connection between Israel's standing in the international community and the status of its relations with its Arab neighbors.

Throughout most of the 1978–88 decade, however, Israel's foreign policy remained singularly reactive, although hardly formless.[41] With very few exceptions (clandestine relations with Iran, arms sales to South Africa and Central American states), until Shimon Peres's unveiling of his peace overture at the United Nations in 1985 and his later campaign for the convening of an international conference on the Arab-Israeli conflict, one would be hard put to point to any serious initiatives on the external front.

Responses to pressures from the outside have ostensibly been determined by the degree to which the desire to pursue perceived interests and assert Israel's autonomy coincided with, or conversely outweighed, the need for external support. The outright rejection by the Begin government of the Reagan peace plan of 1982 (see appendix D), the ambivalence evinced by the Likud government toward the short-lived May 17, 1983, treaty with Lebanon, and the unwillingness until recently to reexamine links with South Africa may be explained in these terms.[42] But more fundamentally, reactions to demands placed on Israel reflected the structure, composition, ideological predisposition, and skills of ruling coalitions in the absence of a domestic consensus on long-range objectives and derivative strategies. As the political repercussions of Camp David demonstrated so convincingly, the successful imposition of external pressures was heavily dependent on domestic approval.

41. Shlaim and Yaniv, "Domestic Politics and Foreign Policy."

42. Naomi Chazan, *Israeli Perspectives on the Israel-South African Relationship*, Research Report 9–10 (London: Institute of Jewish Affairs, 1987).

Those internal divisions that hampered the formulation of a coherent foreign policy also contributed to the greater involvement of external forces in domestic politics. References to outside factors were used to support uncomfortable policy decisions (the 1987 termination of the Lavi project was attributed to the insistence of the U.S. government, for once). Foreign ties were employed to buttress political standing at home. Most important, the extent of international isolation or acceptability became a crucial part of the ongoing ideological debate. Those on the right of the political spectrum who contended that Israel could not rely on props from the outside pointed to the country's troubled international situation and to traditional Jewish isolationism as a vindication of their claims. Those who called for political flexibility based their arguments in part on the connection between Israel's improved foreign standing and the amelioration in its security situation.

Menachem Begin accelerated the process of integrating foreign elements into the domestic political domain by mobilizing the Jewish diaspora (especially in the United States), at first to back the peace negotiations and then to support a series of policy measures (including the extension of Israeli law to the Golan and the Lebanese invasion) while chastising that constituency for any expressions of discontent. He also indirectly responded to Jewish public opinion abroad, as in the case of the creation of the Kahan commission. Partisan groups, from Peace Now and the Civil Rights Movement on the left to Gush Emunim and Kach on the right, later adopted this technique by issuing appeals for financial and substantive support from the outside. In 1986 and 1987 Shimon Peres sought to sway domestic attitudes on an international peace conference by lobbying Jewish organizations and foreign governments to apply pressure on his own cabinet. At the beginning of 1988, once again, Jewish groups became an integral part of the renewed debate within Israel. With the passage of time, the boundary between external recruitment into Israeli politics and external intervention in domestic affairs was blurred.

The successful conclusion of the peace talks between Israel and Egypt depended on the active mediation of the United States (for details see Samuel W. Lewis, "The United States and Israel: Constancy and Change," in this volume). The format of the meetings underscored the interconnection between domestic and external factors in policy formulation. In the ensuing ten years severe ideological, substantive, and institutional constraints were imposed on foreign policymakers, while potential external partners were actively courted. The relationship between the form, the source, and the content of future negotiations still remained open to debate.

ISRAELI PERSPECTIVES ON CAMP DAVID: AN INTERIM ASSESSMENT

The peace treaty between Israel and Egypt has become an integral part of the flow of Israeli politics in recent years. It has had an effect on the values, concerns, modes, structures, and patterns of political interaction in the country. During the 1978–88 decade, the modalities of Israeli political life diverged markedly from former patterns, although these shifts lacked clear direction and purpose. Adherence to old concepts inhibited the translation of new political arrangements into the terms of a coherent policy. How then, in retrospect, were the Camp David Accords perceived in Israel ten years later?

On the substantive level, it was generally acknowledged that the rapprochement with Egypt, by breaking the deadlock between Israel and its Arab neighbors, broadened the range of options available to decisionmakers. For this reason, the reverberations of the peace treaty were felt in every aspect of Israeli life. For this reason, too, the accords could not be divorced from dominant political trends in the country.

On the procedural level, the importance of the Camp David framework was the subject of ongoing debate. Once in power, the main domestic opponents of the agreements (Yitzhak Shamir, Moshe Arens, Ariel Sharon) became the key advocates of its autonomy provisions, which they saw as a means of retaining the West Bank, and repeatedly called for the renewal of direct talks through the good offices of the United States. Camp David proponents (most recently in the person of Shimon Peres), by contrast, sought alternative formulas for the revival of the peace momentum and insisted on the need for negotiations under international auspices. The content of proposed solutions might not always have seemed to vary markedly among these groups, and old approaches appeared to be less viable in the wake of the 1987–88 events; real differences, however, did exist on the path to their realization.

On the operational level, in the eyes of many Israelis, the framework of the negotiations of 1978 failed to provide a compelling precedent. Interim attempts to follow up on the remaining provisions (the Reagan peace plan, the short-lived Hussein-Arafat accords, the Peres-Hussein understanding of April 1987, the Shultz initiative of March 1988) did not yield tangible returns in the decade after

Camp David. As the specific details of the events of 1977–79 began to dim in the collective Israeli memory, the peace with Egypt was slowly being separated from the notion of an ongoing process supposedly set in motion at that juncture.

On the symbolic level, depending on particular ideological dispositions and political propensities, the interpretation of the understanding between Israel and Egypt assumed qualitatively different meanings. No clear consensus on major issues was forged in Israel after the ratification of the accords, and even the myth of consensus was in the process of being abandoned. As long as the task of coming to terms with the anomalies of the Israeli condition was delayed, no operational agreement on national goals was possible.

The Camp David meetings took place at a unique conjuncture in Israel's political history. In domestic terms, the accords could be ratified because on every vital score they offered something to everyone. For Israel, the greatness of these agreements lay in their sensitivity to the domestic politics of the later 1970s. Their endurance is testimony to their internalization within the Israeli body politic. In the coming decade another kind of ingenuity may be called for that will take into account the political transformation that has already occurred and generate a new kind of dynamic in the peace process.

SHIMON SHAMIR

Israeli Views of Egypt and the Peace Process: The Duality of Vision

PEACE CAUGHT Israel by surprise. For most Israelis, Sadat's initiative and the ensuing peace agreement appeared as a veritable deus ex machina. In the decades following the establishment of their state, Israelis had learned to regard peace with a major Arab country as lying outside the range of realizable goals. This conviction was based on a reading of three chief elements in the Arab position toward Israel: the rejection of the legitimacy of the very existence of the state of Israel, which made this conflict qualitatively different from "normal" interstate disputes; the depth of the trauma of 1948, which blended into greater Arab-Islamic historic predicaments; and the belief that the formidable Arab quantitative superiority made the ultimate triumph over the Zionist state a matter of historical inevitability.[1]

Accordingly, the Israeli attitude to peace had been mostly symbolic. The dream of peace—ritualized in songs and speeches and looming large in the Israeli value system and collective self-image—could be cherished without its having any real bearing on concrete political realities. Practical political decisions could be made in total isolation from this vision, for no peace offer from any Arab leader was in the offing. Arab declarations of peaceful intentions had been diagnosed as being no more than exercises in deception.

This paper was submitted for publication before the appointment of its author as ambassador to Egypt and does not represent any official Israeli positions. The views expressed are solely those of the author as an academic researcher.

1. For the most systematic presentation of the Israeli reading of the Arab position, see Y. Harkabi, *Arab Attitudes to Israel*, trans. Misha Louvish (London: Vallentine, Mitchell and Co., 1972).

Therefore, Anwar Sadat's "crossing of the psychological barrier" in his dramatic appearance before the Knesset in November 1977 created a certain cognitive dissonance in the Israeli mind. Politics suddenly became the art of the impossible.[2]

With the subsidence of the initial euphoria, the Israeli attitude was marked by an agonizing sense of suspicion. The trauma of Egypt's surprise attack in October 1973 was still fresh in the collective memory, and for many Israelis Sadat was above all a master of deception. Israelis noted that Sadat's initiative was not preceded in Egypt by any ideological reexamination of the perceptions of the Jewish state and that attitudes prevalent there were hardly compatible with a spirit of genuine reconciliation. Egyptian officials and members of the intelligentsia were often reluctant to interact with Israelis, and two foreign ministers resigned in protest against Sadat's policy. The Cairo press often carried vicious attacks against the Israeli government. Many Israelis—taught by their cumulative historical experience to be distrustful of sudden demonstrations of goodwill—preferred to reserve judgment on the genuineness of the peace offer. On the one hand there was a clear desire by the Israeli public not to miss the historical opportunity offered by Sadat, but on the other, there was a determination not to be trapped by this artful adversary.

This wariness greatly affected the way the Israelis conducted the peace negotiations. They were troubled by the realization that Israel was expected to relinquish concrete assets as a fait accompli in return for an intangible peace relationship that was easily reversible. Accordingly, several issues that eventually turned out to be of little practical import assumed a crucial role in the bargaining process and at some points even threatened to abort it completely. Such issues were the problem of timetables—how much "peace" would be delivered before each phase of withdrawal; the problem of linkage—to what extent the bilateral elements of the agreement would be dependent on the implementation of its Palestinian elements; and the problem of priority of obligations—whether Egypt would be entitled to fulfill its commitments in defense pacts with other Arab states in contradiction of its treaty with Israel. Some of these issues have since been almost forgotten, but they clearly

2. To be exact, there had been some awareness before 1977 among certain Israeli politicians, including Moshe Dayan, that Anwar Sadat's readiness for peace was growing, but they did not consider the change sufficiently profound to justify a change in Israel's policy. The change in Egypt's position was also detected by Israeli academics. See Shimon Shamir, *Egypt under Sadat: The Search for a New Orientation* (in Hebrew) (Tel Aviv: Dvir, 1978).

stressed that the Israeli attitude to peace was apprehensive of dangers no less than it was expectant of benefits.

The successful conclusion of the Camp David Accords in September 1978 and the bilateral treaty in March 1979 did not dispel these fears. The commitment to evacuate Sinai was seen in Israel as a calculated risk abounding with uncertainties. There was no way the Israelis could be completely assured that the peace agreement had not been made merely with Sadat and that it would withstand a change of leadership in Egypt. There was no way of knowing whether Egypt did not harbor a secret intention, or even a well-conceived plan, to renege on its obligations under the treaty once Sinai was returned. Assuming that the restoration of Egypt's relations with the Arab states would become a high national priority after the solution of the Sinai problem, no one could tell how much Cairo would be willing to pay for it "in Israeli currency." The extent to which the Egyptians really adhered to the principle that the validity of the treaty was not dependent on the solution of the Palestinian problem remained an open question. It was impossible to predict the consequences for the peace treaty of a war between Israel and other Arab states or, for that matter, of a major upheaval in the region in general.

This skepticism was of course intensified by the genuine sense of loss generated by the commitment to return Sinai. It was going to deprive Israel of strategic maneuvering space and leverage over its southern neighbors, of major oil fields and areas of considerable development potential, and of the extensive investments that had been made in settlements, air bases, and other facilities. These were some of the chief considerations that motivated a number of Menachem Begin's closest associates and prominent leaders of his party to oppose or abstain in the Knesset vote on the treaty on March 21, 1979.[3]

The subsequent years have not substantiated these fears. The assassination of Sadat and the accession of Husni Mubarak did not affect the peace treaty. Nor was it affected by the completion of the withdrawal from Sinai. In their efforts to restore relations with Arab states, the Egyptians did not yield to what they saw as attempts to dictate to them their policy on the conflict with Israel (and the green light given by the Arab League summit in Amman in

3. On the final phase of the peace negotiations and the vote in the Knesset, see Shiloah Center for Middle Eastern and African Studies, Tel Aviv University, *Middle East Contemporary Survey*, vol. 3: *1978–79*, ed. Colin Legum, Haim Shaked, and Daniel Dishon (Holmes and Meier, 1980), pp. 110–14 (hereafter *MECS*).

November 1987 to resume diplomatic relations with Cairo was not the result of Egyptian concessions on this issue). Although the Egyptians never reconciled themselves to the freeze in the talks on the future of the West Bank and Gaza, they allowed the bilateral treaty to stand on its own. Cairo did react strongly to Israel's war in Lebanon and other military operations in Arab countries but did not let them undermine the foundations of the peace agreement. The various crises that erupted in the Middle East over the years had little impact on the Egyptian-Israeli peace.

As the memory of the traumatic scenes of the evacuation faded and the warnings of the pessimists failed to materialize, even some of the most ardent critics of Camp David had to recognize what Israel had gained by it. These gains appeared on several different levels.

The most important outcome of Camp David for Israel was the removal of the threat of hostilities on its southern border, thus relieving its strategic machinery of the burden of constantly facing a two-front situation. It is true that Israel could not enjoy complete relief from this threat, and its contingency planning had to take into consideration the possibility of the collapse of the peace system or the regime that supported it. Israeli strategists did indeed react nervously to the development of the Egyptian military infrastructure in Sinai, to statements by Egyptian military leaders calling upon their troops to prepare for the eventuality of another war against Israel,[4] and to the effective modernization of the Egyptian armed forces with massive American help. Some strategists would also argue that even without a threat from the south, the situation remained dangerous, for Camp David motivated the Syrians to develop their independent "strategic parity" to such proportions that the overall balance of power did not change much. But the basic improvement in Israel's strategic position was undeniable, and the outstanding fact is that ten years after Camp David, Israel's border with Egypt remained absolutely trouble free for the longest consecutive period since the beginning of the Arab-Israeli conflict.

Camp David also cemented the special relationship between Israel and the United States. Although it was not the only cause of this development, it is a fact that the decade since Camp David

4. The Israelis were particularly annoyed by a press report in January 1987 to the effect that Egyptian Defense Minister Muhammad Abd al-Halim Abu Ghazalah had made a statement to a parliamentary committee labeling Israel as the greatest regional threat that would necessitate military cooperation between Egypt and Syria. See report in *Al-Safir,* quoted in *Ha'aretz,* January 29, 1987.

was a period of unprecedented close cooperation in the political and strategic spheres and of an unprecedented level of American economic aid to Israel. The U.S.-sponsored peace between Israel and Egypt freed the administration from the pressure of the conventional claim that close relations with Israel and with Arab states are mutually exclusive and demonstrated convincingly that disregarding that claim could pay off handsomely. Some critics would argue that this development has dangerously increased Israel's dependence on the United States, but this view was not shared by the country's political elite and aroused little concern in the public at large.

Finally, peace with Egypt established a historic precedent that in a way has changed the terms of reference for the entire Arab-Israeli conflict. This is the least tangible of Camp David's results, but its importance cannot be overstated. Sadat's peace with Israel shattered so many Arab taboos that the previous total rejection no longer seemed viable. Quite a few observers, on both sides of the Middle East conflict, agreed that for many Arabs the dispute today was no longer over the very existence of Israel but rather over the terms of reconciliation with it. Even if this development did not have immediate ramifications, it certainly gave Israel a sense of broader options.

Yet, with all the changes that took place in the Israeli position and outlook, the comprehensive conceptual transformation that some observers and participants (including Sadat) had expected to take place in the fundamental Israeli posture toward the Arabs failed to materialize. When the dust settled after the dramatic initiation of the peace process, it transpired that the overwhelming majority of the Israeli polity managed to set this cataclysmic development within their previous conceptual frameworks, ideological commitments, and political outlooks.

Part of the explanation for this restrained response was self-evident. Whereas the Egyptians could confidently expect that agreement with Israel would allow them to make a complete shift from hostilities to a state of peace, the Israelis knew that they would continue to experience the harsh realities of the conflict with the other Arab countries. The changes produced by the new situation were not sufficiently profound to justify a total reassessment of their position. They thus preferred to view the peace process in the perspective of the overall conflict with the Arabs rather than to look at the conflict in the perspective of peace with Egypt.

There was, to be sure, a considerable readiness to make concessions in order to realize the potential of the peace process, but no structural change took place in basic Israeli positions: there was no reordering of the national priorities, no rethinking of the foundations of Israel's place in the region, no reevaluation of attitudes to the problem of the Palestinians. Israelis did learn some new truths about their neighbors, but old truths were not forsaken. By and large, doves remained doves and hawks remained hawks.

TWO SCHOOLS

In the decade after Camp David, the persistence—or even enhancement—of the basic polarity in the Israeli conception of relations with the Arabs was the most important element shaping Israel's posture in relation to the peace process. The two schools of thought in this polarity, now embodied in the Labor bloc under the leadership of Shimon Peres and the Likud bloc led by Menachem Begin and later by Yitzhak Shamir, confronted each other in that decade in a crucial tug of war. Actually, the polarization into these two credos had already intensified in 1967, when the future of the occupied territories became the principal issue in Israel, and in various forms it had existed in Zionism since the turn of the last century. But before 1977 the contest was mostly doctrinaire, for the Labor camp had completely dominated the scene and the challenge from the so-called Revisionist or "National" camp hardly affected actual policies. This situation was drastically changed in June 1977, just five months before Sadat's trip to Jerusalem, when Begin formed his first government, thus turning the ideological debate into a decisive political struggle that dominated the whole subsequent decade.

The turnabout of 1977 did not neatly substitute a Likud supremacy for that of Labor, for during that decade Likud either held a narrow edge over Labor (1977–84) or achieved a tie with Labor and had to share government with them (1984–88). This situation considerably constrained Likud's decisionmaking on issues of both peace and war and made the programmatic debate between the two camps a critical contest over the actual course that Israel was going to take.

The division into two schools of thought is of course a gross generalization used here for analytical purposes only. The range of diversity over the issues of the peace process was so wide that merely mentioning the various trends would go beyond the scope of this chapter. Nor would it be possible to characterize here the differences of views held by Israeli leaders even within the same political camps—such as Yitzhak Shamir, Ariel Sharon, and David Levy in the Likud bloc, or Shimon Peres, Yitzhak Rabin, and Abba

Eban in the Labor party (not to mention the differences that existed among Menachem Begin, Moshe Dayan, and Ezer Weizman within Israel's team at Camp David). Yet in broad historic terms it would still be possible to speak of a Likud school and a Labor school which, while not necessarily running along strictly partisan lines, enlisted between them the great majority of the Israeli polity.

The views of the two schools on the peace process with Egypt can be summarized as follows. The first school of thought, whose most prominent exponent was Menachem Begin, maintains that this generation's historic mission is to safeguard the integrity of Eretz Israel for the Jewish people. Peace with Egypt must not interfere with this goal. It was achieved at the price of considerable concessions, but it could not have been concluded had it imposed any restrictions on settlements, recognized collective national rights of the Arab population in Judea, Samaria, and Gaza, or compromised the possibility of claiming eventually the annexation of these territories to the state of Israel. Peace with Egypt was a great achievement because it removed the threat of war on one front, separated Egypt from the belligerent Arab camp, and gave Israel a free hand to focus on Eretz Israel. It was also a great step forward on the road to peace, which Israel will continue to pursue whenever it does not threaten Israeli control over the entire land. The agreement on Sinai would not be allowed to serve as a model for agreements with other Arab states, and in the future peace would be sought on the basis of some other principle than "territories for peace." The Egyptians, whose commitment to the Palestinian cause is deemed shallow, would eventually reconcile themselves to this reality.

The second school, best represented in that decade by Shimon Peres, rejects the notion that any goal can supersede the vision of a defensible, Jewish, and democratic Israel, reconcilable with Arab neighbors and acceptable to the enlightened world. The Camp David Accords are significant not only in themselves, but also as a first step in a peace process whose next phase must be conducted with a Jordanian-Palestinian partner. While it is true that the Jewish people have historic rights to all of their ancient homeland, Israel must offer a territorial compromise, giving up the areas densely populated by Arabs. It was probably a mistake not to insist on some territorial compromise in Sinai as well, in return for a more accommodating position on the issues of the West Bank and Gaza. The security of Israel is the supreme consideration. The failure to achieve a more comprehensive settlement, the adherents to this school warned, might not only bring about a conflagration on the eastern front but might also undermine the existing peace with Egypt.

The basic premises underlying this controversy were deeply rooted in the prestate intellectual and political history of Zionism. They had first surfaced in the last phase of the Ottoman period, when the revolutionary concepts of the workers' movement, the forerunner of the Labor party, clashed with the outlook of the farmers in the early Zionist colonies. The former struggled for what was called "the conquest of labor" and sought to realize Zionism by building a new society based on a utopian socialist vision, while the latter focused on a political nationalist solution within an international grand design.

But the full dimensions of this polarity emerged only in the Mandate period with the withdrawal of Ze'ev Vladimir Jabotinsky from the Zionist organization and the establishment of the Revisionist movement (the precursor of Begin's party). The Revisionists were inspired by European nationalism of a more romantic and integral type (notably that of nineteenth-century Italy). They maintained that "nationalism is a supreme value, an expression of cultural progress, of vitality, a realization of uniqueness, selfhood and common destiny."[5] Preaching a separatist and self-centered orientation for the Jewish people, their national myth played on the themes of sacrifice, organic unity, grandeur, and mastership. They defined statehood as the goal earlier and more clearly than many other trends in Zionism, seeking sovereignty and domination over Eretz Israel on both banks of the Jordan. The Revisionists sought to achieve it by military power, which had to be prepared not merely as a contingency option but as an act of self-assertion. Zionism, they argued, could not realistically be achieved through cooperation or compromises with the Arabs, and the notion of the partition of Palestine was rejected by Jabotinsky as completely "senseless."[6]

Conversely, the national vision of the Labor camp, which was the main force in the Zionist movement and whose prominent leader was David Ben-Gurion, had been influenced by the more universalistic perspective of early Russian and Eastern European socialism. They upheld the values of working the land, pioneering endeavors, social egalitarianism, and cultural revival. Regarding the

5. Ya'acov Shavit, "The Attitude of the Revisionist Movement towards the Arab Nationalist Movement," in *Zionism and the Arab Question* (in Hebrew) (Jerusalem: Zalman Shazar Centre for Jewish History, 1979), p. 79. Within Likud circles, Shavit is considered biased against the Revisionist ideology.

6. Yosef Gorny, *Zionism and the Arabs, 1882–1948: A Study of Ideology* (Oxford: Clarendon Press, 1987), p. 267.

establishment of the new society in Palestine as the only channel toward nationhood, they concentrated their efforts on institution-building, settlements, and economic development. A great part of the Labor-Zionist camp propagated solidarity and cooperation with the Palestinian Arab working class and upheld this goal in principle even in periods when it was not deemed practical. The solutions they proposed to the "Arab problem" were more diffuse, indecisive, and fluid than those of their challengers, but they were also more empirical. Of the various models of compromise solutions, partition was finally adopted—opting for the lesser evil and bowing to the unchangeable objective limitations. Attacked by his opponents for not seeking the occupation of the whole land in the 1948 war, Ben-Gurion explained in the Knesset that this could have been achieved only through Deir Yasin-type massacres, mass expulsions, or the renunciation of democracy and of the Jewish character of the state, for "in reality, a Jewish state in the whole of Eretz Israel, or even merely in its western part, without Deir Yasin, a democratic state—is inconceivable."[7]

The examination of the differences between the ideological roots of post-Camp David Likud and Labor should not be construed to indicate a perfect contrast between these two schools of thought. Whereas the Arab observers who tend to dismiss the differences between them as merely tactical and illusory are obviously mistaken, it is equally wrong to play them up to the level of diametrically opposed ideological positions. Such an ideological polarity does indeed exist in Israel, but not between the two major blocs. It rather appears between the two extremes of the Israeli political spectrum where a messianic conception of the redemption of the land confronts the vision of a fully symmetrical reconciliation with the Palestinians. The differences between the two major blocs are much more complex, and they are usually expounded in the public debate in pragmatic rather than ideological terms.

In spite of Likud's emphatic commitment to its ideological tenets, its political campaigns did not depend on them. Both its leadership and membership consisted of many hard-headed and practical-minded persons, for whom the vision of Eretz Israel was not merely an ideological choice but a matter of realpolitik and good sense. They firmly believed that their reading of the Arab side and the political map was more realistic than that of their opponents and

7. Minutes of the twenty-first session of the Knesset, April 4–6, 1949, quoted in Dan Schueftan, *A Jordanian Option* (in Hebrew) (Ramat Gan, Israel: Yad Tabenkin, 1986), pp. 247–48.

that their program better served the national strategic interests. Until 1988 a clear-cut choice between realpolitik and ideology had never been imposed on them (Sinai not being a part of Eretz Israel), but it was clear that ideology did not enjoy an exclusive position in their thinking. Furthermore, the hard-core veteran Revisionists no longer dominated the constituency of Likud, and even in the party machinery their share was diminishing. Votes for the Likud now came mostly from elements whose affiliation with its ideology was quite loose and who were impelled by the wish to protest against the Labor establishment and by other sociocultural motivations. They did identify with the party's basic distrust of the Arabs and its tough posture toward them but not always with the full range of its credo.

Labor's ideological commitments were loose and diffuse to an even greater extent. Its dovish position toward the Arabs was based on predominantly pragmatic arguments and not on a reevaluation of mutual rights and historic relationships—which, as mentioned earlier, had not taken place even in the wake of the Egyptian peace. Many spokesmen of this school readily admitted they would have preferred to see the borders of Israel extend all the way to the Jordan River, but demographic and political realities made this impractical; it would create either intolerable binationalism or an apartheid regime that would isolate Israel internationally and intensify the conflict with the Arabs. Even this narrowly defined compromise program did not enjoy wholehearted support within the Labor party, and many of its members watched Peres's efforts to extend peace with Egypt into the Jordanian-Palestinian area with great wariness. Some elements within Labor shared, at least emotionally, certain premises of the Greater Israel movement. Labor was inseparable from Ha-Kibbutz Ha-Me'uhad and the Moshavim movements that carry the traditions of a frontier spirit focusing on land, settlements, self-reliance, and relentless struggle. Labor had in its forefront veterans of the defense establishment with an orientation toward activism and zero-sum contests with the Arabs. Above all Labor depended on the support of members from sociocultural sectors whose conceptual profile was not very different from that of typical Likud voters and for whom a liberal attitude to the Arabs was the least of Labor's attractions.

But even without full conceptual polarity, the division of the Israeli polity into these two schools of thought was highly significant, possibly the most important single factor affecting Israeli foreign policy. The equilibrium between them produced an uneasy mutual dependence in which the hawkish camp was needed for making peace, and no war could effectively be launched without the doves (as demonstrated by the cases of the peace with Egypt and the war in Lebanon, respectively). Accordingly, every important issue in Israeli politics must always be examined in the dual perspective of these opposing schools of thought.

However, in the crucial stages of molding the peace agreements, Likud was at the helm, and it was thus the irony of history that the task of proposing a solution to the problem of the Palestinians and the West Bank that would be acceptable to the Arab side fell on the shoulders of the element in the Israeli polity that was fully committed to the principle of retaining the whole of Eretz Israel. To cope with this paradox, Begin devised the autonomy plan in late 1977.

AUTONOMY

The concept of autonomy was not entirely new. It had already appeared in the writings of the fathers of the Revisionist trend in Zionism and particularly in Jabotinsky's political thought.[8] It may have also been inspired by the post-World War I period (which apparently shaped many of Begin's basic concepts), in which Eastern European countries like the Ukraine, Lithuania, Latvia, Estonia, and Poland experimented with autonomy for their minorities. Various autonomy plans, for both Jews and Arabs, were discussed in Palestine during the Mandate period. The Camp David autonomy plan must have also been influenced by Dayan's strategy for the West Bank, which sought to keep it under full Israeli control while allowing its inhabitants to manage their own affairs and maintain their ties to Jordan (one variation of the so-called functional partition). Begin's plan was endorsed by his cabinet ministers on December 13, 1977, and personally submitted shortly thereafter to Jimmy Carter in Washington and Sadat in Ismailia.[9] Eventually it provided the foundation of the "framework" for a settlement of the problem of the West Bank and Gaza in the Camp David Accords.

The agreement on the autonomy concept somehow managed to square the circle by postponing the decision on the final status of these territories to the end of the five-year self-rule period and giving each side the right to present its claims in the negotiations leading

8. See Ze'ev Vladimir Jabotinsky's 1912 essay, "Self-Rule of a National Minority," summarized in Shavit, "Attitude of the Revisionist Movement," pp. 80–81.

9. Texts of the original December 13, 1977, autonomy plan, and the revised December 28 plan, are in the appendixes to Uzi Benziman, *Prime Minister under Siege* (in Hebrew) (Jerusalem: Dvir, 1981), pp. 267–71.

to that decision. It promised the Arab inhabitants, for the duration of that transitional period, "full autonomy," the right to elect their "self-governing authority," the participation of their elected representatives in the negotiations to determine their future, withdrawal of the Israeli military government and its civilian administration, and the concentration of the remaining Israeli forces in "specified security locations." Jordan and Egypt were given a role in the negotiations on both the autonomy arrangements and the final status of the territories.

Begin managed to make these concessions, despite substantial criticism in his own party, because he could argue that they did not cross the party's red line. In practice, the agreement left the strategic control of the area in Israeli hands, did not set restrictions on the establishment of Jewish settlements, did not even mention Jerusalem in the agreement's text, and left open the option of demanding the annexation of the territories in the future or at least extending the autonomy arrangement beyond the transitional period. Begin made a point of demonstrating by action, in the wake of Camp David and in defiance of Carter's protests, that the establishment of settlements was definitely continuing.

Even the verbal concessions of recognizing "the legitimate rights of the Palestinian people" and of solving "the Palestinian problem in all its aspects"—not a negligible gesture for a leader and a movement that had always attached great importance to words and symbols—were watered down by Begin's clarification (acknowledged by President Carter) that any usage of the term "Palestinian people" was construed to mean "Palestinian Arabs," and, in Hebrew, "the Arabs of Eretz Israel." Contrary to the teachings of Jabotinsky, who had recognized the collective national identity of the Arab population,[10] Begin did not accept the notion that there was a national dimension to the Palestinian community and their political rights. The guiding principle was that self-rule (or rather self-administration) would not be granted to the territories of Judea, Samaria, and Gaza but only to their Arab inhabitants.

The Labor bloc attacked the autonomy concept "both from the right and the left." Representatives of its more militant wing warned that the Camp David Accords were tantamount to a "Balfour Declaration" for the Palestinians, generating a dynamic that would inevitably lead to the emergence of a sovereign Palestinian state—something to which Labor is formally opposed. They pointed out

10. Gorny, *Zionism and the Arabs,* pp. 268–71.

that the autonomy plan unwittingly consolidated the validity of the 1949 green line, thus impeding any border adjustments in the future. The more dovish wing claimed that autonomy was no more than a verbal exercise whose ambiguous formulations could not conceal the absence of a concrete solution to the problem of the territories and their Palestinian population and were intended merely to perpetuate the occupation. Both wings voiced the criticism that Begin, because of his commitment to Eretz Israel, had narrowed Israel's options. Israel could not offer to adopt a flexible position on the West Bank in exchange for concessions from Sadat concerning the border in Sinai. This option had allegedly existed at the time of the negotiations.

The great majority of the Labor camp remained loyal to the concept of territorial compromise and supported some form or another of the Allon plan, meant to ensure the vital strategic interests of Israel without imposing its rule over large concentrations of Palestinian inhabitants. The contradiction between this concept and that of autonomy was obvious. Nevertheless, given the fact that the Camp David Accords were now the only basis for a peace process agreed on by both states and that autonomy had been designed only as a transitional arrangement, the tendency was to accept them, in spite of their ambiguities. At the same time it was stressed that eventually the solution would have to be sought in cooperation with Jordan, within a Jordanian-Palestinian framework. The Camp David method could be used only for generating movement in that direction.

It was precisely this dynamic that the Likud leaders had to fear. Despite Begin's reassurances, there was no escape from the realization that autonomy could indeed initiate processes over which Israel had little control, that it drove a wedge between Israel and the territories, and that it practically excluded the option of their annexation to Israel.[11] Assuming that Begin had not given up his commitment to Greater Israel, he could count on only two possible scenarios: a restrictive interpretation of the terms of autonomy in a way that would neutralize these risks, or a stalemate in the process of implementation that would freeze the status quo of continuing Israeli control and creeping annexation. Subsequent events developed along both these lines.

Once the peace treaty was signed, Begin drew closer to the

11. See M. Seliger, "The Camp David Accords and Their Political Context" (in Hebrew), Policy Publications 19 (Hebrew University of Jerusalem, Leonard Davis Institute for International Relations, 1987), pp. 2–3.

position of the hawkish group in the cabinet, led by Ariel Sharon, Haim Landau, and Zevulun Hammer. In May 1979 Begin adopted the recommendations of this group, giving a narrow interpretation to self-rule and a broad one to the powers of the Israeli machinery of control and the privileges of the Jewish settlers. He spelled out clearly the intention of claiming, at the end of the transitional period, Israeli sovereignty over the entire territory.[12] The Israeli delegation to the autonomy talks, which started negotiations that month, was given instructions in this spirit, leading eventually to the resignation of Moshe Dayan and Ezer Weizman from the cabinet.

Since a similar process of hardening interpretations took place simultaneously on the Egyptian side, the autonomy talks seemed doomed from the outset. More than a dozen rounds were held through the end of 1981, without achieving a comprehensive agreement. The differences that had not really been reconciled at Camp David resurfaced in these talks with sharper clarity. No agreement could be reached on such key issues as the nature of the self-governing council, its source of authority, its size and powers, the inclusion of East Jerusalem inhabitants, or the role of the Israeli military presence. The total rejection of the autonomy talks by the Jordanians and Palestinians, and the fact that the Israelis and Egyptians tended to use other channels for dealing with immediate problems, further diminished the significance of the autonomy forum, sometimes creating the impression that participants were just going through the motions of diplomatic negotiations.

The last attempt made by the United States to revive the autonomy talks in June 1982 was aborted by the outbreak of war in Lebanon. This caused little regret in Likud circles, particularly since by then the problem of linkage had receded to the background. In Labor circles there was a feeling that their criticism of Begin's approach to the peace process had been substantiated and that the road might now be open for exploring options closer to their own concepts.

NORMALIZATION

Whereas the Egyptians felt disappointed by the failure of the Camp David system to lead toward a solution of the West Bank-Gaza problem, and resented the Israeli policies that imposed on

12. On the recommendations of the Eliyahu Ben Elissar Committee of February 1979 to which Sharon, Landau, and Hammer subscribed, see Shiloah Center, *MECS*, vol. 3, pp. 170–71, 174–75.

them a politically embarrassing separate peace, the Israelis were disappointed by the nature of the bilateral relationship. Many Israelis began to feel that Egyptian behavior did not reflect genuine readiness for a complete reconciliation with Israel and for the implementation in good faith of the normalization agreements.

The concept of "normalization," as understood in the Israeli-Egyptian context, is perhaps unique in international relations. It emanated from the Israelis' awareness that their dispute with the Arabs, unlike other international conflicts, was over the right of their state to exist. Hence what they expected the Arab side to deliver in a peace agreement included such intangible and elusive assets as recognition and acceptance. Since what the Israelis were expected to give constituted concrete territorial concessions that involved serious security risks, they wanted to be reassured that they would get their quid pro quo. Accordingly, normalization was meant to be a concrete embodiment of Egyptian reciprocity, an indication of the sincerity of the Egyptians' readiness to turn over a new leaf in their relationship with Israel, and an expression of a commitment that would be harder to renege on.

For this reason, symbolic and verbal expressions of Egyptian attitudes assumed great importance for Israelis. The process of normalization was expected to eliminate the hostile propaganda and ideological indoctrination that had nourished the conflict and to prove that the Egyptian authorities were indeed educating their public to accept peace with Israel. The introduction of such policies, and particularly the open exchange of information, it was hoped, would transform mutual images and attitudes in a way that would reduce inclinations to return to a state of war. Above all, the normalization agreements were expected to generate an extensive network of economic, social, and cultural interactions that would "humanize" relations and make reversion to hostilities less and less likely. Contrary to the perceptions of Egyptian critics of the process, who saw normalization as an Israeli attempt at economic imperialism and cultural invasion, the Israelis showed little interest in possible material gains from this process. For them it was primarily a test—deficient as it might be, but in the absence of others quite indispensable—of the existence of a readiness for what Golda Meir used to call "real peace."

Thus, in response to Israel's demands, the bilateral treaty contained not only an agreement on the establishment of a "normal relationship," including "diplomatic, economic and cultural relations" and the "free movement of people and goods" (Article 3), but also an annexed protocol that specified methods by which this relationship would be implemented. Until Israel completed its withdrawal from Sinai in April 1982, the two parties had signed more than fifty agreements outlining cooperation in such areas as air transport, agriculture, communications, culture, tourism, police, trade, and transportation.[13]

There was something euphoric in the initial Israeli reactions to the first small steps taken to implement these agreements. Witnessing direct peaceful contacts with Egypt, on the level of daily life, brought the reality of peace closer to the Israelis' minds than the more significant, but less tangible, political and strategic changes. The opening of the borders between the two countries was an exhilarating experience for a society that for thirty years had been living in a state of quasi siege. The first encounters with Egyptians were surprisingly pleasant, and they produced an immediate change in the image Israelis had previously held of them, an image inspired to a large extent by the spectacle of hysterical crowds cheering Gamal Abd al-Nasser's inflammatory speeches. The Egyptians were now seen as a warm, good-natured, and hospitable people who bore the burdens of their daily hardships with admirable patience and a charming sense of humor.

Normalization, however, did not go very far. It evolved gradually toward the completion of withdrawal from Sinai and for a few weeks beyond it, suffered a considerable setback following the outbreak of the Lebanon war, and then leveled off on a more or less stable plateau.

The chief assets of the process of normalization so far have been the operation of embassies and consulates, exchanges of visits by high-level politicians and officials, the sale of Egyptian oil to Israel and trade in oil products, a modest volume of general trade (mostly agricultural products), the use of the Suez Canal (and Egyptian ports) by Israeli shipping, regular flights of commercial airlines, considerable Israeli tourism to Egypt, telecommunications, and the activities of the Israeli Academic Center in Cairo.

To reflect the quantitative dimension of this interaction, the following data may be illuminating. The biggest item in Egyptian-Israeli trade was oil. In the period under discussion, Israel imported crude oil from Egypt on the order of $500 million a year (besides large purchases of Egyptian oil in the spot market) and exported refined products to Egypt on the order of $60 million annually. At

13. For the texts of these agreements, see Arab Republic of Egypt, Ministry of Foreign Affairs, *White Paper on Normalization of Relations between the Arab Republic of Egypt and the State of Israel* (Cairo: Ministry of Foreign Affairs, 1984).

the end of that period these figures declined sharply as the result of the decrease in oil prices and the situation in the oil market. Otherwise the volume of trade between the two countries was very modest. Israeli exports to Egypt in 1981 and 1982 amounted to $15 million to $17 million a year and then declined and leveled off at $4 million to $7 million a year. The figures of Egyptian exports to Israel were even lower. The inclusion of trade through third countries might double or even triple these numbers, but no accurate data are available on this subject.

The statistics on tourism were more impressive. In the years 1980–87 about 300,000 Israeli citizens traveled to Egypt. In a typical year the number stood at 35,000, but in 1987 there was a sharp increase that almost doubled this figure. Over the same period, about 550,000 tourists carrying passports of Western countries crossed into Egypt from Israel (with 1987 again having double the amount of an ordinary year). In addition to that flow, every year an average of about 60,000 Palestinians from the West Bank and Gaza, and 20,000 citizens of other Arab countries, crossed into Egypt from Israel. The sum of these figures amounted to a great share of Egypt's tourist trade, and in 1987 Israel, with the West Bank and Gaza, occupied the fourth place among countries sending tourists to Egypt. Compared with these numbers, the volume of Egyptian tourism to Israel was negligible: no more than 2,000 to 3,000 visitors (of all types) a year.[14]

From the outset Cairo's policy was to use normalization as a lever in its bargaining with Israel, to retain full control of its evolution in the hands of governmental agencies, to keep it away from politically sensitive areas, and to work mostly through official channels and in the least visible types of activities. Nevertheless, in the period before the Lebanon war, Cairo had allowed the emergence of a much wider range of interactions, including various activities that on the level of state-to-state relations seemed modest but in the perspective of the essential purpose of normalization were of the highest import. Such activities included the exchange of youth groups in summer camps, visiting musical performances and art exhibitions, several joint scientific research projects, an exchange of television programs, the examination of textbooks to remove hostile expressions, and pilot studies of large-scale agricultural projects. The de facto suspension of these types of relations in June 1982 left open the question of whether they

14. Figures are from the Israeli Ministries of Energy, Tourism, and Foreign Affairs.

were merely one-time manifestations of goodwill or were the beginnings of a possibly more extensive relationship, which were aborted only when Cairo needed a way to apply sanctions against Israel.

Whatever the case, the bilateral relationship has assumed the form of what Boutros Boutros-Ghali defined as a "cold peace." The term refers to a situation in which a stalemate prevails in the peace process and the level of normal interrelations is deliberately, but not always admittedly, restricted as a reaction to various Israeli policies and actions. Some Egyptians, particularly those critical of the peace process, have explained the lack of progress in normalization by rejecting the notion that normal relations can develop at all with Israel or, as they put it, "be imposed" by Israel, at least at this stage. Egyptians in government circles have tended to explain the stalemate by factors entirely unrelated to the bilateral relationship, but sometimes they would state clearly that the freeze was a deliberate response to Israeli policies and actions that contradicted the Egyptian understanding of the peace agreement. The list of Egyptian grievances was rather long. It included the frozen autonomy talks, annexation of the Golan and Jerusalem, continuation of settlements, treatment of Palestinians, retention of Taba, siding with the Ethiopians against the Copts over Deir al-Sultan,[15] military operations against targets in Arab countries,[16] and most notably, the war in Lebanon—which brought about the strongest measures against normalization.

Seen from Israel, the "cold peace" could be described as a certain political climate in which the Egyptian government's explicit or implicit positions combine with public attitudes, mostly among the intelligentsia, to effectively freeze the development of normalization. Manifestations of the freeze were the discouragement of tourism to Israel, obstacles to trade relations that kept them at a negligible level, boycotts of Israel by professional and academic associations, the channeling of various relations through third parties, and above all the perpetuation of a hostile line in the media that went beyond the criticism of Israeli policies to a total condem-

15. Deir al-Sultan monastery near the Holy Sepulcher in Jerusalem is contested between the Ethiopian and Coptic churches. The Copts complained that the Ethiopians had encroached on their rights, but the verdict of the Israeli High Court of Justice in 1971 did not result in satisfaction of the Copts' demands.

16. The two operations that triggered the sharpest reactions were the bombing of the nuclear reactor near Baghdad in June 1981 (a few days after the Begin-Sadat meeting in Sharm al-Sheikh), and the bombing of the headquarters of the Palestine Liberation Organization in Tunisia in October 1985.

nation of the Jewish state and its people, occasionally still referring to them as the "Zionist enemy."

The impact of these measures on the Israelis was strong. It seems that many Israelis underestimated the intensity of some of the Egyptian grievances, and doubted the validity of others, but at any rate the public at large did not maintain that Egypt's complaints justified measures considered to be a flagrant violation of the peace treaty. Israelis were particularly unhappy with the attacks in Egypt's media, which often touched on historically traumatic sensitivities and nourished the darkest suspicions. Cairo's claim that those denunciations were voiced by opposition circles who were exercising their freedom of expression did not impress the Israelis who pointed out that anti-Semitic and hate-rousing writings could be found in government-sponsored organs as well. These messages, many felt, were the opposite of education for peace; they threatened to undermine its legitimacy and set the ground for its reversal. Accordingly, some Israelis suspected that the Egyptians never intended to respect their commitments under the normalization clauses, no matter what Israel's position on the various controversial issues would have been. Whatever the grounds for the cold peace, there can be no doubt that it has effectively quenched the initial euphoria in the Israeli public for the peace process.

Although this mood was common to most Israelis, there were differences of nuance between the attitudes and reactions of the two major political trends. The Likud camp took a cooler view of the problem. Since it realized that its position on Judea, Samaria, and Gaza was irreconcilable with that of Egypt, it tended to take a certain level of friction for granted. The important thing, according to this view, was the fact that Egypt had abandoned the Arab war camp. Most of the Likud members were not inclined anyway to have excessively high expectations of the potential for interaction between the two societies; therefore the Egyptian restrictions on normalization aroused concern mostly to the extent that they amounted to a violation of the treaty and thus challenged Israel's credibility. Supporters of this trend often maintained that Egyptians must learn to reconcile themselves to certain Israeli actions even if they were not to their liking—sometimes referring to such actions as "tests" that Cairo's commitment to the treaty must stand. Some observers would also argue that in a way the Likud bloc felt quite comfortable with the Egyptians' narrow interpretation of the peace treaty's normalization clauses, because it offset its own narrow interpretation of the Palestinians' legitimate rights included in the Camp David Accords.

Labor put a somewhat greater stress on the role that relations between the two societies played in the development of the dynamics of peace and thus seemed more anxious to see them evolve. Although it, too, maintained that actions that serve national security—such as retaliatory and preemptive military operations in other Arab countries, establishment of settlements in security zones, and strengthening control of the Golan—must take precedence over regard for Egyptian sensitivities, it usually expressed greater apprehension of the danger to peace if relations with Egypt were allowed to deteriorate. Since Labor was more optimistic about the possibility of continuing the peace process toward compromise solutions with Israel's other Arab neighbors, it also believed in the feasibility of more harmonious relations with Egypt and in the importance of such harmony for the process.

Labor's more dovish wing went further and complained that the Egyptians did not adequately understand the interdependence between normalization and the continuation of the peace process. It argued that they should have realized that the struggle over the continuation of the peace process, which is Egypt's foreign policy priority as well, would be decided mostly by the outcome of the internal debate in Israel. Therefore, instead of using normalization to penalize Israel, the Egyptians should have used it to strengthen the Israeli peace camp by conducting an effective dialogue with the Israeli community and making peace more attractive to it. Instead, their policies were nourishing the arguments of the Israeli hawks and undermining the credibility of the doves.

Nevertheless, the Labor camp as a whole tended to show consideration for the constraints that affected the Egyptian decisionmakers and was not inclined to increase the difficulties of maintaining a peace process by pushing too hard for normalization. Thus the two camps, each for its own reasons, felt that the boat should not be rocked too much for the sake of normalization. Moreover, they were also united in the wish to check the deterioration of relations as the result of occasional eruptions of severe incidents. They tried to tone down the public's reactions to such painful events as the shooting of Israeli diplomats and their wives in Cairo or the senseless killings of Israeli tourists at Ras Burka—in spite of the general feeling that the Egyptian authorities handled these affairs in a "cold peace" frame of reference. Evidently, both camps maintained that in the final analysis peace—cold or lukewarm—was a great national asset that must not be jeopardized by too rigid a stand on specific bilateral issues.

THE LEBANON CRISIS

The period of Israel's war in Lebanon neatly divides the decade after Camp David into three phases: the conclusion and implementation of the peace agreement (1978–82); the Lebanon war and the suspension of the peace process (1982–85); and the attempts to revive the process through the concept of an international conference (1985–88). The Lebanon war as such is outside the scope of this chapter, but its relation to the process initiated by the Camp David Accords deserves to be mentioned.

Not all the members of the Likud government, which initiated the war in Lebanon, shared with the architect of that war, Minister of Defense Ariel Sharon, a commitment to all the components of his grand design. Yet the broad conceptual framework of the Lebanon war strategy was derived from the basic tenets of Likud's credo and supported by a consensus in this political camp. According to the planners of the war, its purpose was not merely to remove the menace of the PLO bases in southern Lebanon but primarily to deal the PLO a heavy blow to shatter its influence in the West Bank and Gaza and strengthen the links of these two areas to Israel (which had been somewhat called into question by the Camp David Accords).[17] They also expected the war to cement Israeli-American strategic cooperation in the region and to neutralize the threat of the radical regime in Syria—thus further increasing Israel's freedom of action in those territories. The pax Israeliana designed for Lebanon would prove that the peace process could continue without territorial compromises or substantial concessions to the Palestinians.

Labor found itself in agreement with the war aims as they were initially proclaimed, namely, the removal of PLO bases from the forty-kilometer zone along the Israeli border. Such an operation was compatible with Labor's basic strategic concepts, and it seemed to be similar to other military operations conducted in southern Lebanon in the past and supported by the Labor party. However, as the scope of the war expanded and its far-reaching political goals became evident, Labor stepped up its criticism of the war until finally the two camps confronted each other in a bitter political

17. Seliger, "Camp David Accords," p. 43, regards this aim as a possible explanation for Begin's drifting into the Lebanon war. On Ariel Sharon's grand design, see Ze'ev Schiff and Ehud Ya'ari, *Israel's Lebanon War,* ed. and trans. Ina Friedman (Simon and Schuster, 1984), pp. 31–44.

struggle that opened up the whole issue of the peace process and Israel's policy in the territories.

The effect of the war in Lebanon on the peace with Egypt was an important aspect of this controversy. Egypt saw the Israeli invasion of Lebanon as a flagrant violation of at least the spirit of the peace agreement. It also regarded the invasion as a heavy blow to the credibility of Egypt's arguments in domestic and inter-Arab debates, which had maintained that Egypt's peace with Israel was not a betrayal of Arab solidarity and that it did not expose Israel's neighbors to military attacks. Cairo reacted to the war by suspending the implementation of almost all the normalization projects that were in the pipeline, by sharply reducing trade relations, and by intensifying the attacks on Israel in the media. Otherwise the Egyptian government resisted the external and domestic pressures to withdraw from the basic commitments to the peace treaty; only the uproar produced by the massacres at Sabra and Shatila induced Egypt to add to the sanctions against Israel the recall "for consultations" of its ambassador from Tel Aviv.

The Likud camp was not greatly impressed by these sanctions. It instead stressed that the peace treaty had stood the test of the war and thus vindicated the judgment of its drafters. The Likud school maintained that Egypt had no say in the conflict in Lebanon. The Laborites, on the other hand, tended to acknowledge the legitimacy of Egypt's concern with this conflict and added the need to repair relations with Cairo to the list of considerations necessitating the rapid termination of the war.

REVIVAL OF THE PEACE PROCESS

The initiative was seized by Peres at the end of 1984, following his assumption of the premiership in the national unity government in September. His immediate concern in foreign affairs was to restore some mutual confidence and cooperation with Egypt toward the revival of the peace process. For this purpose he had to cope with the three issues that the Egyptians saw as obstacles to the resumption of a political dialogue with Israel and the return of their ambassador to Tel Aviv: the occupation of Lebanese territories, conditions in the West Bank and Gaza, and the Taba dispute.

The first of these issues was ripe for a solution since by that time there was almost a national consensus supporting withdrawal from Lebanon. The Egyptians, although protesting the continued presence of some Israeli forces in the southern security zone, welcomed the evacuation from Lebanon as a significant improvement in the mutual relationship. The second issue was less tangible, but certain measures taken by the new government, including the authorization of the operation of a Jordanian bank in the West Bank, combined with the de facto freeze on settlements, removed this obstacle as well.

The Taba issue turned out to be the most difficult. The Egyptian demand for Taba had never been popular with the Israeli public, which felt that whatever the merit of Israel's legal case, the Egyptians, whose Red Sea coast extended for hundreds of kilometers, should not have blown up a dispute on a strip of some 800 meters to the proportions of a major national issue. Hence the Likud's reluctance to yield to Mubarak's demand to submit the case to international arbitration enjoyed considerable support. The formulation of agreed terms of reference for arbitration also emerged as a more complicated problem than was previously assumed and was concluded only at the very end of Peres's two-year term in the premiership according to the rotation agreement. The removal of this obstacle was celebrated at the Alexandria summit in September 1986, which among other things proclaimed 1987 as the year of peace negotiations.

All the while it was obvious that these moves were just preparatory steps toward a showdown between the two Israeli camps, which would materialize once a significant plan for resuming the peace process was put on the agenda. For various reasons, the plans that had emerged in earlier stages failed to trigger such a confrontation. The Fahd peace plan of August 1981 and the subsequent Fez resolutions of September 1982 did not bring about a major controversy in Israel because they were seen there as reflecting a quest for Arab consensus rather than a genuine pursuit of a settlement with Israel (see appendix E). Observers in Jerusalem noted that the drafters of the plan hastened to clarify that it did not imply any recognition of Israel or negotiations with it.[18] The two camps in Israel were thus united in rejecting these proposals. The only difference between them was that the doves in Labor added to this evaluation the observation that, at least for a while, there had been some ambiguity about the readiness to recognize Israel and that this attitude was a reflection of some movement in the Arab world toward moderation that Israel should not ignore.

The Reagan plan of September 1982 could have aroused much greater controversy (see appendix D). Since it came from a president who had proved his concern for Israel's security and well-being, and

18. For a discussion of the Fahd peace plan and the Fez resolutions, see Shiloah Center, *MECS*, vol. 6: *1981–82*, pp. 202–07, 790–92, 794–95.

since most Arab governments were careful not to reject it outright, it had to be seriously considered. However, the Begin government saw no alternative but to reject the plan, for it opposed almost everything that Likud stood for. The plan called for autonomy that related to the territory, not just to the inhabitants, and it applied to East Jerusalem as well. Reagan also called for a freeze in settlements and categorically rejected the option of Israeli annexation. Peres could easily criticize Begin's prompt rejection of the Reagan plan, for two reasons. First, the plan's main thrust was based on Labor's concept of a "Jordanian option." Second, the plan also dismissed the possibility of a separate Palestinian state, which would have made it unacceptable to Labor as well. However, Reagan's reluctance to press for the acceptance of his plan prevented, once again, an internal contest in Israel.

Under the national unity government the debate on the desirability of bringing up peace plans was resumed. The Likud bloc felt that the time had come to slow down. Its spokesmen now reminded the Israeli public that an end of the conflict with the Arabs was not in sight and that there were no shortcuts on the road to peace. The Arabs, they said, should be given time to reconcile themselves to the reality of Israel. Any attempt to rush things would inevitably lead to unnecessary concessions. They scorned what they called "the spirit of Now-ism"—the kind of naive impatience that emanated from the Peace Now movement and tended to weaken the resolve of the Israeli public. In Likud's view, peace with Egypt stood on its own. There did exist a kind of de facto peace with Jordan, and the situation in Judea, Samaria, and Gaza was under control.

Conversely, the Labor bloc felt that time was running out. The situation in the territories was becoming increasingly worrying, and the country was moving rapidly, perhaps irreversibly, in the direction of binationalism. The problem was "one of demography—not geography." Peace with Egypt was in danger, for the peace process could either move forward or decline. Israel had no choice but to focus on the Jordanian-Palestinian issue, substantiating what was termed the Jordanian option, for reaching some form of a settlement that might prevent a major conflagration. This position was also based on the evaluation of Peres (supported by various direct and indirect talks with Arab personalities) that the nonradical part of the Arab world was moving toward a readiness for peace agreements with Israel and therefore the continuation of the peace process stood a reasonable chance of success.

The fact that Peres reached what had been planned as the starting point for the revival of the peace process only at the end of his term created a feeling within the Labor camp that a great opportunity had been lost as the result of prolonged bickering over unimportant details of the Taba problem. Nevertheless, the movement toward the revival of the peace process had started in fact before the Alexandria meeting, and it continued well beyond it despite Labor's loss of the premiership in October 1986.

The most significant developments had taken place in Amman. The February 11, 1985, agreement between King Hussein and Yasir Arafat had among its five points several elements that could potentially lead to the emergence of a formula for negotiation acceptable to Labor (see appendix F). It included the concept of peace negotiations in the framework of an international conference; the principle of "territories for peace"; consent to the representation of the PLO within a joint Jordanian-Palestinian delegation; and the pursuit of self-determination within the context of a Jordanian-Palestinian confederation. The agreement had much in it that could not be acceptable to Peres anymore than to Shamir; nor did it solidify into a stable PLO-Jordan accord, and by February 1986, it was no longer considered valid. But nevertheless the agreement did point out a possible avenue for the peace process and made it possible for Hussein to continue on his own in that general direction. Between September 1985 and January 1986, Hussein gradually reversed some of his long-standing positions and crystallized (in coordination with Washington) a concept of direct negotiations between Israel and a Jordanian-Palestinian delegation within the framework of an international conference, convened on the basis of United Nations Security Council Resolutions 242 and 338, and without making negotiations dependent on any preconditions.

At about the same time, Peres formulated his own concept of negotiations, which accepted a certain role for an international forum. In the subsequent years the plan underwent several alterations, but its main concepts remained roughly as follows. The new peace process would be initiated by convening an international conference consisting of the five permanent members of the Security Council, a Jordanian-Palestinian delegation, Syria, Lebanon, Egypt, and Israel. The conference would meet without setting preconditions, on the basis of the participants' agreement, the acceptance of Resolutions 242 and 338, and the renunciation of terrorism and violence. It would aim at solving the Palestine problem in all its aspects. According to Peres, this method would not be inconsistent with the principles of Camp David. This pluralistic forum would admittedly be a problematic channel for negotiations from the Israeli point of view, but it should be accepted out of a realistic recognition of the constraints under which the participation of Jordan could be realized. The international plenum would facilitate the negotiations and provide the opening forum, which would be followed immediately by direct face-to-face negotiations in bilateral geographic committees and possibly also in one multilateral committee, with the participation of Egypt, that would deal with such issues as regional development schemes. The international forum would have no power to veto or impose agreements on the parties, and this restriction would be guaranteed by the United States.

The Palestine problem would be discussed with the Jordanian-Palestinian delegation. Participating in this delegation would be "authentic" Palestinians who would not constitute a PLO delegation. It would not be Israel's concern whether or not they had Arafat's approval, as long as they did not "represent terrorism." Israel's objectives would be to achieve progress toward a settlement primarily through Jordan but in the framework of a concept of Jordanian-Palestinian confederation. An interim period could be envisaged in which Jordan and Israel, forming jointly a steering committee, would play the main role in controlling the territories; the Palestinian population would have autonomy and be represented by an elected council; and the Israelis would have security zones under their control. During that period the permanent settlement would be negotiated, including the determination of borders. Thus a final "territorial" solution would replace the "functional" arrangement of the interim period.[19]

Subsequently, several substantial steps were taken toward the implementation of this strategy. In his talks with Mubarak in Cairo in February 1987, Peres secured the shift of the Egyptian position from insistence on the immediate participation of an official PLO delegation to the acceptance of a phased process. According to that Egyptian concept, the PLO would be told to "hang back but keep a foot in the door," namely, to approve in the initial stage delegates acceptable to Israel, the United States, and Jordan, and to defer the participation of direct representatives to a more advanced stage of the negotiations when the PLO would also be expected to meet the conditions for participating in the conference. Egypt also reiterated its consent to an international conference—on the basis of Resolutions 242 and 338—that would lead to direct negotiations between the parties and would not impose its will on them.

This agreement with Egypt was one of the factors that made it

19. The main points of this plan appear in Shimon Peres's address to the forty-second session of the General Assembly of the United Nations, September 29, 1987.

possible for Hussein to take an additional step to narrow the gap between him and Peres. In April 1987 an understanding was reached between them in London, with the mediation of the United States. According to Peres's aides, the major breakthrough achieved in London was Jordan's withdrawal of its insistence on "referral" to the international conference plenum (see appendix G). Jordan thus agreed to enter into direct face-to-face negotiations for peace with Israel, within the framework of an international conference that would convene according to the terms just listed and would not have the power to impose a settlement or veto agreements reached in the bilateral committees. It also agreed that these committees would be independent of each other.[20]

Peres invested considerable effort to broaden international support for this concept. Talks with King Hassan II of Morocco, with European leaders, and with Palestinian personalities in the West Bank and Gaza were designed to serve this goal. A dialogue with the Soviet Union was initiated, in which the Soviets implied their readiness for flexibility on questions of composition and procedure of the international conference, without, however, agreeing to reduce its role to a merely ceremonial function. The position of the United States was crucial. Washington was, of course, a full partner in the crystallization of the international conference scheme, but for tactical reasons, both domestic and foreign, preferred to keep its public support of the plan at a low profile—thus helping indirectly the critics of the Peres plan in Israel to block it. Peres had obviously realized all along that his plan did not enjoy majority support in the Israeli political system, but he probably hoped that the dynamics of the peace process would increase support for it. Should the plan yield positive results, the public would accept it, as it had done in similar situations in the past.

This was not to come about, and in the course of 1987 the Likud bloc stepped up its objection to the concept of an international conference and effectively froze the whole project. Shamir's school of thought fiercely attacked this concept as damaging the chances of peace rather than enhancing them. Its spokesmen claimed that just as peace with Egypt had been achieved through direct negotiations, so direct talks with Jordan, without any preconditions, were now the correct way to proceed with the peace process. There was no need for a new procedure beyond that which had been established by the Camp David Accords, with autonomy as its key concept.

20. See *Ma'ariv*, May 7, 1987.

The Peres negotiating model was denounced as a violation of Israel's long-standing and irrevocable principle of direct negotiations. There were no adequate guarantees of direct negotiations between the parties and noninterference by the international forum in their resolutions. The various promises on this matter could not be trusted, they said, for the dynamics of the conference were sure to nullify them.

The Shamir school warned that this procedure would open the door to the participation of the PLO, which should be rejected in principle, no matter what verbal concession it might be ready to make. The mention of "the legitimate rights of the Palestinians" in the London agreement, it claimed, was designed to appease the PLO. Even more dangerous was the intention of bringing back the Soviets, through the conference, to a position of influence in Israeli-Arab affairs, while their basic strategy remained damaging and threatening to Israel. At the time, it was recalled, negotiations with Egypt succeeded precisely because the Soviets had been excluded from them. Their participation, with the Syrians and others, would turn the conference into a pro-Arab forum that would either impose its will on Israel or maneuver it into a position in which Israel would be blamed for the collapse of the talks. By consenting to this conference, Israel would be inviting pressure to withdraw to the 1967 borders and establish a Palestinian state. The Peres plan, this school maintained, was hopelessly based on the "territories for peace" concept, while Likud believed in its ability to produce eventually a "peace for peace" settlement, based on a different type of compromise.

If there was a need for a peace procedure at present, the Likud planners suggested, it might be possible to convene a regional conference with the participation of Jordan, Egypt, local non-PLO Palestinians, and the United States. Such a conference would be compatible with the Camp David procedure, which should not be compromised. Alternatively, direct negotiations could be conducted between Israel and Jordan under the sponsorship of Cairo. Another possibility would be to initiate direct negotiations through an opening forum presided over by the leaders of the two superpowers, with the understanding that they will have no further role in the process. The United Nations would not be involved.[21]

21. Yitzhak Shamir expressed his reservations about this plan in a message to Washington on April 24, 1987. George P. Shultz answered, point by point, on May 1, 1987.

For Labor, these Likud schemes and arguments were nothing but efforts to prevent any peace negotiations, out of a fear that they might lead to withdrawal from territories. Yet, in the equilibrium existing in Israel between the two schools of thought, there was no way to get around that objection.

This stalemate was abruptly shaken in December 1987 by the uprising in the West Bank and Gaza, the so-called *intifadah*. The riots in these territories effectively shattered the notion that the continuation of the status quo was the most convenient and the least problematic of all Israel's options, and they invited a reexamination of the fundamentals of Israel's position there.

As a matter of fact, a tendency toward such a reevaluation had been gradually emerging a few months before the uprising, as a result of the growing preoccupation with the "demographic problem." The issue was not a new one in the Israeli political arena, but the increasingly visible quantitative changes in the territories began to assume, twenty years after the occupation, a qualitative nature that was no longer easy to ignore. This tendency intensified the Labor camp's argument for a prompt renewal of the peace process. The effect on the Likud camp was much more complex. While the views of most people at the center of this school remained unchanged, a centrifugal motion became noticeable at the two edges. On the one hand, the concept of a massive "transfer" of Arab inhabitants across the border, through the employment of incentives or force, began to be voiced with increasing boldness by certain party personalities, thus drawing closer to the views of the Tehiya party's militants or even Meir Kahane's fanatics. On the other hand, a readiness to recognize the collective rights of the Palestinians and negotiate a settlement with them, even through the PLO, emerged among some Likud activists, who were promptly denounced by the party's machinery.

The *intifadah* probably intensified these tendencies, but in mid-1988 it was too early to tell what its lasting impact on the various political trends in the country would be. The immediate outcome seemed to be a gravitation toward greater militancy. Labor's "Jordanian option" lost much of its credibility. The fact that a Labor minister, Yitzhak Rabin, was in charge of the efforts to suppress the uprising narrowed the gap between the two camps. The violent clashes in Gaza and the West Bank evidently aroused anti-Arab feelings. Moreover, the conspicuous presence in the forefront of the *intifadah* of frantic youngsters and radical jihadists who showed no interest in a political solution, and raised maximalist slogans, further antagonized or alarmed many Israelis. At the same time, the crisis reactivated dovish groups that opposed the occupation and pressed for its rapid liquidation.

Since it could no longer be claimed that time in the territories was working in Israel's favor, and as the limits of power became increasingly evident, there emerged in Israel a broad consensus on the belief that the only way to cope with the situation was through a "political solution." This new mood precipitated the formation in March 1988 of the Shultz plan—the first official American peace initiative since the Reagan plan in 1982 (see appendix K).

The Shultz proposals laid down a tight timetable according to which the parties would complete the negotiation of interim arrangements and the initiation of talks on the final settlement by the end of the year. Otherwise the plan was essentially identical to the scheme for an international conference worked out between Peres and Hussein in London. Accordingly, Peres had no difficulty in accepting it in principle, while Shamir's problem was how to phrase his rejection in the most positive way possible. Besides his basic opposition to the formula for an international conference, he saw in the plan's rushed schedule and in the active role it prescribed for the United States in the negotiations, a dangerous procedure that might rapidly erode Israel's control of Judea, Samaria, and Gaza. This objection was conceptualized in terms of loyalty to the Camp David Accords that, in Shamir's words, would be completely negated by this plan.

Indeed, the Shultz plan, which was in the spring of 1988 "the only game in town," had come a long way since Camp David. The 1978 accords, which Jordan and the Palestinians had refused to accept and Israel and Egypt had failed to implement in the West Bank and Gaza, could no longer serve as the blueprint for advancing the peace process. Yet their essential contribution to the process is undeniable, and it would be extremely difficult for future peace negotiators to do without their various concepts. The Camp David Accords defined basic rights and legitimate interests, created a distinction between transitional arrangements and final status, suggested a Jordanian-Palestinian partnership, and set full peace as the ultimate objective.

SAMUEL W. LEWIS

The United States and Israel: Constancy and Change

SINCE ISRAEL consolidated its independence in the late 1940s, no prolonged period has exhibited such sharp oscillations in U.S.-Israeli relations as the twelve years that spanned the presidencies of Jimmy Carter and Ronald Reagan. Equally dizzying swings in American policy and tactics toward the Arab-Israeli conflict accompanied those oscillations. At least, that is how it often seemed to the pundits, both American and Israeli. Yet to most Arab observers the often bitter squabbles between Washington and Jerusalem only momentarily obscured the underlying continuity of America's special affinity and "indulgence" for Israel. This affinity, claimed Arab analysts, undermined the broader interests of the United States in the Middle East. The Arab analysis was closer to the mark in stressing the essential continuity of U.S. policy.

Beneath the turbulent political foam, the fundamentals of U.S. policy have been remarkably constant, although diplomatic tactics shifted when political leadership in Washington passed from Democrats to Republicans, as well as within both the Carter and Reagan eras. The fundamentals, however, remained: a unique commitment to the security of the Jewish state and the conviction that only progress toward some peaceful resolution of the Arab-Israeli conflict can safeguard basic U.S. strategic interests in the region, as well as Israel's national future. The tenacious, unavoidable, continuous investment of American diplomacy in the mare's nest called the "Middle East peace process" stems from this duality. The turbulence, as well as the genuine achievements of U.S. diplomacy, reflect the impact of American and Israeli political leaders.[1]

1. As an intimate participant in many of those events, I agree with Steven L. Spiegel, "What has mattered more than the decisionmaking system of the admin-

This explains the seeming contradiction between the Arab analysis and that of Western observers mesmerized by noisy clashes between spokesmen for these two cacophonous democracies. It is the outsized role of political personalities, in both capitals, which accounts for most of the sharp oscillations on the surface of the U.S.-Israeli relationship. Yet they occurred within parameters of a fundamentally stable framework. Clashes may occur over strategy or tactics for confronting Israel's painful security dilemmas; differences are exacerbated or quenched more or less easily depending on the styles of current Israeli and American leaders. Despite the agitation, deeper policy currents flow largely unaffected.

To dissect thoroughly the elements of constancy in the U.S.-Israeli relationship would replough much familiar ground. History, religion, democratic values, family networks, and residual guilt feelings about the fate of European Jewry contribute. As new generations of Americans forget World War II, new techniques of political mobilization arise in the United States to undergird sympathy with political self-interest. Congress has become ever more staunchly supportive of Israel and Israeli security requirements, even as American Jewish citizens have begun here and there to question diffidently the wisdom of Israeli policies toward the Palestinian conundrum. That questioning does not, however, express any basic doubts about the central importance of Israel to U.S. Middle East interests.

During the decade following Camp David, Jewish supporters of Israel have enhanced their political influence in Congress. Their primary vehicle, the American Israel Public Affairs Committee (AIPAC), has grown into a broad-based, mass membership lobbying organization of redoubtable effectiveness. The trend in political campaign financing mechanisms has further enhanced AIPAC's efforts. Moreover, Israel has become a popular cause among many evangelical and fundamentalist Christian religious groups.

Public opinion polls have consistently recorded high support for Israel in the general public, a level that sagged only briefly during the Lebanon war and its immediate aftermath in 1982, rebounding within a few months. Support remained remarkably high thereafter through 1987, despite intermittent unattractive media images of

istration has been the personalities of the critical officials, the relations between them, and—most important—their individual views on Middle East policy." See Spiegel, *The Other Arab-Israeli Conflict: Making America's Middle East Policy, from Truman to Reagan* (University of Chicago Press, 1985), p. 392.

Israeli policy toward the occupied territories, Israel's role in the U.S.-Iranian arms sale imbroglio, and the "Pollard affair," in which a Jewish U.S. naval intelligence official confessed to spying for Israel. The Palestinian "uprising" in Gaza and the West Bank, which began spontaneously in December 1987, sorely tested support for Israel as the U.S. media carried shocking nightly images of Israeli soldiers using lethal or brutal force to try to quell violent resistance to the occupation. Yet the depth of American public support has made it highly resistant to serious erosion, in part because prominent segments of Israel's citizenry have themselves been seen protesting vigorously against the use of excessive force while calling for negotiations and Israeli concessions for peace, thus underscoring the democratic character of the Israeli state and Israeli society.

A broad political base exists for an extraordinarily close U.S.-Israeli relationship, akin to an unwritten alliance, which an American president would ignore only at significant political risk. Congress as well is reluctant to take any action that could be characterized as "anti-Israel" and shows predictable enthusiasm for any initiatives by the executive branch that might advance the prospects for Arab-Israeli peace, so long as Israel's government does not denounce them for jeopardizing Israel's security.

In this domestic American context, great diplomatic triumphs and abysmal failures have marked U.S.-Israeli relations since Camp David. The Camp David Accords and the peace treaty between Egypt and Israel are enduring tributes to President Carter's determination (see appendix C). The de facto strategic alliance between Washington and Jerusalem, which put down deep roots in the second term of the Reagan administration, enjoyed wide political support in both countries. Yet the broader promise of Camp David to open the door for a lasting resolution of the Palestinian-Israeli struggle and for a comprehensive peace between Israel and its other neighbors withered, leaving its swelling legacy of Palestinian bitterness and frustration to water the seeds of eventual rebellion. Israel and the United States stumbled into a Lebanese quagmire that besmirched both nations and accelerated the collapse of a fragile, perhaps doomed, Lebanese nation-state. The historical record will not be kind to some Israeli and American leaders. Yet the peace with Egypt has permanently altered the nature of the conflict and of the Middle East. "Camp David," and what it set in train, defined new parameters for the conflict and changed America's strategic position in the region. In that sense, it was a watershed event for the Arab world, for Israel, and for the United States.

PRELUDE

The 1978–88 decade of U.S. policymaking cannot be understood in isolation. The seeds were planted in the frightful October war in 1973. For the first time since 1948, Israelis came to doubt their leaders' judgment on matters of national survival. A huge expenditure of human and economic assets forced Israel into a heavy reliance on the United States in the war's aftermath. Massive military and economic aid was sought and extended. True independence for Israel became for the first time a receding horizon. Equally important, Henry A. Kissinger's diplomatic wizardry extracted from Egypt and Syria the first steps toward distant peace in the three disengagement agreements he brokered in 1974 and 1975 and established U.S. dominance over the diplomatic process of mediating between Israel and its Arab adversaries.

The war also finally convinced President Anwar Sadat, and perhaps some other Arab leaders, that Israel could not be defeated militarily. Sinai could be regained only at the conference table and only through U.S. intermediation.

Another lesson from the era of Kissingerian diplomacy cast a long shadow: America's senior statesmen would and could invest heavily of their time and personal involvement to mediate Arab-Israeli disputes. Carter and Secretary of State Cyrus Vance would later have to emulate Kissinger to achieve any results, regardless of the cost of diverting time and energies from other global crises. Reagan's subsequent failure to move the peace process further along surely owed something to the tradition started by Kissinger and Carter. Inadvertently, the United States had spoiled Middle Eastern leaders into assuming that peacemaking was more important to the United States than to the protagonists. American journalists fed this conviction by dramatizing Kissinger as "Super-K" and later by assessing the seriousness of an administration's diplomatic efforts according to the frequency of personal trips by a secretary of state to the region.

CARTER AND ISRAEL—PHASE I

By the time President Carter convoked President Sadat and Prime Minister Menachem Begin to Camp David in September 1978, Carter's administration was already battle scarred from dealings with Israel and Israel's supporters in Congress. Carter had invested unprecedented time, effort, and scarce political capital in his determined campaign to bring about an Arab-Israeli peace settlement, ignoring those advisers who urged caution, trampling on Israeli hypersensitivities by expressing new, provocative ideas in public without warning and without care to avoid the loaded code words so prevalent in the thicket of Middle East diplomacy.

Impatient to launch comprehensive peace negotiations at a resumed Geneva conference, Carter tried to ignore the fact that Prime Minister Yitzhak Rabin's cabinet was embroiled in an electoral campaign during the first half of 1977 and in no position to break any new diplomatic ground. By the time Begin unexpectedly surfaced in mid-May as Israel's new leader, Carter's deliberately iconoclastic diplomatic style already had raised the Israeli guard to a high level of nervousness. Suspicions of his ultimate intentions toward Israel had been augmented by Carter's global policy pronouncements on U.S.-Soviet relations and his new arms transfer policies that seemed to bode ill for Israel's security needs in weaponry and military technology. When the flamboyantly rhetorical, ideologically rigid Begin replaced the cool, cautious, analytical Rabin as Carter's chief Israeli interlocutor, fireworks were inevitable.

From Begin's first visit (of ten) to Washington as prime minister in July 1977 until Camp David in September 1978, U.S. policy and U.S.-Israeli relations swung continually between extremes of warm, reassuring statements about shared values and special relationships to cold, angry diatribes about alleged Israeli intransigence. Begin greatly admired the United States, was drawn toward Carter's biblical fascination for the Holy Land, yearned for legitimacy and acceptance as Israel's leader after thirty years in the political wilderness, and believed he could bring Israel peace with Egypt. Yet he was determined to safeguard Israel's political independence from American suzerainty, had a very limited respect for U.S. judgments about the complexities of the Middle East, and was fiercely determined to preserve permanent Israeli control over its historic homeland, the West Bank, known to Begin only as Judea and Samaria. Settling those areas with Jews was the natural corollary to that determination; to Carter those settlements were inflammatory provocations. Begin saw only terrorists and child murderers when the Palestine Liberation Organization (PLO) entered the conversation. Carter was ambivalent, but he tended toward his advisers' view that the PLO was a legitimate spokesman for the Palestinians and in any case a necessary component of any successful peace process.

When Sadat broke the hardening stalemate with his dramatic

flight to Jerusalem in November 1977, Carter first hesitated, then reluctantly shelved his plans for a comprehensive peace to be enshrined at Geneva. Yet he and his advisers worked tenaciously throughout 1978 to try to integrate any bilateral Israeli-Egyptian peace agreement within a broader, comprehensive framework that would address the festering Palestinian problem and thereby protect Egypt from Arab retaliation for breaking ranks to achieve a separate peace. This dogged campaign included a conscious effort in the spring of 1978 to sharpen U.S. differences with Israel over West Bank settlements, the meaning of United Nations Security Council Resolution 242 (see appendix A), and other key issues, so as to rally U.S. congressional, public, and American Jewish leadership support against Begin's recalcitrance, an effort that largely failed. A bruising battle with Israel's supporters in Congress over the sale of advanced F-15 warplanes to Saudi Arabia further strained the Carter-Begin relationship.

Meanwhile, PLO-Israeli clashes north of the Lebanese-Israeli border region had periodically produced dangerous distractions from the business of peacemaking, a harbinger of future tragedies. In March 1978, the dramatic hijacking of an Israeli bus south of Haifa by Palestinian commandos from Lebanon ended in a bloody shootout, and dozens of Israeli civilians died. That prompted a massive Israeli military attack against PLO strongholds in south Lebanon. The aftermath produced a UN peacekeeping force over Israel's objections and unremitting U.S. pressure for prompt Israeli withdrawal. Begin seethed with resentment at Carter's perceived lack of sympathy for Israel's security dilemma.

Although tensions had eased by midsummer, bilateral relations remained strained, and the peace process with Egypt seemed nearly bankrupt. Carter then played his last card to salvage his Middle East policy, the Camp David conference, and it was a long shot indeed. By that time U.S. policy had gradually retreated from Carter's initial ambitions for a comprehensive settlement to a desperate effort to salvage some Israeli-Egyptian agreement that would partly vindicate Sadat's dramatic gamble and Carter's enormous political investment.

By the time Camp David convened, therefore, U.S. policy toward Israel was immersed in the search for peace above all else. The special relationship was intact, but Carter's genuine sympathy for Israel and its security needs had been heavily obscured for Begin and Israel's American supporters by the tactics Carter pursued in conducting his peace diplomacy.

CAMP DAVID—THE AFTERMATH

As Carter, Begin, and Sadat stepped out of the presidential helicopter on the back lawn of the White House on September 17, 1978, with their agreement in hand, Carter's gamble seemed to have paid off. The outcome of the drama of those thirteen days at Camp David temporarily overrode doubts of Americans and Israelis alike. An Egyptian-Israeli peace treaty was there in outline. Moreover, a promising if incomplete approach toward the Palestinian problem had been hammered out, contingent on acceptance by Jordan and the Palestinian inhabitants of the occupied territories, and on some support from other Arab parties, especially Saudi Arabia. Begin and Carter were now "peace partners" with Sadat in a great historic adventure. Unfortunately, Begin had different expectations than Carter about what would follow. And the worm of distrust had already appeared in the apple when, within hours, a bitter dispute erupted over the duration of Begin's crucial promise of a "freeze" on establishing more Jewish settlements in the occupied territories. Carter's conviction that Begin double-crossed him over this issue was never assuaged. It festered throughout the remainder of his presidency and soured their already strained relations despite public appearances to the contrary.

Sensing the fragility of the agreement and Sadat's vulnerability to Arab critics, Carter wanted Begin to help with expressions of statesmanlike restraint to convince the Arab world that the agreements were worthy of support. Jordan had to be enticed to join the next phase of negotiations for autonomy in the territories, as did the Palestinians. The peace treaty with Egypt should present no serious problems; the main elements had all been agreed on. But Carter had to send a bone-tired Vance immediately to the Middle East to lobby for Arab support in Riyadh and Amman. Meanwhile Sadat only made the task harder by indulging in a public pout, offended that Arab leaders did not quickly follow Egypt's lead.

Unfortunately, Begin had different worries and priorities. He was stunned by noisy dissent in his own Herut party over his triumph, furious that many of his oldest political associates opposed his agreements and accused him of selling out Israel's security under Carter's pressure. His immediate preoccupation was to override that opposition at home—which he did by minimizing publicly his compromises and stressing the narrow limits under which the projected Palestinian autonomy would operate.

Demonstrative moves to show that he had not renounced Israel's right to settle Jews across the "green line," thinly veiled threats to move his office to East Jerusalem to dramatize the permanence of Israeli control in all of its capital, angry outbursts at Carter for promising King Hussein more than the Camp David Accords contained to bring him to the negotiating table, disparagement of any possible role for Saudi Arabia in the process—these provocations were largely aimed at protecting Begin's domestic political flanks. But they infuriated Carter and Sadat and undermined whatever slight chance existed to bring Jordan into the game.

Moreover, for Begin and his colleagues, nailing down the peace treaty with Egypt was the first priority, and every "t" had to be carefully crossed because the withdrawal of Israel's now formidable defenses, abandonment of several Jewish towns such as Yamit, and loss of all of the "strategic space" in Sinai was hard even for Labor party doves to contemplate. In any event, that treaty required six agonizing months to complete instead of the planned three. Arcane arguments over legal interpretation of Egypt's other treaty obligations to its Arab League partners consumed weeks, driving Carter to near distraction. Meanwhile, America's close ally, the shah of Iran, was crumbling, and oil prices were again skyrocketing. U.S. strategy in the Middle East seemed hostage to Begin's preoccupation with legalisms.

Apprehensive that his hard-won achievement was slipping away, Carter in March 1979 again invested his maximum political prestige to close the deal. He flew to Cairo and then to Jerusalem for a final round of tense, acrimonious, cliff-hanging negotiations with Begin and his cabinet. Success when it came was sweet, but it was also expensive. Not only did the United States agree to finance a large share of the cost of withdrawal of Israeli military installations and air bases in Sinai, after Carter had vowed privately that he "would not buy their peace," but Egypt joined Israel in the privileged class of aid recipients. Camp David established a level of economic dependency on U.S. aid for both nations that continues a decade later to infect otherwise healthy U.S. ties to its two Camp David partners.

Until he left office in January 1981, Carter continued doggedly to pursue the goal of Palestinian autonomy agreed on at Camp David. His two special diplomatic negotiators, Robert S. Strauss and then Sol M. Linowitz, struggled to infuse the Israeli and Egyptian delegations with the American perception that time was a wasting asset. They failed. Begin was by now fearful that he might have inadvertently planted the seeds for an independent Palestinian state in his autonomy proposal; the criticism of his political friends had left their mark. He inspected each draft with a microscope for telltale flaws. His negotiating team was an unwieldly group of cabinet ministers divided among themselves and operating on a very short leash. (Foreign Minister Moshe Dayan, the intellectual spark plug of the Camp David diplomacy, had resigned in frustration and disgust.) Moreover, Israelis were still skeptical about Sadat's commitment to full peace. Steady progress on "normalization" of bilateral relations had to accompany the autonomy negotiations for the latter to progress. Unfortunately the mood music from Cairo was often unpleasantly dissident.

Egypt's overriding priority was the withdrawal of Israeli troops from Sinai on schedule. Confrontation with Israel over Palestinian autonomy should be avoided if possible so as not to risk a blowup that could abort withdrawal. The United States shared that worry, so Carter's team now also shrank from avoidable blowups with Begin. The absence of Jordanian or Palestinian representatives, however, immobilized Egyptian diplomacy. Egypt's representatives, ill-informed about the realities of life in the territories after twelve years of Israeli rule and fearful of Arab and PLO criticism, would not risk making concessions to adjust Palestinian hopes to those new realities.

As the months lengthened, U.S. policymakers increasingly turned to other crises. Carter's campaign for reelection embroiled him in misunderstandings with Jewish supporters. The growing PLO presence in south Lebanon festered, producing terror attacks and Israeli retaliatory or preemptive strikes at awkward moments, which disrupted Egypt's political equilibrium and the pace of negotiations. New West Bank settlements roiled the waters with Washington and Cairo. On March 1, 1980, a miscalculated U.S. vote in favor of a UN Security Council resolution about West Bank settlements and Jerusalem infuriated Israel and humiliated Carter, who was forced by the Jewish political uproar to disown it. Yet he lost Jewish support and the New York primary to Senator Edward M. Kennedy anyway. Begin's cabinet was maneuvered by a right-wing Knesset member into passing a wholly demonstrative, redundant "Jerusalem law," which then produced a diplomatic fire storm, indefinite suspension of formal autonomy negotiations, and a further worsening of Carter's relations with Begin.

With Iran in turmoil and the U.S. embassy staff held hostage in Tehran, the Russian invasion of Afghanistan, Vance's resignation as secretary of state, and the Kennedy challenge to Carter's renomination, the autonomy negotiations between Israel and Egypt slipped low on the administration's list of priorities. Nonetheless, Carter increasingly blamed Israel in private for undermining the consummation of his Camp David dream: a real beginning of a solution to the Palestinian imbroglio.

Had he been reelected, Carter planned to convene another Sadat-Begin summit to relaunch the process, a problematical venture at best with Begin now increasingly rigid, defensive, and defiant and Sadat hemmed in by Arab animosity. Yet the Camp David peacemakers might have surprised the pundits and their own advisers. All three had great personal stakes in preserving their historical achievement; Begin and Sadat even had Nobel Peace Prizes to defend. Free of political constraints imposed by prospects for reelection, Carter would have undoubtedly pressed Begin harder for flexibility, though Begin would surely have pushed back. U.S. policy toward Israel would have been more insistent in a second Carter term, and, conceivably, more successful in launching the design for autonomy.

But Carter never got the chance. His last meeting with Begin occurred the week after his election defeat. A correct, superficially friendly farewell between old friends, it was in reality for Carter a bitter moment. He was deeply disappointed, convinced that his Middle East peace design remained half finished because of Begin's deception, obstruction, and legalistic rigidities. Carter also believed that American Jewish ingratitude had cost him the election despite his tireless efforts on behalf of Israel's search for peace. He nonetheless treated Begin with extraordinary warmth, dignity, and grace. Carter never appeared more presidential than in that hour of defeat. Meanwhile, many Israelis, having braced to resist unbridled pressure from a second Carter administration, welcomed Reagan's victory.

CARTER AND REAGAN

One could not imagine a greater contrast between two presidents. Carter was a unique amalgam of contradictory tendencies: naval officer, engineer, farmer, self-crafted politician, religious missionary. Devotion to duty, tirelessness and a legendary capacity for work, determination to succeed whatever the odds or the political cost, master of detail, enormous self-discipline, conviction that any problem can be solved with enough goodwill and hard work—all those qualities characterized the man. Sincere and persuasive in small groups, he seemed to shrink on symbolic occasions before large audiences. He was familiar with the Bible but had little prior understanding of Jews, especially the Holocaust-scarred generation that still ruled Israel. A cerebral, inner-directed man, he often understood only too well all sides of every issue.

Reagan embodied, instead, a "laid-back" California style: relaxed, emotional, unconsciously but totally self-assured, optimistic, superficial, amusing, with an actor's instinct for symbolic acts, crowds, the spotlight. He had many American Jewish friends and was early exposed to appalling films of Hitler's death camps the images of which remained vivid in his mind and words. A deeply convinced ideological warrior against world communism, totally suspicious of Soviet intentions, Reagan was the United States' first true ideological president. He saw the world struggle in stark terms: good versus evil, democracy versus dictatorship, allies and friends versus enemies. Only strong military defenses can deter and, if need be, protect against evil aggressors.

For Reagan, Israel automatically fell into the categories of democracy and ally, with an admirable army. Carter, by contrast, had a more complex view: Israel deserved U.S. sympathy and its security merited staunch U.S. support, the Jewish people had suffered enormously and had earned their renewed nationhood, and Israelis deserved to live in peace. Yet the Palestinians too had a valid claim on history. They were a displaced, dispossessed people with a legitimate right to nationhood and a "homeland." Israel, though strong, could only achieve lasting peace by accommodating to this parallel reality. Carter saw it as his personal mission to bring this about, for the peoples of the region as well as in the interests of the United States, but primarily for the former.

Carter immersed himself in every aspect of the history-laden Arab-Israeli imbroglio, to the smallest minutiae. He could debate legal interpretations of treaties with Israel's leading lawyers, and biblical history with Begin or Josef Burg, religious scholar and doyen of Israel's National Religious party. Reagan was often hazy on details. He delivered his prepared talking points to Begin from index cards, even in private, then turned quickly to anecdotes. Carter was alternately warmly sympathetic to Israel and coldly confrontational. Reagan evaded personal confrontation, even when, as during the Lebanon war, he was genuinely if briefly angry. When given sharply critical lines to deliver in person, Reagan invariably softened their impact by a smiling, apologetic demeanor. The truth is that Reagan genuinely admired Israeli strength, courage, democracy, and anti-communist convictions. He saw the PLO and the Arab world quite differently. Carter was more ambivalent.

Finally, their management styles helped produce very different policy outcomes. Carter was quarterback for his Middle East team, on the field, calling his own plays, orchestrating his players' moves, utilizing their special talents to carry out multiple assignments. Unlike the Reagan administration, Carter had a team that was remarkably coherent and internally cohesive, at least on Middle East policy. (The Vance-Brzezinski rivalry that hamstrung Carter's Soviet policy was almost absent with respect to Arab-Israeli issues.) Never in recent history have the secretaries of state and defense and their staffs worked so smoothly in harness. Senior civil servants concerned with the Middle East on the National Security Council staff and in the State Department were old colleagues, as were Carter's career ambassadors in nearly all the important Middle East capitals, and they were also utilized as full members of Carter's policy team. Carter often threw spanners into the diplomatic machinery by his penchant for impromptu public remarks about explosive issues, but his team pulled together. He delegated well, while holding the reins firmly in his own hands. The time consumed cost him heavily in other foreign and domestic issues. But he achieved his Camp David victory. His inability to continue that intense level of personal involvement clearly was one factor in the failure to complete the second phase.

By contrast, Reagan's Arab-Israeli policies were beset with internal contradictions, most glaringly obvious over Lebanon. His own management style was more akin to that of a professional football team's owner than its quarterback. He employed extensive delegation of authority; frequent trades of weak players in his central National Security Council adviser position; a strong preference for staff consensus coupled with enduring reluctance to adjudicate key differences or enforce discipline on strong-minded subordinates like his secretary of defense, Caspar W. Weinberger, and his first secretary of state, Alexander M. Haig, Jr., who approached the U.S.-Israeli relationship from widely divergent premises; and stubborn adherence to his basic sympathy and support for Israel as a genuine ally, punctuated by espousal of punitive acts when pressed by Weinberger or other advisers to react to seemingly irresponsible Israeli actions, such as the bombing of Iraq's nuclear reactor near Baghdad early in his presidency.

These differences in style only reinforced, however, more basic differences in priorities that outweighed the fact that both Carter and Reagan believed in a special U.S. responsibility toward Israel. Carter saw Israel through the warp of biblical history and the weft of hard-ball Jewish domestic power. Reagan looked at Israel through the prism of East-West global confrontation as a natural ally.

Carter's preoccupation with the third world helped put Middle

East peacemaking at the top of his global agenda. He dealt with Israel largely as a crucial player in that game, sometimes as partner, often as antagonist, frequently as road block to be surmounted. Reagan's priorities were elsewhere: domestic policies, economic reforms, and a military build-up to better confront Soviet global assertiveness. For the new president, Israel was a genuine military, strategic asset in the East-West cold war, albeit only in one region. But that region's volatility and vulnerability in the wake of the shah's demise, the Soviet invasion of Afghanistan, and the growth of the Soviet military role in Syria made Israel's demonstrated military and intelligence capabilities attractive assets to Reagan, Haig, and William J. Casey at the Central Intelligence Agency. Unfortunately, Israel looked more like a problem than an asset to Weinberger, NSC Adviser William P. Clark, and others who were more impressed by Israel's capacity for complicating U.S. policies in the Arabian peninsula and other strategic Arab capitals, especially under Begin and Defense Minister Ariel Sharon's increasingly assertive and defiant lead. In retrospect, it is not surprising that the Reagan record in the Middle East demonstrates more failure than success in widening Arab-Israeli peace. However, it cannot be denied that Reagan brought Israel and the United States closer together as strategic and political allies than at any time in history, despite the destructive effects of the Lebanon war. There could be no better evidence that national leaders do ultimately exert the determining influence on relations between nation-states.

REAGAN AND BEGIN—FLIES LAND EARLY IN THE OINTMENT

The Reagan administration took office fully intending to cooperate closely with Israel but in no hurry to pick up the dangling ends of Carter's Camp David process. Secretary Haig had long admired the Israel Defense Forces (IDF) and regarded Begin with more than grudging admiration, unlike Carter and his weary team for whom Begin's charm had long since faded. When Haig made his first Middle East trip in early April 1981, he spoke forthrightly in public and in semiprivate sessions with the Israeli cabinet about Soviet and Syrian threats to the region and the Israeli role in the regional balance, bluntly condemning current Syrian attacks on Lebanese Maronite Christian militia groups in central Lebanon. Haig's militant language made a strongly favorable impact in Jerusalem. It also conveyed a mistaken impression that the Reagan administration as a whole would welcome Israeli military intervention in defense of the Lebanese Christians.

From this early juncture, U.S.-Israeli relations in the Reagan era were repeatedly plagued by mixed signals from Reagan's divided team. Israeli planes downed two Syrian helicopters over Lebanon's Bekaa Valley on April 28, thereby violating an unwritten "red line" agreement brokered by Kissinger in 1976. President Hafiz al-Asad immediately ordered surface-to-air missiles (SAMs) into Lebanon to threaten the Israeli reconnaissance flights that regularly scanned Lebanese terrain for signs of threatening PLO military concentrations.

The fat was now in the fire for both Reagan and Begin. Lebanon would prove to be the dominant issue in U.S.-Israeli relations for the next three years, an issue handled dreadfully by both governments. Though only Begin eventually withdrew from office, in September 1983, under the shadow of Israel's tragic Lebanon adventure, Reagan too suffered a humiliating foreign policy defeat. He eventually committed substantial marine and naval forces to defend a weak Lebanese government against Syrian-supported Muslim militias in pursuit of what he publicly defined as a "vital American interest," only to withdraw them ignominiously in February 1984 as Syria's allies shattered Lebanon's largely Christian army. The myth of American omnipotence, already badly tarnished by Carter's Iran hostage crisis and the failed military rescue attempt, now lay shattered in the ruins of an American embassy and a marine barracks in Beirut. Rulers throughout the region stepped back to assess more carefully the constancy of U.S. security commitments. The cautionary effects of Lebanon on America's friends in the Persian Gulf would condition their initial reactions three and one-half years later, in the twilight of the Reagan presidency, when American naval and air might was again offered to shore up the defenses of weak Arab states, this time against Iranian depredations.

Only a few weeks after Haig's trip in 1981 Begin and Reagan, natural ideological allies, began to quarrel over, of all things, arms supplies. Newly appointed presidential envoy Philip C. Habib at first worked harmoniously with Begin in a high-profile but unsuccessful shuttle attempt to negotiate withdrawal of the Syrian SAM missiles to make unnecessary any Israeli attack on their sites. Then, however, Begin unexpectedly launched his air force in a daring raid on Baghdad to destroy the new Iraqi nuclear reactor before it went "critical." Reagan was astounded, most of all at the seeming absence of any prior consultation with Israel's "close ally" on a matter that clearly affected important U.S. interests in the Arab world. (In fact, there had been extensive secret consultation about the Iraqi nuclear problem during Carter's last months in office. Inexplicably the issue had then been largely overlooked by Reagan's team.) Haig secretly admired Israel's military feat but had to cope with a mushroom cloud of political fallout in Cairo, other Arab capitals, Europe, and the United Nations. Begin had unintentionally humiliated Sadat in Arab eyes by launching the strike only four days after the two leaders had finally, after a long estrangement, met at Sharm al-Sheikh in Israeli-occupied southern Sinai. The reported use of U.S.-supplied F-16 aircraft for the raid stimulated angry outcries in the Pentagon and elsewhere in Washington; the administration ordered an investigation of possible Israeli violations of the Arms Export Control Act and then, more shocking to Begin, took the unprecedented step of suspending shipments of four F-16s already paid for by Israel. The U.S. representative at the United Nations, Jeane J. Kirkpatrick, joined in a unanimous UN Security Council resolution that strongly condemned Israeli action; all this "punishment" for an action Begin believed was justified in order to spare the Jewish people from an Iraqi nuclear bomb, which his intelligence experts told him could be ready in one to three years. The first Reagan-Begin rift had opened; there would be many more.

Those eventful first nine months of Reagan's term established many patterns for subsequent years. Reagan launched his proposal to sell highly sophisticated surveillance planes with airborne warning and control systems (AWACS) to Saudi Arabia, finally prevailing by two Senate votes but only after a bitter struggle with Israel's supporters in Congress. The PLO stepped up pressure on Israel's northern border. Cross border raids, Katyusha rocket attacks, and long-range artillery spurred massive, disproportionate Israeli retaliation on PLO targets inside Beirut, producing hundreds of civilian casualties and triggering more temporary, but infuriating, suspensions of F-16 and F-15 deliveries. By the time the peripatetic Habib had achieved a cease-fire between Israel and the PLO on July 24, 1981, relations between Washington and Jerusalem were significantly strained: an omen of the hot summer in Lebanon to come in 1982.

Yet, all the while, another U.S. envoy, Michael E. Sterner, was successfully concluding arrangements to put in place the key insurance policy for Israel's scheduled withdrawal from Sinai: a multinational peacekeeping force formed under American auspices to replace the planned United Nations force, which the UN, intimidated by the threat of a Soviet veto in the Security Council, would not furnish.

Indeed, two contradictory trends were emerging during Reagan's first months: the peacemakers in Washington, Cairo, and Jerusalem were plodding slowly forward to complete and preserve the Camp David legacy. At the same time, however, war clouds were gathering on the horizon. The hounds of war were barking loudly from PLO strongholds in Lebanon and from Damascus; in certain offices in Jerusalem and Tel Aviv other hounds were straining at their leashes. Two unrelated events combined to tip the scales away from the peacemakers: Begin's unprecedented, come-from-behind victory over the Labor party on June 30 after a bitter demagogic campaign, and the assassination of Anwar Sadat on October 6.

Begin's second term as prime minister began in July 1981 inauspiciously for the Reagan administration. His new cabinet lacked the moderate voices of Moshe Dayan, Ezer Weizman, and Yigael Yadin who had softened the ideological rigidity of his initial coalition. General Ariel Sharon, doughty champion of rapid Jewish settlement in the occupied territories and ruthless foe of Israel's enemy, the PLO, finally achieved his lifelong goal: minister of defense. Subtler but equally significant was a change in Begin's own approach to peacemaking and to Israel's enemies. He had been a political outsider all his life, the loser of six straight elections. He was surprised by his success in 1977 and initially reached out as prime minister for acceptance, approval, and legitimacy. He listened on occasion to cautionary advice from veteran Israeli leaders and even some Americans. Now, however, he had been vindicated by the people, rallying his party from a position far behind in the polls. It was, without a doubt, Begin's personal victory. Moreover, it came after he had also served as defense minister for more than a year, making the lonely decision to launch the dangerous long-distance strike on the Iraqi reactor. Always before somewhat in awe of generals, Begin now felt confident of his military judgments as well as his political mastery. Unfortunately for Reagan, the Begin he now would deal with had largely put aside doubts, moderate advice, and much sense of proportion.

Then there was Sadat's sudden, tragic eclipse only six months before the final Israeli withdrawal from Egyptian soil was scheduled to crown his greatest achievement. In their final meeting at Alexandria only a few weeks before Sadat was killed, Begin and Sadat had finally begun to achieve a certain personal respect and warmth. Had Sadat lived, the relationship between the two men might have provided some insurance that peacemaking would not be totally eclipsed as the PLO's challenge to Israel from Lebanese bases loomed larger in succeeding months. Of the Camp David peace partners, two were now gone.

Reagan's administration eventually endorsed the autonomy negotiations and Camp David but with limited enthusiasm for a symbol that bore the brand of Reagan's defeated opponent. In any case, Reagan's overall approach to the region embodied different priorities. Checkmating Soviet designs and Soviet clients outweighed the search for peaceful accommodations of thorny, perhaps insoluble, regional disputes. And for Begin, Camp David meant primarily achieving a normal peace with Egypt. To the extent that peacemaking continued to compete with Lebanon for the attention of U.S. and Israeli leaders, the primary problem addressed was how to complete Israeli withdrawal from Sinai successfully and achieve full peace with Egypt. Without Sadat, Israeli fears and doubts multiplied far beyond President Husni Mubarak's capacity for reassurance. Frenzied American diplomacy would repeatedly have to plug leaks right up to the moment of final withdrawal in April 1982; only thus could those Israeli "hawks" like Sharon, now hoping to sabotage the treaty and postpone final withdrawal, be thwarted. The rest of the Camp David promise had to wait.

BEGIN AND REAGAN— A SLIPPERY SLOPE OF MISCALCULATION

Begin chafed in frustration for more than half a year after Reagan's inauguration at his inability to sit down face-to-face with the new president. He admired Reagan's speeches and worldview and was confident they would be on the same wavelength about Middle East issues and Israel's role as a U.S. strategic asset. The Israeli electoral campaign had consumed nearly the first half of 1981; to avoid any appearance of intervening in internal Israeli politics, the White House had diplomatically discouraged high-level Israeli visitors until after the election on June 30. Then, because the results were nearly a dead heat, it took Begin more than a month to patch together his new coalition cabinet, with Yitzhak Shamir remaining as foreign minister and Sharon moving into Defense. Finally Begin arrived in Washington the second week of September.

That first day's encounter with Reagan proved to be the high-water mark in official U.S.-Israeli relations during Begin's second cabinet. From that time until Begin dispiritedly left office in September 1983, his cabinet's rapport with the Reagan administration rapidly declined, with only brief temporary upswings. In retrospect, one can see that the misunderstandings, sharp disagreements, suspicions, and bitter personal animosities that increasingly marred the relationship stemmed to a great extent from two factors: Begin's heightened self-confidence and his over-emphasis on his ideological affinity with Reagan, spurred on and heightened by Sharon's condescension and burning ambition; and Reagan's too ready acquiescence to Begin's proposal for a formal "strategic cooperation agreement" with elements of the first, genuine, formal alliance between the two nations.

Begin had always sought, without notable success, to convince Carter that Israel was far more than a client state, more than merely a sentimental responsibility for the United States. He repeatedly argued that Israeli intelligence capabilities and the advanced state of ready professionalism in the IDF were important strategic assets for the United States. Propositions that had seemed highly dubious to Carter now fell on many receptive ears around the cabinet room table, especially Reagan's and Haig's. When Begin proposed to Reagan the elaboration of a formal agreement on strategic cooperation, Reagan casually agreed, believing that this pact would also smooth the road for parallel U.S. strategic arrangements and arms sales to moderate Arab states. The details were to be worked out by Sharon and Weinberger. First, however, at Begin's suggestion, Sharon sketched out for the Americans present in the White House a broad blueprint of potential areas of regional military cooperation of embarrassing pretension. Weinberger and others blanched, but the die was cast for much that unhappily followed.

Begin had scarcely left the Oval Office when a first misunderstanding erupted. Reagan apparently believed he had obtained Begin's private promise not to lobby against the sale of AWACS planes to Saudi Arabia. Begin had indeed promised, but he did not interpret "no lobbying" as a prohibition against expressing his opposition to the sale when queried. When the question was posed to him by members of Congress during his by now ritual meetings with senators and representatives, Begin had responded with habitual forcefulness. Reports of Begin's remarks immediately traveled to the White House where they sparked angry outbursts from Reagan's senior advisers. Haig was left to try to smooth over the misunderstanding. Throughout the next month, a bitter AWACS battle raged in the Senate. Weinberger's clumsy effort to use the negotiations over the strategic agreement as a carrot to weaken Israel's opposition to the sale only worsened things. By the time Reagan had won narrowly in the Senate, much of the good feeling from Begin's meeting had disappeared.

Weinberger finally grudgingly signed with Sharon on November 30 a document replete with the symbolism of Israeli "equality" for Begin but devoid of much substantive content for Sharon; it was a pale version of Israel's original proposal. (To minimize adverse publicity in the Arab world, Weinberger inserted multiple references to cooperation against possible Soviet threats and scheduled the signing ceremony in a locale that was off limits to the press corps.) Sharon had long since concluded that the watered-down agreement was worthless. For Begin, however, it was a symbolic achievement of high order. Sharon was compelled to defend it with glowing phrases in the Israeli Knesset debate that followed.

Meanwhile, Begin had slipped in his bathtub, broken his hip, and been confined to a hospital bed for a prolonged period. Suddenly, without warning, he summoned key associates to his bedside and proposed annexation of the Golan Heights, purportedly in angry reaction to a public statement by President Asad of Syria that rejected indefinitely any idea of peace with Israel. The legislation, which technically only extended Israeli law to the Golan, slid through Begin's submissive cabinet and then the Knesset with such unparalleled speed that the United States had no real chance to intervene diplomatically and thus gain time for more careful reflection. Indeed, Begin seems to have calculated his timing to preclude effective U.S. intervention.

To the Reagan administration, just then coping with a nasty crisis in Poland, the Golan law was an intolerable fait accompli. Though Syria was hardly a favored U.S. Middle East player, nonetheless Israel's preemptive act seemed to foreclose any return to a broader Arab-Israeli peace process, an avowed U.S. policy goal. Most important, the action seemed deliberately provocative to the United States. The administration believed it had finally achieved an understanding with Begin that precluded unilateral surprises on issues, such as the Baghdad reactor strike, that affected broad U.S. interests in the region. In U.S. eyes, the new understanding on strategic cooperation, though it did not refer specifically to "prior consultation" on such matters, embodied an implicit understanding with Israel for full consultation. The United States obviously had a major interest in the peace process and should, at a minimum, have had a proper opportunity to make the case against an action that was seen by Washington to violate various UN resolutions and the Camp David Accords.

The denouement came swiftly. Only nineteen days after signing, the new U.S.-Israeli Memorandum of Understanding on Strategic Cooperation was unilaterally "suspended" by Reagan, pending satisfactory clarification about future consultation on major issues. Two days later, Begin summoned me to his residence in Jerusalem to absorb a fifty-minute tirade bitterly denouncing this action, then immediately had it repeated for the waiting journalists. Begin's command of vituperative oratory has seldom been equaled among contemporary leaders; this was a memorable performance, replete with colorful rhetorical questions such as, "Are we a vassal state? Are we a banana republic? Are we fourteen-year-olds who, if we misbehave, get our wrists slapped?" When my telegram and media accounts of Begin's extraordinary tongue lashing reached the White House, the thermometer plunged to subzero. Needless to say, the suspended memorandum was never revived, and the deep chill spread between Washington and Jerusalem by these events lightened only marginally for short periods during the rest of Begin's period in office.

Yet Israel and the United States are much too entangled to allow their leaders the luxury of prolonged avoidance of one another. Haig and other members of the administration soon tried to repair relations. The darkening cloud of an impending Israeli-PLO clash in Lebanon spurred the United States to try to retain some restraining hand on the increasingly bellicose Begin and his defense minister. Moreover, Washington was determined to ensure full implementation of the treaty of peace with Egypt in April 1982. To thwart the suspected designs of Sharon and others to prevent final Israeli withdrawal, the Reagan administration had to restore a personal rapport with Begin, and with Sharon for that matter. Haig traveled to Jerusalem in mid-January to do so. Meanwhile Begin had made clear that he continued to value his special personal relationship with me and that the "banana republic" lecture was aimed at the Reagan administration in Washington. Channels therefore remained open between the governments. But personalized animus toward Begin grew steadily in Washington, and he was delicately advised against making a planned visit in January. His fond hope of consolidating a close alliance with Reagan dissolved in long-distance exchanges of public diatribes with other members of the Reagan administration. And all the while, as counterpoint, the drums of war grew louder.

THE LEBANESE SWAMP

Israel's disastrous Lebanon war has already spawned a large and growing body of literature. Scholars and journalists have described the military operations, the civilian destruction, the internal debates and miscalculations, and the shattering impact of the war and its prolonged denouement on Lebanon, the PLO, and Israel. Rather than plumb those murky pools again here, I will focus on the effects of the war on U.S.-Israeli relations. Many diplomatic details remain secret, but the outlines of the story are now in the public domain.

Throughout the Carter years, Lebanon had repeatedly intruded into efforts at Arab-Israeli peacemaking. Almost as if by design, critical high-level U.S.-Israeli meetings had to be diverted from key issues in negotiations to cope with the diplomatic fallout from flare-ups along the Israel-Lebanon border. PLO raids, retaliatory strikes by the IDF, UN Security Council emergency sessions, confrontations over U.S. diplomatic responses to Arab pleas for U.S. condemnation of Israel's actions plagued both Carter and Reagan. The Carter administration, however, consistently refused to accord Lebanon any sustained attention. In contrast, Lebanon dominated Reagan's Middle East policy agenda for nearly the entire first term of his presidency.

Begin had reluctantly accepted the cease-fire with the PLO, achieved through Habib's mediation in July 1981, only because the IDF had been unable to silence the elusive sources of PLO's rocket and artillery attacks on Israel's northern towns. He and Sharon seethed at the recognition of the PLO implied in the Habib "understandings." Although, along the border, the cease-fire held in large measure for the next eleven months, Palestinian attacks on Israelis elsewhere and on Jews in European cities continued from time to time, while a buildup of PLO military strength just north of the border went on apace. As 1981 gave way to 1982, Sharon repeatedly warned American officials and journalists that Israel would not long tolerate this state of affairs. In a now well-publicized meeting with Habib and his deputy, Morris Draper, in Jerusalem on December 6, 1981, the defense minister shocked his incredulous listeners with a far-reaching concept for his preferred solution—a large-scale invasion to crush all PLO strongholds in Lebanon and expel the Palestinian fighters once and for all. Though he was careful to stress that these were only his personal views, which he doubted his cabinet colleagues would ever approve, he delivered an ominous warning and ignored Habib's vigorous remonstrations.

In succeeding months the impending attack was telegraphed repeatedly by well-informed Israeli journalists and by Ambassador Moshe Arens in Washington. Begin sent his chief of military intelligence secretly to Washington in early February to warn Haig that, unless the United States took vigorous actions to halt PLO depredations, the IDF would have to act; this time there should be no cause for Washington to complain about being surprised. Indeed, by the time the border erupted with massive PLO rocket attacks in early June 1982 (a predictable response to the heavy Israeli bombing of PLO bases launched to retaliate for a Palestinian assassination attempt on Israel's ambassador in London), a large-scale Israeli attack had clearly become inevitable. Only the triggering incident could have been in doubt. This was a war just waiting to happen.

For six months, Haig, Habib, Draper, other U.S. officials, and I had urged maximum restraint, cautioned against exaggerating the PLO military threat, railed against the danger of triggering a major war with Syria, and stressed the broader international implications of unrestrained Israeli military retaliation. All to no avail. Only a harsh ultimatum from Reagan could have further postponed the increasingly inevitable clash. But Reagan and some key members of his administration understood Israel's security dilemma and sympathized with its frustrations. Believing firmly in the right of legitimate self-defense for the United States as well as for Israel, none of Reagan's representatives would say flatly that Israel must not defend its citizens against attacks. But as Haig stressed to Sharon in their Washington encounter on May 25, it was vitally important that, if Israel had to act, its actions be proportionate to the threat and defensible before the world.

Thus, when the Israeli attack finally came on June 6, Reagan and Haig initially accepted Begin's public and private assurances that Operation Peace for Galilee was intended only to push PLO units out of artillery and rocket range of Israel, approximately forty kilometers, and that Israel had no desire to engage Syrian forces in any way. In the days that followed, it dawned only slowly on the Reagan team, as it dawned slowly on most of the Israeli cabinet, Knesset, and public, that the IDF was courting ground and aerial clashes with Syrian forces in Lebanon and was advancing purposely on PLO headquarters in the Beirut suburbs. Operation Peace for Galilee looked more and more like Sharon's personal grand concept for driving the PLO from Lebanese soil.

With that realization, the Reagan administration became schizophrenic about Israel, Lebanon, and the PLO, a condition from which it did not begin to recover until more than a year later and whose symptoms remained prominent until early in 1984. Though he had tried to discourage any attack, once it was launched Haig saw a strategic opportunity for the United States if the PLO were indeed eliminated from the Lebanese equation and if the Soviet Union's client, Syria, were forced to relax its stranglehold on eastern Lebanon. He maneuvered diplomatically to give the IDF a chance to achieve those goals during the confused weeks that followed. Haig was, however, thwarted by the slowness of the Israeli advance, by a rising public and international uproar as Beirut came within Israeli gunsights, by divided councils within Reagan's team where he usually found the vice president, the NSC adviser, and the secretary of defense arrayed against him, by contradictory signals from the White House to both Israel and the PLO, and eventually by Reagan's decision to drop him from the cabinet in the middle of the Lebanese crisis to restore harmony to his official family.

From the moment it became apparent to Washington that Israeli objectives went far beyond the proclaimed forty-kilometer security zone, U.S.-Israeli relations began to fray. The downward grade steepened once Haig had left the scene. Begin met Reagan in Washington the third week in June; his reassurances about Israel's intentions already met considerable skepticism. Over the next two months, the United States saw countless broken cease-fires, creeping Israeli advances closer to Beirut's core, and heartrending television pictures of civilian casualties from IDF shelling and bombing of the besieged city. Finally, as Habib's desperate efforts to negotiate a PLO withdrawal from Beirut seemed repeatedly sabotaged by Israeli military pressures, the White House mood turned bitter.

Begin's personal loss of credibility with Reagan was the most damaging consequence. Begin had always been prickly and difficult, but he was a man of his word when he gave it. Now, repeatedly, Begin's assurances to Washington about Israeli military intentions in the Beirut battle were exposed to ridicule. Sharon was feeding Begin inaccurate battle information that he passed on uncritically to U.S. leaders. By the time Habib finally coaxed the PLO to leave Beirut in late August, a decision the PLO reached only under the spur of the heavy bombing raids that so angered the White House, Begin's credibility in Washington had nearly dissolved. The last reservoirs were drained during mid-September when, in the wake of Bashir Gemayal's assassination in east Beirut, Begin and Sharon sent the IDF into the heart of west Beirut in violation of a commitment to Reagan. The IDF then stood by passively while Christian Phalangist troops massacred hundreds of Palestinian civilians left undefended after the PLO fighters evacuated the refugee camps of Sabra and Shatila.

The White House quickly digested the damning implications of this atrocity. U.S. good faith assurances had been passed to Yasir Arafat regarding the safety of those Palestinian camps as part of the negotiation leading to PLO evacuation. Those assurances were in turn based on Begin's commitments to Habib that the IDF would not enter west Beirut. So, swept by a wave of guilt for having only days earlier withdrawn the U.S. Marine contingent from the multinational peacekeeping force in Beirut, Reagan made a hasty, ill-advised decision to send them back into the Beirut maelstrom. U.S., French, and Italian units then deployed in west Beirut to replace Israeli forces that Sharon grudgingly pulled back to the city's outskirts under extreme U.S. diplomatic pressure. The stage now seemed set for the United States to take control of Lebanese events, train and equip a Lebanese army capable of ensuring internal security, bring about a prompt Israeli withdrawal, strengthen the new Lebanese government of President Amin Gemayal, and broker an agreement between Lebanon and Israel that would contain the key elements of peace if not the name. What followed produced instead ignominious defeat for both Israel and the United States.

Israel as a truly democratic society regained some credit in Washington when huge popular demonstrations forced a defiant Begin to authorize a thorough judicial inquiry into the tragic events at Sabra and Shatila. Yet the damage to Begin's relationship with Washington was now irreparable. He still hoped to restore it in a visit to the White House in November; that opportunity evaporated when Begin's wife died in Jerusalem while he was in Los Angeles prior to going to Washington. Shattered by her loss, he flew home, never to return. Ten months later he retired from office into permanent seclusion, physically and mentally competent but afflicted with an unshakable depression that destroyed his will to continue in public life.

From the early autumn of 1982 until February 1983, the relationship between Jerusalem and Washington stayed bitterly confrontational as the Lebanon imbroglio deepened. Israel's dream of signing its second peace treaty with an Arab state had exploded with Bashir Gemayal's headquarters, but the hope died hard. Indeed, with Syria temporarily cowed by the IDF's victories over Asad's forces, U.S. and Israeli diplomats cooperated warily but closely to try to persuade Bashir Gemayal's brother, Amin, to negotiate a broad agreement, under which Israeli troops would withdraw, Lebanon would inaugurate normal relations with Israel including open borders, and Lebanese and Israeli military units would collaborate to ensure tranquillity in the border areas.

Meanwhile, however, at the military level, any U.S. cooperation with Israel in connection with Lebanon was strictly verboten. Sharon's high-handed, insulting manner of dealing with American officials, earlier somewhat tempered by Begin's courtesy, now exceeded all bounds. He saw U.S. plots under every rock to "steal from Israel the fruits of its victory" by forcing an Israeli withdrawal without political gains. Moreover, Weinberger and his colleagues were determined to protect the U.S. relationship with strategic Arab nations like Saudi Arabia by ostentatiously differentiating in every way possible between the "peacemaking role" assumed by the U.S. Marines and the role of "illegal temporary occupier" by the IDF. The results were often farcical. One example made worldwide front pages when an American marine officer was photographed apparently halting three Israeli tanks near U.S. lines with his pistol. Though U.S. carrier-based aircraft and the Israeli air force were operating in the same limited air space, the U.S. Air Force was forbidden for weeks by high-level orders from establishing any communications link with the Israeli air force to guard against possibly tragic accidents. Other examples were legion. U.S. diplomacy and military policy seemed to emanate from different governments.

Even diplomatic cooperation proved extraordinarily complicated. Sharon dominated Israeli decisionmaking on Lebanon. He was determined to reach a secret agreement with President Gemayal away from the prying noses of Habib, Draper, and other U.S. diplomats and then flaunt it before them as a surprise, which he did on December 17. While negotiating privately through a trusted Lebanese Christian intermediary, he had raised especially provocative issues in cabinet meetings, such as the proposal that Israel should refuse to negotiate at all unless the Lebanese diplomats would come to Jerusalem. His ploys created endless obstacles to U.S. efforts to bring Gemayal's and Begin's formal representatives together at the negotiating table. Ultimately, Israel lost whatever slim chance there might have been for a durable agreement as a consequence of these stalling tactics. Sharon's compulsion to humiliate the United States led him to leak to a journalist his secret deal with Gemayal, thereby forcing Gemayal to back away from it to protect his political flanks.

By the time formal tripartite negotiations were finally convened at the end of December, Syrian self-confidence had been rejuvenated by a massive resupply of Soviet arms. Syria began to exert pressure on Gemayal to hold back; negotiations were drawn out for more than four months as Begin's negotiators sought to squeeze as many elements of a formal peace treaty into the agreement as possible in exchange for withdrawal. Secretary of State George P. Shultz finally had to join Habib for a shuttle to bring the May 17 agreement to completion, but Syria was by then determined and well positioned to torpedo it, which soon occurred. Indeed, had the commission investigating the Sabra and Shatila massacres not intervened in February to remove Sharon from his powerful Defense Ministry post, it is highly unlikely that the May 17 agreement would ever have been reached at all.

Washington's assessment of Sharon, and indeed of Begin, had by early 1983 become so harsh that the U.S.-Israeli "natural alliance" acclaimed by Reagan and Haig only two years earlier seemed little more than an empty husk. One might argue that was an indirect consequence of Camp David. Unanimous Arab opinion, and some Western analysts as well, are convinced that Israel would never have undertaken its Lebanon invasion had the peace treaty with Egypt not given Begin a sense of security about Israel's southern border. I do not share that judgment. Begin and Sharon were supremely overconfident about the IDF's ability to root out the PLO in a matter of a few days without triggering a wider conflict with Syria. Moreover they judged correctly that Egypt had only a marginal concern about Yasir Arafat and his colleagues. Only a much more cautious leadership team in Jerusalem might have acted differently had the IDF still been encamped close to the Suez Canal.

A FRESH START—A SLOW CONVALESCENCE

The years 1983 and 1984 were years of transition in U.S.-Israeli relations. Suspicion, bitterness, and confrontation began to give way to renewed diplomatic and military cooperation as the months passed. The most important explanation lies in changes of central dramatis personae.

Begin slowly faded as the central Israeli player. Depressed and listless, he withdrew uncharacteristically from active participation in the intricacies of diplomacy. Sharon's departure opened the way for Moshe Arens to return from the ambassador's residence in Washington to the Defense Ministry. Having spent the previous difficult year in the U.S. capital, he knew all too well the damage inflicted on Israel's standing by the war and its aftermath. Moreover, he had been raised and educated in the United States and had a polite, low-key, ingratiating personality that attenuated the impact of his rigid ideology. He was deeply committed to restoring the U.S.-Israeli dialogue to that mode of civility appropriate to the close ties between the two nations. A popular figure in Washington, Arens moved quickly to restore relations with Weinberger and the Pentagon, even as he softened the edges of Israel's demands on the hapless Lebanese.

On the American side, Habib had by now, after two years of

draining frustration, lost some of his professional rudder as a skilled negotiator. The bloody summer of 1982 in Beirut had taken a psychological toll. He had lost some credibility in Israel as a mediator and was by now too openly suspicious of every Israeli move to be fully effective.

Shultz had entered the Middle East scene at a low point in July 1982. His first months as secretary of state produced little but disappointment, and he acquired ample reason to distrust Begin, Sharon, and perhaps Israel. His first major diplomatic initiative, the Reagan peace initiative of September 1, 1982, had met only bitter denunciation from Begin (see appendix D). Yet by early 1983 Shultz and Reagan realized that U.S. policy toward Lebanon would surely fail so long as Israel and the United States were pulling constantly in opposite directions. Moreover, Congress was increasingly unhappy with the administration's approach.

Shultz respected Arens, and as soon as Sharon had left office, Shultz set out to restore a cordial working relationship with Jerusalem. His calm, judicious demeanor and his long experience in labor negotiations facilitated his task and soon gained him great respect from Begin and his colleagues. When Shultz joined Habib at the negotiating table, the May 17 tripartite agreement was soon completed.

The tide then turned. That agreement, never ratified by Lebanon and ultimately repudiated under overwhelming Syrian pressure, was a complete failure in achieving a new, constructive relationship between Lebanon and Israel. But, ironically, the agreement was the bridge back to sanity in relations between Jerusalem and Washington. Once it was signed, Israel and the United States moved finally to the same side with respect to policy toward the crisis with Lebanon and Syria, even though it proved by 1984 to be the losing side. Other elements of the attrited relationship began to heal in the agreement's wake. When Arens and Foreign Minister Shamir visited Washington in July 1983, civilized, far-ranging, productive consultations ensued on the whole range of U.S.-Israeli concerns. For the first time in years, top Israeli and U.S. officials were behaving as friends and colleagues toward one another, wrestling together with the daunting mess that had evolved as an outgrowth of the Israeli invasion. This pattern, with rare exception, now became the norm for the remaining five years of Reagan's presidency.

That pattern survived and indeed deepened despite the slow extinction of hope for the Lebanon agreement; the outbreak of vicious civil strife among Christian, Druze, and Shiite militias after the IDF began to pull back south; the increasing U.S. military involvement in that strife, which led to near, if unwanted, hostilities with Syria; the destruction of the U.S. Marine barracks by a terrorist bomb and the loss of hundreds of marine lives; the collapse of the U.S.-supported Lebanese army and of American and Israeli hopes for seeing a stable government in Beirut that could provide law and order for Lebanon, particularly south Lebanon, to justify total Israeli withdrawal. It even survived the humiliating reversal of Reagan's commitment to uphold Lebanese independence and the withdrawal of U.S. military forces to the offshore fleet, a signal to all countries in the region that Syria had faced down and defeated the United States by proxy war and by tenacious, Machiavellian diplomacy. Indeed, the Lebanese debacle was the nadir in Reagan's presidency prior to the 1986–87 Iran arms sale imbroglio, and many argued that it was Israel's fault. Yet a reborn habit of close collaboration against common adversaries survived and flourished, thanks in large measure to the restraint now exercised by wiser leaders in both capitals. Two bitter years of squabbling had ended, perhaps symbolically, as Begin turned over the prime ministry to Shamir in mid-September 1983. His extraordinary self-imposed withdrawal from public life, accompanied by Sharon's temporary eclipse, permitted the Reagan administration to revert gracefully to its instinctive posture of sympathetic support for Israel.

Shamir and Arens returned to Washington in late November to find concrete reflection of this new era. Collegial discussion of unpleasant choices for both nations dominated the meetings. Shultz offered informal, professional assistance through a joint experts committee to help Shamir come to grips with Israel's escalating inflation. Pentagon purse strings and weapon supply lines reopened. Reagan and Shamir agreed to launch negotiations for a unique bilateral free trade area.

Most significant, the two leaders announced a fresh start on "strategic cooperation" arrangements. Wary of the precedent of the abortive, largely symbolic agreement that Begin and Sharon had obtained in 1981, both sides this time agreed to begin modestly at a professional military level, not to seek any overall agreement. Thus was launched the Joint U.S.-Israel Political-Military Group, which has operated quietly ever since, out of the headlines, with professional staffers exploring areas of overlapping military interests. The results have pleasantly surprised both governments. Shorn of rhetorical political baggage, this effort has proved that it is indeed possible for the IDF and the Pentagon to examine threat contingencies, carry out joint exercises, and coordinate logistical planning in ways that both military establishments find increasingly useful. It has also proved that the United States can work quietly on serious military cooperation with Israel without upsetting parallel strategic relationships in several Arab capitals, including Cairo. Less than a military alliance, this joint effort is strategic cooperation only on subjects on which U.S. and Israeli interests coincide. But the arrangement matches the needs and political limits of the two capitals. Never had Israel drawn so close to its superpower patron as in Reagan's second term. Perhaps the painful lessons from his first term were essential to make it possible, but one thing is certain—it reflects clearly the impact of personnel changes in both governments after the dark days of 1982. Individual leaders, their personalities, and their styles do count.

REAGAN'S APPROACH TO PEACEMAKING

Many Middle Easterners, Europeans, and Americans have criticized Reagan, Haig, and Shultz for allowing the Arab-Israeli peace process to stall. Reagan's administration, it is alleged, emphasized the East-West struggle and strategic-military issues while neglecting to invest enough time, attention, and persistence to carry forward Carter's Camp David legacy. The charge is perhaps partly justified but also exaggerated and unfair. A judgment closer to the mark would be that the Carter administration forced the pace and followed a carefully designed scenario, which, of course, it had to modify and drastically adapt to regional realities after Sadat's Jerusalem trip. With one outstanding exception, Reagan and his advisers followed the peacemakers' vocation only sporadically, in reaction to regional pressures or events. That exception, the so-called Reagan Middle East Peace Initiative of September 1, 1982, carefully crafted in its substance, remained stillborn. Its proposals stayed on the table before the Israelis and Arabs throughout the next six years. Shultz and his State Department associates made strenuous if episodic efforts to convince Jordan, Israel, and some Palestinian elements to espouse it after the Twelfth Arab League summit in Fez, Morocco, early in September 1982 did not explicitly reject it, though the summit adopted the Arabs' own "Fez plan" (see appendix E). But Begin's immediate, intemperate rejection of the initiative chilled Reagan's enthusiasm and doomed its proponents to trudge with it endlessly through the halls of Middle East diplomatic mirrors. That rejection was probably inescapable, but flawed tactics and timing hardened the Israeli reaction and converted a probable failure into a certain one.

Reagan's team had its reasons in late August 1982 for attempting to turn the focus away from Lebanon to the broader problem of peace. The PLO was scattering in disarray; Jordan seemed temporarily better able to respond to a peace initiative without fear of Syrian retaliation; Egypt would be strongly supportive; and, most telling, the looming Arab summit might take decisions that would again preclude any Jordanian role with respect to the West Bank and Gaza. Jordan was the key to further progress now that the Egyptian-Israeli peace treaty had taken hold and had withstood the pressures on Egypt from the Lebanese invasion. Above all, Reagan wanted to recapture the political initiative in the region after U.S. prestige had suffered heavily from the bloody Lebanon summer.

Nonetheless, for Begin the idea of a major U.S. initiative at that moment seemed surrealistic. He had just watched with relish the departure of PLO fighters from Beirut and had gone north to the seacoast resort town of Nahariyya for a week's rest after a long, tumultuous, draining summer, his first vacation in five years. He was preparing to break it briefly to meet the newly elected Lebanese president, Bashir Gemayal, to arrange for the peace treaty Israel had now "won" at heavy cost. When I appeared unexpectedly in Nahariyya on the afternoon of August 31 with Reagan's message describing the proposals he intended to announce publicly almost immediately, a weary Begin was stunned. The content of the message was bad enough, including old issues like a "settlements freeze" and an expansion of the Camp David understanding to include a clear U.S. expression of support for separation of the West Bank from Israel. The realization that the United States had consulted in advance with King Hussein, not Israel, and was even then consulting with Saudi Arabia and Egypt without awaiting Begin's reaction further inflamed him. The result was predictable: fiery denunciation, a hastily called cabinet meeting to ratify Begin's furious reaction, which was subsequently reinforced by a Knesset vote, premature leaks, and demonstrative cabinet announcements about new West Bank settlements.

Beyond these atmospherics, however, the timing was wholly unpropitious for a more fundamental reason. Israel was preoccupied with Lebanon, the overriding, all-consuming, national priority. Until the results of the war were digested, the troops headed home, and a new relationship fixed with Beirut that was at least akin to formal peace, no Israeli leader would have been ready or able to tackle the toughest political nut of all, the future of the West Bank. Shimon Peres as opposition leader could afford the luxury of supporting Reagan's initiative. Had he been prime minister at that time his diplomatic room for maneuver would have been far more restricted.

It was a waste of well-designed proposals. And Reagan's tactics of presentation only increased the likelihood of confrontation between Jerusalem and Washington. No chance would exist for any reconsideration in Jerusalem so long as Begin and the Likud party were in power. All the ensuing months of effort that Shultz expended to elicit a clear acceptance from Hussein were beside the point, and when an answer was finally extracted in April 1983, it was negative.

Having launched the initiative only after being assured by American envoys that Hussein would support it, Reagan and Shultz were left dangling by both key protagonists, Hussein and Begin. No wonder the Reagan administration turned its greatest attention elsewhere thereafter. Contrary to popular mythology, Shultz was not chastened by his failed Lebanon agreement. Rather, he learned some hard lessons about Middle East political realities from that outcome and from the abortive Reagan initiative. When next he entered the peacemaking lists, it would be in support of initiatives generated from within the region, not by Washington.

Peres became prime minister of a new national unity government coalition in September 1984, serving for two years before having to trade jobs with his uncomfortable coalition partner, Foreign Minister Shamir. Much of Peres's energy had to go toward coping with, and eventually containing, a chaotic, runaway inflation and a foreign exchange crisis that were only two of the bitter legacies from the Lebanon war and seven years of Likud economic policies under Begin and Shamir. Nonetheless, peacemaking occupied a high priority for Peres, and he began immediately to engage Shultz and Reagan in a subtle strategy to coax Hussein into negotiations.

He also invited American help to resolve a lingering border dispute with Egypt over the minuscule Taba beach near Eilat. Rekindling some warmth in the by-then frigid Egyptian-Israeli peace was essential to condition the Israeli public for making further concessions for peace with Jordan when that time came, Peres reasoned. U.S. diplomats turned to the task with energy and tenacity, serving repeatedly as "honest brokers" with Egyptian and Israeli negotiators as the months passed. Often stymied by Shamir and his Likud coalition partners, Peres finally achieved agreement with Egyptian President Mubarak only one month before his term as prime minister ended. That agreement required vigorous interventions by Shultz, a shuttle by Assistant Secretary Richard W. Murphy and Legal Adviser Abraham Sofaer, and a personal push from Vice President George Bush. The Reagan team did what was necessary to reinforce Carter's peace treaty.

But King Hussein was Peres's prime target. Operating within the narrow strictures of his coalition agreement with Likud, he employed a multitude of means to persuade Hussein to cooperate in Peres's strategy of launching negotiations in a framework that would initially include his Likud coalition partners. He counted on thus being able to dramatize the chance for peace sufficiently to win a new election and form his own Labor government in order subsequently to reach a peace settlement on terms Hussein might accept, but which Likud would surely never support.[2] Unfortunately for Peres, Hussein was pursuing a different agenda, trying to ensnare Yasir Arafat into playing a subordinate role for a joint approach to peace negotiations. Without Arafat, Hussein did not feel strong enough to risk Syrian opposition to direct Jordanian-Israeli negotiations. By the time Hussein abandoned that effort in disgust in early 1986, Peres's term was nearing its end. Yet Hussein apparently did not credit Peres's warnings that delay could derail the whole strategy.

Peres continued to pursue Hussein energetically, ignoring the fact that his position was much weakened in October 1986 by exchanging the Prime Ministry for the Foreign Ministry. Earlier, secret encounters with the king had convinced him that Hussein needed an international umbrella to risk direct negotiations. Peres had, therefore, begun advocating an international conference, including the Soviet Union and other Security Council members, defying Shamir's adamant opposition to any such Soviet role or indeed any broad conference at all. In London in April 1987, Peres and Hussein finally agreed on arrangements for the conference, but Shamir blocked any implementation (see appendix G).

Throughout all of these maneuvers, Peres assiduously kept Shultz informed, sought his advice and support, and coordinated his moves with Washington. Murphy and other U.S. diplomats shuttled discreetly among Middle East capitals in vain efforts to put together a negotiating framework that could satisfy Peres's complex domestic political constraints, Hussein's need for international and perhaps PLO involvement, and Reagan's resistance to affording the Soviet Union any means of acquiring a major role in Arab-Israeli diplomacy.

As prime minister again after October 1986, Shamir resented Peres's free-wheeling initiatives, though he was confident they would come to naught. By mid-1987, Shamir and Peres were actively competing for Shultz and Reagan's support for their contrasting

2. For a more extensive description of Peres's strategy, Hussein's reactions, and the U.S. role in support of Peres's game plan, see Samuel W. Lewis, "Israel: The Peres Era and Its Legacy," *Foreign Affairs*, vol. 65, no. 3 (1987), pp. 597–602.

approaches to peacemaking. They dispatched separate private envoys to Washington to counter each other's designs. The U.S. administration, bemused and befuddled by this extraordinary diplomacy, moved too cautiously for Peres but too energetically for Shamir. The result was diplomatic motion but little progress.

The dramatic tide of violence in the occupied territories, which rose unexpectedly in December 1987, finally convinced Reagan and Shultz to undertake a high-profile U.S. diplomatic initiative to jump-start the moribund peace process with an American proposal, based on a telescoping of the time frame for negotiations agreed on at Camp David. Prospects for success were dim. Shamir and Peres were at loggerheads and already looking toward new elections. Hussein was wary, Asad opposed, and the PLO unwilling to permit Palestinians in the territories to rise to Shultz's diplomatic challenge. Yet events had forced Reagan's hand, convincing him to make an effort, regardless of the small likelihood of success.

In his potential role as a Middle East peacemaker, Reagan succumbed in his second term to the vicious cross fire of Israeli domestic political rivalry, to Hussein's weak position in the Arab arena, and to a decline in Reagan's political fortunes in late 1986 from the Iran arms sale affair. Lack of U.S. initiative was not the central problem. Interestingly, however, an administration initially disdainful of Carter's Middle East policies had come after eight difficult years to admire the delicate compromises embodied in the Camp David Accords. Reagan had even tentatively come to accept the idea of some U.S.-Soviet sponsorship of Middle East negotiations, with careful safeguards. The key Camp David concept of an interim, transitional regime for the West Bank and Gaza had by 1988 become a central element in the Reagan administration's thinking about possible negotiating outcomes, if negotiations could ever be launched.

THE IMPACT OF ISRAEL'S "SIAMESE TWINS" ON U.S.-ISRAELI RELATIONS

Israel's 1984 election returns had produced a dead heat between Labor and Likud, an outcome that imposed unique complications on U.S. relations with Jerusalem between 1984 and 1988. Labor's large preelection lead had melted during the campaign. Neither Shamir nor Peres could form a majority coalition cabinet. Eventually, with great reluctance, they joined forces to create a broad-based national unity government, adding a unique feature: their personal agreement to rotate their posts halfway through the four-year electoral term. Peres obtained the first stint as prime minister. Rabin became defense minister for the whole four years.

During Reagan's first term he had grappled with a Likud-led cabinet in Israel headed by a charismatic, demagogic, ideologically rigid, prickly, authentic leader, Menachem Begin, and a ruthless, determined war hero, Ariel Sharon. Begin's foreign minister, Yitzhak Shamir, seemed often to be a bit player as he calmly swallowed his resentment at Sharon's overweening style, said little, and loyally supported Begin down the line.

Yet Shamir's grandfatherly mien masks a strong, resilient, tenacious character. Schooled in Israel's pre-state Jewish underground, where he was a major operational commander, and by a long career in the Mossad, Israel's overseas secret intelligence agency, Shamir acquired secrecy, self-control, caution, and suspicion as parts of his second nature. Although ideologically as rigid as Begin about the future of Judea and Samaria, Shamir contrasts with Begin's style. Affable, unassuming, uncharismatic, patient, a good listener, tactically pragmatic, hard to persuade but steady, Shamir was a relief to deal with as prime minister from September 1983 to September 1984, and again beginning in October 1986 for the last two years of Reagan's presidency.

So was Peres. While awaiting his chance through seven painful years as leader of the Labor party opposition, Peres had cultivated relations with American officials and politicians at every opportunity. His conversational agility, charm, wit, intellectual curiosity, and thoughtful analysis of Israel's dilemmas made him a welcome speaker and guest. He could empathize with America's problems as well as those of moderate Arabs like Sadat, Mubarak, and Hussein. He had spent most of his adult life dealing with foreign and defense issues and officials. As prime minister from 1984 to 1986, and then as foreign minister, Peres sought American advice and support, seeking to coordinate his major moves closely with Washington.

Moreover, Israel's two defense ministers during Reagan's second term had both served as ambassadors in Washington, had many friends in administration and congressional circles, including Secretaries Weinberger and Shultz, and understood better than most Israelis the complex, almost uncontrolled and decentralized system by which a president's foreign policy comes into being. Arens was Shamir's closest political ally in the Likud. Rabin, a former Labor prime minister, had long been Peres's bitter rival for party leadership. However, the two had finally reached a modus vivendi during the 1984 campaign and worked smoothly together this time around in government, though with some recurrent wariness.

Changes in Israel's leaders transformed the surface atmosphere of U.S.-Israeli relations during Reagan's second term. This cadre of Israelis dealt with Washington, with rare exception, as the capital of Israel's most crucially important ally and friend. They treated U.S. leaders as friends to convince or as interlocutors in an honest disagreement, not as adversaries. The change of style in the official relationship was soon palpable, even with Weinberger who was the most skeptical member of Reagan's administration about tightening strategic and political links between Jerusalem and Washington. Reagan reverted, relieved, to his original, emotional affinity for Israel as a natural American ally. Shultz spent long hours in private sessions with Shamir or Peres, Arens or Rabin, exploring patiently with them the conundrums of peacemaking, the dilemmas of Israeli security in a dangerous region, and possible avenues of escape from Israel's hyperinflation. Congressional leaders also, overwhelmingly supportive of Israel as they were, had found the Begin and Sharon years difficult. The Lebanon war had bruised their constituents' image of Israel, and Begin's defiant rhetoric, directed at a sympathetic American president like Reagan, had offended many of Israel's strong supporters on Capitol Hill. They too greeted the new Israeli leadership style with great relief. Since Congress was about to be called on to appropriate even more economic aid to help contain Israel's exploding economic crisis, the change of atmosphere was highly fortuitous.

For the most part this arrangement worked surprisingly well while Peres occupied the Prime Ministry. His temperament and background equipped him almost ideally for the leadership of a difficult coalition. Equally important, Shamir's reticence, iron self-control, and personal modesty enabled him to make the difficult transition from the Prime Ministry to the Foreign Ministry with a minimum of obvious resentment. He yielded leadership and limelight to Peres, often swallowing hard, taking few initiatives, going about the foreign affairs routine, biding his time. Extricating the IDF from Lebanon and the country from economic chaos dominated the cabinet's agenda during Peres's tenure. Neither issue divided the coalition along ideological lines. Shamir could cooperate readily with Peres and Rabin on those issues. Peres's peripatetic peace diplomacy went unhappily around in circles. Shamir relied on his own Fabian style to safeguard the Likud's interests.

During Shamir's subsequent two-year term as prime minister, complications multiplied. Peres could not easily adjust to the role of number two. Bored by the foreign ministry routine and determined to push forward his peace strategy, he brushed aside Shamir's reservations, pursued Hussein and Shultz with proposals that Shamir opposed, and operated abroad almost as if no rotation had occurred. For Reagan and Shultz this strange diplomacy eventually became rather unnerving. While the Rabin-Weinberger relationship and IDF-Pentagon links had now settled into a generally productive, professional mode, Shultz had continually to cope with two opposing Israeli foreign policies, at least on the most important and complex issue: how to pursue peacemaking in the region. Peres and Shamir were unable to agree for months on a replacement for Israel's ambassador in Washington, nearly always a crucial link in the chain of the relationship with the administration, Congress, and U.S. public. Yet Peres lacked confidence in the incumbent, a hardworking civil servant and international legal expert, Meir Rosenne, who had been Begin's personal choice for the post. So he bypassed Rosenne, dealing with Shultz through personal emissaries and the U.S. ambassador in Tel Aviv. Shamir responded by sending his own personal emissaries to Washington, including Shultz's friend Moshe Arens, to warn Shultz not to see Peres's proposals as representing Israeli policy. The secretary of state was already preoccupied with Reagan's Iran-Contra crisis, Gorbachev's flamboyant diplomacy, U.S.-Soviet arms control negotiations, and Reagan's fading political influence on Congress. In any case he was highly skeptical about prospects for any breakthrough on the Arab-Israeli diplomatic front, and the mixed signals from Jerusalem reinforced his native caution. Dealing with the two wings of the Israeli cabinet without losing the confidence of either also posed an extraordinary challenge for Ambassador Thomas R. Pickering in Tel Aviv. In summary, then, Israel's national unity government stabilized U.S.-Israeli relations on a macrolevel but posed some insoluble microproblems for Reagan's diplomatic team.

The new era in U.S.-Israeli cooperation paid large dividends in the field of economics. The free trade agreement was completed and ratified. Israel's military industry found doors slowly opening to U.S. military markets. Most important, the Reagan administration and Congress responded tactfully, wisely, and generously to Israel's plea for both advice and financial support to cope with their economic crisis. Peres had taken the helm when inflation was running at an annual rate of over 1,200 percent, fueled by a budget deficit of more than 15 percent. A foreign exchange crisis reflected a widespread loss of confidence by the Israelis in their currency. Within two years, inflation had been brought down to the mid-20 percent range annually and has subsequently been contained well below that, yet unemployment remained within acceptable limits.

Foreign exchange reserves were again ample. The government deficit was nearly eliminated. Significant reforms in taxation and financial markets were launched. Years of low or no economic growth ended. Exports became buoyant. Multiple problems remained, but Israel under the coalition governments achieved a miraculous economic recovery. Skillful U.S. economic diplomacy made a crucial contribution.[3]

Shultz deserves a great share of the credit. Predisposed to admire Israeli democracy and the devotion of its citizens to their state, he came in office to understand that only close consultation between Washington and Jerusalem, as befits allies, could advance U.S. interests in the region. His determined adherence to that course, a course Reagan fully endorsed, enabled the two countries to navigate some stormy seas. As a distinguished economist, accepted at least by 1984 as a genuine friend to Israel, he arranged to provide informal economic advisers and his own counsel to Peres, Shamir, and their finance ministers to reinforce their determination to force tough stabilization measures on a reluctant Israeli cabinet. The sensitive discretion he exercised in his economic diplomacy largely disarmed the inevitable Israeli nationalist reaction to feared "U.S. pressure." Simultaneously, the administration and Congress provided a "financial safety net" to reassure markets while stabilization measures were put into place. Then $1.5 billion in emergency aid over two years was extended in a fashion that encouraged the cabinet to slash expenditures and control credit. It was a virtuoso performance, a model use of U.S. foreign aid to assist an economically embattled ally.

Other issues posed difficult challenges for Washington and Jerusalem during Reagan's last years in office. They have caused so little damage to the relationship because of their careful handling in both capitals. With different leaders, the impact could have been explosive. The administration's desire to sell advanced weapons to Jordan and Saudi Arabia raised inevitable opposition in Jerusalem and on the floor of Congress. A nasty case of Israeli spying in the United States, the "Pollard affair," threatened a harsh confrontation. Israel's large role in Reagan's ill-conceived effort to extract American hostages from terrorists by secretly selling arms to Iran could have scarred relations severely but did not. The two governments labored effectively to contain the political fallout, and congressional investigators followed suit. As both Israel and the United States entered

3. Ibid., pp. 587–93.

their campaign seasons for national elections in November 1988, the relationship between Reagan's administration and Israel's leaders had reached an all-time high of amity.

RETROSPECTIVE AND PROGNOSIS

Twelve turbulent years are ending with a prolonged, daunting crisis over Israel's control of the occupied territories and Shultz's dogged efforts to divert the Palestinian uprising into diplomatic channels toward negotiations for a peaceful settlement. Israel's initially inept and often harsh methods for subduing the uprising's violence have shaken many staunch American friends, especially some segments of American Jewry. Yet the Reagan administration has not faltered in its support for Israel in these months of Israeli frustration, as the IDF strives to restore control and to recreate a status quo ante that probably can never be fully achieved. At the same time, U.S. policy strongly supports Israel in international forums like the United Nations, a quietly expanding set of strategic military cooperation arrangements is in place, a free trade area is beginning to yield solid trading dividends for both countries, and Israel is more secure against external Arab aggression than at any time since independence and is formally at peace with Egypt. The panorama includes a resurgent Israeli economy, some opening of Soviet doors for Russian Jews, fading international isolation for Israeli diplomacy, overwhelming congressional and public support for Israel and its economic and military aid requirements, and as close a working relationship between senior American and Israeli leaders as would be conceivable between two such dissimilar sovereign nations. Yet few Israelis are highly confident that will continue into 1989 and beyond. Both the Carter and Reagan eras were marked by wild swings between angry confrontation and amicable collaboration. What explains this pattern?

The explanation has several elements. First, each capital tends to expect too much of the other. Unrealistic expectations about the model nature of Israeli democracy or about the omnipotence and omniscience of the United States produce frequent disillusionment and suspicion of deliberate ill intent when either government simply errs. Second, the United States is a superpower with global roles and perceived responsibilities. Israel is, at best, a small regional power with a powerful army and air force, preoccupied with immediate security concerns. This different perspective on events can often produce sharp disagreement. Third, the United States has differing impressions of the immediacy of threat to Israel from terror or outright military attack. Jerusalem is close to perceived danger from air bases, missiles, and terrorist bases. Washington is far away from those dangers. U.S. and Israeli analysts making threat assessments will always allow different margins for error. Fourth, Israeli history makes it difficult to accept protestations of the Arabs' peaceful intentions. Moreover, Palestinian voices raised during the 1987–88 uprising that assert that all of Palestine must be Arab only harden Israeli conviction that it is but another battle in Israel's long war for survival. American officials, with ready access to evolving currents in Arab capitals, will often differ sharply with skeptical Israeli analysts about the nature and intentions of the PLO or of countries like Saudi Arabia or Iraq. Fifth, the American and Israeli peoples are entangled by religion, family, and history. That means their national politics are also entangled. Perhaps uniquely, avoiding mutual interference in the domestic politics of the other party is an impossible objective to achieve. Sixth, interaction among leaders and mutual chemistry affects the state of this relationship more than that of other pairs of nations; that reality stems from the previous point about societal interaction. Seventh, Israel's growing economic dependence on the United States since 1973 magnifies the usual sense of vulnerability that characterizes a small nation's view of a larger patron. And Israel as a Jewish state feels particularly vulnerable to swings in policy in the capital of its greatest, and indeed only, ally. Jewish history is unfortunately replete with examples of betrayal by non-Jewish friends and patrons. Only regained economic independence and continued progress toward regional peace can lessen the Israeli habit of overreacting to slight swings in the Washington weathervane.

For these reasons, the oscillating pattern will probably continue in future administrations. Minimizing the sharpness of swings on the graph depends primarily on future decisions of Israeli and American voters. Israeli-American divisions are manageable so long as presidents and prime ministers, secretaries of state and defense, and ministers of foreign affairs and defense seek actively to resolve them as disagreements among well-intentioned friends, rather than as deliberate confrontations among adversaries. The basic elements that undergird the U.S.-Israeli unwritten alliance will remain for the foreseeable future. But deliberately insensitive or demagogic leaders, coming to power in either or both capitals, could again put enormous strain on the alliance.

Finally, what is the legacy of Camp David? It is, above all else, an Arab-Israeli conflict permanently altered in some key dimensions. The psychological barrier walling Israel off from the rest of the region began to crumble and can never be totally rebuilt. When powerful Egypt implicitly acknowledged Israel's permanence, the problem for peacemakers altered from breaking through a solid wall of precedent to finding ways to expand the peace salient. Moreover, Camp David refocused the Arab-Israeli conflict on its essential core: the struggle over the land of Palestine.

Camp David also demonstrated that active, sympathetic involvement by an American president, when the political ground is prepared, can tip the balance to enable an Israeli leader to stretch the extra mile for the sake of agreement. It may, however, yield a mistaken lesson about the need for an American president to become his own chief negotiator. Few if any future presidents would invest their energy and political capital as Carter did.

Camp David's failure to solve the Palestinian problem "in all its aspects" presaged a decade of increasing stalemate and frustration. The Lebanon war and the deep rift it produced between Washington and Jerusalem was one direct result of that failure. So, however, prior to 1988 there seemed to be a slowly increasing understanding among inhabitants of the occupied territories that they had to accept, for the foreseeable future, less than their optimal goal of complete independence. The Camp David concept of autonomy was summarily rejected in 1978 by Palestinians, even as a transition regime. But variants of the idea remained central to most current proposals for progress, suggesting that the concept may be inescapable as a stage in any movement toward a settlement of the conflict. Yet the new mood of defiance among Palestinians, which stems from perceived successes in mounting their uprising in the territories after December 9, 1987, now makes realization of that concept seem more and more problematic.

For Israel, Camp David reinforced psychological and economic dependence on the United States. While it opened the border to Egypt, the aftermath of the "frigid peace" deflated many Israeli illusions about what peace with any Arab neighbor would be like. That disillusion has weakened the case of Israeli doves pressing for far-reaching territorial concessions from the strategic West Bank to obtain a similar peace with Jordan, much less with a PLO still ambivalent about its ultimate objectives toward Israel itself.

Thus the decade now drawing to a close in U.S.-Israeli relations was dominated by Camp David and the eddies it set in motion. Those waves are now nearly spent. The Palestinian uprising of 1987-88 may prove eventually to have been the new catalytic stimulus essential to break the current impasse in Israeli domestic politics and in Arab-Israeli relations. It may, on the other hand, be the first round of another bloody Arab-Israeli war whose outcome could push any prospect for lasting peace even further into the future. Some new political leadership in the Palestinian camp and in Israel as well may be essential elements to unfreeze the diplomatic impasse.

The Israeli election scheduled for late 1988 and the American election occurring at nearly the same time will select those national leaders in Jerusalem and Washington whose interaction will largely determine the future tenor of U.S.-Israeli relations. The unfinished legacy of Camp David will challenge their diplomatic skills. Their personalities and convictions will determine whether cooperation or turbulence will predominate in the relationship as the second decade after Camp David begins.

PART II
OTHER REGIONAL POWERS

RASHID KHALIDI

The Palestine Liberation Organization

LOOKED AT from a contemporary Palestinian perspective, the effect of the Camp David Accords loomed exceedingly large. Camp David obsessed Palestinian leaders and the Palestinian media for years afterward, an obsession reflected in rhetorical denunciations of "the Camp David conspiracy" that were of little analytical value. Even so, some Palestinian criticisms seem remarkably prescient ten years later. Camp David certainly did not usher in a decade of Arab-Israeli peace, even if it did bring peace to the already quiescent Egyptian-Israeli front. This chapter analyzes the impact of the Camp David process on the Palestinians and how they assessed it, thus providing the perspective on this process of one of the parties most affected by it.

STRATEGIC EFFECTS OF CAMP DAVID AND ITS ANTECEDENTS

Among the issues that must be addressed in studying the effect of Camp David on the Palestine Liberation Organization (PLO) is whether the supposed consequences of the agreement should realistically be seen as part of a broad regional trend toward a separate U.S.-brokered Egyptian-Israeli settlement, which began in the aftermath of the October 1973 war. A strong argument can be made that 1973 marked the beginning of this trend, at least in strategic terms. Indeed, events after the October 1973 war seem a logical starting point for many processes related to the strategic situation in the Middle East that is associated with Camp David. This is true whether one is referring to Egypt's disengagement from the rest of the Arab world, to American efforts to play an exclusive brokering role in the settlement process at the expense of the Soviet Union, to the effects on inter-Arab politics, or finally to the redefinition of the Palestine question from an issue between the Arab states and Israel to one essentially between Palestinians and Israelis.

According to this analysis, Syria's (and later the PLO's and the other Arab states') estrangement from Egypt, which culminated in the break after Camp David, had its roots in Anwar Sadat's go-it-alone behavior during the 1973 war. That ranged from his unannounced abandonment of the war aims previously agreed on with the Syrians, documented by his chief of staff, General Saad al-Din al-Shazly, and other sources,[1] to his negotiations with both superpowers toward the end of the war, and to his acceptance of a cease-fire. Sadat apparently did not bother to consult with his nominal Syrian allies about any of these vital matters, let alone take their views or interests into account.

The Kilometer 101 negotiations,[2] Egypt's attendance at the Geneva Middle East peace conference in December 1973, and the first Sinai disengagement accord of January 1974 were all further initiatives in which neither Syria nor other Egyptian allies like the PLO were consulted (although King Faisal of Saudi Arabia in certain cases seems to have been informed). The 1974 agreement was the prelude to the much more significant second Sinai disengagement accord, negotiated in 1975, which alienated virtually the entire Arab world. Here Egypt, for the first time, took substantive steps toward a separate bilateral peace settlement with Israel, detaching itself from other Arab states. In so doing it adopted the approach that was to become the centerpiece of its policy under Sadat, ultimately enshrined in the Camp David Accords and the Egyptian-Israeli peace treaty.

Similarly, the American approach at Camp David and afterward can be seen as having emerged from the policies developed over the preceding five years, whereby Egypt was seduced away from the Soviets (admittedly without putting up untoward resistance), the Soviet Union was systematically and rigorously excluded from a substantive role in the negotiations, and the Palestine issue and the Palestinians themselves were relegated to the back burner.

In the same way, the aftermath of the accord of 1975 prefigured

1. General Saad el-Shazly, *The Crossing of Suez: The October War (1973)* (London: Third World Centre for Research and Publishing, 1980), pp. 24–32. Sadat spelled out his more limited war objectives to Fatah leaders before the 1973 war, as reported by them in 1978 during public speeches in Beirut and cited in interviews with Yasir Arafat (Amman, November 24, 1984), Abu Iyad (Tunis, March 14, 1984), and me.

2. Negotiations to free the Egyptian 3d Army, trapped by the Israeli crossing onto the West Bank of the Suez Canal at the end of the October 1973 war, took place at kilometer 101 on the Suez-Cairo road.

the effect of Camp David on the PLO and on relations among the Arab states. In the earlier instance, inter-Arab polarization replaced the modicum of harmony achieved before the October war, resulting finally in an Arab mini-cold war and the isolation of Egypt for over a year after September 1975. Again in 1978, after Camp David, Egypt was in effect removed from the strategic balance with Israel. In both instances the PLO was deprived of its key Egyptian partner in its inter-Arab balancing act, leaving it much more vulnerable to the sometimes unwelcome influence of Syria.

The events of both 1975 and 1978 were accompanied by conflict in Lebanon involving the PLO. The first outbreak was the ferocious fighting of 1975–76, which began after Henry A. Kissinger's abortive attempt to negotiate Sinai II in March 1975 and flared up again after he succeeded in September. The second outbreak was the Israeli invasion of south Lebanon in the spring of 1978, which took place while the negotiations that ultimately resulted in the Camp David Accords were under way. Indeed, American-Israeli-Egyptian moves toward a separate settlement tended, with monotonous consistency, to be accompanied by fire and brimstone on the ground in Lebanon. That was true for the 1975–76 fighting and Israel's 1978 invasion of Lebanon. Similarly, right after major steps toward peace with Egypt were concluded, Israel flexed its military muscle elsewhere, as with its air, sea, and land campaign against the PLO in 1979 during the six months after the signing of the Egyptian-Israeli peace treaty in March, and with its 1982 invasion of Lebanon after the evacuation of Sinai in April.

Many in the region therefore felt as though each stage of Egypt's peace with Israel was being bought at the price of intensified war by Israel against the PLO along its northern front in Lebanon. Specifically, the strategic effect of the whole trend of separate settlements after 1973 was to free Israel from concern about the security of its western borders, to set obstacles in the path of any Egyptian effort to try to reverse this process and relieve the pressure on the Palestinians, and to isolate the Palestinians in the face of the Israelis, whether in Lebanon or in the occupied territories.

This strategic assessment was somewhat exaggerated. But unquestionably, Lebanon and the Palestinians paid heavily for every step in the Egyptian-Israeli-American rapprochement. Freeing Israel from its earlier strategic concerns with Egypt did not only mean that Israel had more forces at its disposal. It also meant that Syria had to be more afraid of Israel than before, since there was no longer any Egyptian counterweight on Israel's western flanks to bail Syria out as there had been in 1948, 1957–58, or 1966–67. (Resentment about Egypt having played this role in the past, at considerable cost to itself, apparently influenced Sadat's actions in bypassing Syria in 1973.) As a result, the PLO was more naked before an Israel that was far stronger in relative terms than ever before, that had less to fear from Syria, and that wasted no opportunity to test the goodwill and restraint of its new Egyptian "partner in peace" while launching offensives in Lebanon against the PLO.

The strategic effects of the Camp David Accords (including their antecedents of the preceding few years) on the Palestinians can thus be summed up as follows:

—They ended the Arab solidarity, however tenuous, that had prevailed from 1973 through September 1975, and again from October 1976 through September 1977.

—They removed Egypt from the Arab-Israeli strategic equation, putting Israel in its best position militarily since its creation—a position it has exploited repeatedly in Lebanon, and by long-range air and sea attacks against Baghdad and Tunis.

—They left the smaller parties on the "eastern front"—Lebanon, the Palestinians, and Jordan—alone and face-to-face not only with Israel but also with Syria, which now placed far greater demands on those parties in view of its weakened strategic position.

—They caused the Arab-Israeli conflict (together, subsequently, with other conflicts in the region) to be transferred to Lebanon, which became its main arena for the decade after 1978. Lebanon has paid accordingly.

THE POLITICAL EFFECT OF CAMP DAVID ON THE PLO

Besides these regional strategic effects, the Camp David Accords had several specific political consequences for the PLO itself. The actual autonomy agreement, however, had little effect. It was virtually stillborn, never garnered any Palestinian, Jordanian, or Arab support, and was perceived even by many Egyptians who supported peace with Israel as insufficient. They thought the idea of imposing the tutelage of "autonomy" on a people demanding the right of national self-determination seemed like an unacceptable humiliation. The important political effects of the accords have to be looked for elsewhere.

The first of them is that while the PLO was preoccupied with opposing Camp David, and with simultaneously defending itself in Lebanon and struggling with the internal difficulties that emerged, especially after 1982, Israel was free to act in the West Bank and

Gaza. The support of the United States and Egypt at Camp David bought Israel a decade of freedom to deal with the occupied territories. Although Israel failed politically to put out the flames of Palestinian nationalism, it certainly succeeded with the de facto integration of those territories into the Israeli consciousness. Thus most Israelis now consider "Eretz Israel" to include the West Bank and Gaza, and their return to Arab control is seen as "giving up" part of Israel. Particularly during the first five years after the Camp David Accords, the PLO seems to have been successfully distracted from the occupied territories, even while Israel focused on them. That situation has changed over the last five years, but the impression remains that Camp David gave Israel a chance to "impose facts" in the West Bank and Gaza that are only now being questioned by the Palestinians.

A second, more subtle effect of Camp David has become clear only in recent years. While the PLO was busy warding off various challenges in Lebanon, Jordan was slowly being encouraged by the United States, and occasionally by Israel and Egypt, to play the role it abandoned in 1974 at the outset of the separate settlement trend. Thus at times unwillingly, and at others more enthusiastically, the Hashemite regime attempted to stand in for the Palestinians in the settlement process and be the agent of other interested parties in replacing independent Palestinian representation. Jordanian leaders were always ambivalent about such a role. In July 1988, King Hussein rejected the notion that Jordan would speak for the Palestinians, severed links with the West Bank, and declared that henceforth the PLO would bear full responsibility for the future of the occupied territories (see appendix M).

Yet another political effect of Camp David has been to encourage the deeply grounded Israeli-American preference for resolving the Palestine question without the Palestinians, and largely at their expense. This preference was not of course engendered by Camp David,[3] but it received a strong boost from the accords and later from the Egyptian-Israeli peace treaty. Here the leaders of the two countries, blessed by an American president, ended the only conflict that ever seriously threatened Israel in a way that seemed to lay the Palestinian question to rest in line with Israeli wishes. Even after the Lebanon war and the Palestinian uprising in the occupied territories, this preference is still alive and still takes sustenance from the precedent of Camp David.

3. This is shown by Simha Flapan, *The Birth of Israel: Myths and Realities* (Pantheon Books, 1987) and others as going back to at least 1948.

The separate settlement approach begun by Secretary of State Kissinger and continued at Camp David affected the Palestinians in Lebanon in other, more direct ways. The moves by the United States, Egypt, and Israel toward a settlement process that seemed clearly designed to sidestep the Palestine problem, and thus to leave the majority of Palestinians in the diaspora where they were, ended the Palestinian euphoria about a just settlement being within reach. That optimism had started in 1973 after the October war, the brief convening of the Geneva conference, and the first Sinai and Golan disengagement agreements. It gained strength in 1977 when the Carter administration in its first nine months revived the comprehensive settlement approach. Its clear effects can be seen in the radical departure embodied in the program adopted in 1974 at the twelfth session of the Palestine National Council (PNC), and clarified in the following years, when for the first time the PNC called for a Palestinian state alongside Israel as a PLO objective and accepted the principle of a political settlement of the conflict.[4] These important political shifts were a response to what was then seen as the possibility of an imminent settlement.

After Camp David both Palestinians and Lebanese began to realize that no deus ex machina would come to resolve their problems by transplanting the Palestinians in Lebanon to a West Bank-Gaza state. Camp David showed them that they were bound to one another for the foreseeable future. Realization of this fact led to despair, self-delusion, backbiting, and recrimination, and eventually to savage fighting. These conflicts of course had other causes, but a principal one was the frustrating realization that the United States, Israel, and Egypt were now treaty-bound to solve the Palestine question, if they could, in a way that could only work to the detriment of Lebanon and the Palestinians there.

Further, because of the new realities it imposed, Camp David forced the Lebanese to deal with both Palestinians and Israelis differently from before. Many Lebanese were either worried by the

4. For more on this new post-1973 departure in the PLO approach, see Alain Gresh, *The PLO: The Struggle Within: Towards an Independent Palestinian State*, trans. A. M. Berrett (London: Zed Books, 1985), pp. 129–210; and Helena Cobban, *The Palestinian Liberation Organisation: People, Power and Politics* (Cambridge University Press, 1984), pp. 60–63, 79, 84–87. For resolutions of the sixteenth, seventeenth, and eighteenth sessions of the Palestine National Council in 1983, 1984, and 1987, see *Journal of Palestine Studies*, vol. 12 (Spring 1983), pp. 250–54; vol. 14 (Winter 1985), pp. 257–59; and vol. 16 (Summer 1987), pp. 196–204 (see also appendix I for the resolutions of the eighteenth session, minus the final statement). There is an unmistakable evolution in the wording of PNC resolutions on these crucial issues over the period 1974–87.

Palestinians or saw them as allies to be exploited in inter-Lebanese rivalries; others perceived them through an idealized haze that the Palestinians themselves initially did little to dispel, until their own actions revealed them in a colder, less charitable light. Eventually, after much suffering on both sides, it became clear that the Palestinians were in Lebanon on sufferance, however redoubtable their military position; that they were no more the solution to than the cause of all of Lebanon's problems; and that until a solution to their problem was found, they and their Lebanese neighbors would have to work out a modus vivendi that might have to last for a long time.

Finally, Camp David began the process of forcing the PLO to stop using Egypt, or Saudi Arabia or Syria or some other power, as an intermediary in dealing with Israel and the United States, as it had done repeatedly from 1973 until 1977. The PLO has learned that lesson with great reluctance and much backsliding. And at times this reliance on Arab intermediaries was an expedient imposed on the PLO by its foes' refusal to deal directly with it. But the elimination of Egypt from the coalition of states nominally at war with Israel has had a powerful effect on PLO thinking. For there is no possible replacement for Egypt, whether in terms of the weight it carries in both American and Israeli calculations or in its relative disinterestedness as far as the Palestinians are concerned (at least when compared with both Syria and Jordan). This explains why from 1973 to 1977 PLO leaders relied heavily on Egypt to help them obtain a Palestinian state, and explains as well their sense of betrayal when Sadat opted for a separate peace with Israel, in effect abandoning the Palestinians.

Although for most of the past decade neither Israel nor the United States has appeared to want to deal with the PLO, the hope that they did, or might be persuaded to do so, lingered on in some PLO circles. So did the desire to find some Arab state to act as an intermediary. This desire provided the motivation for the "Jordanian option" adopted by the PLO from 1983 until it was repudiated by King Hussein in 1986. Even so, Camp David and the elimination of Egypt from most Palestinian calculations has ended the idea that the PLO could rely on any Arab state—an idea that was rejected by many Palestinians after 1977–78, but that the weakness of the Palestinian negotiating position vis-à-vis Israel and the United States often drove PLO leaders back to in subsequent years.

Seen in historical perspective, the Camp David Accords thus mark a clear victory of an isolationist over a pan-Arab approach in Palestinian councils, in the latest phase of a debate that goes back to well before 1948. The question for the Palestinians has always been whether to rely on their own resources or to depend on others. After Camp David, the PLO had little choice but to go it alone, hard as this was for some Palestinians to accept, since there were in effect no others to help in dealing with Israel and the United States. After its treaty with Israel, Egypt had renounced any role other than offering its virtually useless "good offices"; Saudi Arabia was shown to have no influence on the United States regarding the Palestine question, and as being far more concerned about events to its east than to its northwest; and Syria has always been unwilling to allow its influence to be used for other than Syrian aims.

The PLO leadership, obsessed with hopes for a settlement and traumatized by the 1982 war, turned to Jordan in 1983, and more convincingly in 1985. However, the PLO's hope of riding on Jordan's admittedly abbreviated shirttails was diminished in the face of opposition by both Israel and the United States, before being buried by the king in early 1986. The PLO-Jordanian accord, signed on February 11, 1985, after the holding of the seventeenth session of the PNC in Amman in November 1984, was thus short-lived, and the PLO was left on its own again (see appendixes F and M).

Dealing through Arab intermediaries with the United States, which in turn deals with Israel, has made already difficult negotiations harder by the interposition of regimes that, far from being objective and disinterested, have vital interests of their own at stake and are often malevolently inclined toward the PLO and the Palestinians. But there are signs—such as the April 1987 PNC resolution on contacts with "democratic Israeli forces" (see appendix I), Yasir Arafat's Geneva meeting in September 1987 with Israeli Knesset members and journalists, and several 1987 PLO-Israeli encounters in Eastern European capitals—that after the failure of repeated indirect approaches, PLO leaders have begun to understand the importance of direct openings to Israel. (For example, see the statement of Bassam Abu Sharif, appendix L.)

It is ironic indeed that this recognition comes only after the Israeli Knesset made such contacts illegal for Israelis, and after the U.S. Congress and the Reagan administration, with their closures of PLO offices and other hostile measures, have done their best to prevent PLO contact with the American public. Whether in fact it is now too late for the PLO to attempt the long-delayed direct approach will become clear only in time. What does seem certain is that Camp David made most Palestinians feel that the United States and Israel were irredeemably hostile to them. It delayed their realizing that they need to appeal over the heads of the U.S. and

Israeli governments to the people of those countries, as they have done successfully in the Arab world several times over the past few decades.

PALESTINIAN PERCEPTIONS OF THE CAMP DAVID PROCESS

The PLO immediately assessed the Camp David Accords and the Egyptian-Israeli peace treaty as constituting an unmitigated disaster for the Palestinian cause. Very few Palestinians could be heard dissenting from this general opinion. This new unanimity marked a change in Palestinian political discourse. Ever since Sadat had started to go off on his own several years earlier, some Palestinian critics had described him—and the Arab regimes generally—as being irresistibly drawn to an American-sponsored settlement process, and thus as tending toward abandonment and betrayal of the PLO. This view had adherents both in the mainstream Fatah group and in smaller organizations. An opposing school of thought included the groups headed by Munir Shafiq of the PLO Planning Center as well as most of the Fatah leadership. They agreed that such a "capitulationist" inclination existed but purported to see countervailing "patriotic" tendencies in Egypt and the other "progressive" Arab states (the other face of these regimes). Many of them continued to hope against all the evidence that Sadat had Palestinian interests at heart and at some point would prove it. In the years preceding Camp David, each shift of direction by the Egyptian leader encouraged one of these two opposing schools of thought among Palestinians.

Sadat's visit to Jerusalem in 1977 stilled the voices of those who had illusions about his intentions; the Camp David Accords and the treaty silenced them permanently. The disappointment that resulted was all the greater in that it came after Egypt had supported the PLO while the Carter administration had tried for most of 1977 to revive the idea of a comprehensive settlement that Kissinger had briefly pursued in 1973 before launching the separate settlement approach.

Palestinian hopes, and especially those of the PLO leadership, had been aroused by 1977 American explorations with various Arab states of formulas for PLO involvement in the settlement process, by Carter's own statements about a Palestinian homeland (which were the furthest any U.S. president had gone in this direction), and by the U.S.-Soviet joint statement of October 1, 1977 (see appendix B). The latter marked a high point in PLO euphoria over the prospects of a regional settlement that would take Palestinian interests into account. The Fatah leaders were especially euphoric. But their hopes were undermined only four days later when Israeli Foreign Minister Moshe Dayan, fortified by a wave of outrage at the Carter approach among friends of Israel in the United States, Russophobes, and congressional critics, succeeded in imposing restrictive Israeli conditions on the administration's approach, restrictions that in effect nullified the joint statement.

Some members of the PLO, particularly among the top ranks of Fatah, even as late as Camp David retained hope that Sadat would not completely betray the Palestinians. Besides wishful thinking, they were driven by their reluctance to contemplate dealing with Israel and Syria without the crucial Egyptian counterweight, which had been essential to Palestinian strategy for more than a decade. They therefore did their best to keep lines open to Cairo. But the military blows delivered by Israel in south Lebanon demonstrated that the Camp David process had decisively changed the strategic equation to the disadvantage of the PLO. Coming against the background of the growing new relationship between Egypt and Israel, these attacks bore out the predictions of the most pessimistic, showing that Israel was becoming more aggressive in attacking the Palestinians and Lebanon, while Sadat was even more timid in his reactions. They also showed that without Egypt, Syria and Saudi Arabia were less and less inclined to intervene, whether militarily or diplomatically, whenever Israel attacked Lebanon.

Initially this left the PLO with no place to turn for support, although it did its best to maximize its existing relations on the Arab and international levels. Then in early 1979 the Iranian revolution raised the possibility that the PLO might be able to call in a "new world" to redress the imbalance of the old. This illusion lasted only briefly, essentially until Iraq's attack on Iran buried the always slim possibility of the PLO benefiting from the new circumstances at the eastern end of the Arab world. It is nevertheless testimony to the bleak prospects facing the Palestinians, after what they saw as Sadat's betrayal and the loss of Egypt's strategic weight, that they should have had to look so far, and to such an unlikely source, for support.

The result was a period of drift for the Palestinians that in turn affected their situation in Lebanon. It was one thing for the Lebanese to support them in the 1960s and early 1970s as downtrodden victims and vanguards of the Arab nation, and later, in the 1973–77 period, as possible beneficiaries of a comprehensive settlement that would result in their rapidly leaving Lebanon for their own homeland. It was quite another for Lebanon from 1978 on to pay an enormous price in blood and money for hosting a PLO whose strategy seemed to have little or no chance of success.

Not surprisingly, many Lebanese came to revise their view of the PLO, which was changing from a radical underground movement to a highly visible para-state in de facto control of large parts of Lebanon.[5] This change was reflected in what the Lebanese called the PLO: the complimentary *al-thawra* (the revolution) was replaced by *al-munazzama* (the organization), with all that term's negative connotations. An ascetic core of *feda'iyin* (literally self-sacrificers), who clearly courted great danger for their cause, were perceived as giving way to a bloated, overpaid bureaucracy, some of whose leaders lived in lavish apartments, drove expensive cars, and seemed to be sacrificing little. Of course, just as the initial perception was idealized, hiding the ordinary human failings of members of the early commando organizations, so did the later one overlook the fact that many Palestinians, leaders and followers, ran many risks and often made other notable sacrifices for their cause.[6]

Nevertheless, the change in Lebanese perceptions was deadly to the PLO, slowly sapping the popular support on which it depended to sustain its position in Lebanon. The change in the perceptions of the Maronite community, combined with disappointment in the results of Sadat's separate deal with Israel (which for the Maronites raised the specter of the permanent presence of the Palestinians in Lebanon) provided Israel with an opening. Israel could now fundamentally change the strategic picture of the region by working with the Phalangist party—the party that best expressed the views of the Maronite segment of the Lebanese Christian community. Besides confronting the PLO and its Lebanese allies with the prospect of an Israeli-Phalangist pincer, these changes also imposed difficult new strategic dilemmas on Syria. It now either had to compete with Israel for the favor of the Phalangists by opposing the PLO and its Lebanese allies, or confront a formidable new Israeli-Phalangist alliance, made all the more formidable by Israel's new-found freedom from Egyptian interference.

This new situation created problems that were even worse for the PLO than for Syria. For while Syria had its scrupulously observed

5. See Rashid Khalidi, *Under Siege: P.L.O. Decisionmaking during the 1982 War* (Columbia University Press, 1986), pp. 17–41.

6. Six members of Fatah's Central Committee (which normally numbers fifteen) have been killed since 1970 by the Palestine Liberation Organization's enemies. They were Abu Ali Iyad, Kamal Adwan, Muhammad Yusef Najjar, Majid Abu Sharar, Brigadier Saad Sayel, and Khalil Wazir (Abu Jihad).

1974 disengagement accord with Israel on the Golan Heights, and something of a Soviet guarantee of its own territory in case of Israeli attack, and thus risked only its (admittedly considerable) interests in Lebanon, the PLO had everything to lose. In the wake of the 1975–76 fighting in Lebanon, and of Egypt's abandonment, the PLO's Lebanese base became an objective in itself, to be protected at all costs. After the Israeli invasion of March 1978, Arafat and the mainstream PLO leadership were increasingly willing to crack down on Palestinian military action against Israel that was not strictly retaliatory, in order to preserve the PLO position in Lebanon. Not only did this restraint not placate the Lebanese, who still suffered from Israeli aggression—which the Begin government now announced would be preemptive instead of retaliatory—but they were further infuriated by the fact that the PLO was increasingly committed to the preservation of the status quo in Lebanon.

Although the PLO had built up a position of relative military strength in Lebanon, the attendant alienation of Lebanese public opinion meant that this strength was a diminishing asset. Simultaneously, Palestinian leaders felt under pressure to deliver something to their long-suffering constituents under Israeli occupation. Their resulting sense of urgency and desire for a settlement, even when none seemed in prospect, brought them into confrontation with the Asad regime in Syria. The PLO's attempts to explore any avenue to escape its predicament, combined with a profound reluctance to cede the hard-won independence that its Lebanese base provided, angered Asad and his lieutenants. Their strategy for Syria after Camp David was based in the first instance on control of their immediate environment in Greater Syria—the area consisting of Lebanon, Syria, Jordan, and Palestine. The last thing they wanted in their backyard was Yasir Arafat's unpredictable and often unwelcome involvement in both the settlement process and the Lebanese crisis.

The basic components of the PLO position were thus in conflict with key Syrian desires. The PLO was committed to maintaining its independent Lebanese base against all comers; Syria wanted a Lebanese configuration it dominated. The PLO cherished the freedom of Palestinian decisionmaking; Syria wanted Lebanese, Jordanians, and most of all Palestinians to be subordinate to its strategy as the only remaining state of consequence left in the ranks against Israel. The PLO wanted to explore every opening, however ephemeral, toward a peaceful settlement; Syria argued that this was a mistake until a strategic balance with Israel had been achieved. And while the PLO was convinced that it was essentially alone on the battlefield against Israel, Syria portrayed itself—notably to the Arab oil states that subsidized it—as the outstanding champion of the Arab cause against Israel.

THE EFFECTS OF THE 1982 WAR

Against this background of acrimony in the PLO's relations with various Lebanese factions, ranging from the Phalangists in the north to Amal in the south, and of estrangement in its relations with Syria, Israel launched its 1982 invasion. Palestinian commentators bitterly described the attack as the logical culmination of the Camp David process. It could hardly have come at a worse time for the PLO, which found itself alone on the battlefield for most of the period from June 4, when Israel began its preinvasion air offensive, until the final cease-fire of August 12. Syrian forces in Lebanon were engaged by Israel only from June 9 until the Israeli-Syrian cease-fire of June 26. During this eighteen-day period they bore the brunt of the fighting in most areas. For the remainder of the seventy days of the war, the PLO, its Lebanese allies, and the Syrian units trapped in Beirut fought alone against a large part of the Israeli army. Far from helping them, other Arab states hardly reacted. The Palestinians viewed high-level Saudi and Syrian intercession with Washington as being both self-interested and ineffectual.[7]

The direct effect of the 1982 war on the PLO has been dealt with elsewhere.[8] It suffices here to note that the war reinforced a bitter feeling of isolation and betrayal among Palestinians, a feeling that Camp David had already inflamed. There were several different responses to this feeling. Some, notably within Fatah and in the Popular Front for the Liberation of Palestine, argued that the results of Camp David and the war had shown that the PLO leadership's policy of courting a settlement had been a disastrous failure, and that an entirely new and more radical line was needed. In effect, those who held these views argued, such a policy had led to the PLO estrangement from Syria, a serious problem in 1982, particularly in the absence of the balancing weight of Egypt. These perceptions led to the 1983 split in Fatah and ultimately in the PLO, which lasted for four years.

7. Khalidi, *Under Siege*, pp. 147–65.

8. See Emile F. Sahliyeh, *The PLO after the Lebanon War* (Boulder, Colo.: Westview Press, 1986); and Rashid Khalidi, "Palestinian Politics after the Exodus from Beirut," in Robert O. Freedman, ed., *The Middle East after the Israeli Invasion of Lebanon* (Syracuse University Press, 1986), pp. 233–53.

The PLO mainstream came to the opposite conclusion: if the Palestinians had been variously betrayed by the Egyptian, Syrian, and Saudi regimes, it was imperative for them to practice self-reliance. In effect, this meant relying more on the Palestinians under occupation, moving toward a settlement that took their aspirations into account, restoring relations with Jordan so the PLO could get closer to the occupied territories, and coordinating diplomacy with it. The result was the PLO's "Jordanian option," which had been intensely debated before the 1982 war—with little result—and became the focus of PLO diplomacy for the four years after it.

The Jordanian option had four problems, all of which ultimately proved insurmountable. First, it caused an overt split in Palestinian ranks, and one that sapped PLO strength and credibility. Second, it infuriated the Syrian regime, which could argue plausibly that the PLO was moving toward a separate settlement under U.S. sponsorship, just as Sadat had. Third, King Hussein had his own objectives in entering into such an arrangement, objectives that inevitably came into conflict with those of the Palestinians. And finally, while the PLO may have wanted to move toward a settlement together with Jordan, neither Israel nor the United States ever showed any interest in such a configuration.

Moreover, such an approach had the disadvantage of contradicting all the hard-learned lessons Camp David had taught the Palestinians: do not get into a separate settlement with Americans and Israelis because they will gang up on you; avoid violating the principle of Arab solidarity, which the PLO depends upon more than any other Arab group; do not allow Arab states to act as intermediaries for the Palestinians with the United States and Israel; and avoid alienating the PLO's allies and supporters in the international community.

Even when these "lessons" were of dubious value—Arab solidarity, for example, proved to be ephemeral in the seventy days of war and siege in Lebanon in 1982—they embodied the perceptions of most Palestinians and many Arabs. By ignoring them, the PLO leadership took a risk, even though it was supported by the majority of the seventeenth PNC at the meeting in November 1984. The PLO might have been justified in its actions, and found vindication, had there been a response from the United States and Israel. The cold hostility of both powers fatally wounded the Jordanian option, to which King Hussein eventually delivered the coup de grace in February 1986.

Some argue—usually those who reject dealing with the PLO under any circumstances—that the reunification of the PLO at the eighteenth session of the PNC, held at Algiers in April 1987, moved it away from the peace process. This interpretation is borne out neither by a reading of the session's resolutions nor by PLO actions since then (see appendix I). The resolutions explicitly call for PLO involvement in an international peace conference and for greater contacts with Israeli peace forces. Where they do embody a change is in their insistence that the Palestinians speak for themselves in any negotiations and not allow Jordan or other intermediaries to play such a role, a point now apparently accepted by King Hussein as shown by his July 1988 speech (see appendix M). That seems to be a clear outgrowth of Palestinian perceptions in the wake of Camp David.

CONCLUSION

In sum, how did Camp David affect the Palestinians from 1978 until 1988? It has certainly not affected them in the ways that either its American or Egyptian signatories may have intended. A resolution of the Palestine question is probably further away than in 1978; the Palestinian-Israeli conflict has taken on new and ominous demographic, religious, and Israeli domestic political dimensions, especially after the Palestinian uprising of 1987–88; and the idea of autonomy has proved to be a failure.

Instead it was the Israeli vision—and specifically the Likud vision—that has prevailed on the Palestinian level, not so much in terms of what was explicit in the accords and the treaty, but in terms of what was implicit. And here the Israeli leaders, unlike their American and Egyptian counterparts, seem to have understood exactly what they were getting into, the extent of their leverage and power, and the opportunities that had opened up for them.

With the Camp David Accords, the United States and Egypt set Israel free to deal as it saw fit with both the West Bank and Gaza, and the PLO in Lebanon. The growing number of Israeli settlements and the integration into Israel of the occupied territories began to reveal their full negative impact only a decade after Camp David with the Palestinian uprising. The limits of Israel's freedom to act in Lebanon were only exposed with the 1982 war.

It could be argued that some of these consequences are the result of the PLO's equivocations and hesitations during the crucial first nine months of 1977, before Sadat flew to Jerusalem, when a comprehensive settlement approach was being actively pursued by the Carter administration, the Soviet Union, the Arabs, and Israel. It could also be argued that the PLO weakened itself by the major armed assaults, from the Savoy Hotel attack in Tel Aviv in the spring of 1975 aimed at derailing Kissinger's negotiations for Sinai II, to the March 1978 coastal road attack, aimed at undermining the ongoing United States-Israeli-Egyptian negotiations that culminated at Camp David.

Such assaults had little effect on the PLO's ostensible political objective: both the Sinai II and Camp David agreements were eventually concluded, and were probably not measurably delayed by these actions. But though the assaults undoubtedly further alienated Israeli and American public opinion, and served as pretexts for excluding the Palestinians from any role in the determination of their fate, the question must be asked: would the Palestinians have been included in the settlement process in 1975 or 1978 by the three major participants even had the behavior of the PLO been ideal? Excluded from one round of the peace process, the PLO in the past has resorted to action to derail the process and show that it cannot be ignored—action that is then used to justify its already inevitable exclusion from the next round. The same observation would seem to apply to a number of "missed opportunities" for which the PLO is often berated, such as the Mena House talks proposed by Sadat in December 1977. But would Begin have agreed to sit down with the PLO? And if not, would not Sadat, in his desperation for a settlement, have accommodated the Israeli leader? There can be little doubt, in view of the likely answer to these questions, that the result for the Palestinians would have been much the same as that which actually occurred. The only difference would have been that the American public's image of them might have been slightly less negative.

It is hard to come up with an alternative line that would have worked for the Palestinians in the period after 1978, given the extent, depth, and irreversibility of their desire for national self-determination in their homeland. Most of the PLO leaders seem to have realized the self-defeating nature of certain actions, and to have systematically worked to restrain their followers, beginning in the spring of 1978 right after the Israeli invasion of southern Lebanon that followed the coastal road attack. Palestinian attacks from Lebanon declined, and there was a more active search for a diplomatic approach to a settlement.

All this culminated in the Israeli-Palestinian cease-fire of 1981–82 in southern Lebanon, in PLO support for the Fahd plan and the Fez Arab League peace plan,[9] in the PLO-drafted "Franco-Egyptian"

9. The Fahd plan, announced by Saudi Arabia in August 1981, and the Fez plan,

United Nations Security Council peace initiative put forward during the 1982 war, which was prevented from being brought before the Security Council in July 1982 by the United States,[10] and later in the PLO's opening to Jordan. These were all efforts to behave "moderately" and "responsibly" and even in some measure to conform to stated American concerns. The Jordanian option, and in particular the Arafat-Hussein agreement of February 11, 1985 (see appendix F), can thus be seen as part of an effort to meet the conditions stated in the September 1982 Reagan plan, which by then had long been forgotten in Washington (see appendix D). Needless to say, all these efforts from 1978 on failed, for they coincided first with the election of a Likud government in Israel and later with the arrival of the Reagan administration, which together developed the closest Israeli-American relationship ever, based among other things on a policy of affirming the status quo and eliminating the Palestinians from the settlement process.

Events such as these during the years since Camp David, in particular the past few, have demonstrated to Palestinians the perils of relying on the United States, Egypt, and Jordan—hence the Palestinian preference for a comprehensive settlement approach that includes other parties. Ironically, as far as the Palestine question is concerned, the situation is right back where it was in 1973 or 1977, before the illusion that peace in the Middle East began and ended with Egypt captivated concerned American policymakers and allowed them to be seduced away from a comprehensive approach.

More than ten years after the Camp David Accords, the same questions regarding a settlement remain: which multilateral comprehensive forum is preferable; how to bring together the equally necessary negotiations of bilateral and multilateral issues in such a forum, while at the same time keeping them separate; and finally and most difficult, how to secure authentic full-scale Palestinian representation. Without that, it is ludicrous to claim to settle the Palestine question. Representation has to be achieved, even at the risk of offending Israeli sensitivities that have been allowed to govern American policy since Kissinger's pledge to Israel of 1975.

Camp David, for all the harm it did directly and indirectly to the Palestinians, can also be seen in a broader context as having delayed

approved at the September 1982 Arab League summit, call explicitly for an international negotiating forum to resolve the Arab-Israeli conflict involving *all* parties, and for *all* states in the region to live in peace. In both cases Israel is understood to be included. See appendix E in this volume.

10. Khalidi, *Under Siege*, pp. 135–47.

for at least a decade a solution to the remaining thorny issues in the Arab-Israeli arena, many of which Israel opened up by its hollow victory in the 1967 war and exacerbated by its hollow triumph in diplomacy at Camp David. These issues are a settlement of the problem of the occupied Golan Heights; a final, just disposition of the territory of historic Palestine west of the Jordan River, including a solution to the problem of Jerusalem; and last but not least, the long-belated self-determination of the Palestinian people. The 1987–88 popular uprising in the West Bank and Gaza demonstrates that it is no longer possible to ignore these issues, as has been done for a decade during which the illusion was fostered that Camp David could bring peace to the Middle East.

EMILE SAHLIYEH

Jordan and the Palestinians

TEN YEARS after the signing of the Camp David Accords, an agreement between Jordan, the Palestinians, and Israel over the future of the occupied territories still remains elusive. The opposition of Jordanians and Palestinians to the Camp David Accords is as strong nowadays as it was in 1978. Yet it is wrong to assume that the attitudes of both have remained rigid over the last decade. Many Palestinians, and certainly Jordan, have come to realize that diplomacy is the only option available for the resolution of the Palestinian question. Both Jordan and the Palestinians have also come to accept the need for a transitional regime for the occupied territories as a step toward the final resolution of the Arab-Israeli conflict. A diplomatic breakthrough has so far not taken place. Jordan and the Palestinians, especially those in the occupied territories, operate under severe domestic and external constraints that have limited their freedom to maneuver and the range of options open to them.

JORDAN'S FOREIGN POLICY, 1978–88

Since its independence in 1946, three preoccupations have dominated Jordan's foreign policy: maintenance of the regime and preservation of internal political stability, economic development and modernization of Jordan, and the resolution of the Palestinian

This chapter will concentrate on Jordan in relationship to the occupied West Bank and Gaza. This is not meant to imply that the author or the editor believes that the Palestinian issue must be resolved within a Jordanian framework. For purposes of analyzing the diplomatic moves of the past decade, however, there is merit in focusing on Jordan's relations with the Palestinians, especially those in the occupied territories, since many initiatives have been premised on some degree of Jordanian-Palestinian cooperation.

question. These three objectives are mutually reinforcing and reflect Jordan's core interests.

Jordan's Interest in the West Bank

Jordan's interest in settling the Palestinian problem has stemmed from a complex set of considerations.[1] It was in 1950 that Jordan annexed the West Bank and East Jerusalem. It maintained its claim of sovereignty until King Hussein's decision, in July 1988, to sever ties to the occupied territories (see appendix M). The historic pan-Arab role of the Hashemite family has been another reason for King Hussein's continued interest in resolving the Palestinian problem. The Jordanian monarch has not wanted to be remembered in history as the one who lost the West Bank and East Jerusalem to Israel. For this reason, the king has felt responsible for restoring Arab sovereignty over the area.

Aside from this pan-Arab mission, Hussein's interests in resolving the Palestinian problem are more mundane and practical. National security considerations are important. The prolongation of Israel's occupation will not only radicalize the Palestinians in the West Bank and Gaza but will also politicize those who live in Jordan, especially since the onset of the Palestinian *intifadah* (uprising) in December 1987. The lack of resolution of the Palestinian question will further frustrate the Palestinian refugees who live in the East Bank of the Jordan River. Unlike the class of wealthy Palestinians who live in Amman, the inhabitants of the refugee camps have not developed a stake in the survival of the Hashemite regime. A continuous influx of Palestinians into Jordan from the occupied territories would further tip the demographic imbalance against East Bank Jordanians and compound Jordan's economic problems. The king's sensitivity to this demographic threat has been heightened over the years by the fear that a future Israeli government led by Ariel Sharon could try to settle the Palestinian question on the East Bank at the expense of Jordan's royal family.

The relevance of Jordan to the resolution of the Palestinian question is also sustained by external considerations. The opposition of both the United States and Israel to the inclusion of the Palestine Liberation Organization (PLO) in the peace process points to a central role for Jordan in any future diplomatic round. The two

1. For an elaboration of Jordan's interests in the resolution of the Palestinian question, see El Hassan Bin Talal (crown prince of Jordan), "Jordan's Quest for Peace," *Foreign Affairs*, vol. 60 (Spring 1982), pp. 804–09.

states see Hussein as a natural partner for Israel in any negotiations. Finally, the presence of strong cultural, social, economic, and familial ties between West Bank Palestinians and the population in Jordan also underlines the practicality of involving Jordan in the diplomatic efforts to resolve the Palestinian question.

Despite such motives and interests, Jordan has been reluctant to act independently on the resolution of the Palestinian question. To do so could threaten the attainment of its other two core objectives: the regime's stability and economic modernization. Thus Jordan's treatment of the Arab-Israeli conflict has been characterized by caution, conservatism, and indecisiveness. Whether in regard to the Camp David Accords, the Reagan initiative of September 1982, or the Arafat-Hussein diplomatic accord of February 1985, the Jordanian government has opted not to act against an Arab consensus. When it became clear early in 1988 that no such consensus in favor of a Jordanian role existed, Hussein announced the termination of Jordan's ties to the West Bank.

Constraints on Jordan's Foreign Policy

Over the years, a host of domestic and external considerations has constrained Jordan's freedom of action on the Arab-Israeli dispute. A brief examination of these constraints will not only help clarify the evolution of Jordan's foreign policy between 1978 and 1988, but will also shed some light on the future directions of that policy and the peace process. Jordan's internal political structure, geopolitical and economic position, and constraints imposed by the external environment have limited Jordan's freedom to act on questions related to the Palestinian problem. The constraints make an assertive and independent Jordanian approach to the Arab-Israeli conflict exceedingly difficult.

Jordan's internal political structure and decisionmaking apparatus have affected the government's policy toward the Palestinian question. The king makes the decisions affecting Jordan's foreign and security policy. The centrality of the king in Jordan's decisionmaking process stems from the nature of Jordan's political system, which is characterized by the supremacy of the monarch and a low level of political participation.

Though the king is the final authoritative decisionmaker, policymaking in Jordan is nonetheless complex. The significant decisions about the Palestinian question are not made in a political vacuum. Besides the king, Jordan's top policymaking elite includes the following key participants: the crown prince, the chief of the royal court, the minister of the royal court, the chief of staff of the army, the prime minister, and the ministers of interior and foreign affairs. The influence of these key figures does not stem primarily from their position in the government but rather from their personal relationship with the king. Jordan's Palestinian policy is also shaped by the political stands of influential social groups. The East Bank Jordanians, including the tribal leaders, the army, and the Palestinian wealthy class, are all active in Jordan's complex political life.

Consequently, Jordan's approach to the resolution of the Palestinian problem is far from monolithic. Three tendencies are discernible among the political elite and policy influencers. Advocates of the first tendency do not perceive the Palestinian question as purely a foreign policy issue but more as a domestic problem. The Palestinian demographic threat to East Bank Jordanian national identity and interests is behind the worry of this group of politicians. Though forty years have passed since Jordan and the Palestinians came together in a close relationship, political distrust still exists between the two communities. Profound political cleavages exist between East Bank Jordanians and Palestinians in the occupied territories. With approximately 70 percent of the West Bank population below the age of twenty-five,[2] most of the population has not experienced living under the Hashemite regime and has no political affinity or allegiance to the royal family.

Advocates of this Jordanian nationalist trend do not want to see the reintegration of the West Bank into Jordan. They certainly do not want to assume the difficult task of controlling the West Bank's highly politicized society. This group of politicians wants, therefore, to disentangle Jordan as much as possible from the Palestinian question and devote the government's financial resources to economic development of the East Bank.

The proponents of two other tendencies believe that Jordan, for various reasons, cannot disassociate itself from the Palestinian problem. The two groups, however, differ over who will be Jordan's partners in the search for a political solution of the Arab-Israeli conflict. The advocates of the second trend argue that the Jordanian government should coordinate diplomatic moves with the PLO and the Palestinians in the occupied territories. Their position is predicated on the belief that the future of the West Bank and Gaza is primarily a Palestinian-Jordanian question. These advocates believe

2. Central Bureau of Statistics, *Statistical Abstract of Israel, 1987*, no. 38 (Jerusalem, 1987), p. 702.

that participation of the PLO in the peace process is essential to legitimize any diplomatic solution that may be reached with Israel. Strong ties between West Bank Palestinians and Jordanians, and the large Palestinian community in Jordan, provide the rationale for joint Jordanian-Palestinian diplomatic efforts.

The advocates of the third trend believe that Jordan and the Palestinians on their own cannot negotiate an acceptable deal with Israel. They do not trust the PLO's leadership and consider it weak, indecisive, and lacking in seriousness. Yet because of keen interest in ending Israel's military occupation of the West Bank and Gaza, these politicians advise the king to coordinate his moves with Syria and the other Arab countries.

These three tendencies should not suggest that political debate in Jordan is intense and widespread, rendering the role of the king that of a consensus builder. Rather, such political tendencies among Jordan's political elite and influential social groups leave an impact on the formulation of Jordan's foreign policy. The competing tendencies account, in part, for the ambivalence, indecisiveness, and frequent shifts in Jordan's approach to the resolution of the Palestinian question.

Jordan's Geographic Position and Dependency

Jordan's geopolitical vulnerability and encirclement by militarily and economically superior neighbors (Israel, Syria, Iraq, and Saudi Arabia) have created a deep sense of insecurity among Jordan's policymaking elite. The sharing of borders with these four countries make Jordan susceptible to pressures and penetration, and, from time to time, have rendered it a target of Israel and Syria. Jordan's geopolitical insecurity is reinforced by the small size of its population, which prevents the government from playing a key and continuing role in inter-Arab affairs. Jordan's geographic position has limited its foreign policy options and has often resulted in a foreign policy characterized by caution, ambivalence, and appeasement of its neighbors. Despite this geopolitical weakness, the Jordanian government has, on occasion, been able to play the role of mediator among the more influential Arab states during periods of bitter conflict.

Economic considerations have also constrained Jordan's foreign policymaking behavior. The country's narrow resource base has not allowed the government to pursue an activist foreign policy. Because of its poor economic infrastructure, the Jordanian government relies heavily on foreign aid for economic survival. This situation of economic dependency and weakness heavily influences the goals and substance of Jordan's foreign policy. The country's domestic resources are too poor to be marshaled in support of independent political moves and initiatives. Unlike Egypt, Jordan is a small and weak country with poor material and human resources and cannot afford to be isolated from the Arab world. These prevailing economic realities often compel the Jordanian government to adopt cooperative, conciliatory behavior toward its Arab neighbors and frequently to subordinate its interests and views on the Arab-Israeli conflict to an Arab consensus.

The dictates of the ideology of pan-Arabism and inter-Arab politics reinforce Jordan's sense of geographic and economic insecurity. For a long time the Palestinian question has been seen as a collective Arab responsibility and at the core of Arab concerns. In its search for a solution to the Palestinian question, the Jordanian government has usually not enjoyed collective Arab backing. This situation has meant that Jordan could not successfully initiate its own approach to the complexities of the Arab-Israeli conflict. The centrality of the Palestinian problem to the Arabs constrains Jordan's options.

The Jordanian regime's freedom to maneuver is also influenced by the Palestinians. Since 1974, the PLO has been formally designated by the Arab League as the sole legitimate representative for the interests of the Palestinians in any peace talks. Support for King Hussein in the West Bank and Gaza is very limited. Even the pro-Jordanian West Bank politicians have, over the years, been reluctant to support openly the king's foreign policy moves without the PLO's consent and authorization.

The policies of Israel and the United States are two additional considerations that affect Jordan's foreign policy. Israel's terms for peace have never met King Hussein's minimum requirements for a political solution. The Labor party's concept of territorial compromise promises to return to Jordan only between 60 percent and 70 percent of the West Bank and does not concede to Jordan any right of sovereignty over East Jerusalem.[3] The views of the Likud bloc, Israel's other main political force, are more hostile to Jordan's interests. The leaders of the Likud regard the West Bank and Gaza as parts of the historic "land of Israel," and therefore they are

3. For the official stand of the Labor party on withdrawal from the West Bank, see Yigal Allon, "Israel: The Case for Defensible Borders," *Foreign Affairs*, vol. 55 (October 1976), pp. 38–53.

vehemently opposed to returning any part of these territories to Jordanian sovereignty. The political deadlock in Israel that prevailed after 1984 and the weakness of the Labor party have not given Jordan incentives to begin negotiations.

Another determining factor of Jordan's policy toward the Arab-Israeli conflict has been the pro-Israeli posture of the various American administrations. The Jordanians believe that without a firm American commitment to search actively for a just solution to the conflict it would be too risky to engage in any negotiations with Israel. Jordanian officials have lamented the fact that the United States abstained from using its powerful leverage to induce Israel to make meaningful territorial concessions to its Arab neighbors.

Reaction to the Camp David Accords

Anwar Sadat's trip to Jerusalem in November 1977 and the signing of the Camp David Accords a year later caused a great deal of anxiety among Arab countries. Except for Sudan and Oman, the rest of the Arab countries opposed Egypt's diplomatic moves. The unfolding of such dramatic developments, however, increased Jordan's importance in the Arab political system and King Hussein, who had for a long time been considered an Arab outcast, became an important regional player. Both Egypt and its Arab critics were keen on enlisting his support to their respective sides.

The presence of close ties between Jordan and the occupied territories and Western recognition of Jordan's importance in the resolution of the Palestinian problem were valuable assets that both camps wanted to cultivate. The Egyptians were interested in Jordan in order to broaden the peace process and to undermine the efforts of the Arab countries to isolate Egypt. For this reason the Egyptian government, after November 1977, presented pro-Jordanian demands, including the issuing of a declaration of principles on Israel's total withdrawal from the occupied territories and its acceptance of the Palestinians' right to self-determination. At the same time, Sadat dispatched senior aides to Amman to inform their Jordanian counterparts of the status of negotiations with Israel. In contrast, the opposing Arab camp of Syria, Iraq, Libya, Saudi Arabia, and the PLO were interested in keeping Jordan from joining Egypt's diplomatic venture. Consequently, both the moderate and radical Arab states offered Jordan many types of economic and political inducements.

The Wait-and-See Policy

In response to Egypt's rift with the other Arab regimes, King Hussein's government adopted a cautious, ambivalent posture. Between November 1977 and November 1978, Jordan opted for a policy of wait-and-see about Sadat's diplomatic initiative rather than choosing sides between the two opposing camps.[4] King Hussein was careful not to alienate Jordan from either Egypt or the other Arab countries. For instance, despite the outcry that Sadat's initiative generated in the region, King Hussein did not condemn the Egyptian president for his effort to resolve the Arab-Israeli conflict through diplomatic means. Hussein described Sadat's presentation of pro-Arab demands to the Israeli Knesset as an act of "moral courage."[5] He did not discourage the pro-Jordanian notables in the occupied territories from meeting Sadat during his visit to East Jerusalem. Likewise the king refused to attend the Tripoli conference of December 1977 that led to the formation of the Rejection Front of Syria, Libya, South Yemen, Algeria, and the PLO.

The Jordanians were realistic in assessing their situation as they did not anticipate immediate benefits for their country from Sadat's initiative. They were hoping that Egypt's moves would facilitate the convening of an international peace conference for the resolution of all aspects of the Arab-Israeli conflict on the basis of United Nations Security Council Resolution 242 (see appendix A). In particular, the Jordanians were interested in finding out what territorial concessions the Israelis were willing to make in favor of Egypt.

The signing of the Camp David Accords in September 1978, the Egyptian-Israeli peace treaty in March 1979, and the emerging Arab consensus against Egypt's diplomatic moves caused the Jordanian government to drop its wait-and-see policy and openly side with the Arab opposition. Jordan's rejection of the accords, however, was not total and immediate. In a statement on September 20, 1978, the Jordanian government expressed surprise that Jordan's name was mentioned in the Camp David Accords and stated that it did not consider itself morally or legally bound by the agreement. The

4. For a more detailed account of Jordan's foreign policy during this period, see Adam M. Garfinkle, "Negotiating by Proxy: Jordanian Foreign Policy and U.S. Options in the Middle East," *Orbis*, vol. 24 (Winter 1981), pp. 863–77.

5. "Hussein: 'Close Ranks,' " *Newsweek*, December 12, 1977, p. 59. See also "The Best Contribution Jordan Can Make Is to Ensure Arab Cohesion," *Jordan Times*, December 2, 1977.

cabinet statement lamented Egypt's unilateral move and asserted that it would weaken "Arab rights."[6]

Despite its public criticism, the government of King Hussein expressed some interest in exploring the potential and meaning of the Camp David Accords. Jordan submitted a list of questions to the Carter administration in late September 1978.[7] The Jordanian government wanted to know the Carter administration's interpretation of the Camp David Accords and ascertain the administration's resolve to bring about an Israeli withdrawal from the West Bank and Gaza. Jordan also inquired about the length of the transitional period, the powers of the self-governing authority, the extent of Israel's withdrawal from the occupied territories, and the future of East Jerusalem, Israel's settlers, settlements, and army after the termination of the transitional period.

In response, the Carter administration reiterated past American administrations' stands on the Arab-Israeli conflict. In addition, President Jimmy Carter asserted that his administration would become energetically involved in the next round of diplomacy and that it would support the right of the Palestinian inhabitants of East Jerusalem to vote for the self-governing authority. The Jordanian government did not feel that the American answers offered them sufficient incentives and assurances to join the Camp David Accords. Instead, the government sided with the rest of the Arab world in opposing the Egyptian-Israeli peace process. In early November 1978, King Hussein participated in the Arab League summit in Baghdad that orchestrated a unified Arab opposition to both Egypt's diplomatic moves and the Camp David Accords.

Joining the Arab Consensus

Jordan decided to end its policy of wait-and-see because of several concerns. The country's geopolitical vulnerability and economic dependency compelled the government not to embark on a solution to the Palestinian question that was against collective Arab wishes. In particular, Jordan was careful not to antagonize more powerful neighbors (Syria and Iraq) and not to upset Saudi Arabia (its main financier). The downfall of the shah of Iran during that time

6. "In an Emergency Session of the Council of Ministers Chaired by Hussein Lasting Three Hours: Jordan Defines Its Position concerning the Results of Camp David" (in Arabic), *Al-Dustur*, September 20, 1978.

7. For a list of the Jordanian questions and American answers, see William B. Quandt, *Camp David: Peacemaking and Politics* (Brookings, 1986), pp. 388–96.

heightened King Hussein's fears and anxieties, especially since in the past the king had been the target of several assassination attempts.

In their efforts to keep Jordan from signing the Camp David Accords, the Arab heads of state made special attempts to court King Hussein during their summit conference in Baghdad. The summit pledged to provide Jordan with approximately $1.25 billion annually in economic aid for a period of ten years. In another resolution, the Arab heads of state requested that both Jordan and the PLO form a joint economic committee to distribute the $150 million allocated annually for the West Bank and Gaza by the summit. This move enhanced Jordan's legitimacy and recognized its special role in representing Palestinian interests alongside the PLO. In addition, during that period Jordan's relationship with Syria and Iraq was strengthened and its relationship with the PLO was reconciled.

Jordan's decision not to join the Camp David peace process was also caused by the stand of the Israeli government. Prime Minister Menachem Begin, the leader of the Likud coalition, abandoned the Labor party's search for a resolution of the Palestinian question on the basis of reaching some territorial compromises with Jordan. He also gave a new interpretation of Resolution 242. From his perspective the West Bank and Gaza were no longer occupied territories but were an integral part of the biblical land of Israel and as such were liberated areas. Israel's intensification of settlement activities in the West Bank and Gaza, its narrow interpretation of the concept of autonomy (applicable to the people but not to the land), and its firm opposition to any linkage between the two Camp David agreements convinced the Jordanian government that there was nothing for them in the accords.

Finally, despite President Jimmy Carter's dedication to an Arab-Israeli peace, the remaining years of his administration were not conducive to that goal. Between 1979 and 1980, the American president was preoccupied with the American hostages in Tehran and with getting reelected. Under such circumstances, the Jordanian monarch did not expect Carter to play an active role in the resolution of the intractable problem of the West Bank and Gaza. Carter's reluctance to engage directly in the peace process was evident in his appointment of a personal representative to the autonomy talks.

With Carter's failure to win a second term to the White House, the peace process was placed on the back burner. The Reagan administration did not assign to the resolution of the Arab-Israeli conflict the same urgency. Instead, President Ronald Reagan was interested in building a strategic consensus among U.S. Middle Eastern friends to contain the Soviet Union and to protect the Gulf. It was only in September 1982, after the Israeli invasion of Lebanon, that the Reagan administration introduced a major plan to resolve the conflict over the West Bank and Gaza (see appendix D). In the meantime, major challenges confronted Jordan's foreign policy.

Breaking Away from Neutrality

The new phase that was ushered in after the signing of the Egyptian-Israeli peace treaty in the spring of 1979 witnessed a more assertive Jordanian foreign policy. Between March 1979 and April 1983, Jordan's policymakers were preoccupied with three main issues: management of the outbreak of the new Arab "cold war" and the resulting bitter cleavages, defending against Israel's provocative statements on Jordan's territorial integrity, and restructuring Jordan's relationship with the PLO.

The solidarity among the Arab countries that resulted from their effort to isolate Egypt was short-lived. Inter-Arab rivalries and divisions were soon renewed. In the summer of 1979, the bitter hostility between Syria and Iraq was resumed after a short honeymoon period. With the renewal of tension between these two pan-Arab regimes, Jordan found itself embroiled in the struggle between them. King Hussein sided with Iraq against Syria. Iraq's financial assistance to Jordan's economy and the growing belief that Baghdad would soon replace Cairo as leader of the Arab world led to Jordan's alignment with Iraq.[8] In a defiant gesture against Syrian interests, the Jordanian government in February 1980 supported the pan-Arab National Charter (a document that the Iraqi government sponsored to bring about Arab solidarity).[9] Later that year, after the outbreak of the Iraq-Iran war, the Jordanian government openly sided with Iraq.

The growing intimacy between Baghdad and Amman led to estrangement in Jordan's relationship with Syria. Tension between these two neighboring states was further accentuated by Jordan's complicity and encouragement in the violent activities of the Muslim Brotherhood against President Hafiz al-Asad's regime in

8. For Iraq's growing status at the time, see Claudia Wright, "Iraq—New Power in the Middle East," *Foreign Affairs*, vol. 58 (Winter 1979–80), pp. 257–77.

9. Amman Domestic Television Service, February 10, 1980, in Foreign Broadcast Information Service, *Daily Report: The Middle East and North Africa*, February 12, 1980, p. F1 (hereafter FBIS, *Daily Report: MEA*).

the early 1980s. Between October and November of 1980, the conflict between Jordan and Syria reached a level of brinkmanship. To register his anger against King Hussein's insistence on convening the eleventh Arab League summit in Amman, Asad deployed part of his army along the Syrian-Jordanian border. Jordan's favorable reception of the Reagan initiative in September 1982 and the subsequent Jordanian-PLO dialogue exacerbated the relationship between Damascus and Amman. Hussein's move on both counts clashed sharply with Syria's perception of its role as the key Arab interlocutor in the resolution of the Arab-Israeli conflict.

Israeli Threats to Jordan's Security

Besides the worsening relationship between Jordan and Syria, a second source of anxiety for King Hussein's government came from Israel. Jordan was alarmed by the foreign policy actions and rhetoric of the ruling Likud bloc. Israel's destruction of the Iraqi nuclear reactor in June 1981, aerial bombardment of the PLO's headquarters in Beirut a month later, extension of Israeli law to the Golan Heights in December, and the massive invasion of Lebanon in the summer of 1982 were extremely disquieting to the Jordanian regime. Government officials were afraid that their country would be Israel's next target. Fears were fueled by the statements of key Israeli political leaders including then-Minister of Defense Ariel Sharon and then-Minister of Foreign Affairs Yitzhak Shamir. Both men alleged repeatedly that Jordan was already a Palestinian state. Thus there was no need for a second Palestinian state in the West Bank and Gaza. Such statements, coming on the heels of Israel's heavy-handed provocative practices in the occupied territories and the Arab region, heightened Jordan's security fears. In particular, senior Jordanian officials were worried that Israel might expel a large number of Palestinians to the East Bank in an attempt to resolve the Palestinian question.[10]

To reduce threats emanating from both Syria and Israel, the Jordanian government embarked on several foreign policy moves. First, to check the Syrian menace, Jordan aligned itself with Iraq. But with Iraq's deteriorating position in the war against Iran, a

10. Fears about this possibility were expressed by Adnan Abu Odeh, Jordan's minister of information, in an interview on Radio Monte Carlo on November 26, 1982, and by Crown Prince Hassan in "The Region Is Exposed to Balkanization Not Division and the Alternative Nation Is Not Only in Jordan" (in Arabic), *Al-Hawadith*, no. 1339 (July 2, 1982), pp. 19–22. See also *Al-Ray*, October 25, 1982.

gradual improvement in Jordan's relationship with Egypt was also undertaken. This process culminated in the restoration of full diplomatic relations between the two states in September 1984.

Second, the Jordanian government also envisaged a regional role for its armed forces, including the protection of the oil fields in the Gulf region. Besides enlisting the support of Saudi Arabia and the other Arab Gulf countries for Jordan's national security, the expansion of the role of the Jordanian army was expected to deepen American military commitment to Jordan's security interests and the survival of the Hashemite royal family. To augment the strategic capabilities of his army, King Hussein approached the Reagan administration to purchase ground-to-air mobile missile systems. Congressional opposition led the Jordanian monarch to turn to the Soviet Union to purchase air defense equipment.

Third, Jordan tried to take advantage of the unfolding of political developments in the summer of 1982, including Israel's invasion of Lebanon, the subsequent expulsion of the PLO's troops from Beirut, and the launching of the Reagan initiative. Israel's invasion of Lebanon in June 1982 was received with mixed feelings by Jordan's decisionmakers. The invasion proved again to the Jordanian government the bellicosity of Israel's Defense Minister Ariel Sharon and heightened fears that Jordan might be Sharon's next target. Yet the PLO's vulnerability and political weakness, following the dispersal of its troops from Lebanon, introduced new opportunities to bring Jordan back to center stage. The announcement of the Reagan initiative reinforced that prospect.

In view of these developments, King Hussein felt that his country's relationship with the PLO should assume a new dimension. The cornerstone for this new relationship was to launch a joint Jordanian-PLO initiative to resolve the Palestinian question. The grounds for this initiative would be to associate the West Bank and the Gaza with Jordan and to form a joint Jordanian-Palestinian negotiating team, in line with Reagan's peace proposals.

To pave the way for the restructuring of its relationship with the PLO, the Jordanian government was concerned about preserving a moderate leadership for the PLO during the siege of Beirut in the summer of 1982. Jordan wanted to ensure that the PLO would not be radicalized or subordinated to hostile Arab regimes, so the government declared that it would give refuge to a significant number of PLO fighters. In a letter to the PLO chief, Jordan's prime minister spelled out several conditions regulating the presence of PLO fighters in Jordan. First, those PLO fighters who carried Jordanian citizenship and who were committed to live an orderly civilian life away from armed struggle were allowed to return to Jordan. Second, the government made it clear that it would not tolerate any Palestinian infiltration into the occupied territories or Israel from Jordanian territory. The returning PLO men were required to give up their weapons.[11]

Reaction to the Reagan Initiative and the Rise of the Jordanian-PLO Dialogue

As the drop in the PLO's political weight contributed to the rise in Jordan's political fortunes, the announcement of the Reagan initiative in September 1982 gave Jordan's role in the resolution of the Palestinian question an additional political thrust. The initiative contained several positive points that were congruent with Jordan's political preferences. The Reagan initiative opposed Israel's permanent control or annexation of the occupied territories and expressed opposition to the construction of additional Jewish settlements. President Reagan also declared that the United States would not support the establishment of an independent Palestinian state and proposed instead to give the Palestinians in the West Bank and Gaza self-government in association with Jordan.

King Hussein described the Reagan initiative as "the most courageous stand taken by an American administration ever since 1956." The king also expressed strong interest in seeing the initiative continue and evolve.[12] In a speech to a group of Jordanian politicians on September 20, 1982, King Hussein appealed to the Arab kings and presidents not to reject the Reagan initiative out of hand but rather to consider it carefully.[13]

Despite his favorable reception of the Reagan initiative, the Jordanian monarch was constrained by the 1974 Arab summit resolution in Rabat that gave the PLO the exclusive right to represent Palestinian interests. Jordan's cooperation with the PLO was therefore essential to explore the potential of the American peace plan. The PLO's widespread legitimacy among both the Arabs and the Palestinians was expected to reduce the opposition by the radical Arab countries and Palestinian rejectionists to King Hussein's

11. The content of the prime minister's letter can be found in *Al-Ray,* August 11, 1982. For further elaboration of Jordan's conditions, see Radio Monte Carlo, August 17, 1982, in FBIS, *Daily Report: MEA,* August 17, 1982, p. F2.

12. Hussein's interview with the British Broadcasting Corporation, September 13, 1982, in FBIS, *Daily Report: MEA,* September 14, 1982, p. F3.

13. For the text of the speech, see "Hussein: Jordanian-Palestinian Unity Is the Most Sacred and Successful Example of Unity" (in Arabic), *Al-Dustur,* September 21, 1982.

participation in the peace process. Additionally, the PLO's involvement in any negotiation would open the way for greater flexibility on the issue of territorial withdrawal. The king was aware that in the event of a final political settlement, the Israeli government would insist on keeping some of the territory captured in 1967, especially around Jerusalem. Speaking in the name of the Palestinians, the PLO could put the stamp of approval on concessions of this sort. Jordan could not.

King Hussein invited the PLO chief Yasir Arafat to come to Amman to discuss the federation of the occupied territories with the East Bank of the Jordan River and to form a joint team to negotiate with Israel. In public speeches on September 20, 1982, and January 10, 1983, the king made it clear that his government did not intend to replace the PLO in representing Palestinian interests or to exclude it from any peace talks. On October 9, 1982, a dialogue was started between Hussein and Arafat. After six months, however, the Jordanian monarch ended his talks with the PLO.[14]

The Failure of the First Round of the Talks

A number of conditions accounted for the failure of the Jordanian-PLO dialogue. For example, the concept of federating the occupied territories with Jordan and forming a joint negotiating delegation produced acrimonious debate within the PLO. The dialogue was bitterly denounced by the pro-Syrian Palestinian radical groups, and Arafat's associates in Fatah did not anticipate any clear advantage for the PLO by continuing the dialogue. They were also afraid that their partnership with Jordan would fragment the Palestinians more. King Hussein was angered by Arafat's evasiveness and indecisiveness.

Jordan's decision to end the dialogue was also caused by the absence of any expectation of Israeli political flexibility and the lack of American resolve to press Israel for territorial compromises in favor of Jordan. The Jordanian government was not eager to commence talks with Israeli leaders who maintained inflexible positions over the future of the West Bank and Gaza. Prime Minister Begin categorically rejected the Reagan initiative. Not only did he

14. For the text of the Jordanian official communiqué ending the dialogue, see "Jordan, Citing Return to Square One, Abandons Talks with PLO," *Jordan Times*, April 11, 1983. For a detailed treatment of the success and failure of the Jordanian–PLO dialogue, see Emile F. Sahliyeh, *The PLO after the Lebanon War* (Boulder, Colo.: Westview Press, 1986), pp. 115–38.

oppose any freeze on Jewish settlements in the occupied territories, but he also intensified settlement activity in the area.

Jordan's hopes for an assertive American policy to settle the Palestinian question dissipated soon after the announcement of the Reagan initiative. President Reagan did not follow up on his initiative; instead his administration became embroiled in Lebanon's political and military turmoil. A withdrawal of the Israeli army from Lebanon and a freeze on the construction of Israeli settlements in the West Bank and Gaza were perceived by the Jordanian government as tests of American credibility and resolve in handling the complex issues of the West Bank and Gaza. Israel's unwillingness to withdraw its army from Lebanon raised serious doubts in Jordan about the utility of negotiating with the Likud government and the ability of the Reagan administration to pressure Prime Minister Begin to withdraw from the West Bank, an area that is more valuable to Israel than Lebanon.[15] King Hussein was also warned by Chinese and Soviet leaders not to trust American promises or pledges in a presidential election year.

In fact, Jordan's desire to explore the potential of the Reagan initiative never had Arab support. With the exception of Egypt, the other moderate Arab countries did not openly support the Reagan initiative and Jordan's revived diplomatic role. The conservative Arab countries did not go beyond issuing occasional mild statements of support and declined to use their good offices to bring the Hussein-Arafat talks to a successful conclusion.

Instead of supporting Jordan's initiative, an Arab consensus crystallized around Saudi Crown Prince Fahd's proposal. The twelfth Arab League summit, convening in Fez, Morocco, in early September 1982, endorsed a variant of this proposal, henceforth known as the Fez plan (see appendix E). Among other things, the Fez plan called for the establishment of a fully independent Palestinian state on the West Bank and Gaza with East Jerusalem as its capital. The plan also called for a key role for the PLO in any peace talks. Though the Arab peace plan reflected common Arab stands on a final resolution of the Palestinian problem, the plan did not coincide with Jordan's ideas for the settlement of the Arab-Israeli conflict. Rather than establishing an independent Palestinian state and giving

15. For a criticism of U.S. policy, see King Hussein's interviews in "Hussein's Decision," *Wall Street Journal*, April 14 and 15, 1983; *Al-Nahar*, April 30, 1983, in FBIS, *Daily Report: MEA*, May 2, 1983, pp. F1–F5; *New York Times*, March 15, 1984; and British Broadcasting Corporation, March 20, 1984, in FBIS, *Daily Report: MEA*, March 21, 1984, pp. F1–F2.

the PLO a key role in the resolution of the Arab-Israeli conflict, Hussein wanted a joint Jordanian-Palestinian delegation and a federation of the West Bank and Gaza with Jordan.

The radical Arab countries, particularly Syria, strongly opposed King Hussein's political initiative. President Asad was unyielding in his hostility to the Jordanian-PLO dialogue. In fact, Jordan's diplomatic initiative to resolve the Palestinian question clashed sharply with Syria's image of itself as custodian of the Palestinian question. Syria publicly questioned Arafat's right to speak for the Palestinian people.[16] Damascus also became a source of harsh attacks against both King Hussein and moderate PLO leaders. In addition, Asad sought to enlist Iran and Libya in his campaign against Jordan and the mainstream of the PLO. Finally, Syria encouraged the mutiny that took place in Fatah in the late spring of 1983.[17]

In conclusion, Jordan's geopolitical vulnerability, the lack of Palestinian and Arab support, the rigid stand of the Israeli government, the lack of resolve and energy on the part of the United States to settle the Arab-Israeli conflict, and Hussein's hesitancy were behind the breakdown in the Jordanian-PLO dialogue. The unfolding of political developments in 1984, however, caused the Jordanian government to reconsider its attitude toward the PLO and thus a new round of talks was started.

The Jordanian-PLO Dialogue Revisited

During 1984, the Jordanian government made important domestic and foreign policy decisions. These included the reconvening of the Jordanian parliament, the resumption of the Jordanian-PLO dialogue, and the reestablishment of diplomatic relations with Egypt. Such political moves resulted from the government's optimistic reading and analysis of the situation.[18] Three developments were particularly relevant to the determination of Jordan's foreign policy during that period.

First, the developments within the Palestinian nationalist movement during 1983 and 1984, including the mutiny in the PLO and the subsequent expulsion of Arafat's troops from northern Lebanon

16. Damascus Domestic Television Service, October 12, 1982, in FBIS, *Daily Report: MEA*, October 13, 1982, pp. H1–H2.

17. See Sahliyeh, *PLO after the Lebanon War*, p. 134, and for Syria's involvement in the mutiny, pp. 152–57.

18. For more information on Jordan's attempt to renew discussions with the PLO, see Arthur R. Day, *East Bank/West Bank: Jordan and the Prospects for Peace* (New York: Council on Foreign Relations, 1986), pp. 132–40.

in December 1983, left the PLO chief more isolated and weaker than at any time before. The decline in the PLO's political weight became more serious with the growing schism between Arafat and Asad. The tension between the two leaders culminated in the expulsion of Arafat from Damascus in June 1983. With Arafat's political weakness, the Jordanian government calculated that the PLO chief would be more susceptible to Jordanian pressure and would be compelled to follow a more realistic and pragmatic approach to the resolution of the Palestinian question. From a Jordanian perspective, Arafat was more pragmatic and moderate in his political views than many of his colleagues in the PLO.

Second, Jordan's ruling elite's anticipation of favorable developments in both Israel and the United States prompted the Amman government to reactivate its search for a solution of the Palestinian problem. Public opinion polls in Israel during the spring and early summer of 1984 suggested that the Labor party led by Shimon Peres would win Israel's Knesset elections. The Jordanian government believed that the formation of Israel's next government by the Labor party, which favored territorial compromises, would give a new momentum to the peace process. The inconclusive outcome of the Israeli elections was disappointing to Jordan, as the Labor party did not gain a majority of seats in the Knesset. An agreement between the Likud and Labor parties to form a national unity government occurred in September 1984. According to this agreement, Shimon Peres assumed the prime ministership of the Israeli government for half of the term before Yitzhak Shamir (the leader of the Likud) took over. This transition gave the Jordanians some hope that progress toward a settlement of the West Bank question might be made during Peres's two-year tenure.

Third, Jordan's optimistic definition of the situation was also occasioned by the government's belief that the prospects for settling the Arab-Israeli conflict would be enhanced after the reelection of President Reagan. Jordanian officials believed that during Reagan's second term in office he would work more vigorously to implement his initiative since his administration would be less vulnerable to domestic pressures.

Based on that optimistic reading of the situation, the Jordanian monarch initiated several foreign policy moves. In response to the infighting within the PLO and the growing possibility that the organization might very well come under the complete hegemony of Syria and its radical Palestinian allies, the king issued a royal decree in early January 1984 to reconvene the Jordanian parliament after a suspension of almost ten years. With 50 percent of its members drawn from the West Bank, the reconvened parliament intended to reestablish Jordan's constitutional links with the occupied territories and to communicate Jordan's interest in an active role in the resolution of the Palestinian problem.

Jordanian officials denied that there were any foreign policy implications in their decision to reconvene the parliament. They attributed this measure to the government's desire to avoid a constitutional crisis. Since the last parliamentary elections in 1967, a number of parliament members had died. The government was afraid that it would soon lose the two-thirds majority needed to convene the parliament. Encouragement of participatory politics in Jordan was cited as justification for the reactivation of parliamentary life.[19]

The restoration of full diplomatic relations with Egypt on September 25, 1984, was Jordan's next major foreign policy move. By the mid-1980s, the original reasons that had led Jordan to join the Arab opposition against Egypt had become less relevant. By this time, the Arab countries were preoccupied with the Iraq-Iran war, rising Islamic fundamentalism, the mounting wave of terrorism, and the increasing threats to oil shipping in the Gulf. The urgency of such issues brought the Egyptian government closer to the Arab world. Indeed, Egypt and most of the Arab states had similar positions on many of these issues and had joint interests in limiting the damage of these threats to their societies.

Besides the presence of these common interests that brought Egypt closer to the Arab world, Jordan had other reasons for its rapprochement with the Egyptian government. The Jordanian government needed the backing of a major Arab country like Egypt to neutralize Syria's opposition to its foreign policy initiatives. With the prolongation of the Iraq-Iran war, the Jordanians felt that they could no longer rely on Iraqi support. Together with Egypt, Iraq, Saudi Arabia, and the other Arab Gulf states, King Hussein was hoping to form a nucleus for an alliance of moderate Arab countries against the forces of radicalism and fundamentalism in the Middle East. The restoration of full diplomatic ties between Cairo and

19. Such reasons were advanced by Prime Minister Mudar Badran in a press conference on January 9, 1984, Amman Domestic Service, in FBIS, *Daily Report: MEA*, January 10, 1984, pp. F1–F2, and by Minister of Information Leila Sharif in a press interview on January 12, 1984, Amman *Jerusalem Star*, ibid., January 17, 1984, pp. F3–F4. See also Sahliyeh, *PLO after the Lebanon War*, pp. 186–87.

Amman was also expected to give more credibility and recognition to Jordan's efforts to resolve the Palestinian question. Finally, the disappearance of President Sadat from the political scene removed a major personal obstacle from the path of normalizing relations between Egypt and the rest of the Arab world.

The renewal of the dialogue with the PLO was Jordan's third major foreign policy initiative. In November 1984, King Hussein allowed the PLO leaders to convene the seventeenth session of the Palestine National Council (an equivalent to a Palestinian parliament in exile) in Amman. The government hoped that the convening of the council on Jordanian territory would strengthen the voice of moderation in the PLO and would induce the leaders of the organization to endorse resolutions favorable to Jordan's point of view. In his speech to the council, Hussein urged the Palestinian participants to make the occupied territories their primary constituency and appealed to them to overcome their differences and come up with a plan to save the West Bank and Gaza. He urged them to accept Resolution 242, which embodied the principle of exchanging land for peace, and to work closely with his government to restore Arab sovereignty in the occupied territories.[20] The conferees did not take a clear position on King Hussein's appeal, though they left the issue for the PLO Executive Committee to decide.

On February 11, 1985, three months after the convening of the Palestine National Council in Amman, Hussein and Arafat signed an agreement for a joint diplomatic initiative (see appendix F). The agreement proposed to resolve the Palestinian problem on the basis of exchanging land for peace in accordance with pertinent United Nations resolutions. The agreement also called for the formation of a joint Jordanian-Palestinian delegation and the confederation of a future Palestinian state in the West Bank and Gaza with Jordan. It also called for the convening of an international peace conference that would be attended by the five permanent members of the UN Security Council as well as Israel, the PLO, and other concerned parties.

After signing the accord, Hussein and other senior Jordanian officials visited several Arab and European capitals and the United States to promote the February accord and to enlist support for inclusion of the PLO in the peace process. In particular, the king

20. For the text of the speech, see "King Calls for Joint Jordanian-Palestinian Initiative," *Jordan Times*, November 24, 1984. For additional information about the Palestine National Council meeting in Amman, see Sahliyeh, *PLO after the Lebanon War*, pp. 196–202.

unsuccessfully appealed to the Reagan administration to open direct contacts with the PLO. The American government insisted that for a dialogue to take place, the PLO must recognize Resolution 242, Israel's right to exist, and renounce the use of violence. One year after signing the February accord, however, Jordan's efforts had not yielded any positive outcome and on February 19, 1986, King Hussein ended his dialogue with Arafat, ostensibly because of the PLO's reluctance to accept Resolution 242.

Following the king's announcement, the relationship between Jordan and the PLO deteriorated rapidly. In July 1986 the government closed down the PLO's offices and ordered Arafat's deputy, Khalil Wazir (Abu Jihad), to leave the country. The accord was formally abrogated by the PLO in April 1987 as a price paid by Arafat for reconciliation with his rivals in the PLO.

Collapse of the Dialogue

The collapse of Jordan's dialogue with the PLO was caused by a set of conditions similar to the ones that led to the breakdown of Arafat and Hussein's first round of talks in the spring of 1983. In 1986 the PLO's vacillation and unwillingness to accept Resolution 242 without a reciprocal American commitment to the Palestinian right of self-determination was used as a pretext by Hussein to end the talks. From the beginning, the February 11, 1985 accord generated resentment among the Palestinians. Opposition to the agreement stemmed not only from the PLO's radical groups—the traditional source of opposition to political flexibility and moderation—but also from Fatah Central Committee members, Arafat's own men, who were divided between supporters and critics of the February accord. Salah Khalaf (Abu Iyad), Faruq al-Qadoumi, Rafiq al-Natsheh, and Mahmoud Abbas (Abu Mazin) were all unhappy about the PLO's implied acceptance of Resolution 242 and Arafat's apparent compromise over the PLO's exclusive right to represent Palestinian interests. The idea that Jordan would be the dominant partner in the federal arrangement between Jordan and the West Bank-Gaza entity was disquieting. PLO leaders were also displeased by the ambiguity of the February accord on the establishment of a fully independent Palestinian state and the PLO's direct participation in any peace talks.[21]

21. These reservations were expressed in the interviews of Abu Iyad, Radio Monte Carlo, February 22, 1985; Faruq al-Qadoumi, Radio Monte Carlo, February

Consequently, the PLO's Executive Committee gave a qualified acceptance to the Arafat-Hussein accord. In a statement on February 20, 1985, the Executive Committee insisted on the Palestinians' right of self-determination and underlined the need to establish a fully independent Palestinian state.[22] It also emphasized the PLO's exclusive right to represent Palestinian interests and stressed the need for a joint Arab delegation at an international conference. Over the next few weeks, Jordanian and Palestinian officials negotiated two amendments to the February 11 agreement, one of which reflected the PLO's desire to mention the role of other Arab parties at an international conference (see appendix F).

Some of the PLO's activities in 1985 caused a great deal of consternation in Jordan. Hussein was particularly angered by two developments. The hijacking of the *Achille Lauro,* an Italian cruise ship, by the Palestine Liberation Front (a pro-Arafat group) in October 1985 and the killing of Leon Klinghoffer, an American confined to a wheelchair, undermined Hussein's efforts to depict the PLO as a voice of moderation in the Middle East. In addition, the refusal of the PLO's representatives in the Jordanian-Palestinian delegation to sign a document renouncing the use of violence and accepting Israel's right to exist in return for meeting with the British foreign minister was embarrassing to the Jordanian monarch. After all, the king had arranged the meeting.

Lack of active Arab backing because of Syria's opposition was another reason that King Hussein ended his dialogue with the PLO. The king's hope for a collective Arab endorsement of his initiative was frustrated when the emergency Arab League summit, which convened in Morocco in early August 1985, did not endorse the February accord. Opposition from the Syrian government was particularly detrimental to the Jordanian-Palestinian joint diplomatic venture. In view of its diplomatic gains at the expense of Israel and the United States in Lebanon in 1983–84, the Damascus regime did not tolerate Hussein's quest for an independent foreign policy. Syrian foreign minister Faruq al-Sharaa described the February accord as an alliance between Jordan and the PLO against his country.[23]

13, 1985; Rafiq al-Natsheh, in Hassan al-Bunyan, "No Palestinian Obligation to Any Agreement that Contains Acceptance of Resolution 242" (in Arabic), *Al-Sharq al-Awsat,* February 26, 1985; and Abu Mazin, *Filistin al-Thawrah,* no. 544 (February 9–15, 1985). See also Sahliyeh, *PLO after the Lebanon War,* pp. 207–09.

22. *Al-Dustur,* February 20, 1985, in FBIS, *Daily Report: MEA,* February 20, 1985, p. A1.

23. Al-Sharaa was interviewed in Wadea al-Halw, "The Closing of the Lebanon

Syria's opposition to the February accord went beyond the usual rhetoric and verbal condemnation, as pro-Syrian Palestinian radicals assassinated and injured several Jordanian diplomats and PLO and Palestinian moderate politicians between 1985 and 1986.

Hussein's growing impatience and frustration with the Reagan administration constituted a third reason for the breakdown of the PLO-Jordanian dialogue. Hussein was disappointed by the refusal, in August 1985, of the Reagan administration to meet with the Palestinian members of the Jordanian-Palestinian delegation.[24] The United States was also opposed to the king's idea of convening an international peace conference. Only in 1986–87 did the United States begin to accept Hussein's need for an international conference to legitimize direct talks with Israel. Finally, the Jordanian government was angered when the Reagan administration withdrew Jordan's arms requests from consideration by Congress following mounting congressional opposition to the sale.

Political paralysis and diplomatic immobilization inside Israel also forced the Jordanian government to retreat from its diplomatic initiative. Except for the support of minor leftist Israeli political groups, the Arafat-Hussein February accord was opposed by Labor and Likud, Israel's two main political parties. Jordan's optimistic prognosis of Israel's political scene in early 1984 proved inaccurate two years later. Shimon Peres, the leader of the Labor party, was unable or unwilling to dissolve the Israeli government and call for new elections. Jordanians were also disappointed with his inability to persuade the Israeli government to endorse the idea of convening an international peace conference. Peres was unable to meet Hussein's expectation as he felt obliged to honor the national unity agreement to turn over the prime ministership to Shamir.

Developments in the Middle East region were behind King Hussein's decision to abandon his bilateral venture with the PLO. Because of the drop in the price of oil, the official subsidies from the Arab states to Jordan's economy and the remittances sent by Jordanian nationals working in the Gulf were greatly reduced. Jordan's strained economy also suffered from the cutoff of Iraq's economic assistance following that country's prolonged involvement in the war with Iran. Mounting terrorism and Islamic fundamentalism were also worrying the Jordanian government.

File Is Linked to the End of the Israeli Occupation" (in Arabic), *Al-Nahar al-Arabi wa al-Duwali*, no. 408 (February 25–March 3, 1985), pp. 22–23.

24. See the interview, "King Hussein: Last Chance?" *Newsweek*, September 30, 1985, p. 45.

Toward a New Arab Consensus

These developments led to a redefinition of the situation and rearrangement of Jordan's foreign policy tactics. One could argue that in an economically and politically turbulent period and in the absence of any diplomatic progress, it was natural for the Jordanian government to give priority to the core values of maintaining the regime and preserving internal political stability and economic development. The pursuit of Jordan's third objective of trying to resolve the Palestinian question through forging close diplomatic cooperation with the PLO under conditions of political uncertainty would have been too risky and too costly. As a consequence, the primary goal of Jordan's foreign policy since the breakdown in the Jordanian-PLO dialogue has been to attend to internal political and economic stability while preparing the groundwork at home and in the Middle East region for the next round of diplomacy.

For the time being Jordan has abandoned cooperation with the PLO in favor of Arab solidarity and accommodation with neighboring states. Rather than excluding the PLO entirely from the political game, however, Jordan aimed at increasing the pressure on the PLO so that it would be more committed and serious in any future political talks. Reconciliation with Syria and downplaying of the Palestinian question during the Arab summit conference in Amman in November 1987 were meant by Hussein to force the PLO to accept Jordan's terms for a diplomatic solution, but by mid-1988 these efforts had failed.

Since the mid-1980s, the Jordanian government has been trying to create a new Arab consensus and reduce the intensity of inter-Arab rivalries and divisions. The cornerstone of its policy has been the normalization of relations between Amman and Damascus, Jordan's quest to readmit Egypt to the Arab fold, and its attempt to mediate the conflict between Iraq and Syria. By the end of 1987, the Jordanian government had achieved many of these immediate objectives. To facilitate improvement in his relationship with Syria, King Hussein appointed, in April of 1985, Zaid al-Rifai as Jordan's prime minister. Rifai was known to favor forging closer ties with Syria rather than with the PLO. Prime Minister Rifai abandoned his predecessor's policy of isolating the Syrian government. Under the mediation of Saudi Arabia, Prime Minister Rifai met with his Syrian counterpart in September 1985. These initial contacts culminated in an exchange of visits between King Hussein and President Asad. King Hussein also admitted his country's involvement in the Muslim Brotherhood's violent activities against the Syrian regime in the early 1980s. This admission came in a letter from the king to his prime minister on November 10, 1985, which was published by the Jordanian dailies.

Jordan's decision to reconcile with the Syrians resulted from Hussein's growing conviction that the policy of antagonizing Syria was counterproductive. Asad's vehement opposition to the Jordanian-PLO diplomatic efforts persuaded the king that the road to an Arab-Israeli peace would have to go through Damascus. After all, the Syrian president would not accept any downplaying of his country's role in the resolution of the Palestinian question. Additionally, the limited support that Hussein's diplomatic initiative received from the United States and the moderate Arab countries did not justify the price of antagonizing President Asad.

Besides the resumption of full diplomatic relations between Damascus and Amman and the signing of several economic and trade agreements, Hussein and Asad agreed on a common approach to the Arab-Israeli conflict. Hussein secured Asad's support for convening an international peace conference to find a comprehensive settlement of all aspects of the conflict. In return, the king agreed not to conduct direct and bilateral negotiations with Israel.

After securing President Asad's support for an international peace conference, Hussein discreetly explored the possibility of convening a conference with Israel's foreign minister and the leader of the Labor party, Shimon Peres. The two men worked out the details of an agreement during a secret meeting in London in early April 1987 (see appendix G). This agreement spelled out the rules that would govern the convening and the functions of a conference. Hussein and Peres agreed that the international conference would be divided into three geographical committees in which direct, bilateral negotiations would take place. The three committees would consist of a joint Jordanian-Palestinian-Israeli committee, a Syrian-Israeli committee, and a Lebanese-Israeli committee. It was also agreed that the international conference would not have veto power over any arrangement reached by the bilateral committees. Indeed, the role of the international conference was confined to the task of facilitating the beginning of negotiations and the lending of credibility and legitimacy to any agreement that might emerge from these talks. Finally, Hussein and Peres agreed that acceptance of Resolution 242 and the renunciation of violence were the prerequisites for joining the international peace conference.

Despite the far-reaching implications of the agreement, many obstacles stood in the path of implementation. First, Likud strongly opposed the convening of an international conference, insisting instead on direct negotiations with the Arab countries. Second, despite the Reagan administration's effort to facilitate the conclusion of the Peres-Hussein agreement, the administration did not lend strong and full backing to the convening of a conference. Third, Hussein failed to obtain the approval of President Asad to his agreement with Peres.

In his attempt to forge a new Arab consensus, Hussein managed to convene a summit conference for Arab heads of state in November 1987 after many years of bitter Arab conflicts and rivalries. Besides extending support to Iraq in the Iraq-Iran war, the Arab League summit, held in Amman, allowed individual Arab countries to resume diplomatic relations with Egypt. Yet in deference to Syrian insistence, the Arab heads of state did not permit the readmission of Egypt to the Arab League. The summit conference also endorsed King Hussein's call for convening an international peace conference.

Hussein also managed to arrange a meeting between President Asad and the Iraqi president, Saddam Hussein, during the summit. The meeting was expected to pave the way for a reconciliation between the two rival countries, but as of mid-1988 there was no sign of this occurring.

Hussein also attempted during 1986 and 1987 to rebuild his influence among the Palestinians in the occupied territories and to increase the political weight of pro-Jordanian politicians. He announced a plan in March 1986 to expand the lower house of the Jordanian parliament from 60 to 142 seats. Seventy-one seats were allocated to the population of the East Bank, while 60 were reserved for Palestinians in the West Bank, and 11 were given to the occupants of the refugee camps. In July 1988, however, the king reversed this decision and dissolved the lower house of parliament.

In September 1986 a Five-Year Plan for the economic development of the West Bank was approved by the Jordanian government. The plan envisaged the allocation of approximately $1.25 billion in the coming five years to modernize the West Bank's agricultural, industrial, educational, and health sectors. Yet nearly two years later, the Jordanian government had only been able to collect about $50 million of the planned total. In July 1988, the plan was cancelled and Jordan's ties to the West Bank were broken.

In its quest to rebuild an infrastructure sympathetic to Jordan in the West Bank, the government had the tacit cooperation of the leaders of the Labor party. The Jordanian government convinced four local West Bank politicians to accept mayoral appointments to the West Bank's four leading towns (Ramallah, Al-Birah, Nablus, and Hebron), thus replacing the Israeli military officers who had administered those towns since the early 1980s. The Israeli army's arrest and deportation of pro-PLO activists, the placing of the West Bank Palestinian press under more censorship, and the frequent closure of schools and colleges that expressed pro-PLO sentiments served Jordan's interests in the occupied territories.

Despite these measures, Palestinians in the West Bank and Gaza continued to identify with the PLO and espoused the goals of Palestinian nationalism. The outbreak of the popular uprising in the occupied territories in early December 1987 made the Jordanian government only marginally relevant to politics in the West Bank, which Hussein seemed to acknowledge in his July 1988 speech.

WEST BANK-GAZA POLITICS, 1978–88[25]

By the time of Sadat's dramatic trip to Jerusalem, the subsequent signing of the Camp David Accords, and the Egyptian-Israeli peace treaty, politics in the West Bank and Gaza had changed. One primary feature of that change was the decline in the influence and control of the elite over local politics. Irrespective of their political orientations, elite groups in the occupied territories faced serious challenges from the rapidly growing phenomenon of mass politics. The radicalization of the student movement, the consolidation of the power of the communists, the formation of several labor unions, women's organizations, and professional organizations, as well as the rise of an Islamic fundamentalist movement, especially in Gaza, widened the circle of participatory politics.

Another primary feature of West Bank-Gaza politics in the late 1970s was identification of most Palestinians there with the PLO. Most of the West Bank's public and elite groups espoused the PLO's goal of establishing an independent Palestinian state in the occupied territories. By the late 1970s, as support for the PLO increased, the influence of Jordan and its supporters in the West Bank and Gaza declined. The support for the Jordanian government reached a low ebb during the 1976 municipal elections when the pro-Jordanian politicians suffered major defeats.

Despite the pervasiveness of the sentiments of Palestinian nationalism and support for the PLO, two trends were discernible among the West Bank urban elite at the time of Sadat's trip to Jerusalem. First a number of politicians had moderate ideas about the resolution of the Palestinian question. The mayors of Bethlehem,

25. This section draws on Emile Sahliyeh, *In Search of Leadership: West Bank Politics since 1967* (Brookings, 1988).

Gaza, Hebron, and Tulkarm (Elias Freij, Rashad Shawwa, Fahd al-Qawasmah, and Hilmi Hanoun, respectively) were the main proponents of a pragmatic approach to dealings with Israel. They favored maintaining close ties with Jordan. They were not opposed to U.S. involvement in the search for a resolution of the Arab-Israeli conflict. President Carter's reference in the spring of 1977 to a Palestinian homeland was well received by this group of politicians. In keeping with their pragmatic orientation these politicians did not initially reject the Sadat diplomatic initiative. On the contrary, this group, which also included the most prominent politician in Nablus (Hikmat al-Masri, the former speaker of the Jordanian parliament), praised the Egyptian president for his "courage and political vision."

In contrast, leftist politicians were engaged in activities generating support for the PLO, inciting the local population against Israel and Jordan, and opposing American diplomatic initiatives in the region. They were particularly apprehensive about Sadat's trip to Jerusalem and described it as a "treacherous" act. They also characterized President Carter's reference to the Palestinian right to a homeland as "insincere and deceptive." The coalition included the supporters of the Popular Front for the Liberation of Palestine, the Democratic Front for the Liberation of Palestine, and the communists. The mayors of Ramallah (Karim Khalaf), Al-Birah (Ibrahim al-Tawil), Nablus (Bassam Shaka), and Anabta (Wahid al-Hamdallah) were the representatives of this group of politicians.

Reaction to the Camp David Accords

By late 1978, the political differences between the pragmatists and the leftists blurred. The unfolding of political events sustained the position of power of the leftist politicians and weakened the influence of the pragmatic leaders. Two conditions in particular were responsible for such a development. First, the coming to power of the Likud bloc in Israel in June 1977 narrowed the differences between pragmatic and leftist politicians. The intensification of construction of Israeli settlements in the occupied territories, the expropriation of Arab land, and Prime Minister Begin's consideration of the West Bank and Gaza as "liberated territories" brought the two political groups closer together.

Second, the signing of the Camp David Accords and the Egyptian-Israeli peace treaty blurred the differences between the moderate and leftist politicians. The opposition by the Arab countries to the Camp David Accords and the negative stands of both Jordan and the PLO to those agreements helped to create an anti-Camp David consensus among Palestinians in the occupied territories. As a consequence, most of the urban elite viewed the Camp David Accords as a denial of their national rights and as a sellout by Egypt of the Palestinian cause.

On October 1, 1978, a meeting of West Bank and Gaza politicians took place in Jerusalem to examine the meaning and the potential of the Camp David Accords. The participants formed the National Guidance Committee (a coalition of pro-PLO local politicians) to orchestrate opposition to the accords. This committee sponsored four popular rallies in West Bank and Gaza universities in October and November of 1978 to protest the signing of the Camp David Accords.

West Bank and Gaza politicians articulated five reasons for their rejection of the accords. First, the accords ignored the Palestinians' right for self-determination and statehood. Second, the accords did not acknowledge the PLO's status as being the sole legitimate representative for the Palestinians. Third, the agreements did not address the future of Israeli settlements in the occupied territories and the status of East Jerusalem. Fourth, West Bank politicians also opposed the accords because of their treatment of the West Bank and Gaza as a separate issue from the rest of the Palestinian community outside the occupied territories. Fifth, West Bank and Gaza leaders resented the Camp David Accords' suggestion that the United States, Egypt, Israel, and Jordan would decide the political future of the occupied territories.

West Bank politicians also believed that the autonomy plan would perpetuate Israel's permanent control of the West Bank and Gaza. Begin's narrow interpretation of autonomy as confined to the inhabitants of the West Bank and Gaza, while leaving the control of the land and water resources to Israel, generated an additional reason for the West Bank's opposition to Camp David.

The Eclipse of the Leftist Politicians

By the early 1980s, the power of the pro-PLO politicians in general, and the leftists in particular, was greatly curtailed because of the struggle for power within their ranks. The local politicians were divided between the supporters of the PLO's mainstream (Fatah) and the rejectionist factions.

A more critical factor in the loss of political authority by the pro-PLO politicians was the mounting opposition of the Israeli government to their activities. Between 1976 and 1980, Israel's two defense ministers, Shimon Peres and Ezer Weizman, tolerated the activities of local Palestinian politicians. The two ministers hoped that the new urban elite, particularly the mayors, would evolve into a local leadership independent of the PLO's control. The signing of the Camp David Accords made the task of finding an indigenous leadership more urgent. Thus the mayors were allowed to travel to Arab countries to solicit financial assistance from Arab and Palestinian sources for their towns' local institutions and welfare organizations.

At the same time that Weizman was entertaining the idea of fostering a West Bank and Gaza leadership from among its urban elite, another current of opinion opposed the growing mayoral power. The support for this trend came from military government circles and from Menahem Milson who was the adviser to the military governor on Arab affairs between 1976 and 1978 and the West Bank's civilian governor between 1981 and 1982. Milson believed that the mayors were incapable of providing independent leadership for the Palestinian inhabitants of the occupied territories because of the mayors' subservience to the PLO. He proposed the creation of an alternative leadership of conservative politicians drawn from West Bank rural areas.

Under Milson's guidance, the military government created six village leagues in the districts of Hebron, Bethlehem, Ramallah, Nablus, Tulkarm, and Jenin. The leaders of these leagues were expected to provide an indigenous leadership with whom Israel could negotiate the details of self-government for the inhabitants of the occupied territories. The decision of the military government to allow the village leagues to have their headquarters in West Bank towns was aimed at containing the political influence of the West Bank urban elite.

Additional pressures were placed on the mayors by limiting their municipal budgets, rejecting city development projects, and limiting the flow of money to West Bank towns from outside sources. Restrictive measures against the mayors were intensified under Begin's second term of office, 1981–83. In the summer of 1981, following the appointment of Ariel Sharon as Israel's defense minister, financial assistance to West Bank cities from abroad was terminated. In early March 1982, the Israeli government outlawed the National Guidance Committee and, over the course of the next few months, ousted eight West Bank mayors, including the mayors of its largest towns (Ramallah, Al-Birah, Nablus, and Hebron). The refusal of these mayors to meet with Menahem Milson, the head of the civil administration, to discuss municipal affairs was used as an excuse to remove them from office. West Bank politicians were afraid that the introduction of civil administration in November 1981 was a prelude to the autonomy plan of the Camp David Accords.

Most of the deposed mayors were placed under town arrest and were banned from making political statements or attending political gatherings. The military government appointed local politicians sympathetic to Israel as mayors in several small West Bank towns. The Israeli military officers administered the municipal affairs of the large towns because local politicians refused to accept mayoral appointments.

The Emergence of the Pragmatic Politicians

With the outlawing of the National Guidance Committee and the removal from office of several mayors, the structure of the new nationalist leadership in the occupied territories, particularly the leftist politicians, incurred a serious blow. The dismantling of the PLO's political and military headquarters in Lebanon in the summer of 1982 exacerbated the political losses experienced by the pro-PLO politicians. Despite their political weakness, the leftist politicians continued to seek a more assertive PLO—a PLO that would look toward Syria rather than Jordan, cultivate the support of the Soviet Union rather than seeking collaboration with the United States, and establish an independent Palestinian state rather than link the occupied territories with Jordan.

The unfolding of political events in the early 1980s led to the reemergence of the pro-Jordanian politicians and the crystallization of a less militant brand of pro-PLO pragmatic leaders. The political fortunes of those politicians were significantly enhanced following the dispersal of the PLO troops to several Arab countries as a result of the 1982 Lebanon war. Consequently, the West Bank and Gaza became the PLO's primary constituency and main source of political legitimacy. The new reality compelled the PLO's leaders to be more attentive to the interests and concerns of the Palestinians living in the occupied territories. The enhancement of Jordan's diplomatic stature following the launching of the Reagan initiative in September 1982 sustained the political gains of the pragmatic politicians.

The political support of this group of politicians was crucial to Arafat's political survival in the face of the critical challenges that confronted the PLO between 1982 and 1986. Arafat's diplomatic coordination with Jordan, resumption of political contacts with Egypt, and anti-Syrian posture received full backing from both the pro-Jordanian and pro-PLO pragmatic politicians who held political rallies and frequently issued statements in support of Arafat's policies.

Over time, those politicians developed a system of dual loyalty and acceptance of the Jordanian-PLO diplomatic cooperation. On the eve of Arafat's visit to Jordan in October 1982, twenty West Bank and Gaza dignitaries urged Arafat and Hussein to coordinate their diplomatic moves and reconcile their differences. The members of this pragmatic elite also demonstrated greater flexibility in dealing with the Israeli military administration. To both groups, the PLO's military defeat in Lebanon in 1982 revealed the irrelevance and the elusive character of the strategy of armed struggle to resolve the Palestinian problem. In their opinion, diplomacy was a far more promising instrument to end Israel's military occupation.

The leaders of both camps also welcomed the signing of the February 1985 accord between King Hussein and PLO chairman Arafat. In particular, they were receptive to the idea of forming a joint Jordanian-Palestinian delegation to negotiate the future of the West Bank and Gaza with Israel. They also reacted favorably to the suggestion to confederate a future Palestinian state in the occupied territories with Jordan. Two key figures in the pragmatic camp (Hanna Siniora, the editor of the Jerusalem Arabic daily *Al-Fajr*, and Fayiz Abu Rahmah, a lawyer from Gaza) were nominated by the PLO to participate in the proposed delegation.

Members of the pragmatic camp often served as liaisons between Jordan, the PLO, and Israel. Before the breakdown in the Jordanian-PLO dialogue in February 1986, some of the pragmatic politicians tried to mediate between the two sides and expressed their disappointment over the collapse of the talks. Functioning as liaisons for Jordan, some of the older politicians met frequently with Likud and Labor officials.

Similarly, members of the pragmatic elite served as a conduit between the PLO and individual Israeli politicians. For instance, in the summer of 1987 Sari Nusseibeh, professor of philosophy at Bir Zeit University, and Faisal al-Husseini, the director of the Arab Studies Center in Jerusalem, explored with Moshe Amirav, a young Likud politician, the details of a plan to resolve the Palestinian-Israeli conflict. The two sides agreed that the West Bank-Gaza Palestinians would have a semi-autonomous status, control over land and water resources, and their own passports and flag. In response, the PLO would be expected to renounce the use of violence and accept Israel's right to exist. In turn, the Israeli government would recognize the PLO and stop settlement activities in the occupied territories.[26]

Besides establishing contacts with Israel's two chief political parties, the pragmatic elite in the occupied territories initiated a dialogue with Israeli politicians, academicians, and peace groups to promote mutual understanding between Israelis and Palestinians. The dialogue also served as a sign of appreciation by the pragmatic politicians for the political attitudes and peaceful intentions of moderate Israelis. The pragmatists thought that contacts would advance the popularity of leaders of peace groups inside Israel.

Despite their support for the PLO, the pragmatic politicians in the occupied territories criticized some of the PLO's radical factions and terrorist activities. They deplored the involvement of the PLO in the hijacking of the *Achille Lauro* and blamed it for the failure of a Jordanian-Palestinian delegation to meet with the British foreign secretary in October 1985. The West Bank pragmatic elite were no longer giving automatic and unconditional approval to what they perceived as errors by the PLO.

After clearance from Jordan and the PLO, some pragmatists took personal risks and accepted appointments as mayors to their towns. In late November 1985, Zafer al-Masri was appointed mayor of Nablus; four months later he was assassinated by a follower of the Popular Front for the Liberation of Palestine. In September 1986, three pro-Jordanian politicians accepted mayoral appointments to the towns of Ramallah, Al-Birah, and Hebron (Khalil Musa Khalil, Hassan al-Tawil, and Abd al-Majid al-Zir).

With the prolongation of Israel's military occupation and the diplomatic deadlock, some pragmatists began to advocate new ideas and approaches for the resolution of the Palestinian question that departed sharply from the conventional wisdom. Sari Nusseibeh proposed incorporating the West Bank and Gaza into Israel and demanding equal political rights for the Palestinians in these territories. Nusseibeh's proposal was prompted by Israel's refusal to withdraw from the occupied territories and its opposition to the establishment of an independent Palestinian state. Nusseibeh believed that the incorporation of the Palestinians into Israel would be preferable to the continuation of the military occupation because under occupation the Palestinians were denied their political rights. In his opinion, the Palestinians, in view of their high birthrate,

26. Ibid., pp. 171–72.

would constitute a majority of Israel's population within two decades, thus leading to the establishment of a binational state. The demographic threat had already caused some of Israel's politicians, especially in the Labor party, to advocate some territorial compromise in any future deal over the West Bank and Gaza.

As a practical translation of Nusseibeh's ideas, Hanna Siniora announced in June 1987 his intention to enter the November 1988 municipal elections in Jerusalem at the head of a slate of Palestinian delegates. His decision was made partly because of the diplomatic deadlock in the peace process and partly to press Israel to come up with a solution to the future of the occupied territories. Siniora also believed that running for a municipal seat would reconfirm Arab political rights in Jerusalem and help to expand municipal services to the Arab inhabitants of the city.

The introduction of nonviolence as a technique to resist Israel's military occupation was another manifestation of the new thinking among West Bank and Gaza intellectuals. In 1985 Mubarak Awad, an American citizen of Palestinian origin, opened the Center for the Study of Nonviolence in East Jerusalem and tried to educate West Bank Palestinians about the utility and effectiveness of nonviolent resistance. In January 1988, Awad and some of his colleagues called on the local population to boycott Israeli cigarettes and soft drinks. (Awad was deported to the United States in June 1988.)

The idea of nonviolence and the quest for political equality inside Israel have been primarily circulated among a few West Bank intellectuals. The emotionalism and hostility associated with the Palestinian-Israeli conflict at present limit the appeal of these ideas among the mass public. Such ideas are unlikely to generate official Arab and Palestinian support outside the occupied territories for the time being. Finally, nonviolent tactics clash sharply with the PLO's advocacy of armed struggle as an avenue to end Israel's occupation.[27]

The Youth Uprising (Intifadah)

While Israel's military occupation and the stalled peace process generated innovative approaches among some of the West Bank and Gaza elite, it unleashed a great deal of frustration at the mass level. In the second half of the 1980s, a new phase of political activism by the youth in the occupied territories was ushered in. Young students became actively engaged on the local political scene. In

27. Ibid., pp. 173–74.

the 1977–80 period, 400–500 violent demonstrations occurred annually. Between April 1986 and May 1987 the number of violent demonstrations rose to 3,150.[28] Most of the violence and strikes were spontaneous in nature and not the result of the PLO's incitement. The youths' political activism reached a climax in the outbreak of the large-scale popular uprising that began on December 9, 1987.

A number of tentative conclusions can be drawn from the *intifadah*. The uprising gave the Palestinian question a high degree of political visibility at the local, regional, and international levels. Before the uprising, the future of the West Bank and Gaza was relegated to the sidelines as Arab countries were preoccupied with the Iraq-Iran war. Besides refocusing Arab attention, the youths' uprising compelled the Reagan administration to reactivate the search for a diplomatic solution to the Palestinian question after a long period of neglect. The uprising also led to divisions in the American Jewish community over Israel's harsh treatment of the demonstrators. It showed the Israeli army in a position of using heavy doses of military force against the unarmed civilian population. The wide coverage of the uprising by the world media, particularly by the American television and press, damaged Israel's image, especially in the United States.

To inhabitants of the West Bank and Gaza, such consequences are impressive gains that surpassed the PLO's and Arab countries' political efforts over the last two decades. The *intifadah* revealed the diminishing confidence of the population in the occupied territories in the ability of Arab and PLO leaders to end Israel's military occupation. The uprising gave Palestinians new self-confidence and a sense of victory that would strengthen their bargaining position and their resolve to be more active in any future diplomatic rounds. As a consequence of the *intifadah*, the struggle for the promotion of the Palestinian cause would increasingly come from within the occupied territories. Those Palestinians, however, would be unlikely to break with the PLO as they voice their demands (see appendix J).

The intensity and the large-scale scope of the demonstrations and strikes suggested that the roles of many of the traditional players

28. Meron Benvenisti, *1986 Report: Demographic, Economic, Legal, Social and Political Developments in the West Bank* (Jerusalem: West Bank Data Base Project, 1986, U.S. distribution by Westview Press, Boulder, Colo.), p. 63, and *1987 Report: Demographic, Economic, Legal, Social and Political Developments in the West Bank*, p. 40.

(West Bank politicians, Jordan, the PLO, and the Arab countries) had been seriously challenged. To the West Bank politicians, the increasing politicization of the youth further eclipsed the West Bank local elite. The new generation is dissatisfied with the tactics that the local politicians have used to find a solution to the Palestinian problem. Unlike their parents, the youth do not fear the Israeli army and seem determined to influence the political future of the occupied territories.

The lack of any progress toward a political solution is bound to erode further the remaining legitimacy of the pragmatic politicians. The unrest has already paved the way for the rise of a more militant leadership inside the occupied territories. The nucleus for such a leadership surfaced in February 1988 when an underground committee for the perpetuation of the uprising, the Unified National Command for the Uprising, was formed. This leadership seems to be intimately connected to the PLO.

By seizing the initiative, the young generation increased the political weight of the inhabitants of the West Bank and Gaza and legitimized their political role in the Palestinian nationalist movement. Though the uprising gave the PLO badly needed political mileage to sustain its position in comparison with its Arab rivals, in the long run it could limit the ability of the PLO leaders to dictate their wishes and stands to the Palestinians in the occupied territories.

One could no longer assume political passivity on the part of West Bank-Gaza Palestinians. These Palestinians would insist on having a more influential voice in the determination of their political destiny. The strengthening of that attitude would conflict with the PLO's concept of itself as the only organ that could speak in the name of all the Palestinian people. This observation, however, should not be taken to mean that the Palestinians in the occupied territories are about to abandon the PLO. On the contrary, most of these Palestinians continue to envisage the PLO as the symbol of Palestinian national unity.

The 1987–88 uprising was particularly detrimental to Jordan's interests. Despite the utility of the Jordanian government's role in any final peace settlement, the uprising made King Hussein less relevant to the aspirations of the Palestinians in the occupied territories. More than two-thirds of the Palestinians in the West Bank have never lived under Jordanian rule and do not have any political affinity with the Hashemite royal family. The young people consider Jordan's diplomatic moves irrelevant to their aspirations for a West Bank-Gaza independent state.

Though a high degree of coordination and unity was exhibited among varying West Bank-Gaza political forces, the youth's uprising increased the legitimacy of the Islamic movement—the PLO's serious rival and challenger in the occupied territories. Though young men of different pro-PLO political persuasions participated in the violent demonstrations and strikes, the followers of the Islamic movement played an important role, especially in Gaza, in the December 1987 wave of unrest that continued into 1988. Since the late 1970s, the followers of the Islamic movement have been active in many West Bank-Gaza colleges. Since 1978, the student council of the Islamic University in Gaza has been controlled by the representatives of the Islamic movement. Between 1978 and 1988, for the most part the Islamic groups were the dominant force in the student councils of the Islamic College in Hebron and Al-Najah University in Nablus. A coalition among several pro-PLO student groups kept the Islamic movement from having a representative on the Bir Zeit University student council between 1985 and 1988.[29]

The proponents of the Islamic movement call on their fellow Palestinians to return to Islam and abandon their attachment to secular ideologies. In the opinion of the Islamic groups, Islam alone is capable of ending Israel's military occupation and establishing an Islamic state in all of Palestine. To enhance their popularity and credibility, the followers of the Islamic movement launched several attacks on Israeli targets, including an assault on a group of Israeli soldiers at the Wailing Wall in October 1986.

The prevailing conditions in the occupied territories provide a congenial environment for an increase in Islamic fervor. The poverty of the refugees, the high unemployment within their ranks, the PLO's indecisiveness, the inconclusive diplomatic efforts of the Arab countries, and the current deadlock in the peace process are among the conditions that would strengthen the appeal of Islam to the Palestinians in the occupied territories. Under such circumstances, Islam would offer its adherents a sense of discipline, guidance, and refuge.

The intensity and widespread nature of the 1987–88 demonstrations and strikes clearly indicated that time was not working in Israel's favor. The *intifadah* suggested that the young people were determined to make the price of Israel's military occupation of the West Bank and Gaza morally and politically more costly. The West

29. For further elaboration, see Sahliyeh's chapter on the radicalization of the student movement in *In Search of Leadership*, pp. 115–36.

Bank-Gaza youth began to challenge seriously the deterrent capability of the Israeli army and its ability to control the locally organized riots. In previous encounters with the Arab conventional armies, the Israeli government was able to assert its military superiority. Yet military superiority is of limited utility in the face of protests by unarmed civilians. The deployment of the army against the West Bank-Gaza Palestinians could demoralize the Israeli soldiers and strengthen the resolve of the Palestinians to defy and mock the Israeli military machine.

The uprising has transformed the Arab-Israeli interstate dispute into a Palestinian-Israeli intercommunal conflict, a result that has been in the making since the mid-1980s. With Jordan's increasing irrelevance to the political destiny of the occupied territories, the Palestinians are becoming Israel's direct interlocutors in any future negotiations.

The general strike by Israeli Arabs in December 1987 and the massive demonstrations in Nazareth in January 1988 in support of West Bank-Gaza Palestinians cast doubt about the Israeli government's assumption of the political passivity of its Arab population. Though most Israeli Arabs continue to be loyal to the state of Israel, many of them support the national aspirations of the Palestinians in the occupied territories. In the future, Israeli Arabs will try to make their political weight felt more strongly on Israel's policy toward the occupied territories. The absence of any progress toward a political solution and the continuation of the Israeli military occupation will invite more frequent confrontation with the Israeli army and the hardening of attitudes of both Israelis and Palestinians. Consequently, the hope of achieving a diplomatic solution to the Palestinian-Israeli conflict will diminish.

CONCLUSION

Though ten years have elapsed since the signing of the Camp David Accords, both Jordan and the Palestinians believe the agreements did nothing to advance the peace process for the West Bank and Gaza. Both Jordan and the Palestinians continue to consider the accords an impediment to any new diplomatic round. The Palestinians believe the accords, by taking Egypt out of the conflict, left them more vulnerable and enabled the Israeli government to be more rigid about the future of the occupied territories. The Likud's narrow interpretation of autonomy rendered the plan meaningless. The Likud's insistence on Israel's control over land and water resources generated great hostility among the Palestinians toward the Camp David Accords. Furthermore, developments in the Arab world in the 1980s, including the endorsement of the Fez plan and the call for the convening of an international peace conference, rendered the Camp David Accords irrelevant.

The concept of autonomy as outlined in the Camp David Accords continues to have no attraction to the Palestinians in the occupied territories. A negative attitude may not, however, be an absolute and total one. Should the autonomy plan give the West Bank Palestinians control over the land and water resources, allow for free elections, impose a freeze on construction of Israeli settlements, and recognize the Palestinian right to self-determination, it would be acceptable to many of the West Bank and Gaza Palestinians as a transitional arrangement. Given the current political paralysis inside Israel, however, an autonomy plan of this sort is highly unlikely.

Though Palestinians want to see a quick end to Israel's military occupation of the West Bank and Gaza, they have been unable to develop a concrete political strategy to achieve this goal. The reluctance of West Bank and Gaza politicians to launch their own initiatives has resulted from a number of circumstances. Over the years, Palestinians in the occupied territories have developed strong expectations that political solutions to their problems will come from the initiatives of others. They also do not possess a strong economic base that would enable them to act independently and assertively. West Bank and Gaza politicians lack widespread political legitimacy and domestic support. The 1987–88 popular uprising brought about a change in this situation.

The *intifadah* made the West Bank and Gaza the focal point of the Arab-Israeli conflict. Because of the uprising, the initiative for ending Israel's military occupation may continue to come from West Bank-Gaza Palestinians. The new conditions in the occupied territories have made the local politicians more assertive and have made the flow of influence between West Bank and Gaza Palestinians and the PLO a two-way process.

Most Palestinians identify closely with the PLO and espouse its goal of establishing an independent Palestinian state in the occupied territories. Only a small group of politicians openly supports the Jordanian government. The predicament for both the pro-PLO and pro-Jordanian politicians stems from Israel's intolerance of their political activities and the absence of diplomatic opportunities for the resolution of the Arab-Israeli conflict.

Despite King Hussein's interest in seeing the Palestinian problem resolved, he has apparently decided to remove Jordan from the center stage of future peace efforts. Jordan still supports the exchange of land for peace, a principle that is enshrined in Resolution 242. It also insists on the convening of an international peace conference as necessary for a comprehensive solution of the Arab-Israeli conflict. But the king now wants the PLO to shoulder responsibility for the Palestinians, even though he knows that Jordan and Syria will be actively involved in any comprehensive peace negotiations.

Despite many changes in Jordan's tactical position over the last decade, and Hussein's strong standing in the Arab world after 1985, Jordan cannot act independently in future diplomatic talks. The Jordanians have learned that acting separately against collective Arab wishes, and especially against Syrian interests, and without Palestinian backing, can be hazardous and risky. Thus the Jordanian government will only participate in peace efforts as part of a broad consensus, one that includes the Palestinians.

Only an extremely generous Israeli offer on territory and very strong American commitments could persuade King Hussein to change his mind. And it seems unlikely that these conditions will be met. Thus, as of 1988, the Palestinians and the PLO have broad Arab and international backing to negotiate a settlement with Israel. Whether they can do so, and on what terms, remains to be seen.

GHASSAN SALAME

Inter-Arab Politics: The Return of Geography

THE MAIN FEATURES of inter-Arab relations changed dramatically during the seventies, though it would be hazardous to claim the Camp David Accords, or any other single event, as the main cause of change. Stated simply, the twenty years preceding 1967 were heavily laden with ideology. The 1967–77 decade was a transitional period, in which the effects of the June 1967 disaster were maturing behind a screen of outdated discourse and contradictory moves. The decade that opened in 1977 with Sadat's visit to Jerusalem witnessed the return of geography, or geopolitical calculations, as a primary influence on the political behavior of Arab states. But this shift to geography was soon to reveal its limits, so that, by the end of the 1978–88 decade, a full circle was completed.

The years between 1978 and 1988 were a period of sharp contrasts. The first half was shaped by Camp David, the Iranian revolution, and a huge oil windfall; the second half was dominated by a fall in oil prices, an impasse in the Gulf war, and a cold peace between Egypt and Israel. The 1982 Israeli invasion of Lebanon marked the watershed.

Ten years, almost to the day, after the Egyptian leader's fateful visit to Jerusalem, an Arab summit in Amman was reintegrating Egypt into the Arab family after a decade of ostracism. It is as if the Arabs suddenly concluded that their reliance on geographic considerations had given too much leverage to their mightier neighbors, as if the bonds uniting them had become so dangerously thin that their political and cultural identity was faltering under the combined effect of Israeli supremacy, Iranian nationalism mixed with Islamist militancy, and dependence on the West for bread, motor cars, and weapons. The repudiation of ideologies, so widespread in the past decade, is being gradually replaced with a renewed search for an organizing idea that would help the Arabs face an era of limited oil revenues, continuing military weakness, and short-sighted leaders.

The political atmosphere during the fifties and the sixties was suffused with ideology, be it Arabism, national liberation, or socialism. No distance in miles and kilometers seemed to matter. Arab nationalism was leading Egypt's President Gamal Abd al-Nasser toward unity with Syria, while neglecting the more urgent and probably more fruitful, relationship with neighboring Sudan. Beiruti mobs were thrilled by the Algerian National Liberation Front (FLN) successes. Damascus youth seemed to suffer in response to any action they perceived as hostile to the Arabs, from the Aures mountains to the Iraqi marshes, from the streets of Aden to the Jabal rebellion in Oman. The prevalent idea was that the leaders of Egypt, Iraq, Jordan, Saudi Arabia, and the others all belonged to the same family, with, as in all families, its good guys and its bad guys, depending on one's preferences.

Alignments followed an ideological divide: on the one hand, pro-Western republics and all the monarchies; on the other, the progressive and military regimes. There were, of course, frictions and rivalries within each of the two camps. But the acute ideological polarization helped the members of each camp to overcome their differences. Saudis and Hashemites gradually learned to coexist and even to cooperate despite their old and acrimonious rivalry. On the other side of the divide, Nasser was trying to tame (or at least to coexist with) his fellow progressive and independence-minded leaders: Abd al-Karim Qassem in Iraq, Houari Boumedienne in Algeria, or Salah Jadid in Syria. A quantitative study of the inter-Arab conflicts of the 1945-81 era shows that the most divisive issue by far among the Arab regimes before 1981 was the competition between "progressives" and "radicals." The Palestinian question comes as a distant second in this ranking. Other issues such as border conflicts, Arab unity, economic issues, or common security seem to have been marginal. One other finding of this study is that progressive regimes were much more active in inter-Arab feuds than the conservative ones. The progressives were either opposing the conservatives, or quite often, fighting among themselves.[1]

In these interactions, geography had little influence. Arabs, the

1. Ahmad Yussuf Ahmad, *Inter-Arab Conflicts, 1945–81* (in Arabic) (Beirut: Centre for Arab Unity Studies, 1988).

leaders, as well as the men-in-the-street, felt that they could, or even should, form an opinion on any event taking place in the Arab world, the farther away the better. Ahmad Ben Bella's socialism was feverishly compared with Qassem's flirtation with Marxism. Habib Bourguiba was labeled a pragmatist by some, a lackey of imperialism by others. Byzantine polemics were filling books and pamphlets in which approximately translated quotations from Marx, Engels, Fichte, and Hegel would easily find their place. Binary divisions were paramount: nationalists versus Marxists, local nationalists (later labeled isolationists) versus pan-Arabists, nonaligned versus pro-Westerners or pro-Soviets, pro-Soviets versus pro-Chinese, Ho Chi Minists or Guevarists. More often, the divide was between the listeners to the Cairo-based "Voice of the Arabs" and those listening to the British Broadcasting Corporation (BBC) in Arabic. Contrary to textbook models, acute ideological mobilization did not follow social mobilization; it preceded it by far.

The June 1967 war opened a transitional decade in which few were willing to draw the real lessons of the defeat. Those who did so were too hasty in reaching conclusions about this sudden and devastating blow to the Arabs. Some argued that guerrilla warfare would be more effective than a classical war, that oil embargoes could have a decisive effect on a war's outcome, that army officers were to be blamed for politicians' hasty decisions, or—in a fatalist mood—that defeat was inevitable. Equally hasty conclusions were drawn after the 1973 military half-success and oil embargo, some going so far as to announce the emergence of "the new Arab man," in the aftermath of the "miracle of the crossing," as Anwar Sadat used to call the first day of the 1973 war. Many thought that the then-demonstrated Arab solidarity was unshakable.

The decade from 1978 to 1988 was different. The view of events in this period should not be blurred by official discourse. On the contrary, political statements and joint communiqués are deceptive. Though they do reflect reality, it is often distorted. The most pompous Arabist communiqués went hand in hand with an unprecedented disintegration of inter-Arab relations. However, those who have too hastily concluded that the Arab world has not been, and will never be, more than an abstract idea skillfully used by demagogues have gone too far.

THE DISINTEGRATION OF THE REGIONAL SYSTEM

The Arab world, viewed from a systemic perspective, has disintegrated into local subsystems, loosely connected to one another.

The Camp David Accords undoubtedly accelerated an ongoing process, either by the exclusion of the geographically central piece in the system, Egypt, or by the inability of the other players to devise a new strategy to deal with the undisputed central issue: the Arab-Israeli conflict. Geographic considerations partially explain certain political orientations of the fifties and the sixties, such as Nasser's attempt to establish Egypt's primacy in the region or Syria's obsession with Arab nationalism, not to mention Iraqi isolationism under Qassem. What was once only implied became explicit after 1973. A North African (*maghribi*) or a Gulf Arab (*khaliji*) identity, which had once been an anathema, was no longer so, and the "Egypt first" slogan that had once been held in check gradually became acceptable. Other considerations, such as demography or economics, played a marginal role in this pivotal combination of ideology and geography.

It is evident that this return to an emphasis on geography and on one's particular identity as opposed to the previously dominant dogma of the "superior interests of the Arab nation" was accompanied, and partly triggered, by a greater vulnerability to foreign interference from both neighborly and distant forces. Muhammad Hassanein Heikal has written of the contrast between the Arabs' view of themselves as a single nation with a rich history and the dominant Western view of the Arab world as a weak and vulnerable area with no real unity and no resistance to outside pressures.[2] The Western view seems to have triumphed in the eighties, when Arab governments, with few exceptions, have been trying to react to other actors' initiatives or shows of strength and have not concentrated on building up their own positions in the world system. In fact, the vulnerability of the Arab world has increased. It is challenged not only by the resurgence of the West's influence since Henry A. Kissinger, but also by more immediate sources. Israel, which became part of the domestic political configuration, notably in Egypt and Lebanon, Khomeinist Iran, Marxist Ethiopia, or even militarily respectable Turkey raise serious concerns among Arabs.

The geographical disintegration of the regional system into local subsystems also had a legitimizing ideology but not a vocal one. Subsystems were ostensibly founded on realism, which is an ideology in itself. In fact, this ideology's discourse was produced after these internally integrated and loosely connected local subsystems were established. More often than not, local groupings were formed

2. Mohamed Hassanein Heikal, "Egyptian Foreign Policy," *Foreign Affairs*, vol. 56 (July 1978), pp. 714–27.

around a newly assertive local power. These are what systemic schools in the study of international relations call hierarchical systems, that is, groups of states from which a leading actor has emerged. The dominant state tries to organize its immediate environment into a friendly, or even a submissive, milieu into which it can easily project power. Syria in the Levant, Saudi Arabia in the Arabian peninsula, and to some extent Sadat's Egypt in relation to Sudan and Libya have followed this pattern. By sticking to largely outdated stands and tactics, Iraq was much less responsive to this new trend, pursuing a pan-Arab ideological drive until the eruption of the Shatt al-Arab war.

Arab nationalists often view subsystems as fragments of a pan-Arab regional system that has ceased to exist because of external pressure. Antecedents are found in the pre-Nasserite era, when schemes such as Greater Syria, or a unified Fertile Crescent, were openly discussed and sometimes formally condemned in parliaments. My review of modern subsystems begins with a study of Iraq.

Iraq's Diminished Influence

Soon after becoming president of Iraq in 1979, Saddam Hussein had to concentrate his country's resources on the war with Iran. Books and articles have been written on Saddam Hussein's motivations and expectations. From my perspective, the most important effect of his ascent to the presidency is that Iraq's energy was diverted eastward in an effort to contain the Iranian revolution and to save the Baathist regime. The regime tried, during the first couple of years of the war, to behave as if the war was a marginal factor on the road toward the assertion of Iraq's primacy in the eastern Arab world. But with the success of the Iranian counteroffensive in May 1982, the rapid fall in oil revenues, the depletion of the financial reserves amassed during the years of the petrodollar boom, and the lack of enthusiasm for the Iraqi stand in the Arab world, it was soon clear that the war was affecting Iraq in a much more serious manner. Baghdad had to adapt to a long-term defensive war and to a situation in which choices had to be made between guns and butter.

This eastward diversion should be put into perspective. The seventies saw the buildup of Iraqi influence. Iraq's domestic stability, ensured through a gradual concentration of power in Saddam Hussein's hands, efficient Baathist control of the army, and the crushing of the Kurdish rebellion in 1975, greatly contributed to the country's power. Iraq had a larger share of the oil market, something it had sought for many years. Oil production of 2.0 million barrels a day in 1973 thus rose to 3.5 million barrels a day in 1979,[3] and the oil revenues were consequently (mainly because of the rise in oil prices) boosted from $1.9 billion to $21.0 billion.

These revenues were primarily used to enhance Iraq's capabilities, notably in the military field. By 1980 the Iraqi army had at its disposal some 2,750 main battle tanks, 1,040 major pieces of artillery, 332 combat aircraft, and a fairly respectable navy. In the civilian sector, performance was equally impressive. The gross national product rose tenfold from ID (Iraqi dinars) 1.1 billion in 1970 to ID 10.4 billion in 1979, of which about 80 percent was provided by the public sector.[4] By the late 1970s, about 120,000 Iraqis were working in industry. Mechanization of agriculture was rapid. Education, health, and social services were spreading to the remote rural areas, and several cities were becoming huge building sites.

This sustained effort led to the positioning of Iraq as a major contender for power in the Arab world, and of Saddam Hussein as the most credible successor to Nasser, an expression then repeated ad nauseam. At a minimum, Iraq was "the eastern flank of the Arab world." Others viewed the country as "the West's opportunity" and increasingly as the "New Power in the Middle East." Iraqi-subsidized Arabic publications were even more emphatic.

By 1982, however, rather than pretending to a leading role in the Arab world, Iraqi leaders first had to contain the numerous incursions Iran had made in Arab ranks and to deal with a skeptical and apathetic Arab world. Even the neighboring Arab Gulf countries gave Iraq reluctant and generally unenthusiastic support. In short, the problems caused by Iraq's proximity to an active revolutionary regime outweighed any regional ambitions. Iraq, probably more than any other country, was paying the price of geography.

The Indifference of the Gulf Leaders

The triumph of the Iranian revolution was, of course, contemporary with the signing of the Camp David Accords. Ayatollah Khomeini had arrived in Tehran a few weeks before the official

3. U.S. Department of Energy, Energy Information Administration, *Monthly Energy Review* (GPO, December 1983 [2]), p. 98.

4. Military figures are from International Institute for Strategic Studies, *The Military Balance, 1980–1981* (London: IISS, 1980), pp. 42–43. GNP figures are from International Monetary Fund, *International Financial Statistics: Yearbook* (Washington, D.C., 1986), p. 400; and CIA, National Foreign Assessment Center, *The World Factbook–1981* (GPO, 1981), p. 94.

signing of the formal Egyptian-Israeli peace treaty. This gave the shah's sojourn in Cairo, immediately after his departure from Tehran, a highly political meaning. The triumph of Khomeini and the isolation of Egypt both helped shape the political evolution in the Gulf, though it is difficult to determine with precision the contribution of each of these two factors.

Frightened by the effects of these two important regional events, the Gulf petromonarchies turned their backs on the rest of the Arab world to take advantage of the huge windfall generated by the second oil shock of 1979–80. Though the tendency to develop a "*khaliji*"[5] identity had been there for some time, only a combination of factors that occurred in 1980 could have made a full-fledged subregional institution, the Gulf Cooperation Council (GCC), possible.

But first I will trace the evolution of the regional policy of the GCC's undisputed leader, Saudi Arabia. The first Saudi reaction to the Camp David Accords was one of panic. Some Arab observers were hinting that the Saudis were aware of Sadat's intentions and had encouraged him to go all the way, while others pointed out that Saudi Arabia had condemned Sadat's visit to Jerusalem and cut the aid it was providing to Egypt. The ambiguity of the Saudi reaction was mainly because of the kingdom's extreme embarrassment. On the one hand, the Saudi ruling family did not want to be squeezed into a pariah category with Sadat; but it could not, on the other hand, condemn an initiative taken by a political ally and increasingly welcomed by its American protector.

This problem explains the Saudis' embarrassed silence during the winter of 1977–78. Tensions within the Saudi elite and the desire to assess adequately the other Arab countries' determination to fight Egyptian policies led to passivity and a retreat from regional affairs. Considerable American pressure was necessary to get the Saudis to welcome publicly President Jimmy Carter's call for a summit at Camp David. When the accords were signed on September 17, 1978, the Saudi government reverted to its position of embarrassed ambiguity. The official statement found the results "disappointing," but it also added that the kingdom would not "interfere with the domestic affairs of a country that has decided to recapture her territories through negotiation." One could easily imagine the frustration of both the accords' signatories and of their opponents on reading such a statement.

5. From *khalij*, the Arabic word for gulf.

This was the public stand. In practice, Saudi Arabia had been generally supportive of Sadat's domestic and foreign policies, of an active American role in the peace process, and of a solution reached through peaceful means. Hence the event was basically accepted. When Sadat went to Jerusalem, the Saudi government criticized the trip less in its own right than because "it was harming Arab solidarity." Later, Fahd, then a powerful crown prince, stated repeatedly that Riyadh was expecting a lot from the Camp David talks. But with the triumph of the Iranian revolution, with serious dissension within the royal family (leading to Prince Fahd's self-exile for a few months), and with the confirmation of a wide and militant Arab consensus against the accords, Riyadh could not stick to vague commentaries on events. These three factors, made worse by Sadat's vulgar attacks against the Saudis and Begin's threats against the kingdom, pushed the Saudi leaders to join the Arab mainstream.

This brief description of the Saudi position in the aftermath of Camp David demonstrates that the whole episode was traumatic to the Saudis, leading at the same time to serious tensions within the ruling elite and to an era of mistrust in the pivotal relationship with the United States. Regionally—and that is the main focus of this chapter—the Camp David Accords demonstrated the very narrow limits of Saudi Arabia's leading role in inter-Arab politics. Saudi Arabia was clearly shown to be unable to extract from America (and therefore from Israel) all the concessions it had promised to extract. The kingdom was unable to support Sadat, an ally, or to moderate in a significant way the Arab outcry against the accords, or to devise a "third way" between Sadat and his opponents. So in the end Saudi Arabia resigned itself to a secondary role in the framing of the November 1978 Baghdad summit resolutions.

This poor public showing in regional politics was soon compounded by several unfavorable circumstances. The Saudis witnessed, in January 1979, the shah leaving his country. The Saudis had little admiration for such an ambitious leader, who was arrogant enough to pretend to protect the Saudi oil wells. This feeling had become acute after the U.S. Senate published a report that posited an Iranian role in defending Saudi Arabia.[6] Nor were the Saudi leaders, at that time, very fearful of the Islamic character of the revolution. Their real and growing fear was triggered by U.S. behavior

6. U.S. Senate Committee on Energy and Natural Resources, *Access to Oil—The United States Relationships with Saudi Arabia and Iran,* Committee Print, 95 Cong. 1 sess. (Government Printing Office, 1977).

during that period. Was the American government, under the pretext of concern for human rights, working for the shah's downfall? Was it really unable to help the shah put an end to the insurrection? Was it incapable of rescuing its diplomats? Doubts about American intentions were soon aggravated by an aggressive campaign against the kingdom in leading American newspapers. Was this campaign an indirect American ploy to push the Saudi royal family to liberalize the regime, or was it an Israeli-inspired campaign against a country reluctant to support the Camp David Accords?

The Iranian revolution was followed by several other equally unpalatable events. In February 1979, at the worst possible moment, North Yemeni rebels, supported by South Yemen, began a general offensive against the troops of the pro-Saudi central government in Sanaa. The rebellion scored a number of points on the battlefield. (Worse, instead of being tempted by Saudi money, Aden later confirmed its alignment with the Soviet Union and signed the traditional friendship and cooperation pact with Moscow; shortly thereafter, in December 1979, the Soviet Union invaded Afghanistan, with no immediate or effective reaction from the West.)

By March 1979, the Egyptian-Israeli peace treaty was signed, and Riyadh had to abide reluctantly by the Arab League's anti-Egyptian resolutions. Meanwhile oil prices were climbing rapidly, making a shambles of the subtle, long-standing Saudi strategy to stabilize prices. Radical oil producers happened to be politically radical as well, while some political doves, such as Kuwait, were becoming hawks in oil matters. Crowning this long series of equally threatening regional events was the insurrection in Mecca, which erupted in late November 1979. It took the Saudi authorities some time before they were reassured that this rebellion was not the work of some hostile regional force.

Saudi Arabia was therefore not exclusively preoccupied with Camp David. The Saudis were also facing Israeli threats, American pressures, and Sadat's criticism. The Saudi elite felt much more vulnerable to internal disturbances, Soviet pressure in Afghanistan and South Yemen (accompanied by an astute Soviet "charm offensive" directed at the Saudis), and joint pressure by Syria and Iraq to take a firmer stand against Cairo and, implicitly, the United States.

Some Saudi compromise with this radically different regional environment was necessary. It had to begin with the recognition of the basically defensive Saudi position in regional affairs. Those who had too rapidly spoken of "a Saudi era" in inter-Arab politics were now reviewing their labels. To the Saudis the seventies had been a very favorable decade but certainly not a Saudi era.

The eighties were marked by the newly devised Saudi defensive strategy in Arab affairs. This shift had been affected in two ways by Camp David. First, the Saudis were less certain of American backing for their initiatives now that Washington was fully committed to the Camp David process on the Arab-Israeli issue, and the newly established Reagan administration was reverting to the old and ineffective idea of "a strategic consensus" against the Soviet Union. Second, the Saudis knew that no Arab country could replace Egypt and that they would have to operate in a new environment of power diffused among the various Arab actors, a much more volatile, or at least unpredictable, environment.

This new defensive strategy was best illustrated by the creation of the GCC. The Saudis thought it was imperative to organize the kingdom's immediate environment under Saudi leadership. One long-standing factor in the kingdom's foreign policy has been to try to deny access to the Arabian peninsula to all extra-peninsular actors. If the Saudis had been able to unify only four-fifths of the peninsula under their flag, that did not mean that the remaining fifth would be available to be used as a staging point against them. That was the basic argument for the Saudi opposition to the Egyptian intervention in North Yemen, to Iraqi leader Abd al-Karim Qassem's threats against Kuwait, to Iranian designs on Bahrain, to Iran's intervention in Dhofar, and, of course, to the Soviet presence in South Yemen. These positions demonstrate the well-entrenched Saudi view of the peninsula as a Saudi zone of influence.

Though uniting only the petromonarchies, the GCC clearly reflects this Saudi line of thinking. The creation of the GCC was only possible when the two major powers in the Gulf (Iran and Iraq) were busy fighting each other. Both of them were opposed to a grouping that would affect the old triangular competition for influence over the smaller states of the Gulf among Iraq, Iran, and Saudi Arabia to the benefit of Saudi Arabia. The mounting threats in the Gulf, however, were serious enough to finally convince the smaller states' rulers (notably in Kuwait and Oman) that some institutionalization of the influence that the Saudis already exerted upon them was not such an expensive price for more protection in these troubled years.

To a certain extent, the council has achieved what was expected from it: to encourage and formalize a common *khaliji* stand in comparison with an increasingly unstable regional environment. Geographical proximity has again played a pivotal role in making this endeavor possible. But the GCC has been limited, from its inception, by its own logic. Geographical proximity and social and political similarities do encourage rapprochement, but they are not a guarantee for integration. In other words, similarity does not substitute for complementarity. The six members of the council shared the same dilemma, that of military and demographic weakness coupled with enviable wealth.

The council proved useful in peacetime. Leaders tried to improve their cooperation in political and military affairs, while their aides explored other possible areas of cooperation. But as the threat of the Iran-Iraq war grew, council members tried to cope with the mounting trouble in a much less organized pattern. The Kuwaitis asked the permanent members of the United Nations Security Council to protect oil shipping, and the Saudis pushed for a joint Arab stand against Iran, while other members seemed more eager to find ways to accommodate the ayatollahs. It was soon clear that, with or without the GCC, the six petromonarchies had to depend on foreign protection and on the cooperation of other Arab actors. By 1987 the GCC had come almost full circle from its earlier infatuation with a distinct Gulf identity to a renewed reliance on Arab solidarity against Iran. This evolution was especially notable after Saudi Arabia's loss of its monopoly over traditional Islamic slogans, now used by Iran in a much more effective manner. So when Saudi Arabia uncharacteristically decided to break diplomatic relations with Iran in May 1988, the smaller GCC countries did not follow suit.

Out of concern for the Arab-Israeli conflict, Saudi Arabia came up with a plan that was supposed to be adopted first by the Arab League, then by the Islamic conference, and finally translated into a new resolution of the UN Security Council. The plan stumbled from the beginning at the Fez summit meeting of November 1981. However, a new summit, convened in the aftermath of the 1982 Israeli invasion of Lebanon adopted the Saudi plan with some amendments. At the 1982 meeting, the Arab heads of state were no more impressed with the details of the plan than they had been a year earlier. But they finally adopted the plan (the Fez resolution) because of the summer 1982 trauma in Lebanon and as an answer to the Reagan plan that had been announced a few days earlier. The most important item in the Saudi plan was the first official, though veiled, pan-Arab recognition of Israel's right to exist as a state. Some misreading of the American position then took place. Several Arab leaders (notably King Fahd and Yasir Arafat) were convinced that the Israeli invasion of Lebanon had created momentum for an active American peacemaking initiative in the Middle East. But Washington's lukewarm reaction to the Fez resolution and the American reluctance to work actively for peace, even under the auspices of President Ronald Reagan's plan, soon convinced the Arab leaders that Fez had been a nonstarter. The whole 1981–82 episode had a side effect: it strengthened the hand of those Saudi leaders who were advocating a retreat from regional politics or at least a more determined concentration on peninsular affairs.

What was the Saudi attitude toward Egypt's isolation at this time? Were the Saudis, weakened by Egypt's defection, working for Cairo's return into "the family" during the 1978–88 decade? To many observers' surprise, the answer is no. To explain the Saudi reluctance, and in some instances, open opposition, to seeing Egypt taken back into the Arab realm, one has to speculate, since the Saudi leaders are understandably discreet on this sensitive issue. One thing is certain. Having been accused in 1978 of blocking real sanctions against Egypt, the Saudi leaders did not want to be accused of breaking Arab solidarity. Some observers perceived the Saudi attitude as an indirect attempt to weaken and marginalize the pan-Arab institutions for the benefit of groupings, such as the GCC or the Islamic conference, in which Saudi views were traditionally well received. Finally Riyadh would have had to pay a stiff financial price to impoverished Egypt to rebuild the Saudi-Egyptian relationship.

Despite the Saudi position toward Egypt, Kuwait took the lead in trying to ease Egypt's return to these regional institutions, as shown by the invitation to Egypt to attend the Islamic summit of 1987. The Iranian threat in the Gulf, especially after the events in Mecca and the attempts to destabilize Kuwait and Bahrain, gradually eroded Saudi reluctance. Egypt's relations with the GCC countries were reestablished in the aftermath of the November 1987 Amman summit. In fact, Arab governments were notified, before the summit, that the GCC countries would reestablish their relations with Egypt whatever the results of the summit. This was a setback for the Arab radicals and a real constraint on Syria's maneuvers.

The Levant under Syrian Tutelage

Syria's regional policies have been incomprehensible to many. How could a secular regime, threatened by an Islamist opposition, side with an Islamic regime against another secular regime? How could a country that has earned the title of the "beating heart of Arabism" side with Iran against another Arab country? How could the country that has been uncompromising on Palestinian national rights be so harsh in its treatment of the Palestine Liberation Organization (PLO)? Many hypotheses have been offered to answer these questions. Some stress the particularly sectarian color of the present Syrian regime. Others speak openly of treason. Many are just puzzled.

It is useful to try to find another approach to the Syrian enigma, one that takes into consideration the modern history of that country. Seriously weakened by what many Syrians have perceived as the unjust loss of Lebanon, Transjordan, and Palestine, not to mention Mosul and Alexandretta, Syria has been victimized by plots and schemes hatched in Baghdad, Amman, Riyadh, and Cairo. Nobody would contradict Patrick Seale when he describes the forties and the fifties as an era of "struggle for Syria," when domestic instability, triggered by foreign interference, added to geographic dismemberment by the colonial powers, transformed Syria into a nonentity. "When reduced to terms of power politics," Seale wrote in 1965, "the story of the struggle for Arab unity in the past two decades has been little else than that of rival bids to control Syria."[7]

When Syria was united with Egypt (1958–61), Syria's marginality reached its climax. The country was reduced to a satellite of the then-strongest regional player. But the transformation of Syria, formerly the object of other players' schemes, into an independent player, has been a central theme in Syria's regional policy since the separation from Egypt in 1961. In the sixties, Syria underwent a radical transformation from the ambiguous role of an Arab nationalist country *par excellence* into that of a fiercely independent government, often at odds with everybody, including the other "progressive regimes." Meanwhile, the Syrian government, less affected than Egypt or Jordan by the 1967 defeat, was building up military and economic capabilities, basically with Soviet help.

When Hafiz al-Asad came to power in 1970, he inherited a Baathist line that had been in place for seven years. Luckier than his ideologically activist predecessors, he became president shortly after Nasser's death. The 1973 half-success in the war with Israel strengthened Asad's legitimacy, while Egypt's hasty pursuit of peace greatly enhanced Syria's prestige in the region. In 1974 Asad moved closer to Saudi Arabia and to the Arab mainstream when he disagreed with Sadat about an early end to the oil embargo. The second Egyptian-Israeli disengagement agreement in September 1975—Sinai II—gave Asad the profile of a leader who, unlike Sadat, was

7. Patrick Seale, *The Struggle for Syria: A Study of Post-War Arab Politics, 1945–1958* (Yale University Press, 1987), p. 2.

unwilling to squander the 1973 gains. Camp David was a divine gift to Syria. Asad would henceforth be adopted by both the USSR and the Arab mainstream as the undisputed leader of the struggle against Israel. This regional and international consecration had substantial legitimizing effects on this minority-led regime.

Hence a complex situation resulted, which can be summarized as follows: while pursuing a radical pan-Arab Baathist policy, Asad wanted to be viewed by his fellow countrymen as a Syrian patriot who was giving back to his country the stature it deserved. But if Asad's discourse remained pan-Arab, and if his target was basically domestic, the area of intervention was neither pan-Arab nor domestic. Asad's central regional objective has been pan-Syrian. His aim has been to deny access in what used to be geographic Syria to all other regional actors. In the local subsystem thus formed by Syria, Jordan, Lebanon, and the Palestinians, Syria would have, by far, the strongest position. The other three players are comparatively small and weak.

This means that Lebanon, Jordan, and the Palestinians have to accept this Syrian supremacy, and when possible, hegemony. Left to themselves, these actors have hardly any other option. Only through their alliance with stronger players can they resist it. An association with Israel is politically harmful, though Jordan, indirectly, and the Lebanese Phalangists, openly, have resorted to it. Egypt's waning role in the region and its isolation because of Camp David have made it a much weaker counterweight to Syria's schemes to carve out a large sphere of influence. Saudi Arabia, following a policy of retreat in the peninsula, and because it has systematically chosen to appease the Syrians rather than to oppose them, is of no great help—a realization shared by the Palestinians[8] and by the Lebanese. Both Bashir and Amin Gemayel repeatedly and unsuccessfully tried to draw Riyadh into playing the role of a counterweight to Damascus. The real challenge to this Syrian strategy could come from Iraq—hence the anti-Iraqi line followed by Damascus, probably the most consistent of Syria's policies.

By opposing Iraq, Syria has found its soul. For demographic, financial, and military reasons, Iraq is generally viewed as the stronger party of the two. Hence Syria has consistently followed a policy aimed at isolating Iraq. An assertive Iraq could only project power to the West and by so doing would make Syria a target again instead of a player. No Baathist ideological affinities and no parallel

8. See Rashid Khalidi, *Under Siege: P.L.O. Decisionmaking during the 1982 War* (Columbia University Press, 1986).

political stands could overcome the feeling, on both sides of the border, that the two regimes are irreconcilable. Camp David triggered short-lived cooperation that lasted for less than a year. Iraq could not accept being backed into a corner, while Syria would not give in to Iraqi pressure. With the de facto neutralization of Egypt, an eastern front grouping Syria, Jordan, Iraq, and the Palestinians could not, of course, survive such deep-rooted animosities. In fact, by opposing each other, the two regimes paradoxically became mutually supportive.

By opposing Iraq, even through an alliance with Iran, Syria is trying to redress old grievances including intervention by others in its internal affairs. This is a country that has been threatened by Iraq, dominated by Egypt, and economically bypassed by Lebanon. There are however some short-term elements in Syria's presently enviable position that will not necessarily have permanent effects, since they depend on the political developments in two rival states (Iraq and Egypt) and the decisions made by a formidable enemy (Israel).

Because of Camp David, Egypt was neutralized. This transformed Syria into the major recipient of both Arab financial aid and Soviet military sales. It has been estimated that Syria has received $10 billion in arms imports in the 1979–83 period, and that the USSR has been delivering "over twice the annual value of arms to Syria that the US is delivering to Israel. Similarly, Syria increased its military manning by 82 percent between 1973 and 1982, and then increased it by another 45 percent between 1982 and 1985."[9] In 1985 Syria had 3,700 active main battle tanks, 2,750 major artillery pieces, over 600 jet combat aircraft, and 130 major surface-to-air missile (SAM) units.[10] Iraq, however, because of the eruption of the Iraq-Iran war, was handicapped by years and years of battles. At the same time, Syria was playing the lucrative role of Iran's ally and moderator of Iran's supposedly hostile intentions against the Gulf petromonarchies.

But these are short-term tactics, and while nobody doubts Asad's tactical genius, many are uncertain about his long-term strategy. According to Albert Hourani, "It would be rash to prophesy . . . that the apparent strength of the regime would be real and lasting, and that Syria would never again become a body over which others

9. Anthony H. Cordesman, "The Middle East and the Cost of the Politics of Force," *Middle East Journal*, vol. 40 (Winter 1986), p. 13.

10. Ibid., pp. 13–14.

struggled."[11] If the Camp David stigma were in one way or another removed from Egypt, and if the forty-division-strong Iraqi army comes out of the war undefeated, it would be difficult for Syria, even with Asad as president, to keep the influence it has nowadays.

Paradoxically, Camp David and the Gulf war have played a large role in rejuvenating a regime that was strongly challenged by the Muslim Brotherhood in the late seventies. These positive factors might disappear and Syria could be consequently weakened. But Palestinian and Lebanese daydreamers who are expecting the return of Syria to its position of twenty years ago in the regional balance of power should review their calculations. Both superpowers seem to have been watching the reemergence of Syria as a pivotal regional player with satisfaction. Egypt, now back in the family, could play again the role of a counterweight, more likely in the Gulf than in the more turbulent Levant.

A Modest Role for Egypt

Egypt's first reaction to the outcry against Camp David was extremely arrogant. Sadat and his officially inspired media repeated a number of simplistic ideas. What could Syria alone do against Israel? What was the Saudi contribution to the Arab cause that would justify their opposition to the accords? What was the Arab world without Egypt? To the extent that these statements were aimed at domestic public opinion, they are understandable. But one sometimes felt that Egyptian leaders, beginning with Sadat, took these stands seriously. It seemed that the Egyptian government might have miscalculated the United States' ability and willingness to affect the other Arab governments' attitudes.

A few months after Camp David, the Egyptian government had to face a serious Arab boycott. It seemed that the Arab League was able to survive displacement from Cairo and that nobody was really taking "The League of Arab and Islamic Peoples," which Sadat had created to replace it, very seriously. Arab aid stopped and Cairo was boycotted by Arab public figures. In reaction to this generally hostile attitude, Sadat chose to make a separate deal with Israel. To understand this policy properly, one has to remember the regional environment in which the decision to go to Jerusalem had been taken a year earlier.

By the fall of 1977, the Egyptian elite had had many opportunities

11. Seale, *Struggle for Syria*, p. xv.

to measure their country's declining role in regional affairs. Algiers, not Cairo, brought Saddam Hussein and the shah of Iran together to sign the famous 1975 agreement ending the Kurdish conflict and establishing the border in the Shatt al-Arab area. Syria was almost singlehandedly intervening in Lebanon and containing the Palestinians. Saddam Hussein was actively seeking to become "the new Arab Nasser." Oil countries were being courted by world powers, while the carefully prepared Cairo meeting to organize Arab aid to Africa had been a failure. Even Muammar Qadhafi was now strong enough to resist an Egyptian military operation against him.

Possibly, the Egyptian elite and Sadat himself were unable to adapt to this rapid loss of influence in the region. Frustration with Arab oil countries and, even more, the inability to adapt to unfavorable change partly explain Sadat's sudden decision to "break the psychological wall with Israel." The evident impasse created by Carter's renunciation of the American-Soviet communiqué of October 1, 1977, was only adding to an equally embarrassing though less evident dilemma, that of a leader who was unwilling—for personal and political reasons—to accept his country's downgraded status in the Arab world (see appendix B). This reaction explains Sadat's decision, once the Arab boycott had been adopted, to go all the way. He reasoned that a proud isolation was more palatable than a lower ranking in the Arab pecking order.

This isolation was partly broken as a result of tenuous relations with Oman and Morocco. But the policy, here too, was one of retreat to the immediate geographical environment. Sudan adopted a position ambiguous enough to allow the continuation and even the strengthening of these two countries' relations. Denied a larger role, Egypt concentrated on supporting Somalia in the war with Ethiopia and on resisting Libyan schemes in Sudan and in Chad. By doing so, Egypt was conforming to the general pattern in the region.

Later, with the passing away of Sadat and with the mounting domestic pressure for better relations with the Arab world, Egypt tried to recapture some of its former standing in the region. Though many circumstances combined to make this endeavor possible, the Iran-Iraq war was the single most important factor. The other Arab actors' attitude toward Egypt would probably have continued to be as harsh as before without the multifaceted trauma created by the Iranian revolution.

It would be nevertheless hazardous to think that this return of Egypt to the Arab world was—or is—easy. For a long time to come, the Camp David Accords will be an impediment to the normalization of Egypt's relations with the rest of the Arab world, and, more often than not, an easy pretext to treat Egypt without proper consideration. In the absence of reliable polls, all assessments are impressionistic. But, generally, concerned Arab opinion seems to remain negative toward the accords and will probably continue to be so in the foreseeable future. Egypt has reestablished relations with most Arab countries, but the attempt to bring it back into the Arab League was defeated at the Amman summit. Egypt is back despite Camp David, not because the accords havc suddenly become palatable but because the Arab world had to face new and pressing challenges on its eastern flank.

A return to the Arab realm, however, does not necessarily mean that Egypt will ever recapture the influence it had under Nasser. The new balance of power does not allow for such a pretension. The diffusion of power in the Arab world seems to be the natural order of things. With the passing of time, the Nasserite period looks exceptional in most respects. Most Egyptian intellectuals do not call their country the leader in inter-Arab politics. Instead Egypt is euphemistically described as a "moderator in charge of finding the common denominator among smaller and more agitated brothers" or as "the articulator of Arab consensus." An Egypt readmitted into the Arab family clearly adds to the family's resources but is certainly not able to lead it. The contenders for this position have become too numerous.

The Neutralization of the North African States

Deteriorating into an almost direct confrontation between Algeria and Morocco, the Western Sahara issue erupted in 1975 at a moment when these two leading Maghribi countries were busily building their influence in the eastern Arab world.[12] Moroccan soldiers had fought bravely on the Golan Heights, and King Hassan II was trying to use his newly acquired Arab and Islamic credentials (as host to many Arab summits and chairman of the heavily publicized Jerusalem committee) to strengthen his legitimacy at home. Algiers

12. Morocco and Algeria have clashed over the status of the Western Sahara since Spain's withdrawal in 1975. Morocco considers the territory to be an integral part of the Moroccan nation. Algeria, by contrast, has called for the right of self-determination for the Saharan population, numbering some 200,000 inhabitants. Algeria has supported the Polisario, the armed Saharan group that calls for an independent state. In the spring of 1988, Morocco and Algeria resumed diplomatic relations. This step may open the way for a resolution of the Sahara issue. It may also contribute, along with improved Tunisian-Libyan relations, to a revival of the idea of creating a "Greater Maghrib," or at least to enhanced cooperation among the countries of North Africa.

was investing heavily in a leading role in the eastern Arab world, with an active embassy in Beirut, dealing with almost all Lebanese and Palestinian factions. Algeria was building on its spectacular success in the spring of 1975, when the shah of Iran and Iraq's vice president signed the Algiers Agreement, putting an end—for a time—to the numerous problems facing these two countries.

The Western Sahara issue soon compelled both Algeria and Morocco to devote important political and financial resources to support the Saharan nationalist movement, the Polisario, or, on the contrary, to defeat it. Since a solution to the conflict was pursued within the framework of the Organization of African Unity (OAU), Rabat and Algiers had to concentrate most of their diplomatic capabilities in a non-Arab framework, trying to gain the support of the various African actors. Squeezed into what soon appeared to be yet another political and military impasse, and having to watch unpredictable Libyan moves in the area carefully, it became difficult to ask much of the two Maghribi states on the more central and agitated eastern front.

The de facto neutralization of the Maghribi states partly explains several later events. The Arab reaction to Shimon Peres's visit to Morocco in early 1987, for example, would not have been so mild if the Moroccan influence in Near Eastern affairs had not already been greatly reduced. The fragmentation of the regional system also partly explains the repeated Algerian failures at playing a successful role in the eastern Arab world. Algerian mediation efforts between Iran and Iraq proved fruitless, and Algiers even lost a foreign minister in the process. Though eager to play a role in Lebanon, Algiers could hardly mediate between Christians and Muslims, and even less between Lebanese and Palestinians. Algerian influence has not been completely eradicated, however, as was shown in the weeks preceding the Palestine National Council meeting in 1987 or in the active overtures toward resuming ties with Cairo, but these modest gains were well below Algeria's ambitions.

The two Maghribi powers are again marginal players in the East, while Tunisia, though host to the Arab League and to the PLO, was until 1988 weakened by the succession issue and increasingly challenged by the new fundamentalism.[13]

13. Habib Bourguiba ruled Tunisia from its independence in 1956 until he was deposed by his prime minister in the fall of 1987. During his last months in power, Bourguiba became increasingly arbitrary and despotic, thereby seeming to place in jeopardy the accomplishments of his long rule. In the end, the succession was handled very smoothly.

The fall in oil prices and the war in Chad have seriously curtailed Qadhafi's grandiose schemes. The Libyan colonel was, for a long time, the ardent champion of the struggle against geography, but his setbacks around Aouzou on the Chad border in 1987 could have a more lasting effect than all the unity projects with which he has been associated. He too is now concentrating on his most immediate environment, trying to secure Algeria's support and to avoid a humiliation on Libya's southern borders. Paraphrasing a famous saying, one could easily conclude that, at least for the time being, Mashriq is Mashriq, and Maghrib is Maghrib.

A REGIONAL SYSTEM ADAPTS TO ITS DISINTEGRATION

Although the bond among Arab states is weakened, it still survives. The Arab states are linked by several treaties and inter-Arab organizations that were, of course, largely affected by the Camp David Accords and the subsequent Arab decision to isolate Cairo. To adequately appreciate the effects of Egypt's exclusion, one has to remember the extent to which the Arab League was dominated by Cairo, long before Nasser had transformed it into Cairo's secular hand. The idea of an Arab grouping, as suggested by Britain's prime minister, was presented by Mustapha Nahhas Pasha to the Egyptian Senate in 1943: "When Mr. Eden made his statement, I thought about it and concluded that the best way to achieve it is to let the Arab governments themselves take care of it. I thought that the Egyptian government should take an official initiative by consulting other Arab governments, one by one, then Egypt should coordinate these different views as much as possible. Egypt will then invite Arab representatives to discuss the issue collectively. If an agreement is reached, Egypt will then convene a meeting in Egypt chaired by the Egyptian prime minister."[14] That is what actually took place. The Arab League's protocol was negotiated and signed in Alexandria in 1944. Its charter was signed in Cairo. Nobody dared to contradict Egypt's view that the headquarters should be in Cairo. When the headquarters was built, it was no accident that the building was located a few dozen meters from the Egyptian Foreign Ministry's palazzo. The Egyptians insisted on naming it a *jami'a,* wrongly translated into the much stronger "league," thus rejecting the Syrian

14. Al-Hasani, *History of the Iraqi Cabinet* (in Arabic), 5th ed. (Beirut: Matbaat Dar al-Kutub, 1978), p. 150.

preference for an *ittihad* (union) and the Iraqi insistence on *tahaluf* (alliance). The first general secretary was naturally an Egyptian, and Egyptians dominated the staff. The general secretary was to be replaced by another Egyptian, even more submissive to his government's instructions.

In these circumstances, the mere idea of an Arab League without Egypt seemed utterly absurd. But that is what happened after 1979. How was the league able to survive the severing of the umbilical cord to Cairo and its replacement by one to Tunis? The answer is to be found once again in the pre-Camp David years. Here again, Camp David accelerated an ongoing process. It is true that, after Nasser's death, the league headquarters remained in Cairo and that the third general secretary elected in 1971 was, once again, an Egyptian. The man was not an obscure diplomat. He was Mahmud Riad, the former minister of foreign affairs under Nasser. Though ready and willing to coordinate with his home country's government, Riad was senior enough to stand up to his successors at the Egyptian Foreign Ministry. Moreover, his views on regional issues happened to be different from those of Nasser's successor. More importantly, Riad was shrewd enough to see how the inter-Arab balance of power was shifting, especially after 1973, and to observe that the league's budget would be hereafter from non-Egyptian sources. He led a slow adaptation movement to these new circumstances, playing an active role in inter-Arab politics, recruiting more non-Egyptian Arabs to the staff, and systematically consulting with the new centers of power in the Arab world: Algiers, Riyadh, Baghdad, Damascus, and others.

Camp David led to Riad's resignation, but the league, under his guidance, remained. Sadat had apparently assumed otherwise, having reportedly told many of his confidants that an Arab League without Egypt could not survive. It did, and the Arab governments were unanimous in judging the Camp David Accords contradictory to the league's charter and, more importantly, to the 1950 Arab pact for mutual defense and economic cooperation. Article 10 in this pact, which unambiguously posits that the pact supersedes any past or future treaty signed by a league member, was inevitably used by many Arabs and some Egyptians to contest the legality of the Egyptian-Israeli treaty.

Arab public opinion seemed relieved that pan-Arab institutions could survive a trauma like Camp David. But at what price? Transferred to Tunis, the capital of a state where Arabist ideas are marginal, with a Tunisian general secretary reluctantly backed by his own government, the league saw its political role gradually fade.

It remained the institutional symbol of "the Arab idea," though it did not prevent other regional frameworks from emerging, such as the Islamic conference and the GCC. The league also had to contend with the opposition of some of its members to any attempt to transform the Arab League into a supranational organization—witness the project in 1980 of a new charter for the league. On this occasion Syria and Iraq pushed to have the unanimity rule replaced with a majority one. Saudi Arabia, Morocco, and several smaller states, however, successfully opposed this change. The league, already ineffective in solving inter-Arab conflicts, was now marginal to them. Its inability to do anything for Lebanon was notorious, and though 80 percent of the league's decisions have been unanimous, they are rarely implemented.

Paradoxically, ineffective joint Arab action was matched by official, determined, grandiloquent pan-Arab discourse. While for thirty years the league's charter and resolutions were largely respectful of state sovereignty, the post-Camp David discourse was pompous. In 1980 the Amman summit convened to launch a Decade of Joint Arab Development, adopted a number of resolutions that emphatically and repeatedly stated that the "Arabs form one *umma* (family), with a common destiny and a predetermined solidarity," while the Arab world is referred to as one single *watan* (nation), and full economic integration stated as a "central goal." But Egypt had already been excluded. Syria, Libya, and Algeria chose to boycott the conference, and those countries that were present soon forgot the commitments they had made. Only nine Arab countries ratified the treaty on inter-Arab trade, which was signed the following year. The Amman summit was followed by one in Fez that lasted for three hours. The next summit, also in Fez, adopted the short-lived eight-point resolution on the Arab-Israeli conflict (see appendix E). No Arab summits were convened during the next five years. The inability to implement joint decisions had deteriorated to an inability even to meet. By the mid-1980s, the Arab states, even the richest among them, would not even provide the league with its modest budget (about $33 million in 1986).

Beside the choice of a marginal and uninfluential capital for its seat, the twenty or so sister Arab organizations, previously concentrated in Cairo, are now scattered among eight different Arab capitals, thus providing an additional symbol of the diffusion of power that has taken place in the Arab world. But this is only a symbol, since the league secretariat could hardly be criticized for the deep divisions now prevailing in the region. After years of impotence, which led the present general secretary to concentrate on "information" activities in foreign capitals, the evolution of the Gulf war seemed to give the league an opportunity to add some substance to its activities, as was demonstrated in the Amman summit. But this same summit also decided that the league as such had nothing to do with the bilateral relations of individual countries with Egypt, an issue left to the member states. This was an indirect admission that the league's unanimity rules could be bypassed. It is also proof that the league is only one of several institutions in which inter-Arab politics are conducted, so that a month later, a GCC summit in Riyadh was adopting a line quite different from the one agreed to in Amman on the issue of relations with Iran.

Iran in Inter-Arab Politics

Before the revolution, the Iranian impact on Arab politics was marginal. During the fifties, the domestic problems in Iran and the rapid collapse of the 1955 Baghdad Pact had limited the scope of Iranian influence. The seventies were to witness a much more dynamic Iranian policy, well illustrated by several initiatives such as the attempt to annex Bahrain, the annexation of three islands belonging to the United Arab Emirates, a heavily publicized participation in the war against the Dhofari rebels in Oman, a sudden decision to end support for the Kurdish rebellion as part of the accord with Iraq in 1975, well-publicized visits by the shah to the major Arab capitals—with the provision of some financial aid to Egypt—and finally a repeatedly stated eagerness to intervene in support of any "friendly" Arab regime. With the advent of Khomeini, however, the willingness to intervene in Arab affairs was to be confirmed within a completely different context.

THE DIVISION BETWEEN SHIITES AND SUNNIS. The Iranian revolution has clearly deepened the dormant split between Shiites and Sunnis in the Arab world. This polarization has had mixed results for the Iranians. In the immediate aftermath of the revolution, this split was beneficial to Iran. Quite naturally, many Shiite Arabs identified with the revolution, and Khomeini's picture was hung even in moderate Shiite politicians' homes in Lebanon, Kuwait, and even Saudi Arabia. This was, after all, the first time since the adoption of Shiism by the Safavids that the victimized Shiite Arabs had been given a charismatic figure with which to identify. Moreover the first positive reactions to the revolution in the Arab world, and most notably in Sunni-dominated constituencies, triggered a genuine feeling of pride at being a Shiite, something that neither the Ottoman

Empire nor the modern states that had replaced it had offered to the 10 million or so Shiite Arabs.

Later, it turned out that the Shiite character of the revolution was one of its serious weaknesses. This was evident when the constitution included the principle of *wilayat al-faqih,* which provides for the supreme authority of one learned religious leader over the institutions of the state. This principle is unacceptable to the Sunnis. From then on, Iranian leaders attempted to break the sectarian barrier separating them from 90 percent of the Arabs. The gap was, however, deepening—with marginal exceptions, such as Shaikh Sa'id Sha'ban's movement in Tripoli, Lebanon, and a number of small Sunni fundamentalist groups across the Arab world. This gap was well illustrated in 1987, after the Mecca events in which hundreds of Iranian pilgrims were killed, along with a number of Saudi policemen. The Saudis accused the Iranians of trying to turn the religious event of the pilgrimage to Mecca into an opportunity for political propagandizing. This led to clashes between Iranian pilgrims who were carrying out political demonstrations and Saudi security forces. Arab Shiites—both radical and moderate—supported Iran, while Arab governments and Sunni fundamentalist groups generally supported Saudi Arabia. All in all, Arab governments in the Gulf had a vested interest in exploiting the Shiite-Sunni conflict so that they could portray their opponents as a "fifth column."

In this sense, the Amman summit was a Sunni reaction to a systematic Iranian attempt to "de-Arabize" Islam, that is, to shift the Muslims' center eastward, in the direction of the large Muslim Asian communities. Thus one resolution was adopted in Amman that gave Saudi Arabia a free hand in the organization of the annual pilgrimage to Mecca and the maintenance of the two holy cities of Islam, something strongly contested by the Iranians who insist on the formation of an international Muslim authority to supervise the shrines in what they have come to call, since the Mecca events, "the Hijaz." The Iranian revolution, instead of having sweeping repercussions across the Arab world, may have indirectly given the Arabs renewed reasons to affirm their national and cultural identity.

IRAN AND THE INTER-ARAB BALANCE OF POWER. The first obvious beneficiaries of the revolution were the Palestinians. They went in groups to Tehran where the Israeli embassy had been handed over to the PLO. Many Iranian revolutionary leaders had been trained in the Palestinian camps. So it seemed to some that although Egypt had been lost in the struggle against Israel, Iran had been gained. The Gulf countries partly benefited from the fall of a shah who was becoming increasingly assertive in the region. Though the new leaders in Tehran were not particularly friendly to them, Gulf leaders thought that Iran would be weakened for a certain number of years, which would give them some time to develop their own capabilities, notably within the finally feasible GCC.

More generally the Arab so-called radicals were given a new ally. Despite the religious color of the revolution, it rapidly appeared that Iran's friends in the Arab world (or at least those who were willing to offer a clearly positive assessment of the revolution) happened to be those Arab countries closest to the Soviet Union: Algeria, South Yemen, Syria, and Libya, though there was an obstacle to overcome with Libya on account of the disappearance in Libya of Lebanese Shiite leader Imam Musa al-Sadr. Syria was by far the most skillful Arab country in taking advantage of this new opportunity, despite widespread domestic uneasiness with this stand.

The Syrian-Iranian alliance is related to the systematic Syrian opposition to Iraq. Syria has also benefited financially, as well as through the skillful use of pro-Iranian groups against its enemies in Lebanon and elsewhere. Iran also gave some leverage to Syria in its dealings with Saudi Arabia and the Gulf states. Finally, the Syrian regime, seriously threatened by its Islamist opposition a few years ago, has succeeded in gaining the support of the only country in which Islamic fundamentalism has taken control of the state—no small achievement.

The Syrian game was possible so long as Damascus was able to dissociate itself from the various expressions of Iranian militantism, that is, as long as Iran could be used (as in Lebanon), or appeased (as in the Gulf) while maintaining pressure on Iraq. With the extension in 1987 of Iranian pressure to such places as Mecca and Bahrain and with the targeting of Kuwait, Syria became embarrassed. The Amman summit demonstrated that a pro-Iranian position was becoming untenable. With its clear anti-Iranian line, the summit highlighted Syria's embarrassment and isolation but not its defeat. A month later, the Syrian leaders were shuttling again between Tehran and the GCC capitals, encouraged by Oman, Abu Dhabi, and probably by the other GCC countries as well. In Amman, Syria was able to differentiate between Iranian threats against the GCC, which Damascus opposed, and the broader resolutions on the war between Iran and Iraq to which Syria was only willing to pay lip service.

Has Iran gained any net leverage over Arab politics? The answer depends, of course, on the evolution of the Gulf war and on the future of Islamic fundamentalism in the Arab world, two variables too important to be rapidly addressed here. Some skepticism seems nevertheless justified. Lebanon, for instance, has often been portrayed as the place where the export of the Iranian revolution has been successful. Is it really the case? American envoys have reportedly been amazed to be told by President Asad that he was confident in his capabilities to put an end to Hizbollah activities in Lebanon, whenever necessary. Here again, geography must be taken into account. Without Syria, Iran has almost no access to Lebanon. And if the Syrian-Iranian alliance were to be broken, Tehran could be of little help to its Lebanese followers and friends, as demonstrated during the Tripoli war of 1985, when Syria and Iran were supporting opposite sides. This point was also demonstrated during the camp wars in Beirut, when Damascus easily ignored Tehran's opposition to the fratricidal battles opposing Shiites and Palestinians.

This serious Iranian vulnerability has been well understood by the Lebanese. Though many Lebanese have shown their willingness to work for Iran, they have not necessarily done it through a deeply rooted identification with the Iranian regime. Like many other regional actors (such as Iraq, Libya, or the PLO), Iran has discovered that it is easy to exploit the Lebanese quagmire. The other side of the coin, already experienced by the other actors, is the extreme volatility, not only of the Lebanese scene, but also of Lebanese allegiances. The present trend of cooperation is only partly the result of an infatuation with the Iranian model. A number of militants, today as in the past, are much less fanatic than they would like the world to believe. Iran, like many countries before it, is now pouring huge amounts of money into Lebanon. If Lebanon were to find some civil peace and jobs for the thousands of unskilled children of the war, if Syria were to decide to put an end to pro-Iranian militancy in Lebanon, or if Iran were to interrupt the transfer of money to its supporters, the seemingly entrenched fanaticism could rapidly falter.

Increasing Stability

But Lebanon is a peculiar case. The growing irrelevance of ideology also explains the stability of some regimes. It has been noted that during the last decade the longevity of the average Arab regime has tended to grow substantially. Who could have thought, in the early seventies, that the vulnerable Sadat would remain in power for eleven years, that the embattled Jafaar al-Numeiry would govern Sudan for fifteen years, that countries internationally known for the volatility of their regimes such as Syria or Iraq would have the same leaders for two decades? Not only were the monarchical regimes no longer threatened, but devolution of power was carried out in a peaceful and civilized manner—even when the former leader had been assassinated (King Faysal, Sadat). Stability became the rule, even in the most unlikely places, such as the tribally segmented and coup-ridden North Yemen.

Several factors explain this amazing and widespread stability, to which the Palestinian and the Lebanese peoples are, in a way, the unwilling contrast, the exception that proves the rule. Oil revenues have encouraged widespread political apathy. Authoritarian regimes have devised new, more efficient means of control and repression over societies. Opposition forces are on the whole even less attractive than the leaders in place, triggering, with the advent of many new regimes, a widespread nostalgia for the preceding one. Besides these domestic considerations, several other circumstances account for the present state of inter-Arab relations.

The various Arab regimes are first protected by the triumph of geography. No sweeping trends such as the Nasserite one are emerging. Borders have become much less permeable to ideas originating in other Arab countries. No "Voice of the Arabs" exists anymore; Muhammad Hassanein Heikal has left to others his weekly page in *Al-Ahram*; and the popular Egyptian singer Umm Kalthum has passed away. In their stead are myriads of domestic *Ahrams*, radios, Heikals, and Umm Kalthums. Islamic fundamentalism, though gaining more souls, is less of a devastating wave than the concomitant and parallel return of Islam as a language of politics.

It is also possible to speak of a system of mutually supportive regimes. Political opponents are not taking refuge, as in the past, in the neighboring capital. They know that this is no more a guarantee of safety in an age of opportunistic policies. They either flee to non-Arab countries or, if they remain in the area, they safely quit politics. The Gulf countries are full of former militants recycled into successful businessmen, most of them still eager to count and recount their prowess in politics two or three decades earlier, while stressing their allegiance to one patrimonial Gulf shaikh or the other. Communists are becoming an endangered species. Baathists are in Damascus, in Baghdad, or in business somewhere between London and Sharjah.

Political regimes are harsh with those who dare to challenge them. The Arab Organization for Human Rights, established in Limassol (Cyprus) is now based in Geneva. Even the relatively open Egyptian regime would not allow the organization to be based in Cairo or to have its convention there. The Egyptian government was both irritated by its activity and too eager to please the Arab governments who were unanimously opposed to it. Jails are full of political prisoners who should consider themselves lucky not to have been summarily executed. State terror is often directed against the extended family of a political opponent and thus appears to be more a bloody tribal vendetta than mere repression. Ideological conflicts are often a thin veil for an acute struggle for power among primordial (geographic, tribal, sectarian) loyalties, as experienced in many countries and even in Marxist South Yemen, during a week of terrible fighting in January 1986.

This does not mean that the Arab world has entered an era of permanent stability. Extremely destructive sideshows are still taking place on the periphery: in Yemen, in Sudan, in the Sahara, on the Chadian-Libyan border, and in the internecine and growing terrorist activities. The most striking case is that of Lebanon. It is true that this country is infected with tribal sectarianism and with an incredibly short-sighted political establishment. But Lebanon is also an appendix to the Iraq-Iran war, a battlefield for the Syrian-Palestinian dispute, a place where the flame of the Arab struggle against Israel is artificially, and at high cost, kept alive.

Lebanese tend to portray their wars as the miniature example of what will happen to the other Arab societies—to states that are unable to channel and regulate the conflicts of the civil society. Many outside observers have joined the Lebanese in this assessment and the word "Lebanonization," probably first coined by the *Economist* of London, has already been applied to several other countries ranging from Kuwait to Chad, from Yemen to Syria. The diagnosis might be farfetched. Most Arab societies are more homogeneous, most state structures are better established, most countries are less willing to accept, let alone to invite, foreign interference in their domestic affairs.

It would be nevertheless hazardous to exclude the possibility of events like those in Lebanon occurring in other Arab states. If the Lebanese have been unwilling or unable to build a state of their own, other Arabs have been deeply alienated from their states. Authoritarianism, especially when associated with a government based on kinship, sectarian, or geographic criteria, tends to alienate the society from the state. With representative institutions turned into empty shells to which only impotent walk-ons are "elected," the state gradually loses its organic link with society. The state hangs over society without being identified with it. The state rules without representing society and oppresses without allowing citizens to form and produce an alternative to the ruling group. Such deterioration could lead to a situation that would transform Lebanon from an exception in the present Arab torpor into a Hobbesian model for societies gradually drawn by their despotic rulers into chaos, destruction, and death.

The New Balance of Power

The decade under consideration has, of course, witnessed a wide redistribution of power within the Arab system. For a long while, it has been obvious that nobody could really dispute the Egyptian primacy for (then) obvious demographic, military, and cultural reasons, compounded after 1955, by a political one: the emergence of a strong and charismatic leader. After Egypt's defeat in 1967, Nasser's death in 1970, and the emergence of oil power, the diffusion of power became evident, and no single candidate for succession could really emerge. While some (Heikal among others) were speaking of the coming of a *hiqbah sa'udiyyah* (Saudi era), others were fascinated by Iraq's potential (Lutfi al-Khuli among others), or even by Syria.

The rules of the (inter-Arab) game had changed, but years of Egyptian primacy had poorly prepared the Arabs for new and complex assessments. Demographic factors had for a long while played to the advantage of Egypt and other densely populated countries. But it soon appeared that optimal demographic trends were not necessarily those found in Egypt, and consequently, the 50 million Egyptians were increasingly viewed as a burden on Egypt rather than an asset. Israel, demographically smaller, enjoys unquestioned military supremacy. A much better ratio of resources to population seems to prevail in Morocco or in Iraq, while inflated numbers on Saudi demographics cannot hide the kingdom's sensitive vulnerability in this respect.

Questions should also be raised about the importance of size as a measure of power. This is certainly a problem in Bahrain and the other city-states. But to have a very large area is not necessarily an asset. Sudan, Saudi Arabia, Algeria, Libya, and Egypt have areas ranging between 1.5 million and 2.5 million square kilometers, but the political significance is quite different in mining and agricultural output. Whether a state has 4 percent of its land available for agricultural purposes (Egypt) or 20 percent (Iraq) is an important variable. In military terms, too large an area might be an impediment to an efficient defense, as is clearly the case in a country such as Saudi Arabia.

Economic and financial capabilities are also determinants, and the past decade has been one in which Arab states have been divided not only into "poor" and "rich" but also into the rich enough to sustain low oil prices versus those who are not. Money can buy domestic stability and some security on the regional level too. It seems however that, here again, the optimal level of wealth is not necessarily the highest. Too much money attracts too many pressures to share. This accounts for the Gulf countries' recent tendency to repeat how much they need the oil rent accruing to them. Foreign debt is seriously handicapping Egypt, Algeria, and other countries. For the decades to come, and in view of their limited industrial output, oil will remain the major variable in the economies of Arab countries. But oil revenues will probably be insufficient to keep "welfare" states going. More determined participation by the private sector in economic development is increasingly unavoidable. It will be hard for the regimes, even those of the Gulf, to lure their new middle class into productive activities without offering them some compensation through political participation. It might be that oil has been a pivotal factor in the continuing state control over the society. Some form of democratization seems necessary to smooth the way from an era of easy rents to one of a production-oriented economy.

The most often cited, and possibly the most difficult factor to assess, is the military one. Several studies and annual surveys offer different assessments. The two Arab armies with the best potential in numbers, training, and equipment are those of Syria and Iraq. The Egyptian army is, in comparison with the other armies in the region, much weaker than a decade ago because of overstaffing, dependence on costly Western equipment, and a modest procurement budget. The Gulf armies, including the Saudi one, will remain unable to deal with the huge defensive tasks ahead of them, despite military expenditures per capita that have remained the highest in the world even after the fall in oil prices. In the western Arab world, military expenditures remain relatively modest.

One central factor in these states is the ethnic, linguistic, and religious homogeneity leading to political stability. This is particularly true in the Fertile Crescent. Between the steep mountains of Kurdistan and the flat land in Gaza, and between the unsafe streets of Beirut and the tortured palm groves around Basra, lies the most formidable concentration of weapons, the highest level of military preparedness, and the hottest spots in the Middle East. Despite the military expenditures in the Gulf, the Westernization of the Egyptian army, and the $15 billion paid by Libya for arms during the past decade, the Fertile Crescent remains the area in which military capabilities have most dramatically grown, notably in Israel, Syria, and Iraq. Of course, in this area, the deadliest conflicts are fought: the one opposing Israel to the Arabs, and the Iran-Iraq war, both of which spill over into Lebanon. But the Fertile Crescent is also the Middle Eastern subregion with the least ethnic, religious, and sectarian homogeneity. Hence this frightening mixture of a looming threat of civil wars and a permanent threat of traditional ones, both fought with increasingly huge and sophisticated arsenals. The past decade can be seen as one in which the Fertile Crescent was confirmed as, paradoxically, the most powerful and the most vulnerable subregion in the Middle East. The feeling of weakness naturally stimulated a push for more investment in building power.

Too many books dealing with the Middle East have photographs of Arab leaders on their cover for us to avoid the discussion of the subjective source of strength, that is, the leadership qualities displayed in the region. One is struck by the tactical genius of many leaders, most of them displaying formidable capabilities of adaptation to permanently changing circumstances. President Asad of Syria is one often-cited example. King Hussein of Jordan who has been able to retain his throne since 1951 against many odds is another. Others are positively impressed by President Husni Mubarak's "managerial" qualities or by Saddam Hussein's ability to establish an astute equation between his own political survival and that of his country. But tactical resources cannot replace long-term vision, a quality hardly visible in today's leaders, who seem ready to sacrifice the long-term interests of their countries in order to ensure their immediate survival. More importantly, performance is measured not only by what has actually been accomplished, but also by what would have been done with the same resources by other leaders or other political regimes. Finally, if a last performance criterion, that of the price paid for what has been done, is introduced, the balance sheet would become clearly negative: the schools, the hospitals, and the bridges hide hundreds of billions of dollars spent on luxury items or wasted on white elephant projects. They also hide tens of thousands of political prisoners, of exiles, and whole populations deprived of their basic human rights.

Hence the weakness of a mechanical application of the zero-sum game theory, which would lead me to say that whatever Egypt has lost in influence in the Arab world, other actors have gained. The past decade has in fact witnessed the emergence of both a stronger Arab world, since many new military, financial, and educational resources have been gained by its members, and of a weaker one, since serious differences and acute conflicts have tended to neutralize these gains and to trigger serious doubts concerning the existence of the system.

CONCLUSION

Has the Arab world ceased to exist politically? A number of scholars have announced "the end of pan-Arabism." Is that really the case? One has to dig deeper below the volatile surface of the political scene. Let us first remember that "although contemporary Arab history has witnessed a few attempts at political unification, which either did not last long or did not materialise beyond protocols, Arabs continue to be united as speakers of Arabic."[15] The recurrent idea that local accents are superseding the common quasi-classical Arabic are unfounded. Arabization policies in the western Arab world are strengthening the hold of Arabic while a joint language is emerging. Deutsch remarked in the early 1950s that the Arabic-speaking peoples represent the most successful case of linguistic unification.[16] Arabic has not provided a basis for full political integration, "but it certainly plays a role of paramount significance in the integration and unity of Arab identity."[17]

The policies might not reflect this trend. On Arab television, most of the imported programs have their origin in non-Arab countries. In 1983, for instance, 31 percent of the programs imported were of Arab origin, while those produced in the United States alone represented 32 percent. In the education field, the integrative role of emigrant Egyptian professors is fading away. States are building up their own curricula, and a national university, even in Qatar or in Oman, has become an utmost corollary of national sovereignty. Meanwhile, this inward-looking perspective (as opposed to a pan-Arab one) is leading to the production of school textbooks reflecting each state's particularism.

This tendency toward particularism is confirmed by the economic policies followed during the last decade. In 1983 only 8 percent of total Arab trade was with other Arab countries. Even if oil is excluded, the figures remain modest. The same could be said of

15. Zakaria Abuhamdia, "Speech Diversity and Language Unity: Arabic as an Integrating Factor," in Giacomo Luciani and Ghassan Salamé, eds., *The Politics of Arab Integration*, Nation, State and Integration in the Arab World Series, vol. 4 (London: Croom Helm, 1988), p. 51.

16. Karl W. Deutsch, *Nationalism and Social Communication: An Inquiry into the Foundations of Nationality* (Massachusetts Institute of Technology and John Wiley and Sons, 1953), p. 30.

17. Abuhamdia, "Speech Diversity and Language Unity," p. 51.

inter-Arab capital movements: "The capital markets of the industrial countries act as powerful magnets for investable surpluses; the smaller portion of investment flows to the Arab region are primarily official loans and grants." Only around 15 percent of the Arab oil countries' cumulative current account surpluses were given to other Arab countries as official aid during 1974–81, and much less since then.[18]

Less affected by state policies, inter-Arab migrations are important in shaping the future of the Arab idea. Millions of Egyptian, Sudanese, Yemeni, and Tunisian workers have gone to work in Saudi Arabia, Libya, or Kuwait. Although the size and intensity of this huge social and economic phenomenon can be satisfactorily assessed, little is known about how these migrations have affected the outlook of the political migrants, except in a few special cases such as that of Kuwait's Palestinians. An important study conducted in Egypt during 1985 is the first to deal with the more typical profile of the migrant leaving his home country, without being accompanied by his family, in order to amass some money in an oil country. The results contradict the impression that this movement has strengthened particularisms and alienated the poor Arabs from the rich.[19] A huge bibliography on this topic is increasingly permeated with the idea that this phenomenon has been much more integrative than previously thought.

The past decade has consequently had mixed results: more political disintegration and a higher level of social and cultural interaction. It is remarkable that while ideologues and militants are shunning Arab nationalism, the new generations of Arab professionals, especially in economics, are feverishly looking for joint ventures in the Arab world and interstate integration. The idea has in a way matured. Grandiloquent statements such as those by Sati al-Husri or Michel Aflaq are no longer credible. But governments and societies are increasingly aware of their vulnerability in their present, often artificial, borders. The seventies were marked by a healthy reaction against the general saturation of public discourse with Arabist slogans. The eighties are probably ending with a

18. Samir Makdisi, "Economic Interdependence and National Sovereignty," in Luciani and Salamé, *Politics of Arab Integration*, p. 126.

19. See Nader Fergani, "Egyptian Arab Attitudes in the Mid-1980s and Its Relationship to Work in the Arab Gulf Countries" (in Arabic), *Al-Mustaqbal al-Arabi*, no. 99 (May 1987), pp. 27–53. The complete study was recently published as Nader Fergani, *Making a Living: A Field Study on the Egyptians' Emigration to the Arab Countries* (in Arabic) (Beirut: Centre for Arab Unity Studies, 1988).

rediscovery of the Arab idea, this time without the heavy ideological overtones.

The most disintegrative political events should thus be reinterpreted. The Iraq-Iran war, while weakening Baathism as an ideology, has finally led to the reemergence of an Arab identity in the Gulf, a necessary antidote to the better-established, and historically expansionist, Iranian nationalism. The same could be said of the Camp David Accords. While the Egyptian intelligentsia has, by and large, accepted the basic principle of a unilateral peace with Israel, it has developed a strong feeling of insecurity in view of the acute imbalance in the encounter with a technologically superior and militarily dominant Israel. This feeling has indirectly reintroduced Arabism as, at least, one important dimension of Egyptian regional policies. The Palestinian uprising that began in late 1987 also demonstrates that to involve the Arabs in their struggle, Palestinians have first to seize the initiative, something the PLO has insufficiently done in the past. The enthusiastic response the rebellion has triggered in Arab public opinion has already forced many Arab governments to review their tactics. If pursued, it will no doubt rejuvenate the pivotal place the Palestinian issue has occupied in Arab political culture as the prime example of the struggle for liberation.

Islamic fundamentalism must also be reinterpreted in this perspective. The acrimonious Iranian attacks against Arab nationalism (once portrayed by Bani Sadr as a form of Zionism) blur a much more complex view in which the opposition is much less acute than generally thought. In their insistence on "authenticity," in their opposition to foreign influence over the region, and in their insistence on unity, many Arab Sunni Islamists do not necessarily view their ideology as a negation of pan-Arabism, but rather as a more radical, more authentic nationalism. Has pan-Arabism not been fundamentally "a nationalism explicitly secular but having, like everything in the Middle East, a concealed religious element"?[20]

Geography has reentered politics, but its limits have become apparent. In the late eighties, the Arab world, more than at any time in the past, seems to be in acute need of new ideas. These ideas, pivotal to its future, should articulate, in one way or the other, a concept of at least minimal unity. The Hashemites, the Sauds, and more recently Nasserism and Baathism have tried to cure the fragmentation that followed the collapse of the Ottoman

20. Albert Hourani, *The Emergence of the Modern Middle East* (University of California Press, 1981), p. 16.

Empire. Despite the differences in their tactics, they have all failed to reconcile the widespread, implicitly nostalgic, quest for unity with the reality of postcolonial nation-states. This quest is now compounded with growing modern considerations of the shallowness of almost two dozen underdeveloped, vulnerable Arab states. Camp David has accelerated the disintegration of the Arab system; it has not, however, eliminated the continuing and still unsatisfied quest for unity.

PART III
THE SUPERPOWERS

WILLIAM B. QUANDT

U.S. Policy toward the Arab-Israeli Conflict

It is early October 1977. Imagine a casual observer of the Middle East scene who is trying to follow the intricate diplomacy surrounding the Arab-Israeli conflict. The United States and the Soviet Union have just signed a joint communiqué calling for the convening of an international conference. A glance at the newspaper, however, shows an abundance of unanswered questions about how the Palestinians will be represented at the conference. American officials are spreading the word that Israeli refusal to accept the "territory for peace" equation of United Nations Security Council Resolution 242 could compromise the chances for successful negotiations (see appendix A). Among the Arab parties, Syria seems the most skeptical that an international conference could produce positive results. In Israel consternation and anger are growing over the fact that the United States and the Soviet Union have reached an agreement over Israel's head. And in the United States the powerful pro-Israeli lobby is swinging into action to oppose the U.S.-Soviet communiqué (see appendix B).

Now switch to mid-1988 and stand in the shoes of the same innocent spectator. Once again, the two superpowers are talking about an international conference. The problem of Palestinian representation is still unresolved. Questions abound about whether Israel does or does not still accept the formula of territory for peace as applying to the West Bank. The Syrians, still led by the redoubtable Hafiz al-Asad, are hinting darkly that an international conference is doomed to failure unless there is a closing of Arab ranks—behind Syria—and a redressing of the balance of power. The pro-Israeli lobby, as influential as ever, is predictably warning that pressure on Israel would be counterproductive.

These two snapshots, frozen in time, give the impression that little has changed in the past decade. Some of the same leaders are still in place, including Asad, King Hussein of Jordan, and the chairman of the Palestine Liberation Organization (PLO), Yasir Arafat. In many instances their fundamental positions on the Arab-Israeli conflict have not evolved all that much. But on closer inspection, the scene in 1988 is dramatically different, first and foremost because Egypt is at peace with Israel.

The Camp David Accords, by opening the way to a formal peace treaty between Israel and its largest and most powerful Arab neighbor, radically altered the nature of the Arab-Israeli conflict. So even if many of the players have remained the same over the past decade, and even if some of the formulas from the past are repeatedly repackaged by hard-working bureaucrats and embraced by their easily distracted superiors, the nature of the conflict has nevertheless fundamentally changed.

To the United States, a decade ago the most dangerous dimension of Israel's conflict with its neighbors involved Egypt, the most powerful adversary of the Jewish state. By the 1980s, the Arab-Israeli conflict had been transformed into a regional problem with two main dimensions: an Israeli-Palestinian communal struggle, fought primarily within the area of the historic mandate of Palestine west of the Jordan River; and a military confrontation, for the moment quiescent, between the Israeli and Syrian military establishments, with Lebanon as a testing ground between these two regional rivals.

The Palestinian dimension of the Arab conflict with Israel has always been seen by some observers as central, but in the past it was often overshadowed by the greater danger of war between Israel and the surrounding Arab states. Though war is still a possibility, the more urgent concern—for Israelis, for Palestinians, and even for Americans—involves the conflict between Israeli Jews and Palestinian Arabs in the land they both claim as their own. The Palestinian uprising of late 1987 and 1988, the *intifadah*, dramatically brought this dimension of the Arab-Israeli conflict into focus. The Palestinian issue was left unresolved at Camp David and continues to poison the atmosphere in the Middle East ten years later. How have two American presidents and their aides tried to deal with the Palestinian part of the Arab-Israeli equation over this past decade? How have the stubborn realities of the Palestinian-Israeli conflict forced their way into the thinking of American officialdom, often despite strong predispositions to ignore those realities? This chapter addresses these questions.

THE PALESTINIAN ISSUE AFTER CAMP DAVID

On September 17, 1978, Israeli Prime Minister Menachem Begin and Egyptian President Anwar Sadat signed two "framework agreements," which came to be known as the Camp David Accords (see appendix C). One outlined the principles that should govern negotiations leading to a peace treaty between the two states. This document, on its own, was relatively clear and straightforward. Israel agreed to withdraw from all Egyptian territory in stages and to remove its military bases and civilian settlements. In return Egypt agreed to recognize Israel, exchange ambassadors, accept limitations on force deployments in Sinai, and discuss the possibility of "normalizing" relations in areas such as trade and tourism.

The other part of the Camp David Accords was different in spirit and content. Unlike the bilateral Egyptian-Israeli agreement, which dealt in detail with substantive issues, this broader framework focused more on procedures. To the irritation of many Arabs, Sadat presumed to speak not only on behalf of Egypt, but also for Jordan and the Palestinians, at least in the first stage of developing guidelines for resolving the territorial and political aspects of the Palestinian issue.

The outline for tackling the Palestinian question was procedurally complex, but essentially devoid of content. Egypt and Israel announced their support for the idea of transitional arrangements for the West Bank and Gaza for a period not to exceed five years. Jordan was invited to join negotiations to work out the details of such transitional arrangements. Palestinians could participate in these talks as members of the Egyptian or Jordanian delegations. The parties were enjoined to agree on the powers of an elected Palestinian self-governing authority. Once this authority was elected and established, the transitional period would begin. No later than three years from that point, negotiations should begin on the final status of the territories.

The first big battle over the interpretation of the Camp David Accords took place between President Jimmy Carter and Prime Minister Begin immediately. Carter was persuaded that Begin had promised that Israel would respect a freeze on creating new settlements in the West Bank and Gaza for the duration of negotiations leading to the establishment of the self-governing authority. Begin was equally adamant in maintaining that he had only agreed to a three-month freeze. In the end, Begin prevailed, as he often did in interpreting the meaning of the fine points of the Camp David Accords.[1]

Sadat immediately realized that he would be accused in the Arab world, and by some Egyptians as well, of abandoning the Palestinians. He seemed to count on Carter to deliver Jordanian and Saudi support for the agreements, and when this result was not forthcoming, he was deeply disturbed. His next line of defense was to insist on "linkage" between the two framework agreements. This meant, in essence, that Egypt would hold back on some elements of peace with Israel—such as the exchange of ambassadors—until gains had been made in negotiations for the Palestinians. Sadat and Begin both recognized, in a way that Carter initially did not, that Israel would have a free hand in dealing with the Palestinian issue once Egypt had signed a treaty with Israel. Ultimately, Begin won the argument over linkage. The treaty stood on its own. Egypt thereafter had little direct leverage over Israel to influence negotiations on the West Bank and Gaza.

The Arab reaction to Camp David was almost uniformly hostile from the outset. For several weeks, however, efforts were made by both Jordan and the PLO to clarify some aspects of the accords. Carter put a forthcoming interpretation on the agreements in written responses to questions from King Hussein,[2] a copy of which was passed to the PLO as well. Begin rejected the American interpretations immediately, reducing even further the chance that the Arabs would see the accords as open-ended.

Unable to produce either Jordanian or Palestinian partners for talks with Israel on "autonomy," Carter nonetheless wanted the peace process to move forward. Secretary of State Cyrus Vance, who had been central to the negotiation of the peace treaty, had a backlog of other issues to attend to. In addition, White House aides, joined by Vice President Walter F. Mondale, were eager to get Carter out of the day-to-day haggling with Israel over the Palestinian part of Camp David. They saw no political gains to be scored on Arab-Israeli issues for an already weak president, and reelection was on their minds as early as mid-1979. Thus the two architects of the Camp David Accords, Carter and Vance, were far less involved than they had been previously as they turned their attention toward the thorny problem of persuading Egypt and Israel to reach agreement

1. William B. Quandt, *Camp David: Peacemaking and Politics* (Brookings, 1986), pp. 247–51.

2. Ibid., pp. 388–96, for the texts of the Jordanian questions and President Jimmy Carter's answers.

on the first phase of the autonomy plan. Special negotiators were appointed—first Robert S. Strauss, then Sol M. Linowitz—but little was achieved before time ran out on the Carter administration.[3] It will never be known whether Carter would have chosen to tackle the Palestinian issue with renewed vigor in a second term, although his behavior out of office suggests that he remained deeply concerned.[4]

UNVARNISHED REAGANISM, 1981

One of the earliest and clearest statements of Ronald Reagan's views came in the form of an opinion piece published in the *Washington Post* on August 15, 1979, just as he was launching his bid for the presidency. Not surprisingly, the article was strongly pro-Israeli in tone. But it was more than that. Reagan defined the key issue in the region as the menacing Soviet threat. Only Israel stood as a reliable bulwark in the face of this danger. Inter-Arab quarrels, it was implied, were more dangerous than the Arab-Israeli conflict.

The only mention of the Palestinians occurred in a warning against the creation of a radical Palestinian state on Israel's borders. The words "Camp David," "peace process," and "negotiations" were nowhere to be found. The idea of Israel and Egypt as partners in peace was missing, replaced by the idea of Israel as a formidable strategic asset. Egypt, it was noted, might also be prepared to "take a front-line position in defense of Western security interests," but this possibility was clearly viewed as a "secondary link" that could not "substitute for a strong Israel in the ever-turbulent Middle East."[5]

3. President Carter's last year was also dominated by the crisis of the American hostages held in Iran. For a vivid and accurate account, see Gary Sick, *All Fall Down: America's Tragic Encounter with Iran* (Random House, 1985), especially pp. 218–24.

4. For example, Jimmy Carter wrote extensively about the Middle East, especially in his memoirs, *Keeping Faith: Memoirs of a President* (Bantam Books, 1982), and in *The Blood of Abraham: Insights into the Middle East* (Houghton Mifflin, 1985). The former president also established the Carter Center in Atlanta, Georgia, where two large-scale conferences on the Middle East have been held.

5. Ronald Reagan, "Recognizing the Israeli Asset," *Washington Post*, August 15, 1979. The rhetorical flourishes and the line of argument suggest the influence of Joseph Churba, who became an adviser to Reagan during his 1980 campaign for the presidency. Churba may well have been the ghostwriter for this piece. See Joseph Churba, *The Politics of Defeat: America's Decline in the Middle East* (Cyrco Press, 1977), p. 97, in which the author speaks of "the conflict and tension endemic to the [Middle East] region. This condition is traceable largely to the sectarian and

At one point during his campaign for the presidency, Reagan was quoted as saying, "Let's not delude ourselves. The Soviet Union underlies all the unrest that is going on. If they weren't engaged in this game of dominoes, there wouldn't be any hot spots in the world."[6] Such a perspective, if really an accurate reflection of Reagan's thinking, would have profound implications for dealing with problems of the Middle East.

As president, Reagan's contribution to shaping American Middle East policy probably consisted primarily of injecting this theme of Soviet instigation of regional unrest into the thinking of his subordinates. His secretary of state, Alexander M. Haig, Jr., while much more attuned to nuances than the president, shared the president's view that the Middle East should be viewed primarily through the prism of the U.S.-Soviet rivalry.[7] Surrounding him at the State Department, and clustered at the White House and the Defense Department, was a group of like-minded newcomers with very little experience with the foreign-policymaking process. Most of the officials knew little of the Middle East, even when their job descriptions might have implied otherwise. In such an environment it was easy to hear top officials pontificating that the most serious problem in the Middle East was the presence of twenty-plus Soviet divisions on Iran's northern border.

Early in the Reagan administration, Haig began to speak of the need to try to forge a "strategic consensus" among the pro-Western regimes in the Middle East. If this meant anything at all—and the phrase was never explained very clearly—it presumably meant trying to focus the attention of "our friends" in the region on the Soviet threat, while simultaneously attempting to push parochial local conflicts to the back burner. An early test case arose in the form of a decision to sell a sophisticated radar plane, called airborne warning and control system aircraft (AWACS), to Saudi Arabia.

In normal circumstances, one would have expected the Israelis to put up quite a fight, arguing that the presence of AWACS in

---

fragmented nature of Middle East society." Reagan's article says, "The Carter administration has yet to grasp that in this region conflict and tension are endemic, a condition traceable largely to the fragmented sectarian nature of Middle Eastern society." The near-identity of these two passages suggests either a single author for both or plagiarism.

6. From an interview cited in Karen Elliott House, "Reagan's World," *Wall Street Journal*, June 3, 1980.

7. On Haig's views generally, see Alexander M. Haig, Jr., *Caveat: Realism, Reagan, and Foreign Policy* (Macmillan, 1984), especially pp. 20–33. By the spring of 1982, however, Haig was speaking of the need to address regional issues in the Middle East.

Saudi Arabia could threaten their security. But if Israel and Saudi Arabia were both parts of the U.S.-sponsored strategic consensus, and if both saw the Soviet Union as the primary threat to their security, then the Israelis might be persuaded to allow the sale to go forward in the interests of strengthening the common front against the Soviets and their clients. But there was no such luck. Israel and its supporters in the United States decided to make it an all-out fight. In the end, they lost. The AWACS were sold, but only after Reagan had put his prestige on the line and had gone some distance in meeting Israeli concerns. After the AWACS battle, one heard far less talk of strategic consensus, and Haig himself repeatedly said that the concept had never been correctly understood.

CRISIS IN LEBANON

In the world of pure Reaganism, chronic problems such as those in Lebanon were either not worth much attention, or they were symptoms of Soviet mischiefmaking. No wonder White House aides had little patience for arcane discussions of the internal political dynamics of Lebanon. Who, they seemed to be saying, could keep track of all the sects and their leaders with unpronounceable names?

But Lebanon had a way of forcing itself onto the American agenda because of Israeli concerns. In early 1981, Israeli-PLO clashes had intensified across Israel's northern border. Veteran diplomat Philip C. Habib was then called on by Reagan to try to calm things down. The United States thus found itself negotiating a cease-fire between the two archenemies, and after mid-1981 the Lebanese-Israeli border was quiet.

But Israeli leaders, and especially the powerful Defense Minister Ariel Sharon, had grander plans in Lebanon. For years, the Israelis had been secretly cultivating the tough leader of one of the Christian Lebanese militias, Bashir Gemayal. With presidential elections slated for late 1982, Israelis saw a chance to help bring their man to power. Sharon and his colleagues were also determined to crush the PLO's military presence in south Lebanon. In some of the most dramatic scenarios, Israel might also try to drive Syrian forces out of Lebanon, inflicting a heavy blow on the leading client of the Soviet Union in the process.[8]

8. See Ze'ev Schiff and Ehud Ya'ari, *Israel's Lebanon War,* ed. and trans. Ina Friedman (Simon and Schuster, 1984); Itamar Rabinovich, *The War for Lebanon, 1970–1983* (Cornell University Press, 1984); and Yair Evron, *War and Intervention in Lebanon: The Israeli-Syrian Deterrence Dialogue* (Johns Hopkins University Press, 1987).

These possibilities were risky enough to require careful planning and an attempt at coordination with the United States. On visits to Washington, D.C., in early 1982, Israeli officials outlined their ambitious plan for Lebanon in great detail. State Department officials were appalled and were afraid that Sharon would get the impression that the United States was encouraging, or at least acquiescing, in his plan. What Haig did say, repeatedly, was that the United States would understand such a military move only in response to an "internationally recognized provocation," whatever that might mean.[9] To some, that sounded like an invitation to find a pretext to go to war. Some Israelis have claimed that Haig's statements were indeed interpreted as a "green light."[10]

Whatever Haig's role in precipitating the Israeli decision to invade Lebanon, his career was cut short during the early phase of the war. Already unpopular with some of his colleagues at the White House, Haig was now unable to retain the confidence of the president. At a crucial moment in the crisis that had begun on June 5, 1982, Haig threatened to resign unless he was able to control the conduct of policy toward Lebanon. To his surprise, he was told that the president would accept his letter of resignation, a letter that Haig was then obliged to write.

Haig's successor was George P. Shultz, former secretary of both labor and the treasury, as well as a former top official in the Bechtel Corporation. Because of Bechtel's deep involvement in the Arab world, Shultz had something of a reputation for being pro-Arab. His initial confirmation hearings before the Senate showed a careful, well-informed individual, who seemed attentive to the nuances of the regional setting and was willing to address the Palestinian issue in a forthright manner.

During much of August 1982, the United States participated in intricate negotiations to bring the fighting in Lebanon to an end and to arrange for the evacuation of PLO fighters from Beirut. An American military contingent was even sent to Lebanon as part of an international force to help oversee the PLO departure. Philip C. Habib, who had successfully negotiated the cease-fire in 1981, was instrumental in closing the deal. He also pressed for the election of Bashir Gemayal as Lebanon's next president and made explicit written commitments to the PLO that assurances had been obtained from the Israelis about the safety of Palestinian civilians left behind after the PLO's departure.

9. Haig, *Caveat*, pp. 332–35.
10. Schiff and Ya'ari, *Israel's Lebanon War*, pp. 62–77.

By late August 1982, the Reagan administration seemed to be on the verge of success in the midst of the Lebanese agony, with a pro-Western president about to be inaugurated in Beirut, the Syrians badly battered in the Bekaa valley of eastern Lebanon, and the PLO driven from the country. Playing from a position of apparent diplomatic strength, Shultz persuaded the president to seize the moment to outline a plan for a diplomatic settlement of the Palestinian issue. On September 1, 1982, Reagan gave his first and only major speech on the Arab-Israeli conflict (see appendix D). The core of the initiative was still Camp David, but with important substantive additions. Whereas Camp David had been vague on the so-called final status of the West Bank and Gaza after a transitional period, Reagan said that the United States would oppose both Israeli annexation and an independent Palestinian state. The U.S. preference, he said, was for some form of association between the West Bank, Gaza, and Jordan.

The Reagan initiative clearly shifted the spotlight from Egypt to Jordan and the Palestinians. Syria was left out in the cold. Begin rejected the proposal immediately because it called for eventual Israeli relinquishment of most of the occupied territories as the price for peace. The Arab response was, on the whole, less categorical. Questions were asked, some positive noises were heard, and it was widely rumored that King Hussein had been briefed in advance about the speech and had indicated his approval.

Within days of the Reagan initiative, the Arab states held a summit meeting in Fez, Morocco, and adopted a Saudi proposal that came to be known as the Fez plan (see appendix E). Though different in content from the Reagan proposal, the Fez plan at least gave the United States and the Arabs something to talk about.

The administration's decision to launch an initiative on the Palestinian issue was predicated on the belief that the problems of Lebanon were on their way toward solution. Even before the war in Lebanon, some in the bureaucracy had been making the case for a revived peace effort. Sharon had told the Americans that he would solve the Palestinian issue his way—by moving tanks into Lebanon. The shortcomings of that approach were abundantly clear by September. The time had come for an American diplomatic initiative.

The comforting belief that Lebanon's travails were nearly over was literally and figuratively blown away with the assassination of Bashir Gemayal on September 14, 1982. General Sharon, who had planned to "cleanse" Lebanon of Palestinians once Bashir Gemayal was installed as president, saw a danger that Israel's long-term investment would be lost with Bashir's death. He pressed the leadership of the Lebanese Forces and the Phalange party to respect the deals he had arranged with Bashir. In the circumstances, Israel had great leverage over the Phalange, including the ability to withhold or grant support for the candidacy of Bashir's brother, Amin, as president.

Some of the details of what happened next are not entirely clear, but the broad outline is known. Units of the Lebanese Forces militia under the command of Eli Hobeika moved into two Palestinian refugee camps, Sabra and Shatila, on the southern outskirts of Beirut. There, under the eyes of their Israeli allies, they systematically murdered as many as eight hundred Palestinian civilians. This massacre led to a strong reaction everywhere, including in Israel. Five months later, Sharon and several other officers were censured for their role in not preventing the massacres and were removed from their posts.[11]

The American reaction was to put Lebanon and its ills back at the top of the agenda. American military forces, which had been withdrawn after the departure of the PLO, were returned to the Beirut area to help ensure that there would be no repeat of the horrors of Sabra and Shatila. Negotiation of an Israeli-Lebanese agreement that would lead to the withdrawal of both Israeli and Syrian forces became a priority of U.S. diplomacy.

King Hussein, the object of the Reagan initiative in its first phase, then began to watch how the Americans handled the Lebanese imbroglio as a test of how serious they were likely to be in dealing with the Palestinian issue. He, like many Arabs, felt that unless the Americans could get the Israelis out of Lebanon, there would be little chance of dislodging them from the West Bank. President Reagan further undermined the chances of success for his initiative by saying publicly that nothing could be done on the Palestinian question until agreement was reached on Lebanon.[12] For those who had opposed the Reagan initiative from the outset—and that included Begin, Asad, and the Soviets—this statement was an invitation to make things in Lebanon as difficult as possible to ensure that "another Camp David," as the Syrians labeled the Reagan initiative, would not succeed.

King Hussein visited Washington in December 1982 for talks with President Reagan. In an effort to persuade the King to support

11. For the results of the official Israeli inquiry, see *The Beirut Massacre: The Complete Kahan Commission Report* (Princeton, N.J.: Karz–Cohl, 1983).

12. See William B. Quandt, "Reagan's Lebanon Policy: Trial and Error," *Middle East Journal*, vol. 38 (Spring 1984), pp. 241–42.

the Reagan initiative, Reagan wrote two letters to him spelling out promises and commitments, including a supply of arms, if Hussein would agree to enter negotiations. By all accounts, Hussein was tempted, but he felt the need for Palestinian support. Talks with the PLO took place over the next several months. Finally, in April the king concluded that there was no basis for developing a joint negotiating position with the PLO. Pro-Soviet hardliners in Arafat's entourage were blamed by the Jordanians as responsible for this inability to reach an agreement. Jordan too came under direct Soviet pressure not to go along.[13] On April 10, 1983, the king officially announced that Jordan could not accept the Reagan initiative, stating, "We in Jordan, having refused from the beginning to negotiate on behalf of the Palestinians, will neither act separately nor in lieu of anybody in Middle East peace negotiations."[14]

For much of the remainder of 1983, Arab-Israeli peacemaking became, from the American perspective, synonymous with trying to forge a viable Lebanese-Israeli agreement, as a step toward the withdrawal of both Israeli and Syrian forces from Lebanon. Secretary Shultz, who had shown reluctance to engage directly in the shuttle-style travels of his predecessors, went to the Middle East to put the final touches on the Lebanese-Israeli accord, which was finally signed on May 17, 1983.

The agreement was stillborn. Israeli withdrawal was made dependent on Syrian withdrawal, and the ruler in Damascus (who commanded a sizable constituency inside Lebanon) would not tolerate such a condition. Already the United States and Syria seemed to be on a collision course. In April, the American embassy had been bombed with devastating effectiveness.[15] Americans traced the bombing to Lebanese allies of Iran, perhaps with some Syrian involvement as well. Then in October of that year there was another blow from the same quarter, even more deadly than the first, when

13. The best account of the background to the king's decision can be found in two Pulitzer-prize winning articles by Karen Elliott House, "Hussein's Decision," *Wall Street Journal*, April 14, 1983, and April 15, 1983. According to the king, General Secretary Yuri V. Andropov had taken him aside in early December 1982 during a visit to Moscow to warn, "I shall oppose the Reagan plan, and we will use all our resources to oppose it. With due respect, all the weight will be on your shoulders, and they aren't broad enough to bear it."

14. "Text of Jordan's Statement on Its Refusal to Join the Reagan Peace Initiative," *New York Times*, April 11, 1983.

15. Among the victims of the bombing was Robert Ames, one of the top Central Intelligence Agency officials with responsibility for the Middle East, and one of the core group of officials who had worked closely with Secretary George P. Shultz at the inception of the Reagan initiative.

the compound of the American contingent of the multinational peacekeeping force was destroyed with a truck bomb.[16]

The denouement of these two attacks on the American presence in Lebanon involved one last confrontation between American and Syrian forces, resulting in two American planes being shot down by the Syrians, with one pilot killed and one captured. By early 1984, when the politics of reelection were uppermost in the minds of some of the president's advisers, a decision was made that the marines should be "redeployed offshore." Critics termed the decision "cut and run." Whichever words one chose, the facts were the same. Reagan, who had pinned American prestige on a stable settlement in Lebanon, was removing the most tangible sign of that commitment. Henceforth, Lebanon would be left primarily to the squabbles of its internal factions and its two powerful neighbors.

A MISSED OPPORTUNITY?

Election years rarely witness serious initiatives for Arab-Israeli peace by American presidents. Their priorities lie elsewhere. Controversy, an inevitable corollary of any serious U.S. initiative in the region, is shunned. Pleas from Arab regimes for arms and diplomatic support are put off until after the elections. It was not surprising, then, that by early 1985 there was a large backlog of demands, especially from friendly Arab regimes. By then, too, Israel had gone through its elections and had produced a government headed by Labor party veteran Shimon Peres, a relatively moderate figure within the Israeli political spectrum. Peres was still stuck in an uneasy alliance with the Likud bloc, and he was committed to turning over the job of prime minister to his Likud rival, Yitzhak Shamir, by the fall of 1986. Nevertheless, in 1985 the United States was, for the first time since 1977, dealing with a prime minister of Israel who did not rule out automatically the principle of trading territory for peace as the basis for resolving the Palestinian-Israeli confrontation.

Arab leaders had often expressed the hope that they could deal with a reelected Republican president. This nostalgic view stemmed largely from the perception of the second Eisenhower term, and

16. For an inquiry into the reasons for the vulnerability of the U.S. Marine compound, see U.S. Department of Defense, *Report of the DOD Commission on Beirut International Airport Terrorist Act, October 23, 1983* (Government Printing Office, 1983).

especially Dwight D. Eisenhower's tough treatment of the Israelis during and after the Suez crisis of 1956. Now, in 1985, the Arabs were again dealing with a popular, reelected Republican. So, one by one, Arab leaders trekked to Washington in the first half of 1985. First came King Fahd of Saudi Arabia, followed a month later by Egyptian President Husni Mubarak. Most importantly, King Hussein arrived in Washington at the end of May.

Much of Egyptian and Jordanian policy at the time was aimed at evoking a positive American response to a joint Jordanian-PLO position that had been formalized in a carefully worded statement issued on February 11, 1985.[17] In many ways, the Jordanian-PLO position could be construed as a new attempt to respond to the 1982 Reagan initiative. Both parties announced that their common goal was the creation of a Jordanian-Palestinian confederation, to be established once Israel had fully withdrawn from occupied territory. They pledged to negotiate as a joint delegation within the framework of an international conference.

While the February 11, 1985, agreement raised more questions than it answered in the minds of Americans, the Jordanian attempt at clarification was reassuring. During their visit to Washington in May, Jordanian officials stated that the concept of confederation was really much closer to "federation," with responsibility for foreign affairs and defense clearly understood by both parties to be vested in Amman. In addition, the Jordanians played down the importance of the international conference, stressing instead the need for U.S. contact with a group of Jordanians and Palestinians. The Jordanians also made it clear that they thought the PLO could be brought to the point of accepting Resolution 242, perhaps in return for some form of American recognition of Palestinian self-determination within the framework of a confederation with Jordan.

However tempted some American officials may have been to press forward with an initiative in these seemingly propitious circumstances, there were three offsetting considerations. President Reagan was on record, as recently as March 1985, saying that the United States did not want to participate in Arab-Israeli peace negotiations, despite the Camp David commitment for the United

17. See appendix F in this volume. Both Jordanian and Palestinian sources say that some amendments were later made to the basic text. The authorized English translation of the first principle called for "total withdrawal from the territories occupied in 1967 for comprehensive peace." The Arabic text simply said "land in exchange for peace."

States to be a "full partner" in subsequent phases of the peace talks.[18] Reagan and Shultz repeatedly said that the problem was not for the United States to talk to the parties, but to get the parties to talk to each other. Direct negotiations became something of a slogan.

A second problem in bringing the United States into a more active role in support of King Hussein's approach was reportedly Secretary Shultz's sense of disillusionment with most of the Arab leaders he had dealt with in the 1982–83 period. He seemed to think that they had had their chance and had wasted it; that they had misled him, or even lied, on numerous occasions; and that they were unreliable as potential partners in a complex negotiation. Each of these points was illustrated, according to insiders, with chapter and verse.

The third inhibition was derived from a concern for the political standing of Israeli Prime Minister Peres. During his first year in office he had become popular. The withdrawal of Israeli forces from Lebanon had been welcomed by a war-weary populace. Efforts to curb raging inflation were progressing, though with considerable pain. The management of the economy was turning out to be a plus for Peres. Some American officials wanted to help Peres position himself for a showdown with the Likud. This desire led them to advise against anything that could be viewed as causing a strain in U.S.-Israeli relations, such as American dealings with the PLO.

A practical test of American policy soon emerged. The Jordanians had proposed that the Americans hold exploratory meetings with a joint Jordanian-PLO delegation. The Americans asked what the point of such a meeting would be. The response was a bit vague. Essentially the Jordanians said that the process should be started even if the destination was unclear. As the Jordanians were quick to point out, their reply was almost a verbatim repetition of a long-standing American response to the Arabs' question of what would happen once negotiations with Israel began.

In order to try to organize a preliminary meeting between the United States and a joint Jordanian-Palestinian delegation, the Jordanians forwarded a list of seven names of possible Palestinian members of the delegation. The list was passed by Washington to the Israelis, who said they had no objection to two of the seven names, but who were quick to label the others as PLO. The Americans objected to at least three of the names, but, more

18. Text of "President's News Conference on Foreign and Domestic Issues," *New York Times*, March 22, 1985.

importantly, they kept asking for assurances that any preliminary talks would be accompanied by a clear Jordanian-Palestinian commitment to direct negotiations with Israel. Jordan, eager not to offend Syria, was not prepared to abandon the idea of an international conference in favor of U.S.-sponsored direct negotiations.

Despite these difficulties, there seemed to be a moment in the summer of 1985 when the United States was about to take the plunge. Assistant Secretary of State Richard W. Murphy was sent to the Middle East; the members of a joint Jordanian-Palestinian team were assembled in Amman to meet him; but at the last moment he was told not to proceed with the meeting.

King Hussein made a final effort to persuade the Americans in the fall. He had been told that there was no chance of winning congressional support for a big new arms package for Jordan—something Reagan had promised the king in writing in December 1982—unless Jordan committed itself to direct negotiations. At his speech to the UN General Assembly, the king did make such a commitment, saying, "We are ready to negotiate with Israel under suitable, acceptable supervision, directly and as soon as possible, in accordance with Security Council Resolutions 242 and 338."[19] One month later, the U.S. Senate rebuffed the king's request on arms, stipulating that no major sale could be concluded until "direct and meaningful" negotiations with Israel had begun. In the face of continuing congressional hostility to the sale, the administration finally withdrew the nearly $2 billion arms package for Jordan on February 3, 1986.

October 1985 proved to be a disastrous month for Jordanian-PLO relations, as well as for Hussein's initiative. A minor faction of the PLO had the idea to hijack an Italian cruise ship, the *Achille Lauro.* Before the incident was over, one elderly American, confined to his wheelchair, had been murdered and thrown overboard. (The Syrians, eager to discredit the PLO, recovered the body on their coast and dutifully returned it to the American government, with conclusive proof that the victim had been shot.) In the denouement of the *Achille Lauro* affair, U.S.-Egyptian relations were strained, as American F-14s intercepted an Egyptian airliner carrying the hijackers to Tunis where the PLO would have allegedly put them on trial. The Egyptian plane was forced to land at a NATO base in Sicily, which caused a great outpouring of anger in Cairo and self-congratulations

19. See the text of the September 27, 1985, speech in Amman Domestic Service, Foreign Broadcast Information Service, *Daily Report: Middle East and Africa,* September 30, 1985, p. F3.

and boasting in the United States. Around the same time, Jordan and the PLO failed to reach agreement on terms that would have allowed for a meeting of a joint Jordanian-PLO delegation with the British foreign secretary.

President Asad must have watched all of this with great satisfaction. He had opposed the February 11, 1985, agreement from the outset. He had labeled the U.S. efforts to arrange direct talks under its own auspices as tantamount to another Camp David, and now he found the Jordanian-PLO alliance coming apart. So Asad, working closely with the Jordanian Prime Minister Zaid al-Rifai, encouraged the development of a working alliance with Jordan. The king was obliged to acknowledge past Jordanian misdeeds in allowing anti-Syrian terrorist groups to operate from his territory. Thus the stage was set for Syrian-Jordanian rapprochement and a break between Jordan and the PLO, which was not long in coming. On February 19, 1986, the king spelled out in graphic detail the reasons for the breakdown of coordination with the PLO.[20] The February 11, 1985, accord had barely lasted one year.

In retrospect, it seems clear that the Americans had never been enthusiastic about the idea of dealing with a joint Jordanian-PLO delegation. As one Jordanian minister put it early in the discussions in Washington, Jordan tried to stress that the PLO was relatively weak and therefore could be pressured to make concessions. The American reply, he said, was that if the PLO was weak, it should be excluded entirely from the diplomatic process. Finally, when King Hussein began to conclude that the PLO was a liability in his dealings with Israel, Syria, and Washington, and that it was recreating a substantial presence in Jordan, he moved to sever the tie.

20. The full text is found in Amman Television Service, February 19, 1986, ibid., February 20, 1986, pp. F1–F16. According to American sources who were closely involved in the diplomacy of early 1986, a last-ditch effort was made to find a formula whereby the PLO would accept Resolution 242 unambiguously as the basis for negotiations with Israel, and then would spell out its additional demands. King Hussein told the Americans that the PLO needed a quid pro quo for such a step, and the United States therefore made some concessions on how the PLO would be invited to, and represented at, an international conference. The PLO was still not prepared to accept Resolution 242. Arafat insisted that the United States endorse the Palestinian right of self-determination and open direct channels of communication to the PLO instead of negotiating through the Jordanians. The Jordanians had told the PLO that the United States would not budge on the issue of self–determination and urged the PLO to accept 242 anyway. The final meeting between Hussein and Arafat ended acrimoniously. The Jordanians and Americans concluded that the PLO was neither serious nor trustworthy. This conclusion had a significant impact on subsequent diplomatic moves. Hussein's public account does not cover all of these points, but the tone and substance of his remarks give credence to this interpretation.

REDISCOVERING THE INTERNATIONAL CONFERENCE

Without the PLO to cover his flanks, King Hussein quickly embraced the idea of an international conference with Syrian and Soviet participation. American hostility to the idea had been rooted in the notion that this arrangement would somehow bring the Soviet Union back into the Middle East, from whence they had supposedly been absent since Henry A. Kissinger's brilliant maneuvering of 1973–74. A whole mythology had grown up in Washington about the horrors of the October 1, 1977, joint communiqué issued by the two superpowers (see appendix B). The best thing said about it was that it was so appalling that it had driven Sadat to Jerusalem to avoid dealing with the Soviets.[21]

By late 1985, however, the prime minister of Israel was beginning to speak positively about some form of international forum or sponsorship of direct negotiations. Shortly after this change in the Israeli tune, the United States also began to hint that its previous opposition to the idea of an international conference was weakening. Without much fanfare, the international conference reappeared on the Arab-Israeli diplomatic scene as a potentially live issue. Quiet diplomacy then took over, with professional American diplomats trying to develop a basis of agreement between Israel and Jordan. By April 11, 1987, when King Hussein and Foreign Minister Peres reportedly met in London to sign a document confirming their understanding of how an international conference would work, a fair amount of common procedural ground had been found (see appendix G).

Both Jordan and Israel agreed that a conference would not have plenary powers. It could not impose its views or veto the results of bilateral negotiations that would take place under the umbrella of the conference. Both countries agreed that there would be a ceremonial opening with representatives of the permanent members of the UN Security Council, and those parties to the conflict from the region that had accepted Resolution 242. One sticky issue, the question of what would happen in the event of a deadlock in the bilateral negotiations, the so-called "referral issue," was finessed for the moment.

Clearly, much of what Peres and Hussein had agreed on would be strongly objected to by Yitzhak Shamir, who had been occupying

21. There is no convincing evidence that the October 1, 1977, communiqué played a significant role in Sadat's decision to go to Jerusalem. See Quandt, *Camp David*, pp. 123–25.

the chair of prime minister since the previous fall when "rotation" had proceeded on schedule. How, then, to convince Shamir and at least some of the Likud members of the inner cabinet? Peres's idea, apparently, was to try to enlist the United States as the putative author of the plan. This rather transparent ploy did not fool Shamir, who had been fully briefed on the London meeting, nor did the United States respond by offering full backing for Peres. To some in the State Department, a strong endorsement of the plan would have been seen as blatant interference in internal Israeli politics, something Secretary Shultz was averse to. For a brief moment, Shultz was reportedly tempted to fly to the Middle East to press the case for an international conference of the sort discussed by Hussein and Peres, but he was dissuaded from doing so by the forceful presentation of the former Israeli ambassador to Washington, Moshe Arens, a powerful Likudnik. Once again, moderate Israelis and Arabs complained of a lack of forceful American leadership, while Shamir's political stock rose on his reputation for standing up to the Americans.

As a coda to this phase of diplomacy, a final effort was made, this time in collaboration with Shamir, to find some form of international sponsorship for Israeli-Jordanian talks. Secretary of State Shultz flew to the Middle East in October 1987 while en route to Moscow to put the finishing touches on arrangements for a U.S.-Soviet summit meeting in Washington before the end of the year. While in Jerusalem, he persuaded Shamir to consider the possibility of traveling to Washington at the time of the summit, along with King Hussein, to receive a joint U.S.-Soviet blessing for negotiations. This rather fanciful and ill-prepared idea was then presented to King Hussein, who was about to host an Arab summit in Amman and was politically unable to even hint at an interest in an idea that would be universally ridiculed by the other Arabs. In addition, there was no reason to think that the Soviets would agree to the idea, and the Syrians, who were only mentioned as an afterthought as possible participants in the adventure, would certainly say no. So Jordan found itself put in the position of saying no to the Americans, a fact that was duly leaked to a pro-Israeli columnist a few months later.[22]

In normal times, Hussein's hesitation would have been the last word on the peace process for the Reagan administration. With both

22. See William Safire, "The Little King," *New York Times*, January 13, 1988.

American and Israeli elections slated for November 1988, there was little appetite in Washington for continuing to grapple with the seemingly intractable Arab-Israeli conflict. When the Arab summit was held in Amman in early November, it even seemed as if the Arabs had turned their backs on the Palestinian question. The Gulf, it seemed, was a much greater worry, and Arafat found himself the odd man out among the assembled Arab potentates. Even the acceptance of Egypt back into the fold, which was endorsed by most members of the Arab League, seemed driven more by Gulf concerns than by a desire to coordinate the diplomacy of Arab-Israeli peacemaking with Cairo.

THE UPRISING AND THE SHULTZ INITIATIVE

During Israel's twenty-year domination of the West Bank and Gaza, there had never been trouble-free times. But the costs of the occupation had not been judged excessive and a semblance of normal life existed on most days for the growing numbers of Israeli settlers, and for the Palestinians, some 100,000 of whom had jobs in the Israeli economy as of 1988. Then on December 9, 1987, an unusually nasty series of incidents took place in Gaza, which sparked large-scale Palestinian protests. Within days, West Bank Palestinians joined the "uprising," or the *intifadah,* as it was to be called, and even Israeli Arabs showed support. It soon became clear that something qualitatively new was happening. The previously quiescent Palestinians of the West Bank and Gaza were coming of political age, and with a vengeance (see appendix J).

The PLO was caught by surprise by the timing of the uprising and by how quickly it spread, but the PLO had long been cultivating support in the occupied territories, and pro-PLO networks existed and were supported by the generally pro-PLO sentiment of the population. Before long, coordination between the Unified National Command for the Uprising, as the internal leadership referred to itself, and the PLO seemed to be far reaching.

By January 1988, the Israelis were acknowledging that they had an unprecedented situation on their hands. Defense Minister Yitzhak Rabin took a strong law-and-order approach, publicly sanctioning a policy of beatings and breaking of bones as part of an attempt to frighten the young Palestinians who threw rocks and Molotov cocktails at heavily armed soldiers. Within days, images of savage Israeli beatings of Palestinian youngsters were a part of the American evening television news. The reaction in public opinion was strong.

Even from within the normally pro-Israeli American Jewish community there was an outpouring of criticism and concern.

Several developments then took place that convinced Secretary of State Shultz to reengage his prestige in trying to get Arab-Israeli peace talks started. First, there were hints in a January 17, 1988, letter from Shamir that the Israeli position on "autonomy" for the Palestinians might be softening. Second, American Jewish leaders, as well as some Israeli politicians, began to urge Shultz to become more actively involved. Third, Egypt's President Mubarak came to Washington to make a forceful and convincing plea that American leadership was needed urgently to ward off a radicalization of the entire region.

Shultz approached the challenge methodically. He did not make a flamboyant speech nor did he hold out great hopes of a breakthrough. But he did begin to explore ideas with all the parties, this time including Syria, the Soviets, and some individual Palestinians, as well as Jordan and the Israelis. At the end of his second trip to the region in as many months, Shultz formalized his initiative in a proposal that he described as a "blend of ideas."

The "Shultz initiative," as it was immediately labeled, was certainly the most important involvement by the United States in Arab-Israeli peacemaking since September 1982. In essence, Shultz outlined the conventional goal of a comprehensive peace to be achieved through bilateral negotiations based on Resolutions 242 and 338 (see appendix K).

The Palestinian issue, according to Shultz, should be addressed in negotiations between an Israeli delegation and a Jordanian-Palestinian delegation. Six months would be set aside for negotiating transitional arrangements. In the seventh month, negotiations on the final status of the West Bank and Gaza would start—regardless of the outcome of the first phase of negotiations. A target date of one year for negotiating the final status of the territories was mentioned. Assuming that agreement could be reached on transitional arrangements, a transitional period would begin at an early date and would continue for three years. The United States, Shultz said, would participate in both sets of negotiations and would put forward a draft agreement on transitional arrangements for the consideration of the parties.

Preceding the bilateral negotiations between Israel and a Jordanian-Palestinian delegation, there would be an international conference. The secretary general of the United Nations would invite the regional parties and the permanent members of the Security

Council.[23] All participants in the conference would have to accept Resolutions 242 and 338. While the negotiating parties, by agreement, might report to the conference from time to time, the conference would have no power to impose its views or to veto the results of the negotiations.

Shultz also said that Palestinians should be represented in a combined Jordanian-Palestinian delegation. That delegation would deal with the Palestinian issue in its entirety and those negotiations would be independent of any other negotiation.

In the months that followed his initiative, Shultz doggedly tried to wear down the opponents of his initiative in both Israel and the Arab world. His biggest problem was Israeli Prime Minister Shamir, who blasted the idea of an international conference in no uncertain terms. Shamir also rejected what was called the "interlock," or the linkage between the transitional arrangements and the negotiation of the final status of the territories. This provision, as Shamir correctly noted, was a departure from the Camp David Accords, which had made the so-called "final status" talks dependent on prior success in reaching agreement on transitional arrangements. Finally, as Shamir said publicly, the exchange of territory for peace was foreign to him.[24]

Israeli criticism of the Shultz initiative was well publicized, even though Peres publicly welcomed the American effort. On the Arab side, King Hussein went to great lengths not to be put in the position of saying no to Shultz. He asked questions, sought clarifications, played hard to get, referred publicly to the importance of including the PLO in the game, and generally tried to keep his shrinking options open, until finally he announced his withdrawal from the game in July 1988.

The Palestinian response was more categorical. While pleased to see the United States responding to the uprising, the Palestinian leaders were unhappy with the second-class treatment they were given in the Shultz plan. They saw themselves as being assigned, at best, to the role of junior partner behind Jordan.

The Soviet Union was also unenthusiastic about a central feature

23. The use of the word "parties" instead of "states" suggested that the Palestine Liberation Organization might be invited to the conference.

24. Shamir's statement prompted Senators Rudy Boschwitz, Carl Levin, and twenty-eight other senators, including many friends of Israel, to write a letter to Shultz, dated March 3, 1988, expressing their concern about the Israeli position. Shamir's reply was published in "Text of Letters from Shamir on Criticism from Senators," *New York Times*, March 10, 1988.

of the Shultz plan, the international conference. While Shamir professed fears that the conference would become authoritative and would work to undermine the Israeli position, the Soviet concern was just the opposite. As envisaged by the Americans, the international conference appeared to the Soviets to be only symbolic. The Soviets wanted a real role in the negotiating process, not just an opportunity to legitimize a made-in-America initiative that would ultimately leave them on the sidelines.

In the face of these obstacles, the Shultz plan never had much of a chance of complete success. Nonetheless, it had wide support in American public opinion. There was little criticism of any features of the proposal, with the exception of some sour words from former Secretary of State Henry A. Kissinger about the idea of an international conference. Shultz and his colleagues were no doubt hopeful that they would get a lucky break and that some negotiating process might be started on their watch. But they also spoke of two other purposes behind the initiative. First, they hoped to influence Israeli public opinion. With the prospect of peace negotiations with their Arab neighbors, the Israeli public, it was hoped, would vote for a leadership committed to compromise positions. That possibility may, of course, have been wishful thinking, and much depended on producing an acceptable Arab partner for peace talks. The administration may also have miscalculated the political dynamics in Israel, in that American policies may well have strengthened the hardliners in the Likud instead of the more moderate elements on the other side of the political spectrum. Still, the intention was to help shape the political debate in Israel so that the elections would become a referendum, of sorts, on peace.

The second, perhaps more attainable, goal was to provide the next administration, whether led by a Republican or a Democrat, with a live proposal on the table. Reagan and Shultz were consciously removing certain diplomatic taboos, some of their own design. No longer was it off limits to talk with the Soviets about the Middle East. Some form of international conference was viewed as essential. Dialogue with Syria, even on matters of constitutional reform within Lebanon, was legitimate. A secretary of state could even meet with members of the Palestine National Council, the supreme representative body of the PLO, without setting off more than minor shock waves.

Still, the problem of Palestinian representation was unresolved in the Shultz initiative, and there was no real strategy for persuading the Likud leaders to accept the procedural arrangements that were the essence of the American proposal, let alone to alter their views on the principle of territory for peace. Nor was there enough in the package to draw the Soviets into a cooperative venture, in which they would be called on to use their considerable influence with the Syrians and the PLO to pave the way for successful negotiations. None of these points could be easily resolved, and they would therefore certainly be on the agenda for a new administration to deal with in 1989 and beyond.

CONCLUSION

Compared with the decade that preceded the Camp David Accords, the ten years that followed showed little progress toward the goal of an overall Arab-Israeli peace settlement. True, no full-scale war had erupted that threatened to draw in the superpowers, although the Israeli invasion of Lebanon in 1982 was both dangerous and destructive and might well have escalated if hostilities had spilled over into Syrian territory. But on the diplomatic front, most of the issues that had been on the agenda for negotiation in the immediate aftermath of the Egyptian-Israeli peace treaty were still there. Why was there no further progress, and did the stalemate persist because of the way in which the United States played its role?

First, it must be stressed that the Egyptian-Israeli dimension of the conflict was objectively the easiest to resolve through negotiations. Sinai was a ready-made buffer zone. Egypt was able to act independently of a broad Arab consensus, and Israeli public opinion was overwhelmingly in favor of a bilateral peace with Egypt, in part because it would relieve Israel of pressure to make further concessions on the more difficult issues involving the Palestinians and the Golan. In addition, there was little agreement among the relevant Arab parties—the Palestinians, Jordan, and Syria—on how best to proceed once Egypt had broken ranks.

Thus it might be suggested that the circumstances for further breakthroughs were not particularly propitious in the aftermath of Camp David. Looked at another way, however, one might have reached another conclusion. With Egypt at peace with Israel, the Jewish state no longer faced the danger of a two-front war. In fact, Israel's security was immeasurably improved. In theory, this situation might have made it easier to contemplate making concessions on other fronts, assuming, of course, that security, not territorial aggrandizement, was the primary Israeli concern.

On the Arab side of the conflict, there were also reasons to be somewhat hopeful about the prospects for peace with Israel. Even though Arab opinion was opposed to the Camp David Accords, there were few illusions in the Arab world that Egypt could be forced to reverse course. This reality meant that the Arabs had to think of confronting Israel without the advantage of the weight of the largest and most powerful Arab country. For most Arabs, the military option was now all but irrelevant. One way or another, diplomacy was the only way to recover occupied Arab lands. Certainly King Hussein understood this, as did the mainstream of the Palestinian movement. Only the Syrians continued to talk of the need to restore the military balance with Israel as a precondition for any diplomatic moves.

In brief, then, while the odds were not particularly in favor of further progress in diplomatic negotiations, there were nonetheless large "peace camps" on both sides of the conflict. They lacked leadership, in some cases, and they may have been hesitant and indecisive, but it would be wrong to think that there were no serious openings for peace in the decade after Camp David.

One of the missing ingredients throughout most of this period, however, was active leadership by the United States. No one can say how much this absence mattered, but the record is clear that no Arab-Israeli agreement has ever been reached in the past forty years without a significant involvement of American diplomacy. And during the past decade, American involvement in the peace process has been episodic, at best, and sometimes almost invisible.

There were reasons, of course, for the relative detachment of both the Carter and Reagan administrations from the peace process after the signing of the Egyptian-Israeli treaty in the spring of 1979. For Carter, there was much unfinished business to tend to. There were political considerations as he entered a difficult reelection campaign, and there was the Iranian seizure of American hostages that so thoroughly dominated his last year in office.

For Reagan and his associates, the reasons for a degree of aloofness from Arab-Israeli peace negotiations were different. To put it charitably, President Reagan was not particularly interested in the fine details of Arab-Israeli peace negotiations. Camp David was Jimmy Carter's achievement, and therefore it was only reluctantly embraced by the Reaganites. And the worldview of Reagan and his advisers dictated that priority be given to other issues, first and foremost the Soviet Union.

Apart from these particular perspectives of Reagan and his team, it was plausible, throughout much of the 1980s, to argue that American national interests were not at risk in the Arab-Israeli arena. No danger of large-scale war seemed to exist, with the exception of a brief moment in the midst of the Lebanon crisis. Oil prices were coming down from the record highs of 1980–81 and in any case had little to do with the Arab-Israeli impasse. Egypt, despite unhappiness with the stalemate in the peace process, had few options but to adhere to the treaty and to cooperate with the United States.

American detachment from an activist role also seemed to reflect a deliberate choice by Secretary of State Shultz. From his experience as a negotiator in labor disputes when he was secretary of labor in the Nixon administration, Shultz seems to have concluded that the best time for a mediator to intervene was late in the game. Premature involvement would reduce incentives for the parties to negotiate. They would become dependent on the outside mediator and would adhere rigidly to their positions until the mediator offered a compromise. Shultz seemed to feel that the parties must first show their seriousness and determination to reach a negotiated settlement before it was worth making a high-level American commitment to bridge the remaining gaps. Thus endless fact-finding trips to the region might be authorized. Special emissaries would be dispatched, but the secretary of state and the president held themselves in reserve until the parties to the Arab-Israeli conflict could demonstrate that they had made a serious effort of their own.

This theory of negotiation sounds reasonable when applied to labor disputes, but it has little relevance to the messy politics of the contemporary Middle East. Leaders are often too weak or hesitant to take even the first steps toward compromise. They look to outsiders to provide them with excuses for action. They react more than they initiate. And they have been spoiled, perhaps, by the Kissinger and Carter models of high-level American involvement. With those recent memories still in mind, both Arabs and Israelis tend not to take any American initiative seriously unless the president or his secretary of state is fully involved.

Reasons abound for explaining the broad lines of American policy toward the Arab-Israeli conflict in the 1980s. The Reagan worldview, the perceived national interest, and a predilection for a certain style of negotiations have been emphasized. But a thorough analysis would show that offsetting considerations were also at work and, on occasion, succeeded in provoking a serious debate within the administration about the wisdom of its posture of relative disengagement. And, of course, at the end of the Reagan administration, to the surprise of most observers, there was a sudden burst of energy, a renewed activism, and a full-fledged, if imperfectly crafted, initiative bearing the name of the secretary of state. What, then, were these countervailing considerations?

First, there has always been a bureaucratic impulse, usually focused in the Near East Bureau of the State Department, to do something about Arab-Israeli peace. Conventional wisdom has always held that the conflict could not be contained indefinitely, that it could have regionwide, even global, implications if it continued to fester, and that a semblance of diplomatic activity was needed to give moderate forces straws to grasp at. At worst, this perspective could sound like special pleading for regional clients or an argument for movement for its own sake. But it was also a viewpoint held by those who had a great deal of experience in Arab-Israeli affairs and who rejected the cynical notion that the only time to make peace was in the immediate aftermath of a bloody war.

Second, even when the bureaucracy was quiescent or demoralized, one could count on European allies, especially the British and French, to press the United States to be more involved in Arab-Israeli peace initiatives. In addition, a number of Middle East leaders—especially President Mubarak of Egypt, King Fahd of Saudi Arabia, King Hassan II of Morocco, and, of course, King Hussein—have been persistent in urging the United States to resume leadership in Arab-Israeli peacemaking. These sentiments are also reflected in small, but not insignificant, sectors of American public opinion, including the various Arab-American groups that have organized in recent years. Some Israeli leaders—especially from the Labor party—and likeminded American Jews have also urged American leaders to become more active in the peace process.

Third, and perhaps most important, are the stubborn realities of the situation in the Middle East. Whatever one's ideological predispositions, whatever one's personal preferences, certain courses of action lead nowhere and some assumptions prove untenable. Every administration goes through a learning process. This is not to say that all right-thinking people eventually come to see the issues of the region in identical terms. That is clearly not the case. But views that are wildly divergent from reality eventually are discredited. The range of debate is narrowed as policymakers become increasingly familiar with the issues and the leaders of the region. Blacks and whites are replaced by various shades of grey. Certainties are replaced by an awareness of complexity, of nuance. These developments produce a climate in which policy is debated in less ideological terms than is the case at the outset of an administration. In 1981 Carterites and Reaganites would have found little common ground in discussing the Arab-Israeli conflict. By 1988 the gap between these two perspectives was much narrower.

President Reagan's eight years will not be remembered as a time of great success in America's Middle East policy. Lebanon and the Iran-Contra affair are likely to come more readily to mind than either the Reagan plan or the Shultz initiative, neither of which led immediately to promising results. But future administrations will nonetheless find themselves building on what was done in these years. The U.S.-Israeli relationship has been strengthened considerably, which could provide the next president with great influence in future diplomacy. In addition, Reagan and Shultz have adhered to the main lines of U.S. policy by reaffirming the centrality of Resolutions 242 and 338. On a rhetorical level, at least, the United States remains committed to an overall negotiated peace between Israel and its Arab neighbors.

The Reagan era has also provided a laboratory test of certain propositions. For example, evidence has been accumulated concerning the so-called "Jordan option." It is no longer necessary to ask if King Hussein can or will negotiate on behalf of the Palestinians. He cannot. On at least three occasions in the 1980s, Jordan went as far as it could toward negotiations, only to pull back when it was unable to coordinate with a Palestinian partner. Jordan will not be a substitute for the Palestinians (see appendix M).

The Reagan administration also learned the futility of trying to ignore Syria as a player in both the Lebanese and Palestinian arenas. No future administration needs to go through the same humiliating ordeal of trying to settle things in Lebanon without taking Syrian interests into account. Nor can Damascus be ignored in Arab-Israeli diplomacy.

It also seems clear from the Reagan record that benign neglect from Washington is a recipe for trouble in the Middle East. The United States may be incapable of resolving the Arab-Israeli conflict, but it has certainly made things even worse by standing on the sidelines at crucial moments, especially in mid- and late 1982, again in early 1985, and perhaps in the spring of 1987 as well.

Finally, the Reagan administration has reached the sensible conclusion that the Soviet Union cannot be excluded from the diplomacy of Arab-Israeli peacemaking. Soviet involvement stems from the nature of the relations they have forged with both Syria and the PLO, as well as from the insistence of Jordan and Egypt. One way or another, the United States and Israel will be obliged to deal with the Soviets within some type of international framework if peacemaking is to proceed.

From these perspectives, the Shultz initiative of early 1988 was overdue, but nonetheless welcome. And it contained valuable elements, especially in the emphasis on the need for an international framework, for two stages of negotiations, and for a U.S.-Soviet dialogue.[25] But the initiative fell short in two areas, thus leaving the next administration with formidable challenges. First, the United States has still not faced up to the centrality of the Palestinian issue. Palestinians will have to be invited to negotiations on their own behalf, not as junior partners in a Jordanian delegation. That means dealing, at least indirectly, with the PLO, since no Palestinian will negotiate without its endorsement. And it is futile to ask the PLO to accept Resolution 242 without some clear American or Israeli quid pro quo. Both Americans and Israelis will one day have to overcome their reluctance to deal directly with the mainstream of Palestinian nationalism. That is one lesson of the Palestinian uprising of 1987–88.

A second unresolved issue stems from the post-1977 revision of Israel's terms for peace. Up until that time, Israeli governments were bound by the principle of trading territory for peace as the basis for negotiations. This was, after all, the meaning of Resolution 242.[26] Begin reversed his position on this. Formerly he had rejected 242, saying that it required Israel to withdraw from the West Bank, which he did not want to do. As prime minister, he said that he accepted 242, but it no longer meant what it had in the past. In his view, the withdrawal provision of 242 was fully implemented when Israel evacuated Sinai. In short, withdrawal was not required on each front of the conflict.

The Carter administration tried mightily to convince Begin to revert to the original Israeli interpretation of 242. It failed at Camp David. Begin would not agree that the results of the negotiations concerning the final status of the West Bank and Gaza would be based on the principles of 242, including withdrawal. Since then, Likud leaders have adhered to the Begin line. Some Americans have chosen to interpret this stance as tough, but essentially tactical, a position that could change if negotiations were ever to get under way. On the whole, this was the view of the Reagan administration. In private, it was said, Shamir showed much more flexibility. His rejection of the concept of territory for peace drew some criticism, but Shamir's apologists were quick to point to hints of Israeli willingness to disengage from the West Bank.[27]

25. These points, along with the centrality of Israeli-Palestinian negotiations, are prominent themes in *Toward Arab-Israeli Peace: Report of a Study Group* (Brookings, 1988), published around the time of the Shultz initiative.

26. See the detailed account in David Ignatius, "The 20-Year U.S.-Israeli Battle over Land for Peace," *Washington Post*, April 10, 1988.

27. For example, they noted an article by Yitzhak Shamir entitled "Israel at 40:

Whatever the truth about the Likud position, so far the evidence shows no willingness to relinquish control over the West Bank in any circumstances. No terms of peace, no security arrangements, no political formulations seem to be enough to persuade Likudniks that Israel could and should withdraw from the West Bank. But again reality may assert itself. The Palestinian uprising is having the effect of redrawing the green line that used to separate Israel from the occupied territories. The movement to create new settlements in the West Bank is unlikely to find many new recruits in the future. The need for a political solution to the Palestinian issue is clear to even the most ideological Israelis on the right.

As Professor Yehoshafat Harkabi has persuasively argued, Israel does not face choices between good alternatives in dealing with the Palestinian issue. All of the alternatives entail some risk and some pain. But there are "less bad" outcomes, provided that Israelis are guided by the notion of a "Zionism of quality," not of acreage. A smaller, more Jewish Israel, at peace with its neighbors, he argues, would be more secure than a larger Israel with a sizable Palestinian minority with second-class status.[28]

For a new administration, the challenge of Arab-Israeli peacemaking will be formidable. But no president is likely to be able to ignore the problem for long. The key building blocks for a serious initiative are easily identified. The Shultz initiative contains some of them. But a serious effort will be needed to bring representative Palestinians into the negotiations. And the United States will have to draw on its unique relationship with Israel to try to persuade the Israeli body politic that the risks of standing still outweigh the risks of negotiating on the basis of territory for peace.

The United States can do little to enhance Israel's sense of security in the face of a continuing uprising of unarmed Palestinians. In conditions of peace, however, and once secure and recognized borders have been established between Israel and its Arab neighbors, there would be no reason for the United States not to translate its tacit alliance with Israel into a genuine security treaty

---

Looking Back, Looking Ahead," *Foreign Affairs*, vol. 66, no. 3 (1988), p. 580, where Shamir writes, "But regardless of how the question of sovereignty over Judea and Samaria is resolved, we cannot be barred from Shiloh, Bethel and Hebron any more than we can be excluded from Jerusalem, Tel Aviv and Haifa." This statement could be interpreted as meaning that Israel might accept non-Israeli sovereignty over the West Bank. Or, as Begin might have explained, it could mean that the area would perpetually remain an autonomous area under Israeli control, a region where the issue of sovereignty might never be resolved.

28. Yehoshafat Harkabi, *Israel's Fateful Hour* (Harper and Row, 1988).

offering assurance of American support against any future external threat.

In short, the United States will need to go beyond simply addressing the procedural issues surrounding the Arab-Israeli dispute. Americans should not only be trying to develop an acceptable international framework for negotiations, but also should encourage the discussion of possible visions of the future. The United States can help Israel deal with security problems as it moves toward peace, and the record of the past shows that this potential provides substantial leverage in the course of negotiations. Along with other parties, the United States can also work to bring representative Palestinians into negotiations with Israel. Over the years, Israelis have implied that the lack of progress toward peace could be blamed on the lack of a partner with whom Israel could negotiate. The mainstream of the Palestinian national movement now seems ready to negotiate and can do so with far more legitimacy than Jordan. Encouragement from the United States could help to tip the balance as Palestinians argue over how to turn the uprising into a serious political initiative (see appendix L).

The first decade after Camp David failed to deliver on the explicit commitment to a comprehensive settlement and Palestinian rights that were enshrined in those texts. For the sake of American interests in the area, the next decade should not be similarly squandered.

EVGENI M. PRIMAKOV

Soviet Policy toward the Arab-Israeli Conflict

THE MIDDLE EAST occupies a special place in the hierarchy of Soviet foreign policy interests, and Soviet policy toward the Arab-Israeli conflict, and the Middle East in general, is based on this fact. Sharp conflict, periodically escalating to crisis level, has existed in the Middle East for several decades, causing military and political concern in the Soviet Union. Since the Middle East borders the Soviet Union, Soviet security is adversely affected.

Because of these considerations, the Soviet Union cannot ignore the fact that the Middle East has become a sphere of military and political interest for the West, especially for the main "opponent" of the USSR—the United States. The United States, deeply involved in the Arab-Israeli conflict, has special relations with one of the parties—Israel. The actions of the United States leave no doubt that the chief goal of its military and political domination of the region is the preservation of its position, which, on the whole, it sees in terms of U.S.-Soviet confrontation. Thus the United States strives to minimize the role of the Soviet Union in regional affairs and perhaps even to oust it from the Middle East.

The Middle East has had and continues to have no small economic importance for the Soviet Union. Historically, many Middle Eastern countries have become economic partners of the USSR: Egypt—especially during the time of President Gamal Abd al-Nasser—Syria, Iraq, Algeria, Libya, and the People's Democratic Republic of Yemen (PDRY). Naturally, the USSR is interested in such economic cooperation. Middle Eastern countries are a market for the expanding machinebuilding industry in the Soviet Union. The Soviet Union is also interested in agreements in which Soviet credits are paid off either by the production from enterprises built in cooperation with the USSR or by deliveries of oil.

Despite this arrangement, it is not accurate to assert that the Soviet Union "is hunting for Middle Eastern oil" because its natural reserves, allegedly, are running low. The USSR has sufficient energy resources and is continually increasing the production of oil. However, this does not remove Soviet interest in importing oil from the Middle East, both to satisfy the growing need for it and to supply the consumers in the European part of the USSR who are located near Middle Eastern oil sources. To import oil, however, there is no need for the Soviet Union to have a special position in the region. It is enough to conclude agreements on a normal commercial basis.

In its Middle East policy, the USSR also recognizes the objective interests of the West (including the United States) in the unimpeded export of oil from the region, the guarantee of the safety of international shipping, and the pursuit of multifaceted relationships with countries of the Middle East. But this recognition, naturally, cannot come at the expense of similar interests of the USSR.

Thus, from a political, military, and economic point of view, the Soviet Union is interested in the stabilization of the situation in the Middle East. Such an outcome is impossible without a just and lasting comprehensive settlement of the Arab-Israeli conflict.

In its approaches to this conflict, the Soviet Union bases its position on the following principles:

—The need for a comprehensive settlement of the Arab-Israeli conflict on the basis of a compromise in the interests of all the peoples who have been drawn into the conflict;

—The special importance of resolving the Palestinian problem by granting the right of self-determination to the Palestinian people through the creation of a national state of their own (without this state, the Soviet Union believes that a stable Arab-Israeli settlement is impossible);

—The right to exist for all states in the Middle East;

—The need to create, as part of an Arab-Israeli peace settlement, an arrangement capable of providing stability and security for all states in the region; and

—The importance of keeping the Middle East from becoming a sphere of U.S.-Soviet confrontation.

These principles are derived from a set of interconnected and interdependent Soviet interests: global and regional, state (national) and international, political and military, and economic and ideological. These principles may take on more precise definitions depending on the evolution of the situation in the region and on global developments, but none of them can be ignored or excluded in the formulation of Soviet Middle East policy. In the opinion of the USSR, this comprehensive foundation can secure a stable and just peace in the Middle East.

In the West, it is widely believed that the Soviet Union has an interest in the permanent nonsettlement of the Arab-Israeli conflict, allegedly to give the Soviet Union a chance to "advance its policy." But this argument is based on a misunderstanding of the fundamental interests of the Soviet Union. The location of the Middle East and its global importance unquestionably lead the USSR to work to stabilize the region. Even if one argues, as many in the West do, that the USSR is guided by geopolitical and ideological considerations, the USSR would still strive for peace in the Middle East. Nonsettlement of the Arab-Israeli conflict has not strengthened the position of the USSR in the Arab world, reinforced leftist forces, or weakened conservative trends in the region.

Whether the Soviet Union has always succeeded in making the best of every opportunity it may have had in the Middle East is another matter. In retrospect, one can obviously point to some missed opportunities. Perhaps the Soviet Union did not always act with sufficient initiative but instead responded to changes in the environment. At times, even this reaction could have been more effective. For example, it seems to me that a quicker and more definitive positive reaction to the Fahd plan for a Middle East settlement, which Saudi Arabia put forward in August 1981, would have served Soviet interests. But these details do not challenge the fundamental and obvious conclusion. The Soviet Union has continually worked for a comprehensive settlement of the Middle East conflict and opposed those who have tried to promote partial and separate solutions. Those favoring partial solutions are trying to secure the results of the June 1967 war, that is, they want to preserve the main territorial and political gains that Israel won during this war.

The Middle East policy of the Soviet Union cannot be understood without considering American policy in the region. For this reason, in this chapter I will address Moscow's understanding of American actions in the Middle East, actions that have demanded certain responses from the USSR. But first, I will evaluate the period from the October 1973 war to Camp David, analyzing the significance of this war and its effect on the chances for a peaceful resolution of the Arab-Israeli conflict.

THE 1973 OCTOBER WAR: ITS MEANING AND SIGNIFICANCE

The Soviet Union has never tried to solve its problems by promoting military action in the Middle East. Though the Soviet Union did render essential military aid to the Arab countries opposing the expansionist policy of Israel, it did so to avert the drift toward war. And if war resulted anyway, then the Soviet Union tried to use the situation after the war as a turning point in the search for a lasting, comprehensive settlement. This objective dates from the October 1973 war. I remember that Sadat's order in July 1972 to expel the Soviet military specialists from Egypt was motivated by the restraining influence of the USSR and by his desire to gain a free hand for his complex dealings with the Americans. He repeatedly accused the USSR of being "insufficiently disposed toward a military resolution of the issue."

In contrast, the United States led events to the point of military flare-up, though within certain limits, despite the extremely dangerous potential of such a game. The American hope, it seems, was to produce a separate Egyptian-Israeli settlement.[1]

Thus, on the eve of military operations, Sadat convened the Egyptian National Security Council and informed its members of his intention to start "limited" military operations. When Henry A. Kissinger learned a few days later that military operations were imminent, his reaction, according to one source (the Kalb brothers), foretold his later actions. Kissinger was anxious that Israel not launch a preemptive strike. He mentioned this concern to both the Israeli minister of foreign affairs, Abba Eban, and Israel's chargé d'affaires in Washington, Mordecai Shalev.[2] Later, Kissinger wrote in his memoirs, "Sadat knew from two secret meetings in early 1973 between his national security adviser, Hafiz Ismail, and me that we were willing to engage in the diplomacy of the Arab-Israeli conflict. . . . So Sadat fought a war not to acquire territory, but to restore Egypt's self-respect and thereby increase its diplomatic flexibility."[3]

The hope that the war would be localized was not realized. A real threat arose that it would expand beyond the boundaries of the region. On October 22, 1973, the United Nations Security Council

1. These conclusions are ones shared by both President Hafiz al-Asad of Syria and King Hussein of Jordan, as expressed during discussions with the author.
2. Marvin Kalb and Bernard Kalb, *Kissinger* (Little, Brown, 1974), pp. 459–60.
3. Henry A. Kissinger, *Years of Upheaval* (Little, Brown, 1982), p. 460.

adopted Resolution 338 (see appendix A), in which the cessation of hostilities was linked to the beginning of a political settlement. In the resolution an appeal was made for all parties to prepare for a peace conference, which would be convened to resolve a whole set of issues relating to the settlement of the Middle East conflict and to the establishment of a just and lasting peace in the region.

Intensive discussions between the American secretary of state and Soviet leaders took place in Moscow before the resolution was adopted. The United States, in light of the situation that had arisen, agreed with the idea of concentrating on a comprehensive settlement to end the longstanding and bloody Arab-Israeli conflict. Thus it is possible to say that, at this stage, the Soviet approach gained the upper hand. Moreover, U.S. support for this approach seemed to enhance the possibilities for a political settlement. The failure of Israel's political and military doctrine as revealed by the October 1973 war and the interest of realistic American politicians in reducing global tensions led the leaders in Moscow to agree that a definite possibility existed for a comprehensive Arab-Israeli peace settlement. They also agreed that the mechanism to achieve this objective had been created—the Geneva conference.

Immediately after the approval of UN Resolution 338, however, the United States again began trying to separate the issue of a cease-fire from the process of a comprehensive settlement. Kissinger recounts in his memoirs how the understanding he reached in Moscow had no value for him and how he began deliberately to undermine the efforts to prepare for a comprehensive settlement in the Middle East at the same time as the conditions for such a settlement seemed to be ripening. "The Geneva conference [of December 1973] was a way to get all parties into harness for one symbolic act, thereby to enable each to pursue a separate course, at least for a while. It was as complicated to assemble the great meeting as it was to keep it quiescent afterward while diplomacy returned to bilateral channels."[4]

Thus from the beginning the United States did not consider the Geneva conference a necessity but instead saw it as a way to distract everybody's attention from the deal that was already being made by the Americans in collaboration with Israel and President Sadat. Consequently, the hopes for a Geneva conference began to fade. (After its initial meeting, in late 1973, subsequent meetings never took place.)

4. Ibid., p. 747.

The two disengagement agreements between Israeli and Egyptian forces, and between Israeli and Syrian forces, reflected a different approach to the settlement process. The USSR saw them not as isolated agreements but as links in a single chain leading to a general settlement. Israel and the United States had different ideas. On December 16, 1973, while in Jerusalem, Kissinger described his overall strategy to the Israeli leadership as follows:

> Kissinger explained that the aim of the disengagement talks was to circumvent the need to talk now about borders and final arrangements. The success of the talks [on disengagement] would also lead to another achievement—the lifting of the oil embargo. This would also end Israel's isolation by easing the pressure put on her primarily by the Western European states and Japan. No one in Israel should have the slightest doubt, warned Kissinger, that the failure of the disengagement talks would break open the dam holding back the pressures on Israel, this time not for a partial retreat, but a complete retreat to the June 4, 1967, borders.[5]

Thus the USSR developed its Middle East policy knowing that the October war had created the conditions necessary for a comprehensive settlement of the Arab-Israeli conflict. The USSR worked intensively for the achievement of such a settlement not only with the United States. It arranged consultations with Syria, the Palestine Liberation Organization (PLO), and Jordan about resuming the work of the Geneva conference as well. The composition of the Arab delegation to the Geneva conference was discussed, in particular, and on this complicated issue progress, which could have satisfied all parties, was made. In short, it seemed to the Soviet Union as if the doors to a peace conference on the Arab-Israeli conflict were beginning to open slightly, if only a crack.

However, the U.S. administration directed matters toward exclusively partial and separate agreements. American policy was aimed at alienating Egypt from the Soviet Union and breaking the ties between them, which made Cairo intractable and unresponsive for the time being. In Moscow, it was understood that the United

5. The source for this quotation is a book by the Israeli journalist Matti Golan, who obtained the stenographic records of Kissinger's discussions in Israel and, contrary to the wishes of the Israeli leadership, made them public. See Matti Golan, *The Secret Conversations of Henry Kissinger: Step-by-Step Diplomacy in the Middle East*, trans. Ruth Geyra Stern and Sol Stern (Quadrangle/New York Times Book Co., 1976), p. 152.

States, even if it had not initiated Sadat's decision to end the mission of the Soviet military advisers in July 1972, had certainly urged it upon him. The United States also encouraged Sadat to abrogate the Soviet-Egyptian Treaty of Friendship and Cooperation in March 1976.

PROSPECTS FOR A COMPREHENSIVE SETTLEMENT

With the arrival of the Carter administration, however, there was a certain ray of hope in Moscow. The goal of a comprehensive settlement now seemed more possible. In the summer of 1976, when the presidential election struggle in the United States was in full swing, I had the occasion to meet with one of the advisers to Jimmy Carter, Zbigniew Brzezinski (the future national security adviser), at Dartmouth. Shortly thereafter, I took part in a Soviet-American symposium sponsored by the two nations' United Nations associations. Cyrus Vance, who was also an adviser to Jimmy Carter and later became secretary of state in his administration, participated in that meeting. Both Brzezinski and Vance, when speaking of the Arab-Israeli conflict, said approximately the same thing: the policy of separate deals had exhausted itself. It was now necessary to seek a comprehensive political settlement, and both the United States and the Soviet Union must participate in the Arab-Israeli settlement process by coordinating their efforts.

A publication of the Brookings Institution in Washington on the Arab-Israeli peace settlement had wide repercussions. Among the authors of this report were both Brzezinski and William B. Quandt, who later became Brzezinski's aide for Middle Eastern affairs on the National Security Council staff. These men, as well as other participants in the study, directly participated in the development of President Carter's Middle East policy. In the conclusion of the Brookings report, it was emphasized that there should be an overall settlement, which could not be achieved without the creation of a Palestinian homeland on the West Bank. Two months after taking office, President Carter declared that the Palestinians should have such a homeland. Simultaneously, he made several official statements about the desirability of resuming the work of the Geneva conference on the Middle East.

Contacts then took place between the United States and the Soviet Union and on October 1, 1977, a Soviet-American communiqué on the Middle East was jointly published in which both parties called for a comprehensive settlement of the Arab-Israeli conflict by resolving such key issues as the "withdrawal of Israeli

Armed Forces from territories occupied in the 1967 conflict; the resolution of the Palestinian question, including insuring the legitimate rights of the Palestinian people; termination of the state of war and establishment of normal peaceful relations on the basis of mutual recognition of the principles of sovereignty, territorial integrity, and political independence" (see appendix B).

Later events revealed that even then the United States was not prepared to follow the positions described. A few days before the publication of the joint Soviet-American communiqué, the United States showed its text to Israel. Having become familiar with it, the Israeli leadership, as one ought to expect, activated its lobby in the United States, especially in Congress. An unprecedented attack was soon launched on the communiqué, which Secretary Vance himself had declared was in the interest of peace in the Middle East. The White House wavered. On October 4–5, a few days after the publication of the joint communiqué, Israeli Foreign Minister Moshe Dayan met with President Carter in New York, where both were attending the regular session of the United Nations General Assembly. The talks between Carter and Dayan, which were intended to be relatively short, lasted for many hours, and in the end the United States capitulated to the Israelis. A "working paper" was agreed on in those talks, which amounted to a repudiation of the American signature on the joint Soviet-American communiqué.

From that moment on, American policy, which had already begun to turn against cooperation with the Soviet Union, moved even more firmly in that direction. The Americans abandoned the idea of a comprehensive settlement. Nonetheless, for several months after the signing of the working paper with Israel, the United States would occasionally mention the Geneva conference, mostly because it wanted to find a way out of an awkward situation caused by its renunciation, under pressure, of responsibilities undertaken under the terms of the joint communiqué with the Soviet Union. Soon, however, even routine references to the Geneva conference ceased.

Moscow's study of American policy toward the Arab-Israeli conflict was one reason for the Soviet reaction to the visit of President Sadat to Jerusalem in November 1977. The Soviet Union did not view Sadat's trip to Jerusalem as an isolated phenomenon but rather as a link in a chain forged either directly by the United States or under the influence of American policy. Details that have become clear from a variety of sources about the preparation for this visit confirm this conclusion.

In explaining his decision to go to Jerusalem, President Sadat talked about the need "to break through the psychological barrier."

As a matter of fact, however, he was not so concerned with breaching the psychological barrier as he was with preventing the development of a process that would have led to the Geneva conference. If it had been convened, Sadat's hands would have been tied by the participation in the conference of the USSR, with which he had seriously damaged his relations, and by the active role of Syria and Jordan, as well as by the influence the PLO would have had on the conference.

Although the U.S.-Israeli working paper, as it was called, had signified the repudiation by the United States of the joint Soviet-American communiqué, Sadat at first (that is, when he made the decision to go to Jerusalem) feared that there might be a meeting of the Geneva conference. The upcoming Soviet-American summit obviously also frightened him.

The domestic situation in Egypt had become increasingly charged, exemplified by the bread riots in January 1977 when tens of thousands of Egyptians took to the streets, protesting the decision of the government of Egypt to raise the prices of twenty-five vitally important commodities. The demonstrations were assuming an increasingly anti-Sadat character, and Sadat was deeply worried. His image as the "hero of the October war" had evaporated. Moreover, the turmoil took place just as President Carter was coming to power in the United States. The new president was unknown to Sadat, and during his campaign for the presidency Carter had criticized partial agreements as part of the Arab-Israeli peace process. Sadat had had a deep mutual understanding with President Richard M. Nixon, and Kissinger had brought Sadat close to President Gerald R. Ford. Now, however, both Nixon and Ford had passed from the political scene.

It was in these circumstances that Sadat decided to carry out his visit to Jerusalem in November 1977. His main objective, in the estimation of Soviet specialists, was twofold: the return of the Israeli-occupied Sinai to Egypt and the transformation of Egypt into one of the main partners of the United States. For this, Sadat was ready to sacrifice the interests of all of his allies. But at first he could not, and did not want to, move openly toward a separate deal. To him, rejection of the Geneva conference was not—at that time—synonymous with agreement to a separate deal. Sadat needed the appearance of some movement on the other fronts of the Arab-Israeli conflict. Israel, however, did not permit Sadat to maneuver indefinitely, and in the end he was forced to accept a separate agreement, not only in a de facto sense, but also de jure. Israel, of course, was firmly set on the course of a separate treaty with Egypt from the beginning, since only such a treaty would allow Israel to carry out annexationist policies on the West Bank and Gaza.

The task for the United States during the period after Sadat's trip to Jerusalem consisted mostly of keeping Sadat's initiative alive. However, the United States was not able to support unconditionally Israel's open pursuit of a separate solution, at least not in public. It was forced to consider both the environment in the Arab world, where such solutions were rejected, and the complicated position Sadat found himself in within Egypt.

In light of these considerations, the United States did not try to divert Israel from the pursuit of a separate deal. Instead, the United States tried to facilitate Sadat's acceptance of Israeli demands and to keep his policy alive. In the words of Carter's national security adviser, Zbigniew Brzezinski, "The United States had to help Sadat obtain a justification for a separate accommodation by pressing Israel directly on the West Bank and also, to some extent, on the secondary Sinai issues."[6]

The Americans had to take several issues into account as they moved toward support of a separate Egyptian-Israeli deal. There was an anti-Sadat mood in the Arab world and Sadat's own position in Egypt was not particularly stable. The Israelis were also determined to press their advantage on all fronts, rather than proceed more gradually. This meant that the United States had to take extraordinary measures to facilitate development of the processes that had evolved during Sadat's visit to Jerusalem and to bring about the final Egyptian-Israeli agreement. The United States began to play a central role in Egyptian-Israeli negotiations, no longer just behind the scenes, but openly. It led the negotiations out of numerous blind alleys and ultimately to the signing in September 1978 of the Camp David Accords, and in March 1979 of a separate Egyptian-Israeli treaty.

WHAT THE EGYPTIAN-ISRAELI TREATY REVEALED

Many American experts to this day maintain that the Egyptian-Israeli peace treaty was not a separate deal because its preamble mentions "the urgent necessity of the establishment of a just, comprehensive and lasting peace in the Middle East in accordance with Security Council Resolutions 242 and 338." At the same time, however, in a letter to President Carter dated March 26, 1979, which

6. Zbigniew Brzezinski, *Power and Principle: Memoirs of the National Security Adviser, 1977–1981* (Farrar, 1983), p. 237.

was signed by President Sadat and Prime Minister Begin and affixed to the treaty as an official document, Egypt and Israel not only took upon themselves the obligation to enter into negotiations concerning "self-government" in the West Bank and Gaza within one month of signing the treaty, but they also invited Jordan to join them.

According to the views of several American experts, the treaty became a separate one later on, in part because of the Arab decision to boycott the Camp David process. However, thorough analysis of the treaty as it stood at the moment of signing convinced Soviet experts not only that it was a separate deal but also that it was pro-Israeli and would allow Israel to continue an expansionist course in relationship to other Arab parties. The following examples support this conclusion.

First, despite Sadat's reluctance to admit it, the treaty with Israel would have priority over Egypt's other obligations should there be any conflict between them. This reality was confirmed in an interpretation agreed to by both Israel and Egypt. Egypt, which had the largest military capability of any Arab country, was excluded from the common Arab front even in the event of direct aggression by Israel against another Arab party. Egypt's lack of response to Israel's invasion of Lebanon in the summer of 1982 underscored the practical meaning of this interpretation of part of the Egyptian-Israeli treaty.[7]

Second, the Egyptian-Israeli treaty did not even hint at the right of the Palestinian people to self-determination and in fact stood in the way of its realization. In a joint letter to Carter signed by Sadat and Begin, it was emphasized that "the objective of the negotiations is the establishment of the self-governing authority in the West Bank and Gaza in order to provide full autonomy to the inhabitants" (but not for the territory) and that the Israeli forces would not withdraw from occupied territory but would be redeployed "into specified security locations." To make sure that no doubt would ensue about the final result of self-government for the Palestinians on the West Bank and Gaza, President Carter, on receiving the letter from Begin and Sadat, added an explanatory notation to the copies intended for the United States and Israel: "I have been informed

7. With increasing frequency in 1987 and 1988, Egyptian officials asserted that the treaty with Israel did not prevent Egypt from going to the defense of another Arab state that might be attacked by Israel. This right, it was asserted, was embodied in Article 51 of the United Nations Charter, which recognizes the right of collective self-defense. Some Egyptians even maintained that the United States had agreed with this interpretation of the "priority of obligations" issue at the time of the signing of the treaty (Editor's note).

that the expression 'West Bank' is understood by the Government of Israel to mean 'Judea and Samaria.' "

Third, nowhere in the treaty or the various accompanying documents was there any obligation for Israel, directly or indirectly, to halt the creation of new Jewish settlements in the West Bank or to stop the expansion of those that already existed.

Fourth, "self-government" legitimized the Israeli occupation of the West Bank and Gaza. The concept of self-government also helped advance the Israeli policy of colonizing these two areas, which had been occupied since 1967, since any peace settlement would make it easier for Israel to bring about the economic integration of the West Bank and Gaza with Israel as sources of labor and as an agricultural market.

Fifth, the Egyptian-Israeli treaty indirectly supported a position that allowed for the status of Gaza to be incorrectly interpreted. In Article 2 of the treaty, at the insistence of the Israeli government, it states that "the permanent boundary between Egypt and Israel is the international boundary between Egypt and the former mandated territory of Palestine . . . without prejudice to the issue of the status of the Gaza Strip."

The Egyptian-Israeli treaty also created the conditions for the expansion of a permanent American military presence in the region. Soviet analysts paid particular attention to this fact. As an integral part of the treaty, in the letters to Sadat and Begin dated March 26, 1979, President Carter, on behalf of the United States, undertook to maintain warning stations in the Sinai with the help of American personnel. In these same letters, the United States made a binding commitment to send military personnel to oversee the treaty's implementation should the United Nations be unable to fulfill that mission.

Subsequent events confirmed the initial Soviet assessments of the separate nature of the Egyptian-Israeli treaty. The Camp David deal removed Egypt, the militarily strongest Arab country, and the largest in population and resources, from the struggle to eliminate the results of the Israeli aggression of 1967. Once Sadat had signed the separate Egyptian-Israeli treaty, Israel, as might have been expected, increased its expansionist efforts in all directions.

After the signing of the treaty, decisions were taken by the Knesset that authorized, without any restrictions, the creation of Israeli settlements on the land occupied in 1967. After the signing of the treaty, Israel categorically refused to accept the creation of a Palestinian national state in the West Bank and in Gaza and to conduct negotiations with the PLO, which all Arab countries and most of the other states in the world recognize as the legitimate representative of the Palestinian people.

After Camp David, despite UN resolutions, international law, and world public opinion, the Knesset declared Jerusalem the eternal and indivisible capital of Israel. This action signified the juridical legalization of the annexation of the eastern part of the city, which had been seized by Israel in 1967. After Camp David, Israel carried out a strike against a nuclear reactor not far from Baghdad, Iraq, a reactor that had been built for peaceful purposes. This action flagrantly violated all the norms of international law. After Camp David, the Israeli parliament adopted a resolution extending Israeli jurisdiction to the Golan Heights, which had been seized in 1967. This step signified the de facto annexation of occupied Syrian territory.

Finally, after signing the Egyptian-Israeli treaty, Israel carried out a particularly barbarous attack on Lebanon, which resulted in heavy casualties among the Palestinian and Lebanese populations in that country. It is no wonder that the Soviet Union adopted a negative attitude toward the Camp David process and finds separate solutions completely unacceptable.

AFTER CAMP DAVID

The treaty between Egypt and Israel had become a reality, and the USSR was now compelled to pay attention to the following changes in the region:

—The separate Egyptian-Israeli treaty hardened the position of Israel toward all unsettled problems—Palestinian, Israeli-Jordanian, Israeli-Syrian, and Lebanese—and thereby weakened the possibility of a general and comprehensive settlement.

—The tendencies that developed after the Camp David Accords contained the real threat of an exacerbation and expansion of the Middle East conflict. Consequently, two dangerous new considerations arose: the prospects for the nuclearization of the conflict, now that Israel, according to well-informed opinion, possessed nuclear weapons; and the prospects for the growth of Islamic fundamentalism in the region as a whole, which would be extremely harmful to the possibilities for a political settlement of the Arab-Israeli conflict.

—An intensification of the split in the Arab world also occurred, exacerbated by Egypt's departure from the pan-Arab ranks of opposition to Israeli annexationism and later by the Iran-Iraq war that broke out in September 1980. In such circumstances, the USSR, to preserve its position in the region, was compelled to undertake new measures to counteract the destructive course of Israel that was supported by the United States.

In October 1980, the Soviet Union concluded a Treaty of Friendship and Cooperation with Syria. Since Camp David, Syria had become the focus of strong American and Israeli pressure. Bilateral ties between the USSR and the PDRY, and between the USSR and Libya, continued to develop.

But, as before, the task remained one of achieving a comprehensive and just resolution of the Arab-Israeli conflict and of stabilizing the situation in the Middle East. Such a task became even more urgent in the beginning of the 1980s, when it became especially evident that nonsettlement of the Arab-Israeli dispute encouraged the appearance and ripening of so-called surrogate conflicts in the region.

Soviet experts paid attention to this development for the first time in 1975, when the civil war began in Lebanon. The Soviet Union had already—because of the active Palestinian role in Lebanon—examined the problem of normalizing the situation in Lebanon in the context of the settlement of the Arab-Israeli conflict. Lebanon cannot be stabilized without a resolution of the Palestinian problem, an evaluation that remains true today.

At the beginning of the 1980s, events in the Persian Gulf began to develop along a dangerous path. Of course, the reasons and nature of the Iran-Iraq war do not flow directly from the nonsettlement of the Arab-Israeli conflict. However, if progress had been made in resolving the Arab-Israeli conflict, the Iran-Iraq war might also have been contained and possible paths to a peace settlement might have been pursued. But the armed conflict between Iran and Iraq continued until August 1988, and the potential for other conflict in the Middle East remains.

From the beginning, the Soviet approach to the Iran-Iraq war and to the situation in the Persian Gulf was clear. On the one hand, the USSR has made and continues to make every effort to end the war in the Gulf. On the other hand, it speaks out against any external force being allowed to use the tension in the Persian Gulf for its own interest. Simultaneously, the Soviet Union calls for a recognition of the objective national interests of various states, which include free access to the oil of the Gulf and the guarantee of free shipping.

The well-known Soviet proposals of December 1980 on the guarantee of regional security in the Persian Gulf arose as an expression of such an approach. They were directed at the conclusion of a broad international agreement obligating nations:

—Not to establish foreign military bases or place a nuclear or any other kind of weapon of mass destruction in the Persian Gulf region or on the contiguous islands;

—Not to use, or threaten to use, force against countries of the Persian Gulf and not to interfere in their internal affairs;

—To respect the policy of nonalignment, as established by the states of the Persian Gulf region, and not to involve them in military groupings with the participation of the nuclear powers;

—To respect the sovereign right of the states of this region to their natural resources; and

—Not to create any obstacles or threats to normal commercial exchange or to the use of the sea lines of communication that connect the states of this region with other countries of the world.

Despite the alarming turn of events in the Persian Gulf, the Soviet Union continued to be concerned with the Arab-Israeli conflict. A new, detailed, six-point Soviet proposal on a Middle East settlement was published in September 1982. It recognized the right of all states of the region, including Israel, to a secure and independent existence and development, linked to the principle of the inadmissibility of the seizure of someone else's lands by aggressive means. Again, emphasis was on the need to solve the central problem of the conflict—the Palestinian problem—by satisfying the legal and national rights of the Arab people of Palestine. In these proposals, the Soviet Union called not simply for the end of the state of war between Israel and the Arab states but also for the guaranteeing of peace in the region by the five permanent members of the UN Security Council or by the UN Security Council as a whole. The Soviet Union also proposed a solution to the problem of Jerusalem that took into account the interests of both Arabs and Israelis.

In other words, the Soviet Union was once again calling for a comprehensive settlement. The Soviet proposal could be examined not only as an enumeration of fundamental principles, which formed a compromise "package," but also as an invitation to a dialogue.

This Soviet position could be seen as unrealistic. After all, the aftermath of the Egyptian-Israeli treaty would hardly lead one to be optimistic about a comprehensive settlement. Nevertheless, this interpretation is superficial, since the USSR took into consideration the reassuring change in the position of the Arab countries. This change took shape at a summit conference in September 1982 in Fez, Morocco, when for the first time in history, a collective Arab proposal for a comprehensive settlement with Israel was advanced. As a matter of fact, Israel's right to exist was implicitly recognized (see appendix E). The PLO delegation, arriving in Fez almost immediately after the evacuation of Palestinian fighters from Beirut, completely supported the Fez plan.

One question acquired special significance: how would the United States act in light of this change? An analysis of the 1982 Reagan initiative answers this question (see appendix D). It was published almost simultaneously with the Soviet proposals. Furthermore, according to the testimony of the PLO representative to the United Nations, Zehdi Labib Terzi, the United States had been informed earlier of the Arab plan advanced in Fez. Officially, however, the Fez plan was proposed a week after the Reagan initiative.

President Reagan put forward the following points:

—The rejection of the creation of an independent Palestinian state;

—Self-government for the Palestinians on the West Bank and in Gaza in association with Jordan; and

—A freeze on new Israeli settlements in the West Bank and Gaza. The number of these settlements had already passed one hundred, and no measures were provided to prevent the continuing Israeli acquisition of land in the occupied territories.

Soviet experts concluded that the Reagan initiative intended to take advantage of the situation taking shape after Camp David for the preparation of new separate solutions in the Middle East. Thus the Soviet Union paid special attention to the accompanying line of the Reagan administration on the "globalization of the Middle East conflict."

First of all, the United States accompanied the search for separate solutions with attempts to force the Arabs to turn their back on the Arab-Israeli conflict and to switch their attention to the "Soviet threat." Second, under Reagan, the United States, in a more open manner than under Carter, accompanied its political activity in the Middle East with measures to increase its military presence in the region. The United States organized a way to place its forces permanently in Sinai and brought into Lebanon the so-called "multinational force," the main body of which was the U.S. Marines. A fleet consisting of several tens of ships, including two aircraft carriers, a battleship, and three hundred fighter planes was attached to the battalion of U.S. Marines.

The signing of the U.S.-Israeli strategic cooperation agreement in late 1983 was a benchmark in globalizing the Arab-Israeli conflict. The United States had already concluded a similar agreement with Israel in 1981, but it was suspended after Israel's decision to annex the Syrian Golan Heights. Apparently, the Reagan administration was then trying to downplay its association with Israel, since the administration still had hopes for a successful American policy in the Arab world. By the end of 1983, however, it seemed that the United States was narrowing its attention and focusing on the power struggle in Lebanon and in the region as a whole. The White House also seemed to believe that the international community had acquiesced in the Israeli annexation of the Golan. In any case, the United States no longer saw the annexation as an obstacle to consolidating and legalizing its close military and political ties with Israel. Now more tolerant than ever of Israel's territorial expansion and its refusal to implement UN Resolution 242, the United States was moving even further toward the idea of separate solutions.

In January 1983, I met with Nicolas Veliotes, the assistant secretary of state for near eastern affairs. In response to a question on how the Reagan initiative could be carried out, Veliotes answered that negotiations had to start with Jordan and the other interested parties. Once the negotiations were under way, he said, the logic of the process would make itself felt. At the same time, Veliotes preferred not to say whether Jordan would be invited to join the negotiations under the umbrella of the Camp David Accords. Was the United States trying to promote the creation of self-government for the Palestinians on the West Bank and in Gaza under the control of Israel, or did the Reagan administration have something else in mind? I received the impression that the United States was saying one thing to Israel and another to Jordan. Later discussions with King Hussein confirmed my suspicions. The United States implied to Israel that it was inviting the Jordanians to sit at the negotiating table within the framework of the Camp David process. The Jordanians were told that negotiations would take place outside that framework.

Nevertheless, an American attempt to galvanize the Camp David process by dragging Jordan into it failed. The American initiative to achieve a separate Lebanese-Israeli agreement, which Washington concentrated on after the Reagan initiative failed, met an analogous fate. The Lebanese-Israeli agreement not only sharply encroached on the sovereignty of Lebanon but also turned out to be contrary to the interests of Syria. In the end, that flaw sealed its fate.

Clearly, the trends stemming from the Egyptian-Israeli agreement could not be sustained in the existing conditions. The idea of a comprehensive settlement, which is still being kept alive thanks primarily to Soviet policy and diplomacy, could become the only serious alternative to the Camp David Accords. The Reagan administration, however, following Israel's lead, did not acknowledge this alternative and made no effort to change the Israeli position. One often hears from American officials and specialists that such efforts would be counterproductive. But these a priori judgments do not take into account the serious military and economic dependence of Israel on the United States and its inability to pursue an expansionist course without American backing and assistance.

After the Reagan initiative was rejected by practically all of the participants in the Arab-Israeli conflict, the United States apparently decided not to search for other solutions. Instead it undertook a more careful preliminary study of the Jordanian option embedded in Reagan's ideas. Priority was given to the rapprochement between Hussein and Arafat, which was achieved in a written accord on February 11, 1985 (see appendix F).

The Soviet Union, for historical, political, military, and economic reasons, has always stood for Jordanian-Palestinian rapprochement. The Jordanian and Palestinian leaders have always been well aware of this position. Such a positive attitude toward Jordanian-Palestinian rapprochement did not keep the USSR from taking a negative stand on the February 11, 1985, agreement, precisely because it would be used in the interests of a new separate deal, whatever the intentions of its signatories.

American pressure on the leadership of the PLO—both direct and indirect—aimed at compelling it to renounce the issue of Palestinian self-determination and to virtually abolish itself, again did not produce results. The Palestine National Council annulled its agreement with Jordan after the king suspended cooperation with the PLO in February 1986.

During the mid-1980s, the international climate surrounding the Arab-Israeli conflict gradually developed in favor of convening an international conference. The West European countries, both individually and as members of the European Community, came out in favor of this plan. Syria and the PLO openly favored a conference, a fact that should not be underestimated. This step constituted clear progress on the Arab side.

Palestinian acceptance of the idea of an international conference, for the first time officially approved by the Palestine National Council in Algiers in April 1987, was especially significant (see appendix I). The West tried to ignore this indisputable step forward in the PLO's position and instead focused on the decision of the PLO to break the Amman agreement. This attitude led to the false conclusion that the PLO had rejected a political solution to the Palestinian problem.

The idea of an international conference was even acceptable to some individuals in Israel, such as Shimon Peres, who favored the idea first when he was prime minister and later as foreign minister. The situation in Israel, of course, remained complicated: Prime Minister Yitzhak Shamir and his Likud bloc strongly opposed the convening of a conference aimed at a comprehensive settlement; Peres's position and that of his Maarach (Labor) bloc were not always consistent. Because of these contrasting opinions in Israeli political circles, the situation became fluid.

The idea of an international conference on the Arab-Israeli conflict, however, became widely accepted in the international community. The United Nations General Assembly, as well as the highest forums of the nonaligned movement, favored the conference. The European Community, a group of West European allies of the United States, also favored an international conference. The key opposition came from the United States and Israel. The United States has moderated its approach, albeit slightly. Still, the main purpose of U.S. policy in the Middle East seems to remain the same: preservation of the status quo, perhaps allowing small adjustments, but not allowing for fundamental changes.

Meanwhile, the events that began in December 1987 in the occupied territories, referred to as the "Palestinian uprising," clearly demonstrate the problems of such a policy. The intensity of anti-Israeli protests by Palestinians has not been as strong since 1967. For the first time the Arab inhabitants of Israel came out in support of the demands of the population of the occupied territories for self-determination. At the same time displeasure with the annexationist policy of Israel among the American Jewish community intensified. In these circumstances, the United States suggested new ideas for settling the problem, which seemed to be insufficiently developed. The main principle of addressing the interests of all parties involved in the conflict was not maintained. Many political observers interpreted the new American initiative as motivated by a desire to reduce tension in the occupied territories, to give Israel the opportunity to find a way out of the situation it had created by its illegal, brutal actions.

The American conception of how to resolve the Arab-Israeli conflict is widely regarded as inadequate. The proposed autonomy for Palestinians in the West Bank and in Gaza does not at all mean the settlement of the Palestinian problem. Moreover, the problem cannot be solved without the full participation of the PLO.

Simultaneously, the United States continued strengthening its military presence in the Middle East. In 1987 the United States sent a large number of warships to the Persian Gulf because of the Iran-

Iraq war, and the same was done by some U.S. allies. This deployment had a global pretext. During discussions in September 1987 in Washington with leading members of the State Department and the National Security Council, it was argued that a direct relationship existed between the concentration of more than forty American warships in the Persian Gulf and the Soviet Union's positive response to the request of the Kuwaiti government to provide for the safe passage of Kuwaiti cargoes on Soviet ships. The Soviet-Kuwaiti deal was purely commercial and was carried out between states with long-standing good relations. Moreover, the agreement was reached when the Soviet Union had only a couple of military vessels in the Persian Gulf that were in no way comparable to the number concentrated in the area by the United States and its allies. In addition, the USSR had proposed removing all military ships that did not belong to the states of the Persian Gulf area. One can see that the United States was merely taking advantage of circumstances to build up its military presence in the region, especially because of the strategic stakes there.

CONCLUSION

The process of formulating and conducting the USSR's Middle East policy has been influenced most recently by *perestroika* (restructuring), the democratization of the entire social life of the country, and the widely introduced *glasnost* (openness). These directions were initiated after the April 1985 plenum of the Central Committee of the Communist Party of the Soviet Union and were embodied in the search for new approaches in international affairs—on a global as well as a regional level. The new policies began to have an effect, and prospects for the radical reduction of nuclear arms improved after the Soviet-American treaty on the elimination of intermediate and short-range missiles was signed in December 1987.

However, detailed analysis of those important changes in the USSR, initiated in April 1985, is not my task. The main point is that Soviet Middle East policy is consistent and principled, while at the same time being more flexible and constructive than it has been in the past.

While preserving the definite political priority of relations with Syria, the Soviet Union does not limit its choice of partners in the Middle East by political or, more importantly, ideological criteria (for example, the PDRY). The USSR is tied to Iraq by traditionally friendly relations that by no means signify an identity of views on all questions. Diplomatic relations have been established between the USSR and the United Arab Emirates, Oman, and Qatar. The Soviet Union is prepared to restore and develop ties with Saudi Arabia. The Soviet Union has not only normal but stable and sound relations with the Kingdom of Jordan, Kuwait, the Yemen Arab Republic, Sudan, and others. During the past few years, despite the negative attitude maintained toward the Camp David Accords, the Soviet Union has developed and strengthened ties with Egypt. Therefore the conservative character of these or other Arab regimes is not an obstacle to the USSR's desire to develop full relations with them.

The USSR, keeping in mind that the Palestinian problem is at the heart of the Arab-Israeli conflict, gives great consideration to the role of the PLO—the sole legitimate representative of the Palestinian people, as proven by the difficult and already lengthy history of that organization. Without the resolution of the Palestinian problem, without the recognition of the Palestinian people's legitimate right to self-determination, the Soviet Union believes there can be no durable peace in the Middle East.

The USSR believes that the Palestinian movement and the PLO must remain strong and independent to defend the fundamental interests of the Palestinian people. The Soviet Union has exerted influence in times of discord in the PLO to prevent the development of tendencies leading to a split in that organization, which became universally recognized as the representative of the Palestinian people and won—especially at the end of the 1970s and the beginning of the 1980s—significant international recognition. The USSR emphasizes that the strength of the Palestinian movement depends largely on the settlement of internal disagreements and on united action with Syria, which is on the main battlefront of the struggle against Israeli expansion. Obviously, the discord in the Palestinian movement should in no way be used as a pretext for the rejection of a solution to the Palestinian problem.

The wave of terrorist action that swept the Middle East in the mid-1980s, or that was connected to developments in this region, was not conducive to the creation of favorable conditions for a solution to the Palestinian problem. The Soviet Union repeatedly and clearly expressed a distinctly negative attitude toward acts of international terrorism—both individual and state—and expressed readiness to cooperate in the international struggle against terrorism.

Importantly, the USSR directed its diplomatic activity toward fostering favorable world opinion toward the Palestinians. As a result, with the exception of Israel and the United States, the whole world recognizes the right of the Palestinian people to self-determination.

The position of the USSR toward Israel deserves separate mention. At a reception in the Kremlin in honor of President Hafiz al-Asad of Syria, which took place when he visited Moscow in April 1987, General Secretary Mikhail S. Gorbachev touched on the theme of diplomatic relations between the USSR and Israel, saying, "One cannot consider the absence of such relations as normal" (see appendix H).[8] These relations, however, cannot be restored outside the context of a political settlement in the Middle East. Such a position, naturally, rejects the attempts of some Israeli leaders to make the restoration of diplomatic relations between the two countries a prior condition to the participation of the USSR in the process of Arab-Israeli peacemaking. Besides the inappropriateness of advancing categorical demands on the USSR, the formulation stands everything on its head. Diplomatic relations with Israel were broken not because the USSR committed an aggressive act in the Middle East but because Israel attacked its Arab neighbors in June 1967.

The practical approach of the USSR toward a model or a system for the functioning of an international conference on the Middle East has special significance. The Soviet Union does not support the position of those who want to reduce this conference to a platform on which the USSR and the United States would try to augment their respective positions in the Middle East. To present the USSR's objective in this way is to misunderstand the essence of Soviet Middle East policy. Its main goal is to stabilize the situation in this region and thus contribute to international security.

The idea that the USSR opposes a step-by-step solution of the issues and wants an "all or nothing" approach does not correspond to the facts. The USSR has never opposed step-by-step measures aimed at achieving a comprehensive, just settlement. But a settlement in steps must be part of an overall policy leading to a complete settlement. Once this course is determined, it will be possible to move toward the goal in phases. Thus, for example, the proposals of the Soviet Union on an Arab-Israeli settlement dating from July 29, 1984, envisioned the transfer by Israel of the West Bank and Gaza to the control of the United Nations for a short transitional period.

8. "In a Friendly Atmosphere," *Pravda*, April 25, 1987.

The United States, in contrast, favors partial solutions—not step-by-step, but partial, isolated, separate solutions. In reality, Israel opposes not just one but many Arab countries and the Palestinian movement. Partial, separate acts are proposed not as part of a gradual move toward a comprehensive solution but rather to isolate one Arab party from the others. This objective does not advance the prospects for a settlement. On the contrary, it lessens the prospects, since the side countering Israel becomes weaker as the separate deals are carried out. Simultaneously the pressure on Israel to work toward a full settlement is reduced, and progress toward a comprehensive, just solution is undermined.

It is possible to proceed by combining a comprehensive solution with direct bilateral negotiations between the Arab countries and Israel. One must, as part of this course of action, guarantee real Palestinian representation in the negotiations. Otherwise, a stable settlement cannot be obtained, as events have shown.

Should the principles just mentioned be kept in mind, the following scenario might be possible. After the opening of an international conference in a plenary session attended by all interested parties, as well as the permanent members of the UN Security Council, bilateral commissions would begin to work. In each of these groups, agreements on the issues having a direct relation to the given commission would be worked out. However, certain questions related to a comprehensive settlement would have to be discussed and resolved on a multilateral level. Such a procedure could be productive and eventually lead to positive changes in the situation, which, after forty years of conflict, has begun to look almost insoluble.

Unquestionably, the influence of both the Soviet Union and the United States will be essential for a successful international conference.[9] There is no alternative to this approach. Without it the Middle East will move toward a catastrophe on a scale difficult to predict, bringing new disasters not only to Arabs and Israelis, but to the entire international community as well.

9. The Soviet position was well stated following the meeting of the Politburo on April 14, 1988, when the results of talks in Moscow with the PLO chairman Yasir Arafat were examined. The Politburo reaffirmed that the Arab-Israeli conflict is to be settled "according to the new political thinking, the principle of ensuring a balance between the interests of all parties concerned, and the search for constructive and mutually acceptable solutions to all aspects of the conflict." See "In the Politburo of the CC CPSU," *Pravda*, April 15, 1988.

PART IV
LOOKING AHEAD

HAROLD H. SAUNDERS

Reconstituting the Arab-Israeli Peace Process

THE ARAB-ISRAELI peace process lost momentum after the years of intense activity from 1974 to 1979. Prospects for building new momentum depend partly on understanding what the peace process was. What made it work? What undermined it? To talk in 1988 of "reviving" an approach that has seen no effective agreements in nine years may be unrealistic. To think about how to reconstitute peacemaking on the basis of lessons learned in fifteen years of experience may be wiser.

THE PEACE PROCESS: WHAT IS IT?

The peace process at its best was a series of negotiations embedded in a larger political process that lowered obstacles to agreement and made negotiation possible. Peacemakers set out to change the political environment through specific acts that enabled parties to negotiate alternatives not previously considered negotiable. To make progress, the peacemakers had to build political support for changes in the environment. They had to take concrete steps to erode serious psychological and technical obstacles. Then they had to shape negotiations to consolidate those changes that were achievable at a particular time in the political arena.

Changing the political environment does not suggest a utopian scheme to change human nature. It is part of a real-world effort to move from one situation to another. The politics of Arab-Israeli peacemaking included popular demonstrations and parliamentary decisions, intracabinet maneuver and intergovernment confrontation, press leaks and television interviews, dramatic summits and secret talks, grueling negotiations and triumphant celebrations.

That peacemaking effort produced five Arab-Israeli agreements that changed boundaries, redeployed troops, and led to an exchange of ambassadors.

The peace process was not moved just by a cleverly crafted formula, a procedural maneuver, one interim agreement, or a single political move. It was not advanced just by United Nations Security Council Resolution 242 or 338, nor by Soviet-U.S. cochairmanship of the Geneva Middle East Peace Conference, nor by the Camp David Accords, nor even by Egyptian President Anwar Sadat's dramatic visit to Jerusalem. A single act will not revive it. Momentum will return only gradually as foundations are repaired, new building blocks are laid, and a broadly conceived pattern of political interactions begins to draw the parties into a new effort.

Understandably, by the late 1970s, people thought of the peace process simply as a progression of negotiations. Headlines dramatized the Kissinger shuttles, and front pages displayed pictures of Egyptians and Israelis meeting to negotiate and sign agreements—even a peace treaty in March 1979. The headlines and pictures ignored the plodding work that had laid the political as well as the negotiating foundations over five long years and that had made the peace treaty possible. They rarely highlighted the fact that serious proposals had failed because the ground was not adequately prepared or because those proposals were not diligently pursued with careful attention to the unexciting detail that was not judged newsworthy. Understandably, those who have tried to advance the peace process since have sometimes seen their task as organizing the next negotiation rather than as the larger task of building political foundations.

Experience in the peace process demonstrates that it is more than a negotiation. It is a political process. Formal negotiation is essential, but it is not always the most important instrument. Leaders must constantly move back and forth between the political and the negotiating arenas; they do not move in linear fashion from politics and prenegotiation to negotiation.

At critical points deep divisions have arisen within each party over whether to negotiate at all. Strong feelings have emerged over whether it serves interests to move from the present situation to any other that seems negotiable. Those feelings are best addressed in the political arena. Often the issue of whether to change the situation has been so politically painful and divisive that parties avoid the political issue by arguing over the procedural issues of organizing negotiations.

The peace process at its best presents realistic, substantive alternatives for bodies politic to debate in deciding whether to negotiate. At its most effective, it is a political interaction in which leaders devise steps to meet deeply felt concerns in the political arena that block negotiation. Sadat went to Jerusalem to address Israeli suspicions that no Egyptian leader would make peace with Israel. One aim of the process is to make negotiation possible because negotiation crystallizes new situations and relationships from a changing environment. But negotiation must be an instrument for defining and consolidating change and not an end in itself.

Each of the five Arab-Israeli agreements negotiated in the 1970s involved one or more significant political acts. Presidents Anwar Sadat and Hafiz al-Asad went to war in 1973 to change the political and psychological environment and to draw the Soviet Union and the United States back into the negotiating balance. That act, coupled with the unusual commitment of U.S. prestige by Presidents Richard M. Nixon and Gerald R. Ford through Secretary of State Henry A. Kissinger's shuttle mediation, helped produce the three interim agreements of 1974 and 1975. President Sadat's historic visit to Jerusalem, President Jimmy Carter's invitation to Camp David, President Sadat's and Israeli Prime Minister Menachem Begin's acceptance of that invitation were political acts that changed the political environment for the negotiations that followed. When the Egyptian-Israeli peace treaty negotiations were foundering five months after Camp David, Carter's trip to the Middle East brought the final pieces of the treaty together partly because, as one key Israeli said, it was unwise to "send the President of the United States home with a failure."

Prospects for the peace process in 1988 and beyond will depend on producing the parties' commitment to engage in political interactions that will build relationships in which agreements can be negotiated. The primary question is not whether the parties will agree to one kind of negotiation or another. The agreement to negotiate seriously—for instance, to go to an international conference—may be the vehicle through which a deeper commitment to a settlement is concretely expressed. But the first aim of the peace process is to produce that commitment by understanding and eroding the political and human obstacles to it.

The question is how, and the answer lies in the political arena, not in the negotiating room. The problem is to enable the parties to see the present situation as unacceptable in light of their interests and hopes. The problem is to move them to the point of wanting to change. The problem is to shape realistic opportunities as well as to demonstrate dangers. Prospects for the peace process will depend on the ability of leaders to produce that commitment to change, as well as eventually to build the relationships within which arrangements for change can be negotiated.

This chapter pursues these issues by analyzing the situation in the peace process a decade after Camp David, attempting to define the problem for those who would pursue that process into the next decade, and suggesting elements in a possible approach to the future from the lessons of the past decade.

WHAT RELATIONSHIPS DEFINE THE SITUATION IN 1988?

A serious policy assessment must begin with a probing definition of the situation, identifying the changing interactions and perceptions that have grown around common interests as well as the remaining obstacles and divisions. Given the partial paralysis of the Israeli government and the executive committee of the Palestine Liberation Organization (PLO), that definition will be useful only if it probes the politics behind formal positions. Judgments heard too often are not useful: "Israel will never . . ." or "the PLO will never . . ." An accurate assessment of the prospects for the peace process must be based on an understanding of what political resources the situation does or does not provide.

Did the negotiations at Camp David and the Kissinger shuttles that had paved the way for them fundamentally change relationships among Arabs and Israelis? Some observers are tempted to argue that the peace process fundamentally changed the character of the conflict. Or at least, they say, the situation over these years has changed fundamentally, whatever the cause. Others may ask whether any progress toward peace occurred or whether those five Arab-Israeli agreements between January 1974 and March 1979 were just an elaboration of the armistice agreements of 1949. After all, observers in 1988 see a decade of lost momentum and no agreements since 1979.

My response is twofold: First, the structure and patterns of relationships within bodies politic and across lines have changed in ways that offer opportunities that did not exist before 1967. Second, peacemakers can build on those changes only if they think about how to build working relationships among people who want to negotiate peace. The peace process must be reconstituted as a political process for moving toward some form of reconciliation that can be defined and consolidated through negotiation.

What defines the Arab-Israeli relationship ten years after Camp David, and how much of the change is irreversible? The question of how the situation has changed must be addressed on two levels. One is concrete and easier to observe. The other is more difficult to assess.

The first level is the issue of what relationships the peace process changed. The Egyptian-Israeli peace treaty, for instance, provided for normalization of relations. The elements of that relationship can be analyzed a decade after the treaty. (Even the Israeli-Syrian security interaction on the Golan Heights under the May 1974 disengagement agreement can be assessed as a limited relationship.)

The second level is the issue of what changes in interaction would have happened anyway without the peace process. For instance, the interaction between Israelis and Palestinians after Israel occupied the West Bank and Gaza in 1967 long predated the Egyptian-Israeli treaty and has been far more extensive. The peace process affected the interaction and made it an important subject of discussion in the treaty negotiations and afterwards. But that particular interaction originated and evolved apart from the peace process.

Changes Produced by the Peace Process

The Camp David Accords have been only partially implemented, and formidable obstacles remain in the path to peace. I would argue, however, that the glass is partly full—not completely empty. The argument rests on three main points.

First, the peace process is part of the landscape, and it has produced new arrangements and relationships that now form part of that landscape. Negotiated agreements have changed lines and redeployed troops. The parties involved have concurred on security arrangements, deployed peace observers, agreed on normal relations, and exchanged ambassadors. That was not true in such full measure before 1973—certainly not before 1967. Now it is apparent that negotiated agreements between Israel and its neighbors, changing the interactions between them, are possible. Even a negotiated peace treaty is possible. A decade after Camp David the issue is not whether agreements and changed relationships are possible but what kind of peace process can develop and what further agreements might be reasonable objectives. It is hard to argue that nothing has changed or that change is not possible. We are no longer dealing with peoples who interact only at the points of distant guns.

Second, the strategy of transitional steps established in the peace process and the concepts explicitly recorded in the Camp David Accords have become embedded in practical thinking about how to change relationships and move the peace process forward. That strategy is not universally accepted, but it has been more widely absorbed than is commonly acknowledged.

Experience in the peace process provided a laboratory in which to begin understanding the politics of transition. Those who tried to mediate Arab-Israeli understandings between 1967 and 1973 had attempted to work out a "package deal." The peace process in the mid-1970s demonstrated the practicality of designing politically manageable interim steps that would change the political environment and make it possible to deal with increasingly difficult issues as the parties learned they could deal with lesser ones. Instead of concentrating mainly on final outcomes, much more attention was paid to how to move from here to there. As experience accumulated, it became increasingly clear that the politics of transition had to be right before final arrangements could be negotiated.

The interim agreements of 1974 and 1975 were avowedly devised as building blocks to a larger peace. They enabled negotiators to learn to work with one another; they accustomed bodies politic to seeing agreements signed and kept; they provided for the first steps of Israeli withdrawal from occupied territory and the beginnings of a normal peaceful relationship. The Camp David Accords explicitly provided for a transitional period of five years in the West Bank and Gaza and for three sets of negotiations to change relationships among Israelis, Jordanians, and Palestinians.

Along with the attention given to politically manageable intermediate steps came a recognition that successful intermediate steps depend on assurances that they are not ways of avoiding the issues that must be resolved in a comprehensive settlement. To begin the process, each party wants assurances about the outcome of the negotiation, but smaller steps to build confidence and to change the political environment are necessary before those general assurances can be honestly exchanged.

A fundamental problem in winning support for a step-by-step approach has been mistrust of the other side's intentions. Arabs (and Soviets) are skeptical of "separate deals." They are concerned that Israel will stop serious participation in the process when it gets what it wants (for example, peace with Egypt) and before it is pressed to make concessions it does not want to make (for example, in the Palestinian areas, the Golan Heights, or Jerusalem). Israelis are skeptical of compromise because they believe the Arab side simply wants to improve its position for a later effort to weaken or destroy Israel.

An understanding of the value of interim steps to build confidence in a transitional process has broadened somewhat since 1973, although it continues to be obstructed in some part by the political weakness of leaders in launching the initiatives the peace process requires. Reflection on the experience of the 1970s has led some Israelis, Egyptians, Jordanians, Palestinians, and Americans to understand early stages in the peace process not just as steps in negotiation but also as steps in a political process designed to begin a transition by eroding obstacles to negotiation.

The faltering of the peace process at the end of the 1970s also demonstrated the importance of domestic political environments, both in the countries that are party to the conflict and in those who would mediate such as the United States. After 1980 it became increasingly clear that the Israeli, Palestinian, and Arab nations' bodies politic were deeply divided over the shape of an ultimate Arab-Israeli settlement. The necessity of taking intermediate political steps intended to help reconcile the divisions within each body politic became a recognized element in the peace process. The process is more complex for the nations in the Middle East, but a president of the United States—and perhaps a Soviet general secretary—must consider carefully his own political support for playing a mediator's role.

Third, the Palestinian issue has been returned to the top of the agenda in the Arab-Israeli dispute. The conflict in the middle 1940s had been a conflict between Jewish and Palestinian Arab peoples over their claims to the same land west of the Jordan River. After the partition of Palestine and the armistice agreements between the new state of Israel and neighboring states in 1949, the conflict became a state-to-state conflict. The Arab states administered Arab-controlled areas of Palestine, and the Palestinian people were reduced in most cases to stateless individuals or refugees. The peace process since the mid-1970s has been based on recognition that the legitimate rights of the Palestinian people must be reflected in a final settlement. Some Israelis sharply contest this point, but the Camp David Accords ratified by the Israeli Knesset provided for separate political expression of Israeli and Palestinian identities and for Palestinian participation in negotiations. The issue as defined at Camp David is how to construct arrangements that will enable both peoples to live in the land between the Jordan River and the Mediterranean Sea in security, peace, and dignity to mutual advantage while preserving their separate identities.

Many people see the interim agreements and the Camp David Accords as negative rather than positive developments, and that perspective on the peace process must be addressed. Those who criticize the Camp David Accords argue that the agreements of the 1970s were aberrations resulting mainly from an unusual combination of leaders and circumstances that did not produce fundamental change. The argument rests on three points.

First, the process of the 1970s was an Egyptian-Israeli and not an Arab-Israeli process. Admittedly, moves were made to broaden the process in 1974 with the Israeli-Syrian disengagement agreement in May and with consideration of an Israeli-Jordanian agreement later in 1974. When the process returned to the second Egyptian-Israeli agreement in 1975, according to this argument, it became exclusively tied to the Israeli objective of taking Egypt out of the war and to Sadat's personal interest in ridding Egypt of the conflict to free resources for Egypt's internal problems. The Camp David Accords and the Egyptian-Israeli peace treaty confirmed the limited character of this process.

Second, although the Camp David Accords gave lip service to Palestinian interests, they actually freed the Likud government in Israel to consolidate its hold on the West Bank and Gaza. Evidence shows a major Israeli push to enlarge the program of settlements in the West Bank from the period immediately after Camp David. The United States either acquiesced in that strategy or was powerless to stop Israel from pursuing it. Even some Israeli analysts argue that Israel's occupation cannot be reversed. In the same vein, the Egyptian-Israeli peace freed Israel to invade Lebanon in 1982 to destroy or drive out the PLO.

Third, the United States' attention to interim steps and transitional processes was an admission that no one was able to move Israel against its will. At worst, the U.S. approach was a cynical game of playing with mirrors. At best, it reflected a feeble U.S. effort to keep alive in Israel the forces that favor trading territory for peace. In either case, the U.S. performance since mid-1979 has demonstrated disinterest or political inability to sustain a series of interim steps needed to bring the process to the point of dealing with the difficult issues of an overall peace settlement.

Having participated in the negotiation of the Camp David Accords, I understand the shortcomings of those agreements. Nevertheless, although the situation in 1988 is difficult and disappointing, Arab and Israeli attitudes are different ten years after Camp David from those before 1974. Today discussions focus on how to start a peace process again, not whether such a process is possible. Interested persons are also concentrating on the politics of transition rather than on painting pictures of an ideal solution without regard to how to achieve it. And the Israeli-Palestinian issues would top the agenda in discussions about a just and lasting peace between Israel and neighboring Arab states even if the Palestinian uprising beginning in late 1987 had not taken place.

Changes in the Larger Environment

Most changes in the political environment cannot be attributed primarily to the Camp David process, but many have an intimate relationship with it. Changes in the larger environment especially affect two areas: practical experience in interaction and general changes in perception.

The Egyptian-Israeli experience in interaction cannot be erased. Many Israelis have argued that this state of affairs is a "cold peace" without the fullness of normalized relations that they hoped for. Nevertheless, Egyptians and Israelis have learned to do things together in a matter-of-fact way, much more extensively than before 1973. They now take for granted the peace between their peoples, travel back and forth, and normal diplomatic relations.

As late as 1977, Israeli and U.S. leaders argued with Egypt for a peace that would include aspects of normal international relationships rather than simply an end of the juridical state of belligerency. That debate was resolved by recognizing that a legal document could not create normal feelings of familiarity and harmony between human beings. However, a peace treaty could, and did, create a formal structure in which those relationships could evolve with legal sanction when social and political circumstances seemed appropriate.

Opponents of the peace treaty, both Israeli and Arab, may some day argue that it failed, but they can no longer argue that a treaty of peace is not negotiable. Opponents can argue that Egypt and Israel made a separate peace and failed to build a genuinely comprehensive peace process, but they cannot deny that a peace treaty was negotiated that restored to Egyptian sovereignty all the land Egypt lost in 1967, and produced working relationships between governments and the beginnings of normal contacts between each nation's citizens. No one can argue that negotiation cannot produce results, including Israeli withdrawal from some Arab territory and the establishment of formal diplomatic relations.

A more complex and substantial, yet less dramatic, experience of interaction has taken place between Israelis and Palestinians since 1967 in the West Bank and Gaza. Those sudden steps that removed the barbed wire between Israelis and Palestinians have created an experience for the two peoples in dealing with each other, unmatched even under the Egyptian-Israeli peace treaty.

Although the relationship is between occupier and occupied, two peoples have interacted in ways that pose the Palestine question for both peoples in a new form. Whereas establishing one secular state in Palestine seemed impractical in 1947, by the mid-1980s a one-state solution in Palestine became at least a physical possibility, however unlikely politically. More important, small but significant numbers of thoughtful Israelis and Palestinians have become accustomed to discussing, as a shared problem, how to build a common future in the same land on the basis of mutual respect for separate political identities. A few Palestinians have gone so far as to challenge Israelis to incorporate them into the Israeli body politic with full political rights. Although eventually majorities on each side may choose to live with separate political identities, they will do so having experienced living in direct interaction under one political authority, though in a very unequal relationship.

Israel's interactions with Jordan, Syria, and some other Arab states such as Morocco have been less direct and obvious. In 1974, Syria negotiated a disengagement agreement with Israel. Its military officers sat in an Egyptian-Syrian military working group under UN chairmanship with an Israeli team. The Golan security arrangements have been scrupulously observed. Syria and Israel also carefully managed side-by-side military presences in Lebanon on several occasions, though without direct communication. Syrian officials have stated their readiness to accept Israel behind 1967 boundaries if Israeli troops withdraw from Syrian soil and if a Palestinian state is created. Jordan, in addition to holding unacknowledged meetings over many years with Israeli leaders, signed an agreement on February 11, 1985, with the chairman of the PLO endorsing the principle of exchanging the land Israel had occupied in 1967 for peace and recognition between Israel and a Jordanian-Palestinian confederation (see appendix F). Israeli officials have openly visited Morocco.

Besides these experiences in interaction, certain changes in perception have also taken place. Arab views of the Middle East and Israel's role in it have changed. In 1967 at a summit in Khartoum, Sudan, Arab leaders declared "the main principles to which the Arab states adhere, namely: no peace with Israel, no recognition of Israel, no negotiations with it, and adherence to the rights of the Palestinian people in their country."[1] In contrast, the Arab League summit in Fez, Morocco, on September 9, 1982, declared the

1. See appendix 2 in Harold H. Saunders, *The Other Walls: The Politics of the Arab-Israeli Peace Process* (American Enterprise Institute, 1985), p. 150.

following principles: the withdrawal of Israel from all Arab territories occupied in 1967, including Arab Jerusalem; the dismantling of settlements established by Israel in the Arab territories after 1967; the guarantee of freedom of worship and enjoyment of religious rights for all religions in the holy shrines; the reaffirmation of the Palestinian people's right to self-determination under the leadership of the PLO and the indemnification of all those who do not desire to return; the placement of the West Bank and Gaza Strip under the control of the United Nations for a transitional period not exceeding a few months; the establishment of an independent Palestinian state with Jerusalem as its capital; and Security Council guarantees of peace among all states of the region, including the independent Palestinian state (see appendix E).

In the minds of the Arab leaders gathered in Morocco in 1982, the picture of a just and lasting peace in the Middle East was based on a map that included an Israel within the 1967 borders. While governments may renounce earlier policy statements, the fact remains that the 1982 resolutions were made and can no longer be judged impossible.

Remaining Obstacles

Experience shows that as the peace process comes closer to dealing with the issues in an overall settlement, the divisions within each body politic become deeper and more open. Those divisions constitute and reflect the most difficult obstacles still blocking the path to peace.

Israelis are deeply divided over the future of the Jewish state. Some, particularly in the Likud bloc, want to keep all the land west of the Jordan River—Eretz Israel—and with the passage of time may have made it all but impossible for Israel to relinquish control. Others, particularly in the Labor alignment, argue that maintaining control will destroy the Jewish character of the state. Many of them see Israel well down the road to creating a permanent 40 percent Arab minority now and an eventual Arab majority under Israeli control—either to remain hostile second-class citizens or to hold pivotal power if given the vote. In that context a few Palestinians have fueled the debate by inviting annexation, and they have engaged in open protest to provoke Israeli debate about the consequences for Israel of perpetual occupation. Among those Israelis who would move the peace process forward must be some individuals capable of fashioning a pragmatic compromise built on security interests on which most Israelis can agree and on recognition that Israel can only prosper as a Jewish state if it does not try to exercise absolute sovereignty over all the land west of the Jordan River.

Palestinians are divided along at least two major fault lines. A few extremists flatly reject negotiating peace with Israel, even if they could win recognition of a Palestinian state. But the different perspectives held by the 1.3 million Palestinians living under Israeli occupation and the 2.0 million living outside their homeland are much more significant. Neither group feels that the other can understand or represent its interests. Palestinians living under occupation feel that PLO leaders share neither their sense of urgency about the tightening Israeli grip on the land the Palestinians would like to call their state nor their understanding of the practicalities of moving the Israeli body politic to a decision on the Palestinian question. The Palestinians living in exile fear that those still living in historic Palestine in the West Bank and Gaza have given up the cause of those who lost their homes in 1948. The Palestinian movement has institutions that could provide the forum for working out a common Palestinian position from which to move toward a settlement with Israel. This effort, too, must be taken into account in reconstituting the peace process.

Each Arab state has its own interests that limit the way in which the peace process might be reconstituted. Jordan cannot, although many Israelis believe it can, negotiate on behalf of the Palestinians at the moment when significant concessions will be required. At the same time, Jordan for the sake of preserving the Hashemite monarchy wants to resolve the Palestinian problem west—not east—of the Jordan River but still retain an influence in the formative stages of any Palestinian political entity. Syria also feels the need, for its own protection, to have a voice in the nature of a Palestinian solution.

In sum, while gulfs remain wide and deep, patterns of interaction have grown, creating relationships among Israelis, Egyptians, Jordanians, and Palestinians quite different from those existing before 1973. Each party has experienced interaction—though sometimes at a distance—with the other policymaking communities. Each party is far more sensitive to issues that might move or inhibit other policymakers. Elements in each body politic recognize that, on issues of a peace settlement, they may share more interests with like-minded elements in another body politic than they do with some groups in their own. Publicly unspoken likemindedness—the substance of political alliances—may exist and may have been privately tested across lines in ways generally unthinkable before the post-1973 peace process began. Significant obstacles may over time make this observation academic, but as one assesses what leaders have to work with in the second decade after Camp David, one cannot dismiss the experience in a peace process, the experiences in interaction, and the changes in perception that have evolved. At the same time, not one of the bodies politic centrally involved—Israel, the Palestinian movement, key Arab states as a group—is ready to negotiate. Not one has yet decided to initiate action to change the situation by trying to build relationships of peace that could be captured in negotiation.

ALTERNATIVES FOR THE NEXT DECADE

Further movement in the peace process will depend first on arriving in the political arena at a common definition of the problem. For instance, in late 1973 and early 1974 Kissinger and Sadat decided that the problem was to overcome inertia and impasse by finding a formulation to justify starting some movement. That formulation in the wake of war was "disengagement of forces." It was not an immediate effort to negotiate an overall settlement. Once the problem was defined in that limited way, attention could turn to specific agreements. Discussing how to organize a negotiation—in 1988, an international conference—may prove to be the most useful vehicle for defining the problem in the Arab and Israeli communities, but the first issue is defining the problem in the political arena and not starting a negotiation.

To stimulate public debate over the definition of the problem is more a political than a diplomatic challenge, although the diplomats' substantive contribution is essential. Negotiators will stall if the governments and councils instructing them are so divided over what they see as the purpose of the negotiation that they cannot provide coherent instructions. Producing a common view of the problem is the work of politicians, not negotiators. Establishing a common view of a problem may even include the notion that a body politic is divided but that consensus is needed on how to proceed without being able to agree on ultimate solutions.

The debate that will determine prospects for the peace process includes fundamental questions about how peoples see their interests in relation to a resolution of the conflict. Each body politic needs to define the problem. In doing so, leaders on each side must attend to whether their definition moves away from the other side's definition or provides a basis for building common ground. Then some sort of prenegotiation dialogue among the parties will need to establish a common picture of the problem for negotiators to tackle together. The following questions are posed to help focus the debate.

Is Partition the Governing Concept for a Settlement?

Can each body politic agree on partition as the governing concept for a settlement between the Israeli and Palestinian peoples in the land between the Jordan River and the Mediterranean Sea? When the Palestine question came before the United Nations in 1947, the General Assembly approved the partition of Palestine and the establishment of separate Arab and Jewish states. The essence of a fair settlement remains practical recognition of both peoples' right to political self-expression of their identities. Forty years after the partition vote, the issue is whether or in what form partition is still workable.

The United States has consistently recognized that Palestine is the common homeland of the Jewish and Palestinian peoples and that each people has a right to establish its own homeland there. The United States has supported the principle of a just partition since 1947 through United Nations Security Council Resolutions 242 (1967) and 338 (1973), the interim agreements of 1974 and 1975, the Camp David Accords, and President Reagan's speech of September 1, 1982. Other major powers, including the Soviet Union, have held comparable positions.

The center of gravity in official Arab positions seems to have moved from rejection of partition in 1947 to acceptance of a map of the Middle East that includes an Israel defined by the 1949–67 armistice lines, alongside an independent Palestinian state bounded by those lines and the Jordan River, or a Palestinian state confederated with Jordan. These officials recognize that Israel is an accomplished fact and that Palestine is divided. Whether that recognition includes a lasting willingness to live and let live with Israel, or whether the Arabs would negotiate a settlement with the mental reservation of biding their time to threaten Israel later, remains a key issue. Extremists, at least, remain opposed to partition. But it seems likely that leaders in the Arab mainstream could consolidate political acceptance of partition.

Ironically, as the Arab position has moved toward accepting partition, a growing number of Israelis since 1967 and especially since 1977 seem to have moved away from partition. By mid-1987—the twentieth anniversary of Israel's control over the West Bank and Gaza—a generation of Israelis was coming to maturity knowing only greater Israel. That generation had spent formative years under an Israeli government committed to perpetuating Israeli control over all those lands. In addition, Israel's elaborate settlements and infrastructure in the West Bank and Gaza may have made total Israeli withdrawal and a clean-cut partition politically impossible. Other Israeli leaders still argue that keeping all that land, which would ensure Israel of at least a 40 percent Arab minority, would undermine the Jewish character of Israel. A critical question is how Israelis can resolve this difference.

The political question is whether partition is the issue around which to organize negotiations. Peacemakers must determine whether the formula in Resolution 242—exchanging land Israel occupied in 1967 for peace and security—is still realistic. Do important elements within the Israeli state and the Palestinian movement believe that some form of partition is possible and would serve their interests?

The question does not have to be answered definitively in the political arena before the peace process can resume. But reconstituting the peace process requires addressing in some way the internal differences on this fundamental issue. At Camp David negotiators agreed on a transitional period. They agreed to keep open the basic question of partition while taking steps to give the Palestinians an opportunity to develop institutions that would reflect a political expression of their identity. Currently, if that opportunity were not foreclosed, a transitional process could be designed that would affect the debate on partition. The problem is to begin a process consciously designed to keep the door open.

Are There Alternatives to Partition?

If partition were no longer a viable concept, what serious alternatives would be available?

The binational secular state with individual political, civil, and religious rights protected constitutes one alternative. Some Israelis argue today that Israel's penetration of all the land west of the Jordan River has passed the point of no return. The Israeli-Palestinian relationship has become an internal Israeli problem, they believe, and incorporating a nearly 40 percent Arab minority into the existing state without separate arrangements will transform that state over time. With the long-term historical process as their vision, a few Palestinians have now told the Israelis in effect: "If you don't want us to exist in a separate state of our own, annex us with full rights of citizenship in the Israeli state that exists. What is intolerable is for us to be left stateless, living under authority which we have no voice in shaping." These Palestinians think that engaging in the

Israeli political system may offer the most realistic road to a binational state, but only a small minority shares the view. Most Israelis oppose it.

Menachem Begin's proposal to offer the Palestinians administrative autonomy in the West Bank and Gaza under overall Israeli control, if not sovereignty, reflects another possible arrangement. In Begin's mind, autonomy is a final status, not a transitional one for the Palestinians. Many Palestinians would seriously consider a transitional autonomy if assured of greater freedom after a transitional period, but they would reject it as a cover for perpetual Israeli control.

A variation of this alternative remains a live one not because it is likely to occur through a negotiated agreement in the near future but for two other reasons. First, some Israelis have seriously proposed moving unilaterally to place more responsibility in the hands of West Bank and Gaza officials. Second, such changes may eventually evolve into a new regime, whether transitional or long-term, without negotiation. Moves in this direction could be taken in the context of the commitment to work out an overall long-term relationship. Some have suggested looking at the Swiss cantonal arrangement for possible parallels.

This variation would start from a premise such as the following. It is not possible now to see the basis for partition, but continuing Israeli military occupation in its present form is untenable. Change is necessary, but it probably cannot be negotiated now with any representative group of Palestinians. Consequently, the only viable course is to take one step to change the relationship between Israel and the West Bank and Gaza Palestinians, to let both communities absorb and consolidate the new situation, and then to consider what further steps, if any, might be possible or desirable. The political character of this approach would vary according to whether it seemed to reflect Israeli determination to perpetuate Israeli control or an Israeli commitment to produce separate political identities over time. Where the process ended would depend heavily on the purpose behind the design of individual steps.

Making Partition Acceptable

If partition is still a viable, or at least a preferred principle for governing a settlement, what ideas might make it a workable starting point for moving toward political expression of separate identities? Most Arabs believe that an acceptable partition means the creation of an independent Palestinian state. They want to know what might make that solution politically manageable over time in Israel. The Israelis think a solution, if any, must be found through arrangements other than a separate Palestinian state. Two ideas have received increasing attention during the past decade.

QUALIFIED TERRITORIAL PARTITION. The original principle was clear-cut territorial partition, but establishing agreement on a partition line has not been possible. With Israeli land acquisition and settlements in the territories occupied in 1967 and with concern in Israel for "defensible" borders, there seems to be no consensus in Israel, even among those who favor some withdrawal, about where the partition line might be. As I recall Moshe Dayan in effect telling Egyptians and Americans in 1978 in a meeting just before Camp David: "I've never been able to draw a line through the West Bank that would be secure for Israel and politically acceptable to the Arabs." On the Arab side, most of those who would make peace with Israel call for 1967 borders with reciprocal negotiated changes. The question has arisen whether lines difficult for either side to accept could be made more acceptable by special arrangements for dealing with security apart from borders and for permitting individuals to live, work, and do business on each other's territory.

FUNCTIONAL PARTITION. Because of the difficulty of defining a defensible and politically acceptable border, some have turned to the concept of functional partition. As I recall, Dayan continued in effect: "Therefore we need to develop a relationship between Jews and Arabs in the West Bank [others might say "in Palestine"] the likes of which humankind has never before devised." This plan would mean less attention to exclusive sovereignties and more to political expressions of identities, agreed division of labor and rights to provide security, justice, education, self-government, and administrative and logistical services.

A further notion attached to territorial partition centers on a settlement between Israel and Jordan, with a related agreement for separate status of the Palestinian areas and their confederation with Jordan. Some adherents of this so-called "Jordan option" seem to gloss over different understandings of this approach in Israel and Jordan. Some Israelis speak of the arrangement as a way of avoiding the creation of a Palestinian state. Though Jordan and the Palestinians have not sorted out their exact relationship, they agree that the Palestinians will exercise their right of self-determination, presumably producing a Palestinian state, which will then form a confederation with Jordan. Even in the eyes of those Israelis who would accept partition, that partition is made acceptable only if the Palestinian party to the partition is not accorded equal status with Israel.

One variation of this last view is the concept of shared Israeli-Jordanian sovereignty over the West Bank and Gaza. This is predominantly an Israeli-held idea. It assumes an Israeli-Jordanian condominium in which those two governments would provide for security and together define powers and responsibilities to be exercised by a Palestinian-run government. A more creative variation is the vision of a confederal relationship including Israelis, Palestinians, and Jordanians. This would assume Palestinians acting as partners in their own name to negotiate a complex of understandings in various areas of interaction that would alleviate concerns on all sides about inappropriate infringements on political self-expression.

Virtually all of this discussion poses a fundamental question: Are we who are involved in the peace process seeking these devices to avoid the fundamental issue of a settlement between two peoples, or are we genuinely seeking practical arrangements to enable two peoples to begin developing a relationship for sharing the same area with political expression of separate identities? Much of the talk about qualified territorial partition or functional partition avoids the fact that some lines of geographical and jurisdictional partition would have to be agreed on eventually. Most Arabs have ignored the fact that the Camp David Accords assumed that new arrangements for Palestinian self-government would begin in an area defined as that under Israeli military government—the 1949–67 lines with special arrangements in East Jerusalem and discussion of the status of Israeli settlements, military areas, and state lands.

Much of the talk seems to avoid the central issue of removing obstacles to mutual recognition between the two peoples, which could make questions of practical partition easier to deal with. Some of the talk on the Arab side about partition along the 1949–67 lines avoids questions of how to move an Israel that entrenched itself in the years when Arabs rejected partition. Even those Israelis who accept partition are unwilling to think actively about how they could build political support for negotiating with a Palestinian delegation that will inevitably depend for its authority on the PLO.

In short, the next problem may be not so much to devise the precise formula for a solution as to encourage a commitment to find a formula. It may not be possible to devise a workable formula for partition in some form as long as the political environment is hostile to changing the situation at all to move toward a peace agreement. The problem may be how to design a scenario of political acts leading toward a commitment to reconciliation rather than organizing a negotiation around a formula that bodies politic are still too paralyzed to accept. An Israeli-Jordanian-Palestinian commitment to find a way to peace based on political expression of separate identities could open the door to arranging transitional steps.

Agreeing on Arab Authority in the Partitioned Land

Whatever form a partition might take, to what extent do present realities reflect Arab—and in special ways Palestinian—consensus about what will constitute the Arab authority in the partitioned land?

A settlement between Israel and its Arab neighbors is central to resolution of the conflict. But basic to negotiating that settlement is a supportive political environment for Arab negotiators. Such an environment would include understandings on three other tracks: a Palestinian-Palestinian negotiation on which Palestinians will govern in the Arab portion of a partitioned land west of the Jordan River and how Palestinians not living in that section will relate to political authority there; a Palestinian-Jordanian negotiation to determine the exact relationship between those two Arab authorities; and a Palestinian-Jordanian-Syrian understanding that meets Syria's requirements for influence.

Just as there must be a political strategy for building majority Israeli support for movement, there must be agreement on the Arab—particularly the Palestinian—side on mechanisms for deciding what Arab authority would govern in the land from which Israel would withdraw. In 1978 after Camp David, the United States was charged with trying to drive a wedge through the Palestinian movement by setting up Palestinian leadership in the West Bank and Gaza to the exclusion of the PLO and the Palestinian diaspora. At that time, we discussed such devices as a Palestinian constituent assembly to define the relationships between the diaspora and those living in the Palestinian territories. Other mechanisms would be available.

Given the complexities of these inter-Arab relationships, I cannot envision one negotiation that would settle all the issues. I could envision—at least as a useful framework for planning—trying to construct a political scenario that would take all these dimensions into account, help focus dialogue, and lead to first steps that might begin to change the political environment constructively.

Meeting the Needs of Minority Populations

If the land west of the Jordan River were partitioned territorially, how could the particular needs of minority populations be met for living, working, owning, or renting property in each other's territory? Some Israelis would say their basic requirement in the West Bank is the right of access. Some Palestinians, mindful of their longstanding claim of a "right of return," have asserted a reciprocal right in Israel. Informal practices that accomplish some of those objectives in these areas are already part of the new realities. Israeli settlers live in the West Bank and Gaza, and Palestinian laborers work daily in Israel, although they do not yet have the right to establish themselves there formally.

Thus the range of overlapping political, economic, and social relationships involving Israel, Jordan, and the Palestinians has prompted the discussion of a confederal relationship of some sort among them under an agreement codifying the ways in which the three parties interact. This agreement would define judicial protection and rights for each nationality in each territory, as well as the rules of the interaction. Those rules could develop through stages of transition.

Again, the questions are the following: To what extent must these new relationships be formally negotiated and packaged? To what extent could they evolve as part of a larger political scenario? If evolution seems more likely, then the problem is not first to arrange a negotiation but to design a series of specific steps that would gradually produce a new situation.

Finding Common Interests among the Middle East Communities

If partition remains a preferred principle for governing a settlement, what communities in each body politic—Israeli, Jordanian, Palestinian, Syrian—would support or oppose such an approach to a settlement? What is the nature of common interests and complementary needs shared by these communities?

Each of the two central communities—the Israelis and the Palestinians—is deeply divided within itself over visions of its future. Forming a consensus on any steps in either body politic may not be possible without changes in the political environment. In some cases there is more genuine dialogue between some Israelis and some Palestinians than between some Israelis and other Israelis or some Palestinians and other Palestinians. Identifying steps that these "coalitions" favor, and building political support for them, will be more important in reconstituting the peace process than determining the modalities for an international conference.

Jerusalem

The new realities in Jerusalem since 1967 have caused people to see it as an issue on which no movement is possible, but they have also caused some extensive thinking about how to structure a governing authority that reflects the city's ethnic and cultural diversity. A borough system, a representative city council, a relationship of Arab inhabitants with a neighboring Palestinian authority are just a few of the ideas that have been discussed. In 1987, a few Palestinians discussed the strategy of running in elections for seats on the municipal council. Individual steps could contribute to incremental change, but it has long seemed to me likely that new relationships in Jerusalem would be formalized only when new relationships between Israelis and Palestinians around the city were agreed.

Reviewing the Choices

To recapitulate, those who attempt to reconstitute the peace process in the second decade after Camp David will have to choose between at least the following two definitions of the problem, first in the political arena and then in negotiations:

—A common definition holds that the problem is to negotiate a comprehensive peace agreement that exchanges mutual peace and security for recognition of the 1949–67 borders and creation of a Palestinian state.

—A broader definition might hold that the problem is to generate a commitment to a negotiated settlement and to arrange transitional steps to new practical relationships among Israelis, Jordanians, and Palestinians. The goal should be to promote political self-expression of the three separate identities. The vehicle is a scenario of steps to change the political environment. At an appropriate time, the terms of reference for negotiation of a final peace may be detailed. The steps taken may focus on organizing some form of negotiation such as an international conference, but their main purpose is to ensure the political basis for negotiation. Ten years after Camp David, I believe the realistic definition is the broader one.

A SCENARIO FOR RECONSTITUTING THE PEACE PROCESS

A comprehensive scenario of political as well as preparatory negotiating steps will be a central element in reconstituting the peace process. Political steps will affect prospects for negotiation, and preparations for negotiation affect the political environment. This sounds obvious, but those trying to advance the peace process have not always closely attended to the politics of the process; instead, they have concentrated on trying to begin negotiations.

Judgments about prospects for the peace process do not depend on judgments about whether a formal negotiation can begin. Instead, judgments must be made about whether a broad range of steps can be taken to change the political environment to compel and sustain a negotiated peace. A device to be used in orchestrating a combination of interacting steps is what I call a "political scenario." Most of the "plans" that dot the Arab-Israeli landscape have focused on negotiations and outcomes. Without ignoring their importance, I am concerned in addition with the politics of producing a *commitment* to negotiate agreement.

A comprehensive scenario of political steps serves three purposes. First, as an analytical tool, it identifies the full range of deep-rooted political obstacles to progress and matches those obstacles with acts that might erode them. Second, a scenario specifies a time sequence for actions by each party and responses by other parties that can become mutually reinforcing. For example, one can construct a sequence showing that no party can move immediately to a desired outcome. However, if one party were to take a step to which a second party responded and then the first party responded with the third step, it might be possible to move a step at a time toward the desired destination. It is the dynamic—almost drama-like—quality of the political process of continuous interaction that distinguishes the scenario from a plan for negotiation and agreement. Third, once a scenario begins to take shape, a mediating party can use it in talking with each of the parties and then for establishing informally their agreement to play their respective roles.

This process of scenario-building sounds more technical than it is. During the mediations of the 1970s, the United States as the third party talked through the parties' views on the shape of an outcome for a particular negotiation and the steps that might help get them there. Rarely was this scenario written except for in-house planning and working purposes. That in-house working paper simply served as a starting point for conversations with all parties until everyone was talking about the same goal and the same way of proceeding. Until each party was working from comparable interest in negotiating, from similar pictures of the problem and alternative solutions, and from the same general scenario for proceeding, attempts to negotiate formally were futile.

The purpose of introducing the idea of a scenario at this point is to delineate the full range of elements that in some combination will determine prospects for the peace process. What follows describes choices to be made among the elements that would need to be considered in a first approach to a scenario. They are presented here not as a specific plan of action but as a suggestion from the experience of the 1970s of the breadth of the approach—the scenario—that is necessary for improving prospects for reconstituting the peace process in the second decade after Camp David.

Elements of a comprehensive scenario for reconstituting the peace process might be organized for discussion under the following six headings. These headings do not necessarily represent stages or steps. They are areas of activity. Some actions may have to be taken in sequence; others may have to proceed simultaneously on separate tracks. As they come together they could form a scenario for reshaping the political environment—not just a strategy for structuring a negotiation.

Exploratory Exchanges

In periods of impasse, exploratory discussions about a reconstituted peace process might be conducted in a range of private, quasi-official, or official groups. Many nonofficial exchanges now take place informally between Israelis and Palestinians in the West Bank and Gaza and, less frequently, between Israelis and Jordanians. Organized meetings also take place in international settings with third parties present.

If they are to contribute to influencing the political environment, these exchanges need focus. Dialogue that is relevant to policy is distinguished from casual discussion by its systematic purpose of exploring real interests and what specific steps would help lower the obstacles to progress toward peace. The increased human contact permits each side to convey to the other an air of seriousness about the purposes of the dialogue, but its relevance to policy depends on systematic probing for interests, needs, hopes, fears, pictures of the problem, and alternatives. Sometimes it seems easier to talk about the deep-rooted obstacles and needs in the informal setting of nonofficial dialogue, although there is no objective reason why officials could not open up with each other.

Besides completely nonofficial dialogues, governments could designate a nonofficial group to explore ideas. Such a group would not have the authority to negotiate but might meet with the understanding that the results of the dialogue could be conveyed to governments in the hope that ideas could then be used for quiet official dialogue.

Besides informal meetings and those used in some way to inform governments, officials can arrange secret or open meetings among themselves. The more explicit the purpose of generating new approaches, the closer the informal dialogue comes to engaging governments.

Laying Political Foundations

At some point, the exploratory exchange of ideas could lead to a growing belief among the parties that a serious effort to negotiate a settlement is a real possibility. One of the highest obstacles to negotiation has been the sense on each side that the other is not serious about wanting to reach a settlement. In 1979 and 1980 the Egyptians advanced a long list of measures that Israel could take by itself in the West Bank and Gaza to signal readiness to begin a change in the status of the occupied territories. Similar steps, such as an informal moratorium on violence by the Palestinian side, would signal a Palestinian seriousness about trying to work out a settlement. If some of these steps could be taken by governments as a result of quiet exploratory exchanges, signals could be sent through the same channels that steps being taken were intended to lay the groundwork for an expansion of the dialogue in a more open forum. One purpose of exploratory dialogue would be to identify those steps that would have the most meaning to the people involved.

As unilateral steps are identified and carried out in a pattern intended to produce action and response, further action and further response becomes possible. The shared act of discussing steps and responses begins a direct engagement in a common attempt to change the political environment. As this engagement is established, the public begins to pay attention to the emerging pattern.

Stimulating Domestic Political Debate

Conscious effort to shape constructive debate within each body politic on the need for negotiations and change must occur. The discussion must attend to fundamental interests and how the passage of time affects them. The steps taken to lay the political foundation for negotiation can also be used to direct the domestic debate. For peacemakers the most difficult challenge may be to focus on the following questions: How can the Israeli body politic be persuaded to decide to negotiate changes that could lead to less than complete Israeli control over the West Bank and Gaza? How can Israel be convinced to agree to a settlement recognizing the Palestinians as equally entitled to a homeland in the land west of the Jordan River? And how can the Palestinians, especially those outside the West Bank and Gaza, be persuaded that they could gain something worthwhile from negotiating a settlement with Israel.

Building Political Relationships for Negotiation

As a scenario of foundation-laying steps and public debate proceeds, significant political moves can be made to bring about formal negotiations. These would include statements about readiness for peace; sharing a common homeland; willingness to negotiate on the basis of mutual recognition; recognition of each other's losses, dignity, and need for security; and even readiness to meet in a particular setting for negotiation. Such steps would begin to signal that political leaders are ready to move beyond administrative steps and to test support or build support in the political arena for moving toward a negotiated settlement. It is one thing to talk about negotiation; it requires political steps of a more serious nature to commit a body politic to negotiation.

As efforts to influence attitudes in the political arena proceed, it becomes quickly apparent that words and acts in one body politic begin to influence attitudes in the other. At first, unspoken relationships begin to form among those on both sides who want to move toward negotiation. As those relationships become more explicit, they begin to form the political context in which specific problems can be tackled through formal negotiation.

Precipitating Acts

Eventually, persons will decide on actions that will have the capacity to precipitate change. Sadat's visit to Jerusalem in 1977 or Carter's invitation to Camp David are examples, though precipitating acts need not have the same high drama as those did.

One potential precipitating act, discussed again in the middle 1980s, would be a unilateral Israeli move to open the door in the

West Bank and Gaza for greater Palestinian responsibility for self-government. This step, referred to as "unilateral autonomy," offers a good example of how a precipitating act might have successful or unsuccessful results. If taken in a vacuum, steps toward greater Palestinian self-government under Israeli occupation could be rejected by Palestinians. They could see the effort to move toward autonomy as a final consolidation of Israeli control in the West Bank and Gaza. Such steps taken in the context of detailed discussion that includes commitment to move toward negotiation of further steps could provide assurance of an Israeli commitment to change the situation. Done in that context, unilateral Israeli steps could help catalyze a move toward negotiation.

Similarly, the Palestinian movement has often stated its readiness to move toward negotiation on the basis of peaceful coexistence with Israel, but Israelis have dismissed such statements because they were often equivocal and outside a political context that would pave the way for negotiations. A clear-cut unequivocal Palestinian statement, beamed into Israel in a way that could not be ignored, coupled with a moratorium on violence, could have the impact of a precipitating act.

Not all such acts are peaceful. The purpose of precipitating acts is to change attitudes and cause public debate in ways that lead toward negotiation. Conceivably, precipitating acts could increase the pain of the present situation. The 1973 war served that purpose. An unanswered question at this point is whether the Palestinian uprising beginning in late 1987 might eventually have the same impact.

In the perspective of the next decade, the Palestinian uprising of 1987–88 may seem at a minimum to have refocused attention on the separate identities of the two peoples and on the need to recognize lines between them before negotiation is possible. Even if the uprising is suppressed, it will have changed the relationship between Israelis and Palestinians in those territories and underscored the need to find a solution that recognizes separate identities. A more immediate consequence might result from heightened violence or a major nonviolent campaign in the West Bank and Gaza. For instance, if escalating clashes caused harsher Israeli repression or a dramatic act of retaliation by Israeli settlers, a bloodbath could precipitate sharp reaction in Israel and around the world. Prompt negotiation would then be demanded. The purpose of a political scenario would be to produce acceptance of the present level of confrontation as enough and to avoid further violence on the way to negotiation, but it may be that nothing can happen without more dramatic clashes.

Preparing Negotiation

When a precipitating political act is taken, the mediators and negotiators must have woven into the political scenario those steps that would follow from it leading toward the negotiating room. For instance, important political steps to signify mutual recognition and acceptance would be critical in a scenario to change public attitudes. An invitation from an Israeli official to Palestinian leaders in the West Bank and Gaza to discuss changing Israeli occupation practices matched with a suspension of Palestinian demonstrations could be first practical steps. A sequence of such steps might lead to public statements about the purposes of the meetings that could contain formulations that could eventually be used in setting the stage for negotiations.

A sense of the choices about strategy in the negotiation is also important in preparing for negotiations. For instance, if a step-by-step approach seems to offer the best prospect, can simultaneous political steps be taken to ensure that the long-term objective of an overall settlement remains a commitment on all sides?

The following choices about the international context for negotiation are open to peacemakers in their quest to move toward negotiation:

—A choice open to any party is to attempt a direct negotiation, presumably secret, to try to reach a settlement with one other participant bilaterally and without any broader international involvement. Each party may take the negotiation as far as is politically feasible. Experience suggests that this choice may help to prepare for later understanding. At some point, however, the negotiation must be put into a larger political context.

—A second approach is to continue mediation by one major power—the role the United States served in the 1970s—and to direct that effort at a limited sphere of negotiation. In the 1970s, for instance, most mediation focused on the Egyptian-Israeli front. In the mid-1980s a fundamental question facing the parties has been whether to try to concentrate on an Israeli-Jordanian-Palestinian agreement, depending primarily on U.S. mediation and leaving both the Soviet Union and Syria on the sidelines pending a following round of negotiation between Israel and Syria.

—A third option is to conceive of a reconstituted peace process from the outset as being developed and conducted in a broad regional and international political setting. That approach does not necessarily mean that specific negotiations cannot take place in separate arenas. It does mean that the preparations would include broad understanding that those separate negotiations will take place and that, presumably, at some point there will be provision for incorporating their results into a larger settlement.

In the Middle East, this question has important implications for building a political base both in Israel and in the Arab world. In Israel, opponents of negotiation use Soviet and Syrian involvement as an argument against a broad international effort, although that stance has been changing with the gradual rapprochement between Israel and the Soviet Union. The fundamental question always asked of the Arabs is, can there be a peace process without Syria?

In the larger international environment, the question is whether the Soviet Union and the United States can develop ways of working in parallel, if not jointly. How the Soviet Union and the United States conduct their own relationship will affect their ability to play a third-party role in the Arab-Israeli peace process either individually or together.

In discussing the elements that must be an integral part of a possible scenario I am not prescribing an action plan. That is a task for those in authority. I am saying that the prospects for the Arab-Israeli peace process beyond the tenth anniversary of the Camp David Accords depend on the breadth with which the peace process is reconstituted.

CONCLUSION

The following propositions summarize my analysis:

—The peace process at its best has been a negotiating process embedded in a political process. The fundamental challenge in reconstituting the peace process is not mainly how to organize an international conference or some other form of negotiation. The challenge is to generate a political process that can crystallize, impel, and sustain a commitment to negotiate a settlement. The talk about where, how, and what to negotiate can be an operational focus for debate, but organizing a negotiation without creating a supportive political environment will not give the peace process prolonged new life. First, the commitment to negotiate realistically must be produced.

—A political process involves the interaction of policy-influencing communities on both sides of several relationships. The words and acts of Israelis, Palestinians, and other Arabs influence constituencies on the other side and help shape the political environment in which policymakers act. How these communities interact influences domestic political processes inside each community. A reconstituted peace process will have to be built around a scenario of political acts that will shape that interaction to constitute a new relationship.

—Whatever else may or may not have happened in the peace process since the 1973 war, interaction among Israeli, Egyptian, Palestinian, and Jordanian communities is far more complex and intense in 1988 than in 1973. Relationships have formed across community lines from which new relationships could be built. One aim of the political process is to strengthen those relationships and to make them, in effect, informal coalitions to advance the peace process. Other relationships, such as the interaction between Israeli settlers and Palestinians in the West Bank and Gaza, are potentially destructive and would need to be limited.

—A definition of the problem in light of experience and the situation on the ground suggests that, more than ever, prospects for the peace process will depend first on ability to generate a commitment to a transitional political process for moving from the present situation to a peaceful alternative. That will depend, in part, on strengthening implicit relationships across community lines, as well as on changing attitudes within bodies politic. It will also depend heavily on political steps to ensure that one party will not drop out of the transitional process when it thinks it has what it wants.

—If these propositions are true, then prospects for the peace process in the second decade after Camp David depend on identifying the obstacles in the political arena to reconstituting the peace process and focusing on a scenario of reciprocal steps for eroding those obstacles.

Implicit in these propositions is a fundamental choice about how the peace process is defined—whether as a negotiation to produce a leap to a final settlement or as a political process to begin a transition to new relationships that negotiations one day might define in a final settlement. This choice, to be made by leaders in the second decade after Camp David, will significantly influence the prospects for the Arab-Israeli peace process. Experience shows that negotiators have a chance only when leaders act in the political arena to produce political support, and even pressure, for a negotiated settlement.

PART V

APPENDIXES

APPENDIX A

United Nations Security Council Resolutions 242 and 338

U.N. RESOLUTION 242, NOVEMBER 22, 1967

The Security Council,

Expressing its continuing concern with the grave situation in the Middle East,

Emphasizing the inadmissibility of the acquisition of territory by war and the need to work for a just and lasting peace in which every State in the area can live in security,

Emphasizing further that all Member States in their acceptance of the Charter of the United Nations have undertaken a commitment to act in accordance with Article 2 of the Charter.

1. *Affirms* that the fulfillment of Charter principles requires the establishment of a just and lasting peace in the Middle East which should include the application of both the following principles:

(i) Withdrawal of Israeli armed forces from territories occupied in the recent conflict;

(ii) Termination of all claims or stages of belligerency and respect for and acknowledgement of the sovereignty, territorial integrity and political independence of every State in the area and their right to live in peace within secure and recognized boundaries free from threats or acts of force;

2. *Affirms further* the necessity:

(a) For guaranteeing freedom of navigation through international waterways in the area;

(b) For achieving a just settlement of the refugee problem;

(c) For guaranteeing the territorial inviolability and political independence of every State in the area, through measures including the establishment of demilitarized zones;

3. *Requests* the Secretary-General to designate a Special Representative to proceed to the Middle East to establish and maintain contacts with the States concerned in order to promote agreement

and assist efforts to achieve a peaceful and accepted settlement in accordance with the provisions and principles of this resolution;

4. *Requests* the Secretary-General to report to the Security Council on the progress of the efforts of the Special Representative as soon as possible.

U.N. RESOLUTION 338, OCTOBER 22, 1973

The Security Council

1. *Calls upon* all parties to the present fighting to cease all firing and terminate all military activity immediately, no later than 12 hours after the moment of the adoption of this decision, in the positions they now occupy;

2. *Calls upon* the parties concerned to start immediately after the cease-fire the implementation of Security Council Resolution 242 (1967) in all of its parts;

3. *Decides that,* immediately and concurrently with the cease-fire, negotiations shall start between the parties concerned under appropriate auspices aimed at establishing a just and durable peace in the Middle East.

APPENDIX B

Joint Communiqué by the Governments of the United States and the Union of Soviet Socialist Republics, October 1, 1977

Having exchanged views regarding the unsafe situation which remains in the Middle East, U.S. Secretary of State Cyrus Vance and Member of the Politbureau of the Central Committee of the CPSU, Minister for Foreign Affairs of the U.S.S.R. A.A. Gromyko have the following statement to make on behalf of their countries, which are cochairmen of the Geneva Peace Conference on the Middle East:

1. Both governments are convinced that vital interests of the peoples of this area, as well as the interests of strengthening peace and international security in general, urgently dictate the necessity of achieving, as soon as possible, a just and lasting settlement of the Arab-Israeli conflict. This settlement should be comprehensive, incorporating all parties concerned and all questions.

The United States and the Soviet Union believe that, within the framework of a comprehensive settlement of the Middle East problem, all specific questions of the settlement should be resolved, including such key issues as withdrawal of Israeli Armed Forces from territories occupied in the 1967 conflict; the resolution of the Palestinian question, including insuring the legitimate rights of the Palestinian people; termination of the state of war and establishment of normal peaceful relations on the basis of mutual recognition of the principles of sovereignty, territorial integrity, and political independence.

The two governments believe that, in addition to such measures for insuring the security of the borders between Israel and the neighboring Arab states as the establishment of demilitarized zones

The text of the joint communiqué comes from "U.S., U.S.S.R. Issue Statement on the Middle East," *Department of State Bulletin*, vol. 77 (November 7, 1977), pp. 639–40. The statement was issued in New York City.

and the agreed stationing in them of U.N. troops or observers, international guarantees of such borders as well as of the observance of the terms of the settlement can also be established should the contracting parties so desire. The United States and the Soviet Union are ready to participate in these guarantees, subject to their constitutional processes.

2. The United States and the Soviet Union believe that the only right and effective way for achieving a fundamental solution to all aspects of the Middle East problem in its entirety is negotiations within the framework of the Geneva peace conference, specially convened for these purposes, with participation in its work of the representatives of all the parties involved in the conflict including those of the Palestinian people, and legal and contractual formalization of the decisions reached at the conference.

In their capacity as cochairmen of the Geneva conference, the United States and the U.S.S.R. affirm their intention, through joint efforts and in their contacts with the parties concerned, to facilitate in every way the resumption of the work of the conference not later than December 1977. The cochairmen note that there still exist several questions of a procedural and organizational nature which remain to be agreed upon by the participants to the conference.

3. Guided by the goal of achieving a just political settlement in the Middle East and of eliminating the explosive situation in this area of the world, the United States and the U.S.S.R. appeal to all the parties in the conflict to understand the necessity for careful consideration of each other's legitimate rights and interests and to demonstrate mutual readiness to act accordingly.

APPENDIX C

The Camp David Accords, September 17, 1978

A FRAMEWORK FOR PEACE IN THE MIDDLE EAST AGREED AT CAMP DAVID

Muhammad Anwar al-Sadat, President of the Arab Republic of Egypt, and Menachem Begin, Prime Minister of Israel, met with Jimmy Carter, President of the United States of America, at Camp David from September 5 to September 17, 1978, and have agreed on the following framework for peace in the Middle East. They invite other parties to the Arab-Israeli conflict to adhere to it.

Preamble

The search for peace in the Middle East must be guided by the following:

—The agreed basis for a peaceful settlement of the conflict between Israel and its neighbors is United Nations Security Council Resolution 242, in all its parts.

—After four wars during thirty years, despite intensive human efforts, the Middle East, which is the cradle of civilization and the birthplace of three great religions, does not yet enjoy the blessings of peace. The people of the Middle East yearn for peace so that the vast human and natural resources of the region can be turned to the pursuits of peace and so that this area can become a model for coexistence and cooperation among nations.

—The historic initiative of President Sadat in visiting Jerusalem and the reception accorded to him by the Parliament, government and people of Israel, and the reciprocal visit of Prime Minister Begin to Ismailia, the peace proposals made by both leaders, as well as the warm reception of these missions by the peoples of both countries, have created an unprecedented opportunity for peace which must not be lost if this generation and future generations are to be spared the tragedies of war.

—The provisions of the Charter of the United Nations and the other accepted norms of international law and legitimacy now provide accepted standards for the conduct of relations among all states.

—To achieve a relationship of peace, in the spirit of Article 2 of the United Nations Charter, future negotiations between Israel and any neighbor prepared to negotiate peace and security with it, are necessary for the purpose of carrying out all the provisions and principles of Resolutions 242 and 338.

—Peace requires respect for the sovereignty, territorial integrity and political independence of every state in the area and their right to live in peace within secure and recognized boundaries free from threats or acts of force. Progress toward that goal can accelerate movement toward a new era of reconciliation in the Middle East marked by cooperation in promoting economic development, in maintaining stability, and in assuring security.

—Security is enhanced by a relationship of peace and by cooperation between nations which enjoy normal relations. In addition, under the terms of peace treaties, the parties can, on the basis of reciprocity, agree to special security arrangements such as demilitarized zones, limited armaments areas, early warning stations, the presence of international forces, liaison, agreed measures for monitoring, and other arrangements that they agree are useful.

Framework

Taking these factors into account, the parties are determined to reach a just, comprehensive, and durable settlement of the Middle East conflict through the conclusion of peace treaties based on Security Council Resolutions 242 and 338 in all their parts. Their purpose is to achieve peace and good neighborly relations. They recognize that, for peace to endure, it must involve all those who have been most deeply affected by the conflict. They therefore agree that this framework as appropriate is intended by them to constitute a basis for peace not only between Egypt and Israel, but also between Israel and each of its other neighbors which is prepared to negotiate peace with Israel on this basis. With that objective in mind, they have agreed to proceed as follows:

A. West Bank and Gaza

1. Egypt, Israel, Jordan and the representatives of the Palestinian people should participate in negotiations on the resolution of the Palestinian problem in all its aspects. To achieve that objective,

negotiations relating to the West Bank and Gaza should proceed in three stages:

(a) Egypt and Israel agree that, in order to ensure a peaceful and orderly transfer of authority, and taking into account the security concerns of all the parties, there should be transitional arrangements for the West Bank and Gaza for a period not exceeding five years. In order to provide full autonomy to the inhabitants, under these arrangements the Israeli military government and its civilian administration will be withdrawn as soon as a self-governing authority has been freely elected by the inhabitants of these areas to replace the existing military government. To negotiate the details of a transitional arrangement, the Government of Jordan will be invited to join the negotiations on the basis of this framework. These new arrangements should give due consideration both to the principle of self-government by the inhabitants of these territories and to the legitimate security concerns of the parties involved.

(b) Egypt, Israel, and Jordan will agree on the modalities for establishing the elected self-governing authority in the West Bank and Gaza. The delegations of Egypt and Jordan may include Palestinians from the West Bank and Gaza or other Palestinians as mutually agreed. The parties will negotiate an agreement which will define the powers and responsibilities of the self-governing authority to be exercised in the West Bank and Gaza. A withdrawal of Israeli armed forces will take place and there will be a redeployment of the remaining Israeli forces into specified security locations. The agreement will also include arrangements for assuring internal and external security and public order. A strong local police force will be established, which may include Jordanian citizens. In addition, Israeli and Jordanian forces will participate in joint patrols and in the manning of control posts to assure the security of the borders.

(c) When the self-governing authority (administrative council) in the West Bank and Gaza is established and inaugurated, the transitional period of five years will begin. As soon as possible, but not later than the third year after the beginning of the transitional period, negotiations will take place to determine the final status of the West Bank and Gaza and its relationship with its neighbors, and to conclude a peace treaty between Israel and Jordan by the end of the transitional period. These negotiations will be conducted among Egypt, Israel, Jordan, and the elected representatives of the inhabitants of the West Bank and Gaza. Two separate but related committees will be convened, one committee, consisting of representatives of the four parties which will negotiate and agree on the final status of the West Bank and Gaza, and its relationship with its neighbors, and the second committee, consisting of representatives of Israel and representatives of Jordan to be joined by the elected representatives of the inhabitants of the West Bank and Gaza, to negotiate the peace treaty between Israel and Jordan, taking into account the agreement reached on the final status of the West Bank and Gaza. The negotiations shall be based on all the provisions and principles of UN Security Council Resolution 242. The negotiations will resolve, among other matters, the location of the boundaries and the nature of the security arrangements. The solution from the negotiations must also recognize the legitimate rights of the Palestinian people and their just requirements. In this way, the Palestinians will participate in the determination of their own future through:

(1) The negotiations among Egypt, Israel, Jordan and the representatives of the inhabitants of the West Bank and Gaza to agree on the final status of the West Bank and Gaza and other outstanding issues by the end of the transitional period.

(2) Submitting their agreement to a vote by the elected representatives of the inhabitants of the West Bank and Gaza.

(3) Providing for the elected representatives of the inhabitants of the West Bank and Gaza to decide how they shall govern themselves consistent with the provisions of their agreement.

(4) Participating as stated above in the work of the committee negotiating the peace treaty between Israel and Jordan.

2. All necessary measures will be taken and provisions made to assure the security of Israel and its neighbors during the transitional period and beyond. To assist in providing such security, a strong local police force will be constituted by the self-governing authority. It will be composed of inhabitants of the West Bank and Gaza. The police will maintain continuing liaison on internal security matters with the designated Israeli, Jordanian, and Egyptian officers.

3. During the transitional period, representatives of Egypt, Israel, Jordan, and the self-governing authority will constitute a continuing committee to decide by agreement on the modalities of admission of persons displaced from the West Bank and Gaza in 1967, together with necessary measures to prevent disruption and disorder. Other matters of common concern may also be dealt with by this committee.

4. Egypt and Israel will work with each other and with other interested parties to establish agreed procedures for a prompt, just and permanent implementation of the resolution of the refugee problem.

B. Egypt-Israel

1. Egypt and Israel undertake not to resort to the threat or the use of force to settle disputes. Any disputes shall be settled by peaceful means in accordance with the provisions of Article 33 of the Charter of the United Nations.

2. In order to achieve peace between them, the parties agree to negotiate in good faith with a goal of concluding within three months from the signing of this Framework a peace treaty between them, while inviting the other parties to the conflict to proceed simultaneously to negotiate and conclude similar peace treaties with a view to achieving a comprehensive peace in the area. The Framework for the Conclusion of a Peace Treaty between Egypt and Israel will govern the peace negotiations between them. The parties will agree on the modalities and the timetable for the implementation of their obligations under the treaty.

C. Associated Principles

1. Egypt and Israel state that the principles and provisions described below should apply to peace treaties between Israel and each of its neighbors—Egypt, Jordan, Syria and Lebanon.

2. Signatories shall establish among themselves relationships normal to states at peace with one another. To this end, they should undertake to abide by all the provisions of the Charter of the United Nations. Steps to be taken in this respect include:

(a) full recognition;

(b) abolishing economic boycotts;

(c) guaranteeing that under their jurisdiction the citizens of the other parties shall enjoy the protection of the due process of law.

3. Signatories should explore possibilities for economic development in the context of final peace treaties, with the objective of contributing to the atmosphere of peace, cooperation and friendship which is their common goal.

4. Claims Commissions may be established for the mutual settlement of all financial claims.

5. The United States shall be invited to participate in the talks on matters related to the modalities of the implementation of the agreements and working out the timetable for the carrying out of the obligations of the parties.

6. The United Nations Security Council shall be requested to endorse the peace treaties and ensure that their provisions shall not be violated. The permanent members of the Security Council shall be requested to underwrite the peace treaties and ensure respect for their provisions. They shall also be requested to conform their

policies and actions with the undertakings contained in this Framework.

For the Government of the Arab Republic of Egypt:

A. Sadat

For the Government of Israel:

M. Begin

Witnessed by:

Jimmy Carter
Jimmy Carter, President of
the United States of America

FRAMEWORK FOR THE CONCLUSION OF A PEACE TREATY BETWEEN EGYPT AND ISRAEL

In order to achieve peace between them, Israel and Egypt agree to negotiate in good faith with a goal of concluding within three months of the signing of this framework a peace treaty between them.

It is agreed that:

The site of the negotiations will be under a United Nations flag at a location or locations to be mutually agreed.

All of the principles of UN Resolution 242 will apply in this resolution of the dispute between Israel and Egypt.

Unless otherwise mutually agreed, terms of the peace treaty will be implemented between two and three years after the peace treaty is signed.

The following matters are agreed between the parties:

(a) the full exercise of Egyptian sovereignty up to the internationally recognized border between Egypt and mandated Palestine;

(b) the withdrawal of Israeli armed forces from the Sinai;

(c) the use of airfields left by the Israelis near El Arish, Rafah, Ras en Naqb, and Sharm el Sheikh for civilian purposes only, including possible commercial use by all nations;

(d) the right of free passage by ships of Israel through the Gulf of Suez and the Suez Canal on the basis of the Constantinople Convention of 1888 applying to all nations; the Strait of Tiran and the Gulf of Aqaba are international waterways to be open to all nations for unimpeded and nonsuspendable freedom of navigation and overflight;

(e) the construction of a highway between the Sinai and Jordan near Elat with guaranteed free and peaceful passage by Egypt and Jordan; and

(f) the stationing of military forces listed below.

Stationing of Forces

A. No more than one division (mechanized or infantry) of Egyptian armed forces will be stationed within an area lying approximately 50 kilometers (km) east of the Gulf of Suez and the Suez Canal.

B. Only United Nations forces and civil police equipped with light weapons to perform normal police functions will be stationed within an area lying west of the international border and the Gulf of Aqaba, varying in width from 20 km to 40 km.

C. In the area within 3 km east of the international border there will be Israeli limited military forces not to exceed four infantry battalions and United Nations observers.

D. Border patrol units, not to exceed three battalions, will supplement the civil police in maintaining order in the area not included above.

The exact demarcation of the above areas will be as decided during the peace negotiations.

Early warning stations may exist to insure compliance with the terms of the agreement.

United Nations forces will be stationed: (a) in part of the area in the Sinai lying within about 20 km of the Mediterranean Sea and adjacent to the international border, and (b) in the Sharm el Sheikh area to ensure freedom of passage through the Strait of Tiran; and these forces will not be removed unless such removal is approved by the Security Council of the United Nations with a unanimous vote of the five permanent members.

After a peace treaty is signed, and after the interim withdrawal is complete, normal relations will be established between Egypt and Israel, including: full recognition, including diplomatic, economic and cultural relations; termination of economic boycotts and barriers to the free movement of goods and people; and mutual protection of citizens by the due process of law.

Interim Withdrawal

Between three months and nine months after the signing of the peace treaty, all Israeli forces will withdraw east of a line extending from a point east of El Arish to Ras Muhammad, the exact location of this line to be determined by mutual agreement.

For the Government of the Arab Republic of Egypt:

A. Sadat

For the Government of Israel:

M. Begin

Witnessed by:

Jimmy Carter
Jimmy Carter, President of
the United States of America

LETTER FROM ISRAELI PRIME MINISTER MENACHEM BEGIN TO PRESIDENT JIMMY CARTER, SEPTEMBER 17, 1978

Dear Mr. President:

I have the honor to inform you that during two weeks after my return home I will submit a motion before Israel's Parliament (the Knesset) to decide on the following question:

If during the negotiations to conclude a peace treaty between Israel and Egypt all outstanding issues are agreed upon, "are you in favor of the removal of the Israeli settlers from the northern and southern Sinai areas or are you in favor of keeping the aforementioned settlers in those areas?"

The vote, Mr. President, on this issue will be completely free from the usual Parliamentary Party discipline to the effect that although the coalition is being now supported by 70 members out of 120, every member of the Knesset, as I believe, both on the Government and the Opposition benches will be enabled to vote in accordance with his own conscience.

Sincerely yours,

Menachem Begin

LETTER FROM PRESIDENT JIMMY CARTER TO EGYPTIAN PRESIDENT ANWAR EL SADAT, SEPTEMBER 22, 1978

Dear Mr. President:

I transmit herewith a copy of a letter to me from Prime Minister Begin setting forth how he proposes to present the issue of the Sinai settlements to the Knesset for the latter's decision.

In this connection, I understand from your letter that Knesset approval to withdraw all Israeli settlers from Sinai according to a timetable within the period specified for the implementation of the peace treaty is a prerequisite to any negotiations on a peace treaty between Egypt and Israel.

Sincerely,

Jimmy Carter

Enclosure:
Letter from Prime Minister Begin

LETTER FROM EGYPTIAN PRESIDENT ANWAR EL SADAT TO PRESIDENT JIMMY CARTER, SEPTEMBER 17, 1978

Dear Mr. President:

In connection with the "Framework for a Settlement in Sinai" to be signed tonight, I would like to reaffirm the position of the Arab Republic of Egypt with respect to the settlements:

1. All Israeli settlers must be withdrawn from Sinai according to a timetable within the period specified for the implementation of the peace treaty.

2. Agreement by the Israeli Government and its constitutional institutions to this basic principle is therefore a prerequisite to starting peace negotiations for concluding a peace treaty.

3. If Israel fails to meet this commitment, the "Framework" shall be void and invalid.

Sincerely,

Mohamed Anwar El Sadat

LETTER FROM PRESIDENT JIMMY CARTER TO ISRAELI PRIME MINISTER MENACHEM BEGIN, SEPTEMBER 22, 1978

Dear Mr. Prime Minister:

I have received your letter of September 17, 1978, describing how you intend to place the question of the future of Israeli settlements in Sinai before the Knesset for its decision.

Enclosed is a copy of President Sadat's letter to me on this subject.

Sincerely,

Jimmy Carter

Enclosure:
Letter from President Sadat

LETTER FROM EGYPTIAN PRESIDENT ANWAR EL SADAT TO PRESIDENT JIMMY CARTER, SEPTEMBER 17, 1978

Dear Mr. President:
I am writing you to reaffirm the position of the Arab Republic of Egypt with respect to Jerusalem:

1. Arab Jerusalem is an integral part of the West Bank. Legal and historical Arab rights in the City must be respected and restored.
2. Arab Jerusalem should be under Arab sovereignty.
3. The Palestinian inhabitants of Arab Jerusalem are entitled to exercise their legitimate national rights, being part of the Palestinian People in the West Bank.
4. Relevant Security Council Resolutions, particularly Resolutions 242 and 267, must be applied with regard to Jerusalem. All the measures taken by Israel to alter the status of the City are null and void and should be rescinded.
5. All peoples must have free access to the City and enjoy the free exercise of worship and the right to visit and transit to the holy places without distinction or discrimination.
6. The holy places of each faith may be placed under the administration and control of their representatives.
7. Essential functions in the City should be undivided and a joint municipal council composed of an equal number of Arab and Israeli members can supervise the carrying out of these functions. In this way, the City shall be undivided.

Sincerely,

Mohamed Anwar El Sadat

LETTER FROM ISRAELI PRIME MINISTER MENACHEM BEGIN TO PRESIDENT JIMMY CARTER, SEPTEMBER 17, 1978

Dear Mr. President:
I have the honor to inform you, Mr. President, that on 28 June 1967—Israel's Parliament (The Knesset) promulgated and adopted a law to the effect: "the Government is empowered by a decree to apply the law, the jurisdiction and administration of the State to any part of Eretz Israel (land of Israel–Palestine), as stated in that decree."

On the basis of this law, the Government of Israel decreed in July 1967 that Jerusalem is one city indivisible, the Capital of the State of Israel.

Sincerely,

Menachem Begin

LETTER FROM PRESIDENT JIMMY CARTER TO EGYPTIAN PRESIDENT ANWAR EL SADAT, SEPTEMBER 22, 1978

Dear Mr. President:

I have received your letter of September 17, 1978, setting forth the Egyptian position on Jerusalem. I am transmitting a copy of that letter to Prime Minister Begin for his information.

The position of the United States on Jerusalem remains as stated by Ambassador Goldberg in the United Nations General Assembly on July 14, 1967, and subsequently by Ambassador Yost in the United Nations Security Council on July 1, 1969.

Sincerely,

Jimmy Carter

LETTER FROM EGYPTIAN PRESIDENT ANWAR EL SADAT TO PRESIDENT JIMMY CARTER, SEPTEMBER 17, 1978

Dear Mr. President:

In connection with the "Framework for Peace in the Middle East," I am writing you this letter to inform you of the position of the Arab Republic of Egypt, with respect to the implementation of the comprehensive settlement.

To ensure the implementation of the provisions related to the West Bank and Gaza and in order to safeguard the legitimate rights of the Palestinian people, Egypt will be prepared to assume the Arab role emanating from these provisions, following consultations with Jordan and the representatives of the Palestinian people.

Sincerely,

Mohamed Anwar El Sadat

LETTER FROM PRESIDENT JIMMY CARTER TO ISRAELI PRIME MINISTER MENACHEM BEGIN, SEPTEMBER 22, 1978

Dear Mr. Prime Minister:
I hereby acknowledge that you have informed me as follows:

A) In each paragraph of the Agreed Framework Document the expressions "Palestinians" or "Palestinian People" are being and will be construed and understood by you as "Palestinian Arabs."

B) In each paragraph in which the expression "West Bank" appears, it is being, and will be, understood by the Government of Israel as Judea and Samaria.

Sincerely,

Jimmy Carter

LETTER FROM SECRETARY OF DEFENSE HAROLD BROWN TO ISRAELI DEFENSE MINISTER EZER WEIZMAN, ACCOMPANYING THE DOCUMENTS AGREED TO AT CAMP DAVID, RELEASED SEPTEMBER 29, 1978

September 28, 1978

Dear Mr. Minister:
The U.S. understands that, in connection with carrying out the agreements reached at Camp David, Israel intends to build two military airbases at appropriate sites in the Negev to replace the airbases at Eitam and Etzion which will be evacuated by Israel in accordance with the peace treaty to be concluded between Egypt and Israel. We also understand the special urgency and priority which Israel attaches to preparing the new bases in light of its conviction that it cannot safely leave the Sinai airbases until the new ones are operational.

I suggest that our two governments consult on the scope and costs of the two new airbases as well as on related forms of assistance which the United States might appropriately provide in light of the special problems which may be presented by carrying out such a project on an urgent basis. The President is prepared to seek the necessary Congressional approvals for such assistance as may be agreed upon by the U.S. side as a result of such consultations.

Harold Brown

APPENDIX D

President Ronald Reagan's Speech and Talking Points, September 1, 1982

My fellow Americans, today has been a day that should make us proud. It marked the end of the successful evacuation of the PLO from Beirut, Lebanon. This peaceful step could never have been taken without the good offices of the United States and, especially, the truly heroic work of a great American diplomat, Ambassador Philip Habib. Thanks to his efforts, I'm happy to announce that the U.S. Marine contingent helping to supervise the evacuation has accomplished its mission. Our young men should be out of Lebanon within two weeks. They, too, have served the cause of peace with distinction and we can all be very proud of them.

But the situation in Lebanon is only part of the overall problem of conflict in the Middle East. So, over the past two weeks, while events in Beirut dominated the front page, America was engaged in a quiet, behind- the-scenes effort to lay the groundwork for a broader peace in the region. For once, there were no premature leaks as U.S. diplomatic missions traveled to Mideast capitals and I met here at home with a wide range of experts to map out an American peace initiative for the long-suffering peoples of the Middle East, Arab and Israeli alike.

It seemed to me that, with the agreement in Lebanon, we had an opportunity for a more far-reaching peace effort in the region and I was determined to seize that moment. In the words of the scripture, the time had come to "follow after the things which make for peace."

The text of the speech comes from the *New York Times*, September 2, 1982. The talking points accompanied a letter sent by President Reagan to Prime Minister Menachem Begin of Israel. The same points were presented to Arab governments. See the *New York Times*, September 9, 1982.

U.S. INVOLVEMENT

Tonight, I want to report to you on the steps we've taken and the prospects they can open up for a just and lasting peace in the Middle East. America has long been committed to bringing peace to this troubled region. For more than a generation, successive U.S. administrations have endeavored to develop a fair and workable process that could lead to a true and lasting Arab-Israeli peace. Our involvement in the search for Mideast peace is not a matter of preference, it is a moral imperative. The strategic importance of the region to the U.S. is well known.

But our policy is motivated by more than strategic interests. We also have an irreversible commitment to the survival and territorial integrity of friendly states. Nor can we ignore the fact that the well-being of much of the world's economy is tied to stability in the strife-torn Middle East. Finally, our traditional humanitarian concerns dictate a continuing effort to peacefully resolve conflicts.

When our Administration assumed office in January 1981, I decided that the general framework for our Middle East policy should follow the broad guidelines laid down by my predecessors.

There were two basic issues we had to address. First, there was the strategic threat to the region posed by the Soviet Union and its surrogates, best demonstrated by the brutal war in Afghanistan; and, second, the peace process between Israel and its Arab neighbors. With regard to the Soviet threat, we have strengthened our efforts to develop with our friends and allies a joint policy to deter the Soviets and their surrogates from further expansion in the region, and, if necessary, to defend against it. With respect to the Arab-Israeli conflict, we've embraced the Camp David framework as the only way to proceed. We have also recognized, however, that solving the Arab-Israeli conflict, in and of itself, cannot assure peace throughout a region as vast and troubled as the Middle East.

Our first objective under the Camp David process was to insure the successful fulfillment of the Egyptian-Israeli peace treaty. This was achieved with the peaceful return of the Sinai to Egypt in April 1982. To accomplish this, we worked hard with our Egyptian and Israeli friends, and eventually with other friendly countries, to create the multinational force which now operates in the Sinai.

Throughout this period of difficult and time-consuming negotiations, we never lost sight of the next step of Camp David, autonomy talks to pave the way for permitting the Palestinian people to exercise their legitimate rights. However, owing to the tragic assassination of President Sadat and other crises in the area, it was not until January 1982 that we were able to make a major effort to renew these talks. Secretary of State Haig and Ambassador Fairbanks made three visits to Israel and Egypt early this year to pursue the autonomy talks. Considerable progress was made in developing the basic outline of an American approach which was to be presented to Egypt and Israel after April.

The successful completion of Israel's withdrawal from Sinai and the courage shown on this occasion by Prime Minister Begin and President Mubarak in living up to their agreements convinced me the time had come for a new American policy to try to bridge the remaining differences between Egypt and Israel on the autonomy process. So, in May, I called for specific measures and a timetable for consultations with the Governments of Egypt and Israel on the next steps in the peace process. However, before this effort could be launched, the conflict in Lebanon pre-empted our efforts. The autonomy talks were basically put on hold while we sought to untangle the parties in Lebanon and still the guns of war.

The Lebanon war, tragic as it was, has left us with a new opportunity for Middle East peace. We must seize it now and bring peace to this troubled area so vital to world stability while there is still time. It was with this strong conviction that over a month ago, before the present negotiations in Beirut had been completed, I directed Secretary of State Shultz to again review our policy and to consult a wide range of outstanding Americans on the best ways to strengthen chances for peace in the Middle East. We have consulted with many of the officials who were historically involved in the process, with members of the Congress, and with individuals from the private sector, and I have held extensive consultations with my own advisers on the principles that I will outline to you tonight.

The evacuation of the PLO from Beirut is now complete. And we can now help the Lebanese to rebuild their war-torn country. We owe it to ourselves, and to posterity, to move quickly to build upon this achievement. A stable and revived Lebanon is essential to all our hopes for peace in the region. The people of Lebanon deserve the best efforts of the international community to turn the nightmares of the past several years into a new dawn of hope.

RESOLVING THE ROOT CAUSES OF CONFLICT

But the opportunities for peace in the Middle East do not begin and end in Lebanon. As we help Lebanon rebuild, we must also move to resolve the root causes of conflict between Arabs and

Israelis. The war in Lebanon has demonstrated many things, but two consequences are key to the peace process:

First, the military losses of the PLO have not diminished the yearning of the Palestinian people for a just solution of their claims.

Second, while Israel's military successes in Lebanon have demonstrated that its armed forces are second to none in the region, they alone cannot bring just and lasting peace to Israel and her neighbors.

The question now is how to reconcile Israel's legitimate security concerns with the legitimate rights of the Palestinians. And that answer can only come at the negotiating table. Each party must recognize that the outcome must be acceptable to all and that true peace will require compromises by all.

So, tonight I'm calling for a fresh start. This is the moment for all those directly concerned to get involved—or lend their support—to a workable basis for peace. The Camp David agreement remains the foundation of our policy. Its language provides all parties with the leeway they need for successful negotiations.

I call on Israel to make clear that the security for which she yearns can only be achieved through genuine peace, a peace requiring magnanimity, vision and courage.

I call on the Palestinian people to recognize that their own political aspirations are inextricably bound to recognition of Israel's right to a secure future.

And I call on the Arab states to accept the reality of Israel, and the reality that peace and justice are to be gained only through hard, fair, direct negotiation.

In making these calls upon others, I recognize that the United States has a special responsibility. No other nation is in a position to deal with the key parties to the conflict on the basis of trust and reliability.

The time has come for a new realism on the part of all the peoples of the Middle East. The State of Israel is an accomplished fact; it deserves unchallenged legitimacy within the community of nations. But Israel's legitimacy has thus far been recognized by too few countries, and has been denied by every Arab state except Egypt. Israel exists. It has a right to exist in peace, behind secure and defensible borders, and it has a right to demand of its neighbors that they recognize those facts.

I have personally followed and supported Israel's heroic struggle for survival ever since the founding of the state of Israel 34 years ago. In the pre-1967 borders, Israel was barely 10 miles wide at its narrowest point. The bulk of Israel's population lived within artillery range of hostile Arab armies. I am not about to ask Israel to live that way again.

The war in Lebanon has demonstrated another reality in the region. The departure of the Palestinians from Beirut dramatizes more than ever the homelessness of the Palestinian people. Palestinians feel strongly that their cause is more than a question of refugees. I agree. The Camp David agreement recognized that fact when it spoke of the legitimate rights of the Palestinian people and their just requirements. For peace to endure, it must involve all those who have been most deeply affected by the conflict. Only through broader participation in the peace process, most immediately by Jordan and by the Palestinians, will Israel be able to rest confident in the knowledge that its security and integrity will be respected by its neighbors. Only through the process of negotiation can all the nations of the Middle East achieve a secure peace.

NEW PROPOSALS

These then are our general goals. What are the specific new American positions, and why are we taking them?

In the Camp David talks thus far, both Israel and Egypt have felt free to express openly their views as to what the outcome should be. Understandably, their views have differed on many points.

The United States has thus far sought to play the role of mediator. We have avoided public comment on the key issues. We have always recognized, and continue to recognize, that only the voluntary agreement of those parties most directly involved in the conflict can provide an enduring solution. But it has become evident to me that some clearer sense of America's position on the key issues is necessary to encourage wider support for the peace process.

First, as outlined in the Camp David accords, there must be a period of time during which the Palestinian inhabitants of the West Bank and Gaza will have full autonomy over their own affairs. Due consideration must be given to the principle of self-government by the inhabitants of the territories and to the legitimate security concerns of the parties involved.

The purpose of the five-year period of transition which would begin after free elections for a self-governing Palestinian authority is to prove to the Palestinians that they can run their own affairs, and that such Palestinian autonomy poses no threat to Israel's security.

The United States will not support the use of any additional land for the purpose of settlements during the transitional period. Indeed, the immediate adoption of a settlement freeze by Israel, more than any other action, could create the confidence needed for wider participation in these talks. Further settlement activity is in no way necessary for the security of Israel and only diminishes the confidence of the Arabs that a final outcome can be freely and fairly negotiated.

I want to make the American position well understood: The purpose of this transition period is the peaceful and orderly transfer of authority from Israel to the Palestinian inhabitants of the West Bank and Gaza. At the same time, such a transfer must not interfere with Israel's security requirements.

Beyond the transition period, as we look to the future of the West Bank and Gaza, it is clear to me that peace cannot be achieved by the formation of an independent Palestinian state in those territories. Nor is it achievable on the basis of Israeli sovereignty or permanent control over the West Bank and Gaza.

So the United States will not support the establishment of an independent Palestinian state in the West Bank and Gaza, and we will not support annexation or permanent control by Israel.

There is, however, another way to peace. The final status of these lands must, of course, be reached through the give-and-take of negotiations. But it is the firm view of the United States that self-government by the Palestinians of the West Bank and Gaza in association with Jordan offers the best chance for a durable, just and lasting peace.

We base our approach squarely on the principle that the Arab-Israeli conflict should be resolved through negotiations involving an exchange of territory for peace. This exchange is enshrined in United Nations Security Council Resolution 242 which is, in turn, incorporated in all its parts in the Camp David agreements. U.N. Resolution 242 remains wholly valid as the foundation stone of America's Middle East peace effort.

It is the United States' position that—in return for peace—the withdrawal provision of Resolution 242 applies to all fronts, including the West Bank and Gaza.

When the border is negotiated between Jordan and Israel, our view on the extent to which Israel should be asked to give up territory will be heavily affected by the extent of true peace and normalization and the security arrangements offered in return.

Finally, we remain convinced that Jerusalem must remain undivided, but its final status should be decided through negotiations.

In the course of the negotiations to come, the United States will support positions that seem to us fair and reasonable compromises, and likely to promote a sound agreement. We will also put forward our own detailed proposals when we believe they can be helpful. And, make no mistake, the United States will oppose any proposal—from any party and at any point in the negotiating process—that threatens the security of Israel. America's commitment to the security of Israel is ironclad and, I might add, so is mine.

U.S. Commitment to Peace

During the past few days, our Ambassadors in Israel, Egypt, Jordan and Saudi Arabia have presented to their host governments the proposals in full detail that I have outlined here today. Now I am convinced that these proposals can bring justice, bring security and bring durability to an Arab-Israeli peace. The United States will stand by these principles with total dedication. They are fully consistent with Israel's security requirements and the aspirations of the Palestinians. We will work hard to broaden participation at the peace table as envisaged by the Camp David accords. And I fervently hope that the Palestinians and Jordan, with the support of their Arab colleagues, will accept this opportunity.

Tragic turmoil in the Middle East runs back to the dawn of history. In our modern day, conflict after conflict has taken its brutal toll there. In an age of nuclear challenge and economic interdependence, such conflicts are a threat to all the people of the world, not just the Middle East itself. It's time for us all, in the Middle East and around the world, to call a halt to conflict, hatred and prejudice; it's time for us all to launch a common effort for reconstruction, peace and progress.

It has often been said—and regrettably too often been true—that the story of the search for peace and justice in the Middle East is a tragedy of opportunities missed. In the aftermath of the settlement in Lebanon we now face an opportunity for a broader peace. This time we must not let it slip from our grasp. We must look beyond the difficulties and obstacles of the present and move with fairness and resolve toward a brighter future. We owe it to ourselves, and to posterity, to do no less. For if we miss this chance to make a fresh start, we may look back on this moment from some later vantage point and realize how much that failure cost us all.

These, then, are the principles upon which American policy toward the Arab-Israeli conflict will be based. I have made a personal commitment to see that they endure and, God willing, that they will come to be seen by all reasonable, compassionate people as fair, achievable, and in the interests of all who wish to see peace in the Middle East.

Tonight, on the eve of what can be a dawning of new hope for the people of the troubled Middle East, and for all the world's people who dream of a just and peaceful future, I ask you, my fellow Americans, for your support and your prayers in this great undertaking.

TEXT OF TALKING POINTS SENT TO PRIME MINISTER BEGIN BY PRESIDENT REAGAN

General Principles

A. We will maintain our commitment to Camp David.

B. We will maintain our commitment to the conditions we require for recognition of and negotiation with the PLO.

C. We can offer guarantees on the position we will adopt in negotiations. We will not be able, however, to guarantee in advance the results of these negotiations.

Transitional Measures

A. Our position is that the objective of the transitional period is the peaceful and orderly transfer of authority from Israel to the Palestinian inhabitants.

B. We will support:

The decision of full autonomy as giving the Palestinian inhabitants real authority over themselves, the land and its resources, subject to fair safeguards on water.

Economic, commercial, social and cultural ties between the West Bank, Gaza and Jordan.

Participation by the Palestinian inhabitants of East Jerusalem in the election of the West Bank-Gaza authority.

Real settlement freeze.

Progressive Palestinian responsibility for internal security based on capability and performance.

C. We will oppose:

Dismantlement of the existing settlements.

Provisions which represent a legitimate threat to Israel's security, reasonably defined.

Isolation of the West Bank and Gaza from Israel.

Measures which accord either the Palestinians or the Israelis generally recognized sovereign rights with the exception of external security, which must remain in Israel's hands during the transitional period.

Final Status Issues

A. U.N.S.C. Resolution 242

It is our position that Resolution 242 applies to the West Bank and Gaza and requires Israeli withdrawal in return for peace. Negotiations must determine the borders. The U.S. position in these negotiations on the extent of the withdrawal will be significantly influenced by the extent and nature of the peace and security arrangements offered in return.

B. Israeli Sovereignty

It is our belief that the Palestinian problem cannot be resolved [through] Israeli sovereignty or control over the West Bank and Gaza. Accordingly, we will not support such a solution.

C. Palestinian State

The preference we will pursue in the final status negotiation is association of the West Bank and Gaza with Jordan. We will not support the formation of a Palestinian state in those negotiations. There is no foundation of political support in Israel or the United States for such a solution. The outcome, however, must be determined by negotiations.

D. Self-Determination

In the Middle East context the term self-determination has been identified exclusively with the formation of a Palestinian state. We will not support this definition of self-determination. We believe that the Palestinians must take the leading role in determining their own future and fully support the provision in Camp David providing for the elected representatives of the inhabitants of the West Bank and Gaza to decide how they shall govern themselves consistent with the provision of their agreement in the final status negotiations.

E. Jerusalem

We will fully support the position that the status of Jerusalem must be determined through negotiations.

F. Settlements

The status of Israeli settlements must be determined in the course of the finally status negotiations. We will not support their continuation as extraterritorial outposts.

Additional Talking Points

1. Approach to Hussein

The President has approached Hussein to determine the extent to which he may be interested in participating.

King Hussein has received the same U.S. positions as you.

Hussein considers our proposals serious and gives them serious attention.

Hussein understands that Camp David is the only base that we will accept for negotiations.

We are also discussing these proposals with the Saudis.

2. Public Commitment

Whatever the support from these or other Arab States, this is what the President has concluded must be done.

The President is convinced his positions are fair and balanced and fully protective of Israel's security. Beyond that they offer the practical opportunity of eventually achieving the peace treaties Israel must have with its neighbors.

He will be making a speech announcing these positions, probably within a week.

3. Next Procedural Steps

Should the response to the President's proposal be positive, the U.S. would take immediate steps to relaunch the autonomy negotiations with the broadest possible participation as envisaged under the Camp David agreements.

We also contemplate an early visit by Secretary Shultz in the area.

Should there not be a positive response, the President, as he has said in his letter to you, will nonetheless stand by his position with proper dedication.

APPENDIX E

Resolutions of the Twelfth Arab League Summit, Fez, Morocco, September 9, 1982

The twelfth Arab summit conference convened at Fez on November 25, 1981. The conference adjourned its meetings and later resumed them on September 6, 1982, under the chairmanship of King Hasan II of Morocco.

All Arab countries with the exception of the Socialist People's Libyan Arab Jamahiriyah participated in the conference.

In view of the grave conditions through which the Arab nation is passing and out of a sense of historical and pan-Arab responsibility, their majesties and excellencies and highnesses the kings, presidents and emirs of the Arab nation discussed the important issues submitted to their conference and adopted the following resolution in regard to them:

The conference greeted the steadfastness of the Palestine revolutionary forces, the Lebanese and Palestinian peoples and the Syrian Arab Armed Forces and declared its support for the Palestinian people in their struggle for the retrieval of their established national rights.

Out of the conference's belief in the ability of the Arab nation to achieve its legitimate objectives and eliminate the aggression, and out of the principles and basis laid down by the Arab summit conferences, and out of the Arab countries' determination to continue to work by all means for the establishment of peace based on justice in the Middle East and using the plan of President Habib Bourguiba, which is based on international legitimacy, as the foundation for solving the Palestinian question and the plan of His Majesty King Fahd ibn 'Abd al-'Aziz which deals with peace in the Middle East, and in the light of the discussions and notes made by

Excerpted from Rabat Domestic Service, September 9, 1982, in Foreign Broadcast Information Service, *Daily Report: Middle East and Africa*, September 10, 1982, pp. A17-A19.

their majesties, excellencies and highnesses the kings, presidents and emirs, the conference has decided to adopt the following principles:

1. Israel's withdrawal from all Arab territories occupied in 1967, including Arab Jerusalem.
2. The removal of settlements set up by Israel in the Arab territories after 1967.
3. Guarantees of the freedom of worship and the performance of religious rites for all religions at the holy places.
4. Confirmation of the right of the Palestinian people to self-determination and to exercise their firm and inalienable national rights, under the leadership of the PLO, its sole legitimate representative, and compensation for those who do not wish to return.
5. The placing of the West Bank and Gaza Strip under UN supervision for a transitional period, not longer than several months.
6. The creation of an independent Palestinian state with Jerusalem as its capital.
7. The drawing up by the Security Council of guarantees for peace for all the states of the region, including the independent Palestinian state.
8. Security Council guarantees for the implementation of these principles.

APPENDIX F

The Agreement between Jordan and the Palestine Liberation Organization, February 11, 1985

THE AGREEMENT

Based on the spirit of the Fez resolutions agreed upon by the Arabs, and UN resolutions relating to the Palestinian question, in accordance with international legality, and based on a shared understanding to build a special relationship between the Jordanian and the Palestinian people, the Government of the Hashemite Kingdom of Jordan and the Palestine Liberation Organization have agreed to work together to achieve a peaceful and just settlement to the Middle East issue and to end Israeli occupation of occupied Arab lands, including Jerusalem, according to the following bases and principles:

(1) Land in exchange for peace as called for in resolutions of the United Nations, including those of the Security Council.
(2) The right of self-determination for the Palestinian people. The Palestinians will exercise their inalienable right of self-determination when the Jordanians and the Palestinians can do so in the context of an Arab confederation, to be established between the two states of Jordan and Palestine.
(3) A resolution of the problem of Palestinian refugees in accordance with UN resolutions.
(4) A resolution of the Palestinian question in all its aspects.
(5) On this basis, peace negotiations will take place under the auspices of an international conference, in which the five permanent members of the Security Council and all the parties to the conflict will participate, including the PLO, the sole legitimate representative of the Palestinian people, within a joint delegation (a Jordanian-Palestinian delegation).

AMENDMENTS

(According to official Jordanian sources, two clarifications were subsequently agreed upon by both Jordan and the PLO.)

Point Two: Self-determination for the Palestinian people, in a Palestinian state confederated with the Hashemite Kingdom of Jordan.

Point Five: For this purpose, negotiations will take place under the auspices of an international conference, in which the five permanent members of the Security Council and all the parties to the conflict will participate, including the PLO, the sole legitimate representative of the Palestinian people. Other Arab parties concerned will take part in the conference; among them will be a Jordanian-Palestinian delegation comprising equal representatives of the Jordanian government and the Palestine Liberation Organization.

APPENDIX G

Peres-Hussein Agreement (The London Document), April 11, 1987

(Accord between the Government of Jordan, which has confirmed it to the Government of the United States, and the Foreign Minister of Israel, pending the approval of the Government of Israel. Parts "A" and "B," which will be made public upon agreement of the parties, will be treated as proposals of the United States to which Jordan and Israel have agreed. Part "C" is to be treated with great confidentiality, as commitments to the United States from the Government of Jordan to be transmitted to the Government of Israel.)

A THREE-PART UNDERSTANDING BETWEEN JORDAN AND ISRAEL

A. Invitation by the UN secretary general: The UN secretary general will send invitations to the five permanent members of the Security Council and to the parties involved in the Israeli-Arab conflict to negotiate an agreement by peaceful means based on UN Resolutions 242 and 338 with the purpose of attaining comprehensive peace in the region and security for the countries in the area, and granting the Palestinian people their legitimate rights.

B. Decisions of the international conference: The participants in the conference agree that the purpose of the negotiations is to attain by peaceful means an agreement about all the aspects of the Palestinian problem. The conference invites the sides to set up regional bilateral committees to negotiate bilateral issues.

C. Nature of the agreement between Jordan and Israel: Israel and

The London document was agreed to by Peres and Hussein in their meeting in London in April 1987. See *Ma'ariv*, January 1, 1988, in Foreign Broadcast Information Service, *Daily Report: Near East and South Asia*, January 4, 1988, pp. 30-31.

Jordan agree that: 1) the international conference will not impose a solution and will not veto any agreement reached by the sides; 2) the negotiations will be conducted in bilateral committees in a direct manner; 3) the Palestinian issue will be discussed in a meeting of the Jordanian, Palestinian, and Israeli delegations; 4) the representatives of the Palestinians will be included in the Jordanian-Palestinian delegation; 5) participation in the conference will be based on acceptance of UN Resolutions 242 and 338 by the sides and the renunciation of violence and terror; 6) each committee will conduct negotiations independently; 7) other issues will be resolved through mutual agreement between Jordan and Israel.

This document of understanding is pending approval of the incumbent governments of Israel and Jordan. The content of this document will be presented and proposed to the United States.

APPENDIX H

General Secretary Mikhail S. Gorbachev's Remarks to President Hafiz al-Asad April 24, 1987

The edifice of peace, especially in the nuclear epoch, cannot be durable if at least a part of it remains outside the security system. That is why the USSR strongly favors the settlement of conflict situations, the so-called regional conflicts. A special place among them is occupied by the Middle East problem—one of the most chronic and involved. For two decades now—and if we measure that time from the very outset, even twice as long—it has been crippling the life and destinies of the peoples of the Middle East.

It is impossible to put up with billions spent on military needs, bloody clashes following one another, human casualties almost every day, political and psychological tensions, and an atmosphere of fear and the lack of confidence any longer. This situation affects the economy, hampers development, leads to a drop in living standards, and causes an accumulation of social problems; zones of real calamity for the people are formed.

The dependence on military power in settling the conflict has come to be completely discredited. It would seem that there is more than enough proof of this. The principal source of the persisting conflict is the expansionist policy of the Washington-backed ruling circles of Israel. The U.S. regards the Middle East as a test range for modeling its imperial policy. The U.S., as we have observed, is using regional conflicts in general for manipulating the level of tension and confrontation.

We express solidarity with the Arabs who refuse to recognize the occupation of their lands. We categorically condemn the discrimination against the Palestinian people denied the right to self-

"In a Friendly Atmosphere," Pravda, April 25, 1987, in Foreign Broadcast Information Service, *Daily Report: Soviet Union,* April 28, 1987, pp. H7-H8.

determination and the right of a homeland. In the future, like in the past, we will oppose any separate deals, as they are only holding back and thwarting the search for a genuine settlement.

Israeli leaders are stubbornly clinging to a policy which has no prospects. They are trying to build the security of their country by intimidating their neighbors and are using all means, even state terror, for that purpose. This is a faulty and short-sighted policy, the more so since it is directed against almost 200 million Arabs.

There is another, correct and reliable, way for ensuring a secure future for the state of Israel. It is a just peace and, in the final analysis, good neighborly relations with the Arabs.

Much has been said lately about relations between the Soviet Union and Israel, and a lot of lies have been spread, too. Let me put it straight: The absence of such relations cannot be considered normal. But they were severed by Israel in the first place. It happened as a result of the aggression against the Arab countries.

We recognize without any reservations—to the same extent as with all other states—the right of Israel to a peaceful and secure existence. At the same time, the Soviet Union, as it has been in the past, is categorically opposed to Tel Aviv's policy of strength and annexations. It should be plain—changes in relations with Israel are conceivable only in the mainstream of the process of settlement in the Middle East. This issue cannot be taken out of such a context. This interrelationship has been created by the course of events, by Israel's policy.

We are confident that preparations for an international conference on the Middle East involving all the sides concerned should be a focal point for collective efforts to bring about a settlement.

This idea, as you know, has had a stormy history—it was not accepted at once. But the past years have demonstrated that it is the only road out of the impasse. Today it would not be an exaggeration to say that a substantial part of the international community of nations favors such a conference. Even the United States and Israel cannot maintain an openly negative stand.

The time has come to start careful and painstaking preparatory work. The permanent members of the Security Council could take the initiative in that matter. The Soviet Union, let me reaffirm, is prepared for honest and constructive efforts on a collective bilateral basis.

During our conversations we discussed these issues in sufficient detail. I cannot but express satisfaction at the fact that Syrian leadership is unswervingly following the course toward a political settlement.

It is absolutely obvious that much will depend in this respect on the political activity and persistence of the Arab states, on coordination between them. We are saddened by disunity, frictions and conflicts in the Arab world which are vigorously exploited by imperialists and their henchmen. Naturally we saw a good sign in the current efforts to restore the unity of the PLO.

Making sacrifices and suffering deprivations, the Syrian Arab Republic has for many years now been courageously resisting aggression, the policy of *diktat* and neocolonialist plans. Its vanguard positions in the anti-imperialist struggle are indisputable. Its role is indispensable in consolidating the Arab world along the lines of the Middle East settlement, the most important aim of which is the return of the territories seized by Israel and the exercise of legitimate Palestinian rights.

Now that preparatory work for an international conference on the Middle East appears to be the order of the day, a common Arab stand on that matter is especially important. And here, in our opinion, the activity and authority of the Syrian friends can become a decisive factor.

APPENDIX I

Resolutions of the Eighteenth Session of the Palestine National Council (PNC), Algiers, April 26, 1987

Proceeding from the Palestinian national charter and based on the PNC resolutions, we emphasize the following principles as a basis for Palestinian national action within the framework of the PLO, the sole legitimate representative of the Palestinian Arab people:

I. On the Palestinian Level

1. Adhering to the Palestinian Arab people's inalienable national rights to return, to self-determination, and to establish on Palestinian national soil an independent state whose capital is Jerusalem, and upholding commitment to the PLO's political program which is aimed at attaining these rights.

2. Adhering to the PLO as the sole legitimate representative for our people and rejecting delegation of powers, deputization, and sharing of participation in Palestinian representation, as well as rejecting and resisting any alternatives to the PLO.

3. Adhering to the PLO's independence and rejecting trusteeship, containment, annexation, and interference in its internal affairs and the setting up of an alternative to it.

4. Continuing struggle in all its forms, armed, popular, and political, to attain our national objectives, to liberate the Palestinian and Arab lands from Zionist occupation, and to confront the hostile schemes of the imperialist-Zionist alliance in our region, particularly the strategic U.S.-Israeli alliance, as a genuine expression of our

Edited and excerpted from Sanaa Voice of Palestine, April 26, 1987, in FBIS, *Daily Report: Middle East and Africa,* April 27, 1987, pp. A8-A11.

people's national liberation movement, which opposes imperialism, colonialism, and Zionism.

5. Continuing rejection of Security Council Resolution 242, which is not considered a good basis for a settlement of the Palestine question because it deals with it as if it were an issue of refugees and ignores the Palestinian people's inalienable national rights.

6. Rejecting and resisting all solutions and plans aimed at liquidating our Palestinian question, including the Camp David accords, Reagan's autonomy plan, and the functional partition plan in all its forms.

7. Adhering to the Arab summit resolutions on the Palestine question, particularly the Rabat 1974 summit, and considering the Arab peace plan approved by the Fez 1982 summit and confirmed by the extraordinary Casablanca summit as a framework for Arab action on the international level to achieve a solution to the Palestine question and to regain the occupied Arab territories.

8. Taking into consideration UN Resolutions 3858 and 4148 regarding the convocation of an international conference for peace in the Middle East, and UN resolutions on the Palestine question, the PNC supports the convocation of an international conference within the framework of the United Nations and under its auspices, with the participation of the permanent member states of the UN Security Council and the parties to the conflict in the region, including the PLO, on an equal footing with the other parties. The PNC stresses that the international conference should have full powers. The PNC also expresses support for the proposal to form a preparatory committee, and calls for swift action to form and convene this committee. . . .

9. Enhancing the unity of all the national institutions and forces inside the occupied homeland under the PLO, promoting their joint struggle action against the Zionist enemy, the Israeli iron-fist policy, the autonomy plan, functional partition, normalization, the so-called development plan, and the attempts to create alternatives to the PLO, including the establishment of municipal councils, and supporting the steadfastness of our people who are represented by their national forces and institutions. . . .

II. On the Arab Level

. . . 4. Correcting and establishing relations between the PLO and Syria on the basis of the struggle against imperialism and Zionism, and in accordance with Arab summit resolutions, particularly the Rabat and Fez summit resolutions, and on the basis of equality and mutual respect leading to solid Palestinian-Syrian-Arab relations of joint struggle.

5. The Iraq-Iran war. Working to halt the Iraq-Iran war, because it is a destructive war to the two neighboring Muslim people from which only imperialism and Zionism benefit. This war seeks to exhaust Arab efforts and resources from the principal arena of confrontation of the Zionist aggression, which is backed by U.S. imperialism, against the Arab nation and the Islamic countries. While valuing Iraq's peace initiatives seeking to halt this war, establish relations of good neighborliness between the two countries based on total respect for the sovereignty of each of them, on the noninterference by either side in the domestic affairs of the other, and with respect to their political and social choices, the PNC stands at fraternal Iraq's side in defending its land and any Arab land that is the target of foreign aggression and invasion. The PNC also condemns Iran's occupation of Iraqi territory and the U.S.-Israeli collusion for perpetuating this war through their arms deals with Iran.

6. Jordan. Reaffirming the special and distinctive relations that link the fraternal Palestinian and Jordanian people and working to develop these relations in a manner that will be in line with the national (*qawmiyya*) interests of the two peoples and those of our Arab nation, and consolidating their joint struggle for the enhancement of Jordan's independence and against the Zionist designs of expansion at the expense of its territory, and for the attainment of the Palestinian people's inalienable national (*wataniyya*) rights, including their rights to return, to self-determination, and to establish their independent Palestinian state; abiding by the PNC resolutions pertaining to the relationship with Jordan on the basis that the PLO is the Palestinian people's sole and legitimate representative inside and outside the occupied territories, as was affirmed by the 1974 Rabat summit resolution; and reaffirming that any future relationship with Jordan should be made on a confederal basis between two independent states; and stressing adherence to the bases that were approved by the 15th PNC session and the Baghdad summit resolutions concerning supporting steadfastness, including the work of the Palestinian-Jordanian Joint Committee.

7. Egypt. While stressing the historic role of Egypt and its great people within the framework of the Arab struggle against the Zionist

enemy, the sacrifices of the fraternal Egyptian people and its heroic army in defense of the Palestinian people and their national rights, Egypt's struggle to achieve Arab unity and liberation from imperialism and Zionism, Egypt's struggle to liberate the occupied Arab and Palestinian territories in all circles and arenas, and while also appreciating Egypt's pan-Arab and international position and the importance of Egypt's return to resume its natural role in the Arab arena, the PNC has entrusted the PLO Executive Committee with the task of defining the basis for Palestinian-Egyptian relations in accordance with successive PNC resolutions, especially those of the 16th session, which contain certain positions and principles of Palestinian struggle, foremost of which are the rights to self-determination, return, and to establish an independent Palestinian state and that the PLO is the sole legitimate representative, as well as in light of the Arab summit conferences' resolutions to achieve the Palestinian people's goals and inalienable national rights, which have been stressed by these Arab resolutions in the service of the Palestinian and Arab struggle against the Zionist enemy and its supporters.

III. On the International Level

. . . 3. Strengthening militant relations of alliance with the socialist bloc countries, foremost of which is the Soviet Union, as well as with the PRC. . . .

5. Working with all means in the international arena to expose the Zionist racism exercised in our occupied homeland. This racism was confirmed by the historic UN Resolution No. 3379 in 1975 stating that Zionism is a form of racism, and working to abort the Zionist-imperialist move to cancel this resolution. . . .

8. Developing relations with Israeli democratic forces which support the Palestinian people's struggle against Israeli occupation and expansion, and the inalienable national rights of our people, including their rights to return, to self-determination, to establish an independent state, and recognize the PLO as the sole, legitimate representative of the Palestinian people. Condemning all U.S. imperialist-backed Zionist attempts to compel Jews in a number of countries to emigrate to occupied Palestine, and calling upon all honorable forces to stand up to these feverish propaganda campaigns and their harmful effects. . . .

APPENDIX J

The Fourteen Talking Points of West Bank–Gaza Palestinians, January 14, 1988

January 27, 1988

His Excellency
George P. Shultz
Secretary of State
Department of State
Washington, D.C. 20520

Dear Secretary Shultz,

This meeting takes place at a crucial time when uncivilized and oppressive measures are being employed by Israeli occupation forces to quell the just uprising of our Palestinian people. This uprising comes as the inevitable national expression of our people's will to struggle until we achieve our freedom in our independent Palestinian state under the leadership of our sole legitimate representative, the Palestine Liberation Organization.

Our people are in urgent need of immediate international protection from the brutality of Israel's military authorities which have been unleashed against our unarmed civilian population to kill, maim and terrorize our women and children. To the end, we hope the international community will immediately authorize the provision of an international force to intervene in the occupied territories, to whose trusteeship our population can be delivered, as a first step towards the convening of an international peace conference. This conference is to be held under the auspices of the United Nations, and will be attended by all concerned parties to the conflict, including, foremost, the Palestinian nation through its legitimate representative, the PLO.

We look forward to your personal active involvement and that of the United States Government in the peace process, which we hope will bring an end to the suffering endured by our people for the past 20 years.

Yours respectfully,
Hanna Siniora
Fayez Abu Rahme

Enc.: Copy of statement by Palestinian institutions and personalities from the West Bank and Gaza.

Statement by Palestinian Institutions from the West Bank and Gaza

During the past few weeks the occupied territories have witnessed a popular uprising against Israel's occupation and its oppressive measures. This uprising has so far resulted in the martyrdom of tens of our people, the wounding of hundreds more and the imprisonment of thousands of unarmed civilians.

This uprising has come to further affirm our people's unbreakable commitment to its national aspirations. These aspirations include our people's firm national rights of self-determination and of the establishment of an independent state on our national soil under the leadership of the PLO, as our sole legitimate representative. The uprising also comes as further proof of our indefatigable spirit and our rejection of the sense of despair which has begun to creep to the minds of some who claim that the uprising is the result of despair.

The conclusion to be drawn from this uprising is that the present state of affairs in the Palestinian occupied territories is unnatural and that Israeli occupation cannot continue forever. Real peace cannot be achieved except through the recognition of the Palestinian national rights, including the right of self-determination and the establishment of an independent Palestinian state on Palestinian national soil. Should these rights not be recognized, then the continuation of Israeli occupation will lead to further violence and bloodshed and the further deepening of hatred. The opportunity for achieving peace will also move further away.

The only way to extricate ourselves from this scenario is through the convening of an international conference with the participation of all concerned parties including the PLO, the sole legitimate representative of the Palestinian people, as an equal partner, as well as the five permanent members of the Security Council, under the supervision of the two Super Powers.

On this basis we call upon the Israeli authorities to comply with the following list of demands as a means to prepare the atmosphere for the convening of the suggested international peace conference which will achieve a just and lasting settlement of the Palestinian problem in all its aspects, bringing about the realization of the inalienable national rights of the Palestinian people, peace and stability for the peoples of the region and an end to violence and bloodshed:

1. To abide by the 4th Geneva Convention and all other international agreements pertaining to the protection of civilians, their properties and rights under a state of military occupation; to declare the Emergency Regulations of the British Mandate null and void, and to stop applying the iron fist policy.

2. The immediate compliance with Security Council Resolutions 605 and 607, which call upon Israel to abide by the Geneva Convention of 1949 and the Declaration of Human Rights; and which further call for the achievement of a just and lasting settlement of the Arab-Israeli conflict.

3. The release of all prisoncrs who were arrested during the recent uprising, and foremost among them our children. Also the rescinding of all proceedings and indictments against them.

4. The cancellation of the policy of expulsion and allowing all exiled Palestinians, including the four expelled to Lebanon on January, 13, 1988, to return to their homes and families. Also the release of all administrative detainees and the cancellation of the hundreds of house arrest orders. In this connection, special mention must be made of the hundreds of applications for family reunions which we call upon the authorities to accept forthwith.

5. The immediate lifting of the siege of all Palestinian refugee camps in the West Bank and Gaza, and the withdrawal of the Israeli army from all population centers.

6. Carrying out a formal inquiry into the behavior of soldiers and settlers in the West Bank and Gaza, as well as inside jails and detention camps, and taking due punitive measures against all those convicted of having unduly caused death or bodily harm to unarmed civilians.

7. A cessation of all settlement activity and land confiscation and the release of lands already confiscated especially in the Gaza strip. Also putting an end to the harassments and provocations of the Arab population by settlers in the West Bank and Gaza as well as in the Old City of Jerusalem. In particular, the curtailment of the provocative activities in the Old City of Jerusalem by Ariel Sharon and the ultrareligious settlers of Shuvu Banim and Ateret Kohanim.

8. Refraining from any act which might impinge on the Moslem

and Christian holy sites or which might introduce changes to the status quo in the City of Jerusalem.

9. The cancellation of the Value Added Tax (V.A.T.) and all other direct Israeli taxes which are imposed on Palestinian residents in Jerusalem, the rest of the West Bank, and in Gaza; and putting an end to the harassment caused to Palestinian business and tradesmen.

10. The cancellation of all restrictions on political freedoms including restrictions on freedom of assembly and association; also making provisions for free municipal elections under the supervision of a neutral authority.

11. The immediate release of all funds deducted from the wages of laborers from the territories who worked and still work inside the Green Line, which amount to several hundreds of millions of dollars. These accumulated deductions, with interest, must be returned to their rightful owners through the agency of the nationalist institutions headed by the Workers' Unions.

12. The removal of all restrictions on building permits and licences for industrial projects and artesian water wells as well as agricultural development programs in the occupied territories. Also rescinding all measures taken to deprive the territories of their water resources.

13. Terminating the policy of discrimination being practiced against industrial and agricultural produce from the occupied territories either by removing the restrictions on the transfer of goods to within the Green Line, or by placing comparable trade restrictions on the transfer of Israeli goods into the territories.

14. Removing the restrictions on political contacts between inhabitants of the occupied territories and the PLO, in such a way as to allow for the participation of Palestinians from the territories in the proceedings of the Palestine National Council, in order to ensure a direct input into the decision-making processes of the Palestinian nation by the Palestinians under occupation.

Palestinian nationalist
institutions and personalities
from the West Bank and Gaza

Jerusalem
January 14, 1988

APPENDIX K

The Shultz Initiative, March 4, 1988

I set forth below the statement of understandings which I am convinced is necessary to achieve the prompt opening of negotiations on a comprehensive peace. This statement of understandings emerges from discussions held with you and other regional leaders. I look forward to the letter of reply of the Government of Israel in confirmation of this statement.

The agreed objective is a comprehensive peace providing for the security of all the states in the region and for the legitimate rights of the Palestinian people.

Negotiations will start on an early date certain between Israel and each of its neighbors which is willing to do so. These negotiations could begin by May 1, 1988. Each of these negotiations will be based on United Nations Security Council Resolutions 242 and 338, in all their parts. The parties to each bilateral negotiation will determine the procedure and agenda at their negotiation. All participants in the negotiations must state their willingness to negotiate with one another.

As concerns negotiations between the Israeli delegation and the Jordanian-Palestinian delegation, negotiations will begin on arrangements for a transitional period, with the objective of completing them within six months. Seven months after transitional negotiations begin, final status negotiations will begin, with the objective of completing them within one year. These negotiations will be based on all the provisions and principles of United Nations Security Council Resolution 242. Finally status talks will start before the transitional period begins. The transitional period will begin three months after the conclusion of the transitional agreement and will last for three years. The United States will participate in both negotiations and will promote their rapid conclusion. In particular,

Text of the letter that Secretary of State George P. Shultz wrote to Prime Minister Yitzhak Shamir of Israel outlining the American peace proposal. A similar letter was sent to King Hussein of Jordan. See the *New York Times*, March 10, 1988.

the United States will submit a draft agreement for the parties' consideration at the outset of the negotiations on transitional arrangements.

Two weeks before the opening of negotiations, an international conference will be held. The Secretary General of the United Nations will be asked to issue invitations to the parties involved in the Arab-Israel conflict and the five permanent members of the United Nations Security Council. All participants in the conference must accept United Nations Security Council Resolutions 242 and 338, and renounce violence and terrorism. The parties to each bilateral negotiation may refer reports on the status of their negotiations to the conference, in a manner to be agreed. The conference will not be able to impose solutions or veto agreements reached.

Palestinian representation will be within the Jordanian-Palestinian delegation. The Palestinian issue will be addressed in the negotiations between the Jordanian-Palestinian and Israeli delegations. Negotiations between the Israeli delegation and the Jordanian-Palestinian delegation will proceed independently of any other negotiations.

This statement of understandings is an integral whole. The United States understands that your acceptance is dependent on the implementation of each element in good faith.

Sincerely yours,

George P. Shultz

APPENDIX L

Palestinian Document Circulated at the Arab League Summit in Algeria, June 7–9, 1988, Written by Bassam Abu Sharif, Adviser to PLO Chairman Yasir Arafat

PLO View: Prospects of a Palestinian-Israeli Settlement

Everything that has been said about the Middle East conflict has focused on the differences between Palestinians and Israelis and ignored the points on which they are in almost total agreement.

These points are easy to overlook, hidden as they are under a 70-year accumulation of mutual hostility and suspicion, but they exist nevertheless and in them lies the hope that the peace that has eluded this region for so long is finally within reach.

Peel off the layers of fear and mistrust that successive Israeli leaders have piled on the substantive issues and you will find that the Palestinians and Israelis are in general agreement on ends and means:

—Israel's objectives are lasting peace and security. Lasting peace and security are also the objectives of the Palestinian people. No one can understand the Jewish people's century of suffering more than the Palestinians. We know what it means to be stateless and the object of the fear and prejudice of the nations. Thanks to the various Israeli and other governments that have had the power to determine the course of our people's lives, we know what it feels like when human beings are considered somehow less human than others and denied the basic rights that people around the globe take for granted. We feel that no people–neither the Jewish people nor the Palestinian people—deserve the abuse and dis[en]franchisement that hopelessness inevitably entails. We believe that all peoples—the Jewish and the Palestinians included—have the right to run their own affairs, expecting from their neighbors not only nonbelligerence but the kind of political and economic cooperation without which no state can be truly secure, no matter how massive its war machine, and without which no nation can truly prosper, no matter how generous its friends in distant lands may be.

— The Palestinians want that kind of lasting peace and security for themselves and the Israelis because no one can build his own future on the ruins of another's. We are confident that this desire and this realization are shared by all but an insignificant minority in Israel.

— The means by which the Israelis want to achieve lasting peace and security is direct talks, with no attempt by any outside party to impose or veto a settlement.

— The Palestinians agree. We see no way for any dispute to be settled without direct talks between the parties to that dispute, and we feel that any settlement that has to be imposed by an outside power is a settlement that is unacceptable to one or both of the belligerents and therefore a settlement that will not stand the test of time. The key to a Palestinian-Israeli settlement lies in talks between the Palestinians and the Israelis. The Palestinians would be deluding themselves if they thought that their problems with the Israelis can be solved in negotiations with non-Israelis—and U.S. Secretary of State George Shultz, who will soon return to the Middle East for further discussions on his peace proposals—would be deluding themselves if they thought that Israel's problems with the Palestinians can be solved in negotiations with non-Palestinians, including Jordan.

— The Palestinians would like to choose their Israeli interlocutor. We have little doubt that we could reach a satisfactory settlement with the Peace Now movement in a month. We know, however, that an agreement with Peace Now would not be an agreement with Israel, and since an agreement with Israel is what we are after, we are ready to talk to Mr. Shimon Peres' Labor alignment, and to Yitzhak Shamir's Likud bloc, or anyone else the Israelis choose to represent them.

— The Israelis and Mr. Shultz would also prefer to deal with Palestinians of their own choosing. But it would be as futile for them as for us to talk to people who have no mandate to negotiate. If it is a settlement with the Palestinians that they seek, as we assume it is, then it is with the representatives of that people that they must negotiate, and the Palestinian people, by the only means that they have at their disposal, have chosen their representatives. Every Palestinian questioned by diplomats and the newsmen of the international community has stated unequivocally that his representative is the Palestine Liberation Organization. If that is regarded as an unreliable expression of the Palestinians' free will, then give the Palestinians the chance to express their free will in a manner that will convince all doubters: arrange for an internationally-supervised referendum in the West Bank and the Gaza Strip and allow the population to choose between the PLO and any other group of Palestinians that Israel or the United States or the international community wishes to nominate. The PLO is ready to abide by the outcome and step aside for any alternative leadership should the Palestinian people choose one. The PLO will do this because its *raison d'être* is not the undoing of Israel, but the salvation of the Palestinian people and their rights, including their right to democratic self-expression and national self-determination.

— Regardless of the Satanic image that the PLO's struggle for those rights has given it in the United States and Israel, the fact remains that this organization was built on democratic principles and seeks democratic objectives. If Israel and its supporters in the U.S. Administration can grasp that fact, the fears that prevent them from accepting the PLO as the only valid interlocutor toward any Palestinian-Israeli settlement would vanish.

— Those fears, as far as one can tell from what has been written and said in Israel and the United States, center on the PLO's failure of unconditionally accepting Security Council Resolutions 242 and 338 and on the possibility that a Palestinian state on the West Bank and Gaza would be a radical, totalitarian threat to its neighbors.

— The PLO, however, does accept Resolutions 242 and 338. What prevents it from saying so unconditionally is not what is in the Resolutions but what is not in them; neither Resolution says anything about the national rights of the Palestinian people, including their democratic right to self-expression and their national right to self- determination. For that reason and that reason alone, we have repeatedly said that we accept Resolutions 242 and 338 in the context of the UN Resolutions which do recognize the national rights of the Palestinian people.

— As for the fear that a Palestinian state will be a threat to its neighbor, the democratic nature of the PLO—with its legislative, executive, and other popularly-based institutions—should argue against it. If that does not constitute a solid enough guarantee that the state of Palestine would be a democratic one, the Palestinians would be open to the idea of a brief, mutually-acceptable transitional period during which an international mandate would guide the Occupied Palestinian Territories to democratic Palestinian statehood.

— Beyond that, the Palestinians would accept—indeed, insist on—international guarantees for the security of all states in the region, including Palestine and Israel. It is precisely our desire for such guarantees that motivates our demand that bilateral peace talks with Israel be conducted under a UN-sponsored international conference.

— The Palestinians feel that they have much more to fear from Israel, with its mighty war machine and its nuclear arsenal, than Israel has to fear from them. They would therefore welcome any reasonable measure that would promote the security of their state and its neighbors, including the deployment of a UN buffer force on the Palestinian side of the Israeli-Palestinian border.

— Time, sometimes the great healer, is often the great spoiler. Many Israelis no doubt realize it and are trying to communicate it to the rest of their people. As for us, we are ready for peace now, and we can deliver it. It is our hope that the opportunity that presents itself today will not be missed.

— If it is missed, we will have no choice but to continue to exercise our right to resist the occupation, our ultimate aim being a free, dignified, and secure life not only for our children but also for the children of the Israelis.

APPENDIX M

King Hussein's Speech July 31, 1988

Brother Citizens, I send you my greetings, and I am pleased to address you in your cities and villages, in your camps and dwellings, in your institutions of learning, and in your places of work. I would like to address your hearts and your minds, in all parts of our beloved Jordanian land. This is all the more important at this juncture when we have initiated, after seeking God's assistance and in light of a thorough and extensive study, a series of measures with the aim of enhancing the Palestinian national orientation and highlighting the Palestinian identity. Our objective is the benefit of the Palestinian cause and the Arab Palestinian people.

Our decision, as you know, comes after thirty-eight years of the unity of the two banks and fourteen years after the Rabat summit resolution designating the Palestine Liberation Organization (PLO) as the sole legitimate representative of the Palestinian people. It also comes six years after the Fez summit resolution that agreed unanimously on the establishment of an independent Palestinian state in the occupied West Bank and the Gaza Strip as one of the bases and results of the peaceful settlement.

We are certain that our decision to initiate these measures does not come as a surprise to you. Many among you have anticipated it, and some of you have been calling for it for some time. As for its contents, it has been for everyone a topic for discussion and consideration since the Rabat conference.

Nevertheless, some may wonder: Why now? Why today and not after the Rabat or Fez summits, for instance?

To answer this question we need to recall certain facts that preceded the Rabat resolution. We also need to recall the factors that led to the debate over the objective of establishing an inde-

Edited from text of King Hussein's speech provided by the Jordanian Information Bureau, Washington, D.C.

pendent Palestinian state, which the PLO proclaimed and for which it worked to gain Arab and international support. This meant, in addition to the PLO's ambition to embody the Palestinian identity on Palestinian national soil, the separation of the West Bank from the Hashemite Kingdom of Jordan.

As you recall, I have reviewed the facts that preceded the Rabat resolution before the Arab leaders in the extraordinary Algiers summit last June. It may be important to recall that one of the main facts that I noted was the April 1950 text of the unity resolution of the two banks. This resolution affirms "the preservation of all Arab rights in Palestine and the defense of such rights by all legitimate means—without prejudice to the final settlement of the just cause of the Palestinian people, within the scope of the people's aspirations and of Arab cooperation and international justice."

Another of these facts was our proposal of 1972 outlining alternative forms for the relationship between Jordan and the occupied West Bank and Gaza Strip after their liberation. One of these alternatives was the maintenance of brotherly cooperation between the Hashemite Kingdom of Jordan and an independent Palestinian state, if the Palestinian people so preferred. This means, simply, that we have declared clearly our commitment to the Palestinian people's right to self-determination on their national soil, including their right to establish their independent Palestinian state, more than two years before the Rabat resolution, and we shall adhere to that commitment until the Palestinian people realize their national goals completely, God willing.

The considerations leading to the search to identify the relationship between the West Bank and the Hashemite Kingdom of Jordan, against the background of the PLO's call for the establishment of an independent Palestinian state, are twofold:

I. The principle of Arab unity, this being a national objective to which all the Arab peoples aspire and which they all seek to realize.

II. The political reality of the benefits to the Palestinian struggle that accrue from maintaining the legal relationship between the two banks of the kingdom.

Our answer to the question "Why now?" also derives from these two factors and the background of the clear and constant Jordanian position on the Palestinian cause, as already outlined.

Regarding the principle of Arab unity, we believe that such unity between two or more Arab peoples is a right of choice for every Arab people. Based on that, we responded to the wish of the representatives of the Palestinian people for unity with Jordan in

1950. Within this context we respect the wish of the PLO, the sole legitimate representative of the Palestinian people, to secede from us in an independent Palestinian state. We say this in all understanding. Nevertheless, Jordan will remain the proud bearer of the message of the great Arab revolt, faithful to its principles, believing in the common Arab destiny, and committed to joint Arab action.

Regarding the political factor, it has been our belief since the Israeli aggression of June 1967 that our first priority should be to liberate the land and holy places from Israeli occupation. . . .

Lately it has transpired that there is a general Palestinian and Arab orientation toward highlighting the Palestinian identity in a complete manner, in every effort or activity related to the Palestinian question and its developments. It has also become clear that there is a general conviction that maintaining the legal and administrative links with the West Bank and the ensuing Jordanian interaction with our Palestinian brothers under occupation, through Jordanian institutions in the occupied territories, contradicts this orientation. It is also viewed that these links hamper the Palestinian struggle to gain international support for the Palestinian cause as the national cause of a people struggling against foreign occupation.

In view of this line of thought, which is certainly inspired by genuine Palestinian will and Arab determination to support the Palestinian cause, it becomes our duty to be part of this direction and to respond to its requirements. After all, we are a part of our nation, supportive of its causes, foremost among which is the Palestinian cause. Since there is a general conviction that the struggle to liberate the occupied Palestinian land could be enhanced by dismantling the legal and administrative lines between the two banks, we have to fulfill our duty and do what is required of us. At the Rabat summit of 1974 we responded to the Arab leaders' appeal to us to continue our interaction with the occupied West Bank through the Jordanian institutions, to support the steadfastness of our brothers there. Today we respond to the wish of the Palestine Liberation Organization, the sole legitimate representative of the Palestinian people, and to the Arab orientation to affirm the Palestinian identity in all its aspects. We pray to God that this step be a substantive addition to the intensifying Palestinian struggle for freedom and independence.

Brother citizens, these are the reasons, considerations, and convictions that led us to respond to the wish of the PLO and the general Arab direction consistent with it. We cannot continue in this state of suspension, which can serve neither Jordan nor the Palestinian cause. We had to leave the labyrinth of fears and doubts, toward clearer horizons where mutual trust, understanding, and cooperation can prevail, to the benefit of the Palestinian cause and Arab unity. This unity will remain a goal which all the Arab peoples cherish and seek to realize.

At the same time it has to be understood in all clarity and without any ambiguity or equivocation that our measures regarding the West Bank concern only the occupied Palestinian land and its people. They naturally do not relate in any way to the Jordanian citizens of Palestinian origin in the Hashemite Kingdom of Jordan. They all have the full rights of citizenship and all its obligations, the same as any other citizen irrespective of his origin. They are an integral part of the Jordanian state. They belong to it, they live on its land, and they participate in its life and all its activities. Jordan is not Palestine, and the independent Palestinian state will be established on the occupied Palestinian land after its liberation, God willing. There the Palestinian identity will be embodied, and there the Palestinian struggle shall come to fruition, as confirmed by the glorious uprising of the Palestinian people under occupation. . . .

Safeguarding national unity is a sacred duty that will not be compromised. Any attempt to undermine it, under any pretext, would only help the enemy carry out his policy of expansion at the expense of Palestine and Jordan alike. Consequently, true nationalism lies in bolstering and fortifying national unity. Moreover, the responsibility to safeguard it falls on every one of you, leaving no place in our midst for sedition or treachery. With God's help we shall be as always a united, cohesive family whose members are joined by bonds of brotherhood, affection, awareness, and common national objectives.

It is most important to remember, as we emphasize the importance of safeguarding national unity, that stable and productive societies are those where orderliness and discipline prevail. Discipline is the solid fabric that binds all members of a community in a solid, harmonious structure, blocking all avenues before the enemies and opening horizons of hope for future generations. . . .

Citizens, Palestinian brothers in the occupied Palestinian lands, to dispel any doubts that may arise out of our decision, we assure you that these measures do not mean the abandonment of our national duty, either toward the Arab-Israeli conflict or toward the Palestinian cause. Nor do they mean relinquishing our faith in Arab unity. As I have stated, these steps were taken only in response to the wish of the Palestine Liberation Organization, the sole legitimate representative of the Palestinian people, and to the prevailing Arab conviction that such measures will contribute to the struggle of the Palestinian people and their glorious uprising. Jordan will continue its support for the steadfastness of the Palestinian people and their courageous uprising in the occupied Palestinian land, within its capabilities. I have to mention that when we decided to cancel the Jordanian development plan in the occupied territories, we contacted at the same time various friendly governments and international institutions which had expressed their wish to contribute to the plan, urging them to continue financing development projects in the occupied Palestinian lands through the relevant Palestinian quarters.

Jordan, dear brothers, has not nor will it give up its support and assistance to the Palestinian people until they achieve their national goals, God willing. No one outside Palestine has had, nor can have, an attachment to Palestine or its cause firmer than that of Jordan or of my family. Moreover Jordan is a confrontation state whose borders with Israel are longer than those of any other Arab state, longer even than the combined borders of the West Bank and Gaza with Israel.

In addition, Jordan will not give up its commitment to take part in the peace process. We contributed to the peace process until it reached the stage of a consensus to convene an international peace conference on the Middle East. The purpose of the conference would be to achieve a just and comprehensive peace settlement to the Arab-Israeli conflict and the settlement of the Palestinian problem in all its aspects. We have defined our position in this regard, as everybody knows, through the six principles which we have already made public.

Jordan, dear brothers, is a principal party to the Arab-Israeli conflict and to the peace process. It shoulders its national responsibilities on that basis. . . .

Contributors

ABDEL MONEM SAID ALY, senior researcher at the Al-Ahram Center for Political and Strategic Studies was the general coordinator of *The Arab Strategic Report* of the Al-Ahram Center for 1985 and 1986. Currently he is the head of the International Relations Research unit of the center. His most recent publications are *The Arabs and Their Neighbors: A Study of the Future* (in Arabic) (1987), and *The Arabs and the Future of the World System* (in Arabic) (1987).

NAOMI CHAZAN, senior research fellow at the Hebrew University of Jerusalem is a senior research fellow at the Harry S Truman Research Institute for the Advancement of Peace at the Hebrew University of Jerusalem. She teaches political science and heads the African studies department. She is also a member of the executive board of the International Center for Peace in the Middle East. Among her most recent publications are *The Precarious Balance: State and Society in Africa* (edited with Donald Rothchild, 1988), *Coping with Africa's Food Crisis* (edited with Timothy M. Shaw, 1988), and *Israeli Perceptions on Israel-South Africa Relations* (1987).

ALI E. HILLAL DESSOUKI, director of the Center for Political Studies and Research at Cairo University, is a professor of political science there. He has taught at UCLA, Princeton, and the American University in Cairo. He served as adviser to the Egyptian Ministry of Information (1975–76), member of the editorial board of the *International Journal of Middle East Studies* (1982–87), secretary general of the Arab Association of Political Science (1984–87), and is a member of the Council of the International Institute for Strategic Studies. His most recent publication is *Foreign Policies of the Arab States* (1984).

HERMANN FREDERICK EILTS is distinguished university professor of international relations and director of the Center for International Relations at Boston University. He is former ambassador to Egypt and Saudi Arabia. He participated in all phases of the Egyptian-Israeli peace negotiations from 1973 to 1979.

SAAD EDDIN IBRAHIM is secretary general of the Arab Thought Forum in Amman, Jordan. He is also professor of sociology at the American University in Cairo and author of many books and articles on the contemporary Arab world, including *Egypt's Arabism: The Dialogue of the Seventies* (in Arabic) (1978) and *The New Arab Social Order: A Study of the Social Impact of Oil Wealth* (1982).

RASHID I. KHALIDI, associate professor of modern Middle East history at the University of Chicago, has taught Middle Eastern history and politics at the American University of Beirut, the Lebanese University, and Georgetown and Columbia Universities. He worked at the Institute for Palestine Studies in Beirut from 1976 until 1983. He is the author of *British Policy towards Syria and Palestine* (1980) and *Under Siege: PLO Decision-Making during the 1982 War* (1986), as well as other monographs and articles.

SAMUEL W. LEWIS is president of the United States Institute of Peace. Ambassador Lewis's thirty-one years in the Foreign Service included tours with the National Security Council, as deputy director of the Policy Planning Staff, as assistant secretary of state for international organization affairs, and as ambassador to Israel for eight years under Presidents Carter and Reagan. He participated in the Camp David meetings and all phases of Egyptian-Israeli and Lebanese-Israeli negotiations between 1977 and 1985. Since retirement he has lectured and written extensively on Middle East issues.

EVGENI M. PRIMAKOV is director of the Institute of World Economics and International Relations, Academy of Sciences of the USSR. He is one of the leading Middle East specialists in the Soviet Union. Among his publications are *History of a Deal* (in Russian) (1985), concerning the Camp David negotiations; *The East after the Collapse of the Colonial System* (1983); and *Anatomy of the Middle East Conflict* (1978).

WILLIAM B. QUANDT, senior fellow at the Brookings Institution, was a member of the National Security Council staff from

1972 to 1974 and from 1977 to 1979. During the 1977–79 period, he participated in the negotiations that resulted in the Camp David Accords and the Egyptian-Israeli peace treaty. Since 1979, he has been a senior fellow at Brookings. He has also taught at several universities. His most recent publication is *Camp David: Peacemaking and Politics* (1986).

EMILE F. SAHLIYEH is associate professor of international relations and Middle East politics at the University of North Texas. A native Palestinian, he taught at Bir Zeit University in the West Bank between 1978 and 1984. During 1985, he was a fellow at the Woodrow Wilson International Center for Scholars. During 1985 and 1986, he was a Middle East fellow at the Brookings Institution. In September 1986, he joined the Department of Political Science at the University of North Texas. His most recent publications are *The PLO after the Lebanon War* (1986) and *In Search of Leadership: West Bank Politics since 1967* (1988).

GHASSAN SALAME, director of research at the Centre National de Recherche Scientifique (Paris), has been a professor of political science at Saint Joseph and the American University of Beirut. He was a visiting scholar at the Brookings Institution in 1986. He has also taught at the Panthéon-Sorbonne University in Paris. He is the author of, among other publications, *Saudi Foreign Policy since 1945* (1980), *State and Society in the Arab Levant States* (1987), the editor of *The Foundations of the Arab State* (1987), and the coeditor of *The Politics of Arab Integration* (1988).

HAROLD H. SAUNDERS, visiting fellow at the Brookings Institution, served on the National Security Council staff, 1961–74, and in the State Department, 1974–81. He was assistant secretary of state for Near Eastern and South Asian affairs, 1978–81. He participated in the disengagement negotiations in 1973–75, and helped draft the Camp David Accords and the Egyptian-Israeli peace treaty. He is the author of *The Other Walls: The Politics of The Arab-Israeli Peace Process* (1986).

SHIMON SHAMIR, currently Israeli ambassador to Egypt, was educated at the Hebrew University of Jerusalem and at Princeton.

In 1967, he founded the Shiloah Center for Middle Eastern and African Studies at Tel Aviv University and in 1980 was appointed to the Kaplan chair in the history of Egypt and Israel in the same university. He was the first director of the Israeli Academic Center in Cairo (1982–84). His most recent publication is *The Jews of Egypt: A Mediterranean Society in Modern Times* (1987).

Index